THE EXPRESSION 'SON OF MAN' AND THE DEVELOPMENT OF CHRISTOLOGY

A History of Interpretation

Copenhagen International Seminar

edited by

Thomas L. Thompson

Other volumes in the series include:

Origin Myths and Holy Places in the Old Testament
Łukasz Niesiołowski-Spanò

Japheth Ben Ali's Book of Jeremiah
Joshua A. Sabih

THE EXPRESSION 'SON OF MAN' AND THE DEVELOPMENT OF CHRISTOLOGY

A HISTORY OF INTERPRETATION

MOGENS MÜLLER

Equinox Publishing Ltd

equinox

London Oakville

Published by

UK: Equinox Publishing Ltd., Unit 6, The Village, 101 Amies St., London SW11 2JW
USA: DBBC, 28 Main Street, Oakville, CT 06779

www.equinoxpub.com

First published 2008

Library of Congress Cataloguing-in-Publication Data
A catalogue record for this book is available from the Library of Congress

ISBN 1845533356 (hardback)
9781845533359 (hardback)

Printed by Lightning Source

To the teacher, colleague and friend,
Niels Hyldahl,
in gratitude

Contents

Preface

This book has a long history. The beginnings go back to the early 1970s, but the work was interrupted by other projects only to be partly resumed in connection with the preparation of my doctoral thesis, published in 1984. Here, much of the material from the history of research with regard to the use and interpretation of the expression Son of man in the different periods found its way into a series of excursuses. Then a long pause came, the Son of man theme being not the most relevant topic for my teaching.

The occasion for resuming the work was the publication of Delbert Burkett's *The Son of Man Debate* in 1999. With due respect to all the merits of his investigation, Burkett solved the problem in a way exactly opposite to the one I had intended. Where he thematizes the many different solutions and thus misses the impetus arising from a more chronological approach, my original intention was to write a history of interpretation to show the interaction between the various periods' christology and its impact on their interpretation of the expression Son of man. Thus it would also be a history of christology, trying to elucidate why one interpretation was succeeded by the next.

The present treatise is divided into chapters following the main periods of the history of the Church up to the middle of the 18th century. At that time the picture becomes so complicated that I have chosen to give each different trend in interpretation its own chapter, while at the same time striving to retain a chronological perspective.

It has been my intention to include all scholarly works containing Son of man (or its equivalents) in their titles. I have found them partly through my own reading and partly through bibliographies. As a result, a good many titles not directly interesting or relevant are mentioned. I have also included other works relevant for the theme; any sort of completeness, however, has been impossible. I hope that most of the relevant literature has been included.

A minimal amount of publication data is supplied in the citations appearing in the main text and footnotes. Full bibliographical details for books and articles cited are reserved for the Bibliography.

Practically all quotations in foreign languages within the text are given in English translation, sometimes with key words or important formulations placed in parentheses in the original language. Where it has been possible, I have used existing translations and referred to them. In many cases, where no translation exists, I have made one myself. Only in the footnotes have I allowed myself to supply quotations in other languages, mostly German.

It has been impossible to do justice to everyone involved in the Son of man debate. Through selection and proportion, I have tried to indicate which contributions proved to be innovative and which for other reasons made an impact on research. In many cases, the reference is reduced to a mention of the title in a footnote. If I have misrepresented—or misplaced—any, I apologize. I am only too aware of the unevenness of reference to position, place, and date of scholars and other authors, but I found it more reasonable to offer the information I had access to than to leave it out for the sake of convenience.

A book of this nature would be impossible without libraries and especially librarians. We are fortunate at the Theological Faculty at the University of Copenhagen not only to have a relatively large library, but also to have librarians whose helpfulness in procuring books and articles, not only from Danish libraries but from all over Europe and the United States, has been extraordinary. For this and for their kindness, even in case of longer lists of desiderata, I offer my warm thanks to the leading librarian, Bodil Glenstrup, and the two assistant librarians, Katrine Raatz and Anne Nørgaard-Pedersen.

Of course, I also want to thank my employer of the past nearly 25 years, the Department of Biblical Studies. My teacher, professor, dr.theol. Niels Hyldahl, became not only my colleague but also a dear friend to my wife, Lisbet, and me, a friendship which also includes his wife, Sol. Niels Hyldahl also has been of great help during the preparation of this book, not least through reading the manuscript critically and giving much good advice. Therefore it is only an obvious and dear thing for me to dedicate this work to him.

Last but not least, I want to thank my Old Testament colleague, Professor Thomas L. Thompson, for accepting the manuscript for publication in the Copenhagen International Series, and the Reverend Jim West, ThD, of Petros, Tennessee, for having revised and improved my English. Finally, I wish to thank my faculty and its dean, Professor, dr.theol. Steffen Kjeldgaard-Pedersen, for granting a substantial amount of funding to this project.

Allehelgen/All Saints, 5 November 2006[1]

1. Because of a delay in publishing, it has been possible to include a series of references to books and articles from 2006 and 2007.

Abbreviations

AAR	American Academy of Religion
AB	Anchor Bible
ABD	*Anchor Bible Dictionary*
ABR	*Australian Biblical Review*
AcOr	*Acta Orientalia*
AnBib	Analecta Biblica
ANF	Ante-Nicene Fathers
ANRW	*Aufstieg und Niedergang der römischen Welt*
ANTI	Arbeiten zum Neuen Testament und Judentum
ANVAO	Avhandlinger i norske videnskapsakademi i Oslo
ASNU	Acta Seminarii Neotestamentici Upsaliensis
ASThI	*Annual of the Swedish Theological Institute*
ATD	Altes Testament Deutsch
AThANT	Abhandlungen zur Theologie des Alten und Neuen Testaments
AThD	Acta Theologica Danica
AThR	*Anglican Theological Review*
BBB	Bonner Biblische Beiträge
BBR	Bulletin of Biblical Research
BEThL	Bibliotheca Ephemeridum Theologicarum Lovaniensium
BEvTh	Beiträge zur evangelischen Theologie
BFChTh	Beiträge zur Förderung christlicher Theologie
BHH	Biblisch-historisches Handwörterbuch
Bib.	*Biblica*
BiTod	*The Bible Today*
BiTr	*Bible Translator*
BJRL	*The Bulletin of John Rylands Library*
BR	*Biblical Review*
BS	*Bibliotheca Sacra*
BSNTS	*Bulletin of the Studiorum Novi Testamenti Societas*
BThB	*Biblical Theology Bulletin*
BThS	Biblisch-theologische Studien
BuK	*Bibel und Kirche*
BVC	*Bible et vie chrétienne*
BWANT	Beiträge zur Wissenschaft vom Alten und Neuen Testament
BZ	*Biblische Zeitschrift*

BZAW	Beihefte zur Zeitschrift für die alttestamentliche Wissenschaft
BZNW	Beihefte zur Zeitschrift für die neutestamentliche Wissenschaft
CAT	Commentaire de l'Ancien Testament
CBQ	*Catholic Biblical Quarterly*
DBM	*Deltion Biblikon Meleton*
DDD	*Dictionary of Deities and Demons in the Bible.* Edited by Karel van der Toorn, Bob Becking and Pieter W. van der Horst (Leiden: Brill, 1995, 2nd ed. 1999)
DissAbstr	Dissertation Abstracts
DTT	*Dansk Teologisk Tidsskrift*
EdF	Erträge der Forschung
EHPhR	Études d'histoire et de philosophie religieuses
ET	*The Expository Times*
EThL	*Ephemerides Theologicae Lovanienses*
EThR	*Études théologiques et religieuses*
EvQ	*Evangelical Quarterly*
EvTh	*Evangelische Theologie*
Exp	*The Expositor*
FRLANT	Forschungen zur Religion und Literatur des Alten und Neuen Testaments
FS	Festschrift
FzB	Forschungen zur Bibel
GGA	*Göttingische Gelehrte Anzeigen*
GCS	Die griechischen christlichen Schriftsteller der ersten drei Jahrhunderten
HBTh	*Horizons of Biblical Theology*
HNT	Handbuch zum Neuen Testament
HSM	Harvard Semitic Monographs
HThKNT	Herders theologischer Kommentar zum Neuen Testament
HThR	*Harvard Theological Review*
HUCA	Hebrew Union College Annual
HUTh	Hermeneutische Untersuchungen zur Theologie
ICC	The International Critical Commentary
IDBSup	*Interpreter's Dictionary of the Bible. Supplement*
IKZ	*Internationale Kirchliche Zeitschrift*
Interp.	*Interpretation*
IThQ	*Irish Theological Quarterly*
JBL	*Journal of Biblical Literature*
JBTh	Jahrbuch für Biblische Theologie
JEThS	*Journal of the Evangelical Theological Society*
JJS	*Journal of Jewish Studies*
JNSL	*Journal of North West Semitic Languages*
JPTh	*Jahrbücher für protestantische Theologie*
JR	*Journal of Religion*
JSHRZ	Jüdische Schriften aus hellenistisch-römischer Zeit
JSJ	*Journal for the Study of Judaism*

JSJSup	Journal for the Study of Judaism. Supplements
JSNT	*Journal for the Study of the New Testament.*
JSNTSup	Journal for the Study of the New Testament. Supplement Series
JSOT	*Journal for the Study of the Old Testament*
JSOTSup	Journal for the Study of the Old Testament. Supplement Series
JSP	*Journal for the Study of the Pseudepigrapha*
JThS	*Journal of Theological Studies*
KAT	Kommentar zum Alten Testament
KAV	Kommentar zu den Apostolischen Vätern
KHC	Kurzer Hand-Commentar zum Alten Testament
KEK	Kritisch-exegetischer Kommentar zum Neuen Testament (Meyer)
KNT	Kommentar zum Neuen Testament (Zahn)
KuD	*Kerygma und Dogma*
LCL	The Loeb Classical Library
LThK	*Lexikon für Theologie und Kirche*
LUÅ	Lunds Universitets Årsskrift
LV	*Lumière et Vie*
MGWJ	*Monatschrift für Geschichte und Wissenschaft des Judentums*
MPG	Migne's Patrologia Graeca
MPL	Migne's Patrologia Latina
NedThT	*Nederlands Theologisch Tijdschrift*
NF	Neue Folge
NKZ	*Neue Kirchliche Zeitschrift*
n.s./N.S	novae seriae/new series/Neue Serie
NT	*Novum Testamentum*
NTA	Neutestamentliche Abhandlungen
NTA	*New Testament Abstracts*
NTD	Neues Testament Deutsch
NThT	*NieuwTheologisch Tijdschrift*
NTS	*New Testament Studies*
NTT	*Norsk Teologisk Tidsskrift*
NTTS	New Testament Tools and Studies
OBO	Orbis biblicus et orientalis
OrSuec	Orientalia Suecana
OTA	*Old Testament Abstracts*
OTS	*Oudtestamentische Studiën*
PKZ	*Protestantische Kirchenzeitung*
PrM	*Protestantische Monatshefte*
RB	*Revue Biblique*
RdQ	*Revue de Qumran*
RE	Realenzyklopädie für protestantische Theologie und Kirche
RGG	Die Religion in Geschichte und Gegenwart
RHPR	*Revue d'histoire et de philosophie religieuses*
RSR	*Recherches des science religieuse*
RThR	*Reformed Theological Review*
RV	Religionsgeschichtliche Volksbücher

SBAB	Stuttgarter Biblische Aufsätzbände
SBL	Society of Biblical Literature
SBLDS	Society of Biblical Literature. Dissertation Series
SBLMS	Society of Biblical Literature. Monograph Series
SBLSP	Society of Biblical Literature. Seminar Papers
SBS	Stuttgarter Bibelstudien
SBTh	Studies in Biblical Theology
SBU	Svenskt Bibliskt Uppslagsverk
SCSt	Septuagint and Cognate Studies
SE	*Studia Evangelica*
SémiotBib	*Sémitiotique Biblique*
Ser.	series
SEÅ	*Svensk Exegetisk Årsbok*
SgV	Sammlung gemeinverstädnlicher Vorträge
SHAW	Sitzungsberichte der Heidelberger Akademie der Wissenschaften
SHVL	Skrifter utgivna av k. humanistiska vetenskapssamfundet i Lund
SJLA	Studies in Judaism in Late Antiquity
SJTh	*Scottish Journal of Theology*
SMHVL	Scripta Minora. Kungl. Humanistiska Vetenskapssamfundet i Lund
SNT	Studien zum Neuen Testament
SNTSMS	Society for New Testament Studies. Monograph Series
SNTU	Studien zum Neuen Testament und seiner Umwelt
SS	Second Series
SThU	*Schweizerische Theologische Umschau*
STK	*Svensk Teologisk Kvartalskrift*
StPB	Studia Post-Biblica
STRT	Studia theologica Rheno-Traiectina
StTh	*Studia Theologica*
SUNT	Studien zur Umwelt des Neuen Testaments
SyBU	Symbolae Biblicae Upsaliensis
TANZ	Texte und Arbeiten zum neutestamentlichen Zeitalter
TA-TT	*Teologinen Aikakauskirja-Teologisk Tidsskrift*
TAik	*Teologninen Aikakauskirja*
ThB	Theologische Bücherei
ThBNT	Theologisiches Begriffslexikon zum Neuen Testament
ThDNT	*Theological Dictionary of the New Testament*
ThF	Theologische Forschung
ThLZ	*Theologische Literaturzeitung*
ThQ	*Theologische Quartalschrift*
ThR	*Theologische Rundschau*
ThRv	*Theologische Revue*
ThStKr	Theologische Studien und Kritiken
ThT	*Theologisch Tijdschrift*
ThWANT	*Theologische Wörterbuch zum Alten Testament*
ThWNT	*Theologisches Wörterbuch zum Neuen Testament*
ThZ	*Theologische Zeitschrift*

TRE	Theologische Realenzyklopädie
TTK	*Tidsskrift for Teologi og Kirke*
TU	Texte und Untersuchungen
USQR	*Union Seminary Quarterly Review*
VF	*Verkündigung und Forschung*
VT	*Vetus Testamentum*
VTSup	Vetus Testamentum. Supplements
WA	Weimarer Ausgabe (Luther)
WdF	Wege der Forschung
WThJ	*Westminster Theological Journal*
WUNT	Wissenschaftliche Untersuchungen zum Neuen Testament
ZAC	*Zeitschrift für Antiken und Christentum*
ZAW	*Zeitschrift für die alttestamentliche Wissenschaft*
ZNW	*Zeitschrift für die neutestamentliche Wissenschaft*
ZThK	*Zeitschrift für Theologie und Kirche*
ZWTh	*Zeitschrift für wissenschaftliche Theologie*

Introduction

The shifting understanding of the New Testament expression 'Son of man' through the history of the Church reflects the changing interpretations of the meaning of Jesus of Nazareth in an interesting way. It also reveals shifts in presuppositions for this understanding. The history of the meaning of this expression constitutes an important chapter in the development of Christology.

1. *The Evidence*

Since interest in the historical Jesus arose in the seventeenth century, the expression has often been made the key to Jesus' self-understanding. With some 80 occurrences in the canonical gospels—c. 50 if parallels are not counted—not only is Son of man the expression obviously preferred by Jesus for himself, but it also has nearly maintained a monopoly in sayings in which the evangelists' Jesus declares the content and impact of his messianic task. On the other hand, the expression never turns up in confessional formulas, as, for example, 'Jesus is the Son of man'. Nor is it found in a predicative form, such as 'Jesus, the Son of man'. Apart from Acts 7.56 and the apparent exception of Jn 12.34, the expression, with its characteristic two definite articles (ὁ υἱὸς τοῦ ἀνθρώπου), only occurs in the New Testament on the lips of Jesus. Of the four places in the New Testament where we find it in an indefinite form, only one is in the gospels: Jn 5.27. The three others, Heb. 2.6 (quoting Ps. 8.5) and Rev. 1.13 and 14.14, belong to a different semantic context.

In a dictionary article from 1902, Samuel Rolles Driver established the fact that, 'in considering the *meaning* of the title, it ought to be clearly understood that it is not anywhere *explained* in the New Testament, so that whatever view of it be adopted is based on conjecture and inference'.[1] On the other hand, in the New Testament gospels the expression is used as a matter of course in a way that seems to preclude that it presented any

1. S.R. Driver, 'Son of Man', *Dictionary of the Bible*, IV (1902), p. 584.

difficulties to the evangelists. At the same time, the expression does not seem to be connected with a fixed set of conceptions within the New Testament itself. There is no obvious point of departure for understanding. This raises the question as to whether there is a connection with a distinguishable Son of man tradition outside the New Testament one, which had been presupposed by Jesus or by the authors behind the New Testament gospels.

The Greek expression ὁ υἱὸς τοῦ ἀνθρώπου, with two definite articles, is unknown outside the New Testament and literature dependent on it. The indefinite form, υἱὸς ἀνθρώπου, is only known in pre-Christian times from the Greek translation of the Old Testament, the Septuagint, where it occurs 108 times, 93 of which are in the book of Ezekiel in God's address to the prophet.[2] In other places, the expression appears in most cases in parallelism with ἄνθρωπος.[3] In the Apocrypha, we find it only in Jud. 8.16 and Ecclus 17.20, both referencing Num. 23.19. In the Greek Pseudepigrapha, it occurs in *Testaments of the Twelve Patriarchs*, *Testament of Joseph* 2, and *Joseph and Asenath* 18.9. The plural—in both indefinite and definite forms—is found forty times.[4] There are, however, a number of analogous expressions. They all point in the direction of a rather clear generic understanding.

Coming from the Old Testament, one would expect this to be the case in the New as well. One circumstance, here immediately calling for attention, is the conspicuous double determination, literally '*the* son of *the* man' (ὁ υἱὸς τοῦ ἀνθρώπου). The decisive question is whether this singular way of speaking confers a special meaning to the expression. In Mk 3.28 ('Everything will be forgiven the sons of men', πάντα ἀφεθήσεται τοῖς υἱοῖς τῶν ἀνθρώπων'; cf. the parallel Mt. 12.31, ἀφεθήσεται τοῖς ἀνθρώποις) and in Eph. 3.5 ('Not disclosed to the sons of men', οὐκ ἐγνωρίσθη τοῖς υἱοῖς τῶν ἀνθρώπων), an article is attached to the plural form. It suffices that any postulated difference between the singular and the plural form should be substantiated.

2. Besides the 93 occurrences in Ezekiel, the expression is found in Num. 23.19; Isa. 51.12; 56.2; Jer. 49.18, 33; 50.40; 51.43; Dan. 8.17; Pss 8.5; 79.16, 18; 143.3; Job 16.21; 25.6; 35.8. Except for Ps. 143.3 (MT 144.3), where it renders בן־אנוש, the Hebrew is בן־אדם in all places.

3. Only Isa. 56.2 translates the singular בן־אדם with the simple ἄνθρωπος and only Prov. 15.11 renders the plural בני־אדם with ἀνθρώποι, which Dan. 2.38 uses to render בני־אנשא. In Isa. 53.3, Vaticanus and Lucian read τοὺς υἱοὺς τῶν ἀνθρώπων instead of πάντας ἀνθρώπους, while, e.g., Sinaiticus reads πάντας τοὺς υἱοὺς τῶν ἀνθρώπων.

4. Gen. 11.5; 1 Kgs 26.19; 3 Kgs 8.39, Pss 4.3; 11.2, 9; 13.2; 32.13; 35.8; 52.3; 56.5; 57.2; 61.10(bis); 65.5; 88.48; 89.3; 106.8, 15, 21, 31; 113.24; 144.12; 145.3; Eccl. 1.13; 2.3, 8; 3.10, 18, 19, 21; 8.11; 9.3, 12; Jer. 39.19; Ezek. 31.14; Mic. 5.7; Joel 1.12; Dan. 3.82, and in the Apocrypha Ecclus 36.28, all describing the human race in its weakness before God.

The Gospel of Mark contains fourteen Son of man sayings.[5] Among sayings where Mark's Jesus speaks about his authority, fate and future, only Mk 2.17 lacks the expression Son of man, but it does not turn up in the parallels Mt. 9.13 and Lk. 5.32 either.[6] The same is true of 14.28, where it is also lacking in the parallel Mt. 26.32.

Matthew contains thirty Son of man sayings in all.[7] Thirteen occurrences are taken from Mark and seventeen are new. Only in the parallel to Mk 8.31 does Matthew leave the expression out, changing direct speech to indirect. The one place where Mark lacks the expression in comparison to Matthew, its presence in Mt. 16.13 is more remarkable than its absence in Mk 8.27. Of sayings which could have used the expression, it seems only possible to single out 5.17; 9.13 (cf. Mk 2.17; Lk. 5.32); 10.34 (cf. Lk. 12.51) and 15.24.

Six of the Son of man sayings are special to Matthew.[8] Four times Matthew has inserted the expression in sayings taken from Mark.[9] The expression turns up seven times in sayings with parallels in Luke but without parallels in Mark.[10]

Nine of the 25 Lukan Son of man sayings[11] are taken from Mark, while nine are peculiar to Luke.[12] Seven occurrences have parallels only in Matthew.[13] Three Lukan Son of man sayings have parallels in Matthew, though Matthew's version omits the expression.[14] In six places Luke omits the words Son of man, while they are found in the parallels in Mark and Matthew.[15]

5. See Table 1 at the end of the *Introduction*.

6. For the evidence from the gospels, cf. the relevant passages in M. Müller, *Der Ausdruck 'Menschensohn' in den Evangelien* (1984).

7. See Table 2 at the end of the *Introduction*.

8. 10.23; 13.37, 41; 24.30; 25.31; 26.2.

9. 12.32 (Mk 3.28); 16.13 (Mk 8.27); 16.28 (Mk 9.1); 26.2 (Mk 14.1).

10. 8.20 (Lk. 9.58); 11.19 (Lk. 7.34); 12.32 (Lk. 12.10); 12.40 (Lk. 11.30, in another context, reminding of Mt. 24.30a); 24.27 (Lk. 17.24); 24.37 (Lk. 17.26); 24.44 (Lk. 12.40).

11. See Table 3 at the end of the *Introduction*.

12. 6.22; 12.8; 17.22, 30; 18.8; 19.10; 21.36; 22.48; 24.7.

13. 7.34 (Mt. 11.19); 9.58 (Mt. 8.20); 11.30 (Mt. 12.40; a changed context has altered the meaning); 12.10 (Mt. 12.32); 12.40 (Mt. 24.44); 17.24 (Mt. 24.27); 17.26 (Mt. 24.37).

14. 6.22 (Mt. 5.11); 12.8 (Mt. 10.32) and 24.7 (Mt. 28.6).

15. 9.18 (replacing it with με, Mt. 16.13 having Son of man, Mk 8.27 not); 9.36 (quite a different formulation than Mk 9.9; Mt. 17.9); 17.27 (quite a different construction than Mt. 24.39); 22.22b (impersonal construction, where both Mk 14.21b, Mt. 26.24b have Son of man); 22.27 (ἐγώ, where both Mk 10.45 and Mt. 20.28 have Son of man); 22.30 (Mt. 19.28 has quite another wording).

Passages where Son of man could have been expected are more numerous in Luke than in Mark and Matthew.[16] The author of the Gospel of Luke apparently felt freer than the authors behind the Gospels of Mark and Matthew in allowing Jesus to speak of his vocation and fate in Son of man sayings. This impression is strengthened by the observation that some Lukan Son of man sayings bear a different character than the Markan and Matthean. In 17.22, Son of man figures in an almost predicative way, while in 18.31, in the Passion prediction, a reference to the writings of the prophets is inserted (cf. Mk 14.21a = Mt. 26.24a). The phrase in 21.36, 'to stand in the presence of the Son of man', seems a new way to express a position of heavenly power. Finally, 24.7 is unique in the Synoptic tradition, allowing the expression in an indirect saying, whereby it bears another value and forms a connection to the one and only Son of man saying outside the gospels: Acts 7.56, where Stephen speaks of Jesus as the Son of man.

The Gospel of John indicates that the expression Son of man could function in a tradition extensively formulating its Christology through an independent creation of Jesus-sayings. In John, however, Son of man interacts together with a number of other Jesus-designations, although without unequivocally becoming a christological title. All thirteen Johannine Son of man sayings[17] are without Synoptic parallel. On the other hand, there are parallel formulations for twelve[18] of the thirteen sayings within the Gospel of John itself, where the expression is absent. The exception is 1.51.[19]

With regard to the Gospel of John, it does not make sense to investigate the almost innumerable cases where the expression could have been used. Remarkable is 5.27, where the expression stands without the definite articles. The picture of the use of Son of man in John appears in an exemplary way in John 6.[20] It is never used in sayings where Jesus identifies himself with a noun. For this reason it is not found in the three 'I am' (ἐγώ εἰμι) sayings in vv. 35, 48 and 51 (just as it is not found in the rest of the 'I am' sayings in this gospel). Nor does it turn up in sayings with 'the Father' as subject and is missing in v. 29, vv. 27, 53 and 62 being the only other places in ch. 6, where the expression could have been expected. Neither is it found in sayings where Jesus is made the object, without any further indication. This is seen when comparing v. 62 and v. 40, where 'Son' could have been

16. 4.43; 5.32; 10.22; 12.49, 51; 17.25; 22.15; 24.26, 44, 46; perhaps also 13.32, 33, 34; 21.6; 22.18, 27.

17. In Jn 11.4, a single late witness (0250) reads Son of man instead of Son of God. It would not appear unnatural if 2.25 had been a Son of man saying!

18. 3.13, 14; 5.27; 6.27, 53, 62; 8.28; 9.35; 12.23, 34a, 34b; 13.31.

19. Cf. J. Jeremias, 'Die älteste Schicht der Menschensohn-Logien', *ZNW* 58 (1967), pp. 159-72 (163).

20. Cf. M. Müller, '"Have You Faith in the Son of Man?" (John 9.35)', *NTS* 37 (1991), pp. 291-94 (294).

replaced by 'Son of man'. The expression is used exclusively in general statements, in what could be called theses, but not in conclusions drawn from them (as, for instance, in v. 54).

In these introductory remarks, it should be noted that although a few Son of man sayings are introduced with reference to Scripture (Mk 9.12; 14.21a [= Mt. 26.24b]; Lk. 18.31),[21] none form a quotation. It would be very difficult to point to a specific place in Scripture to determine their content. There is no obvious connection between the expression Son of man and these scriptural references. On the other hand, the at times obvious allusions to Dan. 7.13 (e.g. Mk 13.26 and 14.62 with parallels) are never introduced as quotations. Apparently, it was not so much the expression itself as what is related in Dan. 7.13 about the one like a Son of man which was of interest. As we will see, Justin Martyr is the first to ascertain this reference explicitly, thereby pointing to what in modern times for many was to become the very key to unlocking the meaning of the expression.

2. *The Purpose of this Investigation*

This short sketch of the biblical evidence confirms the claim of S.R. Driver that the meaning of the expression Son of man is not explained anywhere in the New Testament. It is not even established that it was perceived as a title. The following chapters attempt to write the history of the conjectures and inferences made in the interpretation of the expression Son of man through the centuries, relating the conjectures and inferences to the developments in christological thinking.

It is a matter of course that such an undertaking is marked by the preferences of the author. In any event, an agenda is needed if the presentation is not to be amorphous. The *a priori* understanding of the present author is that the expression in the New Testament Gospels is not a title, but originates as a neutral circumlocution for the person speaking.

In spite of the vast Son of man literature, no satisfactorily complete account of the fate of the expression in the history of interpretation is available.[22] There exists a series of articles analyzing shorter periods of this

21. Interestingly, all of these sayings have parallels without reference to Scripture.

22. The first comprehensive exposition of the history of interpretation is found in W. Scholten, *De appellatione ὁ υἱὸς τοῦ ἀνθρώπου, qua Iesus se messiam professus est* (1809). Around 1900, some monographs offer overviews by way of introduction of the interpretion from the patristic literature up to their own time; these included, for instance, H. Appel, *Die Selbstbezeichnung Jesu: Der Sohn des Menschen* (1896), pp. 1-27; H. Lietzmann, *Der Menschensohn* (1896), pp. 1-28; J. Mouren, *Le Fils de l'Homme. Étude historique et critique* (1903), pp. 1-32; P. Tillmann, *Der Menschensohn. Jesu Selbstzeugniß für seine messianische Würde. Eine biblisch-theologische Untersuchung* (1907), pp. 9-60.

history.[23] The only recently published monograph, Delbert Royce Burkett's *The Son of Man Debate: A History and Evaluation* (1999), is too much a catalogue of different opinions, without sufficient regard for their interaction with the christological thinking through the ages.[24] This desideratum required a new and more comprehensive attempt.[25]

The evidence from the Synoptic Gospels is as follows:

Table 1. *Son of Man Sayings in Mark as Compared with Matthew and Luke*

2.10	= Mt. 9.6	= Lk. 5.24
2.28	= Mt. 12.8	= Lk. 6.5
8.31	= (Mt. 16.21)	= Lk. 9.22
8.38	= Mt. 16.27	= Lk. 9.26
9.9	= Mt. 17.9	= (Lk. 9.36)
9.12	= Mt. 17.12	
9.31	= Mt. 17.22	= Lk. 9.44
10.33	= Mt. 20.18	= Lk. 18.31
10.45	= Mt. 20.28	= (Lk. 22.27)
13.26	= Mt. 24.30b	= Lk. 21.27

23. Cf. Chapter 13 n. 6 and 7.

24. It also suffers from other substantial deficiencies, being sometimes too much influenced by the author's preferences and lacking precision. Other written accounts suffer from not being published. This is the case for instance with the otherwise valuable investigations of Christoph Weist, *Wer ist dieser Menschensohn? Die Geschichte der Exegese zum Menschensohn-Begriff* (dissertation from Vienna, 1972), and Werner Bracht, *Der Menschensohn. Eine Untersuchung zum Bedeutungswandel und zur Geschichte der Auslegung und der Erforschung des neutestamentlichen Begriffs* (dissertation from Munich, 1972). Bracht offers both an interpretation and a history of interpretation, the treatment of the patristic material being especially extensive, while the Reformation and onwards is dealt with more succinctly. According to a prefatory remark (p. VI), dated 1986, the manuscript was made ready for publication in 1973 in the series *Biblische Untersuchungen*, but this could not be completed. The dissertation was made available only in typewritten form to fulfil the obligation of publication. It was not possible to get hold of a bound copy in the 1970s, when I began working with the theme. In 2005, however, I was finally able to access the dissertation in the form of a not always easily readable microfiche, the original having disappeared from the University Library in Munich. I owe many references to these two dissertations, not least with regard to patristic and medieval literature. Burkett's work contains several references to older literature—often directly taken over from W. Scholten's exposition—and also includes newer works not figuring in my account. An element of imprecision will always be present when deciding whether or not an item of the vast secondary literature should be examined. The use of 'Son of Man' or one of its equivalents in a work's title cannot be used as the sole guiding principle for its inclusion.

25. A preliminary sketch is found in M. Müller, 'Menneskesønnen og teologihistorien. En kristologisk titels opståen og fald', *Collegium Biblicum Årsskrift 2001* (2001), pp. 31-48.

14.21a	= Mt. 26.24a	= Lk. 22.22a
14.21b	= Mt. 26.24b	= (Lk. 22.22b)
14.41	= Mt. 26.45	
14.62	= Mt. 26.64	= Lk. 22.69

Table 2. *Son of Man Sayings in Matthew as Compared with Mark and Luke*[26]

8.20		= Lk. 9.58
9.6	= Mk 2.10	= Lk. 5.24
10.23		
11.19		= Lk. 7.34
12.8	= Mk 2.18	= Lk. 6.5
12.32	= (Mk 3.28)	= Lk. 12.10
12.40		= Lk. 11.30 (changed context)
13.37		
13.41		
16.13	= (Mk 8.27)	= (Lk. 9.18)
16.27	= Mk 8.38	= Lk. 9.26
16.28	= (Mk 9.1)	= Lk. 9.27*
17.9	= Mk 9.9	= (Lk. 9.36)
17.12	= Mk 9.12	
17.22	= Mk 9.31	= Lk. 9.44
19.28		= (Lk. 22.30)
20.18	= Mk 10.33	= Lk. 18.31
20.28	= Mk 10.45	= (Lk. 22.27)
24.27		= Lk. 17.24
24.30a		= (Lk. 11.30)?
24.30b	= Mk 13.26	= Lk. 21.27
24.37		= Lk. 17.26
24.39		= (Lk. 17.27)
24.44		= Lk. 12.40
25.31		
26.2	= (Mk 14.1)	= (Lk. 22.1)
26.24a	= Mk 14.21a	= Lk. 22.22a
26.24b	= Mk 14.21b	= (Lk. 22.22b)
26.45	= Mk 14.41	
26.64	= Mk 14.62	= Lk. 22.69

26. Text-critically questionable and therefore left out are 18.11 (= Lk. 19.10 + 9.56*) and 25.13 (= 24.44). An asterisk (*) indicates that the saying is text-critically questionable.

Table 3. *Son of Man Sayings in Luke as Compared with Matthew and Mark*[27]

5.24	= Mt. 9.6	= Mk 2.10
6.5	= Mt. 12.8	= Mk 2.28
6.22	= (Mt. 5.11)	
7.34	= Mt. 11.19	
9.22	= (Mt. 16.21)	= Mk 8.31
9.26	= Mt. 16.27	= Mk 8.38
9.44	= Mt. 17.22	= Mk 9.31
9.58	= Mt. 8.20	
11.30	(changed context, cf. Mt. 24.30)	
12.8	= (Mt. 10.32)	
12.10	= Mt. 12.32	= (Mk 3.28)
12.40	= Mt. 24.44	
17.22		
17.24	= Mt. 24.27	
17.26	= Mt. 24.37	
17.30		
18.8		
18.31	= Mt. 20.18	= Mk 10.33
19.10	= Mt. 18.11*	
21.27	= Mt. 24.30b	= Mk 13.26
21.36		
22.22a	= Mt. 26.24a	= Mk 14.21a
22.48	= (Mt. 26.49)	= (Mk 14.45)
22.69	= Mt. 26.64	= Mk 14.62
24.7	= (Mt. 28.6)	= (Mk 16.6)

27. Text-critically questionable and therefore left out are 9.27 (cf. Mt. 16.28) and 9.56 (cf. 19.10 and Mt. 18.11).

1. Early Church

The seeming obviousness of the use of the expression in the New Testament, that is, in the Gospels, stops almost immediately upon leaving them.[1] It is clear that its meaning changes. Apparently, it does not survive in continuous use but primarily in an interpretation of the Son of man sayings in the canonical Gospels.[2] The few examples of a use similar to the one found in the Gospels are exceptions which prove the rule. It comes to be understood genealogically, with a self-contained content. Very soon, the context becomes mostly polemical. Thus Irenaeus' treatment—and a little later Tertullian's—reflects the Gnostic interpretation which, in all its diversity, is uniform in that the genitive 'of man' is generally understood as referring to the divine Anthropos, an interpretation which has its own *ratio* and will therefore be treated separately (see below Chapter 2, 'The Son of Man in Gnosticism'). Besides these, there also exist examples of interpretations which take into account Son of man sayings in the Gospels and what is said about the Son of man. We see this expression in the Gospels about the Son of man introduced in different ways in the often ardent strife about the correct understanding of the nature of Christ and his role in redemption.

1. Bracht, *Der Menschensohn*, p. 405 (assuming Son of man in the Gospels to be a christological title with roots in Jewish apocalypticism and having an eschatological transcendent meaning), remarks that, except for the Gnostic use, most of the authors of this period represent 'die gleiche Auffassung dieses Ausdrucks' and continues: 'Das Merkwürdige dabei ist aber die Unbekümmertheit um seinen ursprünglichen Sinngehalt, der in manchen Perikopen der synoptischen Evangelien noch deutlich genug hervortritt; selbst die Verwendung der Daniel-Vision als christologische Weissagung schon bei Justin führt nicht mehr zu einer messianischen Interpretation des Titels'. This lack of expected continuity is based on a misunderstanding of its original meaning.

2. Cf. Bracht, *Der Menschensohn*, p. 398: 'Die altkirchliche Literatur kennt den Begriff MS [= Menschensohn] zunächst kaum, bis sie ihn durch die Evangelien neu kennenlernt und von einer ganz anderen dogmengeschichtlichen Basis aus neu interpretiert'.

1. *Apocryphal Sayings and the Apostolic Fathers*[3]

The above pertains less to the New Testament Apocrypha and agrapha, where it is difficult to distinguish between quotation and agraphon, as for instance in Clement of Alexandria, *Stromata* IV 6.35: 'The Son of man, on coming to-day, has found that which was lost'.[4]

Other places offer examples of a varied use.[5] In *Acts of John* 109, in eucharistic praise we find it as an apposition to 'the diadem': 'him that for us was called Son of man' (τὸν δι' ἡμᾶς λεχθέντα υἱὸν ἀνθρώπου); *Acts of Peter* 24 quotes Dan. 7.13, while *Acts of Thomas* 66 lets Thomas declare himself in contrast to Jesus to be only a human: 'For I also am a man clothed with a body, a son of man like one of you' (υἱὸς ἀνθρώπου ὡς εἷς ἐξ ὑμῶν); *Apocalypse of Peter* 1 quotes Mt. 24.27, while in *Apocalypse of Peter* 4 it introduces words from Ezek. 37.4 as prophesied by the Son of Man. None of these resembles the use in the New Testament Gospels.

Only in a few places outside the New Testament has the expression survived in apocalyptic sayings, as, for instance, in a saying which stems from James, the brother of Jesus, according to Hegesippus, giving Jesus' reaction to the question of the Scribes and Pharisees:[6]

> 'What is the gate of Jesus?' [cf. Jn 10.9]. And he answered with a loud voice, 'Why do ye ask me concerning [Jesus,][7] the Son of man (τί με ἐπερωτᾶτε περὶ τοῦ υἱοῦ τοῦ ἀνθρώπου)? He himself sitteth in heaven at the right hand of the great Power, and is about to come upon the clouds of heaven (καὶ αὐτὸς κάθηται ἐν τῷ οὐρανῷ ἐκ δεξιῶν τῆς μεγάλης δυνάμεως, καὶ μέλλει ἔρχεσθαι ἐπὶ τῶν νεφελῶν τοῦ οὐρανοῦ).'

The familiarity with texts such as Mk 14.62par. is obvious, the more so if the saying is understood as pointing to the exaltation and not the Parousia. The two parallel participles in the Gospel saying are replaced by two finite verbs (Matthew's 'you will see', ὄψεσθε, is left out) where 'sitteth' refers to the present time, while the Parousia appears in a separately in the future tense. There also seems to be a connection with Acts 7.56. At both places, a persecuted person speaks about the Son of man at the right hand of God.

3. Cf., on the rest of this chapter, Ch. Weist, *Wer ist dieser Menschensohn? Die Geschichte der Exegese zum Menschensohn-Begriff* (1972) pp. 3-16; Bracht, *Der Menschensohn*, pp. 405-17 (notes, pp. 521-33); pp. 464-81 (notes, pp. 574-83). Bracht offers the most extensive treatment of the patristic material and, as mentioned already, I owe much to his work.

4. Translation according to *ANF* 2.

5. The translations are from *The Apocryphal New Testament* (trans. M.R. James, 1924; reprint 1960).

6. Eusebius, *Historia ecclesiastica* II 23.13.

7. The name 'Jesus', included in the translation in *NPNF*, 2nd Series 1, is not in the Greek text, which has Son of Man as the direct object of the question.

Another example comes from the *Gospel to the Hebrews*, from a legend about a meeting between the risen Christ and the same James who 'had sworn that he would not eat bread from that hour wherein he had drunk the Lord's cup until he should see him risen again from among them that sleep'. The risen Christ invites him to supper with the words:

> 'Bring ye, saith the Lord, a table and bread', and immediately it is added, 'He took bread and blessed and brake and gave it unto James the Just and said unto him: My brother, eat thy bread, for the Son of Man is risen from among them that sleep (quia resurrexit Filius hominis a dormientibus).'[8]

The connection with New Testament tradition is obvious, for example, with Mk 14.22par and 8.31par. Both apocryphal sayings probably originate in the second century, the *Gospel to the Hebrews* being known to Hegesippus. There seems no need to take these two instances as evidence of a special Jewish Christian Son of man concept,[9] which is also found in the *Pseudo-Clementine Homilies* and *Recognitions*. The interpretation of the Son of man characteristic of this literature is not present in these sayings.[10]

As will be seen in the next chapter, there are a few instances of a similar, seemingly obvious use of Son of man in Gnostic sources, but the context indicates that it has a special meaning.

Otherwise, outside the New Testament, the expression always occurs with a definition or within an argument, if not directly interpreted.[11] Among the

8. The translation of the quotation, from Jerome, *De viris illustribus* 2, is from James' *The Apocryphal New Testament*.

9. H.-J. Schoeps, *Theologie und Geschichte des Judenchristentums* (1949), pp. 78-82, offers these two sayings as evidence for a special Ebionite apocalyptic-eschatological expectation connected to the 'title' Son of man, which made the 'title' useless for the Church. It presupposes more than what is said in the texts themselves. For a more reasonable judgment, see F.H. Borsch, *The Christian and Gnostic Son of Man* (1970), pp. 49-54. Contesting the existence of a special Jewish–Christian Son of man is also D.R.A. Hare, *The Son of Man Tradition* (1990), pp. 40-42.

10. E.g. C. Colpe, 'ὁ υἱὸς τοῦ ἀνθρώπου', *ThWNT*, VIII (1969), pp. 477-78. Weist, *Wer ist dieser Menschensohn?*, pp. 26-30, also takes these two sayings as indications of a certain Jewish Christian reception of the Son of man in the Gospel tradition: 'Das Judenchristentum hat die in der Urgemeinde herrschende Vorstellung über den Menschensohn wenn auch nicht in statischem Sinn bewahrt und konserviert, so doch ihre Tradition kenntnisreicher und sachgemäßer weitergeführt als dies in der rechtgläubigen Gemeinde, die sich endgültig hellenistischen Denken verschrieben hatte, der Fall war' (p. 26). But this estimation presupposes the existence of a concept which is not obvious in the two sayings which can be looked upon as reflecting the Gospel usage of the expression without any problems.

11. L. Bouyer, 'La notion christologique du Fils de l'Homme a-t-elle disparu dans la patristique greque?', *Melanges Bibliques* (FS A. Robert, 1957), pp. 519-30, only offers a negative answer to his own question, postulating that 'homme céleste' from 1 Cor. 15 is identical with Son of man. Where this idea turns up in the Church fathers, it is therefore the original christological Son of man conception, whereas the Son of man title itself is

Apostolic Fathers[12] it turns up once in the letters of Ignatius of Antioch (died c.110),[13] where in *Ephesians* 20.2, with regard to the breaking of the one bread, 'which is the medicine of immortality (φάρμακον ἀθανασίας)', the congregation is admonished to come together 'in one faith and in Jesus Christ, "who was in the family of David according to the flesh", the Son of Man and Son of God (τῷ υἱῷ ἀνθρώπου καὶ υἱῷ θεοῦ)'. In spite of the indefinite form, the saying seems to reflect the Gospel usage of the expression. On the other hand, it is also clearly understood as a designation for the human nature of Christ. The background should be seen in Rom. 1.3 or in the eventual source for the creedal formula there. Clearly, it is not a title, but a definition.[14]

The same seems true of the use of the expression in the expanded Georgian translation of *Didache* 16.8, with content which differs from the Greek text: 'Then this world will see our Lord Jesus Christ, the Son of man, who (at the same time) is Son of God, (as) coming on the clouds', and so on.[15] In spite of the connection with Mk 14.62par (and Dan. 7.13), the translator obviously felt it necessary to underline that Jesus is Son of God.[16]

This is not quite the case in the *Epistle of Barnabas*. Here, in 12.9, the unknown author points to what Moses said 'to Jesus the son of Naue, after giving him this name, when he sent him to spy out the land, "Take a book in thy hands and write what the Lord saith, that in the last day the Son of God shall tear up the roots of the whole house of Amalek"'. In 12.10, he then urges: 'See again Jesus, not as son of man, but as Son of God, but manifested in a type in the flesh' (ἴδε πάλιν Ἰησοῦς οὐχὶ υἱὸς ἀνθρώπου, ἀλλὰ υἱὸς τοῦ θεοῦ, τύπῳ δὲ ἐν σαρκί φανερωθείς). The expression does not designate the human nature of Christ, but Jesus as human, not with regard to one of his two natures, but exclusively in his human appearance.[17] Thus the

interpreted as meaning the opposite as in the Gospels, where it is not a counterpart to the title Son of God.

12. Text and translation according to LCL.

13. This early date of the death of Ignatius is disputed. R.M. Hübner, 'Thesen zur Echtheit und Datierung der sieben Briefe des Ignatius von Antiochien', *ZAC* 1 (1997), pp. 44-72, is reviving the old argument for a late date.

14. Cf. W. Bauer, *Die Briefe des Ignatius von Antiochia und der Polykarpbrief* (1920), p. 219: 'Die beiden Bezeichnungen Jesu als Menschensohn und Gottessohn werden aus der Doppelseitigkeit seines Wesens erklärt und auf seine beiden Naturen verteilt'.

15. Translated from the German in G. Peradse, 'Die "Lehre der zwölf Apostel" in der georgischen Überlieferung', *ZNW* 31 (1932), pp. 111-16 (116).

16. G. Peradse, 'Die "Lehre der zwölf Apostel"', p. 115, sees in the expansion 'die Spuren der Kämpfe für die Orthodoxie und das Chalcedonense'.

17. Lietzmann, *Der Menschensohn*, p. 58, remarks of Barn. 12.10: 'Wer das schrieb, der kannte den Ausdruck υἱὸς ἀνθρώπου nur in dem Sinne der LXX, nicht aber als Selbstbezeichnung Jesu und auch nicht als Titel der Messias'. Later, not least because of

Epistle of Barnabas (probably from c. 130) rejects, on the basis of Ps. 110.1 and Isa. 45.1, that Christ should be the son of David.

Already in the Apostolic Fathers, Son of man is perceived as an alternative to Son of God. 'Of man' has been ascribed a new and independent signification, qualifying the one so designated as of a different nature than indicated by the title Son of God. Such an understanding is, however, not obvious anywhere in the Gospels, where—with the possible exception of Jn 5.27—the expression never appears with a clear predicative meaning. This contrast, suggesting that Son of God and Son of man say something fundamentally different, became dominant in the interpretation in the following periods and was only neutralized where 'man' was taken as the god 'Man' as in Gnostic texts, the whole expression being seen as a circumlocution with a pronominal meaning or used simply as equivalent to Messiah.

Only if one believes that Son of man was a title with a concept behind it does one miss the expression in those places in the Apostolic Fathers which quote or allude to sayings in the canonical Gospels containing it. In that case, one could[18] point to sayings such as Barn. 15.5 (cf. Mt. 24.30-31; 26.64); 7.9 where Son of man is 'replaced' by Son of God; 12.5-7 (cf. Jn 3.14-15); 2 Clem. 2.7 (cf. Lk. 19.10; 1 Tim. 1.15); 3.2 (cf. Lk. 12.8) and *The Shepherd of Hermas* (*passim*).

2. *Justin and the Early Fathers*

For reasons of clarity, I have made a division in the patristic material at the beginning of the fourth century, allowing the council of Nicea to end the period of the early Fathers. The treatment of the contemporary Gnostic use is offered in the following chapter, before the discussion of the Nicene and Post-Nicene Fathers.

Justin Martyr (died c. 165) is the first to mention Dan. 7.13 explicitly as a prophecy concerning the (second) Parousia of Christ. In *Apology* I 51 and

P.W. Schmiedel, 'Der Name "Menschensohn" und das Messiasbewusstsein Jesu', *PrM* 2 (1898), pp. 252-67 (260), Lietzmann modified his view in, 'Zur Menschensohnfrage', *Theologische Arbeiten aus dem rheinischen wissenschaftlichen Prediger-Verein* NF 2 (1898), pp. 1-14 (8). Cf. also H. Windisch, *Der Barnabasbrief* (1920), p. 373: 'Der evangelische Titel ὁ υἱὸς τοῦ ἀνθρώπου braucht hier nicht desavouirt zu sein; wahrscheinlich ist υἱ. ἀ. hier = ἄνθρωπος ἐξ ἀνθρώπων'. Windisch refers to Justin, *Dialogue* 48-49. However, it is remarkable that the article lacks the genitive. F.R. Prostmeier, *Der Barnabasbrief* (1999), p. 444, also maintains: '"Menschensohn" ist nicht titular verwendet, sondern zielt auf eine Deutung Jesu, die υἱὸς ἀνθρώπου als ἄνθρωπος ἐξ ἀνθρώπων auffaßt'.

18. With Lietzmann, *Der Menschensohn*, pp. 57-59.

Dialogue with Trypho 31, where the whole of Dan. 7.9-28 is quoted,[19] Daniel's saying is used to illustrate how much greater the power of Christ will be at his return than during his earthly life.[20] In *Dialogue* 76 (cf. 79), Justin offers an explanation, stemming from his Logos Christology, as to why Daniel uses the phrase 'like a son of man':

> For when Daniel speaks of 'one like unto the Son of man' who received the everlasting kingdom, does he not hint at this very thing? For he declares that, in saying 'like unto the Son of man,' He appeared, and was man, but not of human seed[21] (ὡς υἱὸν ἀνθρώπου· τὸ γὰρ "ὡς υἱὸν ἀνθρώπου" εἶπειν, φαι-νόμενον μὲν καὶ γενόμενον ἄνθρωπον μηνύει, οὐκ ἐξ ἀνθρωπίνου δὲ σπέρματος ὑπάρχοντα δηλοῖ).

The same understanding apparently lies behind the description in *Apology* I 54.7 of how the demons tried to create a Messiah who could seduce mankind. Among other things, they could not make out 'whether He was the Son of God...or of man (υἱὸς θεοῦ ... ἢ ἀνθρώπου)' and gave out Bellephoron, 'a man born of man (ἄνθρωπον ἐξ ἀνθρώπων)'. But that exactly was what Christ was not.[22]

Justin is also the first to speculate about why Jesus used this expression. Justin understands the genitive as referring to a concrete person, and in *Dialogue* 100.3 he explains the use in the Passion prediction in Mt. 16.21:

> He said then that He was the Son of man (υἱὸν οὖν ἀνθρώπου ἑαυτὸν ἔλεγεν), either because of His birth by the Virgin, who was, as I said, of the family of David and Jacob and Isaac and Abraham; or because Adam[23] was the father both of Himself and of those who have been first enumerated from whom Mary derives her descent.[24]

19. Cf. also *Apology* I 32.1; *Dialogue* 14.8; 76.1; 79.2. Translation according to *ANF* 1.

20. Cf. *Dial.* 32. In *Apology* I 51.8-9, Justin wrongly introduces the quotation from Daniel as from Jeremiah. The Greek text of the quotation is also interesting, confused by him with Mt. 25.31: 'Ιδοὺ ὡς υἱὸς ἀνθρώπου ἔρχεται ἐπάνω τῶν νεφελῶν τοῦ οὐρανοῦ, καὶ οἱ ἄγγελοι αὐτοῦ σὺν αὐτῷ.

21. Although the indefinite form appears in the Greek text, the translation in *ANF* 1 puts a determination before Son of man.

22. Lietzmann, *Der Menschensohn*, p. 70, thinks that because Genesis does not use Son of man, one has to conclude, 'dass Justin die Formel als messianischen Titel kannte und als solchen den Dämonen in den Mund legte'. There is no reason to conclude that Justin should have known the expression as a messianic title.

23. The Greek text here in most manuscripts has 'Αβραάμ, but 'Αδάμ is attested in a single one and is sometimes preferred. Cf. the discussion, Bracht, *Der Menschensohn*, p. 527 n. 47.

24. Lietzmann, *Der Menschensohn*, pp. 70-71, finds that the Son of man in the Gospel quotation not 'schlechthin als Ausdruck der Niedrigkeit, sondern als Bezeichnung des leidenden Messias aufgefasst wird. Justin will sagen: when Jesus von seinem Leiden spricht, so nennt er sich mit guten Gründen ὁ υἱὸς τοῦ ἀνθρώπου, denn—was die

In Justin we see what was to become the two main issues in the discussion of the phrase's meaning; namely, first, that the expression refers to Dan. 7.13 with regard to Christ's second Parousia;[25] secondly, that it is to be understood as a predicative self-designation as used by Jesus concerning his genealogical descent from Mary. Among other things, this means that Son of man sayings, as we know them from the canonical Gospels, are almost entirely absent in the Church Fathers except in quotations. Remarkable also is the fact that the definite articles are normally missing[26]—ὁ υἱὸς τοῦ ἀνθρώπου is replaced by υἱὸς ἀνθρώπου[27]—only to turn up in a few places, particularly in Gnostic literature.

Irenaeus (died c. 200), bishop of Lyon, in his principal work, *Adversus haereses*,[28] from c. 180, like Justin,[29] often uses the expression Son of man about the human nature of Jesus Christ in contrast to his divine nature.[30] That the framework of its meaning is his teaching on recapitulation (ἀνακεφαλαίωσις) is indicated in *Adversus haereses* V 21.1,[31] where Irenaeus

Hauptsache ist—auch hierdurch bekundet er sich als Messias, weil damit auch seine Abstammung von David und Abraham angespielt wird, andrerseits ist der darinliegende Hinweis auf seine menschliche Herkunft, der ja allein seine Leidensfähigkeit verdankt, einem solchen Anspruch besonders angemessen.' It is difficult to imagine that Son of man in *Dialogue* 100.3 should indicate anything but his descendent from the Patriarchs and Mary.

25. Bracht, *Der Menschensohn*, p. 414, remarks that even if Justin in eight out of his twelve Son of man references quotes or alludes to Dan. 7.13, this saying is never related to his being the Messiah, but only to the virginal conception.

26. This does not pertain to quotations from the Gospels as in *Dialogue* 76.7; 100.3.

27. This is not possible to recognize in Latin translations and sources.

28. Translation according to *ANF* 1. Because of the differences in chapter division, references to the edition of Harvey are included.

29. Irenaeus also once quotes Justin as an authority against Marcion (IV 6.2 = Harvey II, p. 158).

30. According to Bracht, *Der Menschensohn*, pp. 527-28 n. 53, Irenaeus uses the expression Son of man 34 times in Books II to V of his *Adversus haereses*, in his argument against the heretics, and five times in Book I in his description of their systems. It is found, moreover, in two places in his later *Epideixis* or *Demonstratio praedicationis apostolicae* (34 and 36). Bracht, p. 531 n. 76, also lists nine New Testament quotations with Son of man in *Adversus haereses*: Mt. 26.24 (II 20.5 = Harvey I, p. 324); Acts 7.56 (III 12.13 = Harvey II, p. 68); Mk 8.31 (III 16.5 = Harvey II, p. 86); Mt. 16.13 (III 18.4 = Harvey II, p. 97); Lk. 18.8 (IV 32.11 = Harvey II, p. 265); Lk. 17.26 (IV 36.3 = Harvey II, p. 279); Mt. 13.41 (IV 40.2 = Harvey II, p. 302); Mt. 9.6 (V 17.2 = Harvey II, p. 370); Mt. 12.40 (V 31.1 = Harvey II, pp. 411-12).

31. Harvey II, p. 381. Cf. also V 21.2 (Harvey II, p. 383): 'et soluta est ea quæ fuereat in Adam præcepti Dei prævaricatio, per præceptum legis, quod servavit Filius Hominis non transgrediens præceptum Dei'.

also establishes a connection between Son of man and the Adam–Christ typology of Paul (Rom. 5.12-21; 1 Cor. 15.21-22, 45-49):

> and therefore does the Lord profess Himself to be the Son of man (et Dominus semetipsum Filium Hominis confitetur), comprising (recapitulans) in Himself that original man out of whom the woman was fashioned, in order that, as our species went down to death through a vanquished man, so we may ascend to life again through a victorious one.[32]

First and foremost, Son of man is employed by Irenaeus to stress, against the Gnostics, Jesus' becoming a real human. Repeatedly, it is formulated in such a way that the Son of God or the Word of God was made Son of man. In *Adversus haereses* III 16.3, it is said for the first time:[33]

> The Son of God being made the Son of man, that through Him we may receive the adoption—humanity sustaining, and embracing the Son of God (Filius Dei, Hominis Filius factus, ut per eum adoptionem percipiamus, portante homine, et capiente, et complectente Filium Dei).

As is the case in several places, Son of man defines the quality of the Son of God through which men may be adopted.[34]

In *Adversus haereses* III 16.7,[35] Irenaeus offers a sort of christological compendium, making the following statement about Christ:

> For He fulfils the bountiful and comprehensive will of His Father, inasmuch as He is Himself the Saviour of those who are saved and the Lord of those who are under authority and the God of all those things which have been formed, the only-begotten of the Father, Christ, who was announced and the Word of God, who became incarnate when the fulness of time had come,

32. O. Cullmann, *Die Christologie des Neuen Testaments* (1957, 3. Aufl., 1963), p. 195, thinks that, Irenaeus is here interpreting a Pauline concept of the Son of man: 'He was the only one of the ecclesiastical writers of the second century to grasp the depth of Paul's idea about the Son of Man'. The following statement is easier to understand: 'His entire Christology is dominated by the contrast between Adam and Christ, and he makes the only attempt in the whole history of doctrine to build a Christology on the concept "Man"' (quoted according to the English translation, *The Christology of the New Testament* [1959, 2nd edn, 1963], p. 189). Bracht, *Der Menschensohn*, p. 418, points to the difference in the use of the Adam–Christ parallel in Irenaeus and Paul: 'denn während Paulus von seiner Christozentrik her Adam als grundsätzlich negativen Faktor ansieht und bei dieser Rückschau Christus als das Gegenbild zum ersten Menschen als δεύτερος ἄνθρωπος bezeichnet, sieht Irenäus ein viel geschlosseneres heilsgeschichtliches System von Schöpfung und Erlösung, in den Christus als MS, und d.h. durch seine Inkarnation den Adam-Anfang aufgreifend rekapitulierte'.

33. Harvey II, p. 84. Also III 17.1 (Harvey II, p. 92); 18.3.4 (Harvey II, pp. 97-98); 18.6 (Harvey II, p. 100); 19.2-3 (Harvey II, pp. 103-104).

34. Also III 10.2 (Harvey II, p. 34); 19.1 (Harvey II, p. 103); 20.2 (Harvey II, p. 107).

35. Harvey II, p. 89.

> at which the Son of God had to become the Son of Man (et Verbum Dei incarnatus, cum advenisset plenitudo temporis, in quo Filium Hominis fieri oportebat Filium Dei).

The context indicates that Son of man stands not as a title, but as a declaration of the true humanity of Christ.[36] Later (18.3.4), Irenaeus practically equates Son of man and Christ and Son of God in his emphasizing of Christ, making it evident 'who it was that suffered',

> indicating that the impassible Christ did not descend upon Jesus, but that He Himself, because He was Jesus Christ, suffered for us. He, who lay in the tomb, and rose again, who descended and ascended—the Son of God having been made the Son of man, as the very name itself doth declare (quemadmodum et ipsum nomen significat)... For when He asked the disciples: 'Who do men say that I, the Son of man, am?' and when Peter had replied [with his confession] he made it clear that He, the Son of man, is Christ, the Son of the living God (manifestum fecit, quoniam Filius Hominis hic est Christus Filius Dei vivi).[37]

But this is done in a way which could be summarized in the sentence: 'Christ is the Son of man'.

In *Adversus haereses* III 16.5,[38] in the context of a Passion prediction, it is maintained that the 'Gospel...knew no other son of man but Him who was of Mary, who also suffered' (Non...alterum Filium Hominis novit Evangelium, nisi hunc ex Mary); and no Christ flew away from Jesus before the passion'. And again, in III 19.3,[39] it is said that Son of man is also an indication of Christ's human nature, pointing to Mary as the one from whom he has received it. The statement occurs in the context of a description of the functions of the two natures:

> He therefore, the Son of God, our Lord, being the Word of the Father, and the Son of man, since He had a generation as to His human nature from Mary—who was descended from mankind, and who was herself a human being—was made the Son of man (quoniam ex Mary, quæ ex hominibus habebat genus,

36. Weist, *Wer ist dieser Menschensohn?*, p. 11, thinks that Son of man is not reckoned 'zu den Würde- und Hoheitsprädikaten' (although his argument from the writing 'filius hominis' with small letters is not convincing). 'Diese vierfache Gleichsetzung läßt sich nach entsprechender Zuordnung der einzelnen Begriffe im Sinn einer Christologie "von oben" und einer Christologie "von unten", nämlich "Sohn Gottes" und "Wort des Vaters" einerseits, sowie andererseits "unser Herr" und "Sohn des Menschen", wiederum reduzieren allein auf die beiden Faktoren "Filius Dei" und "filius hominis". Damit erhalten wir die beiden Seiten einer "Gottmensch"-Vorstellung, für die der Menschensohn-Begriff einmal mehr dazu dient, im Sinn der christlichen Doppelschemas die menschliche Eigenschaft des Erlösers zu erkennen.'

37. Harvey II, pp. 97, 98.

38. Harvey II, p. 86.

39. Harvey II, p. 104.

quæ et ipsa erat homo, habuit secundum hominem generationem, factus est Filius Hominis).[40]

The point here and in many other places is the anti-Gnostic stress on the real humanity of the incarnated. Irenaeus has his reasons for saying Son of man and not 'man', it being important as a reference to Christ's being born of the Virgin Mary. This conclusion turns up again a little later, in III 22.1:[41]

For if He did not receive the substance of flesh from a human being, He neither was made man nor the Son of man (Si enim non accepit ab homine substantiam carnis, neque homo factus est, neque Filius Hominis); and if He was not made what we were, He did no great thing in what He suffered and endured. ... [O]n this account does He confess Himself the Son of man ... [here follow references to Gal. 4.4 and Rom. 1.3, 4].

Son of man in the christological thinking of Irenaeus is completely occupied with his interest in stressing the true human nature of the incarnate Son of God genealogically. As in Justin, Mary is the one from whom Christ inherited his human nature. At the same time, Son of man indicates the very special humanity of Jesus, who is son of a woman but with no earthly father. It enabled him to reverse the disobedience of Adam through his obedience.[42] It also means that even in the two places where Dan. 7.13 is clearly quoted (IV 20.11 and 32.11), it is first and foremost taken as a foretelling of Christ's nature and not framed in the scheme of promise and fulfilment (otherwise prominent in this author). All the same, Irenaeus understands Dan. 7.13 as foretelling Christ's second Parousia as judge (cf. also III 19.2; 33.1).

This is also the understanding of the disciple of Irenaeus, Hippolytus (c. 170–235), presbyter and bishop in Rome, was banished to Sardinia where he died. In his *Contra haeresin Noeti cujusdam* 4,[43] Hippolytus rejects the father of modalistic monarchianism, Noetus of Smyrna (active at the end of the second century), who maintained that there was complete identity between God and Christ, with the consequence that he could not tolerate a real incarnation and therefore had the Father suffering. So Noetus, because of his presuppositions, had to claim that even in heaven Christ possessed human nature, calling in as witness Jn 3.13. Objecting to this, Hippolytus states that Jn 3.13 does not imply the existence of 'flesh' (σάρξ) in heaven before the incarnation. What was in heaven before the incarnation was solely

40. Cf. *Adv. haer*. IV 33.2 (Harvey II, p. 257).

41. Harvey II, p. 121.

42. Cf. the comment of Bracht, *Der Menschensohn*, p. 417: 'Wenn Irenäus die MS-Bezeichnung Jesu auf diese Weise seiner Rekapitulationslehre integriert, so wurde er damit gleichsam zum "Kronzeugen" für spätere Versuche, den MS-Titel der Evangelien im Sinne der Idealmensch-Idee zu deuten, eine Interpretationsrichtung, welche seit dem 17. Jh. bis zur letzten Jahrhundertwende sehr verbreitet war.'

43. The works of Hippolytus are quoted according to the edition in GCS, vols. 1 and 26.

the 'fleshless Logos' (Λόγος ἄσαρκος). When he, nevertheless, was called Son of man from the beginning, it was because of what he was going to be. Thus Daniel also witnesses to the future coming with the words 'like a son of man (ὡς υἱὸν ἀνθρώπου). Rightly then the one in heaven is called by that name, while what was from the beginning, from the beginning is called God's Logos.' This emphasis on the incarnation is also present in the same author's exposition of Daniel from c. 204, the oldest known Christian commentary. Just as Irenaeus and Justin before him, Hippolytus understands Dan. 7.13 as a reference to the second Parousia in glory (IV 10): 'in flesh God and man, Son of God and man, coming from heaven as judge for the world' (ἔνσαρκος δὲ θεὸς καὶ ἄνθρωπος υἱὸς θεοῦ καὶ ἀνθρώπου ἀπ' οὐρανῶν κριτὴς κόσμῳ παραγινόμενος). When Jesus hesitates, it is because he does not want to inflict judgment upon the world before its time.[44] In the following chapter (11), Hippolytus reminds one of Irenaeus when he interprets the Son of man in Daniel as 'firstborn of the virgin, that he in himself could reconstitute the first-created Adam' (πρωτότοκον ἐκ παρθένου, ἵνα τὸν πρωτόπλαστον 'Αδὰμ ἐν ἑαυτῷ ἀναπλάσσων δειχθῇ).[45] Later, in IV 39, he interprets the Son of man in Dan. 10.16 christologically. First, in 10.10, he remarks that a hand of a man touched the prophet, 'a hand of a man, he says, not yet a man'. But the prayer of the just man did make him worthy, having a revelation of things which were not yet visible to the world (τὰ μήπω μέλλοντα φανεροῦσθαι ἐν τῷ κόσμῳ). He now was made wise by the angel Gabriel and afterwards knowledgeable by the Lord and could say (Dan. 10.16):

> 'and I saw, and see, one like a man touched me'. First he said, as a hand of a man, to signify first a part of him, secondly the full incarnation (τὴν καθ' ὅλου ἐνανθρώπησιν). This is because it was preached beforehand [probably in Dan. 7.13] that the Word of God would be revealed as man in human form, as a man in flesh, at that time not yet being (perfect) son of man (ὡς ἄνθρωπος ἐν σχήματι ἀνθρώπου, ἄνθρωπος ἔνσαρκος ἐν κόσμῳ φανησόμενος, οὔπω τότε (τέλειος) υἱὸς ἀνθρώπου ὤν (IV 39).

After quoting Gal. 4.4, Hippolytus summarizes that after Jesus had clothed himself in man, which he got from the virgin, 'he showed himself being both Son of God and Son of man' (υἱὸς θεοῦ καὶ υἱὸς ἀνθρώπου ὢν ἀποδειχθῇ).

The contemporary Latin Church Fathers moved along the same tracks. The North-African lawyer, Tertullian (c. 160–c. 220), in his polemic against the Gnostics, could quote from Irenaeus *Adversus haereses*.[46] Although

44. A similar understanding of Dan. 7.13, about the second coming in glory in contrast to the first in humility, is found in *De antichristo* 44. See further, *In Danielem* IV 18, with references to Mt. 24.27, 30.

45. Cf. *De antichristo* 26.

46. See *Adversus Valentinianos* 5.

Tertullian became a Montanist in the latter part of his life, his writings have survived because of their quality. The expression Son of man is used in the argument against the Gnostics and Marcion, as well as the 'patripassian' Praxeas.

In his *magnum opus* (with regard to anti-heretic polemics), *Adversus Marcionem*, in five books, which he reworked three times, the first edition being from 207, Tertullian argues in IV 10[47] for Christ's right to forgive sins by introducing a lengthy explanation of the description of him as Son of man:

> Concerning the Son of man our rule (praescriptio) is a twofold one: that Christ cannot lie, so as to declare Himself the Son of man (ut se filium hominis pronuntiaret), if He be not truly so; nor can He be constituted the Son of man (neque filium hominis constitui), unless He be born of a human parent, either father or mother.

Since Christ is the begotten Son of God, he is not of a human father. Therefore he must be son of a human mother, who then must have been a virgin. Otherwise, he will have two fathers and the result would be a mythical being like Castor or Hercules:

> Now, if this distinction be observed, that is to say, if he be Son of man as born of His mother, because not begotten of a father, and His mother be a virgin, because His father is not human (si ex matre filius est hominis quia ex patre non est, ex matrem autem virgine quia non ex patre homine) – He will be that Christ whom Isaiah foretold that a virgin should conceive.

Tertullian earlier, in his treatise *De carne Christi* 5, makes the same point about Mary being the person behind 'man' in 'Son of man'.

But back to *Adversus Marcionem*! Against the docetic Christology of Marcion, Tertullian also refers to Daniel 7 in IV 10:

> What now, if Christ be described in Daniel by this very title of 'Son of man' (si ipso titulo filii hominis censetur Christus apud Danielem)?[48] Is not this enough to prove that He is the Christ of prophecy? For if He gives Himself that appellation which was provided in the prophecy for the Christ of the Creator, He undoubtedly offers Himself to be understood as Him to whom (the appellation) was assigned by the prophet.

Tertullian continues:

> But perhaps it can be regarded as a simple identity of names (nominum communio simplex); and yet we have maintained that neither Christ nor Jesus ought to have been called by these names, if they possessed any condition of diversity (diversitatis condicionem tenentes). But as regards the appellation

47. The translations according to *ANF* 3.
48. Is that the first place where filius hominis is called a titulus?

> 'Son of man,' in *as* far as it occurs by accident, in *so* far there is a difficulty in its occurrence along with a casual identity of names. For it is of pure accident, especially when the same cause does not appear whereby the identity may be occasioned. And therefore, if Marcion's Christ be also said to be born of man, then he too would receive an identical appellation (appellationis communionem), and there would be two Sons of man (duo filii hominis), as also two Christs and two Jesuses. Therefore, since the appellation is the sole right of Him in whom it has a suitable reason, if it be claimed for another in whom there is an identity of name, but not of appellation, then the identity of name even looks suspicious in him for whom is claimed without reason the identity of appellation. And it follows that he must be believed to be the One and the Same, who is found to be the more fit to receive both the name and the appellation; while the other is excluded, who has no right to the appellation, because he has no reason to show for it.

In *De carne Christi* 14, Tertullian introduces Ps. 8.6 (cf. 8.5) as a proof from Scripture of Christ's being human:

> Forasmuch, however, as it has been declared concerning the Son Himself, 'Thou hast made Him a litte lower than the angels', how will it appear that He put on the nature of angels if He was made lower than the angels, having become man, with flesh and soul as the Son of man (sic infra angelos deminutus, dum homo fit, qua caro et anima et filius hominis)?

In the following chapter (15), he argues against the Gnostic Valentinus:

> Any one who refused to believe that that flesh was human might pretend it to be anything he liked, forasmuch as (and this remark is applicable to all *heretics*), if it was not human, and was not born of man, I do not see of what substance Christ Himself spoke when He called Himself man and the Son of man (si humana non fuit, nec ex homine, non video ex qua substantia ipse se, Christus hominem et filium hominis pronuntiaret), *saying*: 'But now ye seek to kill me, a man that hath told you the truth'; and 'The Son of man is Lord of the Sabbath-day'.

Besides Jn 8.40 and Mt. 12.8, he also quotes Isa. 53.3 (LXX), Jer. 17.9 (LXX), Dan. 7.13, 1 Tim. 2.5 and Acts 2.22. On the other hand, Tertullian does not give in to Ebionitism. In *De carne Christi* 18, he writes:

> It was not fit that the Son of God should be born of a human father's seed, lest, if He were wholly the Son of a man, He should fail to be also the Son of God (Non competebat ex semine humano dei filius nasci, ne, si totus esset filius hominis, non esset et dei filius), and have nothing more than 'a Solomon' or 'a Jonas,'—as Ebion thought we ought to believe concerning Him.

According to *Adversus Marcionem* IV 10, Jesus is also the one most entitled to both the name Christ and the appellation Son of man. For he was the one seen by the Babylonian king in the furnace as the mystic fourth man, 'who was like the Son of man' (tamquam filius hominis; Dan. 3.25)[49] and was revealed expressly to Daniel as 'the Son of man coming in the clouds of heaven as a Judge' (filius hominis, veniens cum cæli nubibus iudex):[50]

> What I have advanced might have been sufficient concerning the designation in prophecy of the Son of man (Hoc dixi sufficere potuisse de nominatione prophetica circa filium hominis). But the Scripture offers me further information, even in the interpretation of the Lord Himself (Sed plus mihi scriptura confert, ipsius scilicet domini interpretatione).

When the Jews, not recognizing him as God, being Son of God, denied his right as man to forgive sins (Lk. 5.24), a prerogative of God, why—Tertullian asks—did he not tell them that as man he still possessed this power,

> inasmuch as, when He mentioned the Son of man, He also named a human being (quando et filium hominis nominans hominem nominaret)? except it were because He wanted, by help of the very designation 'Son of man' from the book of Daniel (appellatione filii hominis ex instrumento Danielis repercutere), so to induce them to reflect as to show them that He who remitted sins was God and man—that only Son of man, indeed, in the prophecy of Daniel (illum scilicet solum filium hominis apud Danielis prophetiam), who had obtained the power of judging, and thereby, of course, of forgiving sins likewise (for He who judges also absolves); so that, when once the objection of theirs was shattered to pieces by their recollection of Scripture, they might the more easily acknowledge Him to be the Son of man Himself by His own actual forgiveness of sins (eum agnoscerent ipsum esse filium hominis ex ipsa peccatorum remissione).
>
> I make one more observation, how that He has nowhere as yet professed Himself to be the Son of man (professus est se filium hominis)[51] – but for the first in this passage, in which for the first time he has remitted sins; that is, in which for the first time He has used His function of *judgment*, by the absolution.

In his polemic against the modalistic, monarchian 'patripassianism' of Praxeas (active in Rome c. 190), Tertullian uses the expression Son of man

49. The Vulgate reads 'similis filio Dei', whereas the LXX, in Dan. 3.92, has ὁμοίωμα ἀγγέλου θεοῦ ὁμοία υἱῷ θεοῦ. Tertullian repeats the same reading in IV 21 and *Adversus Praxean* 16.

50. Tertullian understands Dan. 7.13 as a prophecy of Christ's second Parousia. Cf. III 7, where a quotation of Dan. 7.13-14 is followed by the comment, 'Then indeed He shall have both a glorious form and an unsullied beauty above the sons of men', along with the quotation of Pss 8.5-6; 95.2-3; Zech. 12.10, 12.

51. *ANF* has 'Son of God'.

rather extensively. In his treatise *Adversus Praxean*,[52] for the first time known to us, Son of man figures in a credo-formula about Christ:[53]

> Him *we believe* to have been sent by the Father into the Virgin, and to have been born of her—being both Man and God, the Son of Man and the Son of God, and to have been called by the name of Jesus Christ (Hunc missum a patre in virginem et ex ea natum, hominem et deum, filium hominis et filium dei, et cognominatum Iesum Christum).

Most of what Praxeas ascribes to the Father is said in reality of the Son, to whom judgment is transferred according to Jn 5.27, '"because He is the Son of Man"—that is, according to the flesh, even as He is also the Son of God through His Spirit (*quia filius hominis est, per carnem scilicet, sicut et filius dei, per spiritum eius*)'.[54] More surprising is the reference to Jn 13.31 in *Adversus Praxean* 23, where the saying 'now is the Son of man glorified, and in him God is glorified' is interpreted as if the God spoken of here is 'certainly not the Father, but the Word of the Father, who was in the Son of man—that is in the flesh (sed sermo patris, qui erat in filio hominis, id est in carne), in which Jesus had already been glorified by *the divine* power and word'. This is elucidated a little later (ch. 27), where the Word which had become flesh is said to be

> certainly in all respects as the Son of God and the Son of Man, being God and Man, differing no doubt according to each substance in its own special property, inasmuch as the Word is nothing else but God, and the flesh nothing else but Man (certe usquequaque filium dei et filium hominis, cum deum et hominem, sine dubio secundum utramque substantiam in sua proprietate distantem, quia neque sermo aliud quam deus, neque caro aliud quam homo). Thus does the apostle also teach respecting His two substances, saying [Rom. 1.3], 'Who was made of the seed of David'; in which words He will be made Man and Son of Man (hic erit homo et filius hominis), 'Who was declared to be the Son of God, according to the Spirit'; in which words He will be God, and the Word—the Son of God. … Neither the flesh becomes Spirit, nor the Spirit flesh. In one *Person* they no doubt are well able to be co-existent. Of them Jesus consists—Man, of the flesh, of the Spirit, God—and the angel designated Him as 'the Son of God' [Lk. 1.35], in respect of that nature, in which He was Spirit, reserving for the flesh the appellation 'Son of Man' (servans carni filium hominis dici).

In his strictly logical argumentation, Tertullian not only points to Mary as the only possible person behind 'man' in Son of man, but also states that the designation stresses the humanity of Jesus. He sees it as relating to the

52. According to Altaner and Stuiber (*Patrologie*, p. 155), this writing is 'die klarste vornizänische Darlegung der kirchliche Trinitätslehre'.

53. This is pointed out by Bracht, *Der Menschensohn*, p. 474.

54. *Adversus Praxean* 21.

prophecy expressed in Dan. 3.25 and 7.13, the last foretelling of the role of the Son of man as judge. To Tertullian, the designation Son of man is also connected with a certain conception that is not derived from the semantic meaning of the word, but from the future role given to the figure in Dan. 7.13. In fact, on the basis of Scripture, Jews should have been able to recognize that Jesus' forgiving sins (i.e. judging) identified him with the Son of man of Dan. 7.13. It is not by accident that Jesus (Mk 2.10, but the same is the case in Lk. 5.24 and Mt. 9.6) uses Son of man for the first time in connection with his forgiveness of sins. In other words, the designation Son of man describes Jesus as the only one on earth having the authority to judge/forgive sins.

The first significant Latin theologian in Rome, Novatianus, known also because of his attitude to the schismatic deserters in the Decian persecution of 250–251, in his *De trinitate* 23-24,[55] argues along the same lines as Tertullian. Writing against any assumption that Christ should not have been man, he expresses a strong dyophysitism. Only as man was Christ able to be mediator between God and man,

> so that reasonably the Son of God might be made by the assumption of flesh the Son of man, and the Son of man by the reception of the Word of God the Son of God (ut merito Filius Dei per assumptionem carnis Filius hominis, et Filius hominis per receptionem Dei Verbi Filius Dei effici possit).

The heretical error consists exactly in their thinking

> that there is no distinction between the Son of God and the Son of man… For they will have it that the self-same that is man, the Son of man, appears also as the Son of God (eundem enim atque ipsum, id est hominem filium hominis, etiam Filium Dei volunt videri); that man and flesh and that same frail substance may be said to be also the Son of God Himself. Whence, since no distinction is discerned between the Son of man and the Son of God, but the Son of man Himself is asserted to be the Son of God (Ex quo, dum distinctio ipse filius hominis Dei Filius vindicatur), the same Christ and the Son of God is asserted to be man only; by which they strive to exclude, 'The Word was made flesh, and dwelt among us'.

The adoptianism against which Novatianus fights takes its point of departure from Lk. 1.35 in the words of the angel to Mary: 'The Holy Spirit shall come upon thee, and the power of the Highest shall overshadow thee; therefore also the Holy Thing which is born of thee shall be called the Son of God'. When the heretics see here a denial of the human nature of Christ, they are deceived. If the angelic word had not contained an 'also', they would be justified in declaring 'that Son of man, in that He is man, is the same as the

55. Translation according to *ANF* 5.

Son of God and man' (*ut hominis filium qua homo est, eundem et dei et hominis filium pronuntiare*). Thus the angelic word in Lk. 1.35 contains

> the proof that the Son of God descended, and that He, in taking up into Himself the Son of man, consequently made Him the Son of God, because the Son of God associated and joined Him to Himself. So that, while the Son of man cleaves in His nativity to the Son of God, by that very mingling he holds that as pledged and derived which of His own nature he could not possess (hic est enim legitimus dei filius, qui ex ipso deo est, qui, dum sanctum istud assumit et sibi filium hominis annectit et illum ad se rapit atque transducit, conexione sua et permixtione societa praestat et filium illum dei facit, quod ille naturaliter non fuit, ut principalitas nominis istius filius in spiritu sit domini, qui descendit et venit, ut sequela nominis istius in filio dei et hominis sit, et merito consequenter hic filius dei factus sit, dum non principaliter filius dei est). And thus by the word of the angel the distinction is made, against the desire of the heretics, between the Son of God and man.

Novatianus takes Son of man as primarily expressing the human nature of Christ, just as he sees Son of God as designating his divine nature. Of course, the incarnation is a part of the concept Son of man, but it does not explicitly express it. As has already been remarked, the goal of the argument is not to divide between the two natures, but to show that their unity in the person of Christ is now the basic assumption.[56] Consequently Novatianus interprets Jn 3.13 and 6.62 as showing that when it is said that the Son of man ascends to heaven, he must also be God, taking on flesh to become Son of man.[57]

Cyprianus (c. 205–258), bishop of Carthage, in his treatise *De opere et eleemosynis* 1, expressly connects the expression Son of man with the incarnation, describing salvation as[58] 'that the Father sent the Son to preserve us and give us life, in order that He might restore us. The Son was willing to be sent and to become the Son of man that He might make us sons of God (*quodque Filius missus esse et hominis filius fieri voluit ut nos Dei filios faceret*)'. On the other hand, quoting Mt. 8.20 in his *Testimoniorum libri III ad Quirinium* III 11, with regard to the conditions of discipleship, and connecting Mt. 12.32 and Mk 3.28 with 1 Sam. 2.25 (III 28), Cyprianus seems to understand *filius hominis* as a reference to man in general and not as a reference exclusively to Christ.[59] As we will see, this understanding is an isolated occurrence in this period.

56. Bracht, *Der Menschensohn*, p. 477: 'Während zuvor die Unterscheidung der Naturen das Beweisziel war, gilt hier die Einheit der Person als Voraussetzung'.

57. See *De trinitate*, respectively, ch. 13 and 14. Cf. also ch. 11 with the allusion to Mk 2.28 par: 'And in the same manner as He was made man "under the law," so as God He is declared to be "Lord of the Sabbath" (ita qua deu sabbati dominus expressus est)'.

58. Translation according to *ANF* 5.

59. Cf. Lietzmann, *Der Menschensohn*, p. 80.

Lactantius, a famous Latin rhetor, called by Diocletian to serve in his new capital Nicomedia in Bithynia, who, later, as an old man (c. 317) was called to educate Constantine's son Crispus, adheres totally to an understanding of Son of man as a description of the human nature of Christ in his main work, *Divinae institutiones* in seven books from 304–313. In IV 12, Lactantius quotes Dan. 7.13-14 and asks:[60]

> How then do the Jews both confess and expect the Christ of God? Who rejected Him on this account, because He was born of man. For since it is so arranged by God that the same Christ should twice come to the earth, once to announce to the nations the one God, then again to reign, why do they who did not believe in His first advent believe in the second?
>
> But the prophet comprises both His advents in few words. Behold, he says, one like a Son of man coming with the clouds of heaven. He did not say, like the Son of God, but the Son of man, that he might show that He had to be clothed with flesh on the earth, that having assumed the form of a man and the conditions of mortality, He might teach men righteousness (non dixit 'ut filius dei', sed 'ut filius hominis', ut ostenderet quod carne indui haberet in terra, ut suscepta homines figura et condicione mortali doceret homines iustitiam).

It is interesting that Lactantius combines an allusion to Acts 1.9 with the words of Dan. 7.14, demonstrating that the coming to the Ancient of Days predicts Christ's exaltation. He adds also the words from Ps. (LXX) 109.2. In ch. 13, he insists that it is befitting that the Son of the Father, born of no one being, was truly named 'fatherless' and 'motherless' according to Trismegistus,

> that the Son also should be born twice, that He also might become 'fatherless' and 'motherless'. For in His first nativity, which was spiritual, He was 'motherless', because He was begotten by God the Father alone, without the office of a mother. But in His second, which was in the flesh, He was born of a virgin's womb without the office of a father, that, bearing a middle substance between God and man, He might be able, as it were, to take by the hand this frail and weak nature of ours, and raise it to immortality. He became both the Son of God through the Spirit, and the Son of man through the flesh—that is, both God and man (factus est et dei filius per spiritum et hominis per carnem, id est deus et homo).

While Clement of Alexandria (died before 215) shows no interest in Son of man in his christological thinking,[61] the other great Alexandrinian, Origen

60. Translation according to *ANF* 7.

61. According to Bracht, *Der Menschensohn*, p. 575 n. 446, Clement quotes Son of man sayings without interpreting the expression. Bracht lists the following sayings: Mt. 11.19 (*Paedagogus* II 2.32.4); Mt. 8.20 (*Stromateis* I 3.23.2); Mt. 24.37, 39par. (III 6.49.4); Lk. 18.8 (III 6.49.5); Mt. 11.19 (III 6.52.4); Lk. 19.10 (IV 6.35.2); Lk. 6.22 (IV

(died c. 253), in accordance with his Logos-Christology, takes the expression Son of man as an indication of the human appearance of the Logos. In his *De principiis* II 6.3, it is said of the Son of God that he has died and that 'He is called the Son of man, who is announced as about to come in the glory of God the Father, with the holy angels' (*et Filius hominis appellatur, qui venturus in Dei Patris gloria cum sanctis angelis prædicatur*). Origen concludes that, 'throughout the whole of Scripture, not only is the divine nature spoken of in human words, but the human nature is adorned by appellations of divine dignity'.[62]

This understanding of the designations Son of God and Son of man as in opposition to each other, also dominates in other places in Origen's writings,[63] for instance, in his commentary on Matthew, where (e.g. 16.27, 28) it is explained that the Logos has the name Son of man because of its residence with men. Thus, *In Matthaeum* 12.29,[64] he comments:

> Now, indeed, the Son of man has not come in His glory; 'for we saw Him, and He had no beauty; but His form was dishonoured and defective compared with the sons of men; He was a man in affliction and toil, and aquainted with the enduring of sickness, because His face was turned away, He was dishonoured and not esteemed' [Isa. 53.2, 3] ..., and having become as they that they may become as He, 'conformed to the image of His glory [Rom. 8.29]', since He formerly became conformed to 'the body of our humiliation [Phil. 3.21]', when 'He emptied Himself and took upon Him the form of a servant [Phil. 2.7],' He is restored to the image of God and also makes them conformed to it.

In 19.28, he declares that the Son of man is the Logos united with man (*In Matthaeum* 15.24).

The same understanding is present in Origen's interpretation in his *In Johannem* 33.35 on Jn 13.31, where the glorifying of the Son of man is seen in the exaltation of the Son of man.[65] He emphasizes that this glory through

6.41.3); Lk. 12.8 (IV 9.70.1); Mk 8.38 (IV 9.70.2); Mk 14.62 (*Adumbrationes* II); Mt. 16.28 (*Excerpta ex Theodoto* 4.3).

62. Translation according to *ANF* 4. Cf. the comment of Weist, *Wer ist dieser Menschensohn?*, p. 14: 'Von einer auf die historische Person Jesu bezogenen doppelten Betrachtungsweise κατὰ σάρκα und κατὰ πνεῦμα oder von einer darauf errichteten "Zweinaturenlehre" ist hier keine Rede. Vielmehr verleiht eben sein Erlösungswerk am Menschen dem verherrlichten Gottessohn den Namen "Menschensohn".'

63. Bracht, *Der Menschensohn*, p. 467, points also to *Homilia in Exodum* V 3 where Jn 3.13 is introduced; *Exhortatio ad martyrium* 35, explaining Lk. 12.8-9, and *Homilia in Ezekielem* I 4 where Origen confronting a docetic Christology, confirms '"filium" eum "hominis" fuisse. Nam qui passiones assumpsit humanas necesse est ut ante passionem susceperit nativitatem.'

64. Translation according to *ANF* 10. Cf. also 12.32.

65. This commentary is quoted according to the edition in GCS.

the death on the cross on behalf of men was not the death of a divine being, but of a man, who was also the Son of man, of the seed of David. The Logos, being from the beginning with God, could not be more exalted. 'But the exaltation of the Son of man (ἡ δὲ ὑπερύψωσις τοῦ υἱοῦ τοῦ ἀνθρώπου), which happened to him when he glorified God with his own death, consisted in that he now no longer is something else than Logos, but the same as this'. This union of the human nature of Jesus (τὸ ἀνθρώπινον τοῦ ᾿Ιησοῦ) with the Logos is closer than the union of the believer with Jesus in the Spirit. Son of man signifies only the human part of Jesus. In another place (*In Johannem* Fragment 71), Origen thinks it right to supplement the faith spoken of in Jesus' question to the man born blind in Jn 9.35: believing first—only—in the Son of man, he had to proceed to belief in the Son of God, so that he—rephrasing 2 Cor. 5.16—could have said: 'If we also once regarded Christ according to the flesh, then we now no longer know him according to the flesh alone, but also as Son of God'.

Other explanations of the use of the expression Son of man are to be found in Origen's writings. Of Mt. 22.2's 'the Kingdom of Heaven is like a king', Origen says[66] that it is for pedagogical reasons that the Saviour persistently calls himself Son of the man, or Son of man (Υἱὸν τοῦ ἀνθρώπου, ἢ Υἱὸν ἀνθρώπου, ἑαυτὸν ὠνομακέναι), thereby signifying that

> just as God is caring for men (ἀνθρωποὺς οἰκονομῶν) when he is called man and in parables, perhaps, somehow, even becomes so, so also the Saviour, being principally Son of God, who also is God, Son of his love and 'image of the invisible God' [Col. 1.13], does not remain what he is principally, but according to the dispensation (κατ᾿ οἰκονομίαν) of the one who is called man in parables, becomes Son of man, although being God, and accordingly, when he cares for men, is imitating God, who is called and somehow becomes a man in parables. One need not seek any man and say that the Saviour is his son, but, holding to this concept of God and the parables statement that he is a man one should wisely listen to him who calls himself Son of man (αὐτοῦ λέγοντος ἑαυτὸν Υἱὸυ τοῦ ἀνθρώπου).[67]

Even if Son of man for Origen first of all designates the human nature, which the Logos took on as Son of God, his understanding of it is not the same throughout.

In *Dialogus de recta in Deum fide*, incorrectly transmitted in Origen's name, but seemingly belonging to the period after 325 and coming from an anti-Origen writer bearing the *nome de plume* 'Adamantius',[68] the meaning

66. In *Matthaeum* 17.20.

67. Lietzmann, *Der Menschensohn*, p. 74, declares this explanation 'für nicht mehr als eine aus der Laune des Augenblicks entstandene geistreiche Spielerei'.

68. Altaner and Stuiber, *Patrologie*, p. 216. It was Rufinus who tried to place the dialogue in his Latin translation to the time of persecution and thus back in Origen's time.

of Son of man is discussed. The confrontation with an explicit Gnostic understanding in I 7 will be referred to in the next chapter. However, even though the argument runs parallel to the rejection of the docetic view of the Valentinian 'Marinus', it will be treated here. In V 4, 'Adamantius' asks 'Marinus' why we hear Christ call himself Son of man: 'If he only seemed to have a human form (εἰ γάρ τῷ δοκεῖν σχήματι ἀνθρώπου ἐφαίνετὸ), why did he need to call himself Son of man? He needed only to say that the man had to suffer much.' Answering as the advocate of orthodoxy, Adamantius declares that Jesus would have been misunderstood

> if he had simply called himself 'man' (εἰ ἁπλῶς ἑαυτὸν ἄνθρωπον ἔλεγεν). However, when he also says he is Son of man (ὅτε δὲ καὶ υἱὸν ἀνθρώπου φάσκει εἶναι ἑαυτόν), how can they who are giving prominence to lies contrive that because the opposite is seen in appearance (σχήματι) it is altogether meant that he is son of a man (νοεῖται πάντως ὅτι ἀνθρώπου ἐστιν υἱός)? And what am I saying with regard to the one appearance? That (they) seem to be not only men in appearance, but they are also men by nature—with regard to essence (ὅτι οὐ μόνον τῷ σχήματι φαίνονται ἄνθρωποι, ἀλλὰ καὶ τῇ οὐσίᾳ, φύσει ἄνθρωποι ὄντες ...).

At any rate, Son of man not only designates the human form (σχῆμα ἀνθρώπινον) but also demonstrates his human descent. Thus, Adam and Eve were not 'sons of men' (υἱοὺς ἀνθρώπων), neither are they so called. The same pertains to angels who are often said to look like humans, but who are never called 'sons of men'. The 'neutral' third person, the pagan Euthropius, suggests that 'son' does not point to the essence of human beings, but to the birth from a human (οὐ τὴν οὐσίαν τῶν ἀνθρώπων δηλοί υἱὸς, ἀλλὰ τὴν ἐξ ἀνθρώπου γέννησιν)."[69]

Although an ardent adherent of Origen, Eusebius of Caesarea (c. 263–339),[70] like Justin, points to Dan. 7.9-10, 13-14 in a Christological discourse of his famous *Historia ecclesiastica* I 2.24-26, saying:[71]

> For instance, Daniel the prophet, under the influence of the divine Spirit, seeing his kingdom at the end of time, was inspired thus to describe the divine vision in language fitted to human comprehension [...]. It is clear that these words can refer to no one else than to our Saviour, the God Word who was in the beginning with God, and who was called the Son of man because of his final appearance in the flesh (υἱὸν ἀνθρώπου διὰ τὴν ὑστάτην ἐνανθρώπησιν αὐτοῦ χρηματίζοντα).

The text is quoted according to the edition in GCS. The Greek text and the Latin translation differ on several points.

69. Cf. V 5, 12, and 6 in the Latin version.

70. Every division into chronological periods has its weaknesses. I have chosen to place Eusebius under the heading Ante-Nicene Fathers, following Altaner and Stuiber, *Patrologie*. This has the result that Athanasius begins the next section.

71. Translation according to *NPNF* 2nd Series 1.

The same line of thought is found in Eusebius' *De ecclesiastica theologia* I 2 (cf. I 6), where it is said that

> It [the Church] only knows of the Son, Jesus Christ, and no other, not according to the birth in flesh, which he took on (what it was taught to call 'form of a slave' [Phil. 2.7] and 'Son of man' (ταύτην γὰρ 'δούλου μορφὴν', καὶ Υἱὸν ἀνθρώπου' καλεῖν δεδίδακται·), but it was according to the [birth] of God and Father himself before all ages.

This understanding of Son of man is maintained against Marcellus of Ancyra, who would not accept Logos being the Son, but who gave the designation Son of God and Son of man identical meaning, being expressions of different places in the economy of salvation.[72] Eusebius connects Son of man in Daniel with 'from the seed of David' in Rom. 1.3, claiming that the prophet clearly emphasizes the real becoming flesh of the Logos and gives him the name employed in the gospels. That the one to whom eternal power is given is not 'the Logos in God' is clear from the fact that he is called Son of man and placed over against the Ancient of Days (cf. *De ecclesiastica theologia* III 17). Eusebius stresses that Logos exists as an independent divine being besides and—according to Eusebian theology—subordinated to God, and that 'Son of man' is used of the human body that Logos took upon itself in Christ.[73] The 'incorporation' in a human body, according to Eusebius' linear understanding of salvation history, is an embodiment of the theophanies in the Old Testament, which prepare for exactly this event. Daniel 7.13 offered both the term Son of man and a forensic context which made it possible for Eusebius to understand Daniel's saying in an eschatological way.[74]

Christ's taking on a human body (ὄργανον ἀνθρώπειον) was a way to be known among men. Accordingly, the Son of God thus had to be one with the Son of David. Eusebius tries to prove this by introducing Scriptural sayings in which it, long before it happened, 'was prophesied that the Firstborn of the whole creation, Himself the Son of God, was to become Son of man'

72. This and the following paragraph heavily depend on Bracht, *Der Menschensohn*, pp. 480-81.

73. Cf. Bracht, *Der Menschensohn*, p. 479: 'Im übrigen aber steht Eusebius bei seinem Gebrauch der Dan[iel]-Stelle als Weissagungsbeweis für die "Mensch-Werdung" des Logos innerhalb der "kirchlichen" Tradition n[eu]t[estament]l[ich] orientierter Interpretationen des AT, bei der—aufgrund der Vorstellung heilsgeschichtlicher Kontinuität—die jüdischen "Offenbarungs"-Schriften gleichsam im Brennpunkt des Christus-Glaubens gesehen werden und so als "Verheißungen" erscheinen oder anders: als sog. "Rückwärtsbegründung" späterer christologischer Erkenntnisse dienen können.'

74. In his *Demonstratio evangelica* IX 17.4-8, where Daniel's vision demonstrates the divine glory connected with Christ's second coming, just as Christ himself taught in Mt. 25.31 (see *Demonstratio* XV).

(*Demonstratio* VII 3.14).[75] Exactly this embodiment caused the Logos to be called Son of man (οὕτω δῆτα ὁ θεὸς ὁ λόγος υἱὸς ἀνθρώπου ἐλέγετο; *Demonstratio* IV 10.19), or, as Eusebius puts it, 'He used to call himself Son of man because of his residence among men' (*De Theophania* IV 34 with reference to Mt. 13.36-43).[76]

75. Translation according to W.J. Ferrar II, *The Proof of the Gospel being the Demonstratio Evangelica of Eusebius of Cæsarea* (1920), p. 88.

76. My translation of the German translation of the Syrian version. The Greek original is lost of this part of *Theophania*. The German text in GCS reads: 'Menschensohn aber pflegt er sich selbst zu nennen wegen seines Durchgangs unter den Menschen'. Cf. Bracht, *Der Menschensohn*, p. 480: 'MS bezeichnet für Eusebius also nicht den Menschen Jesus aus Leib und Seele, sondern nur die unpersönliche Körperlichkeit, deren Subjekt der Logos oder Gottessohn ist'. Bracht also refers to *Contra Marcellum* 1.1 and 2.1. See below, in Chapter 3.

2. The Son of Man in Gnosticism

Before leaving the period of the Early Church, we shall investigate the meaning of the expression Son of man in the more or less contemporary Christian Gnostic sources.[1] Earlier, in the so-called History of Religion School, Gnosticism was treated as a pre-Christian phenomenon, its redeemer figure ('the redeemed Redeemer') being an important source for New Testament christological thinking with regard to the term Son of man. This hypothesis is connected especially with the name Richard Reitzenstein (1861–1931), the famous Göttingen historian of religion.[2] Today the point of view is gaining ground that Gnosticism is a Christian phenomenon.[3] The Church fathers fought it as a heresy rather than as paganism. As a consequence, it is widely agreed that the usage of the expression Son of man in Gnostic sources stems from the gospel tradition.[4] As such, it occurs exclusively in 'Christian' Gnostic writings. Only in a few places do we find the expression in sayings reminding us of what we have in the canonical Gospels.[5] What we see in this literature is a certain Gnostic interpretation of

1. Of the relevant literature, see especially H.-M. Schenke, *Der Gott 'Mensch' in der Gnosis* (1962); C. Colpe, 'ὁ υἱὸς τοῦ ἀνθρώπου', *ThWNT*, VIII (1969), pp. 478-80; F.H. Borsch, *The Christian and Gnostic Son of Man* (1970), pp. 58-121. Borsch's analyses are of great value although his goal is to establish a tradition which, to my mind, is non-existent. See, further, Weist, *Wer ist dieser Menschensohn?*, pp. 36-55; Bracht, *Der Menschensohn*, pp. 418-64 (notes, pp. 533-74). Also Simone Pétrement, *Le Dieu séparé. Les origins du gnosticisme* (1984), esp. pp. 147-81.

2. For more details, cf. below, Chapter 12, 'The History of Religion School'.

3. Cf., especially, Pétrement, *Le Dieu séparé*, where it is the central hypothesis.

4. E.g. Weist, *Wer ist dieser Menschensohn?*, p. 36: 'Obwohl der für die gnostische Glaubenswelt charakteristische Mythos vom Gott "Mensch", vom Ur-Anthropos, eine solche Vermutung naheliegt, ist der "Menschensohn" kein genuin gnostischer Begriff'. Weist refers (n. 142) to the (unpublished) investigation of G. Iber, *Überlieferungsgeschichtliche Untersuchungen zum Begriff des Menschensohnes im Neuen Testament* (1953), pp. 11-17. Cf. Schenke, *Der Gott 'Mensch' in der Gnosis*, p. 154; Colpe, 'ὁ υἱὸς τοῦ ἀνθρώπου', p. 479.

5. Some of them remind us of sayings in the canonical gospels. It pertains to Hippolytus, *Refutation omnium haeresium* V 12.7 (cf. Jn 3.17); V 16.11 (Jn 3.14); *Excerpta ex*

the expression. Although there are differences and exceptions, there is a unifying tendency marking a particular Gnostic contribution. This is found in the understanding of which man the son is a son of, namely the first archetypal man, or god Ἄνθρωπος.[6] It has not been possible to trace what could be identified as a 'developed' Gnosticism, which would include the concept of a redeemer, before the first half of the second century CE[7] (the main source being the so-called *Corpus Hermeticum* and especially its first tract *Poimandres*).

That the Highest God is called Man (Ἄνθρωπος) or the like seems to reflect an interpretation of Gen. 1.26 according to which man is created in the image of God. God must therefore be a man and the next god in the hierarchy may suitably be called Son of man. This does not exclude the possibility that ideas coming from outside the Jewish–Christian tradition have been interpreted by means of the creation story and Christian preaching.

1. *Marcion*

If a primary characteristic of Gnosticism is the distinction between the Highest God and the Creator God (the Demiurge), Marcion is to be reckoned among the Gnostics. Evidently, however, he does not understand Son of man in what was to become the Gnostic manner.[8] In Marcion, it is even possible to detect some reluctance towards the expression.[9] Although he has retained

Theodoto 4.3 (cf. Mt. 16.28); 61.4 (cf. Lk. 9.22); Irenaeus, *Adversus haereses* I 8.3 (Mt. 8.20; Lk. 9.58; cf. *Gospel of Thomas* 86), Clement of Alexandria, *Stromateis* IV 6.35.2, where in traditions ascribed to Matthew we meet a variation of Lk. 19.10. In these five sayings, Son of man appears in all instances with the double determination. Cf. further *Gospel of Mary*, BG 8502 8.17, resembling Lk. 17.21.

6. Cf. Weist, *Wer ist dieser Menschensohn?*, p. 37: 'Durch seine Eigenschaft als der Sohn des Ur-Menschen eröffnet der Erlöser dem wahren Gnostiker die Möglichkeit, sich aus spekulativen Strukturen selbst herzuleiten und zu verstehen. Er zeugt ihm die ersehnte, Ruhe gewährende Heimat der Seele... Und mit alledem führt er ihn zurück zu Gott, zum Gott "Mensch" nämlich, das heißt letztlich zur Selbstvergottung.'

7. See the profound contribution of C. Colpe, *Die religionsgeschichtliche Schule* (1961); idem, 'ὁ υἱὸς τοῦ ἀνθρώπου', pp. 414-18. Cf. Schenke, *Der Gott 'Mensch' in der Gnosis*.

8. Lietzmann, *Der Menschensohn*, pp. 61-62, who dates the formative period of Marcion's theology to 90–115, finds that his gospel contains the oldest traces of knowledge of this formula outside the New Testament. This may be so, but it does not allow Lietzmann's conclusion, that, because of the fact that he seemingly did not share the later interpretation indicating Christ's physical birth, Marcion 'wird demnach noch von dem ursprünglichen, messianischen Sinn Kunde gehabt haben'.

9. A. von Harnack, *Marcion* (2. Aufl., 1924), pp. 123-24: 'Eine Verlegenheit für ihn [scil. Marcion] war auch die Selbstbezeichnung Jesu als "der Menschensohn"; er mußte sie allegorisch verstehen'.

the expression Son of man in twelve places in his 'rewritten' Gospel (of Luke), ten other Lukan Son of man sayings are missing. This evidence does not demand drastic conclusions. In any event, his modalistic Christology did not allow him to understand Son of man (as the fathers of the Church did) as relating to the human nature and descent of Christ. Marcion would have understood it as an allegory as did the fictitious representative of Marcionism, Megethius, in the dialogue *De recta in Deum fide* I 7, which, as mentioned above, has to be dated after 325. The orthodox Adamantius confronts Megethius in the following way, with Euthropius the neutral third party:

> *Adamantius*: Now Christ says: 'I am Son of man (υἱὸς ἀνθρώπου εἰμί)'. Is He according to your view son of a man and not of God?
>
> *Megethius*: Christ is Son of God.
>
> *Euthropius*: You assert that Scripture (τὰ γεγραμμένα) means this. How is He now Son of God, when He calls Himself Son of man (ἑαυτὸν λέγων υἱὸν ἀνθρώπου)?
>
> *Megethius*: He used a parable (Παραβολῇ ἐχρήσατο) when He said Son of man.
>
> *Euthropius*: Is it an intelligible parable or a sensible one (Παραβολῇ νοητή ἐστιν ἢ αἰσθητή)?
>
> *Megethius*: An intelligible one.
>
> *Euthropius*: How then can you say, the contents of Scripture are simple (ψιλὰ εἶναι τὰ τῶν γραφῶν)? This way, they are intelligible and not simple, and where they seem to disagree with the wording, the real meaning (ὁ νοῦς) is to be found.
>
> *Megethius*: Partly intelligible, partly simple.
>
> *Euthropius*: You seem to me to have a changeable opinion.
>
> *Megethius*: Where a parable is assumed, it [Scripture] is intelligible; otherwise, it is simple.
>
> *Adamantius*: Would you make it clear that with regard to the Son of man, a parable is assumed (περὶ τοῦ υἱοῦ τοῦ ἀνθρώπου παραβολὴ ἐπιγέγραπται)? You shall know that a parable is not to be assumed! How do you teach otherwise that he is Son of God? One of the two, you have to admit. According to what you mean, Christ is either found to be a liar, when He calls Himself Son of man, although He was not a human, – or all divine Scriptures are intelligible (ἢ νοηταὶ εἰσι πᾶσαι αἱ θεῖαι γραφαί), also when not assumed to be a parable (thus all Scripture is called inspired by the Apostle). Their meaning is found to be in harmony, and not already what is written is simply what is true and secure.

2. *The Gnostics in the Description in the Anti-Gnostic Fathers*

Passing on to the description in the anti-Gnostic fathers of the Gnostic heresies, we have yet another and clearer picture of the common Gnostic usage of the expression Son of Man. In spite of obvious differences, there are certain common characteristics. Written around 180, the description in Irenaeus' *Adversus haereses* concerns Gnostics who were active before and around the middle of the second century.[10]

We find a representation of the usage of the expression Son of Man by some Gnostics of the *Valentinian* school. The Anthropos, as consort with Ecclesia, is normally seen as part of the primary Ogdoad. From them emanated twelve aeons, one of which separated from the rest, fell out of the Pleroma and produced the rest of the universe.[11] According to this school, Christ was not produced inside the Pleroma, but outside, by his mother, Sophia and with a memory of the heavenly world.

In his description of Valentinian Gnosticism, Irenaeus begins with the system of Ptolemy.[12] We find Son of Man only once in a quotation from Mt. 8.20 = Lk. 9.58.[13] It is a clear example of the new meaning which the expression acquires in a Gnostic context. According to the threefold anthropological division (pneumatic, psychic, and hylic), the man declaring his willingness to follow Jesus belongs to the hylic group. He is warned by Jesus with regard to the material difficulties of his decision. Thus Son of Man designates the visible, bodily existence of Jesus, although, according to the Ptolemaic teaching, it is not at all hylic but of a certain psychic substance.[14]

The next Valentinian to be mentioned is a disciple of Ptolemy, Colorbasus and his pupils. Some of Colorbasus's disciples affirm concerning the Saviour[15]

> that he had his being from those twelve Æons who were the offspring of Anthropos and Ecclesia. On this account, he acknowledges himself the Son of man, as being a descendent of Anthropos (καὶ διὰ τοῦτο υἱὸν 'Ανθρώπου (*adj.* ἑαυτὸν) ὁμολογεῖ, ὡσανεὶ ἀπόγονον 'Ανθρώπου). Others still assert that he was produced by Christ and the Holy Spirit, who were brought forth for the security of the Pleroma; and that on this account, he was called Christ, thus preserving the appellation of the Father, by whom he was produced. There are yet others among them who declare that the Propator of the whole, Proarche, and Proanennoetos is called Anthropos and that this is the great and

10. In the following the translation is according to *ANF* 1.
11. Cf. *Adv haer* I 11.1 (Harvey I, p. 100).
12. *Adv haer* I 1-8.5 (Harvey I, pp. 8-80).
13. *Adv haer* I 8.3 (Harvey I, p. 71).
14. Weist, *Wer ist dieser Menschensohn?*, p. 44.
15. *Adv haer* I 12.4 (Harvey I, p. 113).

> abstruse mystery; namely, that the Power which is above all others and contains all in his embrace is termed Anthropos. Therefore, the Saviour styles himself the 'Son of man' (καὶ διὰ τοῦτο υἱὸν ἀνθρώπου ἑαυτὸν λέγειν τὸν Σωτῆρα).

Son of Man here is clearly an emanation of the Anthropos and of the same substance as his father.

Later, in the description of the system of Marcus, also a Valentinian, after an account of the generation of Jesus through Mary, we are told of the descent of a transcendent power upon him at his baptism. This power was[16]

> the seed of the Father, which had in itself both the Father and the Son...and also all the Æons. And this was that Spirit who spoke by the mouth of Jesus, and who confessed that He was the son of Man (τὸ ὁμολογῆσαν ἑαυτὸν υἱὸν ἀνθρώπου) as well as revealed the Father, and who, having descended into Jesus, was made one with Him. And he says that the Saviour formed by special dispensation did indeed destroy death, but that Christ made known the Father. He maintains, therefore, that Jesus is the name of that man formed by a special dispensation, and that He was formed after the likeness and form of that [heavenly] Anthropos, who was about to descend upon Him. After He had received that Æon, He possessed Anthropos himself, and Logos himself, and Pater, and Arrhetus, and Sige, and Aletheia, and Ecclesia and Zoe.

A docetic christology becomes apparent and the meaning of Son of man seems to be double, namely, as both revealer and man.

The Valentinian Theodotus, in the excerpts preserved by Clement of Alexandria, twice quotes Son of man sayings from the canonical Gospels. The first renders the Matthean version of the statement of Jesus that some of the people present 'will not taste death till they see the Son of man coming in his kingdom' (Mt. 16.28). This saying then is combined with the following story of the transfiguration:[17]

> By reason of great humility, the Lord did not appear as an angel but as a man, and when he appeared in glory to the apostles on the Mount, he did not do it for his own sake when he showed himself, but for the sake of the Church which is 'the elect race', that it might learn his advancement after his departure from the flesh. For on high, too, he was Light and that which was manifest in flesh and appeared here is not later than that above nor was it curtailed, in that it was translated hither from the high, changing from the one place to another, so that this was gain here and loss there. But he was the Omnipresent, and is with the Father, even when here, for he was the Father's Power. And besides, it was necessary that that word also which the Savior spoke should be fulfilled,

16. *Adv haer* I 15.3 (Harvey I, pp. 150-52).

17. *Exc ex Theodot* 4.1-3. Translation according to R.P. Casey, *The Excerpta ex Theodoto of Clement of Alexandria*. Edited with Translation, Introduction and Notes (1934).

> 'There are some of those standing here who will not taste death until they see the Son of Man in glory'. Therefore, Peter, James and John saw and fell asleep.

The other saying is likewise an interesting interpretation, this time of Lk. 9.22,[18] where Theodotus first declares 'That he was other than what he received is clear from what he professes', and quoting Jn 14.6 and 10.30, he points to the difference between the spiritual nature and the psychic appearance. 'When he says "The Son of Man must be rejected and insulted and crucified," he seems to be speaking of someone else; that is, of him who has passion.'[19]

Heracleon (also belonging to the Valentinian school according to the account in Origen, *In Joannem* XIII 49, commenting on Jn 4.36-37) refers to Mt. 13.37, 39 and that the Son of man performs two roles in the interpretation of the parable of the darnel among the wheat. According to Origen, Heracleon thus distinguishes the sower from the reaper, although they have a common goal. He also establishes the truth of the Jesus-saying: 'One sows and another reaps', saying:

> The Son of Man above the Place (of the Middle) sows (ὁ μὲν γὰρ ὑπὲρ τὸν τόπον υἱὸς ἀνθρώπου σπείρει); the Savior, himself also the Son of Man (ὢν καὶ αὐτὸς υἱὸς ἀνθρώπου), harvests and sends as reapers the angels represented by the disciples, each for his own soul.[20]

It is not at all, as he puts it, that there are two sons of man (τοὺς δύο υἱοὺς τοῦ ἀνθρώπου τίνες εἰσίν), of which the one sows, and the other reaps.

The focus is different in the *Ophitic* teaching, which, again according to Irenaeus,[21] maintains that the Father of all is styled the first man:

> They also maintain that his Ennoea, going forth from him, produced a son, and that this is the son of man—the second man (Υἱὸν 'Ανθρώπου καλοῦσι, καὶ δεύτεραν"Ανθρωπος/et esse hanc filium hominis, secundum hominem). Below these, again, is the Holy Spirit, and under this superior spirit the elements were separated from each other, viz., water, darkness, the abyss, chaos...[22]

18. *Exc ex Theodot* 61.4.

19. Cf. Weist, *Wer ist dieser Menschensohn?*, pp. 42-43: 'Ein richtig erkannter exegetischer Tatbestand ist hier einer dogmatischen Voraussetzung dienstbar gemacht'.

20. Fragment 35. Translation from *The Gnostic Society Library. Gnostic Scriptures and Fragments*. Heracleon: Fragments from his Commentary on the Gospel of John <http://www.gnosis.org/library/fragh.htm>.

21. *Adv haer* I 30.1 (Harvey I, p. 227). Also for the following.

22. Colpe, 'ὁ υἱὸς τοῦ ἀνθρώπου', p. 479, sees the Ennoia as identified with the Son of man. It is also the most obvious reading of the Greek, τὴν δὲ Ἔννοιαν αὐτοῦ ... Υἱὸν ἀνθρώπου καλοῦσι, and the Latin, Ennoeam autem ejus progredientem, filium dicunt emittendis, et esse hunc Filium Hominis Secundum Hominem. If so, Colpe might be right in saying that the Son of Man has been added to an existing system. Cf. Colpe, 'New Testament and Gnostic Christology', in J. Neusner (ed.), *Religions in Antiquity: Essays in*

Below them was the Spirit and, delighted by the beauty of this Spirit, being a woman, they shed 'light upon her, and begat by her an incorruptible light, the third male, whom they call Christ, – the son of the first and second man, and of the Holy Spirit, the first woman'. Further below in the system, we meet Ialdabaoth, the Demiurge, who had come into existence by an emanation of Sophia. Looking at the things below him, he boasted and exclaimed with words that remind us of Isa. 45.5-6; 46.9:[23]

> 'I am father, and God, and above me there is no one.' But his mother, hearing him speak thus, cried out against him, 'Do not lie, Ialdabaoth: for the father of all, the first Anthropos (man) is above thee; and so is Anthropos the son of Anthropos'.

Not realizing where the voice comes from, Ialdabaoth thereafter, together with other powers, takes the initiative to create man in his own image. They did not succeed very well, his body being enormously huge and only able to crawl on the ground. By the intercession of Sophia, he becomes the spirit of life. The other qualities enable him to partake in salvation. 'He at once gave thanks to the first Anthropos (man), forsaking those who had created him'. This man obviously is a heavenly figure.

After a long account, which includes figures from the biblical story, we reach the visit of Christ to this world, together with his sister Sophia. It happened in the person of Jesus:[24]

> But Jesus, inasmuch as he was begotten of the Virgin through the agency of God, was wiser, purer, and more righteous than all other men: Christ united to Sophia descended into him, and thus Jesus Christ was produced.
>
> They affirm that many of his disciples were not aware of the descent of Christ into him, but that, when Christ did descend on Jesus, he began to work miracles, and heal, and announce the unknown Father and openly confess himself the son of the first man (Filium Primi Hominis).

The Son of Man is no longer a heavenly figure, co-father of the Christ here, but has descended upon the earthly Jesus.[25]

In Hippolytus' description, *Refutatio omnium haeresium*,[26] of the Naassenes (Ophitic school), we meet the expression Son of Man with a similar

Memory of E.R. Goodenough (1968), pp. 227-43 (238-39). For a critical discussion of this understanding, see Borsch, *The Christian and Gnostic Son of Man*, pp. 62-63.

23. *Adv haer* I 30.6 (Harvey I, pp. 232-33).

24. *Adv haer* I 30.12-13 (Harvey I, pp. 238-39).

25. Cf. Borsch, *The Christian and Gnostic Son of Man*, p. 62: 'Here in a specifically Christian context we again meet a kind of pre-Nestorian or Antiochene Christology making use of the language employed earlier'.

26. *Ref* V 6.4. Translation according to *ANF* 5, which has, however, a different chapter division from the *MPG*-text, for which reason I offer the actual page, here p. 48.

meaning, indicating familiarity between the Naassenes and Monoïmos (see below). Among the Naassenes, the Man and the Son of Man are clearly identified. 'According to the system advanced by them, [they] magnify, (as the originating cause) above all things else, a man and a son of man (ἄνθρωπον καὶ υἱὸν ἀνθρώπου). This man is a hermaphrodite (ἀρσενόθηλυς), and is denominated among them Adam.' In the Naassene system, men reflect the perfect Man.

> That is, from the blessed man from above, or the primal man or Adam, as it seems to them, souls have been conveyed down here into a creation of clay, that they may serve the Demiurge of this creation, Ialdabaoth...[27]

Following a quotation of Eph. 5.14—'Awake you that sleepest, and arise, and Christ will give thee light'—it is said:

> This is the Christ who, he says, in all that have been generated, is the portrayed Son of Man from the unportrayable Logos (υἱὸς ἀνθρώπου κεχαρακτηρισμένος ἀπὸ τοῦ ἀχαρακτηρίστου λόγου).[28]

In Hippolytus' description of the *Peratae*,[29] they claim that 'Christ descended from above from unorigination (ἀπὸ τῆς ἀγεννησίας), that by His descent, all things triply divided might be saved'. Only those borne from above will ascend through him, while beings plotting against those are renounced. In what sounds like an echo of Jn 3.17 or Lk. 9.56a,[30] we find the following saying in this context: 'For the Son of man did not come into the world to destroy the world, but that the world might be saved through Him' (οὐ γὰρ ἦλθεν ὁ υἱὸς τοῦ ἀνθρώπου εἰς τὸν κόσμον, ἀπολέσει τὸν κόσμον, ἀλλ' ἵνα σωθῇ ὁ κόσμος δι' αὐτοῦ).[31] In the Johannine saying, God is the subject and it is the Son of God who is sent. The subject is here the Son of man. For the first time, we meet the familiar double determination. In the Peratic understanding, 'the world' is divided into three parts, of which two are above, the third part being this world, which is going to perish and which is also spoken about in the saying in 1 Cor. 11.32, 'that we may not be condemned with the world', quoted as Scripture (ἡ γραφή).

27. *Ref* V 7.30. Translation according to *ANF* 5, p. 51.

28. *Ref* V 7.33. Translation according to *ANF* 5, p. 51. Cf. Weist, *Wer ist dieser Menschensohn?*, p. 41: 'Der herabkommende Erlöser findet in allen Menschen den Menschensohn als Christus oder "inneren Menschen" "ausgeprägt" vor und kann so mit ihnen einen werden, um sie zu erlösen'.

29. *Ref* V 12. Translation according to *ANF* 5, p. 59.

30. That this saying was circulating also outside the written Gospels in a different form is not only evident from Lk. 9.56a, but also Mt. 18.11. It is a part of the original text only in Lk. 19.10. Cf. 2 Clem. 2.7.

31. *Ref* V 12.7. Translation according to *ANF* 5, p. 59.

Later,[32] we find a word for word quotation of the last part of Jn 3.14, the introduction being only slightly altered. It is remarkable that we have once again two definite articles, as in the canonical Gospels (with Jn 5.27 as the only exception). Interesting also is a saying[33] reminiscent of Col. 2.9 and 1.19—'It pleased him that in him should dwell all fulness bodily and in him the entire Divinity resides'—because in the description in a later book[34] of the so-called Arab Monoïmos the same quotation appears in the form: 'It pleased (God) that all fulness should dwell in the Son of man bodily' (ὅτι πᾶν τὸ πλήρωμα ηὐδόκησε κατοικῆσαι ἐπὶ τὸν υἱὸν τοῦ ἀνθρώπου σωματικῶς).

According to Hippolytus, the same Monoïmos could speak of the highest God as Anthropos as a simple monad, comprising all opposites. This man is the universe which again

> is the originating cause of all things, unbegotten, incorruptible, (and) eternal. And (he says) that the son of (the) man (υἱὸν ἀνθρώπου) previously spoken of is begotten, and subject to passion, (and) that he is generated independently of time, (as well as) undesignedly, (and) without being predestinated. For such, he says, is the power of that man. And he being such constituted in power, (Monoïmus alleges) that the son was born quicker than thought and volition. And this, he says, is spoken of in the Scriptures, 'He was, and was generated'. And the meaning of this is: Man was, and his son was generated.[35]

That Monoïmos' Son of man 'is subject to passion' is probably not meant in the same way as in the canonical Gospels. The predicate is more likely to be understood within the framework of earthly existence as such, in contrast to the heavenly archetype.[36] This also seems evident when, later, just after a quotation—'It pleased (God) that all fulness should dwell in the Son of man bodily'—it is said:

> The Son of man, therefore, he says, has been generated from the perfect man (ἀπὸ τοῦ τελείου ἀνθρώπου ὁ υἱὸς τοῦ ἀνθρώπου), whom no one knew; every creature who is ignorant of the Son, however, forms an idea of Him as the offspring of a woman. And certain very obscure rays of this Son which approach this world, check and control alteration (and) generation. And the beauty of that Son of man (ἐκείνου τοῦ υἱοῦ τοῦ ἀνθρώπου) is up to the present incomprehensible to all men, as many as are deceived in reference to the offspring of the woman. Therefore nothing, he says, of the things that are in our quarter of the creation has been produced by that man, nor will aught (of these) ever be (generated from him). All things, however, have been

32. *Ref* V 16.11. Translation according to *ANF* 5, p. 63.
33. *Ref* V 12.5. Translation according to *ANF* 5, p. 59.
34. *Ref* VIII 13.2. Translation according to *ANF* 5, p. 121.
35. *Ref* VIII 12.2. Translation according to *ANF* 5, pp. 120-21.
36. Thus Borsch, *The Christian and Gnostic Son of Man*, p. 70.

> produced, not from the entirety (ἀπὸ ὅλου), but from some part of that Son of man (ἀπὸ μέρους τινὸς ... τοῦ υἱοῦ τοῦ ἀνθρώπου). For he says the Son of man is a jot in one tittle, which proceeds from above, is full, and completely replenishes all (rays flowing down from above). And it comprises in itself whatever things the man also possesses (who is) the Father of the Son of man.[37]

Monoïmos seems to fight an identification of Jesus with the Son of man, Jesus being born of a woman, as is likewise the case in the Pseudo-Clementine *Recognitiones* I 60.3 (see below).[38] In Monoïmos, we may have a non-Christian Gnostic. On the other hand, this does not mean that the use of the designation Son of man is not of Christian origin. The tittle above is a superscripted mark, which, placed above 'iota', indicates the number ten. 'Thus does the Son of Man, as one uncompounded and simple tittle, yet compound and make multiform.'[39]

In the account in Hippolytus of the teaching of the Gnostic Justin and his *Book of Baruch*,[40] it is related that Baruch, a heavenly messenger, is sent by Elohim to Nazareth, to Jesus, son of Joseph and Mary and announces to him everything that has happened and what was likely to take place, concluding with the warning:

> All the prophets anterior to you have been enticed. Put forth an effort, therefore, Jesus, Son of man (υἱὲ ἀνθρώπου), not to be allured, but preach this word unto men, and carry back tidings to them of things pertaining to the Father, and things pertaining to the Good One, and ascend to the Good One, and sit there with Elohim, Father of us all.

This is the only time we find Son of man in the vocative, the form used 93 times in Ezekiel. But it is not possible to decide whether, in this, Justin ascribes the specific Gnostic meaning to Son of man. If it were of any importance to him, one would expect to find it more than once.

In *Contra Celsum* 8.15, Origen tells us that the Platonic Celsus, in 'A Heavenly Dialogue' of a Gnostic, should have encountered an indication that the Son of man should be Lord and God (according to Origen, with the conclusion that Christians worship Jesus besides or even above God). The quotation runs:[41]

> If the Son is mightier than God, and the Son of man is Lord over Him, who else than the Son of man can be Lord over that God who is the ruler over all things? (Εἰ ἰσχυρότερος ἐστι θεοῦ υἱὸς καὶ κύριος αὐτοῦ ἐστὶν ὁ υἱὸς τοῦ ἀνθρώπου· καὶ τίς ἄλλος κυριεύσει τοῦ κρατοῦντος θεοῦ;)

37. *Ref* VIII 13.3-4. Translation according to *ANF* 5, p. 121.
38. Cf. Borsch, *The Christian and Gnostic Son of Man*, p. 71.
39. Borsch, *The Christian and Gnostic Son of Man*, p. 72.
40. *Ref* V 26.30. Translation according to *ANF* 5, p. 72.
41. Translation according to *ANF* 4.

It is probably correct to conclude that Celsus and, with him, Origen are mistaken about the original meaning of the Gnostic saying.[42] In all probability, it concerns the Demiurge, who, with reference to such Gospel sayings as Lk. 10.22 and 6.5, has been proven to be less than the Son of man.

3. *The Coptic Gnostic Writings Primarily from Nag Hammadi*

The understanding of Son of Man in the Gnostic systems, as reproduced by the anti-Gnostic fathers, finds confirmation in some of the scriptures included in the Coptic Gnostic library found 1945 in Nag Hammadi in Egypt.[43] Here, it becomes crystal clear that 'Man' in 'Son of Man' is the Highest God.

Of special interest, is the *Apocryphon of John* (II, 1.14.14-15), which may be as early as c. 120 CE,[44] containing the teaching of a complete Gnostic system with all its aeons, where the last, the Sophia, brings the Demiurg, Yaltabaoth, into existence, against the will of the Highest God. After having created his world and a host of angels, he thinks in his ignorance that there is nothing beyond his mother and that he is therefore the only god. In an attempt by the other aeons to rescue the repentant Sophia, Christ, her consort in the system of aeons, in an obviously invisible form, is sent to her. The text says (14.14–15.14):

> And a voice came forth from the exalted aeon-heaven: 'The Man exists and the son of Man'. And the chief archon, Yaltabaoth, heard (it) and thought the voice had come from his mother, and he did not know from where she (or: it) came. And the holy Mother-Father taught them, and the perfect, complete foreknowledge, the image of the invisible one who is the Father of the all through whom everything came into being, the first Man, for he revealed his appearance in a human form.
>
> And the whole aeon of the chief archon trembled, and the foundations of the abyss shook. And of the waters which are above matter, the underside was illuminated by the appearance of his image which had been revealed. And when all the authorities and the chief archon looked, they saw the whole part of the underside which was illuminated. And through the light they saw the form image in the water.
>
> And he said to the authorities which attend to him, 'Come, let us create a man according to the image of God and according to our likeness, that his

42. Thus, for example, Lietzmann, *Der Menschensohn*, pp. 67-68.

43. The text references to and quotations from the Nag Hammadi writings are according to the English translation of J.M. Robinson (ed.), *The Nag Hammadi Library* (1977).

44. Schenke, *Der Gott 'Mensch' in der Gnosis*, p. 36, referring to G. Quispel, 'Der gnostische Anthropos und die jüdische Tradition', *Eranos-Jahrbuch* 22 1953 (1954), pp. 195-234 (197).

image may become a light for us'. And they created by means of each other's powers in correspondence with the indications which were given. And each authority supplied a characteristic by means of the form of the image which he had seen in its psychic (form). He created a being according to the likeness of the first, perfect Man. And they said, 'Let us call him Adam, that his name may become a power of light for us'.

I have quoted rather extensively in order to give an impression of a system which reminds us very much of what we found in Irenaeus' description of Ophitic teaching.[45] It shows the intrinsic meaning of the designations Man and Son of Man, where Adam, created by the archons, is a copy of the reflection of the invisible Son of Man seen by the archons in the depth of the water. The expression turns up only once again, in the Apocryphon of John, in 25.1, in a context relating that when Adam 'recognized the likeness of his own foreknowledge, he begot the likeness of the son of man. He called him Seth according to the way of the race in the aeons.'

Of special importance is the *Gospel of Philip*, probably written in the second half of the third century and clearly of Valentinian provenance. Here, we also find Son of man with a clearly Gnostic meaning. The first occurrence (II, 3.63.25-30) is similar in form, but not in content, to the use in the canonical Gospels: the Lord goes into the dye works of Levi, taking 72 different colors and throwing them into the vat, saying, 'Even so has the Son of Man come [as] a dyer'. That that particular designation has a specifically Gnostic meaning is evident from the next occurrence (76.1-2), where it concludes the statement (75.25-36):

A horse sires a horse, a man begets man, a god brings forth a god. Compare [the] bridegroom and the bride. [Their children] were conceived in the [bridal chamber]. No Jew [was ever born] to Greek parents [as long as the world] has existed. And, [as a] Christian [people], we [ourselves do not descend] from the Jews. [There was] another [people and] these [blessed ones] are referred to as 'the chosen people of [the living God]' and 'the true man' and the 'Son of man' and the 'seed of the Son of man'. In the world it is called 'this true people'. Where they are, there are the sons of the bridal chamber.

This seems to mean that the Son of man is son of the God Man and that the seed of the Son of man is the true Gnostic. It could be argued that the three names also designate the chosen race.[46] That the former understanding is

45. *Adv haer* I 30.6 (Harvey I, pp. 232-33). The *Gospel of the Egyptians*, 'an esoteric tractate representing mythological Gnosticism' (Robinson [ed.], *The Nag Hammadi Library*, p. 195), contains only one occurrence of Son of man (III, 2.59.3), a parallel to *Apocryphon of John* (14.14-15).

46. Thus Borsch, *The Christian and Gnostic Son of Man*, p. 80, thinks the titles 'stand in apposition. This would certainly be in keeping with teaching such as that found among the Naassenes... The race is called by the name, as it were, of its divine *eponym*.'

also valid finds confirmation in the *Gospel of Philip*, in a saying famous for speaking of the son of the Son of man (81.14-21):

> There is the Son of man and there is the son of the Son of man. The Lord is the Son of man, and the son of the Son of man is he who is created through the Son of man. The Son of man received from God the capacity to create. He also has the ability to beget...

It should be noted that of the number of other references to 'the Man' in this text, most of them pertain to Jesus.[47]

In the famous *Gospel of Thomas*, in spite of being mostly a collection of sayings of Jesus, Son of man turns up only once, in a passage clearly related to Mt. 8.20 and Lk. 9.58 (logion 86 in 48.1-3). The Gnostic touch, however, is present in the little addition, 'but the Son of Man has no place to lay his head', that is, 'to rest'. It is not possible to determine if the expression has a meaning other than in the canonical Gospels. Perhaps logion 106 (50.20)—'When you make the two one, you will become sons of man'—speaks for understanding Son of Man in logion 86 as Gnostic.[48] In any event, its absence in the rest of the gospel indicates that it had no special interest to the author(s).[49]

47. See Borsch, *The Christian and Gnostic Son of Man*, p. 80, where in n. 93 the following references are given: Perfect Man (55.12; 58.20; 60.23-24; 75.20-21; 80.4; cf. 58.31), Man of Heaven (58.17); Living Man (75.24). I have altered the references to accord with the translation in Robinson (ed.), *The Nag Hammadi Library in English*. According to Borsch, 'This usage might be viewed as a form of christological development in that Jesus is given a title attributed in other Gnostic writings to the high God'.

48. Thus Bracht, *Der Menschensohn*, pp. 456-59, also pointing in support of this view to logion 108 (50.29-30): 'He who will drink from My mouth will become like Me. I myself shall become he, and the things that are hidden will be revealed to him.' This motif is also present at other places (Bracht, pp. 453-59). W. Schenk, *Das biographische Ich-Idiom 'Menschensohn' in den frühen Jesus-Biographien* (1997), pp. 22-23, finds that the plural in logion 106 clears up the semantics of the *singular* specific to this author in logion 86: 'es liegt also bei dem Syntagma hier im EvThom gar kein "Idiom" mehr vor, sondern vielmehr stehen hier nun zwei functional deutlich getrennte Nomina: "Wer ein 'Sohn' (= Schüler) 'des Menschen' (= des präexistenten Pneuma) werden will, der soll sich hier auf Erden nicht ausruhen, sondern die Ruhe als Einung mit dem Pneuma dort suchen, wo sie für den Gnostiker zu finden ist."'

49. One could miss the expression, for example, in logion 44 (40.27-30). On the other hand, it is probably not any special content connected with the expression, which has led to its omission. I, therefore, cannot follow Borsch, when he (*The Christian and Gnostic Son of Man*, p. 84) says: 'We are suggesting...that as Gnosticism fully developed, it inclined to turn away from the presentation of the Son of Man as found in the canonical Gospels and either to omit it or to transform it (and/or to transform a usage which has been inherited from earlier Christian or from non-Christian thought)'. The problem was obviously that Son of Man from the beginning meant something special in Gnostic understanding.

Surprisingly, we find Gospel-like language in a Gnostic writing, which is normally said to be without apparent traces of Christian influence.[50] *Eugnostos the Blessed*, a religio-philosophical epistle, but traditio-historically related to the *Sophia of Jesus Christ*, is a revelation discourse. In spite of their different genres, the two writings seem to be versions of the same original document. Normally, *Eugnostos the Blessed* is seen as the version closest to the non-Christian Gnostic original, the *Sophia of Jesus Christ* being heavily Christianized. Yet, they are apparently not independent versions. Most likely, *Sophia* is a reworking of *Eugnostos*.[51] For that reason we first investigate Eugnostos.

In the first of three (or four) occurrences of Son of Man in *Eugnostos*, we hear of the kingdom of the Son of Man. In a context (III, 3.8.31-9.6) about Man taking his consort and revealing that first-begotten androgyny whose name is 'First-begotten [Son of the Father]' and whose female aspect is 'First-begotten Sophia [Mother of the Universe]' whom some [call] 'Love', it is said (81.10-82.6):

> First-Begetter Father is called 'Adam of the Light'. And the kingdom of Son of Man is full of effable joy and unchanging jubilation because they rejoice continually in effable joy over their imperishable glory, which has never been heard of, nor has it been revealed to all the aeons that came to be and their worlds.
>
> Now Son of Man harmonized with Sophia, his consort, and revealed a great androgynous light. [Some call his] masculine name 'Savior, Begetter of All Things'. His feminine name is called 'Sophia, All-Begettress'. Some call her 'Pistis'.

That we have here the well-known Gnostic scheme is confirmed in the third (and fourth) instance, where it is said (85.11-13):

> Now the first aeon is that of Immortal Man. The second aeon is that of the Son of Man, the one who is called 'First Begetter'. <The third is that of the son of the Son of Man,> the one who is called Savior.

In the *Sophia of Jesus Christ*, there are six occurrences of Son of Man, three of them occurring in doublets with Eugnostos. The first (III, 4.104.1-2) is in a question from Bartholomew to the Holy One: 'How (is it that) <he> was designated in the Gospel "Man" and "Son of Man"? From which of them, then, is this son?' The answer describes how the First Man reflected in his consort, the great Sophia, their union resulting in his first-begotten,

50. For a discussion of the relationship with, and attempts at reconstructing, the original Gnostic myth, see Borsch, *The Christian and Gnostic Son of Man*, pp. 92-101.

51. Thus, for instance, J. Hyldahl, 'Har gnosticismen en filosofisk oprindelse? – det litterære forhold mellem Eugnostos' brev og Sophia Jesu Christi belyst', *DTT* 62 (1999), pp. 203-15.

androgyny with the name 'First-begotten [Son of the Father]'. He is also called 'Christ'. That we should understand this about an emanation of the Son of Man, or the creation of another 'Son' by the Son of Man, seems to be suggested by the content of an answer given later. The surprise is that Son of Man occurs in the question and not the answer (cf. Mt. 16.13).[52]

Sophia (105.19-21), in a way similar to *Eugnostos*, speaks of the 'kingdom of Son of Man', immediately adding: 'the one who is called the Son of God'. The passage about how the Son of Man, harmonizing with his consort Sophia (106.14-24), is nearly identical with that in *Eugnostos*. The enumeration of aeons parallel to *Eugnostos* (85.11-13) in *Sophia* (108.1-17) is introduced (107.17–108.1) with the well-known exhortation: 'Whoever has an ear to hear, let him hear!' But here we find another order, the aeon of the Son of Man coming first:

> The first aeon is that of the Son of Man, the one who is called the 'First Begetter', the one who is called Savior, the one who was revealed. The second aeon is that of Man, who is called 'Adam, the Eye of the Light'. The one who embraces these is the aeon over whom there is no kingdom, (the aeon) of the divine, boundless eternity, the self-begotten aeon of the aeons that are in him...

In a final passage (117.23–118.4), without parallel in *Eugnostos*, about the persons obtaining salvation, it is also said: 'Whosoever knows Son of Man in knowledge and love, let him bring me a sign of Son of Man, so that he might depart to the dwellings with those who are in the Eighth'. There is probably a connection between the sign of Son of Man in this final section and Mt. 24.30, just as the words of the kingdom of Son of Man, although taken over from *Eugnostos*, could have reminded the Christian author of Mt. 16.28 (and 13.49).

Most likely, Son of Man in *Eugnostos* stems from Christian Gnostic use of the title.[53] On reading *Sophia of Jesus Christ*, it is difficult to avoid the impression that the author tries to harmonize what he has found with a more Christian Gnostic understanding by introducing the titles Son of God and the Christ and by making Son of Man the first aeon.

There are a series of other occurrences of Son of man in writings of the Nag Hammadi library. These documents witness to a varied use. The basic

52. Borsch, *The Christian and Gnostic Son of Man*, p. 100, may be right in claiming that this points to 'other accounts and the fact that the title is found in the question furthers our suspicion that the author has borrowed the title from the materials which he used to compose the answer. He thus apparently attempted to make secure the understanding that the one otherwise called the Son of Man is also the Christ, the Son of God.'

53. Of course, this is one of the places adduced by those who postulate that there has been a genuine non-Christian Son of Man, arising within Judaism; cf. Borsch, *The Christian and Gnostic Son of Man*, p. 99, 107-108 and 110-21.

understanding seems at most places, however, to be the same. In the *Prayer of the Apostle Paul* (I, 1.11-15), Jesus Christ as Son of man is obviously identified with the Spirit. Here, invoking the One exalted above every name, through Jesus Christ [the Lord] of Lords, the king of ages, Paul asks for his gifts 'through the Son of man, the Spirit, the Paraclete of [truth]'. In the *Apocryphon of James*, perhaps, but not clearly originating in Valentinian Gnosticism and written in the third century, the Saviour in a passage (I, 2.3.10-20) pointing to the danger of having seen him without having recognized who he is, being not 'filled', uses Son of man two (or three) times, like the canonical Gospels as a third person reference to himself. It is not clear from the context alone if it has only a circumlocutional reference or whether it functions as a title.

In the *Treatise on Resurrection* (also known as the *Epistle to Rheginos*), ascribed by some to Valentinus himself, but probably coming from a late second-century Valentinian Christian Gnostic, Son of Man is clearly used four times as a title, but with similarities to its use in designating the human nature of Christ (I, 4.44.21-36):

> Now the Son of God, Rheginos, was Son of Man.[54] He embraced them both, possessing the humanity and divinity, so that on the one hand he might vanquish death through his being Son of God, and that on the other through the Son of Man the restoration to the Pleroma might occur; because he was originally from above, a seed of the Truth, before this structure (of the cosmos) had come into being.

That it is a title is clear from the third and last occurrence (46.14-15): 'For we have known the Son of Man, and we have believed that he rose from among the dead'. Although reminding one of, for example, Mk 9.9 (and also of Jn 9.35, which speaks of faith in the Son of Man), Son of Man stands with a different meaning than in the canonical Gospels.[55]

The *Dialogue of the Saviour* contains two (or three) instances (III, 5.[131.20-21]; 135.16-17; 136.21) where Son of Man is used as a title for

54. According to Borsch, *The Christian and Gnostic Son of Man*, p. 85, Son of Man in the Coptic here is anarthrous, 'which is unusual if not unique in the Coptic'. It reminds us of the use in Ignatius's *Eph.* 20.2 and *Barn.* 12.10. Cf. Chapter 1, above.

55. Where Borsch, *The Christian and Gnostic Son of Man*, p. 86, because of the last lines, thinks it clear, 'that the author comprehended more than mere humanity when he used the Son of Man designation', D.R.A. Hare, *The Son of Man Tradition* (1990), p. 39, finds that, 'Because of the repeated contrast between Son of God and Son of Man, however, it is better to assume that "Son of man" functions here as a way of referring to the incarnate state of the Son of God; the restoration of human souls to the Pleroma for this author requires incarnation, not simply a docetic revealer'. Thus, although 'the author was aware of Gnostic speculation about "Son of Anthropos", it is clear that he has not allowed such thinking to influence this writing profoundly'.

the Lord without any indications of a special meaning. In the *Second Treatise of the Great Seth*, the picture is more interesting. In a numbering of persons having been made laughingstocks because of the interference of the Hebdomad, we learn that David was made a laughingstock 'in that his son was named the Son of Man...as if he had become stronger than I and the fellow members of my race' (VII, *2*.63.4-9). All the biblical characters from Adam to John the Baptist did not know Seth. 'There is a great deception upon their soul, making it impossible for them ever to find a Nous of freedom in order to know him, until they come to know the Son of Man' (64.7-12). In what follows, the speaker twice presents himself: 'I am Christ, the Son of Man, the one from you (pl.) who is among you'. The second time, 'who is exalted above the heavens' is added (65.18-20; 69.21-22).

The *Apocalypse of Peter* (not to be confused with the apocryphon of the same title) has only one instance with the expression Son of Man (VII, 3.71.12). Not having been known by the former prophets, 'he has now appeared among these, in him who appeared, who is the Son of Man who is exalted above the heavens in a fear of men of like essence'.

In *The Testimony of the Truth*, Son of Man occurs no less than 16 times, some of which are in reconstructions of the text.[56] Throughout, Son of man is used as a designation for the revealer of truth, beginning with the typical statement: 'But the Son of Man [came] forth from Imperishability, [being] alien to defilement'.

In The *Trimorphic Protennoia* there is a saying which echoes 1 Cor. 9.20. Son of Man seems to mean simply a human being (XIII, 1.49.15-20): 'And among the Angels I revealed myself in their likeness, and among the Powers as if I were one of them, but among the Sons of Man as if I were a Son of Man, even though I am Father of everyone'.

Also to be examined in this context is the Coptic *Gospel of Mary*, although it does not belong to the Nag Hammadi library. It contains an interesting saying, resembling Lk. 17.21. Just before his departure, the apparently resurrected Saviour gives a short speech to his disciples, concluding with the words (Codex Berolinensis Gnosticus I 8):

> Peace be with you, Receive my peace to yourselves. Beware that no one is leading you astray, saying, 'Lo here!' or 'Lo there!' For the Son of Man is within you. Follow after him. Those who seek him, will find him. Go then and preach the gospel of the kingdom. Do not lay down any rules beyond what I appointed to you, and do not give a law like the lawgiver lest you be constrained by it.

56. IX, 3.30.8; 31.6; 32.22-23; 36.[24], 37.[10].[27-28]; 38.[4]. 40.[23]; 41.2-3; 60.6; 61.[9]; 67.7; 68.[11]; 69.[15]; 71.[12-13]; 72.[25] (pp. 407-10, 413-15).

This ending of the speech reminds us of a series of sayings known from the canonical Gospels (for the warning, see esp. Mt. 24.5, 23; Lk. 17.23, 21). What is a *possible* understanding of the Kingdom of God in Lk. 17.21 is here *explicitly* the only possible understanding of the Son of man. He is an inward reality. To a certain extent, there is an identity between Son of man and the Gnostic.[57] It is even possible to speak of a 'democratization' of the expression to the effect that in following Jesus, perfect humanity is achieved.[58]

Soon after it is related that the disciples react on the departure of Jesus with grief. 'They wept greatly, saying, "How shall we go to the Gentiles and preach the gospel of the kingdom of the Son of Man? If they did not spare him, how will they spare us?"' We here meet the concept of the 'kingdom of the Son of Man', which could have been inspired by sayings such as Mt. 16.28 (cf. Mt. 13.49, with Dan. 7.13-14 in the background). What pertains to preaching the gospel of the kingdom also reminds us of Gospel sayings, for example, Mt. 24.14.

As is often the case when reading Gnostic sources, their theological content appears surprisingly modern. What the anti-Gnostic fathers found abominable—namely, that the Highest God was perceived as the transcendent and perfect idea of man, the ultimate goal of human existence—is not that foreign to a generation living with the results of psycho-analysis, understanding transcendence not so much as an other-worldly room as a spiritual dimension of this world. With perhaps similar disgust, they found the thought that the Highest God was not the Creator of the world. In the Early Church, this interpretation became a parenthesis, the so-called orthodox faith operating with a two-room concept, with God existing in his Heaven.

57. Cf. Weist, *Wer ist dieser Menschensohn?*, p. 47: 'Vielleicht kann der Schluß gewagt werden, daß wir hier wieder den Gedanken der Vorprägung des Menschensohn-Erlösers im Inneren der zu Erlösenden vor uns haben, wie er schon in der NAASSENER-PREDIGT zu finden war'.

58. Thus Jens Schröter, 'Zur Menschensohnvorstellung im Evangelium nach Maria', in Stephen Emmel, Martin Krause, Siegfried G. Richter and Sofia Schaten (eds.), *Ägypten und Nubien in spätantiker und christlicher Zeit* (1999), II, pp. 178-88 (186): '[Es geht] hier um eine "Demokratisierung" des Ausdrucks in dem Sinne, daß in der Nachfolge Jesu die Erlangung des vollkommenen Menschseins ermöglicht wird. Dabei wird diese Nachfolge offensichtlich stärker von der Erkenntnis bestimmter Zusammenhänge über die Natur der Dinge und des Menschen verstanden als an die historische Person Jesu gebunden.' Schröter thinks it possible that the Johannine Son of man has been the mediator between the Synoptic Son of man and the one in the *Gospel of Mary*, but further, that the Philonic interpretation of the two stories about the creation of man in Gen. 1–2, as reflected in 1 Cor. 15.45-47, could lead to the assumption that 'the Son of man inside you' should be understood in the wake of an interpretation of the impact of Jesus as restoring the image of God in man (cf. pp. 183-85).

As an effort to describe the agent as giving access to knowledge of the Highest God, and thereby able to perform as redeemer, Son of Man was a very apt title. Like the title Son of God, it expressed the moment of redeeming revelation, made possible through the intimate relationship between Creator and his messenger. As Son of the Anthropos, the redeemer was able to offer the gnosis, which alone could liberate the eternal part of the Gnostic from the material world. It seems clear that the title Son of Man, being exclusively used in Christian Gnostic sources, stems from the expression Son of man in the canonical Gospels. This did not happen in form of a continuation of the use of the expression there, but rather as a result of a deliberate interpretation, conveying it in a quite new way.

4. *The Pseudo-Clementine Literature*

A special Jewish–Christian interpretation of Son of man is found in the *Pseudo-Clementine Homiliae* (Greek) and *Recognitiones* (only known in complete form in a Latin translation). This literature is not genuinely Gnostic. Gnostic influence is, nevertheless, traceable in it. The tradition-history of the Pseudo-Clementine literature is obscure. *The Homilies* and the *Recognitions* probably rest independently on a common source, reaching back to the first half of the third century, a source which has already reworked older traditions, among them the *Kerygmata Petrou* from the middle of the second century.[59] In this literature, Son of man is the title of the true prophet who manifested himself in a series of true prophets to find his final form in Jesus.[60] The perception of the true prophet as having revealed himself in a series of figures[61] also manifests itself in the mention of sons of men (υἱοὶ ἀνθρώπων). The singular form always refers to Jesus alone. The meaning of the phrase in this literature appears in *Recognitiones* I 60.1-7, where the claim of Jesus to be the Christ is questioned by a disciple of John the Baptist, quoting the Gospel tradition, but defended by Simon the Canaanite. The logic of the argument is interesting:[62]

> And, behold, one of the disciples of John asserted that John was the Christ, and not Jesus, inasmuch as Jesus Himself declared that John was greater than

59. See Altaner and Stuiber, *Patrologie*, pp. 134-35. G. Strecker, *Das Judenchristentum in den Pseudoklementinen* (1958), also thinks it possible to reconstruct parts of another source; namely, *Anabathmoi Jacobou II* (the numeral indicates that this book should not be confused with the book with the same title mentioned in Epiphany, *Panarion* XXX 16.6-9). Cf. the discussion in J. Neville Birdsall, 'Problems of the Clementine Literature', in J.D.G. Dunn (ed.), *Jews and Christians* (1992), pp. 347-61.

60. *Recogn* I 60.3; III 61.2 (filius hominis) and Homiliae III 22.3 (υἱὸς ἀνθρώπου).

61. *Hom* II 17.2 and III 26.1.

62. Translation here and in the following, according to *ANF* 8.

> all men and all prophets [Mt. 11.9, 11]. 'If, then', said he, 'he be greater than all, he must be held to be greater than Moses, and than Jesus himself. But if he be the greatest of all, then must he be the Christ.' To this Simon the Canaanite, answering, asserted that John was indeed greater than all the prophets, and all who are born of women (omnibus qui sunt filii mulierum), yet that he is not greater than the Son of man (filius hominis). Accordingly Jesus is also the Christ, whereas John is only the prophet: and there is as much difference between him and Jesus, as between the forerunner and Him whose forerunner he is; or as between Him who gives the law, and him who keeps the law.

The logic of the argumentation is that, whereas John is born of a woman, Jesus is Son of a man and thereby belongs to the more important male line of prophecy, whereas John belongs to the less important female line. In the list of the ten pairs (syzygies) in *Recognitiones* III 61.1, the Son of man is paired with the tempter (7th), whereas Christ is paired with Antichrist (10th). This shows that Son of man is exclusively used of the earthly Jesus. In *Homiliae* III 22, we hear about the difference between the first man and the female companion created along with him. She represents the prophecy relating to all who are born of women. 'But the other, as the son of man, being a male (ὡς υἱὸς ἀνθρώπου ἄρσην ὤν), prophesies better things to the world to come as a male (ὡς ἄρσενι τῷ μέλλοντι αἰῶνι)'. *Homiliae* III 23 makes it clear that female prophecy is fraudulent. From *Recognitiones* I 45, it is clear that the Christ title already belongs to the first prophet, appointed by God as 'a man over men, who is Christ Jesus' (hominibus hominem, qui est Jesus Christus). As is said in 47, 'If the first man prophesied, it is certain that he was also anointed' (Si primus...homo prophetavit, certum est quod et unctus sit).

In spite of many traces of Gnostic influence in the Pseudo-Clementine literature, the phrase Son of man is understood distinctly otherwise than in genuine Gnosticism by concentrating on the gender meaning of 'man'.[63] It is not obvious that this use of Son of man should be characterized as a continuation of an apocalyptic tradition. On the contrary, it is an arbitrary exploitation of the wording of an expression for a foreign purpose. Perhaps it should also be said that this 'heretical' use differs from the more 'orthodox' only in having a different content. Principally, the difference is slight.

5. *Conclusion*

The connection between Son of man in canonical texts and Gnostic sources is obvious. The central question is whether there is anything in Gnostic

63. Cf. Colpe, 'ὁ υἱὸς τοῦ ἀνθρώπου', p. 478: 'filius hominis hat deshalb die Bedeutung *Mannessohn*'.

usage pointing in the direction of taking over a set of conceptions originally connected with the expression Son of man, eventually continuing a usage from Christian traditions that developed differently from the one found in the canonical Gospels.[64] The question presupposes that there once existed such a thing as a Son of man concept. As soon as this prejudice is abandoned, the Gnostic use of the designation, Son of man, appears mostly as a special interpretation of the expression as found in the Gospel tradition. This interpretation receives its content from Gnostic cosmogonic and anthropological speculations, which find their confirmation in the use of this term by Jesus. This is the most obvious explanation of what is otherwise a great enigma; namely, how the 'title', which Jesus employed most often about himself, lost its original meaning, shortly after its use in the canonical Gospels.[65]

64. This is the position of Borsch, *The Christian and Gnostic Son of Man*, pp. 110-21 (114): 'We would...suggest that a significant number of the gnostic references to the Son of Man ought not to be regarded as stemming from the influence of canonical materials... We are led...to the second of the possibilities...that gnostic usage of the Son of Man designation, in part, derives from forms of early Christian tradition which then developed differently from those which eventually reached the canonical evangelists.' Borsch thinks of Jewish speculations and Christian 'statements which once had a more decidedly mythological and liturgical frame of reference' (p. 116).

65. Cf., for another understanding, Schenke, *Der Gott 'Mensch' in der Gnosis*, p. 154, where it is said that the Son of Man, originating in speculations in Early Judaism about the first man and the ur-king, was connected by the Gnostics with the conception of the God 'Man'. 'Im frühen hellenistischen Christentum ist nämlich die spätjüdische Messiasbezeichnung "Menschensohn" bald zu einem kaum mehr verstandenen Titel Jesu geworden... Über das Christentum gelangte der Heilands-Titel "Menschensohn" in die Gnosis und gewann hier eine spekulativ-theologische Bedeutung, die ihm in der Kirche vorenthalten worden war.'

3. Nicene and Post-Nicene Fathers

With the establishment of the Christian Church during the reign of Constantine, theology quickly became more or less an 'official' realm, which added a new dimension to the various disputes. A common creed was established at Nicea in 325, asserting that the Son is of the same essence as the Father (ὁμοούσιος τῷ πατρί) and, although this formula was ambiguous, it could be dangerous to dissent![1]

1. *The East*

Beginning in the East, the first person to be mentioned is Athanasius (c. 295–373), who was bishop of Alexandria from 328. Athanasius mediates between the dualistic view of the Antiochenes and the confluence of the two natures in Apollinaris (see below). He takes Son of man as an expression for the human part of the Logos really becoming man by taking on flesh.[2] John 1.14 plays a fundamental role as is seen for instance in his *Oratio contra Arianos* III 30 where it is stressed that while the Logos remained God's Logos, it became Son of man (Υἱὸν ἀνθρώπου γενέσθαι). In *Oratio contra Arianos* I 45,[3] speaking about the exaltation of Christ and its connection with the exaltation he is offering, Athanasius declares:

> For He who is the Son of God, became Himself the Son of Man (αὐτὸς γὰρ ὢν τοῦ Θεοῦ Υἱὸς, αὐτὸς γέγονε καὶ Υἱὸς ἀνθρώπου); and, as Word, He gives from the Father, for all things which the Father does and gives, He does

1. Cf., to this chapter, Weist, *Wer ist dieser Menschensohn?*, pp. 16-25, but especially Bracht, *Der Menschensohn*, pp. 481-517 (notes pp. 583-603).

2. Bracht, *Der Menschensohn*, pp. 488-89, remarks: 'Daß die verschiedenen Gruppierungen alle auch mit dem MS-Titel Jesu argumentierten, lag nicht nur an der allegorischen Methode der Schriftauslegung und der Umdeutung der ntl-christologischen Prädikationen zu Wesensaussagen durch weitgehende Einbeziehung umlaufender philosophischer Vorstellungen in der Schriftinterpretation, sondern ebenso an der noch weitgehend unfixierten Begrifflichkeit, die sich auf die Termini ἄνθρωπος, ἀνθρωπότης, τὸ ἀνθρωπίνον und σάρξ erstreckte, so daß bei wörtlichem Verständnis des MS-Titels dieser ganz unterschiedlichen Ideen als "Schriftbeweis" dienen konnte.'

3. Translation according to *NPNF* 2nd series vol. IV.

> and supplies through Him; and as the Son of Man (ὡς δὲ Υἱὸς ἀνθρώπου), He Himself is said to receive what proceeds from Him after the manner of men, because His body is none other than His and is a natural recipient of grace, as has been said.

In another place, *Epistola de Nicaenis decretis* 14,[4] Athanasius admits that the Son was created too, but first at the incarnation; 'for creation belongs to man'. He proceeds: 'Now as to the season spoken of, he will find for certain that, whereas the Lord always is, at length in fulness of the ages He became man; and whereas He is Son of God, He became Son of man also (καὶ Υἱὸς ὢν τοῦ Θεοῦ γέγονε καὶ Υἱὸς ἀνθρώπου).'

For Athanasius, a consequence of this in describing the human nature of Christ is that Son of man represents the fleshly aspect in such a way that it is indeed inferior to the pneumatic aspect. It stands for human existence in its perishability and mortality. This is seen in *Epistula 4 ad Serapionem* 18–20[5] in an exposition of the saying about blaspheming against the Holy Spirit (Mt. 12.31-32par). The point of departure for the discussion is Mt. 13.54, Jn 8.57, and especially Mt. 12.24, where the adversaries of Jesus accuse him of being an agent of Beelzebul. They hereby sin against the Saviour as a human. On the other hand, the works of Christ witness to his divinity in such a way that they cannot be put aside as the works of Beelzebul without blaspheming. In either case, questions were tolerated as long as the Jews looked at what was human (εἰς τὰ ἀνθρώπινα βλέποντες), even if they thereby sinned against the Son of man. But when they declared his works to be the works of Beelzebul, he condemned them to eternal punishment, because in this they blasphemed against the Holy Spirit. According to Athanasius, the Lord himself indicates this distribution of the two kinds of blasphemy on Son of man and the Spirit, respectively:[6]

> Of himself he says both 'Son of man' and 'Spirit' to show from the one his physical existence (τὸ σωματικὸν ἑαυτοῦ), but from the Spirit to reveal his spiritual and intelligible and most true deity (τὴν πνευματικὴν ἑαυτοῦ καὶ νοητὴν καὶ ἀληθεστάτην θεότητα). And the one [sin] to obtain pardon he assigned the Son of man to signify his bodily existence, but the unforgivable blasphemy he declared to approach the Spirit, for, though saying this with regard to the contradistinction to his bodily existence, to indicate his divinity.

Athanasius also refers to Jn 6.61-63,[7] accentuating the pneumatic aspect at the expense of the fleshly. Again, the Lord distinguishes between his flesh and spirit that they shall learn to believe not only in the visible but also in the invisible part of him, because what he says is not fleshly but spiritual:

4. Translation according to *NPNF* 2nd series vol. IV.
5. Cf. *Epistula 4 ad Serapionem* 16 and *Oratio ad Arianos* I 50.
6. *Epistula 4 ad Serapionem* 19.
7. *Epistula 4 ad Serapionem* 19.

> For this reason, he (sc. John) makes mention of the ascent to heaven of the Son of man to distract them (the listeners) from the corporeal sense (τῆς σωματικῆς ἐννοίας) and finally make them experience the flesh spoken of as the heavenly food from above (βρῶσιν ἄνωθεν οὐράνιον) and the spiritual nourishment given from him.

Returning to Mt. 13.54, Athanasius concludes that he who asks 'Where did he get this wisdom?' sins and blasphemes against the Son of man,

> but he who sees his works done in the Holy Spirit and nevertheless will not acknowledge that he who performs such works is God and Son of God, but ascribes them to Beelzebul, clearly blasphemes in denying his divinity. For, as pronounced so often in the evangelical text, when he is saying 'Son of man', he points to his flesh and humanity (λέγων, 'Υἱὸς ἀνθρώπου', τὸ κατὰ σάρκα καὶ ἀνθρώπινον αὐτοῦ δείκνυσιν), to show that when he is saying 'the Spirit', he possess the Spirit in which he does all these things.[8]

This is also confirmed through the saying in Mt. 26.45 that 'the Son of man is betrayed into the hands of sinners', because his works mean that he has to be believed as the true God while his death shows that he really has a body. 'So he reasonably calls the one betrayed Son of man, because the Logos is immortal and not to be touched, and it is life itself.'[9]

In the so-called *Sermo maior de fide*, falsely ascribed to Athanasius as a *Letter to the Antiochenes*, we find an understanding of Son of man which clearly deviates from the above.[10] The Son of man in this writing is not the Son of God being made man but—in accordance with Antiochene Christology—the human body assumed by the heavenly Logos. Thus the second man from heaven in 1 Cor. 15.47 in par. 8 (9 in the Greek text) 'is to be understood about the Saviour's Man, who is called "Son of Man"' (τὸν κατὰ τὸν σωτῆρα νοούμενον, ὃσ καλεῖται υἱὸσ τοῦ ἀνθρώπου) (cf. 11). This becomes more obvious in par. 14, explaining 1 Jn 3.2:

8. *Epistula 4 ad Serapionem* 20.

9. *Epistula 4 ad Serapionem* 20. Cf. *Oratio contra arianos* I 50. Weist, *Wer ist dieser Menschensohn?*, pp. 17-18, concludes: 'Damit hat der Menschensohn-Begriff alle ihm von Dan 7 her eignende Transzendenz eingebüßt. Gerade infolgedessen bleibt aber unklar, wie ATHANASIUS die Vorstellung der Auffahrt des Menschensohnes mit dem Sterblichkeitsgedanken in Einklang bringt'.

10. I owe this reference to Bracht, *Der Menschensohn*, pp. 491-92. The translation is according to R.P. Casey, *The Armenian Version of the Pseudo-Athanasian Letter to the Antiochenes and of the Expositio Fidei* (1947), where the Greek text of the letter is included (using σ in stead of ς). Bracht, *Der Menschensohn*, pp. 490-91, further refers to some other pseudo-Athanasian writings expressing almost the same view of Son of man. Thus *Oratio contra Arianos* IV 6 (cf. Altaner and Stuiber, *Patrologie*, p. 273), *De incarnatione et contra Arianos* 8 (cf. Altaner and Stuiber, *Patrologie*, p. 273: 'wahrscheinlich ein Werk des Marcellus von Ankyra') and *De incarnatione contra Apollinarem* I 8, 10, 12, 14 and 20 (Altaner and Stuiber, *Patrologie*, p. 274).

> 'When he appears we shall be like him, for we shall see him as he is': It is said that 'until then, no one saw the Son of God as he is until he revealed himself to us. Yet, we have seen the Son of Man, with whom he clothed himself for our sakes… (ὃν δὲ ἐφόρεσεν δι' ἡμᾶσ υἱὸν τοῦ ἀνθρώπου…).

The author further refers to Stephen, who, according to Acts 7.56, did not say that he 'saw the Word or the Father's Wisdom but the Son of Man, the Dominical Man who was from Mary', and to Jn 5.27. And with regard to Prov. 8.22 he claims (20):

> This is related by the Psalm regarding the aspects of the Son of Man, who is from Mary and the Son of God, the Word, who from the beginning is with the Father. He indicates two aspects: one created of Mary and born of man and the other, who has subsisted before the ages by a timeless and eternal generation from the Father.

Verse 27 also serves as an explanation of the saying in Mk 13.32 that not even the Son knows the day or the hour of the Day of Judgment. It is, of course, not valid for the Word or the Holy Spirit but for the Son, meaning the Son of Man. Otherwise

> he might have said that not even the Son of God knows, nor the Holy Spirit or the angels. But when he mentions the angels first and then the Son, because 'he was made a little lower than the angels' [Hebrews 2.7; cf. Psalm 8.5-6] by sufferings and death, he does not recall that he did not say the Holy Spirit did not know, but that the Son of Man did not know the day on which he became the sovereign creator of the universe. For even though he did not say, 'The Son of Man does not know' but merely, 'the Son', he indicates that it was not the divine Word who was ignorant, but the Son of Man.[11]

In this way the unknown author[12] effectively separates the Son of God and the Son of Man, thus laying the groundwork for the much later apologetic idea of *kenosis*.

In the huge collection of letters attributed to Isidor of Pelusium (c. 360-c. 435), suspected to be a forgery,[13] we find in *Epistolarum* I 59 the same explanation as in Athanasius, regarding the possibility of forgiveness for speaking a word against the Son of man in Mt. 12.31-32. It is forgivable because 'for those whose spiritual eye is blessed, it is difficult to comprehend and difficult to observe God indescribably united with the inferiority of

11. The very short Greek text (24) looks like a summary: Εἰ γὰρ καὶ μὴ εἶπεν ὅτι ὁ υἱὸσ τοῦ ἀνθρώπου, ἀλλ' ἁπλῶσ ὁ υἱόσ, δείκνυται μὴ τὸν θεὸν λόγον δηλῶν ἀγνοοῦτα, ἀλλὰ τὸν ἄνθρωπον.

12. Altaner and Stuiber, *Patrologie*, p. 274, mention that *Sermo maior de fide* has been ascribed to Eustathius of Antiochia or Marcellus of Ancyra. Bracht, *Der Menschensohn*, p. 589 n. 617, concludes: 'Die Verwendung des MS-Titels würde eher auf Eustathius hindeuten'.

13. Altaner and Stuiber, *Patrologie*, pp. 267-68.

the visible flesh, his hidden divinity being not recognizable'. In a catena, in connection with Mt. 16.13, there is a repetition of the view of Justin concerning who the 'man' is in Son of man, namely, either Adam or the virgin.[14]

Didymus the Blind (313–398), the famous lay teacher in Alexandria who counted Jerome and Rufinus among his pupils, adhered to some of Origen's ideas, but was condemned for Origenism at the Synod in Constantinople in 553. As a result, most of his writings disappeared into oblivion, until 1941, when a great hoard of papyri was found in Tura near Cairo, which included texts of Origen and several works, among them more Bible commentaries, which can be ascribed to Didymus with more or less probability. One of them is a commentary on Psalms, in which, in his interpretation of Ps. 30.21a (LXX), probably inspired by v. 20d (ἐναντίον τῶν υἱῶν τῶν ἀνθρώπων), he offers an excursus on Jesus' use of the expression Son of man. As has been pointed out, it is one of the oldest treatises on the Son of man.[15] An important feature is Jesus' having both a human soul and preserving the original status of man, that is, sinlessness, a main point in the christological debates of the fourth century.

Didymus offers four reasons for Jesus' right to use this expression, summarizing what is found earlier in patristic literature. The first is the result of a symbolic interpretation, in line with the wording of the Psalm. Because of his care for men, God is often named 'man' in Scripture and it is only natural that his son be called Son of man. The second reason is more to the point and reiterates Irenaeus' concept of *anakephalaiosis*.[16] Thus the words

14. Bracht, *Der Menschensohn*, p. 497 and pp. 501-502, also includes two more Alexandrian witnesses. The first is Peter II of Alexandria, the successor of Athanasius, who, in a fragment of a letter surviving in Facundus of Hermiane, speaks about Christ as having 'persona filii hominis ex Maria, et filii Dei Verbi, quod ab initio erat apud patrem', interpreting Prov. 8.22 and 23.24 as 'duas personas significans' (*MPG* 33, pp. 1292-93). The second is Theophilus of Alexandria, functioning as patriarch (385–412) and especially remembered for his violent fight against John Chrysostom in defence of the true humanity of the one Redeemer. In his festival letter of the year 404, surviving in a letter of Jerome (*Epistula* 100.11), Theophilus maintains in traditional language that the living Word of God was like us in every regard, except sin, and 'was appointed to come to us in a new way, in which he became Son of man while remaining Son of God' (novo modo ad nos venire dignatus est, ut fieret filius hominis et permaneret dei filius). Thus, to Theophilus as to Athanasius, Son of man pertains to the human part of the Son of God becoming man.

15. Thus Bracht, *Der Menschensohn*, p. 498, claiming that it 'in dieser Form als eine der ältesten Abhandlungen über die MS-Prädikation gewertet werden darf'. My exposition of the views of Didymus builds on Bracht, pp. 497-501. The text is according to the edition of Michael Gronewald, *Didymos der Blinde, Psalmenkommentar (Tura-Papyrus) III. Kommentar zu Psalm 29-34* (1969), pp. 108-23. The Text in *MPG* 39, cols. 1315-18 is shorter and does not contain the explanation of Son of man.

16. According to Bracht, *Der Menschensohn* (p. 592 n. 656), this interpretation was resumed a thousand years later by Erasmus in his commentary on Jn 1.1, and since gained ground through J.G. Herder's interpretation of Son of man as 'Idealmensch'.

in Gen. 1.26, concerning man being created in the image and likeness of God, are not seen as related exclusively to the individual Adam, but to the human race as a whole (ὁ καθόλου δὲ ἄνθρωπος). Because Jesus is the only one who has preserved the original type, he is the Son of man, the individuation of the 'ideal' type. 'He who has preserved the original type (πρωτότυπον) as a whole, he is the Son of man.' While the soul of Jesus has preserved what corresponds to the image—because he has not known sin and not committed any—he is named Son of this man, who was 'according to the image and likeness of God' (*Commentary on the Psalms* 152.30-32). The third reason is antidocetic:

> If Jesus as man had no father, he, nevertheless, possessed a mother. Yet the female is also a human being. To abolish the docetism, he is named Son of man. ... For, if he alone was named man, the docetists would have reason to assume that he alone had appeared as man, without having been born a human or having had a beginning. To show that he is from Mary, he named himself 'Son of man' (152.33–153.1 and 153.7-8).[17]

The fourth argument obviously confronts Apollinarism's claim that the body of Jesus was of heavenly origin, which was classified by Didymus as a heresy that revived the Gnostic teaching of Marcion, Basilides and Valentine. It is based on a false interpretation of Jn 3.13, aided by the fact that the Gospels also use the expression Son of man in sayings stressing Christ's divinity. Besides Jn 3.13, 6.62 also creates difficulties when it speaks about the Son of man ascending to where he was before. Didymus, like Diodore of Tarsus and Gregory of Nazianzus, returns to the principle of *communicatio idiomatum*: 'With respect to the composition taken as whole, we often say what is valid in regard to its separate parts' (153.16). This is also the case with respect to the Johannine Son of man sayings. In a fragment of his commentary on John, Didymus explains Jn 3.13's claim that nobody has ascended into Heaven but the Son of God alone, because only he has descended from there, 'the one named Son of man because of the oikonomia (διὰ τὴν οἰκονομία)'.[18]

17. Bracht, *Der Menschensohn*, p. 499, goes on to show how Didymus, like Justin, identifies 'man' in Son of man with Mary, but also tries to prove that the virgin birth does not prevent Jesus from being wholly human by introducing the physiological knowledge of the period according to which women were totally passive in conception, allowing room for the corporality to come from the male alone. Thus he argues from the difference between the prepositions ἐκ and διά. Jesus is not like other humans ἐξ ἀνδρός and διὰ γυναικός (1 Cor. 11.12), but according to Gal. 4.4 and Mt. 1.16 ἐκ γυναικός. Accordingly, he has the whole of his 'materia' (τὴν ὅλην ὕλην) from the female and is therefore named Son of man.

18. According to J. Reuss, *Johannes-Kommentare aus der griechischen Kirche* (1966), p. 177.

Thus Son of man in Didymus could have different content in different contexts. The designation can refer to the body, as is the case when he comments on Ps. 8.5b: when he (the God Logos) explains how he became man with regard to the body, he adds 'or Son of man (ἢ υἱὸς ἀνθρώπου). Because it is according to the body, not according to the soul that one is Son of a man.'[19] Otherwise, Didymus understands Son of man as the human part of the Redeemer, the acting subject of whom is the God Logos.

Cyril of Alexandria (c. 380–444), a sometimes violent bishop in Church politics, builds on Alexandrian tradition for a Christology, in which Logos takes on flesh and thus represents a middle course between the Apollinarian monophysitism and the Antiochene inspired dualism of Nestorius, who became one of the main targets of his polemic.[20] Inspired by Athanasius, Cyril distinguishes between a period before and a period after the incarnation of the Logos in order to preserve the unchangeability of the Logos. Thus Logos is also the subject in the incarnation. In this construction, Son of man designates the singularity of Christ as man. This understanding he sees as confirmed through the determinative:

> When divine Scripture puts articles before the names (τὰ ὀνόματα προταττομένων τῶν ἄρθρων), they signify something unique, which is exclusive and truly second to none as it is... When the Savior with the article (μετὰ τοῦ ἄρθρου) says: '*the* Son of Man', he designates himself in this way as the one selected out of myriads.[21]

Cyril's distinction of the time before and the time after the incarnation results in a distinction of the Son of man sayings between those about the fate of the incarnated and those referring to his glorious state. In either case, Son of man designates the human nature of Christ, emphasizing that it is not merely something external, but expressive of a true and concrete humanity. Cyril operates with a non-confluent (ἄσυγχυτος) union with respect to nature (ἕνωσις φυσικῄ). In an exposition of Jn 3.13—a saying which remains at the centre of the debate—he says:[22]

> About the Logos of God coming down from heaven, it is said that the Son of man came down, avoiding being divided into two persons after the incarnation (διχάζεσθαι μετὰ τὴν ἐνανθρώπησιν εἰς δύο πρόσωπα παραιτούμενος). Not allowing anybody to call one the Son of the Virgin because of the temple, he took on, of necessity, another, the Logos, manifested from God, insofar as it is befitting for each in the division according to nature. For just as the Logos is from God, so also is a man from a woman.

19. *In psalmos*, ad 8.5 (*MPG* 39, col. 1185).

20. The exposition of the views of Cyril owes a lot to Bracht, *Der Menschensohn*, pp. 502-506, where several more references are given.

21. *In Joannem* I 4 (39).

22. *In Joannem* II 1 ad 3.13; cf. IV 3 ad 6.62 and VII-VIII ad 12.23.

That he sees Son of man in this way as similar to man is clear from his explanation of Jn 6.27, admonishing people to work for the food offered them by the Son of man, who had been certified by God: 'Even when I appear to you as one of you, a man and subject to the flesh, I am, nevertheless, anointed and certified by my God, my Father, to unalterable equality with him'.[23] Thus Cyril considers Jn 8.28 as proving that the Son of man is not only man but also truly God.[24] The same clue is seen in the saying in Mt. 9.6, about Christ's forgiving sins; he uses Son of man to show the undivided unity maintaining the divine power within his human nature: 'Thus I am not being deprived of the expressions of the divinity (τι τῶν τῆς θεότητος ἰδιωμάτων); nor have I become meaner, becoming on earth unalterable and truly Son of man according to the flesh'.[25] Of course, this understanding also applies to Dan. 7.13 'describing accurately the mystery of incarnation' where the seer does not simply view the Logos, but one '*like* a Son of man', since because of us he appeared in the form of a man.[26]

In line with contemporary Christology, Cyril also speaks in this context of the two hypostases in Christ. In *Epistula ad Nestorium* 4,[27] in a passage given in a confessional style (which also became influential at the synods in Ephesus and Chalcedon), he writes:

> This the more so, because the Logos, having united itself with the flesh, was animated with a rational soul (σάρκα ἐμψυχωμένην ψυχῇ λογικῇ ἑνώσας), according to its essence (καθ' ὑπόστασιν), beyond thought, incomprehensibly, a man and used the name Son of man (καὶ κεχρημάτικεν Υἱὸς ἀνθρώπου), not only according to the will or satisfaction, but also as a preoccupation with the outward being alone (ἀλλ' οὐδὲ ὡς ἐν προσλήψει προσώπου μόνου).

In the *De recta fide ad reginas* II, one of the chapters (58) has the heading 'that Christ truly is God even when he is called Son of Man'. Here, Cyril adduces Jn 5.26-27; 3.13-14 and Mt. 16.27, summarizing Mt. 16.13 as saying that 'we believe all the more that he is truly God, also when he after being God has become Son of man for our sake, according to the economy of salvation' (πιστεύομεν δὲ μᾶλλον, ὅτι καὶ Θεός ἐστιν ἀληθινὸς, γέγονε δὲ καὶ Υἱος ἀνθρώπου δι' ὑμᾶς οἰκονομικῶς μετὰ τοῦ μεῖναι Θεός).

Finally, that the unity of the two natures established at the incarnation is also insoluble is seen from the apocalyptic Son of man sayings confirming that Christ at his second coming will appear in the same unity of natures.[28]

23. *In Joannem* III 5.
24. *In Joannem* V 5.
25. The fragment is quoted according to J. Reuss, *Matthäus-Kommentare aus der griechischen Kirche* (1957), pp. 185-86.
26. *In Joannem* II 4 ad 3.35.
27. Cf. *Epistula ad Nestorium* 17 and 39.
28. *Adversus Nestorium* IV 6. Cf. *Contra Synousiastas* 6-7.

Much the same line of thought is found in Ammonius of Alexandria (fourth or sixth century). Again Jn 3.13 is the occasion, the Son of man here being connected with an ἐνέργεια. It is said:[29]

> After uniting in substance (μετὰ τὴν καθ' ὑπόστασιν ἕνωσιν) he makes himself common with what belongs to the flesh, and with divinity according to activities, but without a change of those things of which Christ is constituted: the activities, the descending and the ascending. The body of the Lord is not heavenly, because it is exposed to suffering. So the one being according to the flesh is called Son of man, when he is calling the whole of himself after the flawed essence (Ὡς δὲ εἷς ὢν μετὰ σάρκος, λέγεται Υἱὸς ἀνθρώπου, ἀπὸ τῆς ἐλάττονος οὐσίας ὅλον ἑαυτὸν ὀνομάσας).

Quite another point of view is represented by Marcellus of Ancyra (c. 280–374), who sometimes argued with Athanasius against the Arians, but in 336 was condemned for Sabellianism.[30] Asserting strongly monotheistic thinking, he advocated the Nicene ὁμοούσιον in the sense of 'being of the same essence' and accordingly, like nearly all his contemporaries, would not understand Son of God and Son of man as expressions of two different natures. Trying to be strictly a theologian of Scripture, he interpreted the christological titles as functional in regard to the different aspects of the incarnation of the Logos. Thus, to Marcellus, Son of man was not simply a description of the human nature of the Saviour as the first new man as 'mere man (ψιλὸς ἄνθρωπος)'. Son of God and Son of man, as well as the other christological titles, describe the salvation-historical functions of the incarnated Logos. Thus, Marcellus could say that Jesus used to call himself Son of man and not Son of God, 'suggesting with this confession, that man, in community with him by way of adoption, could be Son of God' (καὶ διὰ τοῦτο οὐχ υἱὸν θεοῦ ἑαυτὸν ὀνομάζει, ἀλλὰ πανταχοῦ υἱὸν ἀνθρώπου ἑαυτὸν λέγει, ἵνα διὰ τῆς τοιαύτης ὁμολογίας θέσει τὸν ἄνθρωπον διὰ την πρὸς αὐτὸν κοινωνίαν υἱὸν θεοῦ γενέσθαι παρασκευάσει).[31]

In *De incarnatione Domini nostri, contra Apollinarium* (transmitted in the name of Athanasius, but most probably the work of Marcellus)[32] I 8, it is argued:

29. *In Joannem* ad 3.13; cf. ad 1.51 where the 'man' from whom the Lord had his flesh, is identified as Mary. D. Burkett, *The Son of Man Debate* (1999), p. 8 n. 7, falsely identifies this Ammonius with the Porphyrian philosopher Ammonius Saccas (died 241/242).

30. Some of the references to Marcellus and the description of his position I owe to Bracht, *Der Menschensohn*, pp. 481-82.

31. Fragment 41 = *Contra Marcellum* II 2; *De ecclesiastica theologia* I 16, 20 and II 8 (E. Klostermann, *Eusebius Werke*. IV. *Gegen Marcell*, *Über die kirchliche Theologie, Die Fragmente Marcells* [GCS, 1897]), pp. 192, 42-43, 75-76, 84 and 107-108).

32. Altaner and Stuiber, *Patrologie*, pp. 273 and 289. Lietzmann, *Der Menschensohn*, pp. 74-75, still attributes this text to Athanasius. This is also done by Burkett, without discussion: *The Son of Man Debate*, p. 9.

> The Creator of all things, the Logos, became visible as Son of man, not becoming another, but the second Adam (ὁ γὰρ τῶν ὅλων δημιουργὸς Λόγος ὤφθη υἱὸς ἀνθρώπου, οὐχ ἕτερός τις γενόμενος, ἀλλὰ δεύτερος Ἀδάμ), that we also should learn the truth from the name… But why at all, if he is as you? Was Christ not merely called 'man' as someone new coming from heaven to reside in the world of men, but became Son of man? If accordingly he became Son of man on earth, and indeed was not of human seed, but conceived by the Holy Spirit, he was to be known as son of the one protoplast Adam. Then no other man was registered as being in heaven apart from the Adam of earth, that he also may have a body from heavens, and be Son of a man other than Adam (Οὐ γὰρ ἕτερος τις ἀναγέγραπται ἄνθρωπος ἐν οὐρανῷ ὑπάρξας παρὰ τὸν ἐκ γῆς Ἀδὰμ, ἵνα καὶ ἐξ οὐρανῶν ἔχῃ τὸ σῶμα, καὶ υἱὸς ἀνθρώπου ᾖ παρὰ τὸν Ἀδάμ). For that reason, Matthew describes him as son of Abraham and David according to the flesh, while Luke traces his descent as son of Adam and of God.

Understanding the expression this way from the background of Paul's concept of Christ as the second Adam, he does not describe the human nature but the heavenly origin. This is evident also from the polemic of Eusebius in his *Contra Marcellum* II 1. Here it is said:

> This is the paradox of the Logos: it began all these things for nearly forty years, and it stopped again suddenly after the moment of crisis of the Logos being united with God, as had it been nothing except God; the flesh, which it took on, was left destitute of Logos, as had there never been the Son of God, nor the Son of man who took it on (ὡς μήτε τὸν υἱὸν τοῦ θεοῦ πότε ὑφεστάναι, μήτε τὸν υἱὸν τοῦ ἀνθρώπου ὃν ἀνέληφεν).[33]

A more simplistic view is found in Gregory of Nazianzus (c. 330–390), one of the three famous Cappadocians. Arguing against the Apollinarian understanding of 1 Cor. 15.47 and Jn 3.13 that Christ was Son of man before the incarnation, he claims that what happened was a union of the two natures, the earthly with the heavenly (διὰ τὴν πρὸς τὸν οὐράνιον ἕνωσιν).[34] Thus Son of man describes the human nature which he added to the divine he had from heaven, and to think of a carnal nature before his coming to earth is absurd.[35] In his *Oratio* XXX 21,[36] where Christ is declared to be the son of both Adam and Mary, Gregory further declares that Christ

33. Klostermann, *Eusebius Werke*, p. 32. Eusebius understands the words as a denial of pre-existence and introduces, among other things, Dan. 7.13-14 as a refutation; cf. also *Contra Marcellum* II 2.

34. *Epistola 101 ad Cledonium presbyterum contra Apollinarium* (*MPG* 37, p. 181). This and the following reference I owe to Bracht, *Der Menschensohn*, pp. 496-97.

35. Cf. *Epistola 203 ad Nectarium Constantinopolitanum episcopum* (*MPG* 37, p. 332).

36. Translation according to *NPNF* 2nd series vol. VII. Also with regard to Gregory of Nyssa I owe some of the references to Bracht, *Der Menschensohn*, pp. 494-96.

> is Son of Man, both on account of Adam, and of the Virgin from Whom He came; from the one as forefather, from the other as His Mother, both in accordance with the law of generation, and apart from it (Υἱὸς δὲ ἀνθρώπου, καὶ διὰ τὸ Ἀδὰμ, καὶ διὰ τὴν Παρθένον, ἐξ ὧν ἐγένετο τοῦ μὲν, ὡς προπάτορος, τῆς δὲ, ὡς ματρὸς νόμῳ, καὶ οὐ νόμῳ γεννήσεως).

Gregory of Nyssa (ca. 334–394), another of the great Cappadocians, in *Libri contra Eunomium* I 22[37] (Eunomius was an Arian theologian) understands Son of man about the visible appearance of Christ as a parallel to His naming Himself Son of God:

> Just as when He wished to name His connexion with humanity according to the flesh, He called that phase of His being Son of Man, indicating thereby His kinship with her from whom He was born (ὥσπερ γὰρ τὴν κατὰ σάρκα πρὸς τὸ ἀνθρωπίνον κοινωνίαν σημαίνων, Υἱὸν ἀνθρώπου τὸ φαινόμενον προσηγόρευε, δεικνὺς τὴν κατὰ φύσιν τῆς σαρκὸς αὐτοῦ πρὸς τὴν ἐξ ἧς ἐλήφθη συγγένειαν), so also by the title Son he expresses His true and real relationship to the Almighty, by that name of Son showing this natural connexion.

And in III 4 of the same work, in what is nearly an excursus, Gregory explains his understanding of Son of God and Son of man as together indicating the mixture of natures in Christ. Against Eunomius, who apparently accepted the Virgin birth, claiming that the Lord 'being the Son of the living God, not being ashamed of his birth from the Virgin, often named Himself, in His own sayings, "the Son of Man"', Gregory argues:

> For this phrase [the Son of Man] we also allege for proof of the community of essence, because the name of 'Son' shows the community of nature to be equal in both cases. For as he is called the Son of Man by reason of the kindred of His flesh to her of whom He was born, so also He is conceived, surely, as the Son of God, by reason of the connection of His essence with that from which He has his existence, and this argument is the greatest weapon of the truth. For nothing so clearly points to Him Who is the 'mediator between God and man' (as the great Apostle called him [1 Tim. 2.5]), as the name of 'Son,' equally applicable to either nature, Divine or Human. For the same Person is Son of God, and was made, in the Incarnation, Son of Man, that, by His communion with each, he might link together by Himself what were divided by nature. Now if, in becoming Son of Man, He were without participation in human nature, it would be logical to say that neither does He share in the Divine essence, though he is Son of God. But if the whole compound nature of man was in Him (for He was 'in all points tempted like as we are, yet without sin' [Heb. 4.15]), it is surely necessary to believe that every property of the transcendent essence is also in Him, as the Word 'Son' claims for Him both alike—the Human in the man, but in the God the Divine.

37. Translation according to *NPNF* 2nd series vol. V.

After a longer discourse about different tasting products of wine, sweet and sour, declaring 'that in substance the two are the same, but are distinguished by qualitative differences', it is maintained that:

> Therefore, when we hear from Scripture that the Only-begotten God is Son of man, we learn by the kindred expressed in the name His kinship with true man, so even, if the Son be called, in the adversaries' phrase, a 'product,' we none the less learn, even by this name, His kinship in essence with Him that has 'produced' Him, by the fact that wine, which is called the 'product' of the vine has been found not to be alien, as concerns the idea of moisture, from the natural power that resides in the vine.

In his *Antirrheticus adversum Apollinarem* 6, Gregory polemicizes against the view of a heavenly man, building on Jn 3.13, and asks his adversary: 'But when it is both so, that the Son of man is from heaven (ἐξ οὐρανοῦ Υἱὸς ἀνθρώπου) and the Son of God is from a woman, why should not the same be God and man?' But these two names are not interchangeable but point to the two origins of Christ united in his person. According to Gregory (*Antirrheticus adversum Apollinarem* 57), this also means that the sayings about the apocalyptic Son of man should not be understood literally, but, just as Christ in the Gospels sometimes calls God man (Mt. 21.33; 22.1), so also for pedagogical reasons, Christ, returning as judge could be called Son of man (Mt. 24.30) because of the weakness of men, so that they could see him in a form like themselves.

Eustathius of Antioch (c. 280/288–337 or later?) fought against Arianism and was banned by Constantine to Trace in 336, where he died.[38] He developed a Christology, in which Son of man denoted not only the flesh, but the whole human being of Jesus with both body and soul, in which the Logos had taken up residence. This is already the case in the only complete surviving work of Eustathius, *De engastrimytho contra Origenem* (*About the ventriloquist*, that is, the witch of Endor, 1 Sam. 28), where Son of man obviously is man in Christ. Thus in ch. 18 he interprets Jn 3.13 as a *pars pro toto*-saying, claiming that when Christ witnesses that he was born human and is the only one who has ascended to heaven and descended from there again, and always abides in heaven, then this is said with regard to the soul (ψυχῆς ἀρετῇ ταῦτα ἔπραττεν ὁ ἄνθρωπος ἐκκρίτως). In surviving fragments, it can be observed how Eustathius stresses the independence of the humanity of Christ in relation to the Logos, distinguishing between the divine and human in Christ. He tries to demonstrate this by distributing different Gospel sayings as partly related to the Logos and partly to the human. Here he claims that not only the sayings concerning Passion and

38. I owe the description of the position of Eustathius, as well as the references, to Bracht, *Der Menschensohn*, pp. 482-84.

death, but also those about resurrection, glorification and investment with power pertain to the human, not so much because of the connection with the Logos as because of the virtue of the man Jesus (as it is asserted not least in Lk. 2.52). Thus when, in Mt. 19.28, Jesus speaks of the Son of man in the third person, Eustathius distinguishes between two persons, the one speaking, the other the one spoken of (aliaquidem videtur loqui persona; de altera autem facit manifeste sermonem): the divine Spirit speaks about the Son of man, while he himself speaks about what he will do when he is glorified.[39] This independence of the Son of man as man in relation to the Logos is also clarified through an interpretation of Mt. 24.36 (with parallels), where Eustathius identifies the Son with the Son of man by explaining that the Son of man does not know the day of his coming, because this is hidden from the man in him.[40]

Cyril of Jerusalem (died 386), dismissed and banned by emperor Valens (367–378) because of his loyalty to the Nicene creed, understands Son of man in his *Catecheses* X 4[41] to refer to the Parousia:

> He is called Son of Man, not as having had His generation from earth, as each of us, but as coming upon the clouds to judge both quick and dead (Υἱὸς ἀνθρώπου καλεῖται, οὐχ ὡς ἔσχατος ἡμῶν ἐκ γῆς τὴν γέννησιν ἐσχημὼς, ἀλλ᾽ ἐρχόμενος ἐπὶ νεφελῶν κρῖναι ζῶντας καὶ νεκρούς).

This is a remarkable interpretation. Like Tertullian's interpretation, according to which Son of man refers to Dan. 7.13, the expression is meant to call this vision to remembrance. This is quite in line with *Catecheses* XI 3, where Cyril quotes Mt. 16.13 in the form 'Whom do men say that I, the Son of Man, am?', and adds 'not from vain-glory, but wishing to show them the truth, lest dwelling with God, the Only-begotten of God, they should think lightly of Him as if He were some mere man'. The reference to Dan. 7.13 is also confirmed by *Catecheses* XV, where Dan. 7.9, 13 is quoted and several Gospel Son of man sayings, reflecting v. 13, are taken as descriptions of the glory of Christ's second coming.

Apollinaris of Syrian Laodicea (from 361 bishop in this town; died c. 390) was befriended by Athanasius and fought together with him against Arianism, but not without being influenced by its Christology. Thus, to Apollinaris, Christ was a mixture of God and man, the holding of which view resulted in him being condemned for Docetism as early as the synod in Alexandria in 362 and later, once again, by Pope Damasus (in 377 and 382), as well as at the synod in Constantinople in 381. His point of view is expressed clearly in *Epistula ad Dionysium*, earlier attributed to Pope Julius

39. *MPG* 18, cols. 691-92.
40. *MPG* 18, cols. 691-92.
41. Translation according to *NPNF* 2nd series vol. VII.

I (died in 352), but in reality written by Apollinaris.[42] Again, Jn 3.13 plays a central role, but this time with Lk. 1.35.[43] Son of man turns up in a passage about the Paulians, whose view probably was shared by Apollinaris. After declaring that the divine truth is united with the body (τῆς θεότητος ἀλήθεια μετὰ τοῦ σώματός ἐστι) and not divided into two natures, he writes (ch. 4):

> For nor is it possible to call all what descended from heaven Son of man (τὸ ὅλον υἱὸν ἀνθρώπου καλεῖσθαι καταβεβηκότα ἐξ οὐρανοῦ), and Son of God what was born of the virgin if the division in natures is admitted (εἰ δύο φύσεων διαίρεσιν ἐπιδέχεται). But what descended from heaven is called Son of God and not Son of man; what is born of a woman, is called Son of man, not Son of God. And this division is approved by the Paulian party.[44]

A little later, Apollinaris does not shrink from talking about flesh from heaven, because the divine Scriptures tell us that the Son of man is from heaven.[45] For this reason, he will not distinguish between Son of God and Son of man, allowing the last alone to pertain to the incarnate. Alluding in another place to 1 Cor. 15.47, he claims that 'the man coming down from heaven is not of earth (οὐκ ἐστι...ἐκ γῆς ἄνθρωπος ὁ ἐξ οὐρανοῦ καταβέβηκεν), although also he, who came down from heaven, is man'. And this appellation (προσηγορίαν) is not rejected by the Lord in the Gospels.[46] Apollinaris here distinguishes between Son of man and man. In a fragment of a book against Diodore of Tarsus he states that 'incarnation is abasement; but abasement was shown by him who debased himself not as man but as Son of man according to the covering, not according to a change'.[47] This is

42. Altaner and Stuiber, *Patrologie*, p. 314. In the following, Apollinaris is quoted according to H. Lietzmann, *Apollinaris von Laodicea und seine Schule* (1904, reprint 1970) (page numbers in subsequent references are to this edition).

43. Bracht, *Der Menschensohn*, p. 484, remarks, that Apollinaris 'ist ein weiteres Beispiel dafür, wie durch Selektion der ntl MS-Stellen entsprechend ihren für eine bestimmte Christologie verwertbar erscheinenden Kontexten die MS-Prädikation Jesu bei wörtlichem Verständnis vielfältig allegorisiert und als "Schriftbeweise" eben jener Christologie, welche jeweils die Basis der Auslegung bildet, wieder dienstbar gemacht werden kann'. I owe most of the references to Apollinaris to Bracht's analysis, *Der Menschensohn*, pp. 484-88. This also pertains to the three tracts assumed to come from the Apollinarian school.

44. Lietzmann, *Apollinaris von Laodicea und seine Schule*, p. 258.

45. Lietzmann, *Apollinaris von Laodicea und seine Schule*, p. 259. Here Apollinaris also summarizes his view: he is saying both (ἀμφότερα), because he will not know of any division in the one person (διαίρεσιν τοῦ ἑνὸς προσώπου). Cf. *Apodeixis* fragment 18 (Lietzmann, *Apollinaris von Laodicea und seine Schule*, p. 209) and fragment 165 (from Gregory of Nazianzus, *Epistula 202 ad Nectarius*).

46. *Apodeixis*, fragment 17 (Lietzmann, *Apollinaris von Laodicea und seine Schule*, p. 209). Cf. fragments 25-31 (Lietzmann, *Apollinaris von Laodicea und seine Schule*, pp. 210-11).

47. Fragment 124 (Lietzmann, *Apollinaris von Laodicea und seine Schule*, p. 237).

also expressed by Apollinaris in a detailed declaration of faith (ἡ κατὰ μέρος πίστις) from 380, where he says:

> Further, we declare that the Son of God became Son of man (τὸν υἱὸν τοῦ θεοῦ υἱὸν ἀνθρώπου γεγενῆσθαι), not according to the name, but in truth, taking on the flesh from the virgin Mary and being himself perfect Son of God and Son of man (εἶναι τέλειον αὐτὸν υἱὸν θεοῦ καὶ αὐτὸν υἱὸν ἀνθρώπου), in one person and with the same adoration of the Logos and the flesh, which he took on.[48]

Apollinaris finds this identity of Son of God and Son of man confirmed in Mt. 24.31, because 'if he became God after the resurrection and is no longer man, how then can the Son of man send his angels and how "will we see the Son of man coming on the clouds"'?[49]

Three anonymous tracts, dealing with the Son of man question in the Apollinarian way, are today assumed to come from the school of Apollinaris. Two (*Quod unus sit Christus* and *De incarnatione Dei Verbi*), have survived as pseudo-Athanasian, the third (*De unione corporis et divinitatis in Christo*) under the name of Pope Julius I (337–352).[50] In *Quod unus sit Christus* 5, it is declared that the apostles preached that Christ was not only human, but at one time God and man in so far as they called him Son of God and Son of man, saying he was from heaven and from earth, being both impassable and passable, not another, not two persons (πρόσωπα δύο), not with more than one state of being (οὐχ ὑποστάσεις), not with two sorts of worship (οὐ προσκυνήσεις). In ch. 7, it is repeated that there are not two hypostases in Christ,

> the Son of God being one person, the Son of man being another (ἄλλο πρόσωπον τοῦ υἱοῦ τοῦ θεοῦ, καὶ ἄλλο πρόσωπον τοῦ υἱοῦ τοὺ ἀνθρώπου), the one of the seed of David according to flesh. Thus, neither was the Son of God the Son of man, being of a different substance than David. Nor was one born according to flesh Son of God, being of a different substance than God (ὥστε μήτε τὸν υἱὸν τοῦ θεοῦ εἶναι υἱὸν ἀνθρώπου ἑτεροούσιον ὄντα τοῦ Δαβιδ· μήτε τὸν κατὰ σάρκα γεννηθέντα εἶναι υἱὸν τοῦ θεοῦ, ἑτεροουσίον ὄντα τῷ θεῷ).

48. Lietzmann, *Apollinaris von Laodicea und seine Schule*, p. 177. According to Bracht, *Der Menschensohn*, p. 586 n. 579, Apollinaris is the second (the first being Tertullian) to use Son of man in a declaration of faith. Later, also his pupil, Vitalis, is doing the same (according to Cyril of Alexandria, *De recta fide ad reginas* 10; cf. Lietzmann, *Apollinaris von Laodicea und seine Schule*, p. 273). This understanding Apollinaris also finds confirmed in Mt. 16.27, where Son of man is mentioned together with the glory of his father (see Catene 84 in J. Reuss, *Matthäus-Kommentare aus der griechischen Kirche* [1957], p. 26).

49. *Apodeixis*, fragment 98 (Lietzmann, *Apollinaris von Laodicea und seine Schule*, p. 230).

50. Thus in Lietzmann, *Apollinaris von Laodicea und seine Schule*; cf. Altaner and Stuiber, *Patrologie*, p. 314.

In ch. 8, it is summarized that 'the Son of God was man and Son of man and the one who according to nature was lord was also servant' (ἄνθρωπος καὶ υἱὸς ἀνθρώπου ὁ υἱὸς τοῦ θεοῦ, καὶ δοῦλος κατὰ τὴν μορφὴν ὁ τῇ φύσει κύριος).[51]

In *De incarnatione Dei Verbi* 2-3, Jn 3.13 and 6.62 are introduced among other sayings to prove that the divine and the human were constituted in one person and the opinion is rejected that the Son of man had not come down from heaven, but had risen from earth and received divinity from heaven (ὅτι οὐχὶ καταβεβηκὼς ἐξ οὐρανοῦ υἱὸς ἀνθρώπου, ἀλλ' ἐκ γῆς ἀναστὰς ὑποδέξατο τὸν ἐξ οὐρανοῦ θεόν). In ch. 4, it is declared to be so still, Christ having not stopped being Son of man nor having put off the flesh, because after the only begotten begins to be Son of man, he sends out his angels.[52]

The last of the three tracts, *De fide et incarnatione*, which has only survived in a Syrian translation, contains in chs. 5–8 'a short treatise on the title Son of man'.[53] Here it is claimed that the fact that Christ named himself Son of man does not imply that he was only man. He is always saying something more—whereafter Mt. 25.31 and 16.27 are quoted, the last with the question 'which father? [maybe] Adam's?' Then follows Mt. 18.11, together with the statement: 'And see, when you think to have him among men, then he reels and slides away from you and is from heaven, the one who keeps you through faith. Son of man is also he who is in heaven.' The text continues with quotations from Jn 6.62 and 3.13, Mt. 12.8 and 16.13-17, the last question (Mt. 16.13) introducing a discussion of the impact of Peter's confession. Obviously Son of man in the question of Jesus is not sufficient in itself. For which reason neither is the answer, 'You are the Son of man'. It should be one greater than Elijah and Jeremiah, greater than any of the prophets. As with Daniel and Joseph, enigmatic dreams called for elucidation, so Simon could answer only because of a revelation given by the Father. In his answer, 'he offered the solution and received therefore the beatitude and he learned from the Father and he taught the Church that this Son of man was the Son of the living God, not a prophet, but the Lord of the prophets and the Lord of men'.

Epiphanius of Salamis (died 403) advocates, in his *Ancoratus* 38-39, the view that Son of man points to Jesus' being a human. Thus he interprets the question in Mt. 16.13—'Who do men say that the Son of man is?'—as

51. Quoted according to Lietzmann, *Apollinaris von Laodicea und seine Schule*, pp. 297-98 and 299-300.

52. Quoted according to Lietzmann, *Apollinaris von Laodicea und seine Schule*, pp. 305 and 307.

53. Thus Bracht, *Der Menschensohn*, p. 488. The text is quoted according to the German translation in Lietzmann, *Apollinaris von Laodicea und seine Schule*, pp. 313-16, with my English translation.

parallel to the question of the Father in the Old Testament to Adam: 'Where are you?' As God very well knew the answer to his question, Jesus only uses Son of man to indicate that the disciples should not think he is asking about his divine nature. In *Panarium* II 1.8,[54] Epiphanius resumes older exegesis when arguing against the Noetians:

> What was the One who was in heaven, then, but the Word who was sent from heaven? To show that he was the same divine Word on earth and <in> heaven, changeless and unalterable, he possessed his oneness with the one Godhead, united with it by the Father's might. For he was Word, was God forever, was spirit, was might; and he adopted the name which was common and comprehensible to men, and was called Son of Man, though he was Son of God (Λόγος γὰρ ἤ̓ν, Θεὸς ἦ ἀεῖ, πνεῦμα ἤ̓ν, δύναμις ἤ̓ν, ὥς τὸν κοινὸν ὄ̓νομα καὶ παρὰ ἀνθρώποις χωρετὸν ἀνελάβανεν εἰς ἑαυτὸν, οὕτως καλούμενος Υἱὸς ἀνθρώπου, υἱὸς ὤ̓ν Θεοῦ).

To prove this from Scripture Epiphanius follows Hippolytus in introducing both Dan. 7.13 and Jn 3.13:

> And the name was mentioned beforehand in the prophets because it would apply to him, though it was not yet in the flesh. Thus Daniel said, 'I saw one like unto a Son of Man coming in the clouds'. And the prophet was right to give the Word this name <when he was> in heaven, and call the One he saw by the Holy Spirit Son of Man, since he scrutinized the future before its arrival and named the Word Son of Man before he was made flesh. And thus, although he reverses the order of events, the Only-begotten says, 'No man hath ascended up to heaven save he that came down from heaven, the Son of Man'. He did not mean that he was flesh in heaven, but <that> he descended from heaven, and was to be known by this name.

The founder of the influential exegetical Antiochene School, Diodore of Tarsus (died before 394), shows an understanding of the Gospel Son of man as synonymous with 'man' in the surviving fragments of his interpretations. Thus, in Jn 3.13, he warns against mixing up the natures of Christ by thinking that the seed of Abraham came from above. When God Logos here is called 'man', it is because he resided in the Son of man.[55] This understanding is also present in Diodore's interpretation of Mt. 12.32: if he would

54. Translation according to *The Panarion of Epiphanius of Salamis*. Books II and III (Sections 47-80, *De Fide*, 1994), IV 8.4-8, pp. 96-97. The chapter division in the translation is different from the text edition. Also, the text translated seems somehow different from the Greek text of the text edition.

55. Quoted according to R. Abramowski, 'Der theologische Nachlaß des Diodor von Tarsus', *ZNW* 42 (1949), pp. 19-69: fragment 15 (p. 33). Cf. fragments 24 and 25 (p. 43). The fragments have only survived in a Syrian translation. Bracht, *Der Menschensohn*, p. 492-92, characterizes Diodore as 'Vertreter einer Trennungschristologie vom Typ "Logos-Sarx"'.

have endured an illogical mixture, how then could the Lord say that whoever blasphemes the Son of man will be forgiven, but whoever speaks against the Holy Spirit will not.[56] On the other hand, according to the view of Diodore, Son of man shows the unity of the natures. Thus he has formed the creed: 'I confess that the Son of God became Son of man taking his flesh from the Virgin Mary and that he is complete son and not two, the one Son of God, the other Son of man. A hypostasis and a prosopon.'[57]

Theodore of Heraclea (died 355) of the Antiochene school likewise emphasizes the unity of the Son as Son of God and Son of man. He finds that the reason for Jesus saying Son of man in Mt. 16.13 is to show how he, becoming true man, is also true God, 'not attributing one part to God and another to man specifically, but him some will call Son of man, he will not refuse to believe the same also to be Son of God' (μὴ τεμνόμενος ἀνὰ μέρος εἰς θεὸν καὶ εἰς ἄνθρωπον εἰδικῶς, ἀλλ' ὅν τις υἱὸν ἀνθρώπου προσαγορεύσειεν, οὐκ ἀπιστήσειε τοῦτον αὐτὸν εἶναι καὶ υἱὸν θεοῦ).[58] The same is seen as the presupposition in Jn 6.62 where Jesus speaks of the Son of man ascending to where he was before, although Son of man designates the human nature, in order to make it clear that it is not the body (σῶμα), but the Son of man taking on the body, who deserves faith.[59]

John Chrysostom (c. 344/354–407), also representing Antiochene exegesis, likewise sees Son of man as designating the human nature of Christ. Commenting on Mt. 12.32 in his *Homilia in Matthaeum* XLI 5, he declares that there was forgiveness for words spoken against the Son of man. Christ argued that 'because of the flesh with which I am encompassed' (διὰ τὴν σάρκα τὴν περικειμένην), people can be offended at him.[60] But this is only the case before the cross! And when, in his interpretation of Mt. 16.13 in *Homilia* LIV 1, he remarks that by saying Son of man, Christ is 'signifying how earnestly He desires His Economy to be confessed (τὴν οἰκονομίαν ὁμολογεῖσθαι)...thereby denoting His Godhead (τὴν θεότητα)'. John Chrystotom also refers to Jn 3.13 and 6.62 as similarly pointing to an understanding of Son of man as the incarnated Logos.

In his *Homilia in Joannem* XXI 1, John Chrysostom comments on Jn 1.51 that the elevated situation where angels are ministering to him 'causes him

56. Fragment 20 (p. 39).

57. Fragment 26 (p. 45) in my translation of the German translation of the Syrian version.

58. Quoted according to J. Reuss, *Matthäus-Kommentare aus der griechischen Kirche* (1957), p. 85. The references to Theodore of Heraclea I owe to Bracht, *Der Menschensohn*, pp. 493-94.

59. Quoted according to J. Reuss, *Johannes-Kommentare aus der griechischen Kirche* (1966), p. 76.

60. Translations according to *NPNF* 1st series vol. X and XIV. Some of the references to John Chrysostom I owe to Bracht, *Der Menschensohn*, pp. 506-507.

no longer to imagine Him as merely man (ἄνθρωπον ἁπλῶς)'. That Son of man is so understood of the incarnate is also clear from his remarks on Jn 3.13 in *Homilia* XXVII 1, where he says that

> in this place He called not the flesh 'Son of Man,' but he now named, so to speak, His entire Self from the inferior substance (Υἱὸς δὲ ἀνθρώπου ἐνταῦθα οὐ τὴν σάρκα ἐκάλεσεν, ἀλλ᾽ ἀπὸ τῆς ἐλάττονος οὐσίας ὅλον ἑαυτόν); indeed this is His wont, to call His whole Person (τὸ πάν) often from His Divinity, and often from His humanity.

That Son of man is to be understood in this way, as pointing to the fleshly appearance of the divine Son of God, seems nearly to be forgotten in his explanation of Jn 5.27-29 (*Homilia in Joannem* XXXIX.3), in a discussion with Paul of Samosata (bishop of Antiochia c. 260, but dismissed in 268 because of his 'dynamic monarchism'). Thus John Chrysostom combines Jn 5.27b with 5.28a, saying, 'That He is the Son of Man, marvel not at this' (Ὅτι Υἱὸς ἀνθρώπου ἐστὶ, μὴ θαυμάζετε τοῦτο). But Paul of Samosata put it quite another way: 'He hath given authority to execute judgment, "because" He is the Son of Man' (Ἐξουσίαν ἔδωκεν αὐτῷ κρίσιν ποιεῖν, ὅτι Υἱὸς ἀνθρώπου ἐστίν). Denying this understanding and taking ὅτι to be causal, a reading which is commonly accepted, John Chrysostom argues that Christ does not pass judgment simply because he is man (οὐ γὰρ ἔλαβε κρίσιν ὅτι ἄνθρωπος ἐστιν). That a man should judge would also not be something extraordinary and would logically not justify 'do not wonder at this' in v. 28a. So, according to John Chrysostom, the ὅτι is to be understood as introducing an object-clause:

> For He did not receive the power to judge 'because' He was man (since then what hindered all men from being judges,) but because He is the Son of that Ineffable Essence, therefore He is Judge (ἀλλ᾽ ἐπειδὴ τῆς ἀρρήτου οὐσίας ἐκείνης ἐστὶν Υἱὸς, διὰ τοῦτό ἐστι κριτής). So we must read, 'That He is the Son of Man, marvel not at this'. For when what He said seemed to the hearers inconsistent, and they deemed Him nothing more than mere man, while His words were greater than suited man, yea, or even angel, and were proper to God only, to solve this objection He addeth, Ver. 28, 29. 'Marvel not [that He is the Son of Man,] for the hour is coming in which they that are in the tombs shall hear His voice and shall go forth, they that have done good to the resurrection of life, and they that have done evil to the resurrection of judgment'.

To John Chrysostom, Son of man is obviously not an independent title (cf. also his *Homilia in Matthaeum* 54 [or 55] with regard to Mt. 16.13).

Theodoret of Cyrrhus in northern Syria (c. 393–c. 460), another representative of Antiochene exegesis, has Son of man pertain to visible nature (ἡ ὁρωμένη φύσις). This is seen in his *Eranistes seu polymorphus*, a dialogue directed against monophysitism, where he explains the saying in Mt. 24.30

where Jesus foretells that in the last days they shall see the Son of man coming on the clouds of heaven:

> The prophet [Daniel] did not see the very essence of God (τοῦ Θεοῦ τὴν οὐσίαν), but somehow the pomp of his power happened. But after the resurrection, all shall see the same visible nature of the Judge (ἅπαντες αὐτὴν τοῦ κριτοῦ τὴν ὁρωμένην ὄψονται φύσιν).

And a little later, referring to Acts 7.56, he continues: 'Look at the visible, not at the invisible nature' (Εἶδε δὲ τὴν ὁρωμένην, οὐ τὴν ἀόρατον φύσιν). Accordingly, in his *In Danielem*, he explains Son of man in Dan. 7.13: 'Clearly he calls him Son of man because of the nature he has taken on' (Υἱὸν μὲν ἀνθρώπου σαφῶς ἀποκαλῶν, δι' ἣν ἀνέλαβε φύσιν). And later, commenting on Dan. 11.9, he shows awareness of 'men' (υἱοὺς ἀνθρώπων) and 'prophets' (υἱοὺς προφητῶν) as idioms of the Hebrew dialect, though he does not utilize this knowledge with regard to Son of man in the mouth of Jesus. In *Quaestiones et responsiones ad orthodoxos* (falsely ascribed to Justin, but probably a work of Theodoret[61]), in his answer to Question 66, claiming that the masculine article τοῦ before ἀνθρώπου indicates that Jesus was a product of a conjugal union (ἐκ γαμικῆς συναφείας), Theodoret also denies that the masculine 'man' in Son of man should indicate this. He points to Lk. 3.23, saying, Ὡς ἐνομίζετο, υἱὸς τοῦ Ἰωσήφ, while noting that he was born of the Holy Spirit and Mary. Thus:

> If Christ did not call himself son of man with the female article, it clearly is because he is not son of a female. Likewise also, by not calling himself son of any man, he is not son of any human. But if Christ is not son of any human, of necessity he is not son either (Εἰ διὰ τὸ μὴ εἰπεῖν ἑαυτὸν τὸν Χριστὸν υἱὸν τῆς ἀνθρώπου, οὐκ ἔστι διὰ τοῦτο υἱὸς τῆς ἀνθρώπου δηλονότι· ἄρα καὶ διὰ τὸ μὴ εἰπεῖν ἑαυτὸν υἱὸν τινος ἀνθρώπου, οὐκ ἔστιν υἱὸς τινος ἀνθρώπου. Εἰ δὲ τινος ἀνθρώπου ἐστὶν Χριστὸς υἱὸς, ἐξ ἀνάγκης οὐδε ἐστιν υἱός).

What happened was that Christ was given to Joseph as a son but not as a product of a conjugal union. As it is said (Lk. 1.35): 'the Holy Spirit came over Mary and the power of the Most High overshadowed her, wherefore the child to be born would be called holy, the Son of God'. Accordingly: 'what was born of the wife of Heli was the son of Heli according to the law of God, how much more is that which is born of the wife of Joseph according to the will of God, son of Joseph without conjugal union'. Thus Christ, by calling himself Son of man, indicated that he was a son of Joseph, but only in a metaphorical way.

61. Altaner and Stuiber, *Patrologie*, p. 340.

2. *The West*[62]

Hilary of Poitiers (c. 315–367) was bishop in his town from c. 350, but from 355 to 359 was banished to Asia Minor by emperor Constantius because of his resistance to Arianism.[63] Although deeply influenced by Tertullian, his christological concern was not to stress the true humanity of Christ, but to show the identity between the Son of man and the Son of God. This is seen in his *Commentarius in Matthæum*, written before his exile, where in XVI 5-6, Hilary claims that the question in Mt. 16.13 aims at provoking the disciples to name Christ Son of God: 'Thus it should be concluded from the confession that just as of the Son of God we should also think of the Son of man, because the one does not contribute to the hope for salvation without the other'. A little later he continues: 'And, surely, the contemplation of the body preferred Son of man (Et certe filium hominis contemplatio corporis præferebat); but adding, "who do they say I am", he signified, that, besides what could be seen in him, there was something else to be perceived, because he was Son of man'. The beatitude of Peter shows that the question also signified his being Son of God. In other places in this commentary, he interprets Son of man allegorically. Thus, in VII 10, Mt. 8.20 is applied to faith being obviously put together with 1 Cor. 11.3; and in X 14, Mt. 10.23b is interpreted from the background of Rom. 11.25-26, wherein the eschatological meaning is postponed to a distant future. The human condition of Christ during the incarnation no longer being the problem, the interpretation of the saying about the unforgivable sin in Mt. 12.32 in XII 18 concentrates on the last part of it; thus the unforgivable sin against the Spirit is seen in Christian heretics denying his communion with God (Dei communione).

In his principal work, *De trinitate*, written during his exile, Son of man is employed a great many times by Hilary in his explanation of the incarnation. Basically, in X 20, it is pointed out with regard to his adversaries that 'If they had understood the mystery of the Incarnation, these men would have understood at the same time the mystery that the Son of Man is also Son of God (intelligerent etiam sacramentum ejusdem et hominis filii et Dei filii)'.[64]

62. Bracht, *Der Menschensohn*, pp. 507-508, also mentions Pope Damasus (366–384) as a typical representative. In a synodal paper, Damasus attacks the Apollinarists for claiming an 'imperfectam humanitatem in hominis filius', arguing from Lk. 19.10 that if Christ was an imperfect man, the gift of God and salvation would be imperfect and it would not be the total man which was saved (*MPL* 13, pp. 352-52). Thus, to Damasus, Son of man includes the whole of man.

63. Nearly all the references to Hilary I owe to Bracht, *Der Menschensohn*, pp. 508-11.

64. Cf. X 62 and IX 62. Translation of *De trinitate* according to *NPNF* 2nd series vol. IX.

Again and again, Hilary repeats that the Son of God is also Son of man (III 16; VII 24; IX 40-41; X 15, 19, 21-23, 65-66; XII 48), even in polemical contexts as against Sabellios (I 16), Arius (IX 33) or Apollinarianism (X 50, 52). This identification of Son of Man and Son of God also explains the seemingly contradictory sayings of Christ being sayings pertaining to the one or the other or to the different phases in the fate of the one Christ. As it is said in *De trinitate* IX 5,

> The Only-begotten God...when He was born man of the Virgin, and in the fullness of time was about in His own person to raise humanity to divinity, always maintained this form of the Gospel teaching. He taught, namely, to believe Him the Son of God, and exhorted to preach Him the Son of Man (et hominis filium prædicare admoneret), man saying and doing all that belongs to God; God saying and doing all that belongs to man. Yet, never did He speak without signifying by the twofold aspect of these very utterances both His manhood and His divinity. Though He proclaimed one God the Father, He declared Himself to be in the nature of the one God, by the truth of His generation. Yet in His office as son and His condition as man, He subjected Himself to God the Father, since everything that is born must refer back to its author, and all flesh must confess itself weak before God. Here, accordingly, the heretics find opportunity to deceive the simple and ignorant. These words, uttered in His human character, they falsely refer to the weakness of His divine nature; and because He was one and the same Person in all His utterances, they claim that He spake always of His entire self (cf. I 32, X 62).

Thus, Hilary is able to argue that, while Son of Man designates the true human form of Christ, what is said in this context demonstrates his divine nature (cf. for instance I 32). This pertains for instance to Dan. 7.13 (XII 47), but no less to Jn 3.13 where Son of man cannot be understood in a literal sense. He comments (X 16):

> 'Descended from heaven' refers to His origin from the Spirit: for though Mary contributed to His growth in the womb and birth all that is natural to her sex, His body did not owe to her its origin. The 'Son of Man' refers to the birth of the flesh conceived in the Virgin; 'Who is in heaven' implies the power of His eternal nature... So He descended from heaven and is the Son of Man, yet is in heaven: for the Word made flesh did not cease to be the Word. As the Word, He is in heaven, as flesh He is the Son of Man. As Word made flesh, He is at once from heaven, and Son of Man, and in heaven, for the power of the Word, abiding eternally without body, was present still in the heaven He had left: to Him and to none other the flesh owed its origin (cf. X 34 and *Tractatus super psalmos* II 11).

That Christ as a human possesses divine qualities, Hilary finds confirmed not least in Jn 13.31-32, dividing between the glory which the Son of Man and, in him, also God obtain and the glory which God of himself will give the Son of Man (see IX 40-41, XI 42). The last mentioned glory Hilary sees 'in

Him in the power of the Resurrection' (XI 42). However, also after the resurrection Christ remains Son of Man. Thus in his *Tractatus super psalmos*, interpreting Ps. 2.7, but implying also Mt. 26.64, Hilary calls the resurrection a rebirth by which the Son of Man was born to be what he also was before (Ergo hic resurrectionis suæ ad assumendam gloriam dies est, per quam ad id nascitur, quod ante tempora erat; II 27; cf. LIII 14: per resurrectionis gloriam jam renatus). Having included in this way human nature in the glory of God, Christ remains Son of Man even after the resurrection. In *Tractatus super psalmos* LXX 5, Hilary declares:

> But judgment by power was a necessity in the case of One who being the Son of God was born of a virgin to be Son of Man, and who now being Son of Man was to have the Name and power of the Son of God restored to Him by the power of judgment (ubi Dei filio in filium hominis ex partu virginis nato, rursum ipsi hominis filio per judicii virtutem Dei filii nomen redhibendum esset et virtus).[65]

Among the Latin fathers, Ambrose (333/34, or 339/40–397), bishop of Milan from 374 to 397, in his *Enarrationes in XII Psalmos Davidicos*, ad Psalm 39, also finds the explanation for 'man' in Son of man in Christ being born of a virgin:

> Although born of a virgin and by the Holy Spirit, he is in any case son of man, because a virgin is human (Etsi de Virgine natura est et Spiritus sancto, tamen hominis est filius; quia homo Virgo). Similarly, what is born of flesh is flesh; and he who is born of a human, is called human, the mediator between God and men, the man Jesus Christ.[66]

Accordingly, Lk. 12.10 relates that Christ is *the* Son of man who is born of the Holy Spirit and the virgin (qui de sancto sprititu generatus et virgine est) and thus not inferior to the Spirit and so it is unforgivable to blaspheme against him, because he is Son of God at the same time.[67] Son of God in this manner being the same as Son of man in Mt. 24.36, Christ could use the ambiguous 'Son' saying that not even the Son knows the hour of the end. Since he obviously did know it as Son of God, but not according to his human nature, one has rather to assume that it is said according to his being Son of man (ut magis dictum secundum filium hominis).[68] Ambrose can also say that Jesus asks as Son of man and demands as Son of God.[69] He also

65. Translation according to *NPNF*, 2nd series, vol. IX.
66. Cf. idem, *De fide ad Gratianum Augustum*, IV 32-33; V 221; *De Spiritu sancto*, III 1.
67. *Expositio evangelium secundum Lucam*, VII 19. This and the following references I owe to Bracht, *Der Menschensohn*, pp. 511-12.
68. *Expositio evangelium secundum Lucam*, VIII 34.
69. *De fide ad Gratianum Augustum*, III 4.

claims that when Paul in 1 Cor. 15.28 declares that, in the end, the Son will subject himself to the Father who has subjected everything to him, then the Son is the Son of man and the subjection the incarnation (ergo ut filius hominis subjenctionem, utique per conditionem carnis, non per majestatem divinitatis, agnoscit).[70] Just as Chrysostom earlier, Ambrose finds that the designation of the one nature always also covers the other, as seen in 1 Cor. 2.8 and Jn 3.13.[71]

In *Breviarium in Psalmos*, Jerome (c. 347–420) comments on Ps. 8.5, saying: 'The Son of God is made son of man; that is, son of the Virgin Mary' (Filius Dei, factus est Filius hominis: id est Filius virginis Mariæ). Otherwise, Jerome, like Theodoret of Cyrrhus, exhibits knowledge of the Hebrew origin of Son of man when he, in his *Commentarius in Matthaeum* III 16 ad 16.13, remarks that it is known that, where the Old Testament has Son of man (filius hominis), the Hebrew has son of Adam (in Hebraeo positum sit filius Adam).[72] But, as is seen, he does not let this knowledge influence his view on Christ as Son of man. Thus, he takes it as a sign of humility, when, in Mt. 16.13, Jesus does not ask, 'who do men say that *I* am, but *Son of man*' (quem me dicunt esse homines, sed filium hominis), because he did not want to ask in a boasting manner. Accordingly, Jerome can repeat the sentence originally introduced by Irenaeus: 'Because of our salvation, the Son of God became Son of man'.[73]

Augustine (354-430) summarizes the different meanings attributed to the expression Son of man in Christian theology until his time. And the expression turns up in remarkable numbers. In *De consensus evangelistarum* II 1, Augustine claims that Christ, because of his descent according to the flesh, 'is the Son of Man—a title which He also gives very frequently to Himself' (filius hominis est, quod etiam se ipse saepissime appellat).[74] In a letter to his collegue, the bishop Honoratus (*Epistula* 140.21-22), Augustine interprets the designation Son of man in a singular way through the combination of two sayings, Job 25.5-6 and Ps. 21.7 LXX. Thus, it is said in Job 25.5-6: 'Even if the moon is not bright and the stars are not pure in his sight, how much less a man, who is a maggot and a son of man, who is a worm', whereby man and maggot on the one hand as well as Son of man and worm on the other are put together. Taken together with Ps. 21.7 LXX: 'I am a

70. *De fide ad Gratianum Augustum*, V 12.

71. *De fide ad Gratianum Augustum*, II 7.

72. Later, Erasmus, in his *Annotationes Novi Testamenti* (1516) ad Mt. 8.20, draws attention to Jerome's pointing out in his commentary on Eccl. 9 (vv. 3 and 12) that in Hebrew 'sons of men' designates ordinary people. See below.

73. *Epistula ad Eustacium*, 39.

74. Translation according to *NPNF* 1st series vol. VI. I owe some of the references to Augustine to Bracht, *Der Menschensohn*, pp. 512-16.

worm and not a man' Augustine concludes that the meaning is: 'I am the Son of man and not man'. But because the one, the man, who is not Son of man, must be Adam, then the meaning of the Psalm is: 'I myself am Christ in whom all are vivified, not Adam, in whom all die'. Thus according to Augustine, Christ, 'familiarissime', preferred to name himself Son of man and not man because, through this name, he designated himself as the one in whom such grace was revealed. According to Ps. 35.7-10, he became Lord of those he called sons of men, rather than men (quo se familiarius appellari voluit dominus eorum, in quo talis gratia revelata est, eosque filios hominum potius quam hominess appellavit). That this is the meaning of the self-designation of Jesus, Augustine claims only here.[75]

For Augustine—as for Hilary previously—the expression Son of man is tightly connected with the mystery of the incarnation. Thus, in *Contra sermonem arianorum* I 8, he says that:[76]

> After all, the one Christ is always by nature the Son of God, and he is by grace the Son of Man who was assumed in time. Nor was he assumed in such a way that he was first created and then assumed, rather, he was created in being assumed. And thus on account of the unity of the person that we must understand in the two natures, the Son of Man is said to have come down from heaven, although he was assumed from the Virgin who was already on earth (Ac per hoc propter istam unitatem personæ in utraque natura intelligendam et Filius hominis dicitur descendisse de cælis, quamvis sit ex ea quæ in terra fuerat Virgine assumptus). So too, the Son of God is said to have been crucified and buried, although he did not suffer this in the divinity by which he is the Only-Begotten, coeternal with the Father, but in the weakness of human nature.

In what follows, Jn 3.13 is introduced.[77] The same pertains to *Contra Maximinum Arianum episcopum* II 20.3, where Jn 3.13 inspires him to use Son of man in distinguishing between the two substances in Christ:

> If you pay attention to the distinction of substances (distinctionem substantiarum), the Son of God came down from heaven, the Son of Man was crucified; if you pay attention to the unity of person (unitatem personæ), both Son of Man came down from heaven and the Son of God was crucified...

75. In any case, the interpretation is later resumed by Bonaventura (cf. below).

76. Translation of the following quotations from *Contra sermonem arianorum* and *Contra Maximum Arianum episcopum* is according to *The Works of Saint Augustine* (A Translation for the 21st Century, I.18, 1995).

77. Cf. also *In Joannis Evangelium Tractatus CXXIV*: XIX 15-16, XXI 14, XXII 11, XXVII 3-4. In the last place, it is said: 'Christ, therefore, is one: the Word, soul and flesh, one Christ, the Son of God and Son of man, one Christ; Son of God always, Son of man in time; yet one Christ in regard to unity of person'. Translation according to *NPNF* 1st series vol. VII.

> Because of this unity of person, the Son of Man not only said that he had come down from heaven, but also said that he was in heaven, though he was speaking on earth.

The same line of thought is found in *Epistula* 238.2 (17) and later in the same epistle, 4 (21),[78] where Augustine like Athanasius refers to Mt. 12.31-32. He writes:

> It is more dangerous to sin against a greater than against a lesser, but it is not permissible to separate the Son of man from the Son of God, because it was the very Son of God who became the Son of man, not by changing what He was, but by taking on what He was not (Periculosius enim peccatur in majorem quam in minorem: nec separari fas est Filium hominis a Filio Dei, quia ipse Filius Dei factus est Filius hominis, non mutando quod erat, sed assumendo quod non erat).

In his *De trinitate*, the designation Son of man also plays an important role in describing Christ in his incarnation. Thus, it is said that the presence of the Son of man was a hindrance for the disciples because, looking at his servant form, they could be seduced to think that he was only what could be seen (*De trinitate* I 9 [18]). Again, Mt. 12.32 is also adduced on the same point (I 11 [22]), along with 1 Cor. 2.8 (I 13 [28]), claiming that the Spirit did not assume nature in the same way as the Son of man was assumed, in which form the Word of God itself was presented (assumpta creatura, in qua forma ipsius verbi Dei persona praesentatur—II 6 [11]; cf. also *De praedestinatione sanctorum* XV 31). Because of the two natures in one and the same person, Augustine thinks it possible to explain the different sayings in Scripture. Sometimes it is the human nature, sometimes it is the divine nature to which the sayings pertain. Accordingly, he interprets Jn 12.48: 'I will not judge on behalf of human power, because I am Son of man, but on behalf of the power of the Word, because I am Son of God' (I 12 [27]). On the other hand, Mt. 25.31-32 says that Christ will judge as Son of man. It is possible to say both that the Son of man will judge and also that the Son of man will not judge (I 13 [28-29]). Later Augustine summarizes his view in an interpretation of Jn 1.14 (XIII 19 [24]): 'When I read: "The Word became flesh and lived among us", by "Word", I understand the true Son of God. In "flesh", I see the true Son of man, and both together became the one person of God and man, connected in an effable gift of grace.'

Like Irenaeus, Augustine also uses Son of man to explain the impact of the incarnation on reconciliation. In *Sermones ad populum* 121.5,[79] he argues:

78. Translation according to *Saint Augustine Letters*, vol. V (containing letters 204-70). *The Fathers of the Church* 32 (1956).

79. Translation according to *The Works of Saint Augustine* III 4 (1992).

> For your sake the one who was the Son of God became the Son of man, in order that you who were sons of men might be turned into sons of God... But he differs from us in the way he became the Son of man. We are sons of men by the lust of the flesh; he is the Son of man by the faith of the virgin...; he became the Son of man, but did not stop being the Son of God (Nos filii hominum per concupiscentiam carnis: ille filius hominis per fidem virginis... Factus est filius hominis: sed non cessavit esse Filius Dei).[80]

In *Enarratio in Psalmum* 35.12,[81] Augustine speaks more restrictively about 'the sons of men (filii hominum)', declaring:

> When we bear the likeness of the earthly man, we are men; when we bear the likeness of the heavenly man, we are sons of man; for Christ was called the Son of Man (Quando portamus imaginem terreni hominis, homines sumus, quando portamus imaginem coelestis hominis, filii hominum sumus; quia Christus Filius hominis dictus est (Mt. 8.20 etc.).

For Justin, Irenaeus and Tertullian the virginity of Mary plays an indispensable role. In *Contra Faustum Manichaeum* II 4 (cf. also III 6), Augustine returns to the same line of thought, claiming, not as in Manichean teaching, that Christ is son of the first Man:[82]

> But our Lord and Saviour Jesus Christ, the true and truthful Son of God, the true and truthful Son of man (verus et verax Dei Filius, verus et verax hominis filius), both of which He testifies of Himself, derived the eternity of His godhead from the true God, and His incarnation from true man (de vero Deo divinitatis æternitatem, et de vero homine carnis originem duxit).

This time he also brings 1 Cor. 15.47-49 to bear:

> The first man of the earth, earthy, is Adam, who was made of dust. The second man from heaven, heavenly, is the Lord Jesus Christ; for being the Son of God, He became flesh that he might be a man outwardly, while He remained God within; that He might be both the true Son of God, by whom we were made, and the true Son of man, by whom we are made anew (et ut Filius Dei verus esset per quem facti sumus, et hominis filius verus fieret per quem refecti sumus).

Later, in V 4, the eschatological perspective is included in what could function as a summary of Augustine's understanding of the expression Son of man. After quoting 2 Tim. 2.8, he says that

> it is clear in what sense we must believe Christ to be the Son of man (quemadmodum Christum filium hominis credere debeamus); for being the Son of God by whom we were made, He also by His incarnation became the

80. Cf. *Sermones ad populum* 186.2-3; 342.5; *De civitate Dei* XXI; cf. *Sermones ad populum* 119.5.
81. Translation according to *St. Augustine On the Psalms* (1961).
82. Translation according to *NPNF* 4.

> son of man, that He might die for our sins, and rise again for our justification. Accordingly He calls Himself both Son of God and Son of man (Ideoque utrumque se dicit, et Filium Dei et filium hominis)...[quotation of Jn 5.25-26]. As the Son of man, He has received power to execute judgment, because He will come to judgment in human form, that He may be seen by the good and the wicked.

3. *After Chalcedon*

Ephraem of Antioch (died 545) follows up on this. Adducing Mt. 12.32; 16.27; 17.8 and Rom. 5.15, he comments that 'in all these places the remembrance of the man with the definite article (ἡ τοῦ ἀνθρώπου μνήμη μετὰ τοῦ γενικοῦ προαγομένη ἄρθρου) in no way divides our one Lord Jesus Christ into different states of being (εἰς διαφορὰν ὑποστάσεων)'.[83]

Justinianus (emperor 527–565), eager to show himself a theologian, but probably using the pen of Theodor Ascidas,[84] in *Confessio rectæ fidei adversus tria capitula*, states forthrightly that 'the Son of God became Son of man' (ὁ γὰρ υἱὸς τοῦ Θεοῦ υἱὸς ἀνθρώπου γέγονε).

As has been seen, interpreters in this period, nearly without exception, perceive Son of man as Christ's means of expressing his human nature. The discussion concentrates on the question of the relation between the human and the divine nature. As it is formulated in the Creed of Chalcedon, the human nature is practically swallowed up by the divine or, at least, the creed was interpreted that way. This continued to be the situation in the next period, the Middle Ages, to which we now turn.

83. *Variæ orationes*, in Photius' *Myrobiblion sive bibliotheca*.

84. Altaner and Stuiber, *Patrologie*, p. 513.

4. The Son of Man in Medieval Exegesis

With regard to the understanding of Son of man, the exegesis of the Middle Ages follows in the footsteps of earlier interpretations.[1] The tendency to conserve and carry on existing traditions is effective with respect to the expression Son of man. What we find is mostly repetition. However, even when theologians think they are adhering to 'what—in line with the famous sentence of Vincent of Lerinum (died c. 445)—is believed by all, everywhere, always (quod ubique, quod semper, quod ab omnibus creditum est)',[2] a new theological context gives new meaning to old expressions. Son of man is more and more understood in the light of the Cyrillian monophysitism, which had been victorious at the ecumenical council of Chalcedon in 451. Consequently, Son of man is increasingly seen as an indication of the human nature, more or less swallowed up by the divine nature and as an independent person only by 'heretics'. Nevertheless, it is correct to say that the expression Son of man was not at the centre of the discussion in this period, but rather led a shadowy life.[3]

1. *Early Middle Ages*

In the East, we find Peter of Laodicea (died 735) among the exceptions. He apparently sees Son of man as simply equivalent to man. In his *Commentary on the Gospel of Matthew*, he interprets 12.8 on the basis of v. 7, declaring that 'it is of himself that he says this or of the common nature, while it is because of man that the sabbath and every day exists' (περὶ αὐτοῦ τοῦτο λέγων ἢ τῆς κοινῆς φύσεως, ἐπειδὴ διὰ τὸν ἄνθρωπον τὸ σάββατον συνέστη καὶ πᾶσα ἡμέρα).[4]

1. Cf. especially Weist, *Wer ist dieser Menschensohn?*, pp. 56-74. Bracht, *Der Menschensohn*, pays only passing attention to 'Der MS in der Theologie der nachpatristischen Zeit' (pp. 517-520 and notes pp. 603-605).
2. *Commonitorium* 1.3.41.
3. Thus Weist, *Wer ist dieser Menschensohn?*, p. 56.
4. C.F.G. Heinrici, *Des Petrus von Laodicea Erklärung des Matthäusevangeliums* (1908), p. 131. According to a note, this understanding goes back to Chrysostom: 'περὶ

Next to be mentioned is John Damascene (c. 650–754), who was during final years presbyter in Jerusalem.[5] His understanding of Son of man is literal. In his *Expositio fidei orthodoxae* III.3-4, he argues that sometimes Christ is only mentioned with one of his two natures, even though he was not of a compound nature, but existed in two natures. Because John summarizes the typical christological thinking of this period, he is quoted at some length here:[6]

> Moreover, the Word appropriates to Himself the attributes of humanity: for all that pertains to His holy flesh is His: and He imparts to the flesh His own attributes by way of communication in virtue of the interpretation of the parts one with another, and the oneness according to subsistence (διὰ τὴν εἰς ἄλληλα τῶν μερῶν περιχώρησιν, καὶ τὴν καθ' ὑπόστασιν ἕνωσιν), and inasmuch as He Who lived and acted both as God and as man, taking to Himself either form and holding intercourse with the other form, was one and the same. Hence it is that the Lord of Glory is said to have been crucified, although His divine nature never endured the Cross, and that the Son of Man is allowed to have been in heaven before the Passion, as the Lord Himself said [Jn 3.13]. For the Lord of Glory is one and the same with Him Who is in nature and in truth the Son of Man, that is, Who became man, and both His wonders and His sufferings are known to us, although His wonders were worked in His divine capacity and His sufferings endured as man... Therefore...we sometimes use terms that have reference to His double nature, as 'Christ,' and 'at once God and man,' and 'God Incarnate;' and sometimes those that imply only one of His natures, as 'God' alone, or 'Son of God,' and 'man' alone, or 'Son of Man;' sometimes using names that imply His loftiness and sometimes those that imply His lowliness. ... Likewise also when He is called Man and Son of Man, He still keeps the properties and glories of the divine nature, a child before the ages, and man who knew no beginning; it is not, however, as child or man but as God that He is before the ages, and became a child in the end.

Isho'dad of Merw, modern-day Mary in Turkmenistan, a Nestorian bishop writing c. 850, explains Son of man in Mt. 8.20 as equivalent to 'I'.[7] His commentary on Mt. 16.13, however, shows a more dialectical understanding of the expression. He writes that Christ[8]

ἑαυτοῦ λέγων. ὁ δὲ Μάρκος (2,27) καὶ περὶ τῆς κοινῆς φύσεως αὐτὸν τοῦτο εἰρηκέναι φύσιν. Letztere Ansicht, die Mensch und Menschensohn gleichsetzt, ist bei Petrus bestimmter gefasst.' That the work of Peter of Laodicea really is a commentary is contested in Altaner and Stuiber, *Patrologie*, p. 518: 'Ein sonst unbekannter Petrus von Laodicea ist wahrscheinlich der Kompilator einer *Mt.-Katene* des 7. Jh.'

5. According to Altaner and Stuiber, *Patrologie*, p. 526, John is 'der letzte universal eingestellte Theologe der alten griechischen Kirche.'

6. Translation according to *NPNF*, 2nd Series IX.

7. Quoted according to M.D. Gibson's translation in *The Commentaries of Isho'dad of Merv in Syriac and English* (1911), I, p. 43.

8. *The Commentaries*, pp. 64-65.

calls Himself *the Son of Man*, and not *a Man*, although he was a man according to the flesh, and God according to the spirit, and [He] does not [say] 'whom do they think *I* am?'; first to bridle the chained mouth of Marcion and Manes, who brought upon our Lord an imagination and a hallucination and a flash and a figure; second because the name of *man* was spoken of one who was born of seed like other men; but He says *the Son of Man*, to indicate that He had in truth no personal father in His manhood, like the rest, but was *Son of* the first *Man*, that is to say, Adam the father of the whole community. He does not even call Himself *the Son of David*, because David was included in *the community*; so then our Lord was the Son of the community, and from the community, and for the community, He was deified, etc.[9]

The Nestorian Christology of Isho'dad is clearly present in his comment on Jn 3.13. He stresses that both verbs, ascended and descended, are spoken of both persons 'because of the unity that existed from the first movement of the reception of that holy matter in the womb'. The two persons are conjoined 'into one something and they give names and deeds to each other, in the retention of substances and persons, and in the conversation of the fixed qualities of each of them'. Isho'dad continues:[10]

The Son of Man is a general expression; of Man on the one hand naturally; of the Word on the other hand in the Incarnation; yet He is in Heaven in His Manhood because of His Godhead; but about one Son and Lord and Person we must not say, that half of Him is in Heaven and half on earth; yet just as now the Manhood of our Lord being completely in Heaven, we say that He is also on the earth and in the Church because of the Godhead, so also when He was on the earth in His Humanity, it was said that He was also in Heaven because of His Godhead.

Christ is not to be divided. Therefore, Son of man is not understood as an exhaustive expression. Divinity is supplied to make him fit for ubiquity.

Theophylaktus of Achrida in Bulgaria (c. 1050–c. 1108), who makes use of the insights of Theodoret of Cyrrhus and John Chrysostom, understands Son of man in the human form of Jesus. In his commentary on Mt. 12.32, Theophylaktus explains that it is forgivable to blaspheme against the Son of man, merely 'seeing him living as a human (ἀνθρωπικῶς ζῶντα βλέπων αὐτόν) and calling him a friend of harlots and a glutton and drunkard, because Christ did such things', for they did not comprehend, 'that he was God in his hiddenness' (αὐτὸν Θεὸν ὄντα κρυπτόν).[11] Theophylaktus is faithful to tradition when he interprets Jn 3.13, writing

9. In a remark on Mk 8.31, Isho'dad returns to the Gnostics Manes and Bar Deisan feigning that Christ by calling himself *the Son of Man* point to 'the Son of Man who existed before Adam was created, because he [Adam] was swallowed up and his five sons, there came the Intellectual Lamb to purify them'. See *The Commentaries*, p. 135.

10. *The Commentaries*, pp. 227-28.

11. *Enarratio in Evangelium Matthæi*, ad Mt. 12.32. In *Enarratio in Lucam* (ad Lk. 6.5), Theophylaktus remarks that it is nothing new to replace the personal pronoun with

> that the flesh did not came down from heaven... But because the one substance (μία ὑπόστασις), that is to say, the one person, Christ, was put together of two natures (ἐκ δύο φύσεων σύνθετος), Logos is called by human names, as the names of the Logos are ascribed to the man. Consequently, the Son of man is said to come down from Heaven, as being the one person and one substance.[12]

This understanding, however, causes problems later on with regard to Jn 5.27. With John Chrysostom, he returns to an alternative interpretation: 'Do not marvel at this, that he is Son of man. Even if he is Son of man, he is also God and has, therefore, the right to judge as Son of God' (Εἰ γὰρ καὶ Υἱὸς ἀνθρώπου ἐστιν, ἄλλα καὶ Θεός ἐστιν· ὥστε τὴν κρίσιν εἰκότως ἔχει, ὡς Υἱὸς Θεοῦ). Like Chrysostom, he refutes Paul of Samosota's understanding of this saying as if it spoke of Christ as only a man (ψιλὸν ἄνθρωπον).

Euthymius Zigabenus from Constantinople (first half of twelfth century), who was taken into the confidence of emperor Alexios 1. Komnenos (1081–1118), also adheres to tradition when he, in his *Expositio in Matthaeum* on Mt. 8.20, says:

> He calls himself Son of man (Υἱὸν δὲ ἀνθρώπου καλεῖ ἑαυτόν), confirming that he is in truth incarnated (σεσάρκωται) and not an illusion (κατ' φαντασίαν), as some assume. The human being (ἄνθρωπον) he talks about is his mother. For human being (ἄνθρωπος) is not man alone, but also woman.[13]

In the West, the learned Northumbrian monk Beda Venerabilis (673/4–735), in his commentaries on Mark and Luke, has a few remarks revealing his point of view on Son of man. On the use of Son of man in the Passion prediction in Mk 8.31, he comments that it designates the one who had to suffer much, to be killed and arise, while Christ, although given over to passion in his flesh, according to his divine nature, remains immortal.[14] This division in the person of the Son in Christ and man is also discernable in Beda's exposition of the saying about Christ's authority to forgive sins in Lk. 5.24. It is because God and Son of man are the same that the man Christ was able to forgive sins because of his divinity. The same pertains to the third beatitude in Lk. 6.22, even to the degree that it means a division

Son of man, but that Christ deserved it in a special way because he existed as man in a wonderful way.

12. *Enarratio in evangelium Joannis*, ad Jn 3.13; cf. ad Jn 6.62. Also *Enarratio in Evangelium Matthæi*, ad 26.64 where Dan. 7.13 is understood as a prediction of the one coming in the shape of a servant.

13. Cf. ad 13.37 and 16.13; *Expositio in Joannem* ad Jn 3.13; and ad 5.27-28. N. Schmidt, 'Son of Man', in *Encyclopaedia Biblica* (1903), IV, col. 4715, points to the fact that in the West this understanding caused the translation of 'Son of man' as 'Son of the virgin' in some medieval translations.

14. See *In Marci evangelium expositio*; cf. *In Lucae evangelium expositio*, ad 9.22.

between Christians and other men. The non-Christians, persecuting him who was also Son of man, are called 'men', distinguishing them from the Christians who, thanks to their faith in the Son of man, attain a higher quality than other 'men'. The person who, confronted with the Son of man, believes in Christ obtains a higher life expressed through the appellation 'Christian'.[15] To Beda, Son of man also points to the person from whom Christ gained his 'flesh'. Commenting on Lk. 11.27, with reference to Gal. 4.4, he says that because Christ is conceived by the virgin, he has his flesh from his mother according to the flesh: 'Otherwise no one could, in truth, be called Son of man, who had not his origin from a human' (Alioquin nec vere Filius hominis diceretur, qui originem non haberet ex homine). Son of man thus designates the human part of Christ, which was the opportunity for communication with humanity, but this part stands in direct relation to the divine part in a *communicatio idiomatum*. This is confirmed in Beda's remark on Lk. 19.10, where the usage of Jesus of the designation Son of man is connected to redemption: 'To press the ordinance of his piety upon us, he very often called himself Son of man, commending us to be anxious for what he has done for us in benevolence' (Qui ut pietatis suae nobis dispensationem inculcet, saepissime se Filium hominis appellat, commendans sollicite nobis quod factus est benigne pro nobis). Clearly, this understanding also lies behind his comment on Lk. 22.48, in which Judas betrays Jesus with a kiss: 'You betray, he says, the Son of man, the meaning being the flesh, not the divinity' (Filium, inquit, hominis tradis, quia caro, non divinitas, comprehenditur).

Alkuin (c. 730–804), a pupil of Beda and attached to the court of Charles the Great, adheres to the same understanding in his commentary on the Gospel of John. He contrasts Son of man as Jesus' self-reference in John 1.51 with the title Son of God in the confession of Nathanael in 1.49 and points to the same juxtaposition in the story of Peter's confession in Mt. 16.13-16. The one Mediator consists partly of the Lord himself and partly of a pure human, so that God as man became the fragility of his humanity (Deus homo fragilitatem assumptae), while the man became the quality of eternal divinity. In this concept of a *communicatio idiomatum*, the expression Son of man relates to the humility of Christ.

In the so-called 'adoptionist controversy', the expression Son of man came into the centre of the theological discussion for the first and only time in the Middle Ages. An old tendency in the West to give more place to the Gospel portrait of Jesus, including some limitations and weakness, was revived in what could be called an 'archaic Christology',[16] which differentiated more

15. Weist, *Wer ist dieser Menschensohn?*, p. 58, concludes: 'Mit der Menschensohn-Bezeichnung selbst ist dadurch jedoch implizit eine Niedrigkeitsvorstellung verknüpft.'

16. Thus Weist, *Wer ist dieser Menschensohn?*, p. 60.

strictly between humanity and divinity in the person of Christ than was normally done in the wake of Cyrillian monophysitism, following Chalcedon. Today, we know this reaction mostly from its adversaries, among them Alkuin. Thus, in his *Contra Felicem Urgellitanum Episcopum libri septem*, he attacks the bishop of the Catalonian city Urgel, Felix (died 818), one of the most prominent representatives of the new adoptionism. In the refutation, Felix is presented as follows:

> For you say that the same is Son of God, who is also Son of man and Son of man, who is Son of God, so that, from your words, it can be recognized: He—you say—who from mother's womb, *scil.* from the very conception in one single person so united with and kept to him, that the Son of God became Son of man, not with the changeability of natures, but with the dignity: in the same way also the Son of man is Son of God, not by the changeability of substances, but in that the Son of God is really the Son.

Alkuin responded to this with the accusation that Felix had two deities instead of one Christ. For 'if there are not two Gods, so the true God is not in him and named God, but the true God is one, because God is the truth, and there is no pretence in him, but the whole source of truth'.

The teaching of Felix of Urgel is later refuted also by Agobard of Lyon (died 840), in his *Liber adversus dogma Felix Urgellensis*, dedicated to Ludwig the Pious. His description confirms that adoptionist teaching operates with a double person. So Agobard quotes Felix with the following question and answer (28):

> What is the difference between the proper and natural names of the divinity in the one Son of God, and the accidentals of his humanity?... This is the difference that in the divinity, in so far he is truly Son of God, he is truly God. In true humanity, in so far as he is truly man, he is truly Son of man.

Later on in the account we find this elucidation (33):

> Felix asks saying: 'Do the proper names refer to the accidentals, or the accidentals to the proper names, or not?' He answers: 'Because of the peculiarity of the person, in which the divinity of the Son of God is together with his humanity, they have common actions. For this reason, now and then those which are divine are referred to the human, and those which are done by the human are sometimes ascribed to the divine, and by this arrangement, now and then the Son of God in the Son of man is designated Son of man and Son of man is designated Son of God (et hoc ordine aliquando Dei Filius in hominis filio filius hominis appellari dignatur, et hominis filius in Dei Filio Filius nuncupatur).'

To this, Agobard adds the admonition to his reader that 'he confers this recourse to the names of Felix with the relation of Nestorius and deliberates if they perhaps are not similar' (istum Felicis recursum nominum conferat cum relatione Nestorii, et perpendat ne forte similia sint). Obviously, adoptionists understand Son of man in the same way as orthodox theologians, namely, designating the humanity of Christ. Nonetheless, it is not as a nature within the person of Christ, but as an independent person which, thanks to divine predestination—be it also from the conception—is led to unity with the only begotten Son of God.[17]

Rhabanus Maurus (c. 784–856), in his *Commentarium in Matthaeum* 9.6, again clearly advocates a *communicatio idiomatum*, when he, combining Mt. 9.6 with Ps. 103.12, identifies God and the Son of man as forgiving sins. It is said: 'As Christ as man—thanks to his divinity—has the authority to forgive sins, the same Christ, as God—thanks to his humanity—has the fragility to die for sinners'. That Son of man is to be understood as related to the human nature of Christ is substantiated by Rhabanus in a philological note on Mt. 16.13. Because he does not want to behave ostentatiously, Christ is using Son of man in his question. Thus Son of man really means 'man'. In the Old Testament, Son of man always replaces 'son of Adam', as can be seen in Ps. 11.4, where the Hebrew text reads 'sons of Adam'. Rhabanus also repeats the explanation of Beda, when he adds that men are able to speak only of Son of man, while those who recognize the divinity of Christ, no longer are named 'men', but are divine.

Paschasius Radbertus (c.790–856/859), abbot of Corbie, in his *Expositio in Evangelium Matthaei*, directly emphasizes the polemical meaning in Jesus' use of the designation Son of man. In Mt. 9.6, in the context of the healing of the lame, it serves to prove the divinity of Jesus. But because he does not want to hide his true humanity as assumed by Marcion and his school of heretics, he uses the designation Son of man. Thus Paschasius understands Son of man in a forthright, anti-docetic way. This is also the case in his comments on Mt. 16.13, where he attacks the newly revived error of adoptionism, which divides the one Christ in two persons. It is said:

> Whatsoever therefore anyone thinks about him, he does not ask about anything but the Son of man, to say who he is. Accordingly, in reality he wants to introduce the disciples, whatever other people may think, first to the faith, that they think, believe and understand that he, the very Son of man, in truth is Son of God, and not (as an old error newly come up gain and we suffer removing old potash) divide the one and same Christ in two persons and teach that the humanity of Christ is in God thanks to adoption, as well as that the Word of God which was made flesh is to be confessed the true Son...

17. Thus Weist, *Wer ist dieser Menschensohn?*, p. 62.

2. *High and Late Middle Ages*

Peter Lombard (c. 1095–1160) clearly sees Son of man as a reference to the human aspect of the person of Christ. In his *Sententiarum libri quatuor* III.12.4, under the heading 'If what can be said of God or the Son of God also can be said of this man or the Son of man' (Si ea quæ dicuntur de Deo vel Filio Dei possunt dici de homine illo vel de filio hominis), he says:

> Usually, what is investigated is whether it can congruently be said that the Son of man, or this man, descended from heaven, or whether he is everywhere, so that it could be said that the Son of God, or God, came, and is everywhere. To this we say, if the sayings by the intelligence are related to the unity of the person, it could be said reasonably; if, in reality, to the distinction of the natures, it is by no means to be conceded.

In a commentary to the opus of Peter Lombard, Bonaventura (c. 1217–1274) argues as follows: 'It was more convenient that the Son was incarnated than any other divine person',[18] and, among other things, says,

> that because the Son is born from eternity, and it thus was congruent that God took on flesh to be born of man's kind, and in that way was Son of man (et ita filium hominis); and, for that reason, it was more suitable that he was incarnated than the Father or the Holy Spirit.

In *Vitis mystica seu tractatus de passione Domini*, sometimes ascribed to Bernard of Clairvaux (1090–1153) but most likely by Bonaventura,[19] Christ's use of Son of man is taken as an expression of deep humility. Partly reviving an interpretation of Augustine, in the light of Ps. 22(21).7 ('I am a mere worm and not a man') and Job 25.5-6 ('much more so man, who is but a maggot, son of man who is only a worm'),[20] Mt. 16.13 is understood as distinguishing between man and son of man ('Ecce qualem distinctionem… inter hominem, et filium hominis'). Men are those who descend from the first man, Adam, through corruption.

> But the truly, only pure Christ, the Lord, because he is born without corruption of the virgin Mary, he is not calling himself a man, who at least is a maggot, but son of man, who is a worm. For as a worm is created of earth alone, so Jesus Christ of the virgin alone. Oh what for a humble little worm

18. *Commentaria in quatuor libros sententiarum magistri Petri Lombardi*, lib. III, dist. I, quaest. III. Here according to *Opera Omnia*, III (1887), p. 29.

19. Thus it is printed as a work of Bernard in *MPL* 184 (where the actual text is found in 17) and likewise Bracht, *Der Menschensohn*, p. 519, considers it a work of Bernard. However, it is also contained in *Opera Omnia* of Bonaventura, VIII (1898), pp. 159-229), here the passage is found in *Addimentum* IV 17/59-60 (p. 195).

20. In Augustine, *Epistula* 140.21-22, we thus find the same biblical quotations but with the opposite conclusion: 'Filium hominis dicit magis quam hominem'.

> (vermiculus), Jesus Christ, who was made abused by men, scorned by people (Psalm 22.7), despised by people without reason, without liberation trampled down as a worm.

Nearly contemporaneous with Peter Lombard is Gerhoch of Reichersberg (1093–1169). In a book titled *De gloria et honore Filii Hominis*, from 1163, he defends strongly the equality in glory of Jesus Christ with the Father, also arguing that Jesus Christ in both natures is the entire (unicus) Son of the Father. Therefore those blasphemers should be silenced who claim

> that Son of man is not Son of God according to his being man (quod Filius hominis non sit Filius Dei secundum hominem); I don't say, according to his humanity (secundum humanitatem) that no-one should think me confirming humanity being equal to divinity.[21]

Thomas of Aquino (1226–1274) understands Son of man in accordance with his teaching of the two natures of Christ as constituted by a hypostatic union, where the human qualities do not exist on the same level as the divine, but perform in a passive way (being merely instruments of the divine nature). Although the expression turns up relatively often, it is only explained in a few places.[22] Where this happens it is mostly to substantiate the teachings of the *communicatio idiomatum* and of *ubiquitas*.

In his *Commentary on Matthew*, with regard to the words in Mt. 9.6[23] that the Son of man has authority on earth to forgive sins, Thomas says that this is to prevent two errors; namely, those of Nestorius and Photius. The first claims that Son of God and Son of man are two subjects (duo supposita): what can be said of the one, cannot be said of the other; for example, it cannot be said, this boy has created the stars. For this reason, he says 'of man', because it is God's prerogative to forgive. The second, Photius (probably a pupil of Marcellus), says that Christ first came into existence with the virgin and reached divinity through merit (merito). But as stated in Mt. 28.18, all power in heaven and on earth is given to him. The same view is expressed in a commentary on Mk 2.10. Here it is said:[24]

> that significantly he speaks about forgiving sins on earth to show that human nature and divine authority are united in an indivisible unity. Because even he was made man, he remained the Word of God; even if because of the

21. *De gloria et honore Filii Hominis* 8.3. No wonder that Gerhoch of Reichersberg was sometimes accused of monophysiticism.

22. For a more extensive survey, see Weist, *Wer ist dieser Menschensohn?*, pp. 66-74. The references below I owe to his exposition.

23. The following references to the Gospel of Matthew and the Gospel of Mark are according to the edition *S. Thomae Aquinatis Opera Omnia*, vol. 5 (1980), ad Mt. 9.6, p. 169.

24. *Opera Omnia* 5, p. 250.

> ordinance (per dispensationem), he stayed with men on earth, it did not prevent miracles from being realized, also to establish forgiveness of sins. For nothing human (humanitatis aliquid) diminished anything of the divine qualities, nor did the divinity prevent the Word of God from being Son of man in an unchangeable and true way on earth according to the flesh (nec divinitas impedivit Dei Verbum incommutabiliter & veraciter in terris secundum carnem fieri filium hominis).

This anti-heretical aim also comes to the fore in the comment on Mt. 13.37, where it is said that the Christ called himself Son of man because of his humility (propter humilitatem) and in order to refute future heretics denying either his divinity or true humanity. Therefore, he calls himself Son of man, with regard to what pertains to men, and spiritual seed, in relation to God.[25] With regard to the formulation of the question in Mt. 16.13—'Who do people say that the Son of man is?'—Thomas refers to Hilary of Poitiers for saying that Christ was looked upon as purely human (solum homo). Therefore, he wanted them to recognize that he was something other than simply a human (simplex homo). For that reason he, in this way, revealed that there was something other in him.[26]

In his *Commentary on John*, Thomas returns to the theme of the union of the two natures. As before, his point of departure is Jn 3.13. Opposing the errors of Valentinus and Origen, the one saying that Christ was not born a human, the other that Christ had a pre-existent soul, he says,[27]

> It is not to be understood as if the Son of man descended from heaven according to his human nature, but according to his divine. For when in Christ there is one subject or hypostasis or person of two natures, *scil.* the divine and human, and of each of them that subject is named, they can attribute to him both the divine and the human. We can say that the Son of man has created the stars, and that the Son of God is crucified. However, the Son of God is crucified, not according to his divine nature, but according to his human. The Son of man created the stars according to his divine nature.

Anti-heretical polemic is not the only point in Thomas's understanding of the designation Son of man. He also sees it as a means for God to deal with men, for example, by judging them. It is probably most clearly expressed in Thomas's exposition on Jn 5.27.[28] Here, he discusses and dismisses the interpretation of Chrysostom, placing the full stop before Son of man ('That

25. *Opera Omnia* 5, p. 189.

26. *Opera Omnia* 5, p. 189. Cf. Hilary of Poitiers, *Commentary on Matthew*, ad 16.13 (see above).

27. The references to the Gospel of John are according to *Opera Omnia* 10 (1860, reprint 1949), because I have not been able to verify the quotations in the edition mentioned above. For the comment on Jn 3.13, cf. p. 348.

28. *Opera Omnia* 10, p. 393.

he is the Son of man, marvel not at this') because of his rejection of the understanding of Paul of Samosata (see above). One should rather say, 'that because he is the ineffable Son of God, therefore he is judge'. To Thomas, the very same is the Son of man and Son of God; so of necessity (necessitate) he relates concerning the Lord's proposition:

> As we see, that reasoning in syllogisms with regard to doctrines, they often do not put forward the principal intention (quod syllogizantes in doctrinis frequenter non proponunt intentum principaliter), but with what follows thereof with necessity. Thus the Lord does not say, that he himself is the Son of man, but that the Son of man is of such a quality (quod Filius hominis talis est) so that, at his voice, all dead are wakened. From this that he is Son of God follows with necessity. For to awaken the dead is God's peculiar work (opus proprium Dei).

It appears that Son of man does designate simply one aspect of Christ to Thomas. This conclusion is confirmed by a *dictum* in his *Summa theologiae* 3a 3.5, stating that[29]

> the Sonship in time, whereby Christ is called Son of Man, does not constitute his person, as divine sonship does, but is, instead, a kind of consequence of his birth in time (quod filiatio temporalis, qua Christus dicitur Filius Hominis, non constituit personam ipsius, sicut filiatio æterna, sed est quiddam consequens nativitatem temporalem).

Nicolaus of Lyra (c. 1270–c. 1349), the most important medieval exegete, honoured with the title *Dr. planus et utilis*, claimed a *sensus litteralis*, as well as a *sensus mysticus*, in his interpretation of Scripture. In his *Postillæ perpetuæ sive commentaria brevia in universa Biblia*,[30] he clings, with Peter of Laodicea, to a non-terminological understanding of Son of man, even putting it on the same footing as the personal pronoun 'I'. In his comment on Mt. 8.20,[31] he says: 'But the Son of man etc., means: I am so poor' (filius autem hominis etc. id est ego sum ita pauper). So, too, explaining Mt. 12.32, he declares, that 'he wants to say that a blasphemy, which is against the human, is not unforgivable in the same way as the one against the divine'

29. Quoted according to the 61-volume Latin–English edition (1964–1981): 48 (1976), pp. 100-101. In *Summa theologiae* 3a. 33.4 (49 [1974], pp. 66-67) it is repeated that it was because of his conception in the flesh that Christ is called Son of Man. 'But he is the real and natural (verus et naturalis) Son of Man as he is the real and natural Son of God. Therefore his conception is natural.' Later, in 3a. 10.1 (52 [1972], pp. 102-103), quoting Augustine, it is said that 'what the Son of God has by nature, the Son of Man has by grace'. In 3a. 10.2 (pp. 104-105), there follows a reference to Jn 5.27.

30. Quoted according to the incunabel-edition, *Postillæ perpetuæ sive commentaria brevia in universa Biblia* IV (1472).

31. Leaf 27 verso.

(vult dicere quod blasphemia qua erat contra humanitatem not erat sic irremissibili sicut illa qua erat contra divinitatem).[32] Here we have an example of an understanding of Son of man as equivalent to 'man', although Christ himself is obviously meant.

32. Leaf 40 verso.

5. Reformation, Orthodoxy, Counter-Reformation, and Pietism

1. *The Age of Reformation*

The Reformation, first the Lutheran, then the Calvinist, did not in themselves radically change the understanding of the gospel expression Son of man. But again, the new way of constructing theology had its effect. The more speculative method was replaced by a more biblical-historical reading of the texts. Parallel phenomena can be found in contemporary Catholic exegesis. In this new context, Son of man was understood first and foremost in the light of the teaching of Christ's two natures, that is, as designating his humanity. But there are remarkable exceptions. The strife between the new faith and the old was not centred in christology, but on soteriology and ecclesiology.

The Reformation was connected with, if not partly a child of, the Renaissance, with renewed interest in Antiquity and in reading texts in their original language. After centuries when the Latin Vulgate had more or less been the Bible of the Western church—a fact which was only to be legally ratified as part of the Papal Church's restoration at the Council of Trent—the Renaissance generated renewed study of the Hebrew text of the Old Testament and the Greek text of the New. Where Orthodoxy was not allowed to re-introduce a somewhat scholastic christological thinking, the impetus of the Renaissance led to a preoccupation with Hebrew and Greek philology, developing insights not always easy to neutralize theologically.

This impetus is already felt by one of its initiators inside theology, Desiderius Erasmus (1466–1536), although he was not inclined towards radical conclusions. In his *Annotationes Novi Testamenti* from 1516 in a comment on Mt. 8.20, he explains Son of man as 'son of Adam':[1]

1. Erasmus, *Annotationes Novi Testamenti* (1516, 5th edn, 1535 = facsimile reprint, 1986), pp. 41-42.

> Certainly Christ calls himself Son of Adam, because he is born of his descendents, from whom also the rest of the world's mortals had come. The blessed Jerome explaining (edifferens) the ninth chapter of Ecclesiastes, reminds us that according to the peculiarity of colloquial Hebrew (juxta sermonis Hebraici proprietatem), ordinary men are called 'sons of man' (vulgus hominum *filios hominis* dici). Whereas, in those places, where we read 'sons of men' (filii hominum), the Hebrews have בני האדם, that is, 'sons of man', *scil.* Adam.

Later, in reference to Mt. 11.19, Erasmus—like the earlier Theodoret of Cyrrhus—argues against the idea that τοῦ ἀνθρώπου refers to Mary, the article being masculine.[2]

Martin Luther (1483–1546) is remarkably reticent when it comes to the use of the expression Son of man. It does not play any role in his theological books and pamphlets proper, but sporadically turns up in his sermons. A detailed investigation results at most in the conclusion that Luther avoids thematizing the expression or using it argumentatively.[3] There are not a few examples in his translation of his replacing a Son of man in the text with 'Christ' or 'man' or even 'me'/'him'.[4] There are clear indications, both indirect[5] and direct, of his understanding it as signifying the humanity of Christ. Among the outstanding examples, I will quote two. The first is taken from a sermon on the second Sunday in advent in the *Adventspostille* (1525). The text is Lk. 21.25-36. Here,[6] Luther says of the Parousia:

2. Erasmus, *Annotationes Novi Testamenti* (1516, 5th edn, 1535 = facsimile reprint, 1986), p. 52. Cf. ad Mt. 16.13 (p. 70), and ad Jn 1.1 (p. 220).

3. Cf. Weist, *Wer ist dieser Menschensohn?*, p. 77: 'LUTHER vermeidet es, den Menschensohn-Namen zu thematisieren oder ihn auch nur argumentativ zu gebrauchen.' Cf. also pp. 76-82.

4. Cf. Weist, *Wer ist dieser Menschensohn?*, pp. 76-77 for the following references. For simply omitting the expression: Sermon on Jn 9.1-38 from 1518 (*WA* 1, pp. 267-73), which says nothing about v. 35. Sermon on Lk. 19.1-10 from 1527 (*WA* 17 II, pp. 496-507; 507-14). In a sermon on Jn 6 from 1530 (*WA* 33, p. 11), Luther replaces Son of man in v. 27 with 'I', a sort of parallel to what is found in 'Annotationes in aliquot capita Matthaei' from 1538 (*WA* 38, p. 611), where the question of Jesus in Mt. 16.13 is reproduced indirectly with 'quid homines de se sentient'. Examples of omitting the expression are again seen in a sermon on Jn 3.11-14, also from 1538 (*WA* 48, p. 347), and in a handwritten note on Mt. 11.19 in his personal New Testament, dated 1544 (*WA* 48, pp. 114-15). In a sermon from 1523 on the sign of Jonah and in another sermon from the same year, also referring to Mt. 12.38-40 (*WA* 11, pp. 33-35; 12, p. 427-35), Luther does not comment on the expression, simply replacing Son of man with Christ. The same procedure is used with regard to Mt. 16.13 as in sermons from 1519, 1522 and 1544 (*WA* 2, pp. 244-49; 10 III, pp. 208-16; 52, pp. 655-56).

5. Weist, *Wer ist dieser Menschensohn?*, pp. 79-80, adduces three examples of indirect interpretation of Son of man as signifying the humanity of Christ: from a sermon on Mt. 24 (*WA* 47, p. 604), a paraphrase of Mt. 26.64, in a sermon from the *Hauspostille* (1544) (*WA* 52, p. 763) and an interpretation of Jn 1.51 (*WA* 46, p. 711).

6. *WA* 10 1.2, p. 109.

> And all eyes will see him and also see that he is no one other than the bodily man (leyplich mensch), Christ, in bodily form (leyplicher getallt), just as he was born of Mary (von Maria geporn) and has wandered on earth (auff erden gewandelt); because, otherwise, he would probably have said (wol mugen sagen): They shall see me, which would not clearly be said about the bodily form. But now when he says, they shall see the Son of man, it is clearly expressed that it is a bodily future (eyn leyplich tzukunfft), a bodily seeing (eyn leyplich sehen), a being in bodily form, with great power (in grosser gewallt).

The other example is from a collection of sermons on John 6–8 from 1530. At first, Luther simply replaces Son of man with 'man' (menschen) in his translation of Jn 6.53, but later he returns to the saying with the explanation:[7] 'You have already heard Christ refer to Himself as the Son of Man (des menschen Sohn). With this term, He wants to indicate that He has our true flesh and blood (sei wahrhaftig fleisch und blutt), which he obtained from the Virgin Mary and which contains eternal life.' Therefore,

> we must not let ourselves be taught a god who sits on his Throne up in heaven, one who is to be sought only in the Godhead. If we do, we find ourselves misled. But if you want to escape death and be saved, then admit no god other than the Son of Man. You will find Him in His flesh and blood, for that is where He dwells. In the Son of Man, you will encounter God. The Turk claims that his Mohammed has God. The pope declares that the Carthusians and other monastic orders also have our Lord God. But here it is written: It is the Son of Man. The message, faith, and life of all others are excluded.

The human nature of Christ alone is not able to save. Only in so far as Christ is taken over bodily by the Godhead and Christ is God and man in one person, is the redemption effective and Christ (being called Son of man) also Saviour.

For Luther, Son of man is Christ for us in his human existence. This is the way it is understood in the framework of the doctrine of Christ's two natures. This is confirmed in a Latin note to the words 'on earth' in Mt. 9.6, in a hand-written note in Luther's Bible:[8]

> Therefore, if you want to know, see, touch God, you have to see and touch yourselves, for you are his work, and his works are in you and mutually through you in you. And it is through the Son of man. I do not do this myself in my own unconfirmed majesty (which you are not able to endure), nor through angels (which not even the most holy Moses was able to endure). But the Son of man and after this it is no-one but sons of men who do this for you in you. And on the other side, you sons of men shall do this for other sons of men, until the very day comes, on which God himself will be there without you and do everything for you and you everything in him.

7. *WA* 33, p. 201. Translation according to *Luther's Works* 23 (1959), pp. 129-30.
8. *WA* 48, p. 110.

Son of man is Christ as humans are able to know and see him. It is understandable, then, that this Christology has been described as moderate modalism.[9]

In a commentary on Mt. 9.6, Huldrych Zwingli (1484–1531) remarks that Son of man 'is a periphrasis for man, but this periphrasis explains the peculiarity of the object (proprietatem rei explicat). He so wanted to announce that he was a true man (hominem verum) in everything (except sin) and was similar to us.'[10] In this respect, Zwingli is followed by his successor in Zürich, Heinrich Bullinger (1504–1575), who, however, also thinks that 'filius' in the Hebrew dialect has an intensifying impact pointing to Jesus' taking part in our pitiable human nature.[11] When, in Mt. 24.30, Jesus speaks of the coming Son of man, it shows that he had not abandoned his human nature in heaven.

Like Luther, John Calvin (1509–1564), is very cautious in his use of the expression Son of man,[12] but when he does explain it, directly or indirectly, he too is much indebted to tradition. Thus, in the *Institutio christianae religionis* (1536), he says that it was not a common undertaking, which was up to the Mediator to fulfil, namely

> of sons of men to make sons of God (ut ex filiis hominum filios Dei faceret), of heirs of hell heirs of the kingdom of heaven. Who could do that if not the Son of God made Son of man, and so took on himself what was ours to transfer to ourselves what was his, because what was his nature, he made ours by grace.[13]

Calvin also refers to Son of man as an expression of the humanity of Christ: not being content with the name of 'man' (hominis nomine), he often

9. Thus Weist, *Wer ist dieser Menschensohn?*, p. 82: 'So ahnen wir hier wieder den leisen Modalismus in LUTHERS christologischer Gedankenwelt, auf den es letztlich zurückzuführen ist, daß LUTHER sich dem Menschensohn-Ausdruck gegenüber in einer gewissen Verlegenheit befindet, ihn umgeht, und wenn er ihn doch verwendet, ihn niemals isoliert, sondern ihn allein auf dem Hintergrund des "Gott bzw. Christus für uns" sieht.'

10. H. Zwingli, *Annotationes in Evangelistarum & Apostolorum scripta* (1531; here according to vol. 4 of *Opera D. Huldrychi Zwinglii*, edita per Leonem Iudae 1545), p. 39.

11. H. Bullinger, *In sacrosanctum Jesu Christi Domini nostri Euangelium secundum Matthaeum, commentariorum libri XII* (1542), p. 84b (ad Mt. 8.20): 'significant se esse verum et nobis consubstantialem, ex homine natum hominem secundum carnem'. To Mt. 24.30, see p. 214b. I owe the references to Bullinger to Bracht, *Der Menschensohn*, p. 610.

12. Weist, *Wer ist dieser Menschensohn?*, pp. 82-83, gives examples of how Calvin replaces it either by 'Christ' or by a personal pronoun.

13. J. Calvin, *Institutio christianae religionis* (1536, quoted according to P. Barth [ed.], *Joannis Calvini Opera Selecta* I [1926]), p. 78. A similar understanding in Calvin, *Evangelium secundum Ioannem Commentarius* (1553, 2nd edn, 1560), p. 34, ad Jn 3.13.

used the name Son of man, indicating that he was a man born of human seed.[14] At another place the old juxtaposition of Son of God and Son of man shows that Calvin retained the old doctrine of Christ's two natures, but not so much in a speculative way as to make possible his role as mediator. He says that 'because he had chosen a temple for himself from the virgin's womb in which he lived, he, who was Son of God, was made Son of man, not by confusion of substances, but by the unity of the person'.[15]

In Calvinist exegesis, philology exercised greater influence than in Lutheran. First to be mentioned is one of the pioneers in Hebrew studies, Sebastian Münster (1488–1552), who became a member of the Reformed Church and taught in Basel. He followed an interpretation proposed by the rabbi David Kimchi (1160–1235) of Ps. 49.3, making a distinction between בני אדם (as belonging to a lower class) and בני איש (as belonging to a higher class).[16] Münster, supposing that Jesus had called himself בן אדם, concluded:

> Christ calls himself 'son of man' in the manner of Scripture, which calls the man born of the lowest class 'son of man'. Thus Christ was made in the likeness of men; that is, as if one of the common people of men.

Robert Stephanus (Estienne; 1503–1559), a member of the famous printer's dynasty but also a learned scholar, likewise stresses the aspect of humility in the expression. Thus Jesus employed it according to 'genus dicendi Hebraicum', as in Ps. 8.5 and Job 25.6, to signify his belonging to the lowest class of men and his humility, as taught by Paul in Phil. 2.7.[17]

The successor of Calvin in Geneva, Theodore Beza (1519–1605), understands Son of man as a Hebrew phrase. In a note on Mt. 8.20[18] in his *Novum*

14. Calvin, *Institutio christianae religionis* (8th edn, 1559 = *Opera Selecta* III (1928)), pp. 447-48. Cf. pp. 451-52: 'It is a stinking escape (Puditum est effugium) when they talk nonsense that Christ said Son of man in so far as he was promised to men (Christum dici filium hominis quatenus hominibus promissus est); because it is obvious that, according to Hebrew habit (hebraice more), true man is called son of man (vocari filium hominis verum hominem). It can hardly be doubted that Christ truly insisted on his language's manner of speaking (Christus vero haud dubie phrasin linguae suae retinuit).'

15. Calvin, *Institutio christianae religionis* (8th edn, 1559 = *Opera Selecta* III), p. 458.

16. S. Münster, *Torat Hammaschiach: Evangelium secundum Matthaeum in lingua Hebraica, cum versione Latina atque succinctis annotationibus* (1537), p. 70. I owe this reference and the translation below to D. Burkett, *The Son of Man Debate* (1999), p. 16.

17. Robert Stephanus, *In Euangelium secundum Matthaeum, Marcum, et Lucam commentarii ex ecclesiasticis scriptoribus collecti. Novae glossae ordinariae specimen, donec meliora dominus* (1553), p. 33b (ad Mt. 9.6); p. 32b (ad Mt. 8.20; cf. p. 70b ad Mt. 16.13). I owe these references to Bracht, *Der Menschensohn*, p. 611. Bracht here also (pp. 611-12) introduces the Bern theologian, Benedictus Aretius (Marti c. 1522–1574), *Commentarii in quatuor evangelistas* (2nd edn, 1580), p. 58 (ad Mt. 8.20; cf. ad 16.13 [p. 109b]).

18. *Novum Iesu Christi Domini nostri Testamentum*, p. 31.

Iesu Christi Domini nostri Testamentum, the first edition of which appeared in 1559,[19] Beza refutes those who think that the expression points to a single person, namely, Mary, or to real sons of men (referring to Ezekiel being called so by the Spirit of God). That it should refer to the true human nature of Christ, although true enough, is not substantiated by the Gospel evidence. Thus Beza agrees with those who take it as a Hebrew phrase (Hebraicam phrasim) for 'man' (homine), as when Homer speaks of the Achaians as 'sons of Achaians' (υἱοὺς ἀχαιῶν). It is also normally understood in this way in Jeremiah 49 and other places, where the old translator (Vetus interpres) did not convert a singular into a plural:[20]

> But to this I add that because it is usual for Hebrews (familiare est Hebræis) to speak of themselves in the third person (de se loquantur in tertia persona), I, therefore, accept it instead of the first person pronoun (loco pronominis primæ personæ). In the New Testament, where nobody but Christ alone calls himself Son of man, it is exactly [employed] when he speaks about himself.

In a remarkable way, Beza here stresses the circumlocutional meaning of the expression Son of man used in the Gospels.

In the Lutheran camp, Son of man is predominantly understood as tantamount to 'man'. The reserved attitude of Luther is equally present in the works of Philipp Melanchthon (1497–1560).[21] Nowhere does he offer an explicit account of his understanding of the expression. Perhaps this is due to its use in the tradition as describing one of Christ's two natures (the Christology of Melanchthon being primarily concerned with the salvation of men). Seemingly, he has not found the expression Son of man efficient in his stressing that 'to know Christ is to know his beneficial deeds' (hoc est Christum cognoscere beneficia eius cognoscere).[22]

However, where it is interpreted among the Lutherans, the differences are interesting. Philology and intertextual readings challenge more traditional, doctrinal understandings and there is a slight move away from seeing the expression as an objective description of nature towards a part of Christ's subjective revealing of his role in salvation, a subjective expression of his self-understanding.

19. The full title is *ΤΗΣ ΚΑΙΝΗΣ ΔΙΑΘΗΚΗΣ ΑΠΑΝΤΑ. Novum Iesu Christi Domini nostri Testamentum latine iam olim a veteri interprete nunc denuo a Theodore Beza versum: cum eiusdem annotationibus, in quibus Ratio Interpretationis redditur*. The 1559 edition is the so-called first edition, because Beza introduced text-criticism in his Novum Testamentum only with the later editions (1565 and onwards).

20. In the Vulgate, filius hominis appears two times in Jer. 49 (vv. 18 and 33) in the singular but with a generic meaning.

21. Weist, *Wer ist dieser Menschensohn?*, pp. 85-86.

22. Melanchthon, *Loci communes* (1521, quoted according to Robert Stupperich (ed.), *Melanchthons Werke in Auswahl* 2.1 (1952), p. 7.

Wolfgang Musculus (1497–1563, sometime active in Augsburg), explaining Jn 5.27, states[23] that 'according to the custom of Scripture, to be Son of man is nothing other than to be man, just as to be Son of God is to be God, and son of a horse to be horse, and son of a lion to be lion'. When Christ says Son of man and not merely 'man', it is to emphasize that he really had his flesh from the virgin Mary and, in this way, was of the seed of Abraham, against those who deny he had claimed it from heaven.

The initiator of the Reformation in Strasbourg, Martin Bucer (1491–1551), sees Son of man as designating the humility of Christ. Thus, Son of man in Mt. 8.20 calls for the explanation that[24] 'for Hebrews בן אדם; that is, son of Adam, or man, means nothing other than "man" (homo). However, in Scripture, to call oneself "man", is out of humility (humilitatis), because "every man" would be falsehood and vanity (quod omnis homo mendacium sit & vanitas).' Because the article is *masculinum* τοῦ and not the feminine τῆς, 'man' does not refer to Mary as some falsely take it. That Jesus calls himself Son of man, or Adam, that is, true man and simple man (vere hominem, & plebius hominem), recommends his wonderful combination of both humility and goodness for our sake. For our salvation, he degraded himself to be counted nothing but a human and he even wanted to exist in a truly insignificant and inferior way. Claiming to be son of an outstanding virgin would be more glorious and not increase our faith.

The Church historian, Matthias Flacius (1520–1575, with the byname Illyricus, because he was born in Istrien), father of the so-called Gnesio-Lutherans, points to the use of Son of man in Ezekiel as a parallel to the use of Jesus, both persons employing it in the sense of 'man'.[25] 'In Ezekiel, it often replaces the second person pronoun, signifying the prophet himself, whom God names this way. In the Gospel, Christ, employing the third person instead of the first person, names himself this way.' For the first time, the use of son of man in Ezekiel is introduced in a profound way into the discussion.

Joachim Camerarius (1500–1574), professor in Leipzig, in interpreting Mt. 9.6, takes Son of man as a periphrasis of one born as man (periphrasis hominis nati).[26] Jesus uses it in the gospels when speaking to others. It also turns up very often in the prophecies of Ezekiel. According to Camerarius, it is an elliptical way of speaking (ἐλλειπτικὴ oratio): 'that you may know that

23. *Commentarium in evangelistam Ioannem*. Heptas prima (1545), p. 185.

24. *In sacra quatuor Euangelia, Ennarrationes perpetuæ* (1553), p. 86. Cf. ad Mt. 9.6, p. 91 and ad Jn 3.13, p. 242.

25. *Clavis Scripturæ s. seu Sermone Sacrarum literarum* (1567, 2nd edn, 1609), I, p. 331.

26. *Notatio figurarum sermonis in libris quatuor evangeliorum, et indicata verborum significatio, et orationis sententia, ad illorum scriptorum intelligentiam certiorem, studio* (1572), p. 45. Cf. ad Mt. 16.13, p. 67, and ad Jn 12.34, p. 279.

this Son of man, i.e. me (istum filium hominis, id est me) has authority to forgive sins on earth…' Here it is acknowledged that Son of man sayings constitute a figure of speech, where, obviously, no special speculative meaning is presupposed.

Also to be mentioned in this connection is Johannes Piscator (Fischer, 1546–1625), a reformed theologian, who from 1584 was resident of Herborn. In a scholion on Mt. 8.20. Piscator calls Son of man 'a circumlocution for himself, produced for a reason' (periphrasis sui ipsius a causa procreante). Commenting on Mt. 16.13, he remarks that the two articles limit the common expression to Jesus alone' (ad speciem individuam), thereby meaning 'me, that man' (me illum hominem).[27] Further, Sebastian Pfocenius claims that combinations with υἱός, or a similar word, are idioms in both Hebrew and poetical Greek, having the same meaning as the word itself.[28]

2. *Orthodoxy*

In Lutheran Orthodoxy, the whole weight of theology was placed on the Bible as the inspired revelation. It served primarily as a source of *dicta probantia* in the production of textbooks of Dogmatics, the various philological insights being suppressed. Older schemes of understanding were revived which maintained the revelatory quality of the expression Son of man. Of profound importance was the doctrine of *communicatio idiomatum*. It becomes clear in the *Formula concordia* from 1580 (in article 8), 'Of the Person of Christ (De persona Christi)', that the whole scholastic doctrine of Christ's two natures is again present. In the *Affirmativa* to article 8, it is declared 'that the divine and human nature are personally united in Christ, further means that there exists not two Christs, one the Son of God, the other Son of man, but that the one and same is Son of God and man (unus et idem sit Dei et hominis filius)'.[29]

27. *Commentarius in omnes libros Novi Testamenti* (1621), pp. 92 and 159. This and the following two references I owe to Bracht, *Der Menschensohn*, p. 615.

28. *Diatribe de lingua Graeca N. Test. Puritate* (1648), pp. 30-31. This is refuted by Thomas Gataker, *De novi instrumenti stylo dissertation* (1648), pp. 164-65, who points to the difference between the Greek expressions and Son of man as a Hebraism 'simpliciter pro homine', which does not turn up in Greek literature.

29. *Die Bekenntnisschriften der evangelisch-lutherischen Kirche. Herausgegeben im Gedenkjahr der Augsburgischen Konfession* (1930, 5. Aufl., 1964), p. 805. In the German text the references are Lk. 1[.31-35] and Rom. 9[.5]. Weist, *Wer ist dieser Menschensohn?*, p. 88, refers to Matthias Hafenreffer (1561–1619), *Loci theologici* (1600, 4th edn, 1611), pp. 274-75, and Leonhard Hutterus (Hütter) (1563–1619), *Compendium locorum theologicorum* (1610, later edn, 1855), p. 14, as representatives for an interpretation of Mt. 16.16 that the Son of man is Son of God. Hafenreffer further points to

This understanding is not surprisingly elaborated at length by one of the fathers of the *Formula concordia*, Martin Chemnitz (1522–1586), superintendent in Braunschweig. In his *Harmoniae evangelicae* in comments on Jn 3.13, he begins by repeating nearly verbatim the words from the *Formula*, interpreting the saying as an indication that the words 'the Son of man is in heaven' does not mean that there are two persons in Christ, but that the one person is God and man (unica persona est Deus & homo). Answering the question why Christ employs this expression, he says that there is no doubt, that he has taken the appellation (appellationem) from Dan. 7.13, where the prophet describes the person of the Messiah this way:

> As accordingly this use of the appellation of Messiah is taken from Daniel, so it is out of the same prophet that he commonly calls the Messiah, who was waited, Son of man, him namely, whom Daniel foresaw in a vision, as also the son of David is commonly called Messiah (Sicut igitur ex Daniele sumpta fuit usitata tunc appellatio Messiae, ita ex eodem propheta vulgus Messiam, quem expectabat, vocavit filium hominis, illum scilicet, quem Daniel in visione prospexit, sicut & filium Davidis vulgus Messiam appellavit).[30]

It is probably for the first time here that we meet the assertion that Son of man is a designation (appellatio) for the Messiah.[31]

Chemnitz goes on to define the content of Son of man as used by Christ. He does this in four points. Together with what has been already mentioned, Chemnitz made a number of observations. First, Son of man is an appellation attributed to the Messiah, especially by Daniel. Second, it tells that Christ in truth is man (homo). The Son of God could have created his human flesh of earth in the same way as Adam was made, but he did not call himself merely 'man' (hominem tantum), but rather Son of man, because he took his flesh from Mary and in this manner was made Son of man. Third, in the Hebrew language distinguished and brilliant men, existing in great honour and having authority, are called 'sons of [noble] men' (filii viri),' truly ordinary and insignificant 'sons of men (filii hominum). According to his profound

Jn 5.27, Hutterus (p. 18) to the addition to Lk. 9.56, as indicating a *communicatio idiomatum*.

30. *Harmoniae evangelicae*, ed. posthumously per Polycarpo Lyserum (1593, here according to the edition of 1615), p. 360.

31. Bracht, *Der Menschensohn*, p. 622, also mentions another early spokesman for understanding Son of man as a messianic title, namely Jacques Cappel(lus) (III, 1570–1624, since 1610 professor in theology in Sedan). Thus in *Observationes in Novum Testamentum, exceptis Actibus Apostolorum et Apocalypsi D. Ioannis* (edited by Louis Cappel, 1657), p. 12 (ad Mt. 8.20), he claims that when Jesus so often calls himself Son of man, it seems that he 'ex pluribus elogiis, quae Messiae data fuerant a Prophetis, illud elegit, quod est omnium modestissimum'. Thus Messiah is named Son of man in Ps. 8.5 and Ps. 80.18, where David speaks 'in persona Christi' and in Dan. 7.13. What Jesus has meant is: 'ego sum is, de quo in Vetere Testamento dicatur'.

humility and self-emptying (exinanitionem), taking the form of a servant (forma servi), Christ called himself Son of man. Fourth, and finally, it could be added that Ezekiel, although obviously insignificant, rejected and contemptible, was always addressed by God with the term Son of man when he was sent in a public office or service to the Church. For the same reason with regard to office and service, the Father in Isa. 42.1 refers to the Son with the words: 'This is my servant'.

The author of the famous *Philologia sacra*, Salomo Glassius (1593–1656, from 1640 superintendant in Gotha), also suggests that Son of man means 'man' as in Ezekiel, as well as in the use of the plural form. In the mouth of Jesus, it, nevertheless, designates 'hominem κατ' ἐξοχήν', pointing to his true human nature (ad ipsam humanitatem veram).[32]

The main figure in Lutheran Orthodoxy, Johann Gerhard (1582–1637), professor in Jena, in his famous *Loci communes theologici* (1610–1622) enumerates six reasons for Christ's use of Son of man of himself,[33] including all of Chemnitz's four points, and adding little new. First, Son of man is taken from Daniel 7 as a designation of the Messiah (= Chemnitz 1). Second, it demonstrates Christ's true humanity (= Chemnitz 2, beginning). Gerhard adds the motif 'only begotten' (unigenitus), because, as true God he is born from eternity of the Father.[34] Third, it declares his consanguinity with us, being born by a human and not created of earth like Adam (cf. Chemnitz 2, end). Gerhard adds the motif of consanguinity (consanguinitas) to stress Christ's relation to us by blood. Fourth, it was to show his humility and self-emptying (= Chemnitz 3). Gerhard also (re-)introduces the philological observation that, whereas, in Hebrew, nobles are called 'sons of nobles (בני איש)', ordinary men are called 'sons of man (בני אדם)'. Fifth, it was that he might administer his office (cf. Ezekiel being called Son of man; here Gerhard elaborates on Chemnitz 4). Sixth, it was to show his joy with mankind (cf. Prov. 8.31). The name invites us to consider his philanthropy (considerationem, summæ φιλανθρωπίας), because of which he wanted to

32. The full title is famous, *Philologia sacra, qua totius ss. Veteris et Novi Testamenti scripturae tum stylo et literature, tum sensus et genuinae interpretationis ratio et doctrina libris quinque expenditure ac traditur* (1623–36; quoted according to the later edition by Gottfred Olearius, 1705), p. 671. I owe this reference to Bracht, *Der Menschensohn*, p. 608.

33. *Loci communes theologici*, vol. I (2nd edn, 1667) IV.6, pp. 430-31.

34. Weist, *Wer ist dieser Menschensohn?*, p. 91, draws attention to a place in Gerhard, *Harmonia quatuor Evangelistarum* (1652), p. 242, where, in an explanation of Jn 3.13, he exposes God's plan of salvation: 'Unigenitus igitur filius Dei, qui in coelo est, descendit, factus filius hominis. Atque ita humana natura in Christo per hypostaticam illam cum divinitate verbi unionem ascendit in coelum, ac rursus recuperavit hereditatem ac possessionem regni coelorum, ideo ut nobis, qui ipsius, ut filius hominis fratres sumus, viam in coelum aperirit, et dedicaret.'

be made Son of man. This is the only new element in relation to Chemnitz's four points. Gerhard also refutes those who think Son of man points to Christ's being born of the virgin. It can be used of every man born in humble circumstances.

3. *Testimonies to a Growing Philological Consciousness*

Hugo Grotius (1583–1645), the famous Dutch humanist and member of the Reformed Church, defends the understanding of Son of man as 'man', although he also retains more traditional views. In his *Annotationes in libros evangeliorum* (1641), in a note on Mt. 8.20, he states that the expression is not a denunciation of the virgin birth (repeating the answer of Pseudo-Justin in *Quaestiones et responsitiones* 66). However, as Christ is only called such by himself there must be another reason for the designation, and Grotius points to the fact that Hebrew *adam* and *ben-adam* most often describe a man with a sorry fate (hominem contemtæ fortis). Referring to Judg. 16.7, 11; Ps. 82.7; Gen. 6.2 and Ps. 49.3, he continues, saying that Ezekiel, Daniel and Zechariah, while communicating with angels, were reminded of their fragility by this designation; this also pertains to Dan. 10.16 and to *bar enash* in Dan. 7.13. It is said that he who looks like a Son of man has a sorry fate and is given royal power. Thus, with this designation Christ points to his kenosis, described in Phil. 2.7, in line with the description of the Servant of the Lord in Isa. 53.3.[35] This understanding is applied to Mt. 16.13, where τὸν υἱὸν τοῦ ἀνθρώπου is paraphrased 'i.e. me, me who speaks (id est, me, inquam) (and) who, with regard to every external appearance, prefers nothing to being a common man (plebe hominem)'.[36] In his annotation on Mt. 12.32,[37] he remarks that, in spite of the articles, son of man does not pertain to Christ alone, but to any 'man', Christ not being excepted:

> For the article is often a sign of generality (cf. Mt. 18.17 ὁ ἐθνικός). The meaning is: You shall know that it is a grave crime to injure an innocent man; ... consider therefore how much more serious it is to attack God's own deeds with injuries.

Grotius, however, gives special emphasis to the theme Son of man in a remarkable and often quoted *annotatio* to Mt. 12.8. Here it is said:[38]

> They are mistaken who understand υἱὸν τοῦ ἀνθρώπου at this place especially of Christ. For Christ, acting on earth, is commonly known to submit to the Law, neither abolishing it nor cancelling it, but he has interpreted it according

35. *Annotationes in libros evangeliorum*, p. 176.
36. *Annotationes in libros evangeliorum*, p. 290.
37. *Annotationes in libros evangeliorum*, p. 237.
38. *Annotationes in libros evangeliorum*, p. 226.

> to the meaning, [derived] from the Father. He has confirmed his interpretation with both the authority of the Law and by adducing arguments on equal and good terms. Accordingly this υἱὸς ἀνθρώπου is anybody, as Mark makes it apparent beyond question (Est ergo hic υἱὸς ἀνθρώπου homo quivis, quod ita apertum facit Marcus, ut contradici nequeat). For so Christ speaks by him: '*The Sabbath is because of man, not man because of the Sabbath; therefore son of man is Lord also over the Sabbath*'. These words are not coherent, if you have to interpret son of man as Messiah, sent with power to make the Law obsolete (Haec enim verba non cohaerent, si filium hominis interpreteris Messiam, missum cum potestate legis antiquandae). Add to this that, at that time, Jesus would not proclaim himself either to the people or to the Pharisees as Christ (see below 16.21, Mark 8.30). However, as I have said, it is very clear that for the Hebrews בן אדם designates any man, although now and then, as we have said, it is confined to less noble [people]: it is not [used] otherwise when it is said below [v.] 32: ὃς ἐὰν εἴπῃ λόγον κατὰ τοῦ υἱοῦ τοῦ ἀνθρώπου. ... The meaning of the words of Christ, which are somehow more fully expressed by Mark, is: Because it is compared with the reason for another matter, it should be inferior to him, with whose matter it is compared (Quod alterius rei causa comparatum est, id cedere debet ei, cujus causa comparatum est). When the Sabbath is compared with man's matter, it should accordingly surely be inferior to man, where it is about the salvation of man. κύριος εἶναι in Greek, as in the Hebrew בעל, means that somebody has the right to use something, as man, in such a case, has the right to turn to his use even the day of the Sabbath. It is obviously the same, as when Rabbi Jonathan says that the Sabbath is given into the hands of men, not men into the hands of the Sabbath. Thus to give into hands is the same as to be in [ones] power. Accordingly, it is this rule, also known among Jews, which Christ applies.[39]

The philological observation, that son of man in Mk 2.27-28 obviously means 'man' in general, excludes that, in Jesus' use of the term, it should single him out as the Messiah. In this case, Grotius argues with irresistible logic for the understanding which we have already found less profoundly argued by some exegetes. However, the time was not yet ripe for this acknowledgment. Philological insights alone were not yet able to break down the authority of tradition.[40]

In non-orthodox exegesis of this period we meet sporadically with similar viewpoints. In England, the Anglican clergyman and eminent Semitic

39. Grotius further, in a note to Mk 2.28 (*Annotationes in libros evangeliorum*, p. 536), refers to Mk 3.28 for the meaning of Son of man = 'man'.

40. Cf. A. Meyer, *Jesu Muttersprache*, p. 145, with regard to Grotius' insight: 'Verwundert fragt man sich, wie die hier gebotene Erkenntnis später so gänzlich hat verschwinden können. Der Grund dafür ist aber leicht zu finden. Die ganze Wucht der Tradition stand der hier eingeschlagenen Richtung entgegen, und die auf zwei Stellen beschränkte Anwendung war in ihrer Vereinzelung nicht intensiv genug, um diesen ungünstigen Wind gegenüber sich zu behaupten, so dass das hell aufleuchtende Licht bald wieder verlöschen musste.'

scholar,[41] John Lightfoot (1602–1675), in a commentary on Jn 1.51,[42] remarks that Son of man, which occurs so often in the Gospels and is only used by Jesus himself, does not say more than 'man (hominem)', according to the 'Syriac' idiom of this period (juxta *Syriacam* tunc temporis usurpatam dialectum), בר נשׁא, *Bar nosho*. Lightfoot disputes that it should denote Christ's humility, or, that he was a man similar to us in every regard except sin. It is not always placed in sayings pertaining to humility. The real reason for Jesus' use appears to be that he wanted to proclaim himself the second Adam (indicare *Adamum* seipsum fuisse *secundum*) and call attention to the promise given immediately after the fall of the first Adam, that the seed of the woman shall crush the serpent's head (Gen. 3.15). That is also the reason why Luke has the genealogy go back to Adam. The substance of Jn 1.51, accordingly, is that just as the first Adam closed Heaven, so the second re-opens it. It is, therefore, highly probable, that, in Ezekiel (Ezek. 2.1 etc.) and Daniel (Dan. 8.17), both of these species are called 'sons of man' (filii homines, בני אדם), while in Ps. 62.9 it is a name of nature (*nomen naturæ*). Accordingly, this title of Christ barely denotes the defilement of the human species, but indicates which honour God has granted our nature in him. The fact that Christ so often and so emphatically calls himself Son of man should lead our contemplations to a higher meditation on this.[43]

The Dutch Armenian, Johannes Vorst(ius) (1569–1622) perceived Son of man as a pleonasm for 'man'. To say υἱὸν ἀνθρώπου, instead of ἄνθρωπος, was a Hebraism (ad formam Hebrææ ῥήσεως). This also pertains to Chaldean (= Aramaic), as in Dan. 7.13.[44] Another Dutchman, Johannes Coccejus (1609–1669), professor in Leiden, in a commentary on Mt. 8.20, says that Christ signified nothing except 'this man' (*hic homo*), with this name pertaining to his external appearance (ad externam speciem). 'At that time, Jews said האי בר נשׁא, *this man* for I (*hic homo* pro *ego*) in their everyday language.'[45] Coccejus, however, continues declaring that it is also a very clear name applying to Christ's blamelessness and humility as well as to his kenosis (with references to Isa. 42.2; Phil. 2.6, 7). He is the boy born to us,

41. Cf. W. Baird, *History of New Testament Research* I (1992), p. 12: 'Gibbon is reported to have said of him that "by reading the rabbis, he became almost a rabbi himself"' (with reference to *Dictionary of National Biography*, s.v. 'Lightfoot, John').

42. *Harmoniæ Quatuor Evangelistarum, tum inter se, tum cum Veteri Testamento* I-III (1644–1650, quoted after *Opera Omnia* I [1686]), p. 402.

43. Cf. ad Jn 5.27, p. 528. See also, ad Mt. 16.13, idem, *Horæ Hebraicæ et Talmudicæ* II. *In Evangelium S. Matthæi* (1658; here according to *Opera Omnia* II, 1686), pp. 334-35.

44. *De Hebraismis Novi Testamenti Commentarius* I-II (1658–1665), I, p. 333; cf. pp. 332-34. The reference in the text is to Dan. 7.12.

45. *Scholia in Evangelium secundam Matthæum* (1673; reprint in idem, *Opera Omnia* IV) (1675, 2nd edn, 1689), p. 17.

the son given to us, according to Isa. 9.5, the righteous sprout of David in Jer. 23.5; 33.15 etc. So, after all, it acquires a content of its own according to Coccejus.

Simon Episcopius (1583–1643), like Vorst(ius) a Dutch Armenian and a pioneer in free biblical exegesis, thinks Son of man in some places in the Gospels simply means 'man' (as for instance in Mt. 12.8).[46] In a lengthy comment on Mt. 8.20, Episcopius, however, advocates the view that Jesus also used it with explicit reference to Dan. 7.13 to express his unity with his congregation; that is, it conveys a collective understanding. He writes:

> And so by the 'Son of Man' Christ (Jesus) here designates not only himself, but also all those who were in his service (in famulitio suo erant) or who were ever going to be his disciples; as if it said 'The Son of Man along with his own,' in the manner of the customary diction of Holy Scripture, in which the whole kingdom is sometimes designated by the name of the king and leader alone; as is seen expressly at Daniel 7.13, to which passage the Saviour seems to have referred here when he names himself Son of Man.[47]

Adhering to the tradition much more closely, is the, to my knowledge, first monograph on the Son of man in the New Testament, *Specimen questionum in novum instrumentum de filio hominis* (1684) by the learned minister Jean Gaillard from what in 1830 was to become Belgium.[48] Having predecessors among the Church fathers, he points Eve out as the person whose son Jesus declares himself to be (esse *Hevam*, humani generis matrem). Gaillard also sees the reason for Jesus' use in the prophecy of Daniel (quia Daniel Messiam hoc nomine insignierat). Investigating the question as to why Daniel called the Messiah Son of man and why Jesus wanted to use this rare title so often and sedulously about himself, Gaillard's reasons seem to be the following:

> that he was a man, that he drew his origin from a human, that he was a son of Adam in a singular way, promised because of the fall of this very man, the seed of a woman, who should crush the head of the serpent, and, in turn, be crushed by such a serpent, that he in the same way was promised again to Abraham and David, as he was very often announced by the prophets.[49]

46. 'Notae breves in xxiv. priora capita Matthaei', in idem, *Opera theologica* II (1650), p 70.

47. 'Notae breves', p. 45. I owe to Burkett, *The Son of Man Debate*, p. 35, not only the reference to Episcopius, but also the translation of the quotation in which I have inserted a missing 'Jesus' at the beginning.

48. Being impossible to procure, Gaillard's dissertation is here quoted according to the summary in W. Scholten, *De appellatione* τοῦ υἱοῦ τοῦ ἀνθρώπου, *qua Iesus se Messiam professus est* (1809), p. 163, where the references to Gaillard's work are to pp. 30, 43, *et alibi*.

49. According to Scholten, *De appellatione*, p. 202, in the dissertation of Gaillard, pp. 10-13, 20-51.

At the boundary of a new period stands Johann Jacob Wettstein (1693–1754), a pioneer both in text-criticism and in the use of classical philology in the study of the New Testament. In his famous *Novum Testamentum Graecum* I–II (1751–1752), commenting on Mt. 8.20, he too understands Son of man as a title for Messiah borrowed from Dan. 7.13, and draws attention to the title being used by Stephen in Acts 7.56 (also referring to Rev. 1.13; 14.14) and the rendering of *ben adam* in the Targum to Ps. 80.18 with משׁיאח מלכה, 'King Messiah'. Matthew 8.20 is paraphrased: the Son of man has no home, no mattress, no bed, not even his own tomb where he could be placed after death. The appellation indicates both his humility among people (Phil. 1.7; Ps. 49.3) and the majestic state which was destined for him by God and, accordingly, predicted.

Not even in the period of Orthodoxy is the Lutheran understanding of the expression Son of man uniform. Philological conscience sometimes takes over. Theodor Hackspan (1607–1659), professor in Altdorf, maintains that Son of man is tantamount to 'man' according to the Hebrew language (Hebraica locutio).[50] As an example, Hackspan quotes Ps. 8.5, but also refers to Ezek. 2.1, etc., remarking that Son of man here does not indicate the human origin of the prophet, but merely that he is a man (homo simpliciter). A representative of High Orthodoxy is the Wittenberg professor and superintendedant Abraham Calov(ius) (1612–1686), who, in his refutation of Grotius, similarly claims that Son of man does not merely pertain to 'man having a sorry fate alone (hominem contemtæ fortis)', but that there are also sayings denoting Christ's glory.[51] For this reason, Calov wants to understand it as identical with 'man'. That it could denote man in a low state as in Ps. 49.3 is not to be denied, but that Jesus should have used it in that sense is not self-evident. According to Hebrew usage (usitato Ebraismo), it is 'man' in the same manner as 'sons of Greeks' are Greeks (Joel 3.6) and 'sons of physicians' are physicians.

Christoph Cellarius (1638–1707), professor in Halle, returns to an old position by interpreting Son of man as an indication of the true humanity (vera humanitatis natura) of Christ over against ideas about ghosts (phantasmata) or stars and celestial bodies (quidquid de sidero & cælesti corpore) put forward of Satan's disciples and sectarians.[52] Christ, by this appellation, sought not only to express his true humanity, but also to confirm in the

50. *Notarum philologico-theologicarum in varia et difficilia scripturæ loca* I (1664), p. 51.

51. *Biblia illustrata Novi Testamenti quibus simul Hugonis Grotii annotationes in libros N.T.* I (1676), p. 254.

52. *Exercitii oratorii de humana Christi natura contra haereticos quosvis defenda* (1680; quoted according to reprint in idem, *Programmata varii argumenti oratoriis exercitiis in citicensi Lyceo praemissa* [1689], Programma XXI), pp. 128-36.

highest degree his humble condition being empty of his divinity (humilem exinationis conditionem).[53]

Another representative of High Orthodoxy, Johann Andreas Quenstedt (1617–1688), teaching in Wittenberg, also revives an older tradition when he, treating Mt. 12.32, understands Son of man from the background of the concept of a 'synthetic person':[54]

> The name *Son of man* indicates the union of a compound person (concretum personæ συνθέσου), or a composite (i.e. both of Christ's natures subsisting in one hypostasis) and thus Son of man at this place does not design divinity alone, nor humanity alone, but the whole person composite named according to its human nature (totam personam σύνθεσον ab humana natura denominatam); that is, the total god-man (θεάνθρωπον).

After disputing H. Grotius and G. Génébrard (see below), he continues by saying that Orthodox theologians are in accordance with the truth when they maintain the opinion that Son of man is preferably understood as referring to Jesus Christ.

The learned Danish clergyman Morten Caspar Wolfburg (1686–1729) interprets Son of man as expressing humility, pointing not only to Ps. 49.3 but also to Isa. 53.[55]

Christian Benedikt Michaelis (1680–1764), professor in Halle, in his *Tractatio philologico-theologica de Christo filio hominis* (1736), likewise has Christ called Son of man with respect to his human nature, which he took on in the fullness of time, and also in accordance with the divine promises from of old. It further includes the humility of Christ, because of which Christ preferred to be called Son of man according to his more feeble nature, making him familiar with many and significant weaknesses. As Son of man and 'man' coincide in Hebrew (per Hebraismus), one could be in doubt if somebody, calling himself Son of man, designated thereby his participation in human nature. However, Christ does not speak with the indefinite article (υἱὸν ἀνθρώπου *einen Menschen-Sohn)*, but with the definite τὸν υἱὸν τοῦ ἀνθρώπου (*den Menschen-Sohn*), in this way making the title a *proprium nomen* for himself in a way no other could do. He thereby gives a hint that he is the most excellent person, about whom from the beginning of the world until his incarnation so many earlier divine predictions exist. Michaelis refers to Gen. 3.15; 23.18; Isa. 7.14; 9.5; 11.1; Jer. 23.5;

53. *Exercitii oratorii*, p. 131.

54. *Theologia didactico-polemica theologicum* (1685), pp. 85-86.

55. *Observationes sacrae in Novum Testamentum seu Annotationes theologico-criticae in voces plerasque N.T. ordine alphabetico, et dicta praecipua tam veteris quam novi foederis*. Ed. by Eduard Leigh (2nd edn, 1738; originally 1717), p. 575. This book brought Wolfburg both financial ruin and a bitter conflict with the Theological Faculty in Copenhagen. I owe the reference to Bracht, *Der Menschensohn*, p. 613.

33.15; Ps. 8.5 and Dan. 7.13.[56] It is remarkable that without hesitation Michaelis argues from the Greek text with regard to the difference between the indefinite and the definite form of Son of man, apparently presupposing that Jesus spoke Greek.

J.H. Messerschmidt, in *Commentatio philologica de sacra forma et dictione Ο ΥΙΟΣ ΤΟΥ ΑΝΘΡΩΠΟΥ qua simul sermonis graeci quo N.F. est conscriptum castitatem adserit* (1739), distinguishes between definite and indefinite form in a similar way. The use of the definite article is combined with a certain content distinguishing the one concerned from all others. It is also Christ alone who employs it to draw attention to and denote himself to mortals, not only in his humble condition, but also in his excellent glory and majesty.[57] Messerschmidt, to my knowledge, is the first to contemplate the circumstance that Son of man occurs in the Gospels only (and in Acts 7.56) and not in the New Testament letters, explaining it by the new situation after Jesus' departure, where he was no more visible to mortals.[58] From then on, he was exclusively known through the reading and hearing of the letters of his divine legates. This is also the reason why Rev. 1.13 uses the indefinite form ὅμοιος υἱῷ ἀνθρώπου. It is no longer the familiar and humble figure who stayed with the disciples and apostles on earth whom the divine John sees. Messerschmidt adheres to the many interpreters who understand the expression in the use of Jesus not so much as an indication of his true human nature or his humble status empty of his divine glory, as a declaration and confirmation of the oracles, which the divine prophets pronounced in vaticinations and visions about this name: David in Ps. 8.5, Daniel in Dan. 7.13, but also Moses in the paradisic 'first gospel' (προτευαγγελίῳ) in Gen. 3.15.

Christian Schoettgen (1687–1751), from Dresden, continuing and improving on the work of John Lightfoot, stresses the importance of Son of man in the book of Ezekiel.[59] He also gives a special interpretation of 'man,' אדם, suggesting it indicates love, brotherhood and familiarity (Vox אדם significationem habet dilectionis, fraternitatis & proximitatis).

Christoph August Heumann (1681–1764), professor in Göttingen, in his dissertation, *Solutio quaestionis huius: Cur Filius Dei perfrequenter se appellarit Filium Hominis* (1740), proposes quite another interpretation. His

56. *Tractatio philologico-theologica de Christo filio hominis*, p. 12. In an earlier dissertation, משיח בן אדם *sive Dissertatio philologica ex antiquitate iudaica, de nomine Christi, humanam ipsius naturam designantibus* (1714), Michaelis pointed to Ps. 80.18 and Dan. 7.13 as the background for Son of man in the New Testament.

57. *Commentatio philologica*, p. 14.

58. *Commentatio philologica*, pp. 15-16.

59. *Horae Hebraicae et Talmudicae in universum Novum Testamentum quibus Horae Io. Lightfooti in libri historicis supplentur, epistolae et Apocalypsis eadem modo illustrantur* (1733), p. 90.

originality lies not in his taking Son of man as a description of the *status exinanitionis* (status ἀσθηνείας), signifying his nature as a slave (δούλου μορφήν),[60] but in his arguing for this viewpoint. Seeing the origin of the expression in the Old Testament, but also noting that, in the New Testament, it is exclusively employed by Jesus, Heumann concludes that Son of man was a Pharisaic invective, 'which the Jews gave to Christ in mockery and insult' (quem Iudaei Christo tribuebant per ludibrium et contumeliam), because they would not accept him as Messiah on account of his humble descent from Joseph. That is also the reason for the definite article before ἀνθρώπου: 'that man!' Accordingly, Jesus uses it as if he would say: 'I whom the Pharisees address as the Son of that man'.[61]

Johann Christoph Wilckens, a preacher from Silesia, in a short 'Contemplation on the often used designation in the New Testament of Christ: the Son of Man', from 1741,[62] attempts to include all the positive meanings associated with the expression, seeing it as designating Jesus as an

> un-ending and eminent person who represents and introduces all mankind to the divine judgment and with regard to this is called Son of Man. He always speaks in the third person as often as he uses this name, because in reality another is the same; namely, the whole human race. However, he understands himself as part of it, because he has stepped into their place and overtaken all that they are and have. What they were in Adam before the Fall, the very same is Jesus.

This interpretation is similar to that of Simon Episcopius (see above) and also foreshadows the more speculative to come.[63]

60. Quoted according to *Dissertationum Sylloge diligenter recognotarum novisque illustratorum accessionibus* I (1743), pp. 848-76. See esp. p. 849.

61. *Solutio questionis*, p. 860. This understanding is repeated in idem, *Erklärung des Neuen Testaments I Theil, in welchem die Geschichte des Herrn, wie sie Matthäus und Marcus beschrieben, betrachtet und erläutert wird* (1750), pp. 1694-95, ad Mt. 12.32. Writing under the pseudonym of Lot Ilmar, a certain theologian criticized Heumann in a short article from 1747, 'Bescheidene Vorstellung über die Heumännische Gedancken von dem Namen Christi, da er des Menschen Sohn heisset)', *Heßisches Heb-Opfer*, 4. Band, 39 Stück (1747), pp. 834-46. The author maintains that the expression indicates the human nature of Christ, the man κατ' ἐξοχήν, both in his earthly and exalted state. Among the many scriptural passages he adduces also (p. 843) Acts 17.31, which he combines with Mt. 25.31. In a note attached to an earlier article (Stück 37 [1745], p. 616), it is said of the pseudonym Lot Ilmar: 'Unter diesem Namen liegt ein auswärtiger gelehrter und alter Theologus verborgen'.

62. 'Betrachtung über die im N.T so gewöhnliche Benennung Christi: des Menschen Sohn', *Heßisches Heb-Opfer*. 3. Band, Stück 28 (1741), pp. 696-715; the quotation below, pp. 704-705 (cf. p. 712).

63. The commentary of Johann Christoph Wolf, *Curae philologicae et criticae in IV. ss evangelia et actus apostolicos*, I (1725, 3rd edn, 1739), p. 159, confines itself in a note on Mt. 8.20 to a short survey of the different opinions on the Son of man. The same

4. *Catholic Exegesis*

Contemporary Catholic exegesis shows some of the same trends as the Lutheran and Calvinist. Thus according to Jakob de Vio Cajetan (1468–1534; his Dominican name was Thomas), cardinal from 1517 and not least known for his interrogation of Luther at the 'Reichstag' in Worms in 1521, Jesus employed Son of man 'hebreo modo loquendi' to refute future heretics denying that he was 'man' or son of a virgin[64]

No less interesting is the contribution of Gilbert Génébrard (1537–1597), archbishop of Aix, an eager student of the 'veritas Hebraica' and sometime professor of oriental languages in Paris. In his *De S. Trinitate libri tres* (1569), in an attempt to show the divinity of the Holy Spirit, he adduces Mt. 12.32,[65] interpreting it as saying that sinning against the Holy Spirit is sinning against God himself, a sin which cannot be forgiven. This sin is opposed to the sin against man (filium hominis, id est, hominem) which can find forgiveness. Like the earlier Cyprianus, Génébrard (in this context) refers to the sentence of Eli (1 Sam. 2.25) which offers a parallel declaring that, although using different words, 'If one man sins against another man, God will mediate for him, but if a man sins against the Eternal, who can intercede on his behalf?' In analogy with this saying, Son of man is simply equated with man in general.[66]

In a similar way Juan Maldonado (1533–1583), a Spanish Jesuit, remarks in reference to Mt. 8.20[67] that 'Son of man as a Hebrew idiom signifies nothing but "man"' (filium hominis Hebræorum idiomate, nihil aliud, quam hominem significare). The reason for Christ's use of the expression is the same as in Ezekiel, where it is employed by the angels speaking with him to distinguish him from themselves as not human:

> For a similar reason Christ, because he was God and Son of God, as an antithesis when he spoke of himself as human, called himself Son of man (quasi antithesi quadam cum de se, ut homine, loquitur, filium hominis vocat): Not

pertains to Johann Christoph Köcher, *Analecta philologica et exegetica in quatuor s. evangelia* (1766), pp. 191-93.

64. *Evangelia cum commentario in quatuor Evangelia et Acta Apostolorum* (1530), p. 23 ad Mt. 8.20. Cf. ad 12.32 (p. 31b), 'nam constat significari ipsum Jesum, ut est homo', and ad Jn 3.13 (p. 148b), 'esse hominem natum ex homine, hoc ex matre'. I owe these references to Bracht, *Der Menschensohn*, p. 607.

65. The full title is *De s. Trinitate libri tres contra huius ævi Trinitarios, Antitrinitarios, & Autheanos* (1569, 2nd edn, 1585). See pp. 246-47.

66. A. Meyer, *Jesu Muttersprache* (1896), p. 142, remarks that 'mit der Erwähnung von 1. Sam. 2,25 ist tatsächlich ein glücklicher Griff gethan… Dieser a.t.lichen Stelle ist offenbar Matth. 12,32 nachgebildet.'

67. *Commentarii in quatuor evangelistas* (1596, 3rd edn, 1601), p. 193.

> as of another, but as an otherwise Son of God, because he is God and Son of man, because he is man (non quod alius, sed quod aliter filius Dei, quia Deus, & filius hominis, quia homo esset).

This he did not because of honour, but because of his abjection (abiectionis causa). Maldonado also observes that where Ezekiel never called himself Son of man, but is called so by others, Christ is never called so by others, but only by himself.

Cornelius à Lapide (1567–1637), a Dutch Jesuit, follows an old track when explaining Mt. 8.20.[68] He says that Adam is the one whose son Christ is. In Hebrew, Adam means 'man', and when Christ uses Son of man he alludes to Ezek. 2.1 as a type of Christ (Christi typus) being called Son of man, Hebrew *ben Adam*, son of Adam. But Son of man means much more than 'man', man being created by God as only Adam was. Son of man signifies that he was born of Adam as co-parent (communi parente) and thus shows his immense humility, deeming himself worthy to be born of a sinner, and to suffer and die in his earthly body.

His fellow-countryman, Cornelius Jansen (1585–1638), bishop of Ypern and the father of Jansenism, remarks[69] in connection with Mt. 8.20 that Son of man (i.e. 'I', or 'Christ') is a Hebraism or Hebrew phrase (Hebraïsmus seu phrasis Hebraïca) which simply means 'man', as seen in Ps. 8.5 and Job 25.6. However, it is also a very efficient expression of human misery (quadam efficaviori expressione humanæ miseræ). Therefore, no one in the Gospels calls Christ Son of man, but he does so himself, commending himself to us, because of his mercy to us.

More familiar with mainstream tradition is the Spanish Jesuit, Francisco de Toledo (1532–1596), when he, in the explanation of Jn 3.14,[70] enumerates five reasons for Christ's use of Son of man. For him, the expression: (1) designates not only Jesus' incarnation, but also its manner (modus); (2) describes the conjunction between him and us, because when as Son of man he descends from Adam, it follows that we, also according to the flesh, are his brethren; (3) contains the promises given to the fathers in a complete form, that not only would the Son of God come in flesh, but also be of their seed; (4) is a sign of the new sonship, which should come about, because when the Son of God is made Son of man, man in effect is Son of God; (5) also served to express his humility.

The last Catholic exegete to be mentioned in this chapter, Jean Hardouin (1646–1729), a French Jesuit, somehow anticipated an interpretation to

68. *Commentarius in quatuor evangelia* I-II (1639), I (1639), p. 198.

69. *Tetrateuchus, sive Commentarius in sancta Jesu Christi evangelia* (1639, 2nd edn, 1697), p. 73. Cf. ad Jn 5.27, p. 461.

70. *In sacrosanctum Ioannis Evangelium commentarii* I-II (1589), I, pp. 273-74.

become common in the age of Idealism. In his exegesis of Mt. 8.20,[71] he declares that it is a name of distinction. At every place where it occurs its very beautiful meaning (perpulchrum sensum) should be perceived; 'the most excellent of men with respect to the gifts of nature and grace, commanding the human race (Excellentissimum hominum donis naturæ & gratiæ, Imperantem humano generi), because he is the firstborn among many brethren.'

5. *A Voice from Pietism:* Bengel

I will conclude this chapter with a comment from the greatest exegete of the Pietistic movement in Germany, Johann Albrecht Bengel (1687–1752) from Schwaben. In his famous *Gnomon Novi Testamenti* (1742), in a note on Mt. 16.13, he summarizes much of what has been said already. However, Bengel also makes some new exegetical observations and combines them in a speculative way unknown to Orthodox exegetes and dogmaticians. I offer the note in its totality:[72]

> τὸν υἱὸν τοῦ Ἀνθρώπου, *the Son of Man*) i.e. me, whom I myself am wont to call the Son of Man. Peter gives the right antitheton [in his reply], ver. 16: *Thou art the Son of the living God.*—Cf. John v.19, 27. This title, the Son of Man, which frequently occurs in the Evangelists, should be carefully observed: no one was so called but Christ Himself, and no one, whilst He walked on earth, so called Him except Himself. He first applies this appellation to Himself in John i.51, when they were first found who acknowledged Him as the Messiah and the Son of God (ibid. ver. 50), and thenceforth very frequently, both before and after His prediction of His Passion. For they who expressed their faith in Him, called Him the *Son of David*. The Jews rightly suspected (John xii.34), that by this title He claimed to be the Messiah. For as the first Adam (Adamus I), with all his progeny, is called *Man*, so the second Adam (Adamus II) (see 1 Cor. xv.45) is called *Son of Man*, not with that notion with which בני אדם (filii hominis), that is, the weak are opposed to בני איש (filii viri), that is, the powerful (in Ps. xlix. (xlviii.) 2); or that in which men are called generally, sons of men (*filii hominum*), as in Mark iii.28; Eph. iii.5; Ezek. ii.1, etc; but with the article, ὁ υἱὸς τοῦ Ἀνθρώπου. This article appears to refer to the prophecy of Daniel, vii.13. This, in sooth, is that One Man whom Adam, after the fall, expected by promise for his whole race: ὁ δεύτερος, *the second* (1 Cor. xv.47), to whom every prophecy of the Old Testament pointed, who holds the rights and primogeniture of the whole human race (see Luke iii.23, 38), and to whom alone we owe that we are not

71. *Commentarius in Novum Testamentum* (1741), p. 38. Cf. ad Jn 1.51, pp. 254-56.

72. The full title is *Gnomon Novi Testamenti in quo ex nativa verborum vi simplicitas, profunditas, concinnitas, salubritas sensum coelestium indicatur*. The note is found on pp. 98-99. Quoted according to the English translation, *Gnomon of the New Testament*, vol. 1 (1866, 7th edn, 1877), pp. 320-21.

> ashamed of the name of man: see Ps. xlix (xlviii.) 20, and cf. Rom. v.15. Moreover, our Lord, whilst walking amongst men, by this appellation, both expressed, and as suitable to the circumstance (pro economiâ) of that time, concealed amongst men (cf. ch. xxii.45) and hid from Satan the fact that He was ὁ Υἱὸς, *the Son*, absolutely so called, that is, the Son of God promised and given to man, Gen. iii.15; Isa. ix.6; and sprung from man, Heb. ii.11; and at the same time, as it were, reminded Himself of His present condition, Matt. xx.28; Phil. ii.7, 8. In the same manner, He expressed both His crucifixion and His ascension by one word, ὑψωθῶ, *I be lifted up*, John xii.32. Neither is this appellation suited only to the state of His humiliation, but the expression, the Son of man, is used for every conspicuous situation of His, either in humiliation or exaltation; see John xii.34, and compare therewith, in the following verse, *the light is with you*. And it agrees with the very form of His body, as implying youth, see Dan. vii.13. Consider the following passages: – ver. [Mt. 16.] 27, 28; ch. xii.32, xxiv.27, 30, 37, 39, 44, xxv.31; Luke xvii.22; John xii.23-36, v.27; Acts vii.56. Therefore also this appellation does not once occur in the whole of the twenty-one apostolic epistles, but instead of it, the appellation, *the Son of God*; for in Heb. ii.6 the article is not added, and the words are those of David, not of St Paul, who yet frequently calls Christ both ἄνθρωπος (homo), and ἄνηρ (vir). See the Gnomon on Rom. v.15. And even in the Apocalypse i.13 and xiv.14, as long before in Dan. vii.13, that appellation is only alluded to, not actually applied to our Lord. The agreement of the apostles, even in the case of this single phrase, shows that they wrote by the same Divine inspiration.

A main accent in Bengel's interpretation of Son of Man is placed on his visibility. This aspect also connects the sayings pertaining to Christ in his incarnation to the sayings about his Parousia (e.g. in Mt. 26.64: 'he speaks in the third person: how modest and openly'[73]). According to Bengel, this is also the reason why 'Luke', not seeing Christ, in Acts 7.55, says 'Jesus', while Stephen, seeing the risen Lord, calls him Son of man (v. 56).[74] The teaching of the two natures is here furnished with new clothes.

73. Bengel, *Gnomon*, p. 154. Cf. ad Mt. 12.32, p. 81.

74. Bengel, *Gnomon*, p. 448.

6. Enlightenment, Rationalism, and Idealism

The foundation of modern biblical study was laid in the age of the Enlightenment. With impressive speed, the scene changed from more or less supernaturalistic thinking based on revelatory positivism, which sees the divinity of Christ as directly recognizable in history, to a rationalistic view of Jesus as a more or less purely historical figure. The concept of history no longer took shape according to the biblical story but was emancipated, governed exclusively by human reason without resorting to metaphysical causes. We can observe a movement from an understanding of Son of man as more or less an objective definition to a subjective announcement. Accordingly, the focus of interest moved from the history of the god-man Christ to the interpretation of the faith of Jesus, which viewed him as prophet and teacher. One of the tools in this project was the distinction between the eternal and unalterable message of Christianity and the historical and relative expressions of its truth. Somehow, of course, it is the old problem of defining the two 'natures' of Christ which here finds a new formulation: What is the salvific impact of Jesus Christ?

English Deism marks the beginning of this era. Characteristic of its enterprise, is the famous title of Matthew Tindal's book *Christianity as Old as the Creation* from 1730, in which, among other things, he writes: 'Whatever is true by reason, can never be false by revelation'.[1] This logic had a decisive impact on Christology and, thereby, on the role assigned to the appellation Son of man in biblical theology. What until then was perceived and interpreted as direct revelation, now was more and more viewed as an expression of the self-understanding of Jesus as man and interpreted accordingly as something historical and relative. Somehow, Son of man moved into the centre of interest as the possible key to the revelatory significance attached to the mind of Jesus, the interpretation of the expression indicating what was

1. For a survey of the English Deists, see Baird, *History of New Testament Research* I, pp. 30-57. Quotation from Matthew Tindal, *Christianity as Old as the Creation* (1730), p. 42.

thought important. The meaning of Son of Man often became a pressing question in efforts to reconstruct the historical Jesus, especially with regard to his assumed understanding of himself.

The most radical interpretation with regard to Jesus and the Son of man sayings stems from the Janus-like Hermann Samuel Reimarus (1694–1764), professor of oriental languages in Hamburg. In his published books he appeared as a typical theologian of the Enlightenment, but the influence of English Deism was far deeper than he admitted publicly. This is seen in his manuscript *Apologie oder Schutzschrift der vernünftigen Verehrer Gottes* (*Apology for the Rational Worshippers of God*), which he wrote sometime between 1736 and 1764 and which circulated only among friends.[2] From 1774 to 1778 Gotthold Ephraim Lessing (1729–1781) published anonymously seven fragments of this manuscript as *Fragmente des Wolfenbüttelchen Ungenannten* (*Fragments of an Unknown*), the last being *Von dem Zwecke Jesu und seiner Jünger* (*On the Intention of Jesus and His Disciples*).[3] Here, for the first time, we find the distinction between the teachings of Jesus and the preaching of the apostles which would prove so profoundly important to critical scholarship.[4]

With regard to the Son of man sayings, this distinction made it possible for Reimarus to differentiate the use of Jesus and the apostles respectively. Jesus adhered to the common Messianic expectations calling himself, for instance, Son of God, without thereby making any more than a human claim, performing as a prophet, although the greatest. When he most dearly (am allerliebsten) and often called himself Son of man, it was 'because this appellation (Benennung) shows contempt (Geringschätzlichkeit) for oneself

2. The full text was not published until 1972 (by G. Alexander in two volumes). The division between opinions to be expressed publicly and opinions to be kept private finds its later legitimation in Kant's distinguishing between public use of reason, which has to be free, but directed solely to the reading, learned society, and private use of reason, which has to be regulated according to a person's public duties. Cf. I. Kant, 'Beantwortung der Frage: Was ist Aufklärung?' (1784), in *Kants Werke* (Akademie-Textausgabe, 8; 1912, reprint Berlin: de Gruyter, 1968), pp. 33-42 (37).

3. Here, quoted according to the 5th edition of *Fragmente des Wolfenbüttelschen Ungenannten*, ed. G.E. Lessing (1895). An English translation of the last fragment is available, published as *The Goal of Jesus and His Disciples* (1970).

4. Cf., for Reimarus' intention, (Lessing,) *Von dem Zwecke Jesu*, for example, p. 5 (§3): 'Ich finde groß Ursache, dasjenige, was die Apostel in ihre eignen Schriften vorbringen, von dem, was Jesus in seinem Leben wirklich selbst ausgesprochen und gelehret hat, gänzlich abzusondern'. Cf. the evaluation of A. Schweitzer, in his *Geschichte der Leben-Jesu-Forschung* (2nd edn of *Von Reimarus zu Wrede* [1906], 1913), for example, p. 23: (quoted according to the English translation, *The Quest of the Historical Jesus* [2000], p. 22): 'His work is perhaps the most splendid achievement in the whole course of the historical investigation of the life of Jesus, for he was the first to grasp that the world of thought (Vorstellungswelt) in which Jesus moved historically was essentially eschatological'.

and humility (Demuth), and because Isaiah describes the beloved of God in whom He has delight, according to the quality of humility'.[5]

Accordingly, all the sayings about the Son of man coming in the clouds are creations of the apostles, drafted with the intention of rescuing Jesus as the Redeemer.[6] The background of this concept is Daniel 7 where the description of the coming of the Messiah is different from the common expectation, found in Zechariah 9, to such an extent that some Jews, reasonably enough, comparing the two different descriptions of the coming of the Messiah, concluded that their Messiah would come twice and in totally different shapes. It was this second 'Systema' which the apostles took over because of the failure of the first.[7]

The time was obviously not ripe for the radicalism of the *Fragments of the Unknown*, which saw the transition from Jesus to the apostles as due to fraud and not to the necessity of change resulting from the incorporation of Jesus and his fate in preaching. As a result, Reimarus' achievement became a parenthesis, only to be utilized later, for the first time by David Friedrich Strauss.

Moreover, the understanding of Son of man in this period can be subsumed under the following headings: (1) the expression is equivalent to 'man', but no longer in the context of the doctrine of two natures, but rather in the sense of 'only' a man, or it is simply taken as tantamount to a pronoun. (2) It is seen as a Messianic title, coming from the Old Testament. (3) It is taken as an expression of Jesus' humility. (4) This period, of course, also has representatives of the 'classical' interpretation of Son of Man as signifying Christ's human nature. (5) More philosophically minded authors advanced a speculative interpretation, seeing in 'man' the prototype of mankind as originally designed by God. This idealistic understanding somehow survived in the efforts to write a Life of Jesus which attempted to reconcile history and faith.

1. *Son of Man as Equivalent with 'Man' or the Personal Pronoun*

The first to be mentioned here is the Swiss Neologian, Johann Jacob Hess (1741–1828), the earliest to my knowledge to write a biography of Jesus, *Geschichte der drey letzten Lebensjahre Jesu* I-III (1768). This tome is a paraphrase, which, uncritically, incorporated supernaturalistic traits. In it, Son of man functions much as a disguise. According to his origin, Jesus

5. (Lessing,) *Von dem Zwecke Jesu*, p. 22 (§13).
6. (Lessing,) *Von dem Zwecke Jesu*, pp. 85-87 (§38).
7. (Lessing,) *Von dem Zwecke Jesu*, pp. 84-85 (§37).

should have been named son of Joseph (Benjoseph; cf. Jn 6.42). It turned out, however, that the more general name, Benadam, Son of man, Man, was a better name,

> because it lets His real origin be more indefinite (mehr unbestimmt), and could exist together with the name Son of God, which He sometimes gave Himself, and which His disciples afterwards always gave Him. Son of man was also common among the Jews, and was tantamount to 'man'. Modest and true (Bescheiden und wahr)![8]

Hess is later able to paraphrase Mt. 26.64: 'Yes, I am, said Jesus. – And added: In *this* shape (Gestalt), at any rate, you will not see *this man* (*diesen Menschen*) for long.'[9]

In a note to Mt. 5.16, Johann Adrian Bolten (1742–1807), clergyman in Altona, is the first to argue from Syriac that the term can both mean 'man' (Mensch) and function as an indefinite pronoun: 'man', 'someone', 'one', 'another', 'a certain man'.[10] Bolten understands Son of man in the use of Jesus exactly as a *pronomen indefinitum*. He was a pioneer in pointing back to the language behind the Greek Gospels, presupposing that Son of man in most places in the Gospels was the result of a mistranslation. He himself took to translating Son of man in some sayings according to the Syriac translation; for example, rendering Mt. 5.16: 'So yours also shine for others'. Matthew 26.64, he translates: 'From now on one will be seen by you at the right...'[11] With this understanding of Son of man as not indicating Jesus exclusively, Bolten expands what G. Génébrard had postulated with regard to Mt. 12.32 and H. Grotius with regard to both Mt. 12.32 and 12.8.

One of the most prominent representatives of German Rationalism, Heinrich Eberhard Gottlob Paulus (1761–1851), the so-called Non-Apostle (der Nicht-Apostel), follows the same track. In his commentary on Matthew, on Mt. 8.20, he says 'that υἱὸς ἀνθρώπου Son of man, without any emphasis, is "man" altogether (ohne allen Nachdruck *Mensch* überh[aupt])', referring to Ezek. 2.1. The Oriental avoids using 'I', preferring to speak in the third person. This also pertains to Jesus in the Gospels, where he says instead of 'I', without any emphasis, '"this man", it is he whom you see before you' (Ich ohne alle Emphase 'dieser Mensch', d.h. der, den Du vor

8. J.J. Hess, *Geschichte der drey letzten Lebensjahre Jesu* (4th edn, 1774), I, p. 95 n. 1. Cf. ad Mt. 16.13, I, p. 337: 'Wer glauben sie, daß dieser Mensch, wie ich mich selbst nenne, eigentlich sey?'

9. Hess, *Geschichte der drey letzten Lebensjahre Jesu*, III, p. 242.

10. J.A. Bolten, *Der Bericht des Matthäus von Jesu dem Messia. Uebersetzt und mit Anmerkungen begleitet* (1792), p. 78 n. 19. Cf. ad Mt. 7.9, p. 122, and ad 8.20, p. 137.

11. Bolten, *Der Bericht des Matthäus*, p. 402: 'in der Folge wird man von euch zur Rechten' etc.

Dir siehst).[12] Like Reimarus, Paulus claims a difference between the use of Jesus himself and that of the community later. This time the reason given is not fraud, but

> to the worshipper of Messiah, what by him may have been mostly an adopted manner of speaking, soon became, as it often happens with persons worshipped, more important and significant. They thought of Daniel 7.13, where the Messiah approaches the Godhead as 'Son of man'. According to Matthew 26.64, Jesus interpreted this saying as pertaining to himself. The emphasis is placed on the circumstance, that that Spirit, which they expected at the time when the last chapters in Daniel were composed (in the Maccabean period, towards the end of the persecutions of Antiochus Epiphanes), already was placed very high in the realm of the spirits, or even in the highest place, should appear for the holy people (of the Jews) *as a man* (...) and, *in this way* (v. 14), becoming its Messiah and ruler, a condescension (eine Herablassung), which is also hinted at in Revelation 1.13. Because they remembered that Jesus so often named himself 'this man', many, as it were, found it as a welcome paradox, a hint of that old expectation: 'The exalted Messiah-Spirit and one who has become man'. 'I see that Son of man [him who had become man, that most excellent and genuine man] at the right hand of God', Stephen shouts in ecstasy, Acts 7.56. In the same manner, the more generally meant *man* בן אדם, *whom thou hast made strong for thy service*, in Psalm 80.18, is also in the Targum explained: *the King Messiah.*

This understanding of Son of man, as a circumlocution for 'I' in the mouth of Jesus, is shared by Karl Friedrich August Fritzsche (1801–1846), professor in Rostock, later in Giessen, who stresses the meaning of the definite articles in the use of Jesus, offering the meaning 'this son of human parents' (*filius ille parentum humanorum*), because τοῦ ἀνθρώπου should be taken in a collective sense: 'he who now speaks, that man whom you well know, it is I'.[13] This understanding pertains to Mt. 8.20; 9.6; 11.19; Jn 1.51 and other occurrences. However, the evangelists themselves as well as Jesus' other friends, remembering him using the expression, could introduce it where Jesus was speaking (Mt. 16.13) and add Messianic authority to the formula (formulae ὁ υἱὸς τοῦ ἀνθρώπου *Messiae* potestatem subiicerent). This was easy to do, since the author of Dan. 7.13 had confirmed 'that Messiah had appeared to him in a vision כבר אנשׁ, not dissimilar to the human species (*specie humani non absimili*)'.

12. H.E.G. Paulus, *Philologisch-kritischer und historischer Commentar über das neue Testament I. Der drey ersten Evangelien erster Hälfte* (1800, 2nd edn, 1804), pp. 470-71.

13. K.F.A. Fritzsche, *Evangelium Matthäei. Quatuor N.T. Evangelia* I (1826), pp. 320-21.

2. *Son of Man is Equivalent to Messiah*

More common in this period is the understanding of the expression Son of man as equivalent to Messiah. This pertains, for example, to the famous neologian, Johann Salomo Semler (1725–1791), professor in Altdorf, who took the reference to Dan. 7.13 for granted.[14] Similarly, M.G.W. Rullmann, professor in Rinteln, lets the title of a programma be the question, 'In what sense did Jesus call himself Son of man?',[15] and answers himself that this expression, according to the Jewish and biblical manner of speaking, is a perfect synonym for Messiah (ein völliges Synonymon von *Messias*). Rullmann also combines it with Paul's conception of Christ as the second Man. However, Son of man in Mk 2.28 and Jn 5.27 does not have this meaning.[16] Son of man does not designate the most humble among men, but the Messiah whom Jewish theology, in the words of Eve in Gen. 4.1, imagines as the son of Adam κατ' ἐξοχήν, who is also given this name in Dan. 7.13.[17]

One of the most celebrated, learned and influential men of this period, Johann David Michaelis (1717–1791), son of Christian Benedikt Michaelis (see above Chapter 5) and professor in Göttingen, similarly takes Son of man as used by Jesus as an equivalent of 'Messiah, as he was also perceived by the Jews (Jn 12.34) (although with doubts, because in their language, it was not quite so usual)'.[18] Michaelis rejects the idea that it could be a well-known manner of speaking, meaning nothing more than 'man', because this is always without an article, while as used by Jesus the name always is provided with two articles, '*THE Son of THE Man*' (*DER Sohn DES Menschen*). With regard to the question which man, Michaelis is not in doubt. It is of course Adam, which is confirmed both by Jewish theology and by Paul's speaking of the second Adam in Rom. 5.14-19 and 1 Cor. 15.45.

Eucharius Ferdinand Christian Oertel contributes a new aspect, emphasizing that all attempts to have Son of man express the most noble or the most debased human, or the concept of the second Adam, are only reading into the text what is not there. Even in the vision in Daniel, 'it is not because of the bare expression, but because of the predicates attached to it' (nicht

14. Semler, *Paraphrasis Evangelii Iohannis, cum notis, et Cantabrigiensis codicis latino textu* I-II (1771–72), I, p. 67 ad Jn 1.51, and pp. 101-102 ad Jn 3.14.

15. Rullmann, *In welchem Sinne nennt sich Jesus des Menschen Sohn?*, originally from 1785, here, following the reprint in J.G. Schellenberg (ed.), *Selecta historico-philosophico-theologica* I (1787), pp. 271-85 (79-80).

16. Rullmann, *In welchem Sinne*, pp. 282-83.

17. Rullmann, *In welchem Sinne*, p. 285.

18. Michaelis, *Anmerkungen für Ungelehrte, zu seiner Uebersetzung des Neuen Testaments. Erster Theil, Anmerkungen zu Matthäus, Marcus und Lucas* (1790), p. 111.

wegen des bloßen Ausdrucks, sondern wegen der Prädikate, die ihm dort beigelegt warden)' that it is possible to understand it of the Messiah, because Son of man in itself means 'any man without distinction' (jeden Menschen ohne Unterschied) and can be exchanged with ἄνθρωπος.[19]

This new way of thinking also leads to considering the strategy of Jesus proclaiming himself as Messiah. This happens for the first time to my knowledge with regard to the expression Son of man in an article of Karl Christian Ludwig Schmidt, 'About the Expression "ὁ υἱὸς τοῦ ἀνθρώπου" in the New Testament', from 1798.[20] In the mouth of Jesus

> it was always used as a synonym for Messiah with which he, in a delicate way, referred to the oracle in Daniel 7.13-14. He did not want, nor was he allowed to tell the Jews directly that he was the Messiah, but he wanted and had to lead them towards this thought. For this reason, he appropriately chose an expression, which was already introduced through the oracles of Ezekiel.[21]

Schmidt was very confident that he was correct in his interpretation. Thus he concludes his article saying:[22]

> After all the evidence for the theses proposed above, it occurs to me that only he can be and remain of another opinion who either is too proud and obstinate to admit that he has been wrong, or he who, because of, for instance, age, lacks the flexibility of spirit, or he who rejects anything that does not come directly, from himself.

The rationalist Heidelberg professor, Georg Lorenz Bauer (1755–1806), the first to write a *Biblical Theology of the New Testament*, makes suggestions with regard to Jesus' coming to consider himself the Messiah, the breakthrough being his baptism.[23] Jesus, according to Bauer, did not proclaim

19. E.F.C. Oertel, *Christologie oder die Resultate der neuesten exegetischen Aufklärungen über den Artikel von der Gottheit Christi. Ein systematischer Versuch, besonders den iungen Theologen gewidmet* (1792), pp. 461-66. Bracht—to whom I owe this reference—remarks (*Der Menschensohn*, p. 616) that Oertel's own thesis that Son of man in the New Testament is 'der für einen bloßen, gemeinen Menschen Gehaltene, der in den Augen der Juden verachtete, verkannte Messias' in reality is included in his refusal of interpretations giving it content.

20. The German title is 'Ueber den Ausdruck "ὁ υἱὸς τοῦ ἀνθρώπου" im Neuen Testament', in *(Neues) Magazin für Religionsphilosophie, Exegese and Kirchengeschichte* 8 (1798), pp. 507-26 (511-12).

21. For an exegesis of the Son of man sayings, see Schmidt, 'Ueber den Ausdruck', pp. 513-25.

22. Schmidt, 'Ueber den Ausdruck', p. 526.

23. G.L. Bauer, *Biblische Theologie des Neuen Testaments. Erster Band. Christologie nach den drey ersten Evangelisten* (1800), p. 23: 'Jetzt ereignete sich eine Gelegenheit, die ihn in dem Gedanken stärkte, Gott unterstütze sein Werk, und erkläre ihn feyerlich für den Messias'.

himself the Messiah from the beginning. He was recognized by his disciples to be so and, by oath, he himself confirmed it to the Sanhedrin. Both titles, Son of God and Son of man, are titles of the Messiah among Jews at that time. The expression 'Son of man', which in the Chaldean-Syrian language indeed meant nothing more than 'man', בן אדם or בר אנש, could also be a title of the Messiah because of Dan. 7.13, where 'manlike' correctly has been understood of the Messiah. For that reason, they also gave him the surname 'man', κατ' ἐξοχήν, that is, the prophesied great and excellent, exceptional man, manifesting himself in the clouds of heaven.[24] Bauer is also of the opinion that Jesus interpreted his messiahship, filling in the existing perception of the Kingdom of God with 'a much more precious and exalted conception (eine weit edelere und erhabnere Vorstellung) than the usual. His Kingdom should not be of this world, but one of the future, for which one had to make himself worthy through true virtue and piety (durch wahre Tugend und Religiosität)'.[25] For that very reason, Jesus carefully avoided anything which could give rise to a political revolution and be related to political matters.[26] In this way, Bauer created an important presupposition for the perception of Son of man as the title of an alternative Messiah, as being spiritual, but not political, universal, but not nationalistic. This alternative would prove itself very attractive to many interpreters for a long time to come.

The first real monograph on the Son of man, Wessel Scholten's *De appellatione τοῦ υἱοῦ τοῦ ἀνθρώπου, qua Iesus se messiam professus est*, from 1809, a book which summarizes in a valuable way most of the interpretation of the expression up until the time of its publication, continues along the same lines. Although the expression is a synonym for 'man', and since it is a Hebrew custom to use it that way, it always points to that certain man—the one who, in the New Testament, in a human form (forma humana), is seen by Daniel in his symbolic vision. It means that, as king, he shall reign humanly over humans (humane hominibus); that is, he is the Messiah. On the other hand, to those who did not believe in him, it gave no reason for any accusation, being in itself harmless, which of course could not be said about the title Messiah.[27] The reason why it was not used after the resurrection,

24. Bauer, *Biblische Theologie*, pp. 45-46.

25. Bauer, *Biblische Theologie*, pp. 47-48.

26. Bauer, *Biblische Theologie*, p. 49. The fear of a revolution like the French seems to have had its influence. Cf. pp. 61-62: 'Jesus hat versichert, dass die Absicht seiner Sendung, und der göttliche Plan, den er ausführen sollte, dieser sey, eine richtige Erkenntniss Gottes und Moral zu lehren, die Menschen durch dieselben zur Besserung und zur Tugend zu leiten, und die einen sündlichen Leben ergeben waren, zur Sinnesänderung zu bewegen'.

27. W. Scholten, *De appellatione τοῦ υἱοῦ τοῦ ἀνθρώπου, qua Iesus se messiam professus est* (1809), pp. 67-68.

according to Scholten, is that it did not give satisfactory expression to Christ's new life and exalted condition (nova vita et excelsa conditione).[28] Thus, although Dan. 7.13 is to be interpreted of the Messiah, and Jesus also perceived himself as Messiah, he preferred 'Son of man' to 'Messiah' because it more aptly signified the heavenly character of his reign. In this way, too, it also served as a corrective to the Jewish errors concerning the expected king.[29]

All this witnesses to a growing consciousness of a difference between, on the one hand, the Messianic expectation as found in the Scripture, not to say in the popular elaboration of it at the time of Jesus, and the way Jesus wanted to be the Messiah, on the other. It gave rise to the idea that Jesus himself, from his own understanding, unfolded a particular conception of Son of man to serve this function. This is clearly the opinion of one of the most influential biblical scholars of the nineteenth century, Wilhelm Martin Leberecht de Wette (1780–1849) of Basle, who could say,[30]

> that the teaching of Jesus was the spiritually perceived Messianism (der geistig aufgefaßte Messianismus), or it was the shape in which he introduced it to his nation. This, however, was not accommodation, because he certainly considered and proclaimed himself the Messiah (...often through the conferred designation ὁ υἱὸς τοῦ ἀνθρώπου). Anything but a spiritual Messiah was a nuisance (ein Unding) to him.

In his commentary on Matthew, de Wette elaborates his view in a note on Mt. 8.20.[31] In all Son of man sayings, the connection with Dan. 7.13, repeated in Mt. 26.64, is presupposed, 'so that Jesus thereby indirectly designated himself the Messiah', in accordance with the Jewish custom of calling Messiah *Anani* (Cloud-man), simply because of this occurrence. It should be remarked that it is done in an indirect way, sayings such as Mt. 9.6 and 16.13 not directly fitting with the concept of the Messiah. Jesus wished, according to Dan. 7.13 (and perhaps Ezekiel), to represent the Messiah 'in his human unimpressive individuality'. To those who did not think of Dan. 7.13, Son of man did not mean anything but 'this man' (= 'I'); when read as related to this saying, however, it came to mean 'I, this insignificant man, who, despite his abasement, is determined to be what the prophet had prophesied'.

28. Scholten, *De appellatione*, p. 77.

29. Scholten, *De appellatione*, pp. 136-37.

30. W.M.L. de Wette, *Biblische Dogmatik Alten und Neuen Testaments. Oder kritische Darstellung der Religionslehre des Hebraismus, des Judenthums und Urchristenthums* (1813), quoted according to the third edition (1831), p. 187, where the text differs only a little from the first edition.

31. W.M.L. de Wette, *Kurze Erklärung des Evangeliums Matthäi* (1836, 2nd edn, 1838), pp. 93-94.

Other representatives from this period of a similar view are the famous rationalist dogmatician, Julius August Ludwig Wegscheider (1771–1849) from Halle,[32] Friedrich Lücke (1791–1855), professor in Göttingen,[33] and the eminent Church historian Karl von Hase (1800–1890) from Jena, the author of the first Life of Jesus book (1829), that is, the first attempt at giving a historical-psychological picture of Jesus. Von Hase here concludes that the vacillation with regard to his messiahship, even among those kindly disposed to Jesus (Mt. 12.23; 16.14; Jn 7.24, 26, 31), did not

> prove that there was anything uncertain in the mind of Jesus himself, or that he reluctantly accepted the title of Messiah; for the Messianic office (das Messiasthum) appears, quite evidently, to be the one fixed pivot on which his whole life turned... The true motive and necessity for his reluctance in admitting the name, was this: that he meant to be the Messiah in a wholly different way from that which the people anticipated; so that, if he had announced himself as such without previously preparing their minds, he would have excited hopes he did not intend to gratify, and would have forced the public authorities, who must either acknowledge the Messiah or put him down, into a conflict which he as yet wished to avoid. Therefore, Jesus usually called himself the Son of Man; which expression, alluding to Daniel (vii.13), contains a Messianic meaning (Matt. xxvi.64, John iii.13) and was also intelligible to the people (John xii.34), and found in Jewish writings (see the Book of Enoch), but according to his prohibition, and according to Matthew (xvi.13), is not exactly the same thing as the Messiah, and for that very reason was preferred by Jesus. This phrase only indicated Messiahship in a covert manner, turning attention away from all political expectations to something belonging to universal humanity (compare Mark ii.27 [the text mistakenly has Matt. ii.27!]; 1 Cor. xv.47). This phrase, in the deep significance appropriated by Jesus to express his own individual conception of the Messiah's office and only seldom used by the Apostolic Church (only in Acts vii.56), can only mean the perfect humanity (die Vollendung der reinen Menschheit) of Jesus, and his devotion to the interests of mankind (die Hingabe an die gesammte Menschheit).[34]

32. J.A.L. Wegscheider, *Institutiones theologiae christianae dogmaticae* (1815, 2nd edn, 1817), p. 177 n. d.

33. F. Lücke, *Commentar über die Schriften des Evangelisten Johannes* I (1820), p. 502, ad Jn 1.51.

34. K. von Hase, *Das Leben Jesu* (1829, 3rd edn, 1840), p. 120. Quoted according to the English translation, *Life of Jesus. A Manual for Academic Study* (1860), pp. 135-36. The reference to the book of *Enoch* is probably first present in the 1840-edition, because it is quoted according to the edition of A.G. Hoffmann, *Das Buch Henoch in vollständiger Übersetzung mit fortlaufenden Commentar, ausführlicher Einleitung und erläuternden Excursen* I-II (1833–38). In his later *Geschichte Jesu* (1876), pp. 411-12, von Hase mostly repeats his words from the earlier book, but adds a reference to Ps. 8, saying that because it became his 'Lieblingsbezeichnung' it is adequate to think that he put an ideal meaning into it; namely, 'die Menschheit in sich vollendend und an die ganze Menschheit

Heinrich August Wilhelm Meyer (1800–1873) from Hannover, founder of the famous *Kritisch-exegetischer Kommentar über das Neue Testament*, in his treatment of Mt. 8.20, also considers Son of man an indirect messianic self-reference, understandable to the Jews (Jn 12.34), as a reference to Dan. 7.13, where the Messiah appears in the clouds as a son of man, 'it is, in a form which, although he is more than a mere man is not different from that of a common man'.[35] It was up to the listener to understand this predicate in a Danielic sense or not. Meyer continues in a speculative direction, arguing that Jesus took over this Danielic designation, conscious of its being the antithesis of being Son of God (die Antithese der *Gottes*sohnschaft). More clearly expressed in the Gospel of John as a consciousness of divine pre-existence, the δόξα which he had left to be the Danielic ὡς υἱὸς ἀνθρώπου, it is, to appear in a kind of being not original to him (in einer ihm nicht ursprünglichen Daseinsform). Thus, it is not without good reason that Jesus' use of Son of man is combined with the Pauline thought of κένωσις, in the background of which the consciousness of a pure divine primitive state (Urstand) is to be found.[36]

Daniel Georg Conrad von Cölln (1788–1833) of Breslau is the last to draft a biblical theology from a rationalistic point of view. He also looks to Dan. 7.13 as the source of the expression, understanding it as indicative of not only human abasement, but also of divine glory. That Jesus held to the idea of the perfect man, the prototype of humanity (des Urbildes der Menschheit), is, according to von Cölln, not evident from his speeches.[37]

That the expression Son of man could inspire people other than exegetes and dogmaticians will be demonstrated by several examples. Perhaps the first of this kind is an article by the poet and theologian Johann Peter Hebel (1760–1826).[38] Hebel is in no doubt that Son of man is a synonym of Messiah at the time of Jesus, and that the reason for this is contained in the reference to Dan. 7.13-14. However, Hebel interprets Son of man of the nation, the holy people of God. Hebel is the first to my knowledge to distinguish between the original content of the oracle, how it was understood by the contemporaries of Jesus, and what was said of the holy people, which they transferred to the representative of it, the Messiah. The poet betrays his

hingegeben, wie schon in 8. Psalm der Menschensohn die Menschheit in sich zusammenfaßt, als der von Gott eingesetzte Herrscher der Erde, wenig geringer als Gott'.

35. H.A.W. Meyer, *Kritisch exegetisches Handbuch über das Evangelium des Matthäus* (1832, 5th edn, 1864), pp. 223-24.

36. *Kritisch exegetisches Handbuch*, pp. 224-25.

37. D.G.C. von Cölln, *Biblische Theologie mit einer Nachricht über des Verfassers Leben und Wirken*, ed. D. Schulz I-II (1836), II, p. 16.

38. J.P. Hebel, 'Bar Enasch oder des Menschen Sohn'; quoted from *idem*, *Sämmtliche Werke* IV (1838), pp. 287-95.

deepest feelings when he describes the reason why Jesus preferred this expression, explaining that it was

> because this name addressed the mild son of Mary (den sanften Sohn Mariä) in the most beautiful and lovable way, because he knew that the Bar Enash in the Danielic Vision, placed opposite the beasts was a picture of mildness and goodness, and that he distinctly found and acknowledged the character of this picture in his heart.[39]

Fr. Wilhelm Gass, in his Breslau dissertation, *De utroque Jesu Christi nomine in Novo Testamento obvio Dei filii et hominis* I-II (1839–1840),[40] admits a connection with Dan. 7.13, which he understands as referring to the Messiah, an interpretation confirmed in the book of *Enoch*. However, he does not want to seek the meaning of the expression Son of man as used by Christ in some historical source. Christ did not take it over as something already formed, but employed it in accordance with his own estimation. 'He himself alone is to be heard in relation to the true force and authority of the name (de nominis vera vi ac potestate)'.[41] Gass divides the Synoptic and Johannine Son of man sayings in two groups. The first includes those using the expression more formally, in a periphrastic way, and not as an argument, and, in some cases, even Jesus omits it. He does not employ it as an attribute, but as a surname (non pro attributo, sed pro agnomine), and what is said pertains to himself and not to the appellation (ad se ipsum non ad appellationem enunciata respicerent). The second group consists of those sayings where the appellation, 'besides the simple force of the personal pronoun, introduces something more important and new to the matter of single sayings to be referred to' (praeter simplicem vim pronominis personalis gravius aliquid atque novum ad singulorum dictorum materiam referendum appellatione exhiberi).[42] Accordingly, Gass concludes that, in general, Jesus is Son of man, who, with regard to authority and condition, is separated from other men, but, thanks to his divine birth, is superior in virtue and power and has taken upon himself the duties of God. 'His whole lot, because it would not have befallen the man himself in the same way, had he not come from above, refers, therefore, to the entire weight of the words and the single appellation to Christ, Son of man.'[43] The choice of the expression from Dan. 7.13 is due to the universal aspect of the divine kingdom.[44] The only

39. Hebel, 'Bar Enasch oder des Menschen Sohn', p. 293.

40. In this context only Pars posterior. De nomine ὁ υἱὸς τοῦ ἀνθρώπου, op. cit., pp. 81-168, is of relevance.

41. Gass, *De utroque Jesu Christi nomine*, II, p. 95; cf. pp. 87-95.

42. Gass, *De utroque Jesu Christi nomine*, II, pp. 128-29.

43. Gass, *De utroque Jesu Christi nomine*, II, pp. 141-42.

44. Gass, *De utroque Jesu Christi nomine*, II, p. 143.

difference, then, between Son of man and Son of God is their different accentuation.[45] That is also the reason why the disciples did not make use of it.[46]

The interpretation of Son of man, as primarily deriving from the self-understanding of Jesus, more or less empties the expression of any essential pre-formed content.

3. Son of Man, an Expression of Humility

We also have from this period advocates for an understanding of Son of man as an expression of humility. This pertains, for example, to Gottfried Less (1736–1797), sometime professor in Göttingen. In an essay from 1776,[47] he stresses the meaning of the expression, both in Hebrew and Greek, as equivalent to 'man'—that is, as referring to all who descend from Adam. Less seeks to prove this on the basis on Mk 2.27 and usage in the Old Testament, especially Psalm 8, while Dan. 7.13 is not even mentioned.[48] But then Less proceeds with an important observation, namely, 'that it is from the predicates that one best recognizes what the subjects are' (vero es *praedicata* optime possit cognosci, qualia sint *subiecta*).[49] Jesus did not employ predicates of hierarchy, because such an ἀντίθεσις would awaken the attention of the reader more, and the very combination of the highest and the lowest would exist in a certain way like an ὀξύμερον and, moving the reader, distract him in admiration.[50]

Also to be mentioned in this context is Johann Georg Rosenmüller (1736–1815), professor in Erlangen. Rosenmüller, in his commentary on Mt. 8.20,[51] returns to the distinction between sons of (noble)men and sons of man, derived from Ps. 49.3. He refers to other examples in the Old Testament, where Son of man (*ben adam*) designates man as humble (Dan. 7.13 is not mentioned). Thus Christ has used the term of his κένωσις as described in Phil. 2.7. That is the very reason why the Apostles did not make use of it for the exalted, Stephen being the only exception (Acts 7.56). Rosenmüller

45. Gass, *De utroque Jesu Christi nomine*, II, p. 146.

46. Gass, *De utroque Jesu Christi nomine*, II, pp. 149-50. In an 'Excursus historicus', pp. 151-68, Gass, to my knowledge is the first to analyse the usage of the expression Son of man among the Gnostics.

47. G. Less, '*Nonnulla de* Filio Hominis *praefatus*', quoted according to the reprint in *idem*, *Opuscula theologici exegetici atque homiletici argumenti* I-II (1780–81), pp. 411-38.

48. Less, '*Nonnulla de* Filio Hominis', pp. 413-16.

49. Less, '*Nonnulla de* Filio Hominis', p. 424.

50. Less, '*Nonnulla de* Filio Hominis', p. 425. Less refers, for example, to Mt. 9.6.

51. J.G. Rosenmüller, *Scholia in Novum Testamentum* I (continens Evangelia Matthaei et Marci) (1777), p. 101.

concludes, nonetheless, 'that this phrase is to be taken as replacing the pronoun for the first person ἐγώ, because it is commonplace for the Hebrews to speak of themselves in the third person'.

On the fringes of this understanding, and mostly as a curiosity is the anonymously published pamphlet *Versuch eines schriftmäßigen Beweises, daß Joseph der wahre Vater Christi sey* (1792), where the author—according to a contemporary, Ernst Johann Konrad Walter[52]—tries to prove that the self-designation Son of man in the mouth of Jesus means that he is a son of Joseph. If he had been born in a supernatural way by a virgin, according to Walter, he would not have been able to call himself Son of man, as this expression both means 'man' (as is seen at a lot of places in the Old Testament and in Mk 2.28par.) and speaks of human origin. Thus Adam, who did not descend from a human in Lk. 3.38, was not called Son of man, but Son of God. Neither is it possible to understand τοῦ ἀνθρώπου of Adam or Mary because we have no indication that the contemporaries of Jesus understood it that way. It is only possible to see in this self-designation an affirmation of the opinion of his contemporaries, who 'held him for the true son of Joseph' (für den wahren Sohn Josephs hielten).[53]

4. *An Old Interpretation Revisited: Son of Man Signifies the Human Nature of Christ*

This period also had advocates for the 'classical' position which viewed Son of man primarily as a designation of Christ's human nature. Among the holders of this view was Nikolaj Frederik Severin Grundtvig (1783–1872), a giant in Danish Church and intellectual life, a genius as hymn writer, a pioneer in the enlightenment of the people and an enormously productive author. Parenthetically, it should be noted that, although conservative with regard to biblical studies, one of his theological axioms was the so-called 'unparalleled discovery': the insight that the Church was there from the beginning, with its creed and sacraments, its writings, the New Testament, not coming into existence until later.[54] This discovery could have had a positive effect on the quest of the historical Jesus, as could the related observations of Søren Kierkegaard (1813–1855), elaborating on some

52. Thus E.F.C. Oertel, *Antijosephinismus oder Kritik über eines Ungenannten schriftmäßigen Beweis daß Joseph der wahre Vater Christi sey* (1792).

53. I owe my knowledge of both the pamphlet of Walter and the rejoinder by Oertel to Bracht, *Der Menschensohn*, pp. 626-27 n. 29. For Oertel's own point of view, see above.

54. Cf. M. Müller, 'The Hidden Context: Some Observations to the Concept of the New Covenant in the New Testament', in T. Fornberg and D. Hellholm (eds.), *Texts and Contexts* (FS Lars Hartman, 1995), pp. 649-58.

insights of Lessing on the meaning and impact of historical knowledge in theology. However, it was neutralized by the attempt to identify history and revelation, not distinguishing strictly between historical facts and testimonies of faith.[55] In a series of articles from 1826 to 1827, 'On the true Christianity and On the Truth of Christianity', Grundtvig says that the use by Jesus of the designations Son of God and Son of Man should remind us 'that he on the father's side was Son of God, on his mother's Son of Man, that he had Spirit in common with God, body and heart in common with us'.[56]

A similar position is defended by Friedrich August Gottreu Tholuck and A. Nebe. Tholuck (1799–1877), professor in Halle and very influential in the revival movement, in his commentary on John, denies that Son of man could have been equivalent to Messiah since Jn 12.34 demonstrates that it was not understandable as such to the people and that Dan. 7.13 does not use it as a 'terminus solemnis'. Therefore, it is most likely that the Redeemer chose this designation as Messiah with regard to its definite sense, and in contrast to 'Son of God', in order to stress his true humanity (das 'wahre Menschseyn') as just an essential aspect of being the Son of God (das 'Gottes Sohn seyn').[57] Nebe declares that Dan. 7.13 witnesses to the type of a personal Messiah and that it was from there that Jesus took his favourite designation ('Lieblingsbezeichnung').[58] That it was a designation of the Messiah is confirmed by the book of *Enoch*; however, its pre-Christian origin being dubious, it is an open question whether the Lord found it as a designation of the Messiah or created it as such himself because of Dan. 7.13. At any rate, it seems to have been understandable to the people (cf. Jn 12.34).[59] Nebe draws attention, for example, to J. Hardouin (see above Chapter 5) interpreting Son of man as Man, but adds that this insight was blurred by the dull exegesis of the Enlightenment, equating as it did, Son of man and Messiah or I and Son of man.[60] Refuting both this and the idealistic understanding, Nebe insists that Son of man pertains to the God-man (dem Gottmenschen)

55. Cf. M. Müller, 'Der Jesus der Historiker, der historische Jesus und die Christusverkündigung der Kirche', *KuD* 22 (1976), pp. 277-98.

56. N.F.S. Grundtvig, 'Om den sande Christendom og Om Christendommens Sandhed', *Theologisk Maanedsskrift* 4-9 (1826–27; quoted according to the book of the same title, 1865), p. 13.

57. F.A.G. Tholuck, *Commentar zum Evangelio Johannis* (1827, 5th edn, 1837), p. 80.

58. A. Nebe, 'Ueber den Begriff des Namens ὁ υἱὸς τοῦ ἀνθρώπου', *Denkschrift des herzoglich Nassauischen evangelisch-theologischen Seminars zu Herborn für das Jahr 1860* (1860), pp. 3-56 (15).

59. Nebe, 'Ueber den Begriff des Namens', p. 17.

60. Nebe, 'Ueber den Begriff des Namens', p. 22.

in the position of abasement. 'The incarnated (menschgewordene) Son of God is the Son of man... The oldest churchly perception has passed its exam.'[61]

5. *Son of Man, the Prototype of Man*

Interestingly, some philosophers also paid attention to the possible meaning of Son of man in the mouth of Jesus as a key to the correct interpretation of Christianity. A speculative element in the understanding turns up for the first time here, and is later employed by a large number of exegetes. Immanuel Kant (1724–1804), speaking of Christ as the 'prototype of the humanity pleasing to God' (das Urbild der Gott wohlgefälligen Menschheit),[62] betrays a speculative understanding of Son of man. Thus, he remarks that the judge of the world 'is not represented and named as God, but as Son of man. This seems to indicate that humanity itself, conscious of its limitations and fragility, in this choice is making a statement; this is a goodness, which, however, does not injure the righteousness.'[63]

An anonymous author, writing under the pseudonym *Non quis, sed quid!*, also belongs to this group. Drawing attention, for example, to Gen. 6.2; Deut. 32.8-9; Judg. 9.9 and Ps. 82.6, and in the New Testament Hebrews 1 and 2.5-7, the author understands Jesus' use of Son of man as expressing his opposition to Jewish priests and authorities. They are the gods and sons of god equipped with authority. He is humble, lacking any authority and submitting to them together with other Jews, a poor son of man.[64] This radical removal of 'divinity' from the person of Christ did not find followers, though the way in which the emphasis is placed on 'man' is very characteristic of Idealism.

Following Kant's lead is the poet, philosopher and theologian Johann Gottfried Herder (1744–1803). Herder, from 1776 superintendent in Weimar, also sees in the Son of man an indication that Jesus was the prototype of humanity. Jesus chose this name because it indicated his dissociation from every demand of worldly sublimity, or the usurpation of the name Son of God, because 'his hope, stemming from the mouth of the prophet, expressed exactly that God through the now despised Son of man would show the

61. Nebe, 'Ueber den Begriff des Namens', p. 56.

62. I. Kant, *Die Religion innerhalb der Grenzen der bloßen Vernunft* (1793, 2nd edn, 1794), p. 174.

63. Kant, *Die Religion*, pp. 211-12 note.

64. Anonymous, 'Versuch über den Stellen im N.T. die vom Sohne Gottes, vom Sohn des Menschen, Christus uä. Reden', *Magasin für Religionsphilosophie, Exegese und Kirchengeschichte* (ed. Ph. Henke) 1 (1794), pp. 129-208 (143).

excellence of his reign to the whole world'.[65] He was named Son of God, because to him the will of God was the highest rule. But he did his work 'as Son of man; that is, out of pure duty (aus reiner Pflicht) and in accordance with the highest goal of humanity (zum höchsten Zweck der Menschheit)'. In his effort to redeem humanity from within, he showed goodness, patience and gentleness in an outstanding sense. 'Until his last moment, he was Son of God and Son of man, lamb and lion'.[66] What Herder means, he made clear a few pages earlier.[67] Men should be intertwined[68] with the moral world of God and, in this way, be brethren in a noble tribe of divine nature. In doing good to all in need of mercy, they should do the work with God, and the more hidden, the more unpretentiously it is done, 'the more they are done for pure humanity, for the Son of Man' (Mt. 25.40). At another place, Herder deepens his understanding of Son of man in the usage of Jesus. In a context in which he defines the content of the title Son of God, Herder declares that Jesus hit the very centre of it by calling himself Son of man, 'because the most godly in man (das Göttlichste im Menschen) to him was the very purest and most comprehensive humanity (die reineste, umfassendste Menschlichkeit)'.[69]

Georg Friedrich Wilhelm Hegel (1770–1831) interprets the expression Son of man in connection with his thoughts on the incarnation of God: Jesus does not appear as a teacher with subjective knowledge,

> but as a prophet, proclaiming the demand, in itself immediate, immediate from God, God himself, speaking through it. With regard to the form of this speaking, the main accent is placed on the circumstance that he who speaks this, at the same time essentially is the man, that it is the Son of man who pronounces it, in whom this pronouncement, this activity of what is existing by itself, this work of God essentially happens in a man, not as something superhuman (etwas Uebermenschliches), as something which comes in the shape of an outward revelation (in Gestalt einer äussern Offenbarung), that this divine presence essentially is identical with the human (dem Menschlichen). Christ calls himself Son of God and Son of man. This is to be taken in an exact sense. The Arabs call one another son of a certain tribe; Christ belongs to the human family; this is his tribe.[70]

65. J.G. Herder, *Vom Erlöser der Menschen. Nach unser drei ersten Evangelien* (1796), pp 139-40, quoted according to B. Suphan (ed.), *Herders Sämmtliche Werke* 19 (1880), pp. 135-252 (189-90). Herder refers to Phil. 2.5-7 and Dan. 7.13.

66. Herder, *Vom Erlöser*, pp. 277-78; (1880), pp. 242-43.

67. Herder, *Vom Erlöser*, pp. 272-74.

68. The German word is 'ineinandergreifend'. Weist, *Wer ist Dieser Menschensohn?*, p. 96, kommentiert, 'die Idiomenkommunikation klingt hier nach!'

69. J.G. Herder, *Von Gottes Sohn, der Welt Heiland. Nach Johannes Evangelium* (1797), p. 288; (1880), pp. 253-424 (374; cf. p. 289; [1880], p. 375).

70. G.F.W. Hegel, *Vorlesungen über die Philosophie der Religion. Nebst einer Schrift über die Beweise der Daseyn Gottes*, ed Ph. Marheineke, I-II [= *Georg Friedrich*

The philosophically inspired, highly speculative interpretation of Son of man, is, in the succeeding decades, looked upon with sympathy by a number of exegetes and other theologians who shared his speculative presuppositions. As a consequence, the impact of Dan. 7.13 was toned down, if not simply denied, the source of its usage being primarily seen in the mind of Jesus. This is also openly admitted in an article, 'How Could Jesus Call Himself Son of Man and Son of God at the Same Time?' by Christian Friedrich Böhme, published anonymously in 1802.[71] According to Böhme, Jesus named himself Son of man because he thought of himself and wanted to be thought of as Messiah in the sense (cf. Jn 18.37) of teacher, promoter and practitioner of the truth (esp. the moral-religious truth). In his capacity simply as man (als Mensch schlechthin), without regard to any special and individual conditions, as if he were humanity in person and the representative of the whole mankind, he, however, also spoke and was regarded as the genuine teacher of wisdom.[72] Son of God did not pertain to nature, but to the relationship of Jesus to God. Son of man is he, who did not teach, defend or practice the truth in his capacity of this or that man, as a human individual, but who is perceived as man on the whole, as pure (reiner) man, or as human reason itself in person. Being alone under the authority of God and in his capacity as teacher of wisdom, being God's representative towards all other men; that is, Son of God, the Messiah. According to Jesus, what could he do or be other than what this Son of man did and was? Is it not the same thing to pronounce the judgments of pure human reason, exclusively according to objective arguments and the judgments of God? Is the first not the Truth itself just as the last? 'The pure judgment of reason is to us a judgment of God' (Das reine Vernunfturtheil ist uns ein Gottesurtheil).[73]

Wilhelm Hegel's Werke 11-12] (1832), p. 245. In a work from his youth, *Der Geist des Christentums und seine Schicksal* (probably from 1798–99, published in *Hegels theologische Jugendschriften*, ed. H. Nohl (1907, 2nd edn, 1966), pp. 241-342), Hegel writes that just as Son of God expresses a modification of the godly, Son of man expresses a modification of the human. But 'the man' (der Mensch) is not one nature or one essence (Wesen) as the godhead, but a conception, something thought of (ein Gedachtes); 'and Son of man here means something subsumed in the conception "man". That Jesus is man is a real opinion (Urteil), the predicate being not an essence, but something general (ein Allgemeines).' The Son of God is also Son of man. The divine in a special shape appears as a man. But the connection between the infinite with the finite is a sacred secret.

71. (C.F. Böhme,) 'Wie konnte Jesus sich zugleich Menschensohn und Gottessohn nennen?', *Theologische Monatsschrift für das Jahr 1802*, ed. J.C.W. Augusti, II (1802), pp. 393-411. Cf. Böhme, *Versuch, das Gemeimnis des Menschensohnes zu enthüllen* (1839), pp. III-IV, where he admits to being the author.

72. (Böhme,) 'Wie konnte Jesus sich zugleich Menschensohn und Gottessohn nennen?', p. 399.

73. (Böhme,) 'Wie konnte Jesus sich zugleich Menschensohn und Gottessohn nennen?', pp. 404-405. If the reader is reminded of Kant, it is not an accident. The author

In his book, *Versuch, das Geheimnis des Menschensohnes zu enthüllen* from 1839, Böhme elaborates this understanding. He still claims Jesus' usage to be original, but does not deny a connection with Dan. 7.13. However, Jesus changed the content from being worldly and directed to the Jewish nation. He took over all the predicates from Daniel, but gave them another, non-Danielic subject (ein anderes nichtdanielisches Subject), which endowed them with non-Jewish meaning.[74] Böhme, in the first place, still speaks of Jesus calling himself Son of man in the sense that he, in a manner unlike any other, is the personified idea of man, in one word the ideal of humanity (das Menschheitsideal).[75] Secondly, Jesus was cosmopolitan in the purest sense of this word.[76] And, finally, Jesus is to be perceived as the legislator, primarily in the sense that he is making man holy and blessed, precisely being their Lord and King.[77] How Jesus reached this conviction will probably never be fully known. 'In the history of humanity it is and will remain a miracle.'[78]

The speculative element is obvious in the understanding of Son of man in Friedrich Daniel Ernst Schleiermacher (1768–1834) as well.[79] In *Der christliche Glaube nach den Grundsätzen der evangelischen Kirche im Zusammenhange dargestellt* I-II (1821–1822), he comments on the relation between divinity and humanity in Christ, the human at one and the same time being kept and viewed in relation to the divine. As he writes in the thesis heading §94,

> The Redeemer accordingly is equal to all men through a common human nature, but differs from all through the unceasing strength of his God-consciousness which was a genuine existence of God in him (Der Erlöser ist sonach allen Menschen gleich vermöge der Selbigkeit der menschlichen Natur, von Allen aber unterschieden durch die stetige Kräftigkeit seines Gottesbewußtseins, welche ein eigentliches Sein Gottes in ihm war).[80]

himself refers (pp. 408-409) to *Religion innerhalb der Grenzen der blossen Vernunft*, although he admits that Kant understands the expression Son of man otherwise than he himself does.

74. Böhme, *Versuch, das Geheimnis*, pp. 43-44.

75. Böhme, *Versuch, das Geheimnis*, p. 88.

76. Böhme, *Versuch, das Geheimnis*, p. 90.

77. Böhme, *Versuch, das Geheimnis*, p. 92. The rest of the book, pp. 94-188, contains an exegesis of the Son of man sayings, seeking to prove these three points.

78. Böhme, *Versuch, das Geheimnis*, p. 192.

79. Cf. M. Müller, 'Schleiermacher und der Ausdruck "Menschensohn". Ein typisches Beispiel und ein Ausblick', in D. Lange and P. Widmann (eds.), *Kirche zwischen Heilsbotschaft und Lebenswirklichkeit* (FS Theodor Jørgensen, 1996), pp. 69-80 (= 'Schleiermacher og udtrykket menneskesønnen. Et typisk eksempel og et udblik', in M. Müller, *Skriften i Skriften. Mellem tradition og reception. Fjorten Afhandlinger* [2007], pp. 195-205).

80. F.D.E. Schleiermacher, *Der christliche Glaube* I-II (2nd edn, 1830/31), II, p. 43.

Later in his explication, Schleiermacher applies this to the names Son of God and Son of man:[81]

> This is totally in accordance with the twofold appellation Son of man and Son of God, which Christ used of himself. He could not at all have chosen the first had he not felt himself completely attached to the human nature; still, seizing it would have been without sense, especially had he not viewed himself as a peculiar product of human nature in such a degree that it needed a renewed recollection of his perfect humanity (an seine vollkomne Menschheit). It is precisely this way that the context of the other name in regard to what Christ says of his relation to the Father, shows that he was not using it in a sense in which it could also be used by other people.

In the second edition, Schleiermacher adds a note describing it as a curious idea (ein sonderbarer Einfall) that the expression should refer to the Danielic vision.[82] In his lectures *Einleitung ins neue Testament* (1829 and 1831–1832), Schleiermacher contemplates further on the relation between Christology and messianic expectation, claiming the necessity of a point of contact (Anknüpfungspunct). There we find familiar elements. The connection (Verknüpfung) alone had to be new. Although Christ presupposed and established connections with contemporary messianic concepts, it is a misunderstanding to think that 'the idea of Christ (of what Christ is) was present before his appearance, as if Christ had offered himself as the personal subject of an established concept' (und Christus habe sich nur als das persönliche Subject zu einer ebenso ausgebildeten Vorstellung dargeboten).[83] It is decisive for Schleiermacher's Christian faith that it has its foundation exclusively in the person of Christ and 'in his presentation of himself'. The intention is to make the Christ of faith independent from Judaism, otherwise Christian faith would be nothing other than 'modified Judaism'.[84] Finally, lecturing on the Life of Jesus, Schleiermacher declares that the expression Son of God is

81. Schleiermacher, *Der christliche Glaube* (1st edn), II, p. 245. Cf. Müller, 'Schleiermacher und der Ausdruck "Menschensohn"', pp. 74-75, for a synopsis of the first and second edition.

82. Schleiermacher, *Der christliche Glaube* (2nd edn, 1831), II, p. 99 n. 3. Cf. *idem*, *Einleitung ins neue Testament* (1845), pp. 479-80, where Schleiermacher declares that he would not seek the source of the expression in Daniel, because in Daniel the description pertains to the fifth world monarchy, which contains no personal Messiah. Just as the beasts characterize the four world empires, the Son of man characterizes the fifth.

83. Schleiermacher, *Einleitung ins neue Testament*, p. 479. This is said with reference to Dan. 7.13.

84. Schleiermacher, *Einleitung ins neue Testament*, p. 481: 'Wenn das Christenthum nicht den Grund seines eigenthümlichen Wesen in der Person Christi hätte und also nicht von seiner Darstellung seiner selbst ausginge, sondern wenn es nur entstanden wäre, wie Viele es haben ansehn wollen, durch Nachdenken, Studium oder die natürliche Reinigung, welche andere Vorstellungen erfahren, wenn sie durch ein reinere Gemüth hindurchgehen: so wäre es Nichts, als ein modificirtes Judenthum'.

not to be separated from the expression Son of man. There is 'never a trace that he had separated the divine and the human. He always speaks of himself as complete (er redet immer von sich als ganz). Son of God designates his difference from all; Son of man his connection with all.'[85]

The interpretation of Son of man as solely to be understood dialectically, together with Son of God as expressing the revelatory messianic self-consciousness of Jesus, gained adherents in the following decades. It also produced some forced exegesis. For instance, when Hermann Olshausen (1796–1839), professor in Erlangen and author of a widely distributed New Testament commentary, comments on Mt. 12.8 and Mk 2.28, that paralleling v. 28 with v. 27 says something very unbecoming (etwas ganz Unpassendes). A word like this could only be spoken by someone perfect, the Urmensch. So, according to Olshausen, υἱὸς τοῦ ἀνθρώπου is to be understood in contrast to ἄνθρωπος and seen as an expression of Jesus' messianic dignity.[86] Commenting on Mt. 24.30, Olshausen remarks that Jesus constantly speaks of his future coming as Son of man and not as Son of God, reflecting partly the general usage of the Saviour speaking of himself; partly Dan. 7.13-14, which the Lord may have had in mind:

> But it is significant that this name, designating the ideal humanity (die ideale Menschheit) of the Lord, is also always being used in the description of his future, the reality and corporality (Leiblichkeit) of his appearance being thereby ratified (verbürgt). The return of the Son of man presupposes his ascension in a transfigured body and his sitting at the right hand of God in this transfigured corporality (Leiblichkeit).[87]

August Wilhelm Neander (1789–1850), a Jew converted to Christianity, from 1813 professor in Berlin and especially known as a Church historian, in *Das Leben Jesu Christi in seinem geschichtlichen Zusammenhange und seiner geschichtlichen Entwickelung* (1837), thinks of Jesus' usage of both Son of man and Son of God as coming from a collection of Old Testament messianic designations. Through him, both are transfigured (verklärt) into a more elevated perception (zu einer höheren Auffassungsweise) than was usual among Jews, bearing also an antithetic element. Neander summarizes the content of the expression as used by Jesus:

> He called himself the 'Son of Man' because he had appeared as man, because he belonged to mankind, because he had done such great things even for *human* nature (Matt ix.8) and because he himself was the realized ideal of humanity (das Urbild der Menschheit).[88]

85. Schleiermacher, *Das Leben Jesu*, ed. K.A. Rütenik (1864), pp. 287-88.

86. Olshausen, *Die drei ersten Evangelien bis zur Leidensgeschichte* (1830, 3rd edn, 1837), p. 383.

87. Olshausen, *Die drei ersten Evangelien*, p. 898.

88. A.W. Neander, *Das Leben Jesu Christi in seinem geschichtlichen Zusammenhange und seiner geschichtlichen Entwickelung* (1837), pp. 129-31. English translation

Christian Hermann Weisse (1801–1866), professor in philosophy in Leipzig and the first to elaborate the two-source hypothesis as an explanation for the Synoptic problem, admits that Jesus could have known Old Testament sayings endowing Son of man with a messianic content, but he does not see it as the reason for his employing the term. Similarly, he did not presuppose his listeners' knowledge of this meaning:

> For them [the listeners], according to Jesus' own intention,—he who would declare such a one unworthy of him betrays in this only his own lack of thought,—beyond question the word should have something enigmatic, provoking meditation on his significance. Jesus would not even have forsaken a certain double entendre (Doppelsinn), with regard to its meaning, the less so because it could be presupposed that according to the individual condition of spirit (Geistesbeschaffenheit) and level of culture (Bildungsstufe), different people would understand different things in the concept of his personality and divine destination, and only few (in the early days, perhaps no one) would gain the same insight into it which he himself had.[89]

Jesus used it in contrast to Son of God, designating his human nature, since docetism was not yet a problem. Further, it would presuppose a perception of his divine nature which was not actual at this time. Son of man was meant to conduct one to a higher concept of the nature and origin of Christ, allowing him to appear as the prototype of humanity (das Urbild der Menschheit), which could also be argued from Philo's Platonizing depiction of a prototypical man, but is better seen as founded on the immediate meaning of the expression. According to Weisse, there is an exact parallelism here between Jesus calling himself Son of man and Paul's speaking of Christ as the second man (zweiter Mensch), both aimed at an elevation of the original human nature, a rebirth and transfiguration of natural man to spiritual man, as it were, the second power of humanity:[90]

> But in the choice of this expression, besides elevated self-esteem (Selbstgefühl), a noble modesty is manifested in not trying to press upon anybody the elevated meaning which it wants to express, but, through an ingenious combination, it hides itself in an enigmatic dimness, in such a way, however, that those able to comprehend could not fail to make it out.[91]

(of 4th edn, 1888): *The Life of Jesus Christ in its Historical Connexion and Historical Development*, p. 99.

89. C.H. Weisse, *Die evangelische Geschichte kritisch und philosophisch bearbeitet* I-II (1838), I, pp. 321-22. According to p. 321 n. 1, the paraphrase in Mt. 16.13 of Mk 8.27, substituting με with ὁ υἱὸς τοῦ ἀνθρώπου, shows that the expression was not a satisfying definition of Jesus' dignity.

90. See Weisse, *Die evangelische Geschichte*, I, pp. 323-25.

91. Weisse, *Die evangelische Geschichte*, I, p. 325.

Here we have an early example of the involvement of Son of man in a detailed attempt to elucidate the messianic consciousness of Jesus, seeing himself as the main source of its content, one of the cornerstones in the enterprise in liberal theology (i.e. constructing a life of Jesus reconciling faith and history).[92]

Christoph Friedrich von Ammon (1766–1850), sometime professor in Erlangen and describing himself as a rational supranaturalist, defends an understanding somewhat similar to that of Weisse with regard to Son of man in his Life of Jesus. The expression was neither unambiguous nor wholly intelligible, signifying nearly the same as anonymity. Jesus employed and developed it in his project of religious education (sein religiöser Unterrichtplan). Matthew 16.13 proves that it was not a prevalent synonym for Jesus. On the contrary, he had to develop it step by step and with many modifications following the prophetic suggestion in Daniel (7.13), because its messianic hierarchy was the most spiritual and the most suitable with regard to the divine kingdom.[93] To von Ammon, Son of man is a hidden designation of the Messiah, not to be understood according to the common language of the Jews (Jn 12.34), but according to Dan. 7.13, 14, 27, of the angelic prince, receiving power from God to become the founder of his realm over the whole earth and to introduce it first in his holy and elect people. In this role, Jesus named himself *bar enash*, בר אנש, either because he considered it the only ideal of his messianic mission or because he personally identified himself with him, or yet because he wanted to be perceived as his representative on earth and, accordingly, gifted with a heavenly and earthly existence.[94] Daniel, in his vision, however, had depicted the Son of man as a confidant of the old, most high God—not as a real person (like Gabriel and Michael), but as an ideal man (Idealmenschen) through whom the Kingdom of God should be erected in Judea (Dan. 7.14, 27). Jesus himself felt called upon to realize this ideal. This was the only type of the true Messiah (der einzigen Typus des wahren Messias) to which he persistently dedicated himself.[95] Even when Dan. 7.13 is seen as the source, its Son of man is interpreted according to idealistic philosophy.[96]

92. Later, in *Die Evangelienfrage in ihrem gegenwärtigen Stadium* (1856), pp. 110-14, 225-29, Weisse returns to the Son of man theme, fighting against the attempt to derive Jesus' use of the expression from Dan. 7.13.

93. C.F. von Ammon, *Die Geschichte des Lebens Jesu mit steter Rücksicht auf die vorhandenen Quellen dargestellt* I-III (1842–47), II, p. 288.

94. Von Ammon, *Die Geschichte des Lebens Jesu*, I, p. 334.

95. Von Ammon, *Die Geschichte des Lebens Jesu*, III, p. 243.

96. This also pertains to C.W. van der Pot, 'Iets over den zin en de kracht der benaming, *de Zoon des Menschen*', *Waarheid in liefde: een godgeleerd tijdschrift voor beschaafde christenen* (1846), pp. 74-99 (93).

This is also the case in the *Biblische Theologie des Neuen Testaments* of Christian Friedrich Schmid (1794–1852) from Tübingen.[97] To Schmid, Dan. 7.13 is only 'the occasion for this expression, but not itself the object' (Veranlassung zu diesem Ausdrucke, nicht aber selbst der Gegenstand). To get the full sense, it is necessary to combine the historical explanation with the linguistic ideal.[98] Inspired by Schleiermacher, Schmid reaches the conclusion that the expression conveys two things; first, that, although Jesus was Son of man, he was at the same time something much higher than man; and second, that, although he was something much higher than man, he was nevertheless man, and this in all human abasement, although in himself the most perfect man (der in sich vollkommenste Mensch). Thus, the expression contains a contrast.[99] Schmid also establishes a connection with the messianic symbolic motive of the branch (Jer. 23.5; 33.15; Zech. 3.8; 6.12), where a tiny beginning grows to an indefinable size and fecundity. This is taken as an indication that already the Old Testament promise suggests the element in the messianic personality, which the Lord stresses through the expression ὁ υἱὸς τοῦ ἀνθρώπου, and in such a manner that in 'Branch', צמח, the human dominates in the Danielic Son of man more than the superhuman.[100]

A Danish advocate of a highly speculative interpretation of the expression Son of man is Adolf Peter Adler (1812–1869), today known only because of Søren Kierkegaard's vehement attack on him in his *Papers*. Adler was deeply influenced by Hegel and published the pamphlet *Om Begrebet Menneskens Søn* (*On the Concept Son of Man*) in 1858, claiming that the Son of man is, first of all, Adam created in a perfect condition, and, second, the type of mankind as it should have been; that is, what all of us should have been according to God's will.[101] The Son of man, which mankind itself was not able to produce, was sent by God, and by the death of this man, who was an obstacle for us, the perfect man had left.[102]

Surprisingly, the head of the conservative Erlangen school, Johann Christian Konrad Hofmann (1810–1877), also belongs among the speculative interpreters. In the famous *Weissagung und Erfüllung im Alten und Neuen Testament* I-II (1841–44), he writes that Jesus is Son of man in being Son of God.[103] Hofmann refers to the 'Branch' (צמח) in Zech. 3.8: 'No other man

97. C.F. Schmid, *Biblische Theologie des Neuen Testaments* I-II (posthumously ed. by C. Weizäcker; 1853; English translation, 1870).

98. Schmid, *Biblische Theologie des Neuen Testaments*, I, p. 149.

99. Schmid, *Biblische Theologie des Neuen Testaments*, I, p. 150.

100. Schmid, *Biblische Theologie des Neuen Testaments*, I, pp. 155-56.

101. A.P. Adler, *Om Begrebet Menneskens Søn. En Afhandling* (1858), p. 7.

102. Adler, *Om Begrebet Menneskens Søn*, pp. 16-17.

103. J.C.K. Hofmann, *Weissagung und Erfüllung im Alten und Neuen Testament* I-II (1841–44), II, p. 18.

but the one God produced in a holy way is entitled to an appellation, which designates him as the very descendent of Adam whom the whole history of mankind has moved towards as its end and goal'.[104] The title does not designate the Urmensch, the ideal of humanity, nor is it totally the same as the Pauline expression ὁ δεύτερος ἄνθρωπος:

> much more he [Jesus] compares himself with the rightly interpreted צמח from Zechariah. The Son of man is he, who had to come to fulfil the history of mankind, and in whom is found what all people before him lacked. They lacked a personality, not subjected to the dominion of sin, death, the world and evil. Such a one has turned up in Jesus.[105]

The last to be included here is the outstanding British representative of Christian Platonism, Frederick Denison Maurice (1805–1872). Maurice claims that Jesus was Son of Man before the incarnation and for that reason cannot make any distinction between Christ as Son of God and as Son of man, as respectively the 'representative of God' and 'the representative of man'. In the incarnation (as an historical event), this eternal truth is revealed to man. 'Being the "Archetype of man", "the perfect ideal of humanity", Christ is the creative and life-giving idea of man. Christ, therefore, is the head of mankind and of every man, and it is this fact that has been revealed in the Incarnation.'[106]

104. Hofmann, *Weissagung und Erfüllung*, II, pp. 21-22.

105. Hofmann, *Weissagung und Erfüllung*, II, p. 22.

106. This summary of Maurice's understanding of Son of Man follows T. Christensen, *The Divine Order: A Study in F.D. Maurice's Theology* (1973), pp. 185-96 (185-86). The quotation is from p. 186. Cf. the footnotes in Christensen's study for references to Maurice's works.

7. Son of Man and the Life of Jesus Project

1. *Two Left-Hegelians*

In the preceding chapter, we saw how an idealistic theology involved the expression Son of man in an effort to place revelation in human nature, understood as complementary to divine nature. The next step in the speculative approach turned to the liberation of the revealed idea from its incidental historical covering; that is, to eliminate the friction between historical event and revelation. This prepared the way for radical criticism.

This is exactly what happened in the both famous and notorious *Das Leben Jesu, kritisch bearbeitet* of David Friedrich Strauss (1808–1878), published in two volumes, 1835–36. In contrast to Reimarus, radical criticism functions here as something positive, as an attempt to reach a theological interpretation. The essence of Christian faith: the supernatural birth of Christ, his miracles, the resurrection and ascension are all expressions of 'eternal truths (ewige Wahrheiten), whatever doubt may be cast on their reality as historical facts'.[1] Strauss rejects both Kant's abstract ideal and Schleiermacher's assumption that Christology builds upon the Christian community's creation of an ideal of absolute perfection, occasioned by Jesus' relative excellence (Jesu relative Vortrefflichkeit) and transferred to the historical Christ, where it constantly strengthens and stimulates its consciousness of God (Gottesbewusstsein):[2]

> This is the key to the whole of Christology, that, as subject of the predicate which the Church assigns to Christ, we place, instead of an individual, an idea; but an idea which has an existence in reality, not in the mind only, like that of Kant. In an individual, a God-man (Gottmenschen), the prophecies and

1. Strauss, *Das Leben Jesu*, I, p. VII. The English translation cited here (based on the 4th German edn of 1840) is *The Life of Jesus Critically Examined* (ed. P.C. Hodgson, 1972, 2nd edn, 1994), p. lii.

2. Cf. Strauss, *Das Leben Jesu*, II, p. 719. The treatise is concluded by a 'Schlussabhandlung. Die dogmatische Bedeutung des Lebens Jesu', II, pp. 686-744. English translation, p. 772.

functions which the Church ascribes to Christ contradict themelves; in the idea of the race, they perfectly agree. Humanity is the union of the two natures, God become man, the infinite manifesting itself in the finite, and the finite spirit remembering its infinitude (der zu Endlichkeit entäusserte unendliche, und der seiner Unendlichkeit sich erinnernde endliche Geist).[3]

In the opinion of Strauss, the historical Jesus in this way caused this consciousness to assert itself in humanity. From a modern scientific point of view, there is no doubt that this linking of consciousness with a concrete individual is something typical of the period.[4] According to Strauss, Schleiermacher is right in claiming that not much more is left of the historical person in this understanding than in Ebionitism:

The phenomenal history of the individual, says Hegel, is only a starting point for the mind... But the mind, having once taken occasion by this external fact, to bring under its consciousness the idea of humanity at one with God, sees in the history only the presentation of that idea; the object of faith is completely changed; instead of a sensible, empirical fact, it has become a spiritual and divine idea, which has its confirmation no longer in history but in philosophy (hat sich der Gegenstand vollkommen verwandelt, ist aus einem sinnlich empirischen zu einem geistigen und göttliche geworden, der nicht mehr in der Geschichte, sondern in der Philosophie seine Beglaubigung hat).[5]

I have reported the philosophical presuppositions of Strauss in relative detail in an attempt to show how he managed to set the historical investigation free. With regard to the understanding of the expression Son of man,[6] he rejects both the pronominal and idealistic interpretation. Matthew 16.28, speaking of 'his kingdom', is an occasion for Strauss to suppose that Son of man means Messiah, and that the reason can be found in Mt. 26.64, referring to Dan. 7.13-14, where the man-like should be understood as a personification, though it was normally perceived by Jews as a messianic figure:

If, then, the expression ὁ υἱὸς τοῦ ἀνθρώπου necessarily recalled the above passage in Daniel, generally believed to relate to the Messiah, it is impossible that Jesus could so often use it, and in connection with declarations evidently referring to the Messiah, without intending it as the designation of that personage.[7]

3. Strauss, *Das Leben Jesu*, II, pp. 734-35. English translation, p. 780.

4. Cf. Strauss, *Das Leben Jesu*, II, p. 736: 'Die Wissenschaft unserer Zeit aber kann das Bewusstsein nicht länger mehr unterdrücken, dass die Beziehung auf ein Individuum nur zur zeit- und volksmässigen Form dieser Lehre gehört.' In the English translation, p. 780: 'This alone is the absolute sense of Christology. That it is annexed to the person and history of one individual, is a necessary result of the historical form which Christology has taken.'

5. Strauss, *Das Leben Jesu*, II, p. 737. English translation, pp. 780-81.

6. 'Son of man' is treated in Strauss, *Das Leben Jesu*, I, pp. 463-69. English translation, pp. 281-83.

7. Strauss, *Das Leben Jesu*, I, p. 467. English translation, p. 283.

Sayings such as Mt. 10.23 (cf. Mt. 13.37-41; 16.27-28; 24–25) show that Jesus could speak of Son of man as Messiah, without identifying this figure with himself. To my knowledge, Strauss is the first to offer the theory that Jesus 'might often mean the Messiah when he spoke of the *Son of Man*, without reference to his own person' (er möchte wohl öfters, wenn er vom υἱὸς τοῦ ἀνθρώπου sprach, den Messias, aber ohne Bezug auf seine Person, gemeint haben).[8] This understanding does not pertain to all Son of man sayings; excluded, for instance, are the Passion predictions. Nor does it pertain to sayings if they are together with Son of man sayings, in which Jesus obviously speaks of himself:

> It is possible, however, either that the writer may have misplaced certain expressions, or that the ultimate prevalent conviction that Jesus was *the Son of Man* caused what was originally said merely of the latter, to be viewed in immediate relation to the former (Möglicherweise indessen könnten ja hier von den Referenten entweder Aussprüche in Verbindung gesezt sein, die es ursprünglich nicht waren, oder von der späteren Überzeugung von Jesus als dem υἱὸς τοῦ ἀνθρώπου aus das ursprünglich nur von dem lezteren Gesagte in unmittelbare Beziehung zu dem ersteren gebracht).[9]

The source material which has Jesus speak of the Son of man both of himself and as a figure other than himself raises the question whether there was a period in the life of Jesus, known from his sayings, when he still did not understand himself as Messiah. In that case, the sayings which speak of the Son of man as other than himself could stem from this earlier period. Strauss thinks that the source material shows that Jesus began as a pupil of John the Baptist 'and only gradually attained the elevation of thinking himself the Messiah'. This also explains the prohibition against declaring it publicly: 'For as often as the thought that he might be the Messiah suggested itself to others, and was presented to him from without, Jesus must have shrunk, as if appalled, to hear confidently uttered that which he scarcely ventured to surmise, or which had but recently become clear to himself'.[10] In Strauss, we find a Jesus on his way to himself, a reconstruction which demands extensive confidence in the reliability of the source material if we are to believe they reflect a period in the life of Jesus, where he did not yet consider himself the Son of man. All the same, we see some of the elements in Strauss which later would prove themselves important in the nineteenth century's Life of Jesus enterprise.

8. Strauss, *Das Leben Jesu*, I, p. 467. English translation, p. 283.
9. Strauss, *Das Leben Jesu*, I, pp. 468-69. English translation p. 283.
10. Strauss, *Das Leben Jesu*, I, p. 477. English translation, p. 287. Cf. the title of §58, 'Wie bald Jesus sich als Messias gefasst, und bei Andern als solcher Annerkennung gefunden habe', pp. 469-77. English translation, §62, pp. 284-88.

The idea that the Son of man Christology was first gradually 'internalized' by Jesus could also lead to the conclusion that it was altogether the product of the consciousness of the community. This is apparent in the interpretation of another left-wing Hegelian, Bruno Bauer (1809–1882) in his *Kritik der evangelischen Geschichte der Synoptiker* I-III (1841–42).[11] Bauer is of the opinion that Messiah was not at all a subject of reflection (Reflexionsbegriff) before the age of Christ. The only exception was the book of Daniel, the elevated view of which was not only singular, but also unrecognized,[12] 'until it received further development in the self-consciousness of Jesus and the community and bore fruit'.[13] Because Messiah in both promise and fulfilment was 'an ideal product of the religious consciousness' (ein ideales Product des religiösen Bewußtseyns), it never existed in reality 'as a real individual' (sinnlich gegebenes Individuum). The designation Son of man for Messiah was created for the first time when the Messiah came into existence in Christian consciousness. It happened late, the earliest instance being the Gospel of Mark, with a reference to Dan. 7.13-14.[14] Used of Jesus, its meaning was clear for everyone and a manifestation of 'the highest esteem which, for the first time, saw true man, the true fruit of mankind' (den wahren Menschen, die wahre Frucht der Gattung) in Jesus. In one respect, it was a 'condescension' (eine Herablassung)—one which, however, is important to understand in the right way:

> It signifies the humanization of religion (die Vermenschlichung der Religion), the self-communion (Einkehr) of religion in humanity and the bringing down of Jewish consciousness to which only the highest, who was the One beyond (der jenseitige Eine), to the One who is man here on earth among men.

That is the reason for the attractiveness of the expression. As religious as it is, it alienates at the same time the character of the fruit in which the whole species has laid its dominant force, making the human manifestation in which the religious consciousness of humanity perceives itself to be an object belonging on a metaphysical plane. However, 'all conclusions one would like to draw from Jesus' use of the expression Son of man are unfounded (unbegründet), because Jesus did not use it'.[15] In this way, Bauer is the

11. The third volume has an addition to the title, '*und des Johannes*'.

12. Bauer does not find this denied through the existence of *1 Enoch* ('ein Machwerk wie das Buch Henoch'), because he sees the Son of man therein as a result of Christian reworking of this pseudepigraph. See *Kritik der evangelischen Geschichte*, I, p. 401.

13. Cf. 'Beilage. Die messianischen Erwartungen der Juden zur Zeit Jesu', in *Kritik der evangelischen Geschichte*, I, pp. 391-16 (396).

14. Bauer, *Kritik der evangelischen Geschichte*, III, pp. 14-15, under the heading 'Der Messias als des Menschen Sohn'. The following quotations are from these pages.

15. Bauer, *Kritik der evangelischen Geschichte*, III, p. 15.

first to say that Jesus did not perceive himself to be the Messiah.[16] Later, Bauer denied the historicity of the figure of Jesus.

In Strauss and Bauer, we find a distinction between the teaching of the historical Jesus and Christology as the means by which the believing community interpreted and maintained his significance. Where Strauss allowed Jesus a messianic self-consciousness and the ability to express it by identifying himself with the Danielic Son of man, Bauer considers the identification of Jesus with the Son of man as entirely a product of community theology. With few exceptions, New Testament scholarship tried to overcome this distinction in the following decades through reconstructing the life of Jesus in such a way that their interpretation was essentially anticipated in a messianic self-consciousness that was developed in the historical Jesus himself. The main impetus in the Life of Jesus enterprise was to reconcile history and faith. The many variations cannot hide one common theme: in nearly all of these attempts, Son of man played a key role.

2. *Son of Man—The True Human*

The founder of the 'Tübingen School', Ferdinand Christian Baur (1792–1860), the teacher and promoter of Strauss, follows a different track in his understanding. In *Christentum und die christliche Kirche der drei ersten Jahrhunderte* (1853), Baur sketches an outline of his interpretation. Even if great weight is laid on the personality of Jesus, this had to have a point of departure in some pre-existent conception. It was the only possibility if the individual appearance would result in a development in universal history. The point of contact between Judaism and Christianity was the Messianic idea. Through Jesus' identifying himself with the Messiah in such a way that he was believed to be the fulfilment of the promise, he initiated the development which resulted in Christianity. 'Through the idea of a Messiah, the spiritual content of Christianity first obtained the concrete form in which it could commence the course of its historical development.'[17] On the other hand, nothing of importance could happen in the history of the Jewish people and religion, which was not either attached to the Messianic idea or initiated through it. In this way, the concept determined the course of Christianity. It is in this context that Baur understands Son of man. Jesus uses this 'name' of himself in such a characteristic manner that it seems obvious that he would express some connection with the Messianic idea. The confession

16. Cf. E. Sjöberg, 'Ville Jesus vara Messias? Bestridandet av Jesu messiasmedvetande i det sista seklets forskning' [Would Jesus be Messiah? The Denial of a Messianic Consciousness in Jesus in Scholarship in the Last Century], *SEÅ* 10 (1945), pp. 82-151.

17. Baur, *Christentum und die christliche Kirche* (1853), p. 36; cf. pp. 36-39.

of Peter at Caesarea Philippi made it an obvious fact, for himself as well as the disciples, that Jesus was the Messiah. Yet Jesus' death made it impossible to reconcile his being Messiah with popular Jewish Messianic expectations. It meant a total rupture between Jesus and Judaism. From now on only faith in the resurrection could conquer the barrier of death.

Later, in an article from 1860, 'Die Bedeutung des Ausdrucks: ὁ υἱὸς τοῦ ἀνθρώπου,'[18] Baur seeks to detect a development in the understanding of Son of man in the Gospels. Because Johannine use, with the exception of 5.27, reflects a later stage, in which the divine and the human was looked upon as a unity, the Synoptic Gospels are the only reliable source of the use of the term by Jesus himself. Matthew 16.13 shows that it could not have been synonymous in the mouth of Jesus with Messiah, and for that reason, was not the familiar and common Messianic designation as is often assumed. 'It leaves one with a choice, either to take the expression in an emphatically high or in an emphatically low sense.'[19] The first possibility is excluded because it does not fit into the nature of Jesus as portrayed in the synoptic gospels. When he preferred to designate himself as man, it was because he was everything man is, including suffering. In the development of his Messianic consciousness, it was his means to take over the national Messianic idea as the only way to gain common acceptance, and perform a real, nationalistic deed. On the other hand, he had to avoid looking like the Messiah of vulgar expectation. Matthew 16.13 gives the clue: Jesus calls himself Son of man in contrast to Son of God. Son of man did not apply to the vulgar Messianic expectation as Son of God did. However, it included a quiet proviso claiming the Messianic idea, and, as soon as it was sufficiently prepared and motivated, he revealed it. Baur writes:[20]

> In contrast to a Messiah appearing with earthly power and glory to set up a kingdom of earthly faith and worldly rule, he wished only to be a man, in the simple, unassuming sense belonging to the concept of a human subject as such; man in the most authentic and broadest sense as one who holds nothing remote from himself and deems nothing foreign to himself which in a human existence belongs to the lot of human life, be it the least and lowliest.

Baur finds this original meaning in sayings such as Mt. 8.20 ('as pure and simple man [als schlechthinniger Mensch]'), and it is possible to see it also in Mt. 9.6 and 11.19. In the last-mentioned saying, Bauer thinks it possible to render the meaning with a quotation from Terence: *homo sum, humani*

18. Baur, 'Die Bedeutung des Ausdrucks: ὁ υἱὸς τοῦ ἀνθρώπου', *ZWTh* 3 (1860), pp. 274-92.

19. Baur, 'Die Bedeutung des Ausdrucks', p. 278.

20. Baur, 'Die Bedeutung des Ausdrucks', p. 280. Translation according to Burkett, *The Son of Man Debate*, p. 17.

nihil a me alienum puto.[21] In other pericopes, such as Mt. 12.1-8, arguing *a minori ad maius*, the Danielic notion of the Son of man has been substituted by the community, which 'was accustomed to see in him alone the Messiah proclaimed by the prophet and elevated to his higher dignity'.[22] Baur concludes:[23]

> With regard to the name υἱὸς τοῦ ἀνθρώπου, the same progress appears which on the whole so much of primitive Christianity has made, that the original and plain is gradually replaced by concepts and opinions through which the natural was subordinated to the supernatural, the true human to the transcendent divine, the ethical to the dogmatic, as the first was totally superseded by the last.

According to Baur, what was only an indirect allusion for the historical Jesus in his substituting the Messiah of vulgar expectation, refining the Messianic idea through his life and not least his death, becomes a direct Messianic designation in the interpretation of the Church, identifying Jesus with the Danielic transcendent figure.[24]

In contrast to Baur, and in a profound criticism of Baur's 1860 article, Adolf Hilgenfeld (1823–1907), a pupil of Baur and professor in Jena, emphasizes the Messianic meaning of Son of man as used in the Gospels. For example, in the Gospel of Matthew, it functions as a reference to Daniel.[25] On the other hand, Hilgenfeld admits that 'would Jesus, through the appellation Son of man, really make reference to the Danielic vision?... [H]e however neither denied the more common meaning of the expression, nor did he find it a current designation of the Messiah'.[26] In spite of so much consensus with the Old Testament, there is a contrast to the current Jewish concept of Messiah, because an earthly man, weak and fragile as all others, more homeless and unpropertied than they, comprehends the whole of the supernatural glory of the Messiah in his religious consciousness. His

21. Baur, 'Die Bedeutung des Ausdrucks', p. 283.

22. Baur, 'Die Bedeutung des Ausdrucks', p. 290. Cf. also pp. 283-85. This pertains to Mt. 12.40.

23. Baur, 'Die Bedeutung des Ausdrucks', pp. 290-91.

24. Cf. Baur, *Vorlesungen über neutestamentliche Theologie* (posthumously edited by F.F. Baur, 1864, reprint, 1973), pp. 75-82, where Baur refers to pre-Christian *1 Enoch* as an instance where ὁ υἱὸς τοῦ ἀνθρώπου 'eine bei den Juden nicht ganz ungewöhnliche Bezeichnung des Messias war' (p. 77). However, Baur is not totally sure that the relevant passages are not Christian interpolations.

25. A. Hilgenfeld, 'Die Evangelien und die geschichtliche Gestalt Jesu', *ZWTh* 6 (1863), pp. 311-40. In this article Hilgenfeld attempts to prove the priority of Matthew over against Mark. The Son of man problem is treated on pp. 327-34.

26. Hilgenfeld, 'Die Evangelien', p. 333. According to Hilgenfeld, Dan. 7.13 speaks of a personal Messiah, but *1 En.* 37–71 'ist eine christliche Einschaltung in dem sicher vorchristlichen Buche' (p. 333).

kingdom, and the judgment he had to exercise, belonged to the future. 'The name "Son of man" in the mind of Jesus had exactly this meaning: that it included the humility of the external appearance in the glory of the Messiah' (Der Name 'Menschensohn' im Sinne Jesu hat eben diese Bedeutung, dass er die Niedrigkeit der äussern Erscheinung in die Hoheit des Messias einschliesst).[27]

In the rewritten version of his Life of Jesus from 1835–36, *Das Leben Jesu für das deutsche Volk bearbeitet* (1864), Strauss, inspired by F.C. Baur, leaves his original position with regard to the Son of man. He now questions whether Jesus really advertised himself from the beginning to be Messiah by using an expression that was not yet a Messianic title. On the occasion referred to in Mt. 16.13, it seems more likely that the disciples had, until then, perceived the expression according to its use in the book of Ezekiel, that is, as a formula of humility (Demuthsformel), 'in which Jesus spoke of himself as a weak receptacle of Divine Revelation'.[28] The influence of Baur is not only aknowledged but also clear in the following quotation:[29]

> For some time Jesus followed this calling before the eyes of his disciples and his nation; he exhibited himelf as the Son of Man and the Friend of man (Menschensohn und Menschenfreund), who regarded nothing human as too petty for him, nothing human as foreign to his interests, who as little despised innocent human joys as he turned away from the sorrows of human life when they lay on the path of his calling. And it was not until he had done all this that it appeared to him to be time to drop the veil, and to assume the title of messiah, at least before his friends.

With Hilgenfeld and the later Strauss, we stand on the threshold of the period that is chiefly dominated by the attempt to reconstruct a life of Jesus, which could reconcile faith and history. A radical historical criticism is here held in check for some decades by making the messianic self-consciousness of Jesus the point of departure in attempting to interpret the theological significance of Jesus. The presupposition in this enterprise is, of course, that there exists a real possibility for a reliable historical reconstruction of the self-understanding of Jesus. Naturally, in this endeavour, Son of man stands at the centre as the most frequent self-designation of Jesus in the Gospels. Heinrich Julius Holtzmann expresses the case very precisely, writing that[30]

27. Hilgenfeld, 'Die Evangelien', p. 334.

28. Strauss, *Das Leben Jesu für das deutsche Volk bearbeitet*, I, p. 227. Quoted according to English translation, *The Life of Jesus for the People* (1879), I, p. 309.

29. Strauss, *Das Leben Jesu für das deutsche Volk bearbeitet*, I, p. 228. English translation, I, p. 311.

30. H.J. Holtzmann, 'Ueber den NTlichen Ausdruck "Menschensohn"', *ZWTh* 8 (1865), pp. 212-37 (213). The translation of the last part of the quotation is according to Burkett, *The Son of Man Debate*, p. 1.

> in reality it is a significant fact that to the extent a real 'science of the life of Jesus (Wissenschaft vom Leben Jesu)' is made possible, the interest of research mostly concentrates on fathoming the Christ-designation which most decidedly can be dated back to Jesus himself, in order to produce the picture in which his consciousness has become an object to him... Nothing can be more certain than that he himself chose it as the most apt where it applies to designate what was typical of his personal essence (persönlichen Wesens), what was characteristic of his appearance and calling. Therein is contained the entire importance of the name.

Because the content of the expression is understood, not so much from the background of existing concepts as from a result of a development in the consciousness of the man Jesus in the reconstruction of the interpreter, this point of departure results in a nearly endless range of variations on the same theme. One constant is a pronounced unhistorical spiritualization of the Messiah concept. Only a more intensive interest in comparative religious studies (Religionsgeschichtliche Schule), conceiving Jesus as more a child of his own age, and, accordingly, more foreign to the modern mind, or a renewed occupation with the possible Aramaic original behind the Greek expression, were able to disturb this whole enterprise at the end of the day.

3. *Son of Man Mainly Expressing the Human Essence of Jesus*

A number of scholars chose to let the very wording of the expression and the self-consciousness of Jesus be the only source of its meaning. This pertains to the founder of the Strasbourg school and mediator between French and German scholarship, Eduard Reuss (1804–1891). Reuss was influenced by Albrecht Ritschl (1822–1889) and adhered to his 'liberal theology', believing that reason should be combined with faith. Reuss thinks that Jesus adopted the title Son of man as his distinctive messianic self-designation, describing himself as the model human, 'the realization of the moral ideal in the person of Him who assumed such a name'.[31] Reuss also thinks that the non-apocalyptic picture of Jesus in the Gospel of John is closer to the historical Jesus than were the Synoptics.[32] A similar view is taken by Daniel Schenkel (1813–1885) from Heidelberg. Schenkel denies that Jesus should have used Son of man in the meaning of the book of Daniel, declaring it

31. E. Reuss, *Histoire de la théologie chrétienne au siècle apostolique* I-II (1852, 3rd edn, 1864), quoted according to W. Baird, *History of New Testament Research* (2003), II, p. 97, using the English translation of Reuss's work, *History of Christian Theology in the Apostolic Age* (1872), I, p. 199.

32. Cf. Baird, *History of New Testament Research* (2003), II, p. 97, quoting the following question from Reuss, *History of Christian Theology in the Apostolic Age* (1872), I, p. 215: 'Can His religion, else so pure, so spiritual, so essentially free from all alloy of earth, have been consummated by an eschatology so grossly material?'

fairly unlikely, 'as, from this book, the "Son of man" suits very little the personal characteristics of Jesus... Jesus could only have designated himself as Son of man in opposition to this picture of the Messiah.'[33] He used the expression to show exactly how far he was from every undue self-conceit. At any rate, he was not only a man as any other man, but the man who would lead misguided and trampled down human nature back to the right way and raise it to God.[34]

W.S. Tyler, an American scholar, does not deny a certain connection of the concept to the Old Testament, but 'cannot fail to observe the marked peculiarity of our Saviour's appropriation of this title to himself... He is in some peculiar sense *the* Son of *mankind*, the child of humanity, the son of the race.'[35] He is 'the prototype of all that man is capable of becoming, all that a pure heart can wish or a holy imagination can conceive in the future progress of the race'.[36] Another American, G.F. Wright, sees Jesus using Son of man to express 'the great idea of the humiliation of his deity into humanity'.[37] In this way, it 'is a more exalted expression than "Son of God". But the exaltation arises from the height of the point of view from which the conception underlying the appellation proceeds',[38] which in a simple way explains why the apostles never used this designation. A third American scholar, Orello Cone, rejects the idea that Jesus should have used Son of man in an apocalyptic sense. 'That Jesus could have identified himself, the compassionate Son of Man, with the awful Messiah of the Enoch-Parables is more than improbable', which means that the apocalyptic Son of man sayings are to be charged to the account of the generation following him.[39] Son of man indicates in the use of Jesus the mere humanity of Jesus.

The idealistic note is even clearer when H. Burton writes that, although the Son of man was among men, he was 'separated by infinite distances from all other sons of men'.[40] As the last Adam, 'He comes to repair the ruin of the fall, steps into the place of the first Adam, as Head and Representative of the race'.[41] Also the Swiss Franck Coulin (1828–1907), writing, not a

33. D. Schenkel, *Das Characterbild Jesu. Ein biblischer Versuch* (1864, 2nd edn, 1872), pp. 77-78.

34. Cf. Schenkel, *Das Characterbild Jesu*, p. 376, and 'Menschensohn', in idem, *Bibel-Lexicon: Realwörterbuch zum Gebrauch für Geistliche und Gemeindeglieder* (1872), IV, pp. 170-75.

35. W.S. Tyler, 'The Son of Man', *BS* 22 (1865), pp. 51-78 (54).

36. Tyler, 'The Son of Man', p. 59.

37. G.F. Wright, 'The Term "Son of Man" as Used in the New Testament', *BS* 44 (1887), pp. 575-601 (585). Wright is here quoting J. Morgan.

38. Wright, 'The Term "Son of Man" as Used in the New Testament', p. 595.

39. O. Cone, 'Jesus' Self-Designation in the Synoptic Gospels', *The New World* 2 (1893), pp. 492-518 (511).

40. H. Burton, 'The Son of Man', *Exp* 5.4 (1896), pp. 388-400 (391).

41. Burton, 'The Son of Man', p. 399.

monograph on the expression, but a life of Jesus titled *Le Fils de l'homme* (1866), belongs in this context, since he has Son of man designate the uniqueness of Jesus among men.[42] The same is true of Brooke Foss Westcott (1825–1901), one of the Cambridge Three, who considered the title to be 'a new one', and depicted Christ as 'the representative of the whole race'. Son of man described his self-humiliation at the same time as it raised him 'immeasurably above all those whose nature he had assumed'.[43]

Two Danish voices are also heard in this choir. Frederik Christian Krarup (1851–1931), a theologian who, although he never possessed a chair at the university, became a very influential spokesman for a Ritschlian, so-called liberal theology, in Denmark, in his thesis from 1885, concerning the divine and the human in the person of Christ, also discusses Son of man. Denying that it was an understandable messianic title derived from Daniel 7, Krarup takes it as an equivalent to 'man' used by Christ as much to veil as to reveal his true essence.[44] Thus also he reaches an idealistic interpretation, maintaining that 'the real essence of Christ must be subsumed under the designation of him as ὁ υἱὸς τοῦ ἀνθρώπου, not only hinted at, but really expressed therein; but his essence, as it comes to the fore here, must be truly divine and not only ideally human. This is the double demand placed on this expression through the New Testament use of it.'[45] The divine is included in the expression, although it points to his human nature. 'While his internal divine fullness is presumed, it is its external form as an intensive development through a poor, concrete human life, which here is displayed. He calls himself ὁ υἱὸς τοῦ ἀνθρώπου as one, who, although divine according to his essence, nonetheless according to the necessity of this very essence, has to go through an intensive human development.'[46]

Another Danish theologian, Anders Andersen (1846–1919), in a book which attempts to underline the basic unity of the portraits of Jesus in the

42. F. Coulin, *Le Fils de l'homme* (1866), p. 6; 'Le Fils de l'homme, c'est celui, qui est unique entre les hommes, quoique réellement et fondamentalement homme'.

43. B.F. Westcott, *The Gospel According to St. John: The Authorised Version with Introduction and Notes* (1882, 18th edn, 1937), pp. 34-35. Cf. also the hermeneutical reflections ending the note: 'It may well be admitted that the early disciples did not at first apprehend all that the later history of the race enables us to see in the title... But we cannot be bound to measure the interpretation of Scripture by that which was at once intelligible. The words of the Lord are addressed to all time. They stand written for our study, and it is our duty to bring their interpretation whatever fulness of knowledge a later age may have placed within our reach.'

44. F.C. Krarup, *Om forholdet mellem det guddommelige og det menneskelige i Kristi person* [*On the Relation Between the Divine and the Human in the Person of Christ*] (1885), pp. 320-30 (323).

45. Krarup, *Om forholdet mellem*, p. 325.

46. Krarup, *Om forholdet mellem*, pp. 325-26.

Gospels, assigns the expression Son of man a central role in this enterprise.[47] According to Andersen, the expression is created by Jesus himself to designate his perceiving himself as a human, as one deriving from man, thus emphasizing his human origin. The definite article, however, leads Andersen to understand it in line with 'a son of Abraham', interpreting 'man' in 'Son of man' to be the progenitor, whose nature with respect to spirit and body he is carrying in a special way. Jesus also has stressed the first part of the expression, 'Son'.

> He is a child of man; this means, first of all, that in all points in his life, he experiences that it is an inherited nature which he carries; secondly, it means that in his life he is driven by this nature which he has inherited, to be a child to his father, to love the nature, the human life from which he descends. This is the basis for the love with which he loves his neighbour as himself. Finally, it means that, in this filial love, he does not want to rule, but to serve his human life, from which he derives, to serve it by honoring it according to the desire of the child, leading it to glory and honor. All this he has collected and expressed through the name 'the Son of Man'.[48]

F. Sieber, taking his point of departure in the messianic consciousness of Jesus and not in the messianic expectations of Judaism, finds the meaning of the expression Son of man through a back-translation to Hebrew בן האדם or Aramaic בן האנש [*sic*], claiming the characteristic to be the second article, meaning that, rightly understood, it has to be translated 'the whole world's man or universal man' (Allerweltmensch oder Universalmensch).[49] This meaning is not derived from anywhere in the Old Testament, as no Old Testament expression is congruent with the self-consciousness of Jesus. Moreover, the decision for his self-designation cannot at all have been something acquired in a certain moment of awakened consciousness.[50]

The last to be mentioned is Friedrich Nietzsche (1844–1900). In *Der Antichrist*, in a description of Jesus as preaching a new way of life and not a new

47. Thus A. Andersen's *Menneskets Søn. Evangelieopfattelsernes Enhed fremstillet i Grundtræk* [*The Son of Man: The Unity of the Gospel Perceptions Represented in Outline*] (1894) is not a monograph on the Son of Man, but the author's conclusion in four books, published in the years 1878 to 1890, treating each of the Gospels' perception of Jesus separately. In a way, Andersen anticipates redaction criticism. However, he is to be characterized as a conservative scholar. For the Son of man, see pp. 156-69.

48. Andersen, *Menneskets Søn*, pp. 164-65.

49. F. Sieber, 'Über die Selbstbezeichnung Jesu als des Sohnes des Menschen', Appendix I in Georg Schnedermann, *Jesu Verkündigung und Lehre vom Reiche Gottes in ihrer geschichtlichen Bedeutung* (1895), II, pp. 257-69 (265). Cf. Lietzmann's harsh remark, *Der Menschensohn*, p. 23 n. 34: 'Der Versuch F. Sieber's...die Formel aus dem Aramäischen resp. Hebräischen zu erklären, ist nur im Princip zu loben: die Ausführung leidet unter der Unbekanntschaft des Verfassers mit der ersten Sprache ganz wesentlich'.

50. Sieber, 'Über die Selbstbezeichnung', p. 269.

faith, Nietzsche claims 'that the concept "Son of Man" is not a concrete person, who belongs to history, something singular, once for all, but an "eternal" reality, a psychological symbol, redeemed from the conception of time' (nicht eine concrete Person, die in die Geschichte gehört, irgend etwas Einzelnes, Einmaliges, sondern eine 'ewige' Thatsächlichkeit, ein von dem Zeitbegriff erlöstes psychologisches Symbol).[51] Nietzsche continues the tradition of Kant and Hegel.

4. *Son of Man—Taken from the Old Testament but Transformed by Jesus*

The following solutions, with regard to the meaning of the expression Son of man as used by Jesus, are characterized by the tendency to allow Old Testament content to be more or less neutralized by the self-consciousness of Jesus as the dominant factor in deciding its significance. The Dutch scholar J. Tideman has Jesus take the expression from Dan. 7.13, but uses it with regard to his being a true human.[52] This understanding could mean that other Old Testament texts besides Daniel 7 are applicable. That is, for instance, the case when the Old Testament scholar Franz Delitzsch (1813–1890), who ended his career in Leipzig, while not excluding influence from Daniel 7, thinks Psalm 8 more important. In Jesus, according to Delitzsch, the congregation experiences what in this Psalm is said about man. 'For this reason, he is the ideal, but, at the same time, outstanding man, because the divine essence which he brought with him at the incarnation signifies a superabundance with regard to the idea of man' (indem die zu seiner Menschwerdung mitgebrachte göttliche Wesenheit einen Ueberschwang über die Idee des Menschen mit sich bringt). What the Psalm says of contemporary men 'becomes a promise of the Son of man κατ̓ ἐξ[οχήν] and the new humanity' in the light of the salvation history of the New Testament.[53] In this, Delitzsch is followed by a professor in Strasbourg, Timothée Colani (1824–1888),[54] who argued that no concept of the Son of man existed at the time of Jesus. Son of man in Dan. 7.13 was a symbol and the Parables in the book of *Enoch* proved nothing, being of a later date.[55] Theodor Keim

51. F. Nietzsche, *Der Antichrist. Versuch einer Kritik des Christenthums* (Umwertung aller Werthe. Erstes Buch) (1888, first published 1895), reprinted in *Nietzsche's Werke*. Erste Abteilung, 8 (1906), pp. 259-60.

52. J. Tideman, 'De Zoon des Menschen', *Waarheid in liefde: én godgeleerd tijdschrift voor beschaafde christenen* (1862), pp. 559-86 (577): 'De Zoon des menschen, dat was, mag ik het zoo noemen, een zoo bescheiden, stille Messias-naam, dat hij als naam, dien Hij zelf bezigte, reeds hierom den Heer welgevallig wezen moest'. Cf. p. 579.

53. F. Delitzsch, *Commentar über den Psalter* (1859), I, pp. 67-68.

54. T. Colani, *Jésus-Christ et les croyances messianiques de son temps* (1864), p. 81.

55. Cf. Colani, *Jésus-Christ et les croyances messianiques*, pp. 15-24.

(1825–1878), professor in Giessen, also sees Psalm 8 as the main inspiration for Jesus' use of Son of man, but he includes Daniel 7 as well (Son of man not yet being a title of the Messiah).[56] Psalm 8 encouraged Jesus because it spoke of his destiny as it could be grasped by human consciousness; that is, as proceeding from below to above, from the lesser to the greater, from earth to divinity. Jesus wanted to state his affiliation with humanity in being the Messiah. For this reason, 'he called himself not only a son of man (einen Sohn von Menschen), but *the* Son of man (den Sohn des Menschen)'.[57]

The Danish Old Testament scholar, Frants Buhl (1850–1932), eventual successor of Delitzsch in Leipzig, but later to return to Copenhagen, suggests that the influence is mainly from Psalm 8. To him, it is a mistake to think that the expression Son of man should be equivalent to Messiah (Dan. 7.13 not referring to Messiah, and the allegories in the book of *Enoch* being later, while Mt. 16.13 shows that Christ himself did not use it in this sense).[58] Buhl also distances himself from a 'modern-abstract' understanding, such as 'the true man, the ideal man' or the like. More obviously, the expression derives from Psalm 8 and is chosen by Christ, 'because this Psalm expressed the paradoxical antithesis between the humble, despised and overlooked appearance, and the huge task and promised sovereignty'. Describing the last position, the expression could, of course, easily be combined with Dan. 7.13 (as, for instance, in Mt. 24.30; 25.31), but as a derived use and not as the original conception—which can be seen if one replaces Son of man with Messiah, here.

In pointing to Psalm 8 as the main inspiration for Jesus' use of Son of man, Buhl is followed by the Copenhagen New Testament professor, Frederik Torm (1870–1953).[59] Torm thinks that even if Son of man was applied to Messiah before the time of Jesus, it did not play any significant role. In contrast to Buhl, Torm (re-)introduces an idealistic element in his understanding, claiming that Jesus thereby demonstrated that he was the scion of the human race in whom human nature had achieved its perfection. This suggests that Jesus could also employ the name when speaking of himself as the Messiah of the Jews, because of the way Dan. 7.13 spoke of him, who is like a Son of man and coming on the clouds of heaven and receiving an eternal kingdom.

56. T. Keim, *Der geschichtliche Jesus* (1865), p. 105. Later he clarifies his position in *Geschichte Jesu von Nazara in ihrer Verkettung mit dem Gesammtleben seines Volkes II. Das galiläische Lehrjahr* (1871), pp. 65-76.

57. Keim, *Geschichte Jesu von Nazara*, pp. 72-73.

58. F. Buhl, *De messianske Forjættelser in det gamle Testamente* [*The Messianic Promises in the Old Testament*] (1894), p. 236.

59. F. Torm, 'Hvad mente Jesus af Nazareth om sig selv?' [What Did Jesus of Nazareth Think of Himself?], *Theologisk Tidsskrift for den danske Folkekirke* 11 (1896), pp. 557-605; 12 (1897), pp. 1-47 (11 [1896], pp. 593-600).

The introduction of Ps. 8.5, although not quoted anywhere in the Gospels (and in the New Testament as a whole, only in Heb. 2.6), seems to be founded in openness towards either an idealistic or paradoxical interpretation of the expression Son of man, of which the content was not fixed beforehand.

In contrast, Ernest Renan (1823–1892), philologist, religious historian and philosopher, understands Son of man in the mouth of Jesus in his famous *Vie de Jésus* from 1863 exclusively in relation to Dan. 7.13. In Aramaic the expression was equivalent to 'man', but because of the Danielic saying

> the words, *Son of Man*, became, at least in certain schools, one of the titles of the Messiah, regarded as judge of the world, and as king of the new era about to be inaugurated. The application which Jesus made of it to himself was therefore the proclamation of his Messiahship, and the affirmation of the coming catastrophe in which he was to figure as judge, clothed with the full powers which had been delegated to him by the Ancient of days... The name which he preferred himself was that of 'Son of man,' an apparently humble title, but one which connected itself directly with Messianic hopes. This was the title by which he designated himself, and he used 'The Son of Man' as synonymous with the pronoun 'I,' which he avoided. But he was never thus addressed, doubtless because the name in question would be fully applicable to him only on the day of his future appearance.[60]

It does not seem incidental that, as a religious historian, Renan lets the content of Daniel 7 decide the meaning of Son of man in Jesus' use to such a degree that he comes near to the consequent eschatological interpretation of Johannes Weiss and Albert Schweitzer of some decennia later. The difference is obvious when we move to the successor of Baur in Tübingen, Carl Weizsäcker (1822–1899), who postulated a development in Jesus' use of the expression. Trying to increase its likelihood, Weizsäcker introduces, besides Daniel 7, the book of Ezekiel as a presupposition. Seeing Jesus as creating something new out of already existing concepts, he thinks that by this designation 'he may also have envisaged the view, which had made its way into Jewish apocalyptic because of the Danielic promise, and which served the higher tendency in messianic belief, the expectation of a heavenly renewal in contrast to an earthly reign and victory'.[61] That Jesus meant this is beyond doubt. But one may wonder how he could do so without perceiving it as a messianic notion. This shows that it had not been a common and proper title for the Messiah. Therefore, Weizsäcker concludes:

60. E. Renan, *Vie de Jésus*, pp. 87-88. Quoted according to English translation *The Life of Jesus* (1935), pp. 85-86.

61. C. Weizsäcker, *Untersuchungen über die evangelische Geschichte, ihre Quellen und den Gang ihrer Entwicklung* (1864, 2nd edn, 1901), p. 274

> Just as in former times the prophets had spoken of themselves as sons of men, expressing humility, being aware in their intercourse with God of human feebleness and divine condescension, this name could now be used with its changing meaning as a prophetic self-designation, in a context where it was used to invoke divine revelation and divine authority, and was therefore not striking. At the same time, the more elevated use in apocalyptic gradually gave occasion to messianic self-revelation.[62]

There was something, however, enigmatic about the title that challenged those who listened to Jesus to detect the ambiguous depth of the expression. This development did not happen only in the mind of Jesus, but by means of his self-disclosure.

The highly influential Strasbourg New Testament scholar, Heinrich Julius Holtzmann (1832–1910), in the previously mentioned article from his time in Heidelberg, 'Ueber den NTlichen Ausdruck "Menschensohn"',[63] summarizes the mainstream understanding of the period in a useful way. According to Holtzmann, Jesus uses Son of man to point himself out 'as the present reality of Daniel's messianic vision' (als erschienene Wirklichkeit der Danielischen Messiasvision).[64] This, however, raises three questions: (1) Was this an interpretation which Jesus took over? (2) Did he use the expression to hide or to reveal his messiaship? And, (3) did he endow it with an understanding of his own? To the first question, Holtzmann's answer is that, whatever one may think about the sayings in *4 Ezra* and the book of *Enoch*, Gospel usage makes it clear that the name 'Son of man' was no widespread and popular designation for the Messiah. The second question is already answered through the correct insight that Jesus did not want to act as the Messiah from the beginning. 'When he used the name Son of man at all, he wanted merely to express a riddle.'[65] The answer to the third question is that Jesus did use the expression to designate 'the servant figure in his messianic appearance' (die Knechtgestalt seines messianischen Auftretens), desiring to suppress the current expectation of the messianic idea through such a self-designation.[66]

Holtzmann also points to what he perceives as a false presupposition held by many interpreters, namely, to take the Gospel of Matthew as the oldest of the Synoptic Gospels and therefore Mt. 8.20 as the point of departure for an understanding of Son of man. As an example, he refers to F.C. Baur's calling it 'the first place' (erste Stelle):[67]

62. Weizsäcker, *Untersuchungen über die evangelische Geschichte*, p. 274.
63. See n. 30, above.
64. Holtzmann, 'Ueber den NTlichen Ausdruck "Menschensohn"', p. 219.
65. Holtzmann, 'Ueber den NTlichen Ausdruck "Menschensohn"', p. 226.
66. Holtzmann, 'Ueber den NTlichen Ausdruck "Menschensohn"', p. 231.
67. In Baur, *Vorlesungen über neutestamentliche Theologie*, p. 81.

> But also apart from this, it is not possible to comprehend why exactly the saying in Matthew 8.20 should contain an analytical proposition in the sense of Kant, when its pathos seems to consist in the fact that the assertion is not at all already included in the concept of the subject, but much more contradicts it.

It also follows from Mk 2.28 that when the Sabbath is a servant for men, 'the Son of man, the bearer of all human dignity and all human rights (der Träger aller Menschenwürde und aller Menschenrechte)', is thus certainly Lord of the Sabbath.[68] Holtzmann concludes:

> As a result, Jesus resorted to the discussed self-designation, not to characterize himself in contrast to υἱὸς τοῦ θεοῦ, but to designate his peculiar and central position in the circle of υἱοὶ τῶν ἀνθρώπων. Daniel's expression is reflected in his consciousness in the universal and humane meaning, which Paul later develops in his teaching about the ἄνθρωπος ἐπουράνιος and δεύτερος' Αδάμ (Romans 5.12-21; 1 Corinthians 15.47).[69]

Willibald Beyschlag (1823–1900), professor in Halle, avoids the difficult concept of a development in Jesus' use of Son of man. He too sees Daniel 7 as the only source for the Gospel expression, which in his opinion speaks of the Messiah. 'The Son of man, in the mouth of Jesus as well as in the meaning of Daniel's saying, is the ideal, heavenly, divine (gotteinige) man who is the Messiah in exactly this way.'[70] This also includes the thought of pre-existence. That Son of man in this way was a designation of Messiah at the time of Jesus is seen from the book of *Enoch*. Thus it did not express the lowliness of his human nature, which was never questioned by his Jewish contemporaries. With regard to the Passion predictions, Beyschlag remarks that they also contain a prediction of the resurrection. However, the messianic interpretation is not the only possible one; the expression could also be understood as in the book of Ezekiel. The motive of challenging the hearers to the right understanding is present, but the pedagogical motif was not the only one. Using the expression Son of man, Jesus declares himself a man:

> In the very same breath in which he places himself side by side with all of us as his brothers, however, he separates himself from all of us—he is the man katexochen, the ideal, absolute, heavenly man, who reflects the whole of his heavenly father's face and includes the whole fullness of divinity in himself, who, before his earthly appearance, pre-existed with God, by God. He is sent by God into the world to found in it the kingdom of God and he will be sent once more to complete what he began, the quintessence of all divine revelation, the A and Ω of humanity and world history.[71]

68. Holtzmann, 'Ueber den NTlichen Ausdruck "Menschensohn"', p. 234.
69. Holtzmann, 'Ueber den NTlichen Ausdruck "Menschensohn"', p. 235.
70. W. Beyschlag, *Die Christologie des Neuen Testaments. Ein biblisch-theologischer Versuch* (1866), p. 25. The section on the Son of man appears on pp. 9-34.
71. Beyschlag, *Die Christologie des Neuen Testaments*, p. 33.

The advantage of Beyschlag's understanding is that he not only takes Daniel 7 as his only source, but also allows Jesus to take over Daniel's Son of man without postulating any transforming reinterpretation and is able to show the possibility that is in all the Gospel Son of man sayings. The price he pays is a not too convincing idealistic interpretation of Dan. 7.13.[72]

In principle, Beyschlag is followed by Ludwig Theodor Schulze (1833–1918) in his *Vom Menschensohn und Logos. Ein Beitrag zur biblischen Theologie* (1867). For Schulze, the content of the expression Son of man is to be found through an exegesis of Daniel 7. 'Jesus shared, developed and clarified the views revealed through the Old Testament, but did not provide them with a substantially other meaning',[73] since they had something enigmatic about them, only being understood rightly when the connection to Dan. 7.13 was seen.

On the other hand, the Rheinish minister, Carl Wittichen (1833–1882), gets around Beyschlag's mistaken interpretation by assuming that Jesus took over Daniel 7 in the interpretation of the book of *Enoch*, where Daniel's symbol of the ethical character of future Israelite world dominion has been personified. However, Jesus modified and developed Enoch's concept by completing its ethical content. Realizing its (until then) abstract definitions, he related them to an Old Testament context, with an unthinkable connection with the Suffering Servant of the Lord, and introduced the thought of the second coming.[74] Wittichen retains the idealistic interpretation when he concludes that the crucial word is 'man', the other qualities being only different moments, conditions and aspects of it. These qualities are of two sorts: as the concept of the ideal, divine idea of the true man, the Son of man represents God himself on the one hand, and the human species on the other and, therefore, is spokesman for both. Behind these stands the idea of man, 'in so far as the same constitutes a moment in both the consciousness of God and

72. Cf. Lietzmann, *Der Menschensohn*, where a very sympathetic review (pp. 9-12) ends in the verdict: 'Das πρῶτον ψεῦδος der Construction liegt in der Danielexegese'. Later, in *Neutestamentliche Theologie oder Geschichtliche Darstellung der Lehren Jesu und des Urchristenthums nach den neutestamentlichen Quellen* (1891, 2nd edn, 1896), I, pp. 62-70, Beyschlag has considerably moderated his views. Now it is said, that 'der Gedanke selbst behält im Geiste Jesu etwas abstract Dogmatisches, Befremdliches' (pp. 63-64). Dan. 7.13 is interpreted as an emblem of the kingdom of the holy ones (see p. 67), and, of Jesus, it is said that he, calling himself Son of man, knows himself as that man who in himself carries the power of the kingdom of heaven, in whom the Kingdom of God and the community with God has come down to earth (see pp. 69-70).

73. L.T. Schulze, *Vom Menschensohn und Logos. Ein Beitrag zur biblischen Theologie* (1867), pp. 40-41.

74. C. Wittichen, *Die Idee des Menschen, zweiter Beitrag zur biblischen Theologie hauptsächlich der synoptischen Reden Jesu* (1868), pp. 60-146.

in the human consciousness of Jesus'.[75] The connection of Son of man and Isaiah's Servant of the Lord is something new. With this understanding, Wittichen would find many followers.

The Dutch scholar H.H. Tijssen was certain that the expression in the Gospels is taken from Dan. 7.13, which text he interprets in a collective way, seeing the Son of man as one realizing the messianic kingdom. *First Enoch* and *4 Ezra* do not prove that Son of man had grown into a messianic title before New Testament times. In using it, Jesus did not openly declare himself the Messiah, but showed, in an enigmatic way, that he considered himself as one bringing the Kingdom of God.[76]

Karl Friedrich Nösgen (1835–1913), who ended his academic career in Rostock, maintains in *Christus der Menschen- und Gottessohn* (1869), against Beyschlag and Schulze, that only an analytic interpretation is satisfactory. 'Jesus can only have designated himself Son of man in a way in which others in Scripture could also be designated sons of man.'[77] He looks at Old Testament usage without excluding Dan. 7.13, which did not constitute an exception, according to Nösgen. In Jesus' use of the term, Son of man designates his feebleness and powerlessness, in both psychical and ethical respects. In Daniel 7, however, it pertains only to the psychical, the result of his subjection to suffering because of the dominion of sin. In this way, it was precisely Daniel's picture of the Son of man that made it possible for Jesus to use it of himself, because it did not include subjection to sin. Nösgen summarizes:

> Choosing this expression as his self-designation, which was comprehensible on the one hand to every Israelite from knowledge of the Old Testament, but, on the other hand, through Daniel's saying, was supplied with a highly significant stamp of the human essence of the Messiah, he never needed to explain it.[78]

According to this understanding Jesus' use of the expression is not subject to any recoining, but only emphasizes the special content it had in Daniel's vision.

75. Wittichen, *Die Idee des Menschen*, p. 157. Later, in *Das Leben Jesu in urkundlicher Darstellung* (1876), pp. 110-11, 140-41, 338-39, Wittichen returns to the question, also supplying a description of later development (p. 141): 'Erst eine spätere Zeit hat unter Einfluß polytheistischer Anschauungsweise, welche die ideale Menschheit nur in der Form der Gottheit fassen vermag, aus der Gotteskindschaft Jesu das Dogma von seiner Gottheit entwickelt und dann beide Begriffe so coordinirt, daß sie die Gottessohnschaft auf die göttliche, seine Menschensohnschaft aber auf die menschliche Natur Christi bezog.'

76. H.H. Tijssen, 'De Zoon des Menschen', *Geloof en vrijheid* 2 (1868), pp. 1-22.

77. Nösgen, *Christus der Menschen- und Gottessohn. Eine Erörterung der Selbstbezeichnungen Jesu Christi in ihrer grundleglichen Bedeutung für die Christologie* (1869), p. 14.

78. Nösgen, *Christus der Menschen- und Gottessohn*, p. 25.

A similar view is found in the work of the Catholic exegete Adam Krawutzcky, who suggests that Jesus used Son of man by pointing precisely to Daniel's figure, thereby trying to teach his adversaries that, though he was a man, he also was Son of God. Daniel 7.13 contained the promise that the Messiah and Son of God was to be thought of and expected as Son of man.[79] Not only did Jesus imply the Danielic meaning, but he also pointed back to the promised Son of Adam in Paradise. It is not difficult, of course, to see a connection of this premise with the Pauline teaching of the second Adam. In this way, Jesus, in his person, subsumed the whole meaning and task of the original man, from whom the woman had been formed. 'Just as our kind falls subject to death through a defeated man, we reach life through a victorious man.'[80] In contrast, another catholic scholar, J.K. Zenner, points out that the article before the genitive is a serious mistake in Classical Greek, but understandable as a Hebraism or Aramaism. For that reason it should not be given any specific meaning. It does not single out a certain man, but has its origin in Dan. 7.13. In the mouth of Christ, it refers to 'his higher mission and divinity'.[81]

The Bonn professor, Wilhelm Julius Mangold (1825–1890), combines, as others before him, a highly idealistic interpretation of Jesus' use of Son of man with a derivation of the expression from Dan. 7.13, 14. Jesus proclaims himself 'as the true son of humanity in whom the idea of humanity has appeared'.[82] It was, however, Jesus himself who made it a messianic designation, using it as 'a riddle, through the deciphering of which, they (that is, his disciples and the people) should come to recognize the special content of his messianic self-consciousness'.[83]

In a less idealistic way, the 'Ritschlian' Hans Hinrich Wendt (1853–1928), professor in Jena, states in his two-volume treatment *Die Lehre Jesu* (1886–1890), that Jesus' use of Son of man points to Dan. 7.13. Nevertheless, he maintains that this self-designation was not a clear indication of a messianic claim. Jesus employed it in a paradoxical way to show

79. A. Krawutzcky, 'Ueber die Bedeutung des neutestamentlichen Ausdrucks Menschensohn und sein Verhältnis zur paulinischen Bezeichnung Christi als des zweiten Menschen', *ThQ* 51 (1869), pp. 600-57 (603-604).

80. Krawutzcky, 'Ueber die Bedeutung des neutestamentlichen Ausdrucks', pp. 656-57.

81. J.K. Zenner, 'Der Menschensohn, Ὁ υἱὸς τοῦ ἀνθρώπου', *Zeitschrift für katholische Theologie* 16 (1892), pp. 567-73 (573).

82. W.J. Mangold, 'Ueber die Bedeutung des Ausdrucks ὁ υἱὸς τοῦ ἀνθρώπου', *Theologische Arbeiten aus dem rheinischen wissenschaftlichen Prediger-Verein* 3 (1877), pp. 1-25 (13).

83. Mangold, 'Ueber die Bedeutung des Ausdrucks', p. 17.

> divine action and heavenly glory in a man. Human experiences, human suffering and death in a Messiah destined to heavenly glory are in accordance with Scripture. Daniel 7.13f. offered him the example. It was the only saying in the Old Testament which so energetically stressed the human essence of the Messiah, while also speaking of his heavenly power and glory.[84]

Another advocate for seeing Dan. 7.13 as the background for Jesus' use of Son of man, without postulating that it was a messianic title, is the conservative Basel professor Georg Schnedermann (1852–1917), who later taught in Leipzig. Schnedermann is of the opinion that if the Jewish background of Jesus' teaching is visible anywhere, it is palpable in his use of the expression 'Son of man'.[85] The expression, according to Schnedermann, stems from Daniel 7, but that the Danielic saying was little known among the Jews at the time of Jesus, is shown from Jn 12.34. Exactly for this reason, it was suitable for Jesus to make it his 'personal property', using it of himself in a suggestive and enigmatic way. According to Schnedermann, it was no concept: it only occurs as subject in sentences, never as a predicate, because these sentences never serve to elucidate the expression. Because there is no concept, it also cannot be determined. Designations such as Messiah or Son of God are predicates in such sentences, in which the expression Son of man is a suitable subject. 'The sentence: "the Son of man is made known as the Messiah", expresses in the briefest possible way the meaning of Jesus, as it, *mutatis mutandis*, also corresponds to the context of Daniel 7.13f.'[86] This would only be understood by people in apocalyptic circles. Other experienced listeners could also combine it with the Son of man in the book of Ezekiel, or the collective interpretation of Son of man in Dan. 7.18, as the true humanity or the ideal man.[87] Schnedermann concludes:

> It is reasonable to think that, in the loneliness and hardship of his messianic vocation, Jesus has been pleased and encouraged exactly thereby that according to this highly normative prophecy of Daniel, it is about such a messiah who would be as any other man and would all the same be elevated to incommensurable honor, power and glory.[88]

The Catholic scholar F.S. Trenkle, in a pamphlet titled *Der Menschensohn. Eine exegetische Untersuchung* (1888), cannot believe that the first

84. H.H. Wendt, *Die Lehre Jesu* (2nd edn, 1901), pp. 435-36.

85. G. Schnedermann, *Jesu Verkündigung und Lehre vom Reiche Gottes in ihrer geschichtlichen Bedeutung* I-II (1893–95), II, pp. 206-209.

86. Schnedermann, *Jesu Verkündigung und Lehre*, p. 208.

87. Cf. Lietzmann's remark, *Der Menschensohn*, p. 23, of this 'catalogue': 'Deutlicher kann die völlige Hülflosigkeit der Exegese nicht ausgesprochen werden, als durch diese den Eindruck abschliessender Zusammenfassung machende Aufreihung der verschiedenartigsten bis dahin ersonnenen Hypothesen'.

88. Schnedermann, *Jesu Verkündigung und Lehre*, p. 208.

hearers of Jesus understood Son of man as a messianic title, arguing that the point of the sayings was about the present Son of man not being messianic. The sayings about the future Son of man, on the other hand, are messianic, although that is only perceived through what is said about Son of man in, for instance, Mt. 26.64. The ambiguity reflects two different sources. With regard to the sayings about the present Son of man, he points to the book of Ezekiel, and with regard to the future Son of man, to Dan. 7.13, although Son of man was in no way a *nomen proprium* for the Messiah.[89]

Wilhelm Brückner (1832–1925), minister in Karlsruhe, likewise sees the point of departure in Jesus' use of Son of man in Dan. 7.13, a saying which he understands as expressing 'origination on the soil of Israel and the growing ideal of humanity from faith in Yahweh', as opposed to the Greek, moving to conquer all people and nations.[90] Jesus proclaims himself to be Christ in the sense of Dan. 7.13-14. What is future to Daniel, however, is also future to Jesus as the Son of man who gives up his life for the sake of humanity. Brückner spiritualizes the concept of the second coming. In his sayings about the second coming, Jesus clings to the Danielic cloud-man in such a way that he never uses the pronoun 'I', so that one may understand that Jesus did not mean primarily his own 'I', the human Jesus, but rather the ideal, which he, as Son of man, carried in his heart and, with which, he, in the depth of his spirit, felt himself in concord.[91] In this interpretation, Brückner comes close to the later understanding of the Son of man in the mind of Jesus, as a future vindicator of his action.

A French contribution to the debate, Emile Carrairon's *Essai historique et critique sur le titre de Fils de l'homme* (1886), postulates a development in the meaning of the expression within Judaism, concluding with its being a messianic title at the time of Jesus. Linguistically, it only means 'man'. 'It is, moreover, *the* Son of man, because, in him, the character of man, the human stamp, is found in a superior and unique degree... Further, it presents him whom the Old Testament predicts shall personify the ideal of Son of man.'[92] Carrairon sees the development running from Ps. 8.5 through the book of Ezekiel to Dan. 7.13; a saying which he understands symbolically.

89. Trenkle, *Der Menschensohn*, p. 33. L. Paul, *Die Vorstellungen vom Messias und vom Gottesreich bei den Synoptikern* (1895), pp. 42-43, sees Jesus in a similar way, using the expression Son of man not only to confront his hearers with a problem, but with the question, if Daniel's oracle pointed at him, a question which for himself was first answered along the way through revelation, for the hearers through his achievements. For this reason, the expression is used from the beginning in an indefinite way (Mt. 8.20), first later to be filled with a messianic content.

90. W. Brückner, 'Jesus "des Menschen Sohn"', *JPTh* 12 (1886), pp. 254-78 (264).

91. Brückner, 'Jesus "des Menschen Sohn"', p. 272.

92. E. Carrairon, *Essai historique et critique sur le titre de Fils de l'homme* (1886), pp. 21-22.

He also points to the book of *Enoch*, which proves that it became a title for the Messiah. Jesus, however, used it according to his understanding of his messianic vocation: 'Always and everywhere, the title implies two things: the human nature of the Messiah, and the Messiahship of the man Jesus'.[93]

The titular meaning is also assumed because of its usage in the book of *Enoch* by the Oxford professor William Sanday (1843–1920), who combines it with an idealistic and paradoxical interpretation.[94] Jesus preferred it to Messiah because it expressed his self-understanding 'in a veiled and suggestive way, which characterized the whole of His teaching on His own person'.[95] This also pertains to G. Runze, professor in Berlin. He understands Son of man as deriving from 'apocalyptic school language', with Jesus using it as 'the genuine man, the Urbild of whom is realized in person by the "Son of man"', being himself, in his life, the perfect manifestation of the will of God.[96]

J.-J. Nandrès, in *Jésus-Christ le Fils de l'homme* from 1867, concedes that, in using the expression, Jesus had in mind Dan. 7.13, but only to show the contrast between this expected figure and himself. Literal speech about the coming Son of man is due to the evangelists. Jesus himself perceived it in accordance with the thought of a 'realized eschatology'; that is, spiritually: 'the day when the kingdom of God is realized, that day will be the coming of the Son of man in his glory'.[97] Thus it is not a plain designation of the Messiah. Along the way, Jesus filled it with content for his disciples. 'It is a progressive revelation of his messianic consciousness. The title is, at first, in his mouth, not a synonym for Messiah; it became as a development in his own understanding.'[98]

Coming from a more conservative position, the Königsberg professor R.F. Grau (1835–1893), in his *Das Selbstbewusstsein Jesu* of 1887, does not want to see one or more isolated Old Testament text as the background for Jesus' use of Son of man, as though Scripture functioned for him as a

93. Carrairon, *Essai historique et critique*, p. 83.

94. W. Sanday, 'On the Title "Son of Man"', *Exp* 4.3 (1891), pp. 18-32 (29).

95. Sanday, 'On the Title "Son of Man"', p. 30.

96. G. Runze, *Das Zeichen des Menschensohnes und der Doppelsinn des Jonâzeichens. Glossen und Materialien zur Erklärung des Herrensprüche vom 'Zeichen'* (1897), p. 21. The sign-problem, Son of man, is only touched upon peripherally. An article with the same title in *ZWTh* 41 (1898), pp. 171-85, is a summary of the book, defending it against an unfavourable review.

97. J.-J. Nandrès, *Jésus-Christ le Fils de l'homme* (1867), p. 55.

98. Nandrès, *Jésus-Christ le Fils de l'homme*, p. 61. Cf. p. 55: 'En un mot, il est le Messie; mais, entre "le Fils de l'homme" et "le fils de l'homme" de Daniel (comme l'interpretaient les Juifs) il n'y a qu'une seule analogie, celle du mot: Jésus est le Messie chrétien, le Christ.'

goldmine of learned combinations.[99] As Son of man in a totally unique way, he is the one of whom the Law and Prophets; that is, the whole of the Old Testament, as one great promise, speaks. Grau evades the widespread spiritualization of the concept and so has Jesus, as Son of man, summarize all the offices in the Kingdom of God. All these offices Jesus subsumed under the name Son of man.

In quite another direction we find Vernon Bartlet, who rejects the idea that Son of man in the mouth of Jesus designates an apocalyptic figure like the one in the book of *Enoch*, which he looks upon as 'esoteric in its origin'. Instead, he sees it as 'a constant implicit reference' to the Servant of the Lord in Isaiah 53.[100] Bartlet tries to demonstrate 'the affinity between the Son of Man of the Gospels and the Servant of Jehovah in Isaiah, xl–lxvi... the Archimedean point of positive proof' being Mk 9.12-13.[101] Daniel 7.13, accordingly, should be understood in the light of the other Old Testament texts where the expression is found and as a testimony of Jesus' 'strikingly original attitude to Scripture'. In Jesus' use, the title 'had primary reference to Himself as the unique personalized type of the Kingdom of God'.[102]

The parables of the book of *Enoch* play a growing role in the discussion concurrently with a more open attitude towards non-canonical writings. We are nearing the break-through of a more realistic religio-historical way of looking at the Bible in general and at Jesus in particular. Thus, it was a decisive step when some exegetes began to argue that this pseudepigraph witnesses to a development or interpretation of Dan. 7.13, attributing a meaning to the Son of man figure not inherent in the book of Daniel itself, and that it was possibly with this interpretation that it was taken over by Jesus. For instance, the influential editor and specialist of the non-canonical Jewish writings, Robert Henry Charles (1855–1931) of Oxford, known as the editor and main contributor to the standard work *The Apocrypha and Pseudepigrapha of the Old Testament* I-II (1913 and several reprints), claims that we find true understanding of the expression in the mouth of Jesus,

> if we start with the conception as found in Enoch, and trace its enlargement and essential transformation in the usage of our Lord. In this transformation it is reconciled to and takes over into itself its apparent antithesis, the conception of the Servant of Jehovah, while it betrays occasional reminiscences of Dan. vii., the ultimate source of this designation.[103]

99. R.F. Grau, *Das Selbstbewusstsein Jesu* (1887), p. 182. The section on Son of man appears on pp. 178-218.

100. V. Bartlet, 'Christ's Use of the Term "The Son of Man"', *Exp* 4.6 (1892), pp. 427-43 (427).

101. Bartlet, 'Christ's Use of the Term', pp. 430-32.

102. Bartlet, 'Christ's Use of the Term', p. 437. The italics are original.

103. R.H. Charles, 'Messianic Doctrine of the Book of Enoch, and its Influence on the New Testament', *ET* 4 (1892–1893), pp. 301-303 (302). The italics are original.

Blending together of the 'Son of man' and the 'Servant of the Lord' has happened 'in a Personality transcending them both', explaining why, on the one hand Son of man has no place to rest his head (Mt. 8.20), and, on the other hand, is Lord of the Sabbath (Mk 2.28).[104] In another article, Charles claims that the influence from the book of *Enoch* on the writers of the New Testament 'has been at times so direct and powerful that it is impossible to understand many New Testament passages without knowledge of Enoch...one of the most carefully studied books in the library of the writers of the New Testament'.[105] Here, also, for the first time, Son of man appears as a 'definite personality', and Charles finds that some of the Son of man sayings in the Gospels are direct quotations from the book of *Enoch*.[106] That Jesus used such a messianic title as Son of man from the beginning of his ministry, 'implies that *from the very outset He had claimed to be the Messiah*, but—we cannot emphasize this point too strongly—not the Messiah according to any pre-existing Apocalyptic or Pharisaic school'.[107] Thus, it is not the self-consciousness of Jesus which undergoes a development, but the disciples' understanding of him as the Messiah.[108] It is interesting to observe that the emphasis on the influence from the Enochic Son of man in the Gospels, in Charles' interpretation, is neutralized through the transformation of Jesus' use of it.

5. *A Symbolical or Collective Understanding*

The difficulty in assuming that the content of the expression Son of man as used in the Gospels or by Jesus himself could be radically different from its postulated background in the Old Testament, may have been a deciding factor for the few scholars choosing to understand it symbolically of a

104. Charles, 'Messianic Doctrine', p. 303.

105. Charles, 'The Son of Man', *ET* 4 (1892–93), pp. 504-506 (504-505). This article is an answer to V. Bartlet, 'Christ's Use of "the Son of Man"', *ET* 4 (1892–93), p. 403, denying that Son of man was an open title of the Messiah.

106. Charles, 'The Son of Man', p. 505. Thus Jn 5.22, 27 should quote *1 En.* 69.27, while Mt. 19.28 quotes *1 En.* 62.5, and Mt. 11.19 'may be a reminiscence' of *1 En.* 62.14.

107. Charles, 'The Son of Man', p. 506. V. Bartlet, '"The Son of Man": A Rejoinder', *ET* 5 (1893–1894), pp. 41-42 (42), still disagrees with Charles, doubting that Jesus 'could or would *count at once upon such a similar transformation in its associations to the mind of His hearers at large*, as to justify His own attribution of the title in an Enochic (*i.e.* explicitly Messianic sense) to His own person'. According to Bartlet we should here discern 'between an implicit and an explicit Messianic claim'.

108. Cf. Charles, *The Book of Enoch* (1893), Appendix B, 'The Son of Man: Its Origin and Meaning', pp. 312-17. See also 'Book of Enoch', in *idem* (ed.), *The Apocrypha and Pseudepigrapha of the Old Testament* (1913, 6th edn, 1969), II, pp. 163-277 (175-76).

corporate entity when it is found in the mouth of Jesus. As we have seen, an early representative of this interpretation was Simon Episcopius (cf. above Chapter 5).

Sytse Hoekstra (1822–1898), teaching at the Mennonite Seminar in Amsterdam, in *De benaaming 'de Zoon des menschen'. En historisch-kritisch onderzoek* from 1866, says that, just as in contemporary Judaism, Jesus has understood the Danielic Son of man symbolically of the saints of the Most High. For this reason, in his use of this name, Jesus has not thought of the Messiah, but of the new community of God (Godsgemeente) to which the kingdom would be given.[109] This original meaning is lost, however, in the Gospel of John, but also in the three other Gospels, and we can observe a development towards seeing it as a designation of Jesus himself. Hoekstra will not categorically reject the possibility that, in using the expression Son of man, Jesus would also emphasize his humanity. But this is not demonstrable. His only certainty is that Jesus, by this expression, 'has thought of the heavenly, spiritual character of the community of God'.[110] Another Dutch scholar, H.N. van Teutem, likewise emphasizes the collective meaning of Daniel in the use of Jesus.[111]

J. Estlin Carpenter (1844–1927), professor at the Unitarian Manchester College in Oxford, in a somewhat apologetic voice, asks if Jesus was mistaken when speaking of a coming Son of man or if he used the expression as an 'apocalyptic symbol' signifying for him 'the entrance of the eternal agencies of truth and equity, mercy and peace, into the scene of Israel's life', because 'of their approach of which he had been the herald'.[112]

Likewise the Danish scholar, Alfred Christian Larsen (1840–1914), in a pamphlet titled *Om Menneskesønnen* [About the Son of man] of 1902, speaks of the Danielic picture as 'a poetical vision serving to clothe the certain hope of the impending entrance of a better and true human order in humanity'.[113] Because the key to the expression in the mouth of Jesus is to be found in Mt. 26.64, it stems beyond doubt from Dan. 7.13. For this reason, Larsen is convinced that Jesus did not think of himself alone in

109. S. Hoekstra, *De benaaming 'de Zoon des menschen'. En historisch-kritisch onderzoek* (1866), p. 44.

110. Hoekstra, *De benaaming 'de Zoon des menschen'*, p. 71.

111. H.N. van Teutem, 'Van waar, dat Jezus zich bij voorkeur den Zoon des Menschen noemde?', *Geloof en vrijheid* 2 (1868), pp. 301-29 (303): 'Als deze nu de uitdrukking Zoon des Menschen aan DANIËL ontleent om daarmede zichzelf aan te duiden, dan wijzigt Hij haar door er het collective uit weg te nehmen'.

112. J. Estlin Carpenter, *The First Three Gospels: Their Origin and Relations* (1890, 4th edn, 1906), pp. 389-90.

113. Alfred Christian Larsen, *Om Menneskesønnen* (1902), quoted according to the reprint in *idem*, *Gennem mange Aar. Foredrag og mindre Afhandlinger* I-II (1915), II, pp. 170-94 (180).

speaking of Son of man, 'but of a whole class of people to which he himself belonged and, as the representative of which he appeared at the time and by chance'.[114] Larsen is aware that the understanding of Dan. 7.13 is different in the book of *Enoch* and that this book exerted influence on the shape in which many of the sayings of Jesus appear. It is only a question whether Jesus would acknowledge this. The decisive problem in the perception of Jesus is whether he took the Danielic or the Enochian attitude. Larsen is in no doubt, assuming that Jesus did not know the book of *Enoch*.[115]

6. *Son of Man—A Title Deriving from Early Christian Theology*

Some exegetes—like Bruno Bauer—drew the consequences of the messianic interpretation of Dan. 7.13 in the Gospels, suggesting that it could not originate in Jesus but only arose as a result of the identification of the early community of the man-like figure in Daniel with the exalted Jesus.

Among those assuming that Jesus did not employ Son of man to express his self-consciousness, we find Gustav Volkmar (1809–1893), professor in Zürich. According to Volkmar, Jesus first became Son of man in the belief of the early community after his resurrection and exaltation to the right hand of God. 'Of the υἱὸς τοῦ ἀνθρώπου—a human—now comes into being "ὁ υἱὸς τοῦ ἀνθρώπου", the one man who fulfils the Danielic hope, the human destined to sovereignty, the resurrected Jesus as ruler of the world in the sense of Daniel.'[116] That is the reason why it is not found in the other writings of the New Testament. As a designation of the Messiah, it is only comprehensible on the basis of Dan. 7.13. As such, it is created by Mark. First, in Mk 8.38, it performs as a direct designation of Messiah. The other evangelists have taken it over from Mark, not from the book of *Enoch*, where its appearance is assumed to be a result of Christian interpolations.[117] An apologetic ulterior motive comes to the fore when Volkmar assumes: 'What Daniel once saw in a dream, was now fulfilled in daylight, but who dares to ascribe the thought of a flight on the clouds (einen Wolkenflug-Gedanken) to Jesus himself?'[118]

114. Larsen, *Om Menneskesønnen*, p. 178.

115. Larsen, *Om Menneskesønnen*, p. 182. In Chapter 12 we shall meet A.C. Larsen as the author of a critical commentary on Daniel.

116. G. Volkmar, *Die Evangelien oder Marcus und die Synopsis der kanonischen und ausserkanonischen Evangelien nach dem ältesten Text mit historisch-kritischem Commentar* (1870), p. 198.

117. Volkmar, *Die Evangelien*, pp. 199-200. Cf. *idem*, *Jesus Nazarenus und die erste christliche Zeit, mit den beiden ersten Erzählern* (1882), pp. 145-55.

118. Volkmar, *Jesus Nazarenus*, p. 154.

August Jacobsen likewise dismisses the idea that Jesus used Son of man of himself: 'Jesus had surely better and more important things to do than to seek out Old Testament ideas and types he could employ for himself'.[119] Jacobsen goes on to establish the hypothesis that the phrase Son of man turns up for the first time in New Testament writings in Revelation. It is the author behind this book that produced that 'magnificently ingenious idea', which saw the second coming of Jesus prophesied in Dan. 7.13. From here, the idea has penetrated into the later tradition of the Gospels:

> If Jesus had called himself without further ado Son of man, the apocalypticist's way of expression would be totally unintelligible. Turned around, it is very likely I repeat that as soon as the fortunate interpretation of the Danielic saying about Jesus was offered, as soon as Christianity had felt this interpretation as somehow a redeeming word, which adequately rendered the thoughts of many, the abstruse presentiments of many, the inclination made its appearance and contiued to spread.[120]

Otto Pfleiderer (1839–1908), professor in Berlin, revives an idea of D.F. Strauss when he declares that Son of man is a messianic title in the Gospels stemming from Dan. 7.13. However, because the return of the present (gegenwärtigen) Jesus is never spoken of, but always about the coming of the Son of man (as a third person), one gets the impression that, because Jesus could not have spoken this way of himself and of his second coming, a 'foreign word, an apocalyptic citation is placed in his mouth'.[121]

Likewise Henricus Lucas Oort, in *De uitdrukking Ο ΥΙΟΣ ΤΟΥ ΑΝΘΡΩΠΟΥ in het Nieuwe Testament* from 1893, finds that Son of man is a messianic title in the Gospels. However, the fact that neither the letters of the New Testament nor the oldest Church Fathers know the expression forces the interpreter to choose between assuming either that the authors of these writings really did not know it or that Jesus has in fact not used it. Oort is convinced that the latter is the case. The Passion predictions are *vaticinia ex eventu*, and other sayings are spurious for internal reasons. Perhaps the sayings concerning the second coming and some other 'neutral' sayings rest on genuine tradition. Thus, it is a possibility that Jesus has used Son of man

119. A. Jacobsen, 'Die Johannes-Apocalypse und die canonischen Evangelien', *PKZ* 33 (1886), pp. 563-68, 583-88, 606-11, 630-33 (567).

120. Jacobsen, 'Die Johannes-Apocalypse und die canonischen Evangelien', p. 567.

121. Otto Pfleiderer, *Das Urchristenthum, seine Schriften und Lehren, in geschichtlichen Zusammenhang* (1887), p. 387. According to Pfleiderer, Dan. 7.13 probably concerns 'ein persönliches Haupt des theokratischen Volkes', the apocalypticist also elsewhere speaking of guardian angels and the like of the peoples (cf. *Das Urchristentum*, p. 308). Later, in the 2nd edn (1902), I, p. 671, Pfleiderer changed his view to a collective understanding.

as a metaphor, but never as a title of the Messiah. Oort's conclusion is that the early Church, under the influence of apocalyptic literature, made it a messianic designation and that the evangelists introduced it as a self-designation in the mouth of Jesus.[122]

Wilhelm Brandt (1855–1915), professor in Amsterdam, is more radical. The definite form, which can only refer to a certain Son of man, does not likely originate with Jesus. It is not to be found except according to an individual perception of the one coming with the clouds of heaven in Daniel's figure.[123] The absence of the title outside the Gospels and Acts also is hardly compatible with the assumption that Jesus should have employed it as an especially apt way to express his non-national and non-earthly vocation as Messiah. This means that the most acceptable hypothesis is that the evangelist Mark introduced it, influenced by the apocalyptic *Parables* (*of Enoch*). This was more so, according to Brandt, because it is highly questionable that the pericope of the book of Daniel, from which it comes, existed already at the time of Jesus.[124] It is a later writer who ascribed Son of man to Jesus, presuming that he was Daniel's Son of man, and, to such a degree, it was important to this writer that he thought it right to do so with the authority of Jesus himself. This is easy to understand, since no other Old Testament conception of the Messiah is more in accordance with Christian faith than the Danielic. Brandt also has an apologetic concern when he declares it a psychological absurdity to think that Jesus explicitly claimed to be Messiah, because 'a decided self-promotion (in eigener Sache) is by far foreign to the character of really pious sentient natures: what they expect for themselves, they hand over to Him, in the providence of whom they trust'.[125]

122. H.L. Oort, *De uitdrukking Ο ΥΙΟΣ ΤΟΥ ΑΝΘΡΩΠΟΥ in het Nieuwe Testament* (1893), p. 101. A.J.Th. Jonker, 'De Zoon des Menschen. De uitdrukking ὁ υἱὸς τοῦ ἀνθρώπου in het Nieuwe Testament', *Theologische Studiën* 13 (1895), pp. 228-60, is a critical review of Oorts' thesis, maintaining Son of man as a genuine messianic self-designation in the mouth of Jesus.

123. W. Brandt, *Die evangelische Geschichte und der Ursprung des Christenthums auf Grund einer Kritik der Berichte über das Leiden und die Auferstehung Jesu* (1893), p. 564.

124. Brandt, *Die evangelische Geschichte*, p. 566. With regard to a late dating of the book of Daniel, Brandt refers to Paul de Lagarde's review, 'Havet, Ernest: Études d'histoire religieuse. La modernité des prophetes, 1891', *GGA* 2 (1891), pp. 497-520. Among other things, it is here said (p. 510): 'Daniel 7 gehört mithin in das Jahr 69 nach Christus... Immerhin sind alle Daniel 7 benutzenden Stücke des neuen Testaments jünger als 69.'

125. Brandt, *Die evangelische Geschichte*, p. 476. Cf. p. 478.

7. *The 'Synthetical' Solution: What is Said of the Son of Man?*

Bernhard Weiss (1827–1918), from 1876 professor in Berlin but earlier in Kiel, representing a mediating theology,[126] initiates a new direction in the interpretation of the expression Son of man. According to Weiss, Son of man was not a common designation of Messiah. It confronted the audience with one who was not Son of man in the same manner as all others, but the Son of man, who through his uniqueness demanded to be known by all. The question in Mt. 16.13, rightly rendered only in Matthew's Gospel, shows that Jesus did not assume that it was an intelligible designation of his Messiahship. 'When he himself, through his use of it, drew attention to Dan. 7.13, it could be perceived as such.'[127] Peculiar to the expression is not the article before the genitive, but the article before the nominative which points to a specific Son of man. It designates him to all who knew the Scripture as the one called by Yahweh to fulfil the messianic mission. What in this way is indirectly done in the sayings concerning the mission on earth of the Son of man, is spoken of directly in the sayings of his second coming, which allude openly to Dan. 7.13. In the Gospel of John, the accent has been altered. Here, Son of man designates his heavenly origin, not his Messiahship.[128]

As noticed by Lietzmann,[129] we have here, for the first time, an exposition of the concept Son of man, which takes all the Son of man sayings as synthetical and not analytical propositions. An adequate understanding is only achieved from what is said about the Son of man, not from the wording of the expression itself. The only reason for Jesus' choice of this unusual title is that it could lead the thoughtful to Dan. 7.13 and, thereby, to the concept of a second coming.[130]

126. Cf. the remark in Baird, *History of New Testament Research*, II, p. 101: 'Like a horse and buggy in the age of the locomotive, Bernhard Weiss looks out of place in a survey of liberalism'. But, thanks to his Life of Jesus book, it is where he belongs (see below).

127. B. Weiss, *Lehrbuch der biblischen Theologie des Neuen Testaments* (1868, 5th edn, 1895), pp. 54-55.

128. Weiss, *Lehrbuch der biblischen Theologie*, p. 605. Cf. also *idem*, *Das Leben Jesu* I-II (1882, 3rd edn, 1888), I, pp. 429-31, and *Die Religion des Neuen Testaments* (1903), pp. 141-42.

129. Lietzmann, *Der Menschensohn*, p. 14.

130. When Lietzmann, *Der Menschensohn*, p. 15, characterizes Weiss' exposition as lacking, in that he believes to have communicated the thoughts of Jesus, where he in reality has stated the view of the evangelists. Today, this is not felt as a serious problem. That the Gospels really communicate the thoughts of Jesus is also defended by H. Gebhardt, 'Die Zukunft des Menschensohns nach den Synoptikern', *Zeitschrift für kirchliche Wissenschaft und kirchliches Leben* 6 (1885), pp. 449-61, 505-22, claiming

The work of the Swiss scholar Johann Martin Usteri (1848–1890) is in a similar vein. To him, Dan. 7.13 is only the external cause for Jesus' use of Son of man. Even if this saying does not speak of a person, Jesus could have interpreted it this way in a spiritual development of the Danielic idea.[131] In the mouth of Jesus, however, it was not equivalent to Messiah. 'It is conspicuous that if one takes the concept "Son of man" as it is used, in all the sayings in which it appears as subject, it is a synthetical and not an analytical proposition (Urteile).'[132] Son of man in Old Testament usage can only describe man in his natural essence, perhaps even in his ideal dignity. Accordingly, Jesus could not think of it as signifying any certain direction for his life. On the other hand, so many characteristic sayings about his person and mission are connected with Son of man that one may assume that Jesus wanted to stamp this name on his self-revelation. But this self-revelation is totally his own achievement. It does not concern his essence, since it is so much more a concept of office (ein Amtsbegriff). Therefore, it would not be as adequately explained through an equation with Messiah as B. Weiss thought. On the contrary, Jesus chooses this name with the intention that people should receive his self-testimony and his personality in an unprejudiced way. 'Here, he thought of his *peculiar vocation as he identified it through his incarnation* and used the name when he wanted to characterize *it*. It was, all the same, the vocation of the Messiah, but in the Christian sense of saviour of the world (des Weltheilandes).'[133]

In a lengthy article from 1891, 'Die Bedeutung der Ausdrucksform ὁ υἱὸς τοῦ ἀνθρώπου im Bewußtsein Jesu', Carl Holsten (1825–1897), Professor in Heidelberg from 1876, the last major representative of the Tübingen

that the 'future' of the Son of man begins with the resurrection, to be completed only at his second advent. To Gebhard, it is obvious that Jesus took the title from Dan. 7.13 because it expressed his messianic consciousness as the one also to come in glory (esp. p. 458). Likewise, the conservative Oslo professor Daniel Andreas Frøvig (1870–1954), in his 'Jesu ord til ypperstepresten om sit komme paa himmelens skyer (Mt 26,64). Til belysning av de synoptiske utsagn om Menneskesønnens snarlige komme' [Jesus' Words to the High Priest concerning his Coming on the Clouds of Heaven (Mt. 26.64). Elucidation of the Synoptic Sayings about the Son of Man's Immediate Coming], *Theologisk Tidsskrift for den danske Folkekirke* 4/1 (1920), pp. 257-79, speaks of a successive expansion of power (p. 275).

131. J.M. Usteri, 'Die Selbstbezeichnung Jesu als des Menschen Sohn', *Theologische Zeitschrift aus der Schweiz* 3 (1886), pp. 1-23 (5-6).

132. Usteri, 'Die Selbstbezeichnung Jesu', p. 14.

133. Usteri, 'Die Selbstbezeichnung Jesu', p. 14 (author's italics). To be listed here is also A.B. Bruce, 'The Kingdom of God: The Son of Man and the Son of God', *The Monthly Interpreter* 3 (1886), pp. 278-93, likewise prioritizing what is said of the Son of man by Jesus announcing 'a Messiah appointed to suffer, richly endowed with human sympathy, and destined to pass through suffering to glory' (p. 286).

School,[134] illustrates the impasse in which the Son of man discussion found itself in the nineties of the nineteenth century in a clear way.[135] Characteristic, also, is his lament over the situation regarding the expression Son of man:

> The precariousness and the poverty of our historical knowledge of this personality come together on hardly any other point than this so burdensome one, on spirit and mind. Not only that, the results of scholars time and again abolish and contradict those of others—any new attempt to solve the riddle (Rätselfrage) evokes new riddles, the solution of which we still trouble ourselves over in vain.[136]

In the first part of his investigation, Holsten produces a series of what he calls 'facts' (Thatsachen). Claiming, with Weiss, that Mt. 16.13 with Son of man is the only correct rendering of Jesus' question—' the purpose of the question is if people and the disciples have, in their consciences, completed the unification of the two expressions ὁ υἱὸς τοῦ ἀνθρώπου and χριστὸς ὁ υἱὸς τοῦ θεοῦ'[137]—he summarizes his results in six conclusions:[138] (1) Jesus used the name before the incident at Caesarea Philippi, (2) but had not employed any other known messianic name. (3) From the use of Son of man the people could have deduced his Messiahship, and such was intended and expected by Jesus. (4) All the same the expression could be perceived in the meaning 'man', thus, it was not a pronounced messianic concept (Messias-Begriff). For that reason, Jesus had not before been asked if he was the Messiah. (5) Jesus had his reasons to maintain the messianic secret during his Galilean ministry. In this period he had appeared as a teacher in the eyes of the disciples. (6) After the episode at Caesarea, there was no reason to keep the secret from the disciples.[139] There must have been a reason to maintain it with regard to the people.

134. Cf. H. Harris, *The Tübingen School* (1975), p. 247: 'The theologian who could best lay claim to Baur's mantle was Carl Holsten, who only became well known twenty years after Baur's death.'

135. Published as 'Biblisch-theologische Studien III', *ZWTh* 34 (1891), pp. 1-79.

136. C. Holsten, 'Die Bedeutung der Ausdrucksform', p. 1. Cf. the evaluation of Weist, *Wer ist dieser Menschensohn?*, p. 156. The situation has not altered decidedly since the contribution of Holtzmann in the same journal in 1863. 'Seitdem...hat die Menschensohn-Forschung...ungeheuren Scharfsinn aufgewendet, Theorien aufgestellt, sie verworfen, mit anderen Theorien kombiniert oder kompiliert, und hatte doch—sofern sie wenigstens kritisch vorging—das längst zuvor von HERDER und SCHLEIERMACHER, STRAUSS und BAUR abgesteckte Terrain so gut wie nie verlassen.'

137. Holsten, 'Die Bedeutung der Ausdrucksform', p. 29.

138. Holsten, 'Die Bedeutung der Ausdrucksform', pp. 30-33.

139. How far psychologizing exegetes could go is exemplified in Holsten's remark on this point ('Die Bedeutung des Ausdrucksform', p. 32, n. 1): 'Wie fremd aber muß Jesus während seiner galiläischen Wirksamkeit diesen Jüngern in der Tiefe seines Selbstbewußtseins gegenübergestanden sein!'

Holsten then turns to the question of whether Jesus' use of Son of man sought to express his messianic consciousness exclusively. He draws attention to the peculiarity in Jesus' use, speaking in both the first or the third person, although it is always clear from the context that he means himself. However,

> in this peculiar usage, all the predicates belong, not to the individuality of Jesus, but to the personality of the ὁ υἱὸς τοῦ ἀνθρώπου, in so far as they are not deduced from the essence of the Son of man in itself (an sich), but from a special salvation historical mission, destiny and position of this Son of man as the Messiah, and belongs to Jesus only in so far as his individuality has passed away in the figure of this Messiah-Son of man (Messiasmenschensohnes)... Thus, we have the fact that all predicates which are connected with 'the Son of man' can be traced back to propositions (Urteile), the subject of which in the consciousness of Jesus is the concept of Messiah. From this follows...that all that Jesus says of the Son of man is not taken from the concept of this word (dem Begriffe dieses Wortes), but comes from his Christ consciousness (Christusbewusstsein) and is connected with this mode of expression (Ausdrucksform). All of it appears as a predicate of a synthetical, not an analytical proposition (dass alles sich als Prädikat eines synthetischen, nicht analytischen Urteiles darstelle).[140]

Holsten here joins Usteri. In this way he succeeds in reaching a common denominator of the two modes of existence, the worldly and the coming one. In this world, the Messiah-Son of man is only inwardly the Messiah through the Spirit of God; functioning in him, and only in the coming world, does this inward essence (Innerlichkeit) become visible.

With regard to this interpretation of the facts, it is said that Son of man designates man in his human condition. This is confirmed through a 'grammatical-logical analysis'.[141] The article before the genitive does not point back to Jesus himself or designate the ideal man, but emphasizes ὁ υἱός as belonging to a species. This being so, Jesus could only employ the self-designation ὁ υἱὸς τοῦ ἀνθρώπου if he carried the peculiar consciousness in himself that as one begotten of a man and belonging to the human species, representing the specific species (Gattungswesen) of man. This designation of essence is also accurate if one wants to understand the Son of man as a title (Amtsbezeichnung). Then, 'only because the Messiah, as begotten through a man in the messianic consciousness of Jesus, belonged to the species of man, could the expression, ὁ υἱὸς τοῦ ἀνθρώπου, be for him a title (Amtsname) for the Messiah'.[142]

140. Holsten, 'Die Bedeutung der Ausdrucksform', pp. 34-37.
141. Holsten, 'Die Bedeutung des Ausdrucksform', p. 47.
142. Holsten, 'Die Bedeutung des Ausdrucksform', p. 47.

The article before υἱός points back to the son of man in Dan. 7.13. In this way the two articles are explained. When it can be proven that during his Galilean ministry, Jesus could have, should have and, in fact, had reached this conclusion, then, and only then, are the two articles explained.

This is substantiated through 'a religious interpretation', the point of departure being that the messianic consciousness of Jesus came into being during the Galilean ministry as an experience of God's giving him his spirit. Polemicizing againt W. Baldensperger (see below) and his denial of a clear messianic consciousness during the Galilean ministry (Baldensperger only wants to speak of the 'lively feeling [lebhafte Empfindung]' of an inward God-relation experienced by Jesus in his baptism), Holsten here distinguishes between a 'Messianic feeling' (Messiasgefühl) and a 'Messianic consciousness' (Messiasbewußtsein):

> Feeling is only awareness of myself in an elevated or diminished condition of life. Messianic feeling is a consciousness, a knowledge of myself as the Messiah, a consciousness which then evokes a feeling high (Hochgefühl) in the mind (im Gemüte). But consciousness is formed knowledge.[143]

This consciousness, which Holsten calls 'consciousness of experience' (Erfahrungsgewißheit) is seen in contrast to the Davidic expectation of a Kingdom of God, replacing worldly empires in a violent way. 'It is hardly possible to show how the break (with the Davidic ideal) came about in the mind and consciousness of Jesus.'[144] This Messianic consciousness was to Jesus 'pure fervor (reine Innerlichkeit)', for which he had confirmation only by seeing the results of his ministry. It is 'a testimony of the soberness of his spirit that Jesus never rushed to find proof through self-assurance, until the moment where the invocation of the high priest forced him to this self-assurance, Matthew 26.63, 64'.[145] The real proof was the future intervention of God.

This Messianic consciousness was followed by the conviction that, just as the messianic kingdom was realized in two steps, so also the Messiah had to pass through two ways of existence (Daseinsformen); that is, the one which Jesus experienced in his earthly life, where the outward life did not correspond to the inward, and the other, the future one, that would be according to the promise founded on the hope evoked by experience. For this idea of the Messiah, Jesus needed a suitable name and a prophetic confirmation. 'He

143. Holsten, 'Die Bedeutung des Ausdrucksform', pp. 55-56 n. 2. Understandably, Weist (*Wer ist dieser Menschensohn?*, pp. 261-62 n. 637) notes that Holsten here introduces a distinction, 'deren psychologischer Dilettantismus sicherlich einen Tiefpunkt in der Geschichte der Exegese zum Menschensohn-Begriff darstellt, sofern man hierbei überhaupt noch von Exegese sprechen kann'.

144. Holsten, 'Die Bedeutung des Ausdrucksform', p. 57 n. 1.

145. Holsten, 'Die Bedeutung der Ausdrucksform', p. 58.

found both the form and the justification in the apocalyptic prophecy of Daniel and in the perception offered there of the בר אנש, the υἱὸς ἀνθρώπου, the Son of man.'[146] According to Holsten, the direction of the movement in Daniel 7 is from earth to heaven, the Son of man himself being a personification of Israel. The argumentation, however, is surprising: 'That Daniel did not see and speak about the beginning of this movement from earth and upwards, is a consequence of his seeing a heavenly scene and only the end of the movement, the arrival of the Son of man in heaven'.[147] Although according with the original meaning of Daniel 7, it is only the 'form' which is employed by Jesus. In this reading, the consciousness of being Son of God precedes the consciousness of being the Son of man. Because of the certainty of the experience of the spirit of God dwelling in him, Jesus must have judged: 'I am chosen by God, ὁ υἱὸς τοῦ θεοῦ and this "I am" in the form of ὁ υἱὸς τοῦ ἀνθρώπου'.[148]

With regard to the historicity of the Synoptic picture of the Messianic consciousness of Jesus, Holsten believes that although Jesus was convinced that he had to die, the concept of a redeeming death is to be seen as a product of the later community (as is the concept of Jesus as judge of the world). Otherwise, it is true that whatever meaning is attached to Son of man in the consciousness of the Synoptic Jesus, the same is to be assumed for the consciousness of the historical Jesus.[149]

Two more contributions in the same direction remain to be mentioned. Martin Kähler (1835–1912), conservative professor from Halle, was also of the conviction that it is not the predicate that gives the subject its content, but the subject that gives the predicates their content. Thus, we are justified in giving it the content which it has been given through the life of Jesus as the Messiah.[150] That earliest Christianity did not use the expression Son of man is, for Kähler, a sign of the Apostolic Church identifying it totally with

146. Holsten, 'Die Bedeutung des Ausdrucksform', p. 60.

147. Holsten, 'Die Bedeutung der Ausdrucksform', p. 66. Weist, *Wer ist dieser Menschensohn?*, p. 161, is not impressed: 'Auf dieser eigentümlichen, letztlich eine Eisegese darstellenden Danielexegese, die HOLSTEN erst am Ende seines Aufsatzes bietet, basiert eigentlich seine gesamte Erklärung des Begriffs. Sie allein steht hinter sämtlichen vorgeschalteten komplizierten und weitschweifigen Erörterungen des neutestamentlichen Befundes, die er anstellt, und sie ist auch das schwächste Glied seines Beweiskette, an welchem dieser letzte großangelegte Versuch einer Lösung des Menschensohn-Problems mit historischen Mitteln schließlich zu Fall gebracht wurde.'

148. Holsten, 'Die Bedeutung des Ausdrucksforms', p. 71.

149. Holsten, 'Die Bedeutung des Ausdrucksform', p. 79. Cf. *idem*, 'Zur Entstehung und Entwicklung des Messiasbewußtseins in Jesus. Biblisch theologische Studien IV', *ZWTh* 34 (1891), pp. 385-449.

150. M. Kähler, *Der Menschensohn und seine Sendung an die Menschheit* (1893), p. 7.

Messiah, 'Christ' having lost all of its contemporary Jewish content and having taken over the whole content of Son of man. Kähler even declares that the Apostles' preaching of Christ in the Gentile world is the confessing interpretation (bekennende Auslegung), which they give the self-predication of Jesus, Son of man. In other words, 'The mission validates this self-designation of Jesus'.[151]

The second and last contribution to be mentioned is *Die Selbstbezeichnung Jesu: Der Sohn des Menschen. Eine biblisch-theologische Untersuchung* from 1896 by Heinrich Appel. To Appel, Son of man, in both Old and New Testaments, characterizes man in his relation to God. This also pertains to Dan. 7.13, which speaks of a Messiah coming from earth to heaven.[152] The human nature of the Messiah is also confirmed in Dan. 9.24-27, which concerns the death of the Messiah (as in *4 Ezra* 7.29; what is said of the Son of man in the book of *Enoch* surpasses by far Daniel, though, for none of these Pseudepigrapha, should we count on Christian influence). Jesus' use reflects his seeing himself as man in relation to God. On the other hand, he also combines it with predicates suitable only for God himself. This is emphasized through the article ὁ before υἱός. Daniel 7.13 is probably the source of the expression in the mouth of Jesus, the Danielic Son of man also transcending the rest of humanity. All the same, it is crucial for our understanding to set to work synthetically and not analytically.[153] Jesus was the first to combine it with Son of God. This meant a re-interpretation of Son of man, showing the whole life and ministry of the Messiah ceasing to be humanly orientated. Appel sees the following development in the use of Jesus: before the episode at Caesarea, Son of man served to emphasize the differences between him and other men and, in this way, to prepare for the recognition of his being Son of God. After Caesarea, it was important to the Lord, because in the best possible way, it was apt to enlighten how these differences constituted a profound contrast between Son of man and other men.[154]

8. *Conclusion*

The common denominator among the different interpretations of Son of man in this chapter is the constant reference to the self-consciousness of Jesus, the variable being the assumed influence from one or more Old Testament sayings or concepts, sometimes mediated through an extra-biblical interpretation

151. Kähler, *Der Menschensohn und seine Sendung*, p. 8. Cf. *idem*, 'Christologie, Schriftlehre', *RE* 4 (1898), pp. 4-16 (8-9).

152. Kähler, *Die Selbstbezeichnung Jesu*, pp. 44-45.

153. Kähler, *Die Selbstbezeichnung Jesu*, p. 64.

154. Kähler, *Die Selbstbezeichnung Jesu*, p. 139.

and sometimes evaluated in a negative way; that is, the decision that Jesus himself could not have used it because of its content or connotations. The confidence in the possibility of reaching into the mind of Jesus, sometimes even into his secret intentions and conscious progressive revelation, because of the abilities of his disciples to grasp his divine mission and office, is fundamental. Whereas a number of exegetes have had difficulties in accepting a radical difference between the original meaning of the Danielic saying and the content it assumes in the use of Jesus, others show themselves freer in this regard. Even those who notice the impact of the evangelists' developments on the meaning of Son of man in the Gospels, find themselves capable of distinguishing between these later additions and the original meaning.

At the same time, two movements in scholarship at the end of the nineteenth century opened up new perspectives. The first was a relativizing interpretation from the perspective of the growing knowledge of contemporary religious thought. The Old Testament was also no longer looked at in isolation, but to some extent through its reception in contemporary Judaism; that is, first of all in the Pseudepigrapha, but also in other Jewish writings from the period, partly as witnessing to influence from other religions and traditions. This religio-historical approach would prove very influential, not least with regard to the understanding of the expression Son of man. The other movement was the profound work on the mother tongue of Jesus, which opened up Aramaic studies. However, the radical consequences of this approach—as will be seen—were soon neutralized.

8. The Emergence of a Specific Apocalyptic Son of Man Concept

Until the beginning of the second half of the nineteenth century, interpreters had usually been content to point out one or other Old Testament saying as the possible background for Jesus' or the evangelists' use of Son of man. Following the rediscovery of Pseudepigrapha, such as the book of *Enoch*, and a renewed interest in *4 Ezra*, other non-canonical material began to be taken into consideration. Although we see a tendency to let this use follow the original meaning of the sayings—sometimes in the form of having them determine their true meaning—the Messianic consciousness of Jesus or the Messianic belief of the New Testament authors was considered as transforming the content in such a way that this consciousness or belief may be described as the real determinative factor.

Albert Schweitzer, in his history of the Life of Jesus project, characterized the situation as follows:

> It had become a dogma of theology that Jesus used the term Son of man to veil his messiahship; that is to say, every theologian found in this term whatever meaning he attached to the messiahship of Jesus: the human, humble, ethical, unpolitical, unapocalyptic or whatever other character was held to be appropriate to the orthodox 'transformed' messiahship.[1]

The second half of the century witnessed a movement towards an increasing desire to understand Jesus from the background of contemporary Jewish Messianic expectations. A growing religio-historical approach had, as one of its important results, an ever more consequential attempt to reach a historical understanding of Jesus and the traditions and interpretations contained in the New Testament. As we have seen, opinions had been divided concerning the understanding of Dan. 7.13, as to whether the Son of man was a messianic figure or a symbol. But only a few of the adherents of the symbolical understanding stretched this to cover the use of Jesus. Increasing awareness of the

1. A. Schweitzer, *Geschichte der Leben-Jesu-Forschung* (1913), p. 257. Quoted according to the English translation, *The Quest of the Historical Jesus* (2000), p. 219.

impact of apocalyptic thinking in the centuries around the beginning of the Common Era opened up gradually to an understanding of Jesus' messianic consciousness as formed by apocalyptic thinking and an eschatological attitude.

Excursus I: The Interpretation of Daniel 7.13 until ca. 1850[2]

a. *The Messianic Interpretation of Daniel 7.13*

Approaching the subject from the point of view of the New Testament, Christian interpreters normally understood the saying in Dan. 7.13 as a prophecy of the second coming of the Messiah. Among the Church Fathers, this interpretation is almost universal.[3] However, there are exceptions. For example, Cyprianus's understanding of the prophecy in Dan. 7.13 is not about the second coming but about the exaltation to God just after the resurrection.[4] Much later, Cosmas Indicopleustes construed Dan. 7.13 of the first coming of Christ and interpreted the clouds of the virgin birth, and, like Cyprianus, also took v. 14 of the exaltation following the resurrection.[5] The messianic understanding prevailed also in Judaism.[6]

In the Reformation period, we find Calvin repeating the Fathers: when '*as* a son of man' (*tamquam* filius hominis) is used, it is because Christ has not yet assumed our flesh. He appears to Daniel as a son of man, because he later should be true and fully son of man (postea fuit vere & reipsa hominis filius).[7] Martin Chemnitz, as we have already seen, could say that Son of man was Daniel's designation for the Messiah. Later, the Leipzig professor, Johann Benedikt Carpzov (1639–1699), further developed this interpretation in the first (to my knowledge) monograph on this question, *Dissertatio de Filio Hominis ad antiquum dierum delato, ad Daniel. VII: 13, 14* from 1679[8]. The saying is a

2. Cf., on the following, M. Müller, *Der Ausdruck 'Menschensohn' in den Evangelien* (1984), pp. 33-38 (Excursus B. Die messianische Deutung von Dan. 7,13). A comprehensive history of the interpretation of Dan. 7 from the Church Fathers and onwards is in Bracht, *Der Menschensohn*, pp. 65-205.

3. Thus Justin, *Apology* I 51, *Dialogue* 31-32; Irenaeus, *Adversus haereses* III 19.2; Hippolytus, *In Danielem* IV 10-11; Tertullian, *Adversus Marcionem* IV 10; Eusebius, *Historia ecclesiastica* I 2.24-26. All five see Dan. 7.13 as a prediction of the second coming of Christ. Cf. M. Casey, *Son of Man: The Interpretation and Influence of Daniel 7* (1979), pp. 92-93, for a list of quotations and allusions to Dan. 7.13-14 in patristic literature until Eusebius. Casey (pp. 57-77) also produces Aphrahat, Ephraem, Jerome, Polychronius, and Theodoret of Cyrrhus as representatives for this interpretation. I owe most of these and the following references to Casey's work.

4. Cf. *Testimoniorum libri III ad Quirinium* II 26. In this Hippolytus was partly followed by Lactantius, *Divinae institutiones* IV 12-21.

5. *Christian Topography* II 69. This work is from c. 550.

6. Cf. Casey, *Son of Man*, pp. 80-84.

7. J. Calvin, *Praelectiones in librum propheticarum Danielis* (1561, 2nd edn, 1571), pp. 89 (2), 90 (1).

8. Here according to the reprint in *Thesaurus theologico-philologicus, sive Sylloge dissertationum elegantiorum ad selectiora et illustratiore Veteris et Novi Testamenti loca* (1701), I, pp. 887-901.

description of the revelation of the glorious coming of the Messiah. The prefixed *kaph* is, accordingly, a *kaph similitudinis* and not a *kaph veritatis*:

> It was not a true man who appeared to Daniel in this vision, but a sort of φάντασμα pointing to the human species, just as he did not see real beasts suggesting the four kingdoms, but their picture shown to his imagination. This prefiguring does not preclude the real humanity of Christ. Because one thing is the real thing prefigured (*res ipsa praefigurata*), another, the prefiguring of this thing (*rei illius praefiguratio*).[9]

Until then, the Messiah was not a real person, but became so at the incarnation. Carpzov also discusses the interpretations of Jewish sages.[10] This also pertains to Christian Benedikt Michaelis (1680–1764) in his משיח בן אדם *sive Dissertatio philologica ex antiquitate iudaica, de nominibus Christi, humanam ipsius naturam designantibus* (1714).

In Holland, the reformed professor Hermann Venema (1697–1787) stresses that Messiah in Dan. 7.13 is called Son of man because of the nature he—the Son of God—was going to have and the character of his reign.[11] 'The holies of the Most High', according to Venema, are not an interpretation of Son of man, but his helpers; that is, angels.[12]

Leonhard Bertholdt (1774–1822), in a commentary on Daniel, writes that the comparison כבר אנש later produced the predicate Son of man for the Messiah. As such, it seems it was employed by Jesus. In Daniel, we also have a description of a Christophany, but the Messiah is not called Son of man, but merely compared to one. The concipient thereby thought of an exalted heavenly being who would come from heaven and erect his eternal and imperishable reign on earth without having any real body—a view later shared by some Jewish Christians (as seen from the polemic of the apostle) (1 Jn 1.1; 4.1-3). 'The Name υἱὸς ἀνθρώπου, used of the Messiah, is thus, originally, only an abstract expression (ein abstrahierter Ausdruck), the meaning of which is not to be obtained etymologically (as has happened for a long time among the dogmaticians), but historically from this text.'[13] In Bertholdt, we can detect the beginning of the claim that a Son of man concept was a special supranatural variant of the more earthly-national Messiah concept.

Other representatives of this view are, for instance, Wessel Scholten[14] and W.M.L. de Wette.[15] The conservative Heinrich Andreas Christoph Hävernick (1811–1845), ending up as professor in Königsberg, sees Son of man as depicting the true character of the

9. J.B. Carpzov, *Dissertatio de Filio Hominis ad antiquum dierum delato, ad Daniel. VII: 13, 14* (1679), p. 888.

10. Carpzov, *Dissertatio de Filio Hominis*, pp. 889-91.

11. H. Venema, *Dissertationes ad vaticinia Danielis emblematica Cap. II, VII, et VIII. De quatuor orientis regnis, ordine sibi successuris, et quinto Messiæ* (1745), pp. 541-42.

12. Venema, *Dissertationes ad vaticinia*, p. 550.

13. L. Bertholdt, *Daniel aus dem Hebräisch-Aramäischen neu übersetzt und erklärt* I-II (1806–1808), II, pp. 463-65 n. 21.

14. W. Scholten, *De appellatione τοῦ υἱοῦ τοῦ ἀνθρώπου, qua Iesus se Messiam professus est* (1809), pp. 89-101.

15. W.M.L. de Wette, *Biblische Dogmatik des Alten und Neuen Testaments* (1813, 3rd edn, 1831).

Messiah: 'True God and true man, he also appears here'.[16] The famous, and similarly conservative Berlin professor Ernst Wilhelm Hengstenberg (1802–1869), finds Dan. 7.13 pointing directly to the employment by Jesus of Son of man with an apologetic meaning: nobody should be embarrassed by his human debasement.[17]

C. von Lengerke finds that Son of man in Dan. 7.13 can only be the Messiah, just as the reign spoken of in vv. 14, 18 and 23 can only be the reign of Messiah. It cannot be pure fiction. 'Thus the Messiah is indisputably ascribed a higher, superhuman nature'.[18] Lengerke produces three arguments for the choice of Son of man. The human form was only accessible if the seer wanted to depict him as a person, which, accordingly, is the case in the depiction of angels (cf. Dan. 8.15; 10.16). He had to find a suitable predicate for the Messiah, partly because he was fond of circumlocutions, partly because there was not yet any common name for the Messiah and Son of David was not suitable in this circumlocutional and symbolic context.[19] Jesus' giving preference to the expression points back to Dan. 7.13 and to its ideal meaning.[20]

The last to be mentioned in this context is Bruno Bauer, who even claims that, to the author of the book of Daniel, the Messiah has become a free object of contemplation in contrast to the other prophets.[21]

It is significant that the various aforementioned interpreters of Daniel also take Jesus' use of the expression Son of man into account. The connection between the two testaments of the Christian Bible is still seen as essential and bi-directional.

b. *The Symbolic Interpretation of Daniel 7.13*

However, a pure historical or symbolical understanding of Daniel's Son of man shows up very early.[22] The philosopher and anti-Christian polemicist, Porphyry (died c. 305), in his *Against the Christians* XII (c. 270), reflects this in all likelihood in understanding the figure as representing the Maccabean Jews.[23] But long before that, there existed explicit

16. H.A.C. Hävernick, *Commentar über das Buch Daniel* (1832), p. 242.

17. *Christologie des Alten Testamentes und Commentar über die messianischen Weissagungen* I-III (1829–35, 2nd edn, 1854–57), III.1, pp. 6-19 (17). Dan. 7 is only included in the 2nd edn. Cf. III.2, p. 30.

18. C. von Lengerke, *Das Buch Daniel. Verdeutscht und ausgelegt* (1835), p. 336.

19. Lengerke, *Das Buch Daniel*, pp. 337-38.

20. Lengerke, *Das Buch Daniel*, p. 339.

21. B. Bauer, *Kritik der evangelischen Geschichte der Synoptiker* I (1841), p. 396.

22. Cf. Müller, *Der Ausdruck 'Menschensohn' in den Evangelien*, pp. 39-42, the beginning of Excursus C, 'Die symbolische Deutung von Dan. 7,13'.

23. It was assumed earlier that Porphyry himself had invented this interpretation, even that he had meant that Daniel's Son of man was Judas Maccabaeus. Jerome was guilty of this mistake when he referred to Porphyry in his *Commentarium in Danielem prophetam*, *MPL* 25, cols. 491-583 (533). Today, it can be proven that Porphyry, in reality, referred to the Maccabean Jews, and that his interpretation originates in an older Syrian exegetical tradition, also witnessed in Aphrahat, *Demonstratio* V 21. See P.M. Casey, 'Porphyry and the Origin of the Book of Daniel', *JThS* NS 27 (1976), pp. 15-33; *idem*, *Son of Man*, pp. 59-62. Among other things, it is said (p. 59): 'This theory began in the pre-critical era, and that is where it belongs'. An attempt to refute Casey's understanding, A.J. Ferch, 'Porphyry: An Heir to Christian Exegesis?', *ZNW* 73 (1982), pp. 141-47, was aptly answered in Casey's rejoinder, 'Porphyry and Syrian Exegesis of the Book of Daniel', *ZNW* 81 (1990), pp. 139-42.

testimonies of a Jewish collective interpretation.[24] It also seems to have gained support in the Syrian Church,[25] as seen especially in Aphrahat (died after 345).[26] Later, it is also witnessed in Ephraem (died 373), Theodore bar Koni (c. 790) and Isho'dad of Merw (c. 850), all three dividing between the literal meaning and the essential. In his commentary on Dan. 7.13, Ephraem writes: 'While the significance of this was prefigured in the sons of the People, in that they subdued the Greeks and the surrounding kingdoms, its consummation was perfected in Our Lord', while Theodore expresses the same thought by saying that 'their essential quality is fulfilled in Our Lord the Christ'. Isho'dad, in his commentary on Daniel, simply asserts: 'This refers to the Maccabees, but in truth it refers to Christ.'[27] Finally, Polychronios (died c. 430) and Cosmas Indicopleustes (sixth century), though both interpreted Dan. 7.13 of the Messiah indirectly, witness to the existence of the symbolic understanding.

The Medieval Jewish scholars, Rashi (1040–1105) and Ibn Ezra (1092–1167), think of the holy people of Israel.[28] This interpretation characteristically gains a foothold in Christian exegesis with the arrival of critical scholarship. Thus, Hugo Grotius looks at the reign of the Son of man as the Roman Empire,[29] while Coccejus takes the figure as signifying 'the people of the holies, who are holy to the Holy God, whose πολίτευμα is in heaven'.[30]

In the nineteenth century, the expression is interpreted about the Maccabees by J. Jahn[31] and as referring to the nation of God's holy people by J.P. Hebel,[32] F.D.E.

24. Cf. M. Casey, 'The Corporate Interpretation of 'one like a son of man' (Dan. vii 13) at the Time of Jesus', *NT* 18 (1976), pp. 167-80; *idem*, *Son of Man*, pp. 81-83. Here Casey adduces the rabbinic places, *Midrash Psalm* 21.5 and *Tanchuma Toledot* 20. Casey's interpretation of the last text is contested by J. Coppens, 'L'interpretation collective du Fils d'homme daniélique', *EThL* 53 (1977), pp. 189-91.

25. Casey, *Son of Man*, pp. 51-70.

26. Cf. Casey, *Son of Man*, pp. 58-59: 'Aphrahat's fifth Demonstration thus provides clear evidence that there were exegetes in A.D. 337 who held a pure form of the Syrian tradition, an accurate outline of the original author's interpretation of Dan. 7. This must have been transmitted to them by the Jewish communities in Syria. Edessa is the obvious centre for the whole area where Jewish communities are known from pre-Christian times. Some of their members were subsequently converted to Christianity, and the Jewish communities continued alongside the newly formed Christian groups. Hence, the Syrian Churches had so much more exegetical material in common with Jews than did the Churches in the West. This is the path travelled by the authentic interpretation of the Book of Daniel.'

27. I owe these three references and the translation of the quotations to Casey, *Son of Man*, pp. 64-65. Cf. also the refusal in Theodoret of Cyrrhos, *In Danielem* ad 7.13, of an interpretation seeing behind Son of man in Dan. 7.13 the Maccabeans.

28. References in Casey, *Son of Man*, pp. 84-85, where it also is remarked that Ibn Ezra, who, in a shorter commentary from c. 1142 had interpreted Dan. 7.13 messianically, in his longer commentary from c. 1153 has changed his mind.

29. H. Grotius, *Annotata ad Vetus Testamentum* II (1644), p. 438.

30. Coccejus, *Observationes ad Danielem* (1666), quoted according to *idem*, *Opera omnia theologica, exegetica, didactica, polemica philologica* (2nd edn, 1689), III, p. 356.

31. J. Jahn, *Einleitung in die Göttlichen Bücher des Alten Bundes* (2nd edn, 1803), II, p. 616.

Schleiermacher,[33] and J.Ch.K. Hofmann.[34] The Zürich professor Ferdinand Hitzig (1807–1875) also belongs in this company, claiming that only in the book of *Enoch* and the New Testament, does it come to have a personal messianic understanding.[35] During the Maccabean era, there did not exist any expectation of Messiah. The Son of man signifies the reign, consisting of the Saints of the Most High, inasmuch as he reigns over the pagans. Whereas this reign comes down from Heaven, the pagan stems from Hell.[36]

***

Around the mid-nineteenth century, Jewish apocalyptic was taken up as a theme in its own right. A main reason was naturally the study of the Pseudepigraphic literature, not least after the rediscovery of the book of *Enoch*.[37] With regard to the second Pseudepigraphon to be claimed as a witness to a Son of man concept, *4 Ezra*, it had been known all along as an appendix to the Vulgate. The discovery of an Ethiopic manuscript resulted in a new edition in 1820.[38]

The first substantial monograph on apocalyptic is by Adolf Hilgenfeld, *Die jüdische Apokalyptik* (1857). In this it is maintained that

> Jewish apocalyptic is the historical mediation between the religion of the Old Testament and Christianity, because there existed from the beginning an intimate contact between the messianic hope of late Judaism (des späten Judenthums) and the Messianic belief of Christianity... In this broader form, Jewish apocalyptic is the whole pre-history of Christianity, because another branch of late Judaism, Jewish Alexandrianism, penetrated by Hellenistic education, intervened emphatically in the development of Christian doctrine first with the Letter to the Hebrews.[39]

32. J.P. Hebel, 'Bar Enasch oder des Menschen Sohn', *Sämmtliche Werke* IV (1838), p. 291.

33. F.D.E. Schleiermacher, *Einleitung ins neue Testament* (1845), pp. 479-80.

34. J.Ch.K. Hofmann, *Weissagung und Erfüllung im alten und neuen Testamente* I (1841), pp. 290-91.

35. F. Hitzig, *Das Buch Daniel* (1850), p. 114.

36. Hitzig, *Das Buch Daniel*, p. 117.

37. At the suggestion of a capuchin working in Egypt, the British explorer James Bruce brought three Ethiopic manuscripts of *1 Enoch* to England in 1733. The first to translate it into a modern language was C.R. Laurence, *The Book of Enoch, an apocryphal production, now first translated from an Ethiopic MS. in the Bodleian Library* (1821). Following this came A.G. Hoffmann, *Das Buch Henoch in vollständiger Übersetzung mit fortlaufendem Commentar, ausführlicher Einleitung und erläuternden Excursen* I-II (1833–38). It was not until the text-edition of August Dillmann, *Liber Henoch Aethiopice ad quinque codices editus* (1851), and *idem*, *Das Buch Henoch übersetzt und erklärt* (1853), that a scientific edition was published.

38. C.R. Laurence, *Primi Ezrae libri, qui apud Vulgatam appellatur quartus, versio aethiopica, nunc primum in medium prolata et latine anglique reddita* (1820).

39. A. Hilgenfeld, *Die jüdische Apokalyptik in ihrer geschichtlichen Entwickelung. Ein Beitrag zur Vorgeschichte des Christenthums nebst einem Anhange über das gnostische System des Basilides* (1857), pp. VIII-IX.

A presupposition for the emerging interest in apocalypticism was the assurance,

> that as sure as Christianity, in the infinity of its essence, supersedes the preceding development of Judaism, as a genuine historical phenomenon at any rate, it joins intimately the thought-world and the conditions of later Judaism.[40]

In the beginning, this did not mean much with regard to the understanding of the problem of the Son of man. The discussion concerning Son of man in the book of *Enoch* concentrated on the question whether Enoch's Son of man was really the result of a Jewish interpretation of Dan. 7.13 or if this figure was a product of Christian interpolation. The Berlin professor August Dillmann (1823–1894) advocated the first view. Dillmann evaluates the Messianic concept of the book of *Enoch*

> as a substantial further development of Jewish christology and by far the most exalted doctrine known to us of the Messiah, which pre-Christian Judaism has brought about. We also confess that it is a christology in which the Jewish point of view has not yet been transcended and where there are no marks of making the Messiah a divine being or an incarnation of God.[41]

That the concepts of Son of man and Kingdom of God should be Christian interpolations is rejected with the argument that exactly these concepts are presupposed as known by people in the speeches of Jesus.[42]

On the other hand, the Jewishness of Enoch's Son of man is contested by, for instance, Hilgenfeld, who sees only the development of the Messianic concept in the book of *Enoch* possible inside Christianity.[43] James Drummond, in *The Jewish Messiah*, from 1877, thinks the messianic passages in the *Similitudes* are 'probably of Christian origin; and that, therefore we cannot safely appeal to them as evidence of pre-Christian Jewish belief'.[44]

The importance of the book of *Enoch* was pre-eminently seen in its making Son of man a messianic title in applying it to an individual and thereby producing possible pre-Christian evidence for Son of man as a title.

A step in the direction of giving more importance to existing Jewish concepts and, correspondingly, diminishing the degree in which Jesus transformed them, letting his messianic self-consciousness be the deciding factor, is found in the important book, *Das Selbstbewusstsein Jesu im Lichte der*

40. Hilgenfeld, *Die jüdische Apokalyptik*, p. 1.

41. A. Dillmann, *Das Buch Henoch* (1853), p. XXIV.

42. Dillmann, *Das Buch Henoch*, p. XLIX.

43. Hilgenfeld, *Die jüdische Apokalyptik*, pp. 157-58. Hilgenfeld was certainly not alone in German scholarship in this. Above, in Chapter 7, for instance, we found a representative in B. Bauer.

44. J. Drummond, *The Jewish Messiah: A Critical History of the Messianic Idea among the Jews from the Rise of the Maccabees to the Closing of the Talmud* (1877), p. 73; cf., however, pp. 48-73.

messianischen Hoffnungen seiner Zeit from 1888[45] by Wilhelm Baldensperger (1856–1936), who, from 1890 to 1916, was professor in Giessen. Baldensperger suggests that the symbolic meaning of Dan. 7.13 is an exegetical fact, but then remarks that

> for the historian, here, the more important point is, not how the author himself understood Son of man, but how the schools and thus the contemporaries of Jesus have since interpreted it.[46]

Like Dillmann, Baldensperger takes the *Similitudes* in the book of *Enoch* as a testimony of the high level of Jewish messianism in the period immediately before the appearance of Jesus. In this book, in importance second only to the book of Daniel in this connection, 'the messianic expectations of Judaism had reached their highest intensity'.[47] The Messiah in the *Similitudes*, being until then only a larva, comes out as the Son of man, at the same time, coming near to God and participating in supramundane glory, having power as judge. Added to this was the concept of pre-existence:[48]

> First, when it is realized how this whole complex of ideas organically and suitably had to grow out of Judaism, one gains the conviction that the expression 'Son of man' which Jesus took over and which was combined with it, is, in fact, a pre-Christian Jewish-apocalyptic (jüdischapokalyptische) designation of the Messiah. Also, if it were not a current title for the common people, men familiar with Scripture surely were able to expound it.[49]

Baldensperger also finds it attested in Rabbinic sources.[50] This would be incredible if it had been an invention of Christians (ein Fündlein der Christen).

With regard to Jesus' use of Son of man, Baldensperger is confident that 'seldom is it possible to discern more clearly the continuity in the development of a concept than in the transition of the designation "Son of man" from Judaism to Christian documents'.[51] The double character of the

45. W. Baldensperger, *Das Selbstbewusstsein Jesu im Lichte der messianischen Hoffnungen seiner Zeit* (1888), quoted according to the 2nd edn, 1892. A 3rd edn, from 1903, contains only the description of the Jewish expectations: *Die messianisch-apokalyptischen Hoffnungen des Judenthums*.

46. Baldensperger, *Das Selbstbewusstsein Jesu*, p. 75 n. 1.

47. Baldensperger, *Das Selbstbewusstsein Jesu*, p. 84.

48. Baldensperger, *Das Selbstbewusstsein Jesu*, pp. 84-85; cf. the summarizing of the results pp. 91-92.

49. Baldensperger, *Das Selbstbewusstsein Jesu*, p. 90.

50. Baldensperger here refers to *Targum Psalm* 80.18, *Midrash Psalm* 2.7, sayings about the coming of the Messiah on the clouds of heaven, and polemical utterances, *y. Taan.* 65b and *4 Ezra* 13.2, 12, 25, where *ille homo* is seen as a deliberate attempt to escape the expression.

51. Baldensperger, *Das Selbstbewusstsein Jesu*, p. 171.

Synoptic Son of man, being both in accordance with Daniel's and Enoch's concepts and a more inwardly religious term, combined with debasement and suffering, contains no contradiction. When combined with the more triumphant features, it must be concluded that it is an integrated element of the messianic dignity. 'For Jesus, the contrast is deliberate and intentional, an open protest against the Jewish ideal of ruling.'[52] In the use of Son of man, we see the same realignment in the mouth of Jesus as with regard to the concept 'Kingdom of God', a realignment having its cause in his religious consciousness, in his consciousness of being God's Messiah. Baldensperger is convinced that the only safe point of departure for an understanding of the use of Jesus is the form which the Son of man concept had in pre-Christian Judaism.[53] Polemicizing against C. Holsten's grammatical-logical interpretation (cf. Chapter 7 above), he advocates the understanding of Daniel in Judaism contemporary with Jesus; that is, in the *Similitudes*. 'He who does not assume this, but lets Jesus approach Daniel's Son of man in a reflective and critical way, not only is building on sand, but causes the whole Messiahship of Jesus to be absorbed once again into an idea.'[54]

The consciousness of being the Son of man for Jesus also included the concept of a second coming in glory to execute judgment.[55] Jesus received it through a revelation at his baptism, but it came to be an open Messianic confession for the first time at Caesarea Philippi. Until then, there had been a period of preparation for the messianic task, characterized objectively through a growing emphasis on the spiritual signs of the kingdom and resignation, with regard to outward glory, subjectively through a struggle in his religious certainty of being the Messiah with the traditional, rational Messianic belief.[56] Here, Jesus reached the conviction that he should die in

52. Baldensperger, *Das Selbstbewusstsein Jesu*, p. 172.

53. Arguing like Volkmar (see above, Chapter 7), that the disappearance of the Son of man in Judaism was a reaction against the Christian use of this concept, is to assume too much Jewish indulgence towards Christians. Nevertheless, according to Baldensperger (*Das Selbstbewusstsein Jesu*, p. 181, n. 1), this is little if compared with the surprising confidence on behalf of the community which after cross and death ascribed to the Lord a dignity which he had never claimed: 'It seems almost as if the whole of the Christian spiritual movement (Geistesbewegung) has to be deduced, not from Jesus, but from an inexplicable enthusiasm for his person'.

54. Baldensperger, *Das Selbstbewusstsein Jesu*, p. 184. On p. 187, Baldensperger ridicules Holsten's interpretation of Dan. 7.13, seeing the movement from earth to heaven (see above): 'So wird in das durch und durch transcendent gedachte Gemälde Daniel's, in diese erhabene Himmelsscene, ein Erdgeborener, ein Schwacher, der ohnmächtig ist durch sich, eingeschmuggelt. Vielleicht dürfte es aber Manchen dünken, dass dieser Gast ohne hochzeitliches Gewand doch nicht dahin gehöre.'

55. Baldensperger, *Das Selbstbewusstsein Jesu*, p. 212.

56. Baldensperger, *Das Selbstbewusstsein Jesu*, pp. 253-54.

fulfilment of his messianic task. Accepting the thought of death, he avoided uncertainty with regard to the question of how and when God would fulfil his promises:

> One may imagine what a happy solution it was to the spiritual tension, what a reassurance had set in, how, as a consequence (and moreover because of the consent to the sacrificial death), the religious feeling of Jesus increased, and one may find it intelligible that he in cloudless, triumphant and full consciousness (Vollbewusstsein) about his position as Messiah, he grasped the title Son of man. It was the quintessence, at the same time the synthesis, of his present soul condition (Seelenzustandes), the point of conjunction where the elevated self-consciousness, death and parousia of the Messiah converged. One may notice that Daniel offered the same combination of ideas: not only in the title itself and the office of judgment, but also in the ruin of the anointed.[57]

Baldensperger's assertion that Jesus in his use of Son of man took over a concept is not a little counterbalanced by his strongly psychologizing reconstruction of the religious consciousness of Jesus. Thus, Baldensperger also concludes that, in the mouth of Jesus, it was in reality an innovation (Neuschöpfung). The impact of his interpretation can be seen in the reaction of A. Hilgenfeld. In a review, Hilgenfeld describes it as a parallel to the view of Bruno Bauer, namely, that Jewish Christology reached such a high level that nothing more was left of Christianity than 'that Messianism flourished on the stem of the Christian religion'.[58]

A consequent eschatological understanding of Jesus employing Son of man for the first time is present in the epoch-making investigation *Die Predigt Jesu vom Reiche Gottes* from 1892,[59] by Johannes Weiss (1863–1914), professor in Heidelberg, having also taught in Göttingen and Marburg. According to Weiss, the form in which Jesus visualized the picture of the Messiah was Daniel's and Enoch's Son of man; it was a religious and transcendental expectation, where nothing human, but a divine intervention alone, could determine the issue. The point of departure is the question of how it is that Jesus, when talking about the Son of man, always does so in the third person, speaking objectively about himself. The answer is that, in

57. Baldensperger, *Das Selbstbewusstsein Jesu*, p. 259. In n. 2, Baldensperger refers to Dan. 9.26.

58. A. Hilgenfeld, 'Jüdische Apokalyptik und Christenthum', *ZWTh* 31 (1888), pp. 488-98 (493). The review is of the 1st edn. In a review of the 2nd edn, 'Der Menschensohn-Messias', *ZWTh* 35 (1892), pp. 445-64 (462), Hilgenfeld ironically remarks that what happened was that the Jewish concept of the Son of man/Messiah disappeared as soon as the true Messiah had appeared as Son of man. 'Ein kurzes Stilleben innerhalb des Judenthums, vielleicht eher in der gelehrten Welt!'

59. The 2nd edn, 1900, is rewritten and strongly expanded. The 3rd edn of 1964 is a reprint af the 2nd edn, but '...erweitert um einen Anhang mit wichtigen Stücken aus der ersten Auflage von 1892', pp. 215-47.

the sayings about the Parousia, Son of man in most cases functions as an abbreviated reference to Daniel's prophecy, whereas those speaking of the present and suffering Son of man get their meaning from the contrast. Weiss continues:

> But in none of these cases is the predicate a plain and simple self-designation. This is not surprising, however. In fact, from the Jewish standpoint, such a usage would have been grotesque. For how can a man, a simple rabbi in Jesus' situation, regard himself as the Son of man? One could not imagine a greater contrast between this name and reality. Therefore Jesus' employment of this title seems to be meant more as a claim than as an actual self-designation.[60]

This is what is said in John 3.14 where, however, the interpretation which implies a death originates with the evangelist. The *tertium comparationis* with regard to the brazen serpent, then, is not death but exaltation. 'When Jesus used the title, therefore, it is to be understood only in the sense of a claim, the certain hope that this office would be conferred upon him.'[61] It bears another meaning, as when he called himself Son of David or a prophet. 'He *is* a prophet before the eyes of all. But he is to *become* the Son of man, whether at some point during his lifetime, or, as he became ever more convinced, after he had passed through death.'[62] There are also sayings where the expression is secondarily introduced by the evangelists' replacing a personal pronoun, as in Mt. 11.19; 16.13; Lk. 7.34, and sayings where the expression did not have any messianic meaning, but originally meant 'man', as in Mk 2.10, 28. All things considered, the facts are that

> he is not yet 'Son of man' so long as he has not received the full authority of messianic judgment. On the other hand, he has claim to this full authority, because he is 'Son of man'. We see, therefore, that even in his lifetime, Jesus has this office, but it is the office of the claimant (des Prätendenten), of the heir. The rule, the inheritance, already belongs to him, but he has not yet taken possession of it.[63]

In this way Weiss succeeds in keeping separate the historical person, Jesus, and the apocalyptic-eschatological concept of the Son of man. That certainly is a fruit of the emergence of a specific concept of the apocalyptic Son of man.

60. *Die Predigt Jesu vom Reiche Gottes* (1892), pp. 53-54 (= 1964, p. 237). Quoted according to English translation of the 1892 edition, *Jesus' Proclamation of the Kingdom of God* (1971, 2nd edn, 1999), p. 119.

61. Weiss, *Die Predigt Jesu vom Reiche Gottes* (1892), p. 54 (= 1964, p. 238). English translation, p. 120.

62. Weiss, *Die Predigt Jesu vom Reiche Gottes* (1892), p. 54 (= 1964, p. 238). English translation, p. 120.

63. Weiss, *Die Predigt Jesu vom Reiche Gottes* (1892), p. 59 (= 1964, p. 239); the reference is to Jn 5.26-27. English translation, pp. 126-27.

In contrast to the exposition of Weiss, the explanation of Wilhelm Bousset (1865–1920) in his programmatically titled book *Jesu Predigt in ihrem Gegensatz zum Judentum. Ein religionsgeschichtlicher Vergleich*, also published 1892, is seen as a counter-motion. Bousset, then teaching in Göttingen, but later professor in Giessen, claims that it is insufficient to understand Jesus exclusively from the background of contemporary Judaism (in German then labelled 'Spätjudentum', today a politically incorrect term). The study of contemporary Judaism can only be a beginning, the purpose of which must be to detect, not only common features, but contrasts, in order to see where Jesus was original in his thinking and preaching. Only through religio-historical comparisons aimed at detecting the important, the originally effective and real meaning and value of the single feature in the history of religions,

> can we hope that the little we know of the life of Jesus will coalesce into a lively unity, to grasp this little in its full meaning, to comprehend how the greatest turn that world history has experienced, is connected to the name Jesus.[64]

Bousset is in no doubt that Jesus used the expression and did so, connecting it to Dan. 7.13. But he opines that it was an understandable concept. To introduce the book of *Enoch* and *4 Ezra* is of no help, because Son of man there is the result of interpolations:

> The confidence in having found a reliable point of departure in the hypothesis of a ready christological ideal picture of the Messiah, already prevailing in Judaism, with regard to the interpretation of Son of man as used by Christ, is without foundation.[65]

Thus, the only available material is the Synoptic tradition, offering the impression that Jesus has used Son of man without any fixed messianic content. This unique use leads to the assumption

> that in the use of Son of man as self-designation we have in Jesus an original innovation of the messianic ideal—which has come about all the same in connection with Daniel—the content of which we have to investigate, not through some concepts common to the time, but through the suggestions given by Jesus himself.[66]

According to Bousset, Jesus has unquestionably employed Son of man as a title, claiming thereby the dignity of Daniel's Son of man, a position at the judgment and a coming on the clouds of heaven in the glory of the Father, which at the same time implied a protest against the more popular earthly

64. W. Bousset, *Jesu Predigt in ihrem Gegensatz zum Judentum* (1892), p. 9.
65. Bousset, *Jesu Predigt*, p. 109.
66. Bousset, *Jesu Predigt*, p. 110.

messianic expectations. There are also sayings about his special authority on earth, his debasement, poverty, his Passion and death. These sayings not only express something paradoxical about the heavenly Son of man; they say much more that his unique task, dignity and right are also included in this; that he has come to serve, not to rule, and that he will give his life as ransom for many. All of this confirms

> that Jesus employs the expression Son of man in a wholly individual, original way. He makes it something present, he uses the phrase in the present, designating a wholly transcendent figure, belonging to the world to come, as a designation and characterization of his peculiar position and dignity, his unique task in the world to come.[67]

Seeing Jesus' original self-consciousness in this way as the real common denominator of the different Son of man sayings brings Bousset into the company of those exegetes advocating a synthetic understanding. On the other hand, Jesus' Messiah-Son of man consciousness is, according to Bousset, best taken as a process lasting all of his life and suggesting a continuous readjustment of existing concepts.[68]

In spite of Bousset's countermotion, Son of man was regarded by a growing number of scholars from this time on as a title of an apocalyptic concept of Messiah, the connection to Dan. 7.13 being considered a fact. For many, the assumption of such an alternating Messianic expectation was confirmed by the attempt of the History of Religion School to combine it with an Oriental myth of a Primordial Man or Urmensch—an enterprise in which no other than Bousset himself became a leading figure.

67. Bousset, *Jesu Predigt*, p. 111.

68. Bousset, *Jesu Predigt*, pp. 124-27. A similar understanding with regard to Jesus' use of the image from Dan. 7.13 to express his future role in his Father's kingdom is found in F.J. Krop, *La pensée de Jésus sur le Royaume de Dieu d'après les évangiles synoptiques avec un appendice sur la question du 'Fils de l'Homme'* (1897), pp. 127-32; *idem*, 'Jezus, de "Zoon van David?"—De Zoon des menschen.—De Zoon van God', *Geloof en Vrijheid* 37 (1903), pp. 434-45.

9. The First Aramaic Stage in the Son of Man Research

Even before the critical distinction between the meaning of Son of man in the mouth of Jesus and in the Gospels was made, advocates were found of a more or less pronominal understanding of the expression based on Hebrew or Aramaic usage. This understanding was strongly accentuated through the monograph of Hans Lietzmann, *Der Menschensohn*, in 1896, which eventually initiated what a few years later was called by W. Baldensperger 'the Aramaic stage' (das aramäische Stadium).[1]

There had been a few forerunners of this view, having their antecedents in Rationalism. Thus C.B.E. Uloth, in an article from 1862,[2] tried on the basis of Mt. 16.13-16; 9.6 and Lk. 22.67-70 to show that Son of man cannot have been a messianic designation in the mouth of Jesus, because in Aramaic it is a simple expression for 'man'. Uloth refers to the usage in 2 Cor. 12.2 and Ezekiel. Rather than superiority, the word articulated inferiority and meekness (nederrigheid en zachtmoedigheid).[3]

The famous Göttingen orientalist, Paul de Lagarde (1827–1891), is mentioned in this context for his sporadic remarks that, for the Indo-Germans, 'human' is an honorary (ehrendes) adjective; but, for the Semites, it is a depreciatory (tadelndes) comment, so that Jesus was the first to ennoble ברנשׁ = υἱὸς τοῦ ἀνθρώπου.[4] This interpretation was, by the way, part of de Lagarde's problematic racial theory.

1. W. Baldensperger, 'Die neueste Forschung über den Menschensohn', *ThR* 3 (1900), pp. 201-10, 243-55 (203). Cf., to this chapter, the beginning of Excursus I, 'Die Versuche, den Ausdruck "Menschensohn" in den Evangelien vom hebräischen und aramäischen Sprachgebrauch her zu verstehen', in Müller, *Der Ausdruck 'Menschensohn' in den Evangelien*, pp. 219-32.

2. C.B.E. Uloth, 'De beteekenis van de uitdrukking "Zoon des menschen"', *Goodgeleerde Bijdragen* 36 (1862), pp. 467-87.

3. See especially Uloth, De beteekenis', pp. 474-75.

4. P. de Lagarde, *Gesammelte Abhandlungen* (1866), pp. 25-26 n. 1. Cf. *idem*, 'Die religion der zukunft', *Deutsche Schriften* 1 (1878), pp. 229-30, where Lagarde claims that

However, only with the successor of de Lagarde in Göttingen, Julius Wellhausen (1844–1918), did this understanding prevail. In the first edition of his classic *Israelitische und Jüdische Geschichte*, appearing in 1894, Wellhausen categorically states that

> because Jesus spoke Aramaic, he has not named himself ὁ υἱὸς τοῦ ἀνθρώπου, but barnascha. However, this means 'man' and nothing more, the Arameans having no other word for this conception. Moreover, in Daniel 7, it is not at all a name for Messiah and was never perceived to be so by the Jews. It only functions there as a comparison, in an absolute and not in an emphatic state. The pagan realms appear in bestial and, in contrast, the future Jewish in human form. The first Christians did not understand that Jesus simply named himself 'man'. They took him for the Messiah and made Barnascha a designation for the Messiah. They did not translate it with ὁ ἄνθρωπος, as they should have done, but totally wrongly with ὁ υἱὸς τοῦ ἀνθρώπου (not yet by Paul). The Syrians followed them as well as they could (breh d'nascha instead of barnascha).[5]

More to the point is the work of the Leiden professor Bernardus Dirks Eerdmans (1868–1948), in an article on the origin of the designation Son of man as messianic title in the Gospels (1894). Eerdmans claims that the Aramaic expression behind 'Son of man' simply meant 'man', and neither in the use of Jesus, nor in apocalypses, such as the Book of Daniel or the book of *Enoch* was it a messianic designation. On the contrary, Jesus employed it to stress that he was only a man, in a polemical address to the messianic expectations of his surroundings. He, thereby, caused it to develop into a messianic designation, because the direct translation of בר אנש, υἱὸς ἀνθρώπου, and בר אנשא, ὁ υἱὸς τοῦ ἀνθρώπου were obscure in Greek. Here, it was understood as a messianic title, with its root in Dan. 7.13.[6]

Jesus would not be the Messiah: 'er nennt sich einen menschen—denn das ist der sinn des schon frühe verkannten namens menschensohn'.

5. J. Wellhausen, *Israelitische und Jüdische Geschichte* (1894), p. 312 n. 1. Wellhausen goes on to say that when this misunderstanding is found in a part of the book of *Enoch*, it is an indication of Christian influence, because it is fully unthinkable that Jesus should have read this book and appropriated this misunderstanding. In the 2nd edn from 1895 (p. 346 n. 1), Wellhausen also refers to Rev. 1.13 and Mk 2.27-28. The curious reasoning with regard to the book of *Enoch* has disappeared and is now replaced by the remark that 'Son of man' in this book must be left out of consideration as long as it cannot be made clear whether Jesus knew or could know the relevant part of it.

6. B.D. Eerdmans, 'De oorsprong van de uitdrukking "Zoon des menschen" als Evangelische Messiastitel', *ThT* 28 (1894), pp. 153-76. In a Nachschrift (Response), pp. 177-87, W.C. van Manen (1842–1905) objects that we cannot get behind the existing written sources and that the expression in the Gospels is a messianic title which he finds confirmed in the book of *Enoch*. Eerdmans, 'De uitdrukking "Soon des menschen" en het boek "Henoch"', *ThT* 29 (1895), pp. 48-71, answers with a lengthy argument for a non-titular understanding of Son of man in the book of *Enoch*. As is seen from W.C. van

The American scholar Nathaniel Schmidt (1862–1939) reaches the conclusion that, although it is apparent that Son of man is a title in the Synoptic Gospels, the expression cannot have been a title in the Aramaic original. 'In the Galilean dialect בר נשׁא meant "man", "the man".'[7] The reason for its becoming a title can be seen in sayings such as Mt. 17.22 and 26.64. With regard to Jesus' use of the expression, Schmidt claims

> that it is his eternal glory that with unremitting zeal he sought to find what man should be; that, with deep intuition, he discerned what man is in the truest sense, and that, faithful unto death, he realized what man may be on the highest side of his nature.[8]

More radical consequences of detecting Aramaic roots are drawn by Arnold Meyer (1861–1934), then professor in Bonn, but ending up in Zürich. In his pioneering work, *Jesu Muttersprache*, from 1896, Meyer sets forth the alternatives with regard to uncovering Aramaic as the mother tongue of Jesus.[9] When Jesus says ברנשׁ in all Son of man sayings (with the exception of those where the evangelists themselves have replaced it by 'I'), including those with an affinity to Dan. 7.13 and the Passion predictions, he speaks of man generally. Or, instead of 'I', he says 'a man', precisely when he implies a contrast to God, other beings or animals.[10] Here, Meyer does not see a cryptic self-designation, not even where he paraphrases an 'I' with the more accentuated 'man'. For

> he thereby has, truly enough, not designated himself as a superhuman being (übermenschliches Wesen). He has also not said 'the man' and designated himself as 'only man' (blossen Menschen). Surely, he did not need to stress his humanity and would not have succeeded in doing so by using a common mode of speaking. It is not in the bar-nasch that we find a statement of Jesus about himself, but in what is said of this man; that is, that, in him, the sin-remitting and saving grace of God has appeared (Nicht in dem bar-nasch liegt eine Selbstaussage Jesu, sondern in dem, was von diesem Menschen ausgesagt wird, nämlich dass in ihm die sündenvergebende und heilsame Gnade Gottes erschienen ist).[11]

Manen, 'De "Zoon des menschen" bij Henoch', *ThT* 29 (1895), pp. 263-67, he did not convince his opponent.

7. N. Schmidt, 'Was בר נשׁא a Messianic Title?', *JBL* 15 (1896), pp. 36-53 (38).

8. Schmidt, 'Was בר נשׁא a Messianic Title?', p. 53. Mt. 26.64 is understood symbolically and as an authentic saying (p. 51).

9. The full title of Meyer's work is *Jesu Muttersprache. Das galiläische Aramäisch in seiner Bedeutung für die Erklärung der Reden Jesu und der Evangelien überhaupt*. For an evaluation of this book with regard to the study of the Aramaic background of the Gospels, see M. Casey, *Aramaic Sources of Mark's Gospel* (1998), pp. 12-15.

10. Meyer, *Jesu Muttersprache*, p. 93. Among the first are reckoned Mk 2.27, 28; Mt. 12.32; Mk 2.10par, and, among the last, Mt. 8.20par; 11.18, 19par.

11. Meyer, *Jesu Muttersprache*, p. 98.

The expression was not a problem for the contemporaries of Jesus, but it became so in the Greek Gospels. To the community from which these Gospels came, Son of man was a deeply significant (tiefbedeutsame) name for the Messiah whom they knew and who on this earth was only a poor Son of man. However, in Daniel 7 it was predicted that he should come on the clouds of heaven. 'Thus ὁ υἱὸς τοῦ ἀνθρώπου is wholly a regula fidei with regard to Christ, a preliminary stage to the Apostolicum which, in essentials, only added the miraculous birth.'[12] As a messianic name, it had its origin in Daniel 7.[13]

In the same year, 1896, appeared a dissertation, *Der Menschensohn. Ein Beitrag zur neutestamentlichen Theologie*, by the then twenty-one year-old Hans Lietzmann (1875–1942), later to become the successor of Adolf von Harnack in Berlin. This book marks the climax of the (first) Aramaic stage of the Son of man-Forschung, according to Albert Schweitzer, 'to the great surprise of the theological world' (zur großen Ueberraschung der theologischen Welt).[14] In it he tried to prove Son of man impossible as a messianic title in the mouth of Jesus by way of an analysis of its possible Aramaic linguistic background. First of all, Lietzmann finds a blunder in many interpretations that they have built on the basis of the Greek Gospel text and not on Aramaic, the language of Jesus. Secondly, he also deems insufficient the various attempts to include Aramaic, because their claim that the expression was a synonym for 'man' is much too imprecise, its meaning varying from 'man' to 'anybody'. It is also insufficient because the non-canonical Christian literature has not been taken into account.

Lietzmann starts his investigation of Son of man in Aramaic by claiming that there is only one Aramaic term which might serve as a potential background to the Greek expression; considering the Galilean dialect that Jesus would have spoken, this term was בר נשא: 'Thus when the ὁ υἱὸς τοῦ ἀνθρώπου of the Gospels renders an authentic self-designation of Jesus, it

12. Meyer, *Jesu Muttersprache*, p. 99.

13. Meyer, in an appendix—Anhang B. Geschichte der Deutung: Menschensohn = 'Mensch' oder 'Ich' (*Jesu Muttersprache*, pp. 140-49)—offers a short history of the non-titular interpretation of the expression. Later, in *Die moderne Forschung über die Geschichte des Urchristentums* (1898), p. 75, he faces the question as to what stems from later apocalypticism and what comes from Jesus himself, because in some sayings it can be shown that Son of man has replaced an original 'I'. In other sayings, the coming of the Son of man is identical with the coming of the Kingdom (compare Mt. 16.28 with Mk 9.1 and Lk. 9.27), seemingly because the sign of the coming Kingdom is the Son of man (Mt. 24.30). In *Das 'Leben nach dem Evangelium Jesu'* (1905), p. 4, Meyer also speaks of Son of man as an eschatological sign, which disappears when it has fulfilled its mission. Only Christians identify it with Jesus.

14. Schweitzer, *Geschichte der Leben-Jesu-Forschung*, p. 266.

has thereby placed בר נשׁא in the mouth of the Lord'.[15] That בר נשׁא has been the only common expression for 'man' in that dialect is seen from the *Evangeliarum hierosolytanum*, where the Greek translation, now understood as a title, is rendered with the monstrous ברהדברנשׁא, an expression not witnessed before, just as ὁ υἱὸς τοῦ ἀνθρώπου did not exist before it became a translation of בר נשׁא. Where the expression and its equivalents are rather seldom in the singular in the Judean Aramaic represented in the targums of Onkelos and Jonathan, there,

> through the usus tyrannus, בר נשׁא became in Galilea the most employed and, at the same time, the least emphasized word for 'man', in such a way that, in the majority of cases, it does not say more than a pronomen indefinitum: it is the most colourless and undetermined designation for the human individual (es ist die farbloseste und unbestimmteste Bezeichnung des menschlichen Individuums).[16]

Whereas, in Greek, Ἄνθρωπος could be a name for a god, because of a development in the philosophical tradition, the opposite was the case in Aramaic where 'man', through generalization, became equivalent to 'any-body' (jemand). It cannot, therefore, in any language designate a specific man. In Dan. 7.13, it is not a title, but a symbol for Israel. Nor is it a title in *4 Ezra* or in the book of *Enoch*. On the other hand, it is clearly a messianic title for Jesus in the Gospels, where, without question, it could be rendered with Messiah. However, it is not (with Acts 7.56 as the only exception) found outside the Gospels, nor does it turn up in the Apostolic Fathers. All this leads Lietzmann to the somewhat surprising conclusion that the oldest traces of information of the formula are found in Marcion's gospel. Because his theological understanding has probably been formed in the period 90–115, there must have existed a gospel which used the expression, perhaps a gospel in use in Marcion's hometown, Sinope. This would mean that this gospel came into existence between the activity of Paul and the year 90.[17] Where Son of man in Marcion's gospel seems to have retained its messianic content, we find the earliest traces of its interpretation in gnostic systems. This points to Christianity in Asia Minor and Alexandria as the places where ὁ υἱὸς τοῦ ἀνθρώπου was first conceived as a messianic title. According to Lietzmann, it is also a messianic title in Ignatius, Justin and Hegesippus, but, since Irenaeus, it was taken as designating the human nature of the Saviour.

On the one hand, it is obvious that the Gospel sayings about the Parousia, glory and suffering are to be understood in their actual shape as sayings of Jesus about his messianic dignity. On the other hand, it is equally clear

15. Lietzmann, *Der Menschensohn*, p. 30.
16. Lietzmann, *Der Menschensohn*, p. 38.
17. See Lietzmann, *Der Menschensohn*, pp. 61-62; cf. p. 95.

> that בר נשא could be neither a self-designation nor a messianic title. Accordingly, all the sayings where ὁ υἱὸς τοῦ ἀνθρώπου can only be explained as a circumlocution for 'Jesus the Messiah'—and this is the vast majority—the Greek formula does not originate in the analogous Aramaic word. In its transmitted form it is not from the mouth of Jesus. Jesus never attributed to himself the title Son of man, because it never existed in Aramaic and, for linguistic reasons, it never could have existed.[18]

In a number of sayings (Lk. 6.22; Mt. 16.13; Mk 10.45 par.; Mt. 16.28; Mk 14.21; Lk. 22.29), it seems likely according to Lietzmann that the messianic interpretation of Son of man is secondary. In some other sayings the original reference probably had not been to Jesus, but to man in general. For this reason, it should have been rendered ἄνθρωπος (Mt. 12.32 par.; Mk 2.10 par.; Mk 2.27-28 par.; Mt. 8.20 par.; Mt. 11.19 par.). The failing knowledge of the formula in the earliest Christian literature, in the sayings of the Synoptic Gospels containing it, shows the existence of a pre-canonical evangelical tradition that had not yet used the formula as a self-designation of Jesus. This raises the question of how it arose in the canonical text and from where, as it was not from the mouth of the Lord. The answer to the question, of how a circumlocution for the singular ἄνθρωπος became a designation for the Messiah, is that

> υἱὸς ἀνθρώπου in Greek—in quite another way than בר נש in Aramaic—had a totally foreign and unusual ring. Thus, a priori, there is the linguistic possibility that it could be a special designation for one singular person. When the Messiah in just one case had been designated υἱὸς ἀνθρώπου, then, in Greek, the step was not a difficult one to call him ὁ υἱὸς τοῦ ἀνθρώπου and to give him this designation as a title precisely because it was so unusual. An example of this is found in Daniel 7.13.[19]

In this way, Dan. 7.13 is the creative saying (die schöpferische Stelle) and, for this reason, the Christian apocalypses are the earliest places where this title had been employed as a designation for the Lord (for instance Mk 13.5-27; Mt. 24.4-31; Lk. 21.8-27). Because these sayings were transmitted as sayings of the Lord, it shifted from being a designation for Jesus Son of man to become a self-designation of the Lord. At the same time, it became a Christian title for the Messiah, necessarily combined with the specifically Christian element in the concept of the Messiah: suffering. The bridge can be seen in Lk. 17.24, 25, where suffering becomes the necessary step on the way to the glorious second coming. From here, the expression also penetrated into sayings where בר נש in the Aramaic text invited a change to a saying about the Messiah. Thus, Lietzmann concludes his investigation by arguing that in the formula ὁ υἱὸς τοῦ ἀνθρώπου we have a terminus

18. Lietzmann, *Der Menschensohn*, p. 85.
19. Lietzmann, *Der Menschensohn*, pp. 91-92.

technicus of Hellenistic theology, which had perhaps been created previously in Jewish circles, but was willingly taken over by the primitive Greek community, and marked as a designation of Jesus.[20]

With Lietzmann, it became nearly a fact that the Greek ὁ υἱὸς τοῦ ἀνθρώπου was the result of an over-literal rendering of the Aramaic בר נש. Only in its Greek form did it become an unusual expression. That it also became a title equivalent to Messiah is an inference rather than a necessary consequence. In the Gospels, the expression was reserved for Jesus in sayings where the emphasis is placed on the person speaking.

Of course the thesis of Lietzmann was met with both applause and opposition. In the third edition of his *Israelitische und Jüdische Geschichte* from 1897, Wellhausen alters his explanation to state that 'the messianic interpretation of the expression Son of man first originates with the Greek translators of the gospel'.[21] On the other hand, Hilgenfeld is not convinced. He points to the rendering in *Peshitta* and *Syrus Sinaiticus* of Mt. 17.9 and Mk 9.9 as evidence that Jerome must have translated filius hominis in *Liber de viris illustribus* 2 from ברה דאנשא, since he would have otherwise chosen aliquis.[22] Paul Wilhelm Schmiedel (1851–1935) thinks, with regard to the quotation from Psalm 8 in 1 Cor. 15.25, that it is exactly the expression Son of man which occasioned its use by Paul. But that Paul related Son of man to Jesus, while Jesus did not use it himself, would only be explicable if there had existed a tradition for interpreting Psalm 8 in relationship to Messiah on the basis of Dan. 7.13. This tradition then would also have been known to Jesus. For this reason, it must be concluded that Jesus must already have named himself Son of man in a messianic way, with the definite article pointing precisely to the figure predicted in Daniel.[23]

20. Lietzmann, *Der Menschensohn*, p. 95.

21. J. Wellhausen, *Israelitische und Jüdische Geschichte* (3rd edn, 1897), p. 381 n. 1, where some of the argumentation of Lietzmann is repeated. Wellhausen also says that the transition from messianic people to a personal Messiah was easy, as seen not least in Ps. 80.18 where Israel is named 'man': 'Wichtig ist es, dass Paulus den Ausdruck noch nicht gebraucht.'

22. A. Hilgenfeld, 'Hans Lietzmann. Der Menschensohn. Ein Beitrag zur der Neutestamentlichen Theologie, 1896', *Berliner Philologische Wochenschrift* 17 (1897), cols. 1520-25 (1521). Referring to Heb. 2.6, Hilgenfeld also claims that בר אנשא or ברה דאנשא have been understandable references to Dan. 7.13. See, further, *idem*, 'Johannes und Jesus nach J. Wellhausen's Darstellung', *ZWTh* 41 (1898), pp. 481-501 (498).

23. P.W. Schmiedel, 'Der Name "Menschensohn" und das Messiasbewusstsein Jesu', *PrM* 2 (1898), pp. 252-57. In 'Bezeichnet Jesus den Menschen als solchen durch "Menschensohn"? Zugleich ein Beitrag zur Verständigung über einige Grundsätze der Evangelienkritik und der Erforschung des Lebens Jesu', *PrM* 2 (1898), pp. 291-308 (p. 303), Schmiedel leaves Mk 2.28 as the only saying where the Aramaic use of Son of man seems obvious. L.A. Muirhead, 'The Name "Son of Man" and the Messianic Consciousness of Jesus', *ET* 11 (1899–1900), pp. 62-65, warmly supports Schmiedel in his

In an article from 1898, Lietzmann answers some of his critics, especially Schmiedel and Hilgenfeld. He rejects both the assumption that the author of Hebrews and Paul should have known the title and the retrograde translation of Hilgenfeld, arguing that nobody then would have sensed the reference to Daniel.[24]

If Lietzmann had stirred the waters by making the Aramaic usage the point of departure for the understanding of 'Son of man' and trying to render it impossible as a messianic self-designation in the mouth of Jesus, the Old Testament scholar Gustaf Dalman (1855–1941), at the time in Leipzig, but ending his professional career in Greifswald, attempted by the same token to pour oil on these troubled waters. This he did in his classic work *Die Worte Jesu* I, from 1898.[25] From Biblical Hebrew and Aramaic, Mishnaic Hebrew, *Targum Onkelos*, the Samaritan Pentateuch targum, the Prophetic targum and Aramaic inscriptions, Dalman thus deduces that only Jewish-Galilean had, like Christian-Palestinian, בר אנש for 'man'. Thus the material accessible to him led to the conclusion that the older Jewish-Palestinian Aramaic had אנש for 'man', only occasionally designating a plurality of men בני אנשא. The singular form בר אנש was unfit for use and only employed in imitating the Hebrew of biblical texts, where בן אדם belonged to poetical language, but not in normal use.[26] This also seems to have been the case for Galileans at the time of Jesus and the use of it is therefore a novelty. When determined, the determination had to be placed with אנש, just as בן אדם was determined בן האדם. But neither בר אנשא nor בן האדם could be translated

rejection of the understanding of Wellhausen that the expression has not been a designation for the Messiah among the Jews. Cf. also Muirhead, 'Schmiedel on the Name "Son of Man"', *ET* 11 (1899–1900), p. 124.

24. H. Lietzmann, 'Zur Menschensohnfrage', *Theologische Arbeiten aus dem rheinischen wissenschaftlichen Prediger-Verein* NF 2 (1898), pp. 1-14. On the question of whether it is not a horrible act of violence (ein furchtbarer Gewaltstreich) to obliterate Son of man totally from the Gospel tradition, the answer decidedly is no, if the name itself bears witness to its spuriousness (p. 13). Hilgenfeld, 'Noch ein Wort über den Menschensohn', *ZWTh* 42 (1899), pp. 149-51, is a rejoinder to Lietzmann. Later, first in *Der Weltheiland* (1909), pp. 29-31, Lietzmann is not so sure any more, and in his *Geschichte der alten Kirche 1. Die Anfänge* (1932), his conclusion is that, although the philological problems attaching to this word had not yet been solved, the trustworthiness of the tradition and the messianic meaning of the word cannot be doubted. On the other hand, it is also obvious that it was not a common messianic title. Early Christianity no longer understood the word and has avoided the use of it, 'and it has been an enigma until this day' (und es ist ein Rätsel geblieben bis auf den heutigen Tag).

25. The full title of Dalman's work is *Die Worte Jesu mit Berücksichtigung des nachkanonischen jüdischen Schrifttums und der aramäischen Sprache I. Einleitung und wichtige Begriffe* (1898, 2nd edn, 1930 [= reprint 1965]). For the treatment of Son of man, see pp. 191-219.

26. Dalman, *Die Worte Jesu*, p. 194.

'the man', but only 'Son of man', if the peculiarity of the expression was not to be lost.[27] In Greek, ἄνθρωπος is neither a collective concept, like אנשׁ and אדם, nor does υἱός designate the individual who bears the traits of the collective. For this reason, the translators chose to render the meaning which the determined בר אנשׁ evoked in Aramaic, with the strongest possible determination of the combined expression. In this way, they avoided a misunderstanding, since only 'man' as such was meant, suggesting the possibility that Jesus could have used it as a self-designation. However, it is only too likely that, from the beginning, Hellenists did not understand the expression in a Semitic manner, but in a Greek one, as if Jesus should somehow have designated his humanity.[28] Thus, Dalman is not denying the proposed understanding of בר נשׁ, but only that Jesus would have used it in this indeterminate way.

In Dan. 7.13, Son of man is described as one who himself cannot take dominion of the world, but can become lord of the world if God makes him so. In *1 Enoch* 37–71, Son of man is clearly not a title, just as *4 Ezra* does not suggest anything other than dependence on Dan. 7.13. Thus, it was not a common Jewish name for the Messiah. To the evangelists behind the Synoptic Gospels, Son of man was, as in the Early Church, not a designation of glory, but 'a diligent wrapping of Messiahship behind a name which stressed the humanity of its bearer' (eine geflissentliche Verhüllung der Messianität hinter einem Namen, welcher die Menschheit seines Trägers betont), as it would appear to a Hellenist.[29]

It is more difficult to determine the understanding of the phrase for Jesus himself. The fact that it was not a common designation for 'man' among Palestinian Jews, but belonged to poetical and prophetical language meant that a Jewish audience would primarily seek its meaning in Holy Scripture, where only Dan. 7.13 had the same Aramaic expression. Because of Jesus' obvious reference to this saying in his apocalyptic speech and in his confession before the Sanhedrin, there is no doubt that he took it from this saying. 'When he named himself בר אנשׁא, he only said that he was the one in whom this Danielic vision of the "one like unto a man" came true.'[30] It is not certain that Jesus employed it before the episode at Caesarea Philippi, but, thereafter, he used it in the presence of the disciples as a name taken from Dan. 7.13, designating the one assigned for world dominion. The reason for choosing exactly this prophecy is, according to Dalman, that nowhere else is it said more clearly that the necessary change of all things on earth is to be expected from God alone:

27. Dalman, *Die Worte Jesu*, p. 196.
28. Dalman, *Die Worte Jesu*, pp. 196-97.
29. Dalman, *Die Worte Jesu*, pp. 209-10.
30. Dalman, *Die Worte Jesu*, p. 211.

> When Jesus attaches the first announcement of his violent death to the Messianic confession of Peter, it was to make clear that the accession to dominion was still far remote, and that Jesus' Messiahship did not include, but excluded, self-help. The 'one like unto a man' in Daniel 7.13 is also one who alone is going to attain dominion.[31]

The conclusion is that

> Jesus designated himself בר אנשא not as the 'debased' (Niedrigen), but as, according to its nature, the weak human being (Menschenkind), whom God is going to make the Lord of the world. It is very probable that Jesus found the Son of man from Daniel also in the Psalm (8.5-6).[32]

That, by going back to Aramaic usage, Dalman tries, in this way, to reintroduce all which seemingly was lost, is confirmed by the six consequences he draws. These consequences are: (1) that the way Jesus uses the designation is special to him and not parallel to what is found in *1 Enoch* and *4 Ezra*; (2) that abasement and Passion sayings are combined with בר אנשא just as well as sayings about exaltation (Hoheitsaussagen); (3) that the meaning which the word had for those who did not catch the connection with Daniel 7 was not false because they would, at any rate, be aware that Jesus was not a usurper, depending on his own might; (4) that it was possible that the disciples were satisfied from the beginning with this meaning and did not demand any further elucidation from Jesus; (5) that the understanding which the Hellenistic Synoptics and the Early Church reached with regard to the expression, although false on a closer look, was not false, insofar as they saw here a confession of Jesus of his humanity; (6) that the Church nevertheless acted correctly when it did not use the designation on its own behalf—because after 'the human being' (das Menschenkind) had taken his place on the throne of God, he really is no longer so (only a man), but ruler of heaven and earth, 'the Lord' (as Paul in the Thessalonian letters and the *Teaching of the Apostles*, respectively, in their apocalyptic sayings rightly name the one coming with the clouds of heaven).[33]

If Dalman had tried to weaken the impact of the Aramaic solution through neutralization, Wellhausen, in a treatise on the Son of man appearing in the sixth volume of his *Skizzen und Vorarbeiten* from 1899, wanted to draw the full consequence of the insights of Lietzmann. In the Preface, he rejects Dalman's assertion that the word did not exist in Judean Aramaic. The

31. Dalman, *Die Worte Jesu*, p. 217.

32. Dalman, *Die Worte Jesu*, p. 218.

33. Dalman, *Die Worte Jesu*, p. 218. In an appendix, 'Nachträge und Berichtigungen', to the 2nd edn (1930, pp. 383-97), Dalman maintains this understanding in a discussion with later contributions. D. Eaton, 'Professor Dalman on "The Son of Man"', *ET* 10 (1898–1899), pp. 438-43, is an uncritical summary of the understanding of Dalman.

contrary is shown in Dan. 7.13, the *Jerusalem Evangeliar* and parts of the old Jewish (spätjüdischen) literature, which bears witness to special Galilean Aramaic. When Dalman denies this, it is only because the texts do not say what he wants them to say.[34] Wellhausen adheres to Lietzmann's act of violence as the only way out, but he has serious objections against the use of the linguistic material. However that might be, the whole investigation is unnecessary. 'Barnascha exists in all Aramaic dialects and means no more and no less than ὁ ἄνθρωπος in Greek or the man (der Mensch) in German.'[35] Because of this, Jesus has not at all been able to express the difference

> which the gospels made between ὁ ἄνθρωπος and υἱὸς τοῦ ἀνθρώπου. This difference is not authentic, but only established by later interpreters and redactors of the gospel tradition. In the mouth of Jesus, ὁ υἱὸς τοῦ ἀνθρώπου must have meant the same as ὁ ἄνθρωπος. It is of particular importance to stick to this. Son of man is nothing other than the man. It is a seemingly literal but, in reality, misleading translation. In the gospels, it is restricted to one certain application. There, Son of man is only used as a name for Jesus, which he ascribes to himself.

According to Wellhausen, it has not been a title; which is also clear from Dan. 7.13; *4 Ezra* 13 and *1 Enoch* 37–71. On the other hand, Wellhausen cannot agree with A. Meyer's claim that Son of man would have been a totally empty circumlocution for 'I'. In the mouth of Jesus it must have been emphatic. And Wellhausen does not find it credible that Jesus should have designated himself in this way as the fully human being (Vollmenschen) who, on the one hand, was not foreign to anything human, and, on the other, fulfilled the idea of humanity. 'He was no Greek philosopher, nor a modern humanist, and he did not speak to philosophers or humanists.'[36] For this reason the tradition itself must be viewed suspiciously:

> Because when the only possibility left by philological exegesis leads to totally unacceptable results, it follows that the basis presupposed by exegesis is false, namely the trustworthiness of the tradition. If the name barnascha does not suggest any meaning in the mouth of Jesus, he cannot have used it. Much more, this alleged self-designation either rests on false interpretation or has been placed arbitrarily.[37]

An investigation of the use in the Gospels, according to Wellhausen, shows that Son of man is an equivalent to Messiah. 'Throughout, the predicates stand with nearly the same content and in such a necessary connection

34. J. Wellhausen, 'Des Menschen Sohn', *Skizzen und Vorarbeiten* 6 (1899), pp. 187-215. Foreword, p. VI.
35. Wellhausen, 'Des Menschen Sohn', p. 196; cf., however, pp. 194-96.
36. Wellhausen, 'Des Menschen Sohn', pp. 200-201.
37. Wellhausen, 'Des Menschen Sohn', p. 201.

with the subject that they stand or fall with them.'[38] Wellhausen finds the origin of this usage in the introduction of Dan. 7.13 in connection with the concept of a second coming. In the oldest stratum of the Gospel tradition, there was a certain reserve against depicting Jesus as identifying himself with this coming Son of man. Jesus only quotes the words of Daniel, the meaning of the word being a secret and, therefore, in need of an authentic Christian interpretation to be identified with a certain person. From there came the custom of substituting Son of man, in sayings about the second coming, for 'I' as subject. Thereby, the expression lost its secret meaning in the mouth of Jesus and has become a simple equivalent for the first person singular. As such, it was later used in non-eschatological sayings, mostly, however, with a messianic content. That it does not originate with Jesus himself, is, according to Wellhausen, confirmed from the *argumentum e silentio* that it is not found in Paul.

Surprisingly, Wellhausen ends his treatise by posing the question: Did the bipartition of not only the word, but also concept, originate with the Greeks? He answers:

> I rather believe that in many sayings barnascha, already in Aramaic, has been employed in the specific (that is, messianic) meaning. The Greeks, then, have dotted the yod and introduced a special word. It is possible, then, that ὁ υἱὸς τοῦ ἀνθρώπου originally replaced barnascha everywhere, but later was only left where it should mean Messiah; while otherwise it was replaced by ἄνθρωπος. One could be inclined to detect a trace of the earlier usus promiscuus in Mark 3.27.[39]

This means that the decisive obstacle for Jesus' not having employed the expression as a messianic title has in reality been removed. Wellhausen, however, admits that it is still not possible to arrive at answers to such subtle questions with regard to the redaction, and perhaps it never will be. But 'the homo unius libri, still not extinct among professionals who know of nothing but the New Testament and the more recent specialist literature, would certainly not move us forward'.[40]

38. Wellhausen, 'Des Menschen Sohn', p. 206.

39. Wellhausen, 'Des Menschen Sohn', pp. 214-15. Wellhausen here thinks of the use of 'nobody' (οὐδείς).

40. Wellhausen, 'Des Menschen Sohn', p. 215. Wellhausen from this point on maintains this understanding; see his *Israelitische und Jüdische Geschichte* (4th edn, 1901) p. 387 n. 1 (in the 5th edn of 1904, p. 387 n. 1, he only refers to the treatment in *Skizzen und Vorarbeiten*, and, in addition, in his *Das Evangelium Marci* [1903], pp. 68-69 [ad Mk 8.27]). In the 6th edn of 1907, as in the 7th edn of 1914, there is no mention at all of Son of man. In *Das Evangelium Marci*, pp. 66-69, and in *Einleitung in die drei ersten Evangelien* (1905), pp. 39-40, Wellhausen briefly summarizes his understanding. In the 2nd edn of of *Das Evangelium Marci* (1909), pp. 19-20 (ad Mk 2.10), he only

In a review article on the Son of man debate from 1900, Baldensperger tried to draw a picture of what he named 'the Aramaic stage' (das aramäische Stadium) and which he understood as a threat to his own apocalyptic interpretation: 'Thus the, until then, more exegetical-critical and historical-psychological Son of man problem became a philological, linguistic question'.[41] To Baldensperger, this approach loses its credibility because of the mutual disagreement between its advocates. The apocalyptic material is not easily displaced. Moreover, the results of a capacity for linguistics like Dalman's 'ought to cause an early end to the Aramaic stage of our problem'.[42] Baldensperger summarizes that the debate leaves one with the impression that the respective result depends on the overall view of the person and work of Jesus, if one takes seriously his Messiahship as a historical reality, as the centre of his internal life, or simply sees it as a mere accident. 'Weakening interpretations of the Son of man will gain willing hearers, where emphasis is put on rational motives just so the rapid blossoming of the "Aramaic" solution is greatly indebted to the rationalistic leaven still effective in the theological world.'[43]

The last major contribution in the first round of the debate about the Aramaic background of Jesus' use of the expression Son of man was a monograph from 1901, *Der Menschensohn. Jesu Selbstbezeichnung mit besonderer Berücksichtigung des aramäischen Sprachgebrauches für 'Mensch'* (*Son of Man: Jesus' Self-designation with Special Regard to the Aramaic Usage of 'Man'*) by Paul Fiebig (1876–1949). In this work, Fiebig praises Lietzmann for raising the problem, but blames him for not adequately distinguishing between plural and singular forms. This was done by Dalman, though Wellhausen pointed out important weaknesses in Dalman's exposition. This alone explains the reason for a new examination.[44]

First, Fiebig states that ὁ υἱὸς τοῦ ἀνθρώπου is the determinate form of υἱὸς ἀνθρώπου, meaning 'human being' (Menschenkind) while the determined form should be rendered 'the human being' (das Menschenkind) not 'the Son of man' (der Sohn des Menschen). Speaking Aramaic, Jesus is best

refers to it, the full explanation being now included in the 1911 2nd edn of *Einleitung in die drei ersten Evangelien*, pp. 123-30. Here Wellhausen also launches a severe attack on Dalman for being tendentious. He continues (p. 125): 'Manche Neutestamentliche Forscher haben die Entdeckung Dalmans mit Freuden begrüßt, aus dem selben Motiv, welches ihn darauf geführt hat; für die Blößen, die er sich gibt, haben sie kein Auge. Sie suchen sich eine Autorität aus, die ihnen zusagt; oder sie konstatieren mit Vergnügen, daß die Gelehrten nicht einig seien, und halten es inzwischen, wie es sie lüstet.'

41. W. Baldensperger, 'Die neueste Forschung über den Menschensohn', *ThR* 3 (1900), pp. 201-10, 243-55 (204).

42. Baldensperger, 'Die neueste Forschung', p. 251.

43. Baldensperger, 'Die neueste Forschung', pp. 254-55.

44. Fiebig, *Der Menschensohn*, pp. IV-V.

imagined to have employed the corresponding determined Aramaic בר אנשא.[45] An extensive investigation leads Fiebig to the conclusion that it has been up to the translator whether this expression should be rendered determined or undetermined. And it is not only בר אנשא which is ambiguous. The same pertains to בר נשא which can mean both 'a man' (ein Mensch), 'anybody' (jemand) and even 'the man' (der Mensch). Assuming a correct translation, the linguistic investigation suggests that ὁ υἱὸς τοῦ ἀνθρώπου early on is already = בר אנש(א) = 'the man' (der Mensch), not equal to 'the human being' (das Menschenkind) as maintained by Dalman.

True enough, the Greek expression is an exact, but only a formally exact rendering of Aramaic, which to the Greek reader introduces a distinction between ὁ ἄνθρωπος and ὁ υἱὸς τοῦ ἀνθρώπου not necessarily present in the Aramaic. In Aramaic, the expression with בר meant exactly the same as without. At the time of Jesus, accordingly, there were two expressions for 'the, respectively a, man': אנשא and בר אנשא. Assuming an exact translation, ὁ υἱὸς τοῦ ἀνθρώπου in the original texts would imply the form with בר.[46] As regards אנש, אנשא, בר (א)נש and בר נשא, none is unambiguous and all have a common range of meaning. According to Fiebig, this has to be emphasized because Lietzmann, Dalman and Wellhausen all neglect to stress this ambiguity.[47]

Examining the New Testament material, Fiebig claims the genuineness of the sayings, assumed by Wellhausen, Lietzmann and Meyer to have Son of man because of a mistranslation. The question as to why it has come to 'this painfully literal and un-Greek translation (sc. ὁ υἱὸς τοῦ ἀνθρώπου) of the Aramaic', leads to the suggestion that the translator wanted to establish a connection with Dan. 7.13. This is confirmed by an investigation of the bulk of the Gospel Son of man sayings: 'ὁ υἱὸς τοῦ ἀνθρώπου is equal to the man from Dan. 7.13 equal to the Messiah'.[48] However, that Dan. 7.13 is the point of departure for Jesus' use of the concept does not imply a limiting of his thoughts. Furthermore, it is his point of departure only insofar as he excluded all the particularistic features in Daniel's concept. That 'the man' (der Mensch) was really a designation of the Messiah, is confirmed, according to Fiebig, especially in *4 Ezra* and *1 Enoch*. New Testament evidence gives the solution to the seeming contradiction that the expression at one and the same time is used as a known designation for Messiah and in a satisfactory way

45. Fiebig, *Der Menschensohn*, pp. 2-3.

46. Fiebig, *Der Menschensohn*, pp. 55-56. For the investigation of the linguistic material, see pp. 8-53.

47. Fiebig, *Der Menschensohn*, p. 60. On pp. 56-60, Fiebig compares his results with those of his predecessors.

48. Fiebig, *Der Menschensohn*, p. 75.

can be understood in the meaning 'man'. The contradiction can only be resolved in this way: as often as Jesus used the expression, it must have been possible to believe that one understood it if one had also misunderstood it.[49] Jesus may even have exploited the ambiguity inherent in the Aramaic expression:

> You could understand more or less: 'the man in a collective sense' or 'a man' or 'somebody' while Jesus himself did not mean that at all. Jesus also had to keep all thought of an eschatological character out of the way, or the linguistic ambiguity would not be effective.[50]

This expression made it possible for Jesus to speak objectively of Messiah as if he did not mean to refer to himself, even though he had. The originality in Jesus' use is not in the employment of Daniel's 'man' as a messianic title, nor in the enrichment of the Danielic image. He is original in his connecting Passion sayings, which use Daniel's 'man', both in removing all particularistic traits of this image and in applying it to himself. Reasons for his choice could be precisely its ambiguity, eventually hiding the fact that he spoke of himself as Messiah, avoiding the particularism inherent in, for instance, Son of David, enlarging Daniel's 'man' in apocalypticism with more and more divine traits and a place ever more near to God, corresponding to his messianic consciousness. In any event, Daniel's image was dear to Jesus because 'the figure of Jesus in it is again brought near to us in a human way (menschlich)'.[51]

49. Fiebig, *Der Menschensohn*, p. 100.

50. Fiebig, *Der Menschensohn*, p. 100.

51. Fiebig, *Der Menschensohn*, p. 118. In an appendix (pp. 121-27) Fiebig analyses the Johannine and other New Testament Son of man sayings only to find his conclusions confirmed. The reason why Paul did not make use of the expression is that it was 'a specific Jewish designation of Messiah' (p. 127). J. Croskery ('Recent Discussions on the Meaning of the Title "Son of Man"', *ET* 13 [1901–1902], pp. 351-55) is a presentation partly of Baldensperger's review article from 1900, and partly Fiebig's treatise; the results of which he welcomes. Later Fiebig returns to the theme in 'Der "Menschensohn" als Geheimname', *PrM* 6 (1902), pp. 431-37, defending himself against W. Staerk, 'Jesu Stellung zum jüdischen Messiasbegriff', *PrM* 6 (1902), pp. 297-309, who finds it a mistake to attribute to Jesus a messianic consciousness. It is everywhere a product of the thinking of the community. 'Nun wohl, dann höre man auch endlich einmal auf, von dem Messiastum Jesu zu sprechen und ziehe ihn nicht länger in die Atmosphäre etnischer Religiosität herab... Jesus nicht der Messias, sondern der Zeiten Wendepunkt, weil der Erlöser der Welt durch Befreiung der Religion aus den Banden des Materialismus, gleichviel ob gesetzlicher, kultischer oder chauvinistischer Art—in hoc signo vincemus!' (p. 309). In 'Der Menschensohn und Wellhausen', *PrM* 8 (1904), pp. 12-26, Fiebig once again repeats his conclusions after the appearance of Wellhausen, *Das Evangelium Marci* (1903).

With the conclusions of Dalman and not the least of Fiebig,[52] the main source of understanding the Gospel Son of man sayings was again found in the messianic consciousness of Jesus. Lietzmann's effort to classify any Son of man christology as community theology could now be dismissed, for instance, with the retort that 'It may be reckoned among the ghosts which appear for an hour on the stage of learning, attracting attention and admiration, but having no permanent connection with reality'.[53] Actually, Lietzmann's insight was threatened in several ways, one being the admission of the possibility that the Aramaic expression could function quite early as a messianic designation. P.W. Schmiedel, for instance, is not hesitant in exploiting Wellhausen's surprising remark in this regard, claiming that it removes the whole basis of the assumption that Jesus could not have employed the expression as a title because, in Aramaic, it only meant 'man' and nothing more.[54] The adherents of the thesis that it could not have been the messianic title in the mouth of Jesus were relatively few and marginal, some of the more well-known exceptions being Nathaniel Schmidt[55] and,

52. Cf. Ch. Weist, *Wer ist dieser Menschensohn?* (1974), p. 190: 'Dieses philologische Resultat FIEBIGS ist nicht mehr überboten und bis heute anerkannt worden'. This is said without knowledge of the second Aramaic stage, initiated in 1967.

53. J. Stalker, 'Son of Man, The', *The International Standard Bible Encyclopaedia* (1915, 2nd edn, 1925), V, cols. 2828-30 (2828). Cf. M. Kähler's similar remark ('Christologie, Schriftlehre', *RE* 4 [3rd edn, 1898], pp. 4-16 [p. 8]): 'Es sei gestattet, hier die Vermutung und Hoffnung auszusprechen, dass das Rezept sich bald verbraucht erweisen werde, das geschichtliche Christentum aus lauter litterarischen Missverständnissen zu erklären; eine "Buchreligion" ist es eben nicht'.

54. P.W. Schmiedel, 'Die neuesten Auffassungen des Namens "Menschensohn"', *PrM* 5 (1901), pp. 333-51 (345).

55. In 'Son of Man', in *Encyclopedia Biblica* (1903, 2nd edn, 1907), IV, cols. 4705-40, containing a scrutinizing examination of the whole linguistic material and the other problems; in *The Prophet of Nazareth* (1905), pp. 94-134, his earlier thesis that Jesus should have used Son of man symbolically of the Kingdom of God (see above) is now abandoned (G. Meloni, 'Filius Hominis', *Saggi di Filologia Semitica* [1913], pp. 315-19, offers an objection to the conclusion of the encyclopedia article); third, in 'Recent Study of the Term "Son of Man"', *JBL* 45 (1926), pp. 326-49. Others are: R. Rhees, 'A "Striking Monotony" in the Synoptic Gospels', *JBL* 17 (1898), pp. 87-102; P. Haupt, 'The Son of Man', *The Monist* 29 (1919), pp. 125-33; *idem*, 'Hidalgo and Filius Hominis', *JBL* 40 (1921), pp. 167-70, and *idem*, 'The Son of Man = hic homo = ego', *JBL* 40 (1921), p. 183; R. Boehmer, 'Zum Verständnis des "Menschensohnes"', *Die Studierstube* 3 (1905), pp. 411-18; Emil G. Hirsch, 'Son of Man', in *Jewish Encyclopaedia*, IX (1905), pp. 461-63; Primo Vannutelli, *Il figlio dell'Uomo. Studi sugli Evangeli* (1923). (The latter was critically reviewed in W.M. Macgregor, 'Il figlio dell'Uomo, studio sugli Evangeli. By P. Vannutelli. The Messiah and the Son of Man. By A.S. Peake', *Exp* 9.2 [1924], pp. 229-31 [230]; cf. Vannutelli's rejoinder, '"Il Figlio dell'Uomo" [Critica ad una critica]', *La Scuola Cattolica* [1925], pp. 456-60.)

later, George Dupont.[56] A typical reception of the outcome of the first Aramaic stage is also represented by the Manchester professor Thomas Walter Manson (1893–1958) who suggested that:

> It may now be regarded as extremely probable, if not absolutely certain, that ὁ υἱὸς τοῦ ἀνθρώπου in the Gospels is nothing but a slavish rendering of an original Aramaic *bar nasha* (בר נשא or בר אנשא) and that the idiomatic translation of *bar nasha* would not have been ὁ υἱὸς τοῦ ἀνθρώπου but simply ἄνθρωπος, 'the man'.
>
> A second fact, which may help to solve our problem, is that the word 'man' was taken up into the esoteric vocabulary of the apocalyptic literature and used, not in its literal sense but as a symbol for something else,

as is the case in Dan. 7.13.[57] But then, in connection with Lk. 7.34 (= Mt. 11.19), Manson argues further that:

> In Galilean vernacular the expression *hahû' gabra* (ההוא גברא) 'that man', 'a certain man' is used as a substitute for 'I' in certain cases. The idiomatic rendering of the expression would be ἐγώ; a literal translation would be ὁ ἄνθρωπος ἐκεῖνος (οὗτος) or ἄνθρωπος τις. Now the same effect could be produced by the use of the indeterminate form *bar nash* instead of *bar nasha*. *Bar nash* means simply 'a man': and in the context before us it could be used as a substitute for 'I' in the same way that the *hahû' gabra* is used in Rabbinic writings of Palestinian origin. If this be granted, it is possible to see how ὁ υἱὸς τοῦ ἀνθρώπου has got into our Greek text. It is a misunderstanding of *bar nash* which could have been more correctly translated by ἄνθρωπος τις, 'a certain man' (i.e. Jesus himself).[58]

In this way, Manson tries to escape the effect of the Aramaic approach, making the Aramaic expression in its definite form (if at all possible) a comprehensible symbol and having the indefinite form used solely as a circumlocution for the person speaking, equivalent to ההוא גברא.[59]

56. See below, in the next chapter.

57. T.W. Manson, *The Teaching of Jesus* (1931, 2nd edn, 1935 = 8th edn, 1959), p. 212. For Manson's interpretation, see also below Chapter 14.

58. Manson, *The Teaching of Jesus*, pp. 217-18. Cf. K.A. Fox, 'The Son of Man. Criticism of Dr. Manson's Exposition in "The Teaching of Jesus"', *ET* 57 (1945–46), p. 328, and Manson's rejoinder, 'The Son of Man. Some Observations on Mr. Fox's Criticism in the September Number', *ET* 58 (1946–47), p. 83.

59. This understanding was somehow anticipated by the Basel professor F. Schulthess (1868–1922), in his 'Zur Sprache der Evangelien', *ZNW* 21 (1922), pp. 216-36, 241-58: Appendix C, 'Menschensohn' (pp. 247-48). Thus Schulthess thinks Jesus' use of Son of man reflects an emphatic Aramaic *hahû barnasha* or *hahû gabra* replacing an 'I'. That was, according to Schulthess, at the time of Jesus, a way of speaking among Rabbis, and Jesus employed it because, when he spoke he always kept God in view. In spite of the emphasis in the mouth of Jesus, it is a 'Bescheidenheitsformel'. The double determined Greek expression is not a translation of the expression used by Jesus but deliberate exegesis, it is a messianic interpretation of the Danielic saying.

10. The Eschatological Interpretation

The Aramaic stage did not cause a decisive and lasting rupture in the understanding of the Son of man as used by Jesus, and the discussion soon returned to well-known tracks. The importance of Lietzmann's attempt with regard to an examination of the Gospel use as a product of community theology, which could have been supported by the insights of the Breslau professor, William Wrede (1859–1906), in his classic *Das Messiasgeheimnis in den Evangelien* from 1901, was, however, mostly neglected. Neither did Wrede commit himself to a more specific understanding of the expression and restricted himself solely to the mention of the difficulties which the Life-of-Jesus-*Forschung* had with Mk 2.10, 28:

> Nowhere is there even a note telling us that people were brought up sharply by this title and did not understand it, or that Jesus chose it with a definite purpose in mind. From the Gospel, as distinct from any theory about it, the reader gets the impression only that Jesus at the beginning described himself as the Son of man, and that he does the same later—and more frequently—in the presence of his disciples—but also in the presence of his opponents.[1]

A non-titular understanding of the expression in the Gospels was next to non-existent, the question being primarily if—when and how far—Gospel use reflected the understanding of Jesus himself. Many interpreters continued

1. W. Wrede, *Das Messiasgeheimnis in den Evangelien. Zugleich ein Beitrag zum Verständnis des Markusevangeliums* (1901, 3rd edn, 1963), p. 18. Translation according to the English version, *The Messianic Secret* (1971), p. 20. Wrede returns to the problem in a short note, 'Zum Thema "Menschensohn"', *ZNW* 5 (1904), pp. 359-60, where he says that the most decisive reason for Jesus not having used the self-designation is the impossibility of comprehending that he should have spoken of himself as he does in the Gospels. It would only be understandable and thinkable if it could be shown that the Aramaeans had the habit of saying 'the man will, knows, does' instead of 'I will, know, do'. It is not correct to translate with 'this man' or 'this woman' because, with the Son of man the demonstrative is lacking, which alone could include the reference to the first person. In that case, the translators probably could render it with 'I' in Aramaic.

to look for the key to the self-understanding of Jesus in this expression. At the same time, the thought of a special preformed concept of Son of man gained ground because comparative religious studies could establish how speculations attached to a human figure, the original man, flourished in some pagan religions, particularly Gnosticism. This also had its influence in partly neutralizing the attempt to see the origin of the Gospel expression in an Aramaic manner of speaking. To this we will return in the next chapter.

Here, we follow the thread from Chapter 8, considering the role of the expression Son of man in a consequent eschatological interpretation of Jesus' self-understanding. The founder of this 'school', Johannes Weiss, develops his views in the second edition of his *Die Predigt Jesu vom Reiche Gottes* from 1900.[2] According to Weiss, the attempt of Lietzmann and Wellhausen to show that Son of man was not a messianic designation at the time of Jesus is superfluous and only serves to veil the problem. It is only a supposition that, at the time of Jesus, the appearance of the Messiah was often supposed to follow Dan. 7.13. *4 Ezra* and *1 Enoch* only refer to Daniel's saying, Son of man not really being a 'name', but a 'type' of Messiah.[3] Weiss gladly agrees with Wellhausen, claiming that these texts refer exclusively to Daniel and adds that exactly the same is the case in the Gospels: 'Jesus in this case was able to express exactly what we mean through the status emphaticus ברנשא'. The evangelists were familiar with it insofar as they distinguished sayings where they thought to do their best in translating the determinate 'man' with ὁ υἱὸς τοῦ ἀνθρώπου and sayings where they simply wrote ἄνθρωπος (Mt. 10.36; 11.8; 12.35), even if in many places they were mistaken (as for instance in Mk 2.10, 28).[4] In reality, the problem is not linguistic, but psychological. It is deemed unthinkable that Jesus should have identified himself directly with the heavenly appearance because of the enormous gap between himself and the wonderful glory of this image:

> Because he had the certainty of being the elect of his Father, and because, on the other hand, it was certain that the Messiah was going to appear in such glory, it was self-evident that he was not already, for the time being, the Messiah, the Son of man in the meaning of Daniel, but that he only could become so… The real problem is not at all the choice of this remarkable expression, but the indirect form and way in which Jesus speaks of this entity.[5]

2. J. Weiss, *Die Predigt Jesu vom Reiche Gottes* (2nd edn, 1900), esp. pp. 159-75, and 'Excurs V. Die nichtmessianischen Aussagen vom Menschensohn', pp. 201-10.

3. Weiss, *Die Predigt Jesu vom Reiche Gottes*, p. 162 n. 1.

4. Weiss, *Die Predigt Jesu vom Reiche Gottes*, p. 164 (both quotations).

5. Weiss, *Die Predigt Jesu vom Reiche Gottes*, pp. 165-66. Weiss here refers especially to Mt. 10.32-33par.; Mk 8.38par. (p. 167: 'Die Art, wie hier das Ich und der Menschensohn scharf zusammenrücken, zeigt um so deutlicher, dass Jesus ausdrücklich vermeidet, sich mit dem erhöhten Messias zu identificieren').

According to Weiss, only the Son of man sayings which relate to Parousia and Passion bear the stamp of authenticity. He also speaks of a certain shyness on behalf of Jesus:

> The shyness of Jesus to speak directly and exposed about these things is fully understandable. It was motivated by the concern that he could not himself say that he already was the Messiah in the present and in the full sense of the word. The possibility to speak of this in a circumlocutional and instructive way must have been a help to him.[6]

This eschatological interpretation was intensified by Albert Schweitzer (1875–1965), then in Strasbourg. In *Das Messianitäts- und Leidensgeheimnis Jesu. Eine Skizze des Lebens Jesu* from 1901, Schweitzer states: 'The coming of the "Son of Man" signifies—*the dawning of the Kingdom of God with power*'.[7] Matthew 10.23 was central in this understanding. 'His eschatology is the apocalyptic of the Book of Daniel, since the Kingdom is to be brought about by the Son of Man when he appears on the clouds of heaven (Mk 8.38, 9.1).'[8] Jesus' attitude is characterized by a 'now and then (jetzt und dann)'. '*If the kingdom was future, so also was the Messiah.*'[9] For this reason Jesus does not appear as the Messiah—it is his secret that he is the Messiah. Only after the episode at Caesarea Philippi, only after the 'yes' of Jesus, could the disciples and High Priest know of the identity of the Son of man. Before the people, Jesus only hinted at the Son of man as being in solidarity with him who preaches him. For this reason, Schweitzer regards only the future Son of man sayings as genuine:

> 'Son of Man', accordingly, is the adequate expression of his messiahship, so long as he, in this earthly æon as Jesus of Nazareth, has occasion to refer to his future dignity... The problem about the Son of Man is herewith elucidated. It was not an expression which Jesus commonly used to describe himself, but a solemn title which he adopted when in great moments of his life he spoke about himself to the initiated as the future Messiah, while before others he spoke of the Son of Man as a personality distinct from himself.[10]

Early Christianity, however, experienced an intervening time, for which Jesus had not taken account and, in which, he was looked upon as Messiah

6. Weiss, *Die Predigt Jesu vom Reiche Gottes*, p. 175.

7. Schweitzer, *Das Messianitäts- und Leidensgeheimnis*, p. 16. The translation is from the English translation, *The Mystery of the Kingdom of God: The Secret of Jesus' Messiahship and Passion* (1914, paperback edn, 1964), p. 88.

8. Schweitzer, *Das Messianitäts- und Leidensgeheimnis*, p. 28 (English translation, pp. 114-15).

9. Schweitzer, *Das Messianitäts- und Leidensgeheimnis*, p. 38 (English translation, p. 135).

10. Schweitzer, *Das Messianitäts- und Leidensgeheimnis*, p. 67 (English translation, pp. 192-93).

in heaven, sitting at the right hand of God. He was already the Messiah, but he did not become Son of Man before coming with the clouds of heaven. This also answers the problem regarding why the expression disappeared in the Early Church. It is due to the fact that

> Son of Man was the messianic expression for a clearly defined episode of the messianic drama... Jesus would have expressed himself inaccurately had he said, I am the Messiah—for that he was to be only when he appeared in the glory of the Son of Man.
>
> The primitive Church would have expressed itself inaccurately had it said, Jesus is the Son of Man—for after the Resurrection he was the Messiah at the right hand of God, whose coming as the Son of Man the Church expected.[11]

In *Geschichte der Leben-Jesu-Forschung* (1913; 2nd edn of *Von Reimarus zu Wrede*, 1906),[12] besides a repetition of his consequent eschatological interpretation of Jesus' use of the expression, Schweitzer also reviewed the Aramaic stage in the Son of Man debate.[13] According to Schweitzer, the conclusion of the philological discussion is that Jesus' messianic use of the expression cannot be denied on linguistic grounds:

> Thus, by a long detour, criticism has come back to Johannes Weiss. His eschatological solution to the Son of man question—the elements of which are to be found in Strauss' first Life of Jesus—is the only possible one...
>
> Broadly speaking, therefore, the Son of Man problem is both historically solvable and has been solved. The authentic passages *are* those in which the expression is used in that apocalyptic sense which goes back to Daniel.[14]

11. Schweitzer, *Das Messianitäts- und Leidensgeheimnis*, p. 71 (English translation, pp. 200-201).

12. In the meantime Schweitzer also discussed the specific use of the expression Son of man in the Gospel of John; namely, in the posthumously published inaugural lecture at the Theological Faculty in Strassbourg, 1 March 1902, 'Die Bedeutung der Logosspekulation für die historische Darstellung des Lebens Jesu im 4. Evangelium mit besonderer Berücksichtigung des Ausdrucks "Menschensohn"', in *idem*, *Straßburger Vorlesungen* (ed. Erich Grässer and Johann Zürcher, 1998), pp. 27-41 (36-40). Thus Schweitzer (pp. 36-37) describes the Johannine use this way: 'Es handelt sich für ihn nicht um die zwecklose Verwendung einer überlieferten Bezeichnung Jesu, als einer Ausdrucksweise neben anderen, sondern um die bewußte Umbiegung der Vorstellung des Kommens des Menschensohns zum Gericht dahin, daß die irdische historische Erscheinung Jesu dieses Kommen des Menschensohns zum Gericht schon in sich beschließt und darstellt'.

13. Schweitzer, *Geschichte der Leben-Jesu-Forschung*, pp. 266-75 and 390-443, respectively (English translation, *The Quest of the Historical Jesus* [2000], pp. 226-33 and 315-54).

14. Schweitzer, *Geschichte der Leben-Jesu-Forschung*, p. 272 (English translation, p. 230). In n. 1 (English translation, p. 507 n. 19) Schweitzer complains that Weiss, in the 2nd edition of his *Die Predigt Jesu vom Reiche Gottes*, has been seduced by the

'The stumbling block of tradition has become the cornerstone of the tradition (Der Stein des kritischen Anstoßes ist zum Eckstein der Ueberlieferung geworden).'[15] Schweitzer also draws a picture of the messianic expectations at the time of Jesus and of how he thinks of Jesus as the one who probably created his own synthesis of the prophetic and the Danielic-apocalyptic concept, a synthesis later established by the authors of *4 Ezra* and *2 Baruch*.[16] Thus, like *1 Enoch*, Jesus identifies the anointed with the Son of Man, although giving the latter aspect prominence:

> At any event the work is that of a brilliant and sovereign spirit (genial und souverän gestaltenden Geistes)...
>
> This is so profound and grandiose in its way that in the end it can be understood only as the result of a deliberate shaping of a superior and thoughtful spirit...
>
> Thus Jesus is the only one among the scribes of the time who dared to occupy himself with the central problem in which all the difficulties of the eschatological notion of the time came together. He recognized it and solved it in the only possible way. In so doing he proved himself to posterity to be the greatest of the rabbis.[17]

In this manner Schweitzer dared to allow his historical Jesus to possess a highly apocalyptic Son of man consciousness.[18] In this regard, Jesus failed. But that does not make Schweitzer abandon the Jesus of history. The attempt to modernize Jesus has failed, but the historical figure stands out in his heroic greatness. Thus Schweitzer describes his aim in the book of 1901: '*to depict the figure of Jesus in its overwhelming heroic greatness and to impress it upon the modern age and upon modern theology*'.[19] In 1913, he further develops his view, declaring that:

Urapostels of modern theology (Lietzmann, Wellhausen and Dalman) to explain the speaking of the Son of Man in the third person as 'humble reverence' (demütige Scheu).

15. Schweitzer, *Geschichte der Leben-Jesu-Forschung*, p. 275 (English translation, p. 232).

16. Schweitzer, *Geschichte der Leben-Jesu-Forschung*, pp. 276-316 (English translation, 233-59).

17. Schweitzer, *Geschichte der Leben-Jesu-Forschung*, pp. 313, 314, 316 (English translation, pp. 257 and 259).

18. In a little book from 1913, *Die psychiatrische Beurteilung Jesu* (2nd impression 1933), his medical dissertation, Schweitzer argues that this does not mean that Jesus was mentally insane. Schweitzer returns to the eschatological interpretation in the posthumously edited *Reich Gottes und Christentum* (the first part of which appeared in 1967, the full manuscript was published by Ulrich Luz, Ulrich Neuenschwander and Johann Zürcher in 1995), pp. 127-49.

19. Schweitzer, *Die Messianitäts- und Leidensgeheimnis*, p. 109 (English translation, p. 274). Cf. his *Geschichte der Leben-Jesu-Forschung*, p. 638 (English translation, p. 484).

> Jesus' action consists in the way in which his natural and profound moral consciousness (Sittlichkeit) adopts late-Jewish (spätjüdischen) eschatology, thus expressing in the ideas of that time the hope and desire (Wollen) for an ethical consummation of all things (Weltvollendung).[20]

While some interpreters follow Schweitzer in seeing Son of man in this way reflecting the Danielic figure in its transcendent and future aspect, viewing it as part of the self-consciousness of Jesus himself, others resumed the old position initiated by Strauss, namely, that Jesus spoke of the Son of man as other than himself.

Thus Wilhelm Bousset changed his mind, and in his *Jesus* in the series Religionsgeschichtliche Volksbücher from 1904, he saw Jesus' use of Son of man in intimate connection with his realization of his upcoming death and Passion. This opens readers to 'the final understanding of the concept of the Son of man, or better, the Son of man presentiments (Menschensohn-Ahnungen) of Jesus'.[21] As the expression now stands in the Gospels, it conveys a community theology (Gemeindetheologie).[22]

Adolf von Harnack (1851–1930), in his *Lehrbuch der Dogmengeschichte*, gave up the view that Son of man in the mouth of Jesus simply was a title for Messiah.[23] He claimed that Jesus, after the confession of Peter at Cesarea Philippi, employed it 'with growing clarity, so as to reveal himself as the Son of Man (= the Son of God = the Messiah) and, thereby, as the one who will come again and erect the Kingdom of heaven in the future. In his earthly life, he is only Messias designatus'.[24]

20. Schweitzer, *Geschichte der Leben-Jesu-Forschung*, p. 635 (English translation, p. 482).

21. W. Bousset, *Jesus* (2nd edn, 1907), pp. 83-89 (p. 88). Cf. *idem*, *Die jüdische Apokalyptik, ihre religionsgeschichtliche Herkunft und ihre Bedeutung für das Neue Testament* (1903), p. 58. This connection between Passion and Parousia sayings as originating in Jesus himself is also claimed by Wilhelm Heitmüller (1869–1926, then teaching in Marburg, but ending up in Göttingen), *Jesus* (1913), pp. 79-86; cf. *idem*, 'II Menschensohn im NT', *RGG*, IV (1913), cols. 297-300, and the Basel professor Paul Wernle (1872–1939), who, in his *Jesus* (1916), pp. 351-55, emphasizes that the 'man' coming from heaven in Daniel is another, although it will be Jesus.

22. The expression in the mouth of Jesus relating to his future position is also advocated by the Danish scholar P.O. Ryberg-Hansen (1860–1911), in *Evangelierne som Kilder til Jesu Liv. Hovedtræk i den nyere Forskning* (*The Gospels as Sources to the Life of Jesus: Main Features in Recent Research*) (1904), pp. 128-32, and by Hermann Freiherr von Soden (1852–1914) in the booklet *Die wichtigsten Fragen im Leben Jesu* (1904), pp. 101-103.

23. Thus, in his famous *Das Wesen des Christentums* (1900), pp. 82-83, Harnack mentions the kingly and the prophetic aspect but not the future one.

24. A. von Harnack, *Lehrbuch der Dogmengeschichte* (4th edn, 1909), I, pp. 73-74.

In this new context of a consequent eschatology, a number of interpreters re-activated the old idea of D.F. Strauss that Jesus preached a coming Son of man without identifying himself with this messianic figure.[25] The Amsterdam professor Daniel Völter (1855–1942), in *Das messianische Bewusstsein Jesu* (1907), took the position that Jesus, like the author of the Revelation (in 14.14-16), spoke of the Son of man as a heavenly figure who would appear at the end of days.[26]

Two Danes adhered to a related interpretation. The first, the Copenhagen professor of classical philology, Anders Bjørn Drachmann (1860–1935), saw Jesus' preaching of Son of man as a heavenly Messiah, which, for him, was part and parcel to his concept of the coming kingdom.[27] The second Dane, an otherwise nearly unknown private scholar, Johannes Schousboe (1879–1964), thought that Jesus looked upon himself as the heir of John the Baptist; that is, as the prophet of the Son of man. Schousboe also finds clues of what he calls 'the Son of Man religion' where the Son of man figured with the God Yahweh in a way which implied a departure from monotheism. Because of this, Jesus first took the place of the Son of man in the history of the community relatively late. This was not possible as long as the memory of Jesus and his view of himself was alive.[28]

Benjamin Wisner Bacon (1860–1932), professor in Yale, argued from the presupposition 'that the messianism of Jesus was pre-eminently ethical and religious'.[29] Besides the sayings of Jesus about the future Son of man as someone other than himself, the occurrence of the expression in the Gospels also rests on sayings of Jesus employing it 'in the ordinary Old Testament sense of an every-day mortal in contrast to God'.[30]

25. Cf. Excursus H: 'Die Hypothese, Jesus habe den "Menschensohn" als eschatologische Gestalt verkündigt, ohne sich mit dieser zu identifizieren', in Müller, *Der Ausdruck 'Menschensohn' in den Evangelien*, pp. 163-67 (164-65).

26. D. Völter, *Das messianische Bewusstsein Jesu*, p. 9. It is a rejoinder to the book of H.J. Holtzmann with the same title of the same year (see below). Völter here sees the source of the messianic consciousness of Jesus in Isa. 53. With regard to the changed position of Völter later on, see below.

27. Anders Bjørn Drachmann, 'Messiasproblemet', *Tilskueren* (1908), quoted according to reprint in *idem*, *Udvalgte Afhandlinger* (1911), pp. 108-23 (117).

28. J. Schousboe, *Om den christne Eschatologis Forhold til den jødiske* (*On the Relation of the Christian Eschatology to the Jewish*) (1915), *passim*.

29. B.W. Bacon, 'Jesus as Son of Man', *HThR* 3 (1910), pp. 325-40 (325).

30. Bacon, 'Jesus as Son of Man', p. 337. Later, in 'The "Son of Man" in the Usage of Jesus', *JBL* 41 (1922), pp. 143-82, Bacon changes his view, claiming that after the episode at Caesarea Philippi, Jesus identified himself with the coming Son of man: 'On the testimony of Mark we may well believe that Jesus himself, in these days of preparation for the great tragedy spoke among his intimates those reassuring words which pointed to the vision of Daniel and which in due time were to be recalled as proof that all

A similar position is taken by the Jena professor Heinrich Weinel (1874–1936), who leaves out the Passion predictions as *vaticinia ex eventu*, deeming the future Son of man sayings as solely authentic. When the later tradents have Jesus speak of himself as the Son of man, they were probably not mistaken. 'He not only called himself so, but spoke of the Son of man as something exalted and distant, because it was to him the object of his most intimate experience and belief, of what, in advance of the others, he experienced as his call and the secret of his essence.'[31] Thus, Weinel did not accept the genuineness of the sayings containing Son of man as a circumlocution, because he cannot imagine how two such different usages could be employed by the same person. 'He could speak only of the coming Son of man. Yet later Christianity also has this way of speaking; it has retained it, but surely not invented it.'

This view is also represented by Kirsopp Lake (1872–1946), professor at Harvard, in his contribution to *The Beginnings of Christianity*,[32] Rudolf Bultmann (1884–1976), in his classic of form criticism, *Geschichte der synoptischen Tradition*[33] (I shall return to Bultmann in Chapters 12 and 14), the Cambridge New Testament professor Francis Crawford Burkitt (1864–1935)[34] and the Strasbourg professor Jean Héring (1890–1966).[35] The last two mentioned also suggest influence from a primeval Man conception, transcending a purely Jewish sphere (see Chapter 12).

The last to be mentioned is Martin Werner (1887–1964), professor in Bern and profoundly inspired by Albert Schweitzer. In his monumental *Die Entstehung des christlichen Dogma*, from 1941, Werner considers Son of man as belonging to the higher angelic world. As seen, for example, from Mk 8.38, Jesus did not directly identify himself with the Son of man, but expressed solidarity. 'The real meaning of this relationship of solidarity is obviously that Jesus, according to his own perception, as an earthly and historical man, is certainly not yet the heavenly Messiah-Son of man, but one who, in the future, somehow will be exalted to the nature and dignity of

his earlier impersonal references to the coming of the Son of Man were mysterious "self-designations"' (p. 182).

31. H. Weinel, *Biblische Theologie des Neuen Testaments. Die Religion Jesu und des Urchristentums* (1911, 3rd edn, 1921), pp. 208-19 (218).

32. K. Lake, *The Beginnings of Christianity: Part I. The Acts of the Apostles*, vol. I (1920), pp. 368-84 (378).

33. R. Bultmann, *Geschichte der synoptischen Tradition* (1921), pp. 73-74, 92 (2nd edn, 1931 = 6th edn, 1964), pp. 127, 130, 163.

34. F.C. Burkitt, *Jesus Christ: An Historical Outline* (1932), pp. 34-36, and p. 38 quoting Schweitzer.

35. J. Héring, *Le royaume de Dieu et sa venue. Étude sur éspérance de Jésus et le l'apotre Paul* (1937, 2nd edn, 1959), pp. 111-12.

this Son of man.'[36] The precondition for this thought was already present in a branch of late-Jewish apocalyptic, with which Jesus was very familiar—the Enochian. Thus, the transformation of Enoch to the Son of man (*1 En.* 71) played a decisive role.[37]

36. M. Werner, *Die Entstehung des christlichen Dogma* (1941), p. 312.

37. Werner, *Die Entstehung des christlichen Dogma*, pp. 313-14. Werner was met with strong opposition with regard to his angelic christology by Wilhelm Michaelis, in *Zur Engelchristologie im Urchristentum. Abbau der Konstruktion Martin Werners* (1942).

11. Mostly Backwater

The positions described in the previous chapters had but a moderate following after their first blossoming. The period from the end of the nineteenth century to the Second World War witnessed a series of contributions to the Son of man problem, which repeated old positions, particularly by combining an Old Testament background with the creative transforming mind of Jesus, letting his self-consciousness be the real source of the content of the expression. These interpretations reflect a theology built on an assumed historical reconstruction of the mind of Jesus. More radical, even fantastic, solutions were promoted within this framework. What is new in this period is that critical scholarship is no longer restricted to continental exegesis. English and American voices are now increasingly making themselves heard.[1]

1. *In his Use of Son of Man Jesus is Alluding to and Transforming One or More Old Testament Sayings*

In a relatively long list of contributions to the Son of man debate in this period, the interpretive varieties of the use of the term in the gospels point more or less to the Danielic Son of man. Variation lies in the degree to which interpreters think Jesus transformed the concept. Not a few find confirmation for a messianic understanding in the gospels in *1 Enoch* (and *4 Ezra*) and also see influence from other Old Testament sayings or ideas.[2]

1. Cf. the remark in W. Baird, *History of New Testament Research* (2003), II, p. 55: 'Since the days of the deists, nothing startling had taken place in British biblical studies. NT research in the main had been conservative resistant to the Enlightenment methods'. The words are found in an introduction to the 'Cambridge Three'. With a few remarkable exceptions, critical exegesis first influenced British and American scholarship in the twentieth century.

2. Some of the interpreters mentioned in this chapter also note some influence from foreign concepts of Primeval Man as proposed by the History of Religions School, but without making it a principal thing. Scholars more strongly influenced by this approach will be discussed in the following chapter. But of course it is debatable where a particular scholar might be placed.

Among those seeing Daniel 7 as the primary source of Jesus' use of Son of man,[3] the 'veteran' Heinrich Julius Holtzmann deserves closer examination.

In *Das messianische Bewußtsein Jesu. Ein Beitrag zur Leben-Jesu-Forschung* (1907), Holtzmann returns to the theme Son of man,[4] stressing that Jesus on the one hand is presented as Son of Man where he preaches and furthers the Kingdom of God through forgiving sins, healing, teaching and suffering, and, where he, on the other hand, coming on the clouds, is going to complete the kingdom.[5] Besides these two groups of Son of man

3. Other representatives enumerated chronologically only are the Königsberg professor A. Klöpper (1828–1905), 'Der Sohn des Menschen in den synoptischen Evangelien. Ein Beitrag zur Deutung dieser Selbstbezeichnung Jesu', *ZWTh* 42 (1899), pp. 161-86; V. Rose, 'Études évangelique III, Fils de l'homme et Fils de Dieu', *RB* 9 (1900), pp. 169-99; C.G.M. Quack, 'Waarom gaf Jezus de voorkeur aan den naam: "Zoon des menschen", en niet aan den naam "Zoon van God"?', *Geloof en Vrijheid* 36 (1902), pp. 356-72; E. Schürer (1844–1910), *Das messianische Selbstbewusstsein Jesu Christi* (1903); J. Mouren, *Le Fils de l'Homme. Étude historique et critique* (1903); J. Kipp, '"Des Menschen Sohn"', *Evangelische Kirchenzeitung* (1904), pp. 437-45, 459-63; the Uppsala professor A. Kolmodin (1855–1928), 'Jesus—människosonen', *Kyrklig Tidskrift* 11 (1905), pp. 289-311 (309); G. Peloux, *Valeur et contenu du terme: le Fils de l'homme dans la bouche de Jésus. Essai de théologique biblique* (1906); the archdeacon of Manchester W.C. Allen, *A Critical and Exegetical Commentary on the Gospel According to S. Matthew* (1907, 3rd edn, 1912), p. lxxiv; S.L. de Skibniewski, *De* בר נשא. *Filio hominis* (1908; according to the summary in *RB* NS 3 [1910], p. 145); J. Derambure, 'Le "Fils de l'homme" dans les Évangiles', *Revue Augustinienne* 13 (1908), pp. 708-20; 14 (1909), pp. 319-40; M. Sardi, 'Il "Figlio dell' Uomo"', *Revista storico-critica delle scienze teologiche* 5 (1909), pp. 12-19 (according to the summary in *RB* ns 3 [1910], p. 145); L. ten Bokum, 'De Zoon des Menschen', *Nederlandsche Katholieke Stemmen* 9 (1909), pp. 2-10; V. Hartl, 'Anfang und Ende des Titels "Menschensohn". Ein Beitrag zur Lösung der johanneischen Frage', *BZ* 7 (1909), pp. 342-54; H.H. Meulenbelt, 'De Zoon des menschen, de Zoon, de Zoon van Gods', *Theologische Studiën* 29 (1911), pp. 388-438 (390-410); the Copenhagen New Testament professor and later bishop P. Madsen (1843–1911), 'Menneskets Søn', *Kirke-Leksikon for Norden*, III (1911), pp. 228-29; J.W. Graham 'The Mind of the Son of Man', *The Interpreter* 8 (1911–12), pp. 289-302; J. Stalker (1848–1927), 'Son of Man, The', *The International Standard Bible Encyclopaedia*, V (1915, 2nd edn, 1925), cols. 2828-30; F.W. Grosheide 'Υἱὸς τοῦ ἀνθρώπου in het Ev. naar Johannes', *Theologische Studiën* 35 (1917), pp. 242-48; the Swedish bishop E. Billing (1871–1939), '"Människosonen" och "Gudsriket" i Jesu förkunnelse', in *För Tanke och Tro* (FS Oscar Ekman, 1923), pp. 241-83 (253-57); the Jewish scholar J. Klausner (1874–1958), *Jesus of Nazareth: His Life, Times, and Teaching* (1925), esp. pp. 256-57; F. Roslaniec, *Sensus genuinus et plenus locutionis 'Filius Hominis', a Christo Domine adhibitae* (1920); H. Dieckmann, '"Der Sohn des Menschen" im Johannesevangelium', *Scholastik* 2 (1927), pp. 229-47; P. Joüon, 'Appendice A: le Fils de l'homme', in *idem*, *L'Evangile de Notre-Seigneur Jésus-Christ* (1930), pp. 601-604; J. McNaugher, 'Son of Man', *BS* 88 (1931), pp. 90-104.

4. Cf. also H.J. Holtzmann's *Lehrbuch der neutestamentliche Theologie* (1896, 2nd edn, posthumously edited by Adolf Jülicher and Walter Bauer, 1911), I, pp. 313-35.

5. Holtzmann, *Das messianische Bewußtsein Jesu*, p. 67; the same words appear in *Lehrbuch*, p. 327.

sayings, a third describes what is characteristic for him. The connection to Dan. 7.13 is original: 'He wants to be the Messiah exactly in the sense of Daniel's Son of Man.'[6] In Jesus' use of the term, we see a development towards referring explicitly to himself as the Son of man and are reminded of voices from the nineteenth century, as Holtzmann continues:

> The gradual harmonization of the third and first person address invites us to think that in the consciousness of the speaker, Son of Man first functions as an objective entity determined by the scriptural (schriftmässig) eschatological program, in which he only reluctantly and reservedly dared to recognize himself and, accordingly, confess himself. Thus, [it occurred] in response to the same authority of Scripture, by which his being the Messiah was put upon him.[7]

This confession of Daniel's apocalyptic belongs to a late period of Jesus' life. It occurred after the episode at Caesarea Philippi. The expression was not a formal title for the Messiah. Thus people, listening to Jesus, had to detect the deeper meaning of the expression for themselves. In 'his creative religious originality, the messianic consciousness of Jesus received its stamp of contemporary concepts (ihre zeitgeschichtliche Prägung)', first when the old was connected with the new:

> The possibility of such a mixture (Ineinander) of both factors resulted in the concept of Son of Man as the Christus futurus. Thus, the Messiahship of Jesus implied his experience of God, projected from the present into the future. The Son of God is in accordance with contemporary experience the Son of Man a postulate of the future... The older elements form the cover, under the protection of which new forces dared to turn up in the light. These destroy the older cover without further ado, without for that reason feeling them too restraining and immediately to be rid of.[8]

As an example from the Catholic camp, Fritz Tillmann (1874–1953), later professor in moral philosophy in Bonn, is totally confident in his *Der Menschensohn. Jesu Selbstzeugnis für seine messianische Würde*, in the virtues of Roman Catholic exegesis that he perceives the Holy Scriptures of the Old

6. Holtzmann, *Das messianische Bewußtsein Jesu*, p. 70; cf. *Lehrbuch*, p. 320: 'Der Ausdruck signalisiert ihn eben als Messias. Es ist nur zu verstehen als Abbreviatur.'

7. Holtzmann, *Das messianische Bewußtsein Jesu*, p. 84. Holtzmann also remarks that it helps to understand the custom of that time of speaking in the third person, adducing 2 Cor. 12.2-5 as an analogy.

8. Holtzmann, *Das messianische Bewußtsein Jesu*, pp. 98-99. Holtzmann did not totally abandon his former idealistic understanding. Cf. further *idem*, *Die Synoptiker* (1890, 2nd edn, 1901), pp. 53-54 and p. 124 where, with regard to Mk 2.28, it is said: 'Nicht etwa als Vertreter echter Menschenrechte und Menschenwürde...zerbricht hier Jesus das Joch des Sabbatszwanges, sondern als Vertreter der väterlichen Liebe Gottes; ähnlich also, wie er 2,10 als Menschensohn den Menschen auch Sünden vergibt'.

and New Testament as a unified revelatory organism (einheitlichen Offenbarungsorganismus), guaranteed in its fundamental views by the Church itself. It is the dogma of a purely human development in Jesus in non-Catholic exegesis which is to blame for the failure to achieve lasting results.[9] The *ke* before Son of man in Dan. 7.13 does not indicate a symbol, but the difference between this man and all other men.[10] Roman Catholic exegesis is correct in assuming the Danielic saying describing the divine and human nature of the Messiah. The Parables of *1 Enoch* show the development towards the messianic title it has become in the gospels. Son of man was a messianic title and the only reason it was not always immediately understood was the great distance between Daniel's Son of man and the earthly Jesus. As shown in his writing about a δεύτερος ἄνθρωπος and the messianic exegesis of Psalm 8 in 1 Cor. 15.27 and Heb. 2.6-8, Paul was acquainted with the title.[11]

Some scholars distinguish themselves from others because of their peculiar points of views. This is true, for instance, of J. Courtenay James' proposal that Jesus himself 'intentionally translated the elastic בר נשׁא in a rather over-literal fashion, and Himself introduced the somewhat mystical, yet very suggestive, Greek expression ὁ υἱὸς τοῦ ἀνθρώπου' into the Gospel tradition'.[12] The Erlangen professor Otto Procksch (1874–1947), like Hilgenfeld earlier (see above), thinks that the Aramaic expression behind the use of Jesus was ברהדאנשׁא, *breh de'anasha*, 'his son, it is, the man's', being not at all equivalent to 'man', which is the case for ὁ υἱὸς τοῦ ἀνθρώπου, designating Jesus alone. In Jesus' use, it has a *double entendre*, designating his highest self-revelation. Jesus fills the heavenly appearance of Daniel with an earthly content, when he, as son of God (Mt. 16.13-16), speaks of his coming death from the very moment he is recognized as the Son of man (Mt. 16.13-16). He did not choose 'Messiah' but precisely 'Son of man' because in this

9. F. Tillmann, *Der Menschensohn. Jesu Selbstzeugnis für seine messianischen Würde* (1907), pp. 3-4, where it is also said: 'Es ist methodisch und logisch nicht zulässig, a priori selbst die Möglichkeit des Transzendentalen zu leugnen'.

10. Tillmann, *Der Menschensohn*, p. 95; cf. p. 83: 'So klein auch ein einzelner Zug der Offenbarung erscheinen mag, in der Vorbereitung des Christusnamens durch die Danielische Prophetie eröffnet sich uns ein Blick in den wundersamen Pragmatismus der göttlichen Heilsgeschichte'.

11. Tillmann, *Der Menschensohn*, pp. 172-75. Further the conclusion p. 176. In 'Hat die Selbstbezeichnung Jesu "der Menschensohn" ihre Wurzel in Dn 7,13?', *BZ* 5 (1907), pp. 35-47, Tillmann objects to Th. Zahn's denial of Dan. 7.13 as the background for Jesus' use (see below). The pamphlet *Jesus, der Menschensohn* (1908) is a popular summary of the investigation from 1907.

12. J. Courtenay James, 'The Son of Man: Origin and Use of the Title', *ET* 36 (1924–1925), pp. 309-14 (313). Because of Dan. 7.13 and *1 En.* 37–71 one can assume 'that the term "Son of Man" was understood Messianically at the time of Christ's advent, but it was not a current and generally recognized title of the Messiah' (p. 310).

designation alone are the apocalyptic and universal aspect of his appearance clear, together with his metaphysical being as Son of God.[13] A. McCaig follows the same line of thought where he finds that '"*the* Son of man" must be equivalent to The Man, the man pre-eminently, the distinguished Man'. Thus it 'trembles with all the signification of full Divinity'.[14] The influential Copenhagen professor in history of religions, Vilhelm Grønbech (1873–1948), also belongs here, claiming that Jesus as religious genius in fact took over Daniel's figure and transformed it into something unrecognizable: 'I am the greatest—that he knows—the outstanding, the world-transforming, the innovative. In his mouth Son of man and I become equivalent words. Everything which has been augured about the future of Israel, everything the prophets have spoken about, stands here—I am that.'[15]

Because the mind of Jesus is assumed to be the real creative factor behind the messianic concept in the Gospels,[16] a number of scholars thought it possible to reckon with an explicit connection between the use of Daniel's Son of man and Isaiah's Suffering Servant.[17] A spokesman for this view is James Drummond.[18] Drummond considers the Aramaic solution but because

13. O. Procksch, 'Der Menschensohn als Gottessohn', *Christentum und Wissenschaft* 3 (1927), pp. 425-43, 473-81 (481). Cf. *idem*, 'Christus im Alten Testament', *NKZ* 44 (1933), pp. 57-83, where he rejects any religio-historical material pointing to Primeval Man and also offers Exod. 24.16 and Ezek. 1.26 as places where the divine figure in the likeness of man is in the centre, to be taken over by Jesus, who uses it about himself.

14. A. McCaig, 'The Title "Son of Man" in its Lofty Associations', *Biblical Review* 12 (1927), pp. 44-56 (45 and 56).

15. V. Grønbech, *Jesus Menneskesønnen* (1935), p. 131; cf. pp. 131-34 and the notes, pp. 162-63, where it is said that we cannot know to what extent Jesus himself has employed the name Son of man, because it has become a cliché in the gospels. Undoubtedly this way of speaking goes back to Jesus himself. Grønbech's *Jesus Menneskesønnen*, a trilogy with a second volume about Paul and a third about Christ the Risen Lord, is not a monograph on the Son of Man, although the title is indicative of Grønbech's basic understanding of Jesus.

16. A few interpreters even operate with a concept of a suffering Son of man in Judaism, as will be seen in the next chapter.

17. This pertains, among others, to M.G. Evans, 'The Title "the Son of Man"', *BS* 57 (1900), pp. 680-95; G.P. Gould, 'Son of Man', in *A Dictionary of Christ and the Gospels* (1909), II, pp. 659-65; the conservative Halle New Testament professor Paul Feine (1859–1933), *Theologie des Neuen Testaments* (1910, 2nd edn, 1911 [in several editions, the last posthumously edited by Kurt Aland, 1948 = 1953]), pp. 119-37; and the Swede Henrik Steen, *Jesu ställning till judafolkets nationnella messiasförhoppningar* (*Jesus' Position to the National Messianic Expectations of the Jewish People*) (1910), esp. pp. 180-201; J. Moffatt (1870–1944), *The Theology of the Gospels* (1912, 5th edn, 1948), esp. pp. 150-63; the Manchester professor A.S. Peake (1865–1930), 'The Messiah and the Son of Man', *BJRL* 8 (1924), pp. 52-81 (reprint in idem, *The Servant of Yahweh* [1931], pp. 220-37); A. Ross, 'The Title "Son of Man"', *EvQ* 6 (1934), pp. 36-49.

18. J. Drummond, 'The Use and Meaning of the Phrase "The Son of Man" in the Synoptic Gospels', *JThS* 2 (1901), pp. 350-58 and pp. 539-71.

of the disagreement of its detractors he rejects it. All the same, he is sure that the Greek expression goes back to Aramaic *barnasha*, which could mean 'man' but 'it is surely not impossible that "the Man", pronounced with a little emphasis, might be used to denote the figure in Daniel's vision. Our reasoning must, I think, adapt itself to this conclusion'.[19] However, it was not a common messianic title but could easily lend itself to such an interpretation. The various ways in which Jesus employs it indicates that he 'did not use the term in a very strict or limited sense, and that He might have given it a somewhat varying application according to circumstances.' If he started from Daniel, it could stand for the true representatives of humanity, 'the people of the saints of the Most High', which could be connected with the Isaianic servant of God. Being 'conscious of His own Messianic calling, He must have regarded Himself the head of this ideal class—the Son of Man in a pre-eminent sense—the one in whom (though not in whom exclusively) prophecy found its fulfilment'. Perhaps he has not identified himself with the conquering Son of man, but saw the prophetical vision 'as a poetical description of the spiritual conquest of the world's brute forces by a divinely commissioned humanity, personified as the Son of Man'.[20] Another, the Oxford scholar A.E.J. Rawlinson,[21] thinks that at least certain circles in Judaism identified the human-like figure in Dan. 7.13 with a heavenly, pre-existent figure, a superhuman 'Man', to be revealed in the last days (as seen in *1 Enoch* and *4 Ezra*, an identification with a possible scriptural basis in Ps. 80.17). That the title turns up in different categories of sayings, Rawlinson supposes to be the result of a melting together in the mind of Jesus of the role of the Son of Man with the role of the Lord's Servant. To Jesus, however, it was equivalent to Messiah. The Baptist scholar E.A. McDowell aptly sums up the position.[22] The original Son of man concept was transformed in the mind of Jesus, who preferred it because (1) it was not a common messianic title, (2) its enigmatic character would appeal to the curiosity of spiritually minded people, (3) in later times, it could preserve his self-understanding and (4) it allowed combination with the concept of the Suffering Servant. Jesus was not the apocalyptic Son of man in the way Albert Schweitzer thought. But '[b]y this close attachment of the consummation of all things to the present, Jesus infused his teachings with an eternal quality that

19. Drummond, 'Use and Meaning', p. 358.

20. Drummond, 'Use and Meaning', p. 568.

21. A.E.J. Rawlinson, *The New Testament Doctrine of Christ* (1926, 2nd edn, 1929), pp. 242-50: Appended Note III, 'On the Meaning and Use of the Title "Son of Man" in the Gospels'.

22. E.A. McDowell, *Son of Man and Suffering Servant: A Historical and Exegetical Study of the Synoptic Narratives Revealing the Consciousness of Jesus Concerning His Person and Mission* (1944, 2nd edn, 1946), p. 115. Cf. the later study of *idem*, 'The Kingdom of God and the Day of the Son of Man: A Study of Luke 17:20-37', *Review and Expositor* 39 (1962), pp. 54-64.

gives them an urgency and an importance which they could not have otherwise'.

At least two can be mentioned who, in addition to Dan. 7.13, look to Psalm 8. The famous pietistic Tübingen New Testament professor Adolf Schlatter (1852–1938) also sees Ps. 8.5 as constituent and of no less importance than Daniel 7, because the scriptural promise is perceived as a unity (die Weissagung wird als eine Einheit aufgefasst).[23] The Oslo New Testament professor Lyder Brun (1870–1950) sees both Ps. 8.5 and the book of Ezekiel with Daniel 7 as pointing to the paradoxical contrast between human inferiority and divine election.[24] Some few scholars even look to Psalm 80 as a main presupposition for the use of Son of man in the mouth of Jesus. This pertains for instance to Heinrich Holzinger (1863–1944), who thought that Jesus takes up the Psalter in his effort to address the normal understanding of the Messiah. The Son of man of Ps. 80.18 is of special importance as it is not apocalyptic, but in full accordance with Deutero-Isaiah's Servant of the Lord. 'If this is to be taken as messianic, the Son of man, like the Servant of the Lord, is nothing other than the bearer of true religion and its mission to represent it in the world.'[25]

Others look for an un-apocalyptic background for Jesus' use of Son of man, pointing to the book of Ezekiel as the main presupposition, the Danielic link being first introduced by the later community. As we have seen earlier, some interpreters included the book of Ezekiel in this context as part of the explanation. Some, however, assume that it is the primary source. First to be mentioned is Edwin A. Abbott. In his huge investigation *'The Son of Man' or Contributions to the Study of the Thoughts of Jesus* from 1910,[26] Abbott thus claims that Jesus

> was not influenced by the Book of Enoch, but by the scriptures and the whole of the scriptural conception of 'man' and 'the son of man', or, as the Hebrew Bible would mostly put it, of 'Adam' and 'the son of Adam', from Genesis to

23. A. Schlatter, *Die Theologie des Neuen Testaments. Erster Teil: Die Worte Jesu* (1909), pp. 462-67. Cf. *idem*, *Der Evangelist Matthäus. Seine Sprache, sein Ziel, seine Selbständigkeit. Ein Kommentar zum ersten Evangelium* (1929, 5th edn, 1959), pp. 285-87 (Mt. 8.20).

24. L. Brun, *Jesu Evangelium. En historisk fremstilling av Jesu forkyndelse* (1917, 2nd edn, 1926), pp. 545-62.

25. H. Holzinger, 'Zur Menschensohnfrage', *Beiträge zur alttestamentlichen Wissenschaft* (FS Karl Budde, 1920), pp. 102-106 (p. 106). Earlier also Eberhard Nestle (1851–1913), 'The "Son of Man" in the Old Testament', *ET* 11 (1899–1900), p. 238, and later M. Wagner, 'Der Menschensohn', *NKZ* 36 (1925), pp. 245-78, and *idem*, 'Der Menschensohn des 80. Psalms', *ThStKr* 104 (1932), pp 84-93.

26. *Diatessarica VIII* (lii + 873 pages!). A popular summary is found in *The Message of the Son of Man* (1909).

> Malachi, not indeed excluding the vision of Daniel but including a great deal more. In particular... He had in view the appellation 'son of Adam', given to Ezekiel, between whom and Himself there [are] many parallels.[27]

That Jesus really spoke of himself as son of Adam Abbott sees confirmed in Paul's speaking of the second Adam, originating 'from an inspired insight into Christ's self-appellation'.[28] Thus Jesus, in his use, includes first of all 'the much grander, more original and more wide-reaching vision of Ezekiel, to which Daniel seems to have given a special application'.[29] In both places we find the contrast between the beasts and the one in human form; and Jesus identified the spirit he had received

> with the Spirit of humanity in heaven controlling or subjugating animate and inanimate nature for the purposes of divine order and for the conformation of Man to God... He preferred to call Himself Son of Man, as if to say 'Keep constantly in view my human nature, that you may perceive how divine a thing human nature may be, and that you may be led through the knowledge of the divinity of Man to the knowledge of the humanity of God'.[30]

An even more outspoken representative of understanding of Son of man as mainly confined to the use of ben Adam in God's addressing the prophet Ezekiel is Daniel Völter,[31] who, later, also maintains that Jesus could not have had an apocalyptic-heavenly Son of man concept because this only arises in connection with the belief in his resurrection and his Parousia.[32]

27. E.A. Abbott, *'The Son of Man' or Contributions to the Study of the Thoughts of Jesus* (1910), p. xvii. Abbott himself sums up his results in the introduction, from where this and the following quotations are taken.

28. Abbott, *'The Son of Man'*, p. xviii.

29. Abbott, *'The Son of Man'*, p. xix.

30. Abbott, *'The Son of Man'*, pp. xix-xx.

31. D. Völter, *Jesus der Menschensohn oder das Berufsbewußtsein Jesu* (1914). Völter has given up the consequent eschatological interpretation he earlier adhered to (see above): 'The Son of man is primarily nothing other than a man, who has a special prophetic task from God. No messianic meaning is attached to it' (p. 64). This only arose when Jesus came under the influence of Isa. 53. It is the same understanding which we find in Rom. 5.15-17 and 1 Cor. 15.21-22. Other Pauline letters (for instance 1 Cor. 1.7, 8; 15.48, 49) show that here the soteriological Son of man concept of Jesus himself is connected to the apocalyptic eschatology of Daniel. In 'Opmerkingen tot de Menschenzoon-kwestie', *NThT* 3 (1914), pp. 379-83, Völter maintains this view against the criticism of H.A. van Bakel, 'De Carne Christi', *NThT* 3 (1914), pp. 254-87. In 'Noch ein Wort über den Menschensohn. Neutestamentliche Streitfragen III', *NThT* 4 (1915), pp. 143-47, Völter continues the debate because of renewed objection from H.A. van Bakel, 'Ezechiel's Menschenzoon', *NThT* 4 (1915), pp. 36-42.

32. D. Völter, *Die Menschensohn-Frage neu untersucht* (1916). This is not contradicted by Dan. 7.13 because there we only witness the employment of a thought or picture from Ps. 80.18 for which reason Son of man in Daniel also stands for Israel.

This should be welcomed all the more because it liberates us from the not very satisfactory assumption that Jesus, in a moment of distress, should have taken refuge with and sought consolation in the fantastic hope of becoming the Son of man in the apocalyptic-heavenly sense.[33] Pierson Parker claims that Son of man is not a messianic title and that the three passages in the Synoptics where the interpretation functions as an apocalyptic discourse (Mk 13.26; 14.62; Mt. 24.30) are not authentic. In the few other passages where such an interpretation is possible, it is unnecessary. Messianic understanding seems to be the result of 'a Christian process, without warrant from either himself or his predecessors'. The prerogative connected with it then should be seen in the use in Hebrew poetry where the concern is nearly always with God's relation to man (Job 25.5, 6; Pss 8.4; 80.17; Isa. 56.1, 2). 'The phrase is not technical, but it echoes with a prophetic ring.' This is confirmed by the fact that the three men to be called Son of man in pre-Christian times—Ezekiel, Daniel and Enoch—are all receivers of divine revelation. 'Then Jesus, in taking the title, will have marked himself not as Messiah, but as one who, in the line of Enoch, Daniel and Ezekiel, envisioned the Kingdom.'[34]

2. *Son of Man in an Idealistic Interpretation*

This period also witnesses a series of interpreters who still maintain an outright idealistic understanding of Son of man as used by Jesus.[35] As mentioned above, it is also often present in the work of those claiming one or more Old Testament text as the imagery's main source. There are some who take their point of departure exclusively in the wording of the expression and

33. See Völter, *Der Menschensohn-Frage neu untersucht*, p. 56. This understanding is still present in the last (to my knowledge) utterance of Völter in this debate, *Die Grundfrage des Lebens Jesu* (1936). See also Karl Bornhäuser (1868–1947), *Das Wirken des Christus durch Taten und Worte* (1921), esp. pp. 30-32.

34. P. Parker, 'The Meaning of "Son of Man"', *JBL* 60 (1941), pp. 151-57 (156-57).

35. A list includes: Gross Alexander, *The Son of Man: Studies in His Life and Teachings* (1900), pp. 307-17 (I owe this reference to D. Burkett, *The Son of Man Debate* [1999], p. 14 n. 3); A. Carr, 'The Son of Man as the Light of the World', *Exp* 7.1 (1906), pp. 115-23; F. Bard, *Der Sohn des Menschen. Eine Untersuchung über Begriff und Inhalt und Absicht solcher Jesusbezeichnung* (1908, 2nd edn, 1915), esp. p. 29; H. Gottshed, *Der Menschensohn* (1908), p. 23 (not a monograph on the expression Son of man, but a Life of Jesus book); J. MacRory, 'The Son of Man', *IThQ* 10 (1915), pp. 50-63; T. Stephenson, 'The Title "Son of Man"', *ET* 29 (1917–18), pp. 377-78; H.O. Cavalier, 'The Gospel of the Son of Man', *Theology* 6 (1923), pp. 218-21; A.M. Sanford, 'Did Jesus Call Himself the Son of Man?', *JR* 3 (1923), pp. 308-11 (this work is a rejoinder to C.S. Patton; see below).

do not allow any Old Testament saying to constitute the real significance of the term. The Oxford Old Testament professor Samuel Rolles Driver (1846–1914)[36] could write:

> The title, as it seems to the present writer (though he would avoid such expressions as the 'ideal' or 'representative' man), designates Jesus as *the* Man in whom human nature was most fully and deeply realized, and who was the most complete exponent of its capacities, warm and broad in His sympathies, ready to minister and suffer for others, sharing to the full the needs and deprivations which are the common lot of humanity, but conscious at the same time of the dignity and greatness of human nature, and destined ultimately to exalt it to unexampled majesty and glory.[37]

The highly influential, conservative professor in Erlangen, Theodor Zahn (1838–1933), refuses to see any connection with Dan. 7.13, which would suggest that the expression Son of man functions as a learned abbreviation. When the alternative is either to understand it in the mouth of Jesus as meaning the species (Gattung) 'man' or as designating the man κατ' ἐξοχήν, the last mentioned is the only real possibility.[38]

Finally, this period also sees a number of Life of Jesus books choosing 'Son of man' as their title in order to indicate the true humanity of the person of whom they write a biography.[39]

36. 'Son of Man', in James Hastings' *A Dictionary of the Bible* (1902), IV, pp. 579-89. 'The title may have been borrowed by our Lord from Dn 7,13; but He did not, at least when first using it, intend to bring before His hearer the figure there portrayed: He adopted it as a mere shell or form, suggestive of His humanity, into which He threw a new import and content of His own' (p. 587).

37. Ibid.

38. T. Zahn, *Das Evangelium des Matthäus* (1903, 3rd edn, 1910), pp. 351-62 (Mt. 8.20), especially p. 356.

39. See K. Gibran, *Jesus, the Son of Man: His Words and his Deeds as told and Recorded by Those who Knew Him* (1928); E. Ludwig (*nome de plume* of Emil Cohn [1881–1948]), *Der Menschensohn* (1928); E. Ellwein, *Der Menschensohn* (1934); the Swede S. Lønborg, *Jesu från Nazara* (1931), which in the Danish translation became the title *Jesus Menneskesønnen* (1932); H. Ussing, *Menneskesønnens Liv paa Jorden* (1936). The book of V. Grønbech, *Jesus Menneskesønnen* (1935), could also be mentioned here (cf. above).

Mainly edifying are the following articles: E.W. Winstanley, 'Days of the Son of Man', *ET* 24 (1912–13), pp. 533-38; R. Somerwell, 'The Son of Man', *ET* 29 (1917–18), pp. 522-23 (an apologetic warning against putting Son of man in connection with Adam whom most people would no longer recognize as a historical figure); M.A. Hopkins, 'The Son of Man: John 12:34', *The Union Seminary Review* 39 (1927–28), pp. 145-57, being fundamentalistic in its approach; H.C. Phillips, 'Jesus, Son of Man', *Religion in Life* 5 (1936), pp. 207-15.

3. *Some 'Outsiders'*

Besides the more 'classical' views, the period also has representatives of some new interpretations, looking for a meaning for the expression in quite other directions. D. Smith claims that leaving out of account every link to apocalyptic literature and, consequently, every messianic understanding the Old Testament material, together with the New Testament, points in one certain direction: Jesus was 'a son of man! one of the common people, the עם הארץ, whom the rulers despised (Jn 7.49)'.[40] In this way 'the title "Son of Man" served as a continual protest against the secular ideal of the Messiahship which more than anything else hindered His recognition and acceptance'.[41] 'If this were indeed the origin of the title "Son of Man", it was in the first instance an opprobrious epithet, in fact a nickname; and Jesus transfigured it by wearing it'.[42] Its being 'a name of scorn' is also the reason why the disciples never use it.

E. Kuhnert takes his point of departure from a profane Greek idiom, witnessed in many Greek inscriptions from the period, using υἱός in connection with a town or an association as a title of honour (Ehrentitel). When Jesus called himself *ben adam* or *barnasha*, he used a predicate understandable to any Jewish hearer as a title of the coming saviour of the world, in Greek ὁ υἱὸς τοῦ ἀνθρώπου. For that reason, the evangelists never explain it.[43]

Walther Bleibtreu will not accept that in his use of Son of man Jesus should have taken over any meaning from either Scripture or the street, from Judaism or the pagan world. This title is entirely his original creation, although within the framework of Old Testament thinking.[44] It belongs exclusively in the mouth of Jesus, 'a sacred thing not to be approached by any other, *a Noli me tangere*, demanding veneration in the highest degree'.[45]

40. D. Smith, 'The Nickname "Son of Man"', *ET* 18 (1906–1907), pp. 553-55 (554). Although Smith is rather alone with his understanding, he is not totally without predecessors. It reminds one partly of the interpretation of Sebastian Münster in the sixteenth century and those following him (see above Chapter 5, Section 1) and partly of the interpretation of C.A. Heumann (see above Chapter 5, Section 3).

41. Smith, 'The Nickname "Son of Man"', p. 554.

42. Smith, 'The Nickname "Son of Man"', p. 555.

43. E. Kuhnert, ''Ο υἱὸς τοῦ ἀνθρώπου', *ZNW* 18 (1918), pp. 165-76 (170). Thus there is no reason to deny that Jesus should have used the expression (p. 175). E. Hertlein, ''Ο υἱὸς τοῦ ἀνθρώπου', *ZNW* 19 (1920), pp. 46-48, is a counterplea against Kuhnert based on his own very special understanding (see below), and the same pertains to H. Dieckmann, ''Ο υἱὸς τοῦ ἀνθρώπου', *Bib* 2 (1921), pp. 69-71, pointing both to the obscurity of the definite article in Kuhnert's understanding and to the failing explanation of why the title disappeared so soon; this is understandable from the Aramaic.

44. Walther Bleibtreu, 'Jesu Selbstbenennung als der Menschensohn', *ThKrSt* 98–99 (1926), pp. 164-211 (182-83).

45. Bleibtreu, 'Jesu Selbstbenennung als der Menschensohn', pp. 184-85.

Its meaning is, in reality, Son of God in human form, and Bleibtreu finds it reasonable that the Church later found confirmation in this title for its teaching of the two natures of Christ. Thus Jesus also could have recognized himself in the one like a Son of man in Dan. 7.13.[46]

Also to be mentioned in this context is C.H. Valentine, who thinks that when Jesus spoke of the Son of man coming in the clouds, he did so in a figurative sense with reference to the coming of the Holy Spirit.[47] This theory, however, was not grasped by the scholarly community.

4. *The Son of Man in a Corporate Interpretation*

If the new interpretations listed above are to be characterized as singular appearances on the stage of exegesis, another attempt gained more adherents, namely, the collective interpretation which we have already seen in the work of Simon Episcopius in 1650 (see above Chapter 5).[48] The acknowledgment that the one like a Son of man in Dan. 7.13 is not a messianic figure, but a symbol of 'the holies of the Highest', convinced some exegetes of a symbolic understanding in the Gospels. Normally, this interpretation is maintained with regard to the historical Jesus and not the expression Son of man as it now stands in the Gospels. There are exceptions. We already witnessed above a symbolic understanding in the mouth of Jesus, represented by S. Hoekstra, J.E. Carpenter and A.C. Larsen.

A new beginning was initiated by the Halle professor Ferdinand Kattenbusch (1851–1935). He remarked, for instance, that when Jesus interprets himself as the one Daniel beheld, he saw himself forced to interpret himself according to what Daniel had experienced about the Son of man; that is, not what he was as an individual alone, the personal Son of God, but also as representative, appointed Lord of a certain people, the 'people of the holies'.[49] This was possible only because he recognized that Daniel's Son of man was at the same time Isaiah's Suffering Servant.[50]

46. Bleibtreu, 'Jesu Selbstbenennung als der Menschensohn', p. 210.

47. C.H. Valentine, 'The Son of Man Coming in the Clouds. Mark xiii.26; Matthew xxiv.30; Luke xxi.27', *Theology* 23 (1931), pp. 14-21.

48. On the following, cf. the first part of Excursus G: Kollektive Deutung des Ausdrucks 'Menschensohn' in Jesu Mund und in den Evangelien, in Müller, *Der Ausdruck 'Menschensohn' in den Evangelien*, pp. 157-63.

49. F. Kattenbusch, 'Der Quellort der Kirchenidee', *Harnack-Ehrung* (1921), pp. 143-72 (160); cf. *idem*, 'Das Messiastum Jesu', *ZNW* 12 (1911), pp. 270-86.

50. Kattenbusch, 'Der Quellort der Kirchenidee', p. 161. This interpretation was taken up by K.L. Schmidt (1891–1956), in 'Die Kirche des Urchristentums. Eine lexicographische und biblisch-theologische Studie', *Festgabe für Adolf Deissmann* (1926), pp. 258-19 (294-95); *idem*, ''Εκκλησία', *ThWNT*, III (1938), pp. 502-509. For a positive evaluation, see O. Linton, *Das Problem der Urkirche in der neueren Forschung. Eine kritische Darstellung* (1932), pp. 148-49; for a more critical one, see W.G. Kümmel,

A very similar understanding was proposed in England, first by A.T. Cadoux[51] and N. Micklem,[52] but with far more impact by the Manchester professor Thomas Walter Manson (1893–1958) in his classic *The Teaching of Jesus: Studies in its Form and Contents* (1931), which gave the thesis a broad foundation. Manson accounts for the presuppositions of his understanding of Son of man in the Gospels as follows:

> It...is the final term in a series of conceptions, all of which are found in the Old Testament. These are: the Remnant (Isaiah), the Servant of Jehovah (II Isaiah), the 'I' of the Psalms, and the Son of Man (Daniel)... It is the idea of the Remnant which is the essential feature about each of these: and it is now suggested that the Son of Man in the Gospels is another embodiment of the Remnant idea. In other words, the Son of Man is, like the Servant of Jehovah, an ideal figure and stands for the manifestation of the Kingdom of God on earth in a people wholly devoted to their heavenly King. [That the expression 'Son of Man' became also a Jesus-designation, is because it is connected with] the outcome of the prophetic ministry of Jesus. His mission is to create the Son of Man, the Kingdom of the saints of the Most High, to realise in Israel the ideal contained in the term. This task is attempted in two ways: first by public appeal to the people through the medium of parable and sermon and by mission of the disciples: then, when this appeal produced no adequate response, by the consolidation of his own band of followers. Finally, when it becomes apparent that not even the disciples are ready to rise to the demands of the ideal, he stands alone, embodying in his own person the perfect human response to the regal claims of God.[53]

On the cross, he alone is the 'Son of man'. This should have been the end of his story, but it was not.

> The sufferings and death of Jesus are the birth-pangs of the Son of Man. The cross proves to be the key that opens the Kingdom of God to men. The death of Jesus accomplished what his teaching could not... By dying Jesus has brought the Son of Man into existence, given to that dream-figure a body, a local habitation and name. It is the Church, his own body, of which he is the head.[54]

'Die Eschatologie der Evangelien. Ihre Geschichte und Sinn', *ThBl* 15 (1936), pp. 225-41, quoted according to reprint in *idem*, *Heilsgeschehen und Geschichte. Gesammelte Aufsätze 1933–1964* (1965), pp. 48-66 (55-56); idem, *Kirchenbegriff und Geschichtsbewußtsein in der Urgemeinde und bei Jesus* (1943, 2nd edn, 1968), pp. 33-34. Cf. also R. Bultmann, 'Die Frage nach der Echtheit von Mt 16,17-19', *ThBl* 20 (1941), pp. 265-79, quoted according to reprint in *idem*, *Exegetica. Aufsätze zur Erforschung des Neuen Testaments* (1967), pp. 255-77 (273-75).

51. A.T. Cadoux, 'Son of Man', *The Interpreter* 18 (1920), pp. 202-14.

52. N. Micklem, 'The Son of Man', *Queen's Quarterly* 36 (1929), pp. 205-24 (217).

53. T.W. Manson, *The Teaching of Jesus: Studies in its Form and Contents* (1931), pp. 227-28.

54. Manson, *The Teaching of Jesus*, p. 235. Later, in the article 'The Son of Man in Daniel, Enoch and the Gospels', *BJRL* 32 (1949–50), pp. 171-93, quoted according to

Manson's understanding of the Son of man was later taken up by a number of scholars.[55]

5. *Son of Man as a Title Ascribed to Jesus by the Community*

Some interpreters (some, belonging to the History of Religion School, which will be discussed in the next chapter) continued the tiny thread of seeing Son of man in the Gospels as the outcome of community theology; that is, regarding its content as determined by the Messianic belief of the primitive Church.[56] F.P. Badham sees its presupposition in the use by Jesus of the 'almost colourless expression' *bar-adam*, son of Adam.[57] This, however, is no longer the case in the Gospels.

reprint in *idem*, *Studies in the Gospels and Epistles* (ed. by Matthew Black, 1962), pp. 123-45 (143), Manson introduces the concept 'corporate personality'. He claims that 'this corporate entity is embodied, *par excellence*, in Jesus himself in such a way that his followers, who constitute with him the Son of Man as a group, may be thought of as extensions of his personality, or, as St. Paul puts it later on, limbs of his body'. Cf. further *idem*, 'Mark ii.27f.', *Coniectanea Neotestamentica* 11 (FS Anton Fridrichsen, 1947), pp. 138-46; and *The Servant-Messiah: A Study of the Public Ministry of Jesus* (1953), pp. 72-74, 80.

55. Among those publishing before and during the Second World War were B.H. Bulcock, 'Was the Double Use of "Son of Man" a Factor in the Deification of Jesus?', *The Congregational Quarterly* 17 (1939), pp. 44-55; C.J. Cadoux, *The Historic Mission of Jesus: A Constructive Re-examination of the Eschatological Teaching of the Synoptic Gospels* (1941), esp. pp. 90-103; Å.V. Ström, *Vetekornet. Studier över individ och kollektiv i Nya Testamentet med särskild hänsyn till Johannesevangeliets teologi Joh 12:20-33* (*The Grain of Wheat: Studies in the Individual and Collective with Special Regard to the Theology of the Gospel of John, John 12.20-33*) (1944), pp. 136-38, 223-24; H.H. Rowley, *The Relevance of Apocalyptic: A Study of Jewish and Christian Apocalypses from Daniel to Revelation* (1944, 2nd edn, 1947), pp. 30, 56-59, 102-103, 120-23; T.F. Glasson, *The Second Advent: The Origin of the New Testament Doctrine* (1947, 2nd edn, 1947), pp. 54-55.

56. An example of one hoping that an original Son of man saying has been altered in transmission to a general saying is B. Violet, 'Die Verfluchung des Feigenbaums', in *ΕΥΧΑΡΙΣΤΗΡΙΟΝ* (FS Hermann Gunkel, 1923), pp. 135-40. Violet sees in the curse of the fig tree a misunderstood Son of man saying, because, as it now stands, the story seems absurd. It is clear from the Peshitta that the word of Jesus need not be a curse, but could be a prophecy. When Jesus, in fact, did not say *nash*, but *barnasha*, the Greek translator should not have rendered μηκέτι ἐὶς αἰῶνα ἐκ σοῦ μηδεὶς καρπὸν φάγοι but οὐ μὴ ἐὶς τὸν αἰῶνα ὁ υἱὸς τοῦ ἀνθρώπου ἐκ σοῦ καρπὸν φάγεται (p. 137). If it can be claimed that Son of man has been introduced in the tradition at passages originally having only 'man', the opposite could be claimed with even greater confidence. The intention of Violet is 'aus Liebe zu meinem Heilande' to preserve Jesus from having said something so absurd.

57. F.P. Badham, 'The Title "Son of Man"', *ThT* 45 (1911), pp. 395-448.

Hyper-radical in his interpretation and pathetic in his style, Eduard Hertlein does not even see the presupposition for the New Testament Son of man to have existed at the time of Jesus.[58] Hertlein will not base his solution on intuition but on facts, and facts in this connection must be of a literary kind. He is sure that Daniel 7, the source of the 'title', as earlier assumed by P. de Lagarde, belongs to a later period.[59] The first phase in the understanding of the Son of man was the dogmatic, the second the historical and this third the last and final. What happened was that the author behind the Gospel of Mark drew the Son of man figure from Daniel 7, a text deriving from around 70 CE, the figure being as a symbol of the holy people. His was a messianic interpretation, although such that the use of Son of man alone was an indirect designation for Jesus as the supernatural Son of God and Messiah. From here, the expression penetrated the whole Gospel tradition, whereby an original motive for secrecy was lost. Thus it is not possible to speak of a Son of man concept at the time of Jesus at all.[60]

C.S. Patton is on more familiar ground when he says that, whatever the meaning of the expression in Aramaic, there is no doubt that it is a messianic title in the Gospels. Because we know that Jesus did everything to avoid being known as the Messiah, it must be secondarily introduced to an original logion or be present in sayings belonging to a later period. According to Patton, 'many or most of those messianic conceptions which are most materialistic and most obnoxious to modern minds' are found in passages with the phrase Son of man. 'The present study does certainly throw doubt upon the authenticity of those passages as coming from Jesus, and therefore relieves him of the responsibility for the grosser elements of the messianic conception.'[61]

In the monograph *Le Fils de l'homme. Essai historique et critique* (1924), George Dupont sums up what for some was to be the basic understanding.[62] Son of man was not a messianic title at the time of Jesus. Daniel 7 is to be

58. E. Hertlein, *Die Menschensohnfrage im letzten Studium* (1911). In the introduction, he declaims that 'es hier zum erstenmale unternommen wird, die Frage nach dem neutestamentlichen "Menschensohn" unter der Voraussetzung zu betrachten, daß die Ursprungstelle dieses Ausdrucks im nachchristlicher Zeit entstanden ist' (p. III).

59. Hertlein refers to Lagarde's review of E. Havet, *Études d'histoire religieuse. La modernité des prophetes* (1891). *GGA* 2 (1891), pp. 497-520 (510) (see also above), and to the results of his own earlier book, *Der Daniel der Römerzeit* (1908).

60. In 'Die Wolken des "Menschensohnes" (Dan 7,13)', *ZAW* 37 (1917–18), pp. 134-36, Hertlein attempts to show that the clouds of Dan. 7 have their source in Isa. 60.8a. They do not prove any superhuman character of the Son of man (the whole religio-historical enterprise, being deprived of its foundation).

61. C.S. Patton, 'Did Jesus Call Himself the Son of Man?', *JR* 2 (1922), pp. 501-11 (511).

62. In fact, Dupont could have been placed above, in Chapter 8.

understood symbolically, and Son of man in *1 Enoch* is to be understood due to Christian interpolations, while *4 Ezra* also shows Christian influence. In Aramaic, the possible candidate בר אנשׁ, like אנשׁ, signifies humanity in general, a meaning still to be seen in some Son of man sayings in the Synoptic Gospels, where it has, however, become a messianic title. The messianic content, therefore, has to be attributed to the community having committed 'a philological blunder' (une erreur philologique).[63] The concept of Jesus as Messiah is due to a transformation of a prophet announcing the kingdom into the Son of God.[64]

The Chicago professor Shirley Jackson Case (1872–1947) proposes the philologically less reasoned opinion that Jesus in no way named himself Son of man, because

> the Semitic tongue, whether Hebrew or Aramaic, framed the expression 'son of man' as easily as English says 'mankind' (literally 'man's child') or German 'Menschenkind'—with the same generic meaning. Of course, no one in his right mind goes about calling himself 'the Mankind,' 'the Human Race'.[65]

Thus, Case also thinks it improbable that Jesus should have used Son of man in the third person, just as he did not think of himself as the Messiah.[66] Hans Windisch (1881–1935), interpreting Jn 1.51, also sees this unique saying as a creation, whose background lies in early Christian Son of man mythology.[67] 'There exists a Son of man theology in the gospels, *a vita filii hominis Jesu Christi*, an account of the πράξεις and λόγια of Jesus, perceived as manifestations of the apocalyptic Man on earth,' of which Jn 1.51 is a fragment.[68]

The last to be mentioned under this heading is Henry Burton Sharman. In his *Son of Man and Kingdom of God: A Critical Study* (1943), he makes an observation that is taken up by others after the Second World War. According to Sharman, the whole Son of man tradition belongs to a time after the resurrection. The disciples of Jesus had hoped that he was the one who should redeem Israel (Lk. 24.21), but the crucifixion destroyed that expectation:

63. G. Dupont, *Le Fils de l'homme. Essai historique et critique* (1924), p. 162.

64. G. Baldensperger, 'Le Fils de l'homme. Essai historique et critique par George Dupont, 1924', *RHPhR* 5 (1925), pp. 262-73, offers a thorough critique from his own point of view (see above), which he finds confirmed by the results of the religio-historical school, of which he blames Dupont for not having taken any account.

65. S.J. Case, 'The Alleged Messianic Consciousness of Jesus', *JBL* 46 (1927), pp. 1-19 (17-18).

66. Cf. also S.J. Case, *Jesus: A New Biography* (1927), pp. 360-71.

67. H. Windisch, 'Angelophanien um den Menschensohn auf Erden. Ein Kommentar zu Joh 1,51', *ZNW* 30 (1931), pp. 215-33 (229-30).

68. Windisch, 'Angelophanien um den Menschensohn', p. 231.

> But the disciples of Jesus had experiences presently which led them to believe that he had not been utterly extinguished but was potently existent. When appearances were no longer reported, it became their conviction that he had departed to the right hand of God. Henceforth he was considered to be the Danielic-apocalyptic Son of Man, and in that revised form declared to be the Messiah of God—destined ultimately to return in glory as the Judge of Mankind.[69]

Sharman further sees his interpretation confirmed by the circumstance that there does not seem to be any relation between Son of man and Kingdom of God: 'They create the impression of two foci that do not belong to the same ellipse… The Son of Man has no kingdom and the Kingdom of God has no Son of Man.'[70] This is wholly in contrast to the understanding of Rudolf Otto (see below).

69. H.B. Sharman, *Son of Man and Kingdom of God: A Critical Study* (1943), p. 83.
70. Sharman, *Son of Man and Kingdom of God*, p. 86.

12. The History of Religions School

Nearly simultaneously with the Aramaic stage, another attempt at understanding the term gained a foothold, challenging the interpretation of Son of man from another angle, as merely equivalent with 'man'; not to say merely as a circumlocution for the person speaking. This understanding presupposed that the man-like figure in Dan. 7.13 was not an *ad hoc* invention, created merely as an apt contrast to the beasts, but that the figure had its background in ancient pagan mythology. The leading force behind this attempt was the so-called History of Religions School, which had its main base in Göttingen and which enjoyed its widest influence between 1890 and 1930 (although with a sequel also in the following decades). The assumed mythological background added a new dimension to the understanding of the impact of a reference to Daniel's Son of man and its employment in *1 Enoch* 37–71 and *4 Ezra* 13, eventually offering the possibility of seeing testimonies of a special Jewish variant of a pagan mythological figure in these texts. It mediated the old alternative between a messianic and a symbolical understanding, still actual in the exegesis of Daniel. For some, however, it offered new life to a psychologizing understanding in line with what we have seen in the previous chapter.

Excursus II. *The Interpretation of Daniel 7.13,* 1 Enoch *37–71 and* 4 Ezra *13 from c. 1850 to the Second World War*

Of course, interpreters in the period from c. 1850 to 1945—and the Second World War is here used as a limit for practical reasons—were still divided on the question whether Son of man in Dan. 7.13 is to be understood as a personal Messiah or as a symbol, and how the relation to the Son of man/Man figure in *1 Enoch* 37–71 and *4 Ezra* 13 should be perceived.[1]

1. Cf. on the following, Excursus B: Die messianische Auslegung von Dan. 7,13, and Excursus C: Die symbolische Auslegung von Dan. 7,13, in Müller, *Der Ausdruck 'Menschensohn' in den Evangelien*, respectively, pp. 33-38 and 39-44.

a. *The Messianic Interpretation of Daniel 7.13*

A number of commentators adhere to a messianic interpretation of Daniel's saying. Among these, we find Adolf Hilgenfeld postulating that, even if the figure symbolizes the people, it remains true that the 'Messiah alone is head of this people'. He finds this figure again in Dan. 8.15-17; 10.5-6, 9, 11-14, 19-21; 11.1-2 and 12.6-7.[2] Georg Behrmann (1846–1911) reminds us of the dictum of le roi soleil: 'L'état c'est moi'.[3] The series can be continued with J. Boehmer,[4] Georg Beer (1865–1946),[5] Paul Riessler (1865–1935),[6] Conrad von Orelli (1846–1912)[7] and Marie Joseph Lagrange (1855–1938).[8]

As a variant of this interpretation, Paul Haupt claims that Judas the Maccabee stands behind the man-like in Dan. 7.13.[9] A few suggest a known or unknown angel. While the first is the conjecture of H. Gressmann[10] and F. Stier,[11] Nathaniel Schmidt refers to the description of Gabriel in Dan. 8.15, 16; 9.21; 10.5, 16, 18; 12.6, 7, and maintains that 'the "one like unto a son of man" in Dan. 7,13 is an angel, and more particularly Michael, the guardian angel of Israel'.[12] In this, he was followed, for instance, by A. Bertholet.[13]

Among those adhering to the results of the religio-historical approach, Paul Volz finds that the meaning and function of the visional man is that of the Ruler-Messiah (Herrschermessias),[14] while Hugo Gressmann argues that, just as in old Israelite opinion, the Messiah was at the head of the new era, where all people would submit to him, so the 'Man' is a figure parallel to the Messiah.[15]

2. A. Hilgenfeld, *Die jüdische Apokalyptik* (1857), pp. 46-49.

3. G. Behrmann, *Das Buch Daniel* (1894), p. 48. Nonetheless, it was not a common designation for the Messiah at the times of Jesus, before he himself revealed it in Mt. 24.30 (cf. p. Preface, XLII).

4. J. Boehmer, *Reich Gottes und Menschensohn im Buche Daniel* (1899), pp. 139-45.

5. G. Beer, 'Das Buch Henoch', in E. Kautzsch (ed.), *Die Apokryphen und Pseudepigraphen des Alten Testaments* II (1900, 2nd edn, 1921), pp. 217-310 (p. 262).

6. P. Riessler, *Das Buch Daniel* (1902), pp. 70-71.

7. C. von Orelli, 'Messias', *RE* 12 (3rd edn, 1903), pp. 723-39 (727).

8. M.J. Lagrange, *Le Messianisme chez les Juifs (150 av. J.-C. a 200 ap. J.-C.)* (1909), p. 66, where Lagrange points to the heroes of the Maccabean revolt, the Hasideans and the Hasmoneans as possible candidates. Cf. also pp. 224-28, and *idem*, *Le Judaïsme avant Jésus-Christ* (1931), pp. 66-68, 383-84, and further *idem*, 'L'Avénement du Fils de l'Homme', *RB* NS 3 (1906), pp. 382-411, 561-74.

9. P. Haupt, 'The Son of Man', *The Monist* 29 (1919), pp. 125-33 (130).

10. H. Gressmann, *Der Ursprung der israelitisch-jüdischen Eschatologie* (1905), p. 348. Cf. below.

11. F. Stier, *Gott und Engel im Alten Testament* (1934), p. 129.

12. N. Schmidt, 'The "Son of Man" in the Book of Daniel', *JBL* 19 (1900), pp. 22-28 (26); cf. *idem*, 'Son of Man', in *Encyclopaedia Biblica*, IV (1903, 2nd edn, 1907), cols. 4705-40 (4710).

13. A. Bertholet, 'M(enschensohn) im AT und Judentum', *RGG*, IV (1913), cols. 296-97.

14. P. Volz, *Jüdische Eschatologie von Daniel bis Akiba* (1903), p. 11. Cf., however, the 2nd edn, *Die Eschatologie der jüdischen Gemeinde im neutestamentlichen Zeitalter* (1934 = 3rd edn, 1966), p. 13, where Volz speaks of the 'Man' in Dan. 7.13 as 'das eschatologische *Gottesreich*, zugespitzt in dem *eschatologischen Herrscher*'.

15. H. Gressmann, *Der Ursprung der israelitisch-jüdische Eschatologie* (1905), p. 342; cf. pp. 36-37.

Denying foreign influence on the Son of man portrait in Dan. 7.13, Heinrich Junker admits that the concept presents a totally new picture of the Messiah, which is comprehensible from internal Israelite presuppositions as a consequence of the still more transcendent picture of the kingdom of the Messiah.[16] Werner Küppers would not exclude any influence from the outside world, but also sees no reason to distinguish between a transcendent Savior figure, the Son of man and a political-national Messiah. What we witness here is a tension within Messianic expectation of Late Judaism.[17]

b. *The Symbolic Interpretation of Daniel 7.13*

The argument that a messianic kingdom includes a king brings us near to the purely symbolic understanding maintained, among others,[18] by James Drummond,[19] A.C. Larsen,[20] Frants Buhl,[21] Emil Schürer,[22] Karl Marti (1855–1925),[23] Joseph Klausner,[24] Eduard König (1846–1936),[25] H. Rongy,[26] George Foot Moore,[27] J.A. Montgomery,[28] R.H.

16. H. Junker, *Untersuchungen über literarische und exegetische Probleme des Buches Daniel* (1932), pp. 55-65 (64).

17. See W. Küppers, 'Das Messiasbild der spätjüdischen Apokalyptik', *IKZ* 23 (1933), pp. 193-256; 24 (1934), pp. 47-72, especially the first part.

18. Not a few interpreters have already been mentioned above, for instance Baldensperger, Wellhausen and Lietzmann.

19. J. Drummond, *The Jewish Messiah* (1877), p. 284.

20. A.C. Larsen, *Profeten Daniel og Esters Bog oversatte of forklarede for Lægfolk* (1893), p. 102.

21. Frants Buhl, *De messianske Forjættelser i det gamle Testament* (1894), p. 175; idem, 'Daniel, der Prophet', *RE* 4 (3rd edn, 1898), pp. 445-57 (456).

22. E. Schürer, *Geschichte des jüdischen Volkes im Zeitalter Jesu Christi* (4th edn, 1907), II, p. 614.

23. K. Marti, *Das Buch Daniel* (1901), p. 52. With regard to the expression in the Gospels, Marti assumes that the evangelists have placed it in the mouth of Jesus because of his reference to Dan. 7.13 in Mk 13.26, understanding the saying in its original sense.

24. Thus Son of man is not mentioned in his *Die messianischen Vorstellungen des jüdischen Volkes im Zeitalter der Tannaiten* (1903, reworked and included as Part III [pp. 387-517] in *idem, The Messianic Idea in Israel from Its Beginning to the Completion in Mishnah* [1956]). With regard to Dan. 7.13, see anyway *The Messianic Idea*, pp. 229-31, in Part I, 'The Messianic Idea in the Period of the Prophets' (pp. 1-243; in its original form published in 1909).

25. E. König, 'Der Menschensohn im Danielbuche', *NKZ* 16 (1905), pp. 904-28. When Jesus took it over, it was interpreted already as a designation for the Messiah. He established the connection to Dan. 2.44, including in it the Kingdom of God. His use witnesses to his sovereignty with regard to the Prophets.

26. H. Rongy, 'Le Fils d'homme dans Daniel VII,13', *Revue Ecclesiastiques de Liége* 14 (1922–23), pp. 96-100. The symbolic understanding does not exclude a king: 'Pouvait-il s'imaginer un royaume sens roi?' (p. 100).

27. G.F. Moore, *Judaism in the First Centuries of the Christian Era: The Age of the Tannaim*, II (1927, 11th edn, 1970), p. 334.

28. J.A. Montgomery, *A Critical and Exegetical Commentary on the Book of Daniel* (1927), pp. 319-20. Cf. p. 323: 'If we admit that the term "son of man" is not in itself mysterious, and if we avoid confounding it with later interpretations, there is nothing

Charles[29] and H.H. Rowley, who argued that Son of Man 'represents the coming empire', not being held to 'stand for the saints, as such, but for the *Kingdom*, or *rule* of the saints'.[30]

c. *Other Interpretations of Daniel 7.13*

The then Berlin rabbi Leo Baeck (1873–1956) sees an impassable gap between the original significance of the word in Hebrew and Aramaic and what it becomes in the Greek Gospels. The interpretations in *1 Enoch* and *4 Ezra* cannot bridge this gap, just as it is impossible to conclude that Judaism, before the destruction of the Second Temple, had designated the expected Messiah Son of man.[31] It is an old biblical word equal to '*ish, enosh, gewer*'. In Dan. 7.13, the idea of the pre-existent Messiah and the pre-existent people of Israel were joined so that the result of 'the ideal Israel or, in the language of Daniel, the *Sfar*, the Archont, the Aeon of Israel has become Messiah and Messiah the ideal Israel', which is even clearer in *1 Enoch*.[32]

Another Jewish scholar, Moses Gaster, delivers 'a new interpretation', drawing the conclusion from a comparison between Dan. 7.9-18 and Deut. 33.2-4 and the haggadic interpretation in three targums that 'there can be no doubt that the Son of man must be Moses, who is represented in his true character, coming on the clouds of heaven to the throne of glory, there to plead with God'.[33]

d. *The Significance of* 1 Enoch *37–71 and* 4 Ezra *13*

With regard to the Son of man texts in *1 Enoch* 37–71[34] and *4 Ezra* 13, the point of view gains ever more force that these passages are the result of Jewish interpretation of Daniel 7 and not of Christian interpolation. While the latter opinion is still maintained by, for instance, F. Buhl,[35] Emil G. Hirsch (with regard to *1 Enoch*),[36] Daniel Völter[37] and Nils

strange in its use as the type of Israel. It belongs to the Semitic genius to personify the people, as in the "I"-Psalms.'

29. R.H. Charles, *A Critical and Exegetical Commentary on the Book of Daniel* (1929), p. 187.

30. H.H. Rowley, *Darius the Mede and the Four World Empires in the Book of Daniel: A Historical Study of Contemporary Theories* (1935), pp. 61-66 (62-63 n. 2).

31. L. Baeck, 'Der "Menschensohn"', originally in *MGWJ* 81 (1937), pp. 12-24; reprinted in *idem*, *Aus drei Jahrtausenden. Wissenschaftliche Untersuchungen und Abhandlungen zur Geschichte des jüdischen Glauben* (1938, 2nd edn, 1956), pp. 187-98 (187).

32. Baeck, 'Der "Menschensohn"', p. 195.

33. M. Gaster, 'The Son of Man and the Theophany of Daniel, Ch. VII.: A New Interpretation', *The Search* 1 (1931), pp. 15-30 (29).

34. L. Gry, 'La dénomination messianique "Fils de l'Homme" dans la Bible et les Apocryphes éthiopiens', in *XENIA. Homage international à l'Université nationale de Grèce* (1912), pp. I-XII, investigates the different expressions for Son of man in the Ethiopic rendering, arriving at the conclusion that it is the result partly of a literal translation of the Greek, partly due to influence from Aramaic documents, and partly because of a 'manifeste l'interprétation chrétienne d'un traducteur isolé' (p. XI).

35. F. Buhl, *De messianske Forjættelser i det gamle Testament*, p. 232.

36. E.G. Hirsch, 'Son of Man', in *Jewish Encyclopaedia* (1905), IX, pp. 461-63 (462).

Messel,[38] the Jewish origin of the interpretation in the two Pseudepigrapha is defended by a number of outstanding scholars.[39] With the rise of the religio-historical approach and its attempt to connect the Son of man of Jewish apocalyptic with pagan concepts of a Primeval Man, the New Testament evidence of the Son of man expression loses interest as the possible source for the figure in the Pseudepigrapha. Attention is absorbed by the religious concepts of the surrounding world.

e. *The Quest for the Religio-Historical Background of the Son of Man in Jewish Apocalyptic*[40]

The first to propose such an origin in mythology outside Israel was Hermann Gunkel (1862–1932), then teaching in Berlin but ending his career in Halle. In *Schöpfung und*

37. D. Völter, 'Die Gesicht vom Adler und vom Menschen im 4. Esra nebst Bemerkungen über die Menschensohn-Stellen in den Bilderreden Henochs', *NThT* 8 (1919), pp. 241-73.

38. N. Messel, *Der Menschensohn in den Bilderreden des Henoch* (1922). Messel, however, thinks *1 En.* 46.2-4 and 48.2 to be original, but here the expression is equivalent to 'the Chosen', a personification of the Jewish people. The evidence from *1 Enoch*, therefore, cannot be used to prove Son of man to be a name for Messiah in Judaism.

39. This was already maintained by F.G. Gass, *De utroque Jesu Christi nomine in Novo Testamento obvio Dei filii et hominis*, I-II (1839–40), II, p. 95; A. Dillmann, *Das Buch Henoch* (1853), p. 156. Later also W. Baldensperger, *Das Selbstbewusstsein Jesu im Lichte der messianischen Hoffnungen seiner Zeit* (1888), p. 69 (2nd edn, 1892, pp. 80-81); H. Lietzmann, *Der Menschensohn* (1896), pp. 42-48; J. Wellhausen, 'Des Menschensohn', *Skizzen und Vorarbeiten* VI (1899), pp. 198-99; J. Weiss, *Die Predigt Jesu vom Reiche Gottes* (2nd edn, 1900), p. 162 n. 1; G. Beer, 'Das Buch Henoch', in E. Kautzsch (ed.), *Die Apokryphen und Pseudepigraphen des Alten Testaments*, II (1900 = 2nd edn, 1921), pp. 217-310 (231-32) (with regard to *1 Enoch*); H. Gunkel, 'Das vierte Buch Esra', in E. Kautzsch (ed.), *Die Apokryphen und Pseudepigraphen des Alten Testaments*, II (1900 = 2nd edn, 1921), pp. 331-401 (350-52) (with regard to *4 Ezra*). E. Schürer, *Geschichte des jüdischen Volkes im Zeitalter Jesu Christi*, II (4th edn, 1907), pp. 614-15 n. 13 (English: *The History of the Jewish People in the Age of Jesus Christ*, II [revised by Geza Vermes *et al.*, 1979], pp. 520-21 n. 27); M.-J. Lagrange, *Le Messianisme chez les Juifs* (1909), p. 88; *idem*, *Le Judaisme avant Jésus-Christ* (1931), pp. 242-43; R.H. Charles, 'Book of Enoch', in *idem* (ed.), *The Apocrypha and Pseudepigrapha of the Old Testament*, II (1913 = 6th edn, 1969), pp. 163-277 (184-85) (with regard to *1 Enoch*). On p. 171, Charles argues for assigning the Parables 'either to the years 94–79 or 70–64' B.C.; G. Box, 'IV Ezra', in Charles (ed.), *The Apocrypha and Pseudepigrapha of the Old Testament*, II, pp. 542-624 (616) (with regard to *4 Ezra*); J. Klausner, *The Messianic Idea in Israel from Its Beginning to the Completion of the Mishnah* (1956), Part II: 'The Messianic Idea in the Books of the Apocrypha and Pseudepigrapha' (originally 1921), pp. 245-386 (291-92) (*1 Enoch*) and pp. 358-59 (*4 Ezra*); G.F. Moore, *Judaism in the First Centuries of the Christian Era: The Age of the Tannaim*, II (1927 = 11th edn, 1970), pp. 333-35.

40. A summarizing catalogue (without much evaluation of the different attempts to discover a background for the Son of man in the history of religions) is J. Eggler, *Influences and Traditions Underlying the Vision of Daniel 7:2-14: The Research History from the End of the 19th Century to the Present* (2000), especially pp. 55-110.

Chaos in Urzeit und Endzeit from 1895, he claimed that the enigmatic Danielic Son of man was taken over from tradition. The author did not himself invent this picture of Israel. 'In the myth "Son of man" became the title of the God-conqueror.'[41] So even if Son of man for the seer was a picture for Israel, Gunkel sees its background all the same in the Babylonian chaos-myth which—in the meantime—had become a promise and was traditionally interpreted in a political context. Thus Daniel 7 ultimately stems from the Babylonian Tiamat-myth.

This widening of the perspective to include pagan mythology, of course, raised the question of the reach of religio-historical parallels in the interpretation: whether it should influence understanding or be considered wholly domesticated by its biblical context. Julius Wellhausen deemed Gunkel's conclusions all too far-reaching:

> The Protos Pseudos is that he assigns great importance to the question of origin. It is of methodical importance to know material that actually is present in the apocalypses, [material] which is not always wholly saturated by the concept of the author, nor always fully absorbed in his casting, but more often leaves an opaque rest for our explanation: anyway, from where this material originally stems is totally unimportant in regard to method.[42]

The original meaning was of no importance to the authors. For interpretation, the important thing is to see how it is used. 'Gunkel thinks he has to correct them and to confront their interpretation with the correct understanding. This may have antiquarian interest, but it is not the task of the theologian and the exegete.'[43]

In a rejoinder, Gunkel takes his point of departure precisely in the Son of man problem. The Gospels show that the term was known in Jewish eschatological tradition, or at least in some parts of it, as a name of Christ. If we could not find a source for this, the conclusion would be that for the time being we are too badly informed about the Judaism at the time of Jesus.[44] Gunkel also complains that many interpreters are only too willing

> immediately to presume, as soon as two writings somehow are in contact, a pure literary connection between both of them, without even thinking of the oral tradition! This habit which plays such an uncommonly fatal role and deprives the interpreter of the knowledge of a great part of the spiritual life of antiquity, that which is not witnessed directly in books, [this habit] one always must confront with the evidence that the world does not consist exclusively of authors and books.[45]

Because, according to Gunkel, it can be concluded from the Gospels that Daniel 7 cannot be the only background for the expression Son of man, because *1 Enoch* 37–71 and

41. H. Gunkel, *Schöpfung und Chaos in Urzeit und Endzeit. Eine religionsgeschichtliche Untersuchung über Gen 1 und Ap 12* (1895), pp. 328-31 (331).

42. J. Wellhausen, 'Zur Apokalyptischen Literatur', *Skizzen und Vorarbeiten* VI (1899), pp. 215-49 (233).

43. Wellhausen, 'Zur Apokalyptischen Literatur', p. 234.

44. H. Gunkel, 'Aus Wellhausen's: neuesten apokalyptischen Forschungen. Einige principielle Erörterungen', *ZWTh* 42 (1899), pp. 581-611 (585).

45. Gunkel, 'Aus Wellhausen's: neuesten apokalyptischen Forschungen', pp. 587-88.

4 Ezra 13 are dependent not only on Daniel, but, in addition, on a tradition at present unknown to us (auf eine uns zunächst unbekannte Tradition), we have to conclude, 'that Daniel 7 also is based on this tradition of the heavenly figure of "the Man"'.[46]

Johannes Weiss was not convinced by Gunkel's reasoning and maintained that 'in Daniel the picture of "Man" grows from the opposition to the pictures of animals', so that it is possible to see how it comes into existence and therefore to conclude that it really is original at this place.[47] However, other interpreters showed themselves far more positive toward the possibility of reaching the sources of the figure in Dan. 7.13.[48]

While Gunkel had pointed to the Babylonian creation-myth in an indefinite way, Fritz Hommel (1854–1936) was more exact when attempting to show the similarities between Son of man and Adapa-Marduk. Characteristic for the period is the description of the use of the expression by Jesus: 'He took the vessel of Babylonian mythology, otherwise so unclean, and hallowed it for ever in this matter where its searches had lead to a presentiment of the truly divine'.[49] Of others, who likewise pointed to the Babylonian creation-myth as the background for the expression Son of man, could be mentioned the Leipzig professor Heinrich Zimmern (1862–1931),[50] the Berlin professor Hugo Winckler (1863–1913),[51] Nathaniel Schmidt,[52] the Norwegian born professor of history and philosophy of religion in Leiden, William Brede Kristensen (1867–1953),[53] the Halle professor in Old Testament Gustav Hölscher (1877–1955),[54] E.G.H. Kraeling,[55] the Norwegian H. Ludin

46. Gunkel, 'Aus Wellhausen's: neuesten apokalyptischen Forschungen', p. 588.

47. J. Weiss, *Die Predigt Jesu vom Reiche Gottes* (2nd edn, 1900 = 3rd edn, 1964), p. 162 n. 1.

48. Of the vast literature on this theme only those contributions are included which either deal with the religio-historical background of the expression Son of man in a monograph, or have played an important role in the discussion. In this context, it first bears upon the background of Dan. 7.13 and thereby also of *1 En.* 37–71 and *4 Ezra* 13. Therefore, the consequences drawn of the different interpreters with regard to the impact on the understanding of the New Testament expression are only touched upon sporadically.

49. F. Hommel, 'The Apocalyptic Origin of the Expression "Son of Man"', *ET* 11 (1899–1900), pp. 341-45 (345).

50. In E. Schraeder, *Die Keilinschriften und das Alte Testament*. 3. Auflage mit Ausdehnung auf die Apokryphen, Pseudepigraphen und das Neue Testament neu bearbeitet von H. Zimmern und H. Winckler (1903), II. Religion und Sprache, pp. 343-653 (391-93; cf. 520-22).

51. H. Winckler, 'Des menschen sohn = erlöser', *Altorientalische Forschungen* III.2 (1904–1905), pp. 296-301.

52. N. Schmidt, 'The "Son of Man" in the Book of Daniel', *JBL* 19 (1900), pp. 22-28 (27).

53. W.B. Kristensen, 'De term "Zoon des Menschen"; toegelicht uit de antropologie der ouden', *ThT* 45 (1911), pp. 1-38. Kristensen especially points to the Babylonian King-Ideology where the king is both the first typical man and son of god, where a soteriological aspect was within reach (cf. p. 37).

54. G. Hölscher, 'Die Entstehung des Buches Daniel', *ThStKr* 92 (1919), pp. 113-38. Hölscher separates Dan. 7 from both the visions, chs. 8–12 dating from Maccabean times, and the legends, chs. 1–6, dating from third century BCE. Also in ch. 7, he finds interpolations from the same redaction which added chs. 8–12. All allusions to Antiochus IV Epiphanes are secondary and the original parts of ch. 7 took its material from Babylonian mythology. What we find is thus the myth of chaos-beast connected with the myth of the

Jansen[56] and the famous Baltimore professor of archaeology, William Foxwell Albright (1891–1971).[57]

Most of the hypotheses regarding the origin of the Son of man resulted in a personal-messianic interpretation of the figure—if not in Daniel 7, at least in the basic concept. An exception is the proposal of Daniel Völter, who looks for the background in the concept of *Khsahathra vairyia* in Parseeism. According to Völter, this was not only an abstract concept but was perceived also as a person, as one of the Amesha Spentas from the immediate heavenly surrounding of Ahura Mazda. As in Daniel 7, the Kingdom of God in Parseeism also has a personal heavenly representative, although he was not expected to be visible at the realization of this kingdom as its present king or as a personification of the people to whom this kingdom belongs.[58]

four kingdoms and the heavenly Primeval Man (himmlischen Urmenschen). The Bern professor Max Haller (1879–1949), 'Das Alter von Daniel 7', *ThStKr* 93 (1920–21), pp 83-87, building on Hölscher's presuppositions, wants to date ch. 7 before chs. 1–6, also because this chapter does not seem to know anything concrete about the fourth kingdom. Likewise Martin Noth (1902–1968), later professor in Königsberg and Bonn, in 'Zur Komposition des Buches Daniel', *ThStKr* 98–99 (1926), pp. 143-63, isolates vv. 9, 10, 13 and 14 in Dan. 7 as secondary, offering a new meaning from the context of this chapter. As in *1 En.* 37–71, the Son of man was originally the Messiah coming to judge the world. A comparison of the two 'Son of man' passages leads to the conclusion that both come from the same source, from which *1 Enoch* has preserved the original meaning, while Daniel has reinterpreted it.

55. E.G.H. Kraeling, 'Some Babylonian and Iranian Mythology in the Seventh Chapter of Daniel', in *Oriental Studies: In Honour of C.E. Pavry* (1933), pp. 228-31. Kraeling draws the attention to 'the Babylonian New Year's myth' and to Marduk as 'prototype' (p. 230). However, he admits that 'the possibility still exists that the designation "manlike one" was not of foreign origin, but rather a Jewish formulation. There is one circumstance favourable to this latter view, viz. the arrival of this individual on the clouds of heaven. This motif seems to presuppose the idea of a translation. Thus Moses and Elijah can appear on earth because they were taken away in supernatural fashion, and Jesus, too, comes back on the clouds of heaven, because he departed from earth in this fashion. The title "one like a son of man" might then simply point to *the previous earthly life* of this celestial figure, i.e. the idea of the David redivivus, but in a vague, non-dynastic form' (pp. 230-31).

56. H. Ludin Jansen, *Die Henochgestalt. Eine vergleichende religionsgeschichtliche Untersuchung* (1939), p. 110. The Son of man is seen as a sort of an antitype to the Babylonian-Chaldean Ea-Oannes. Ludin Jansen thinks the Son of man of the book of *Enoch* is created on Jewish soil, which has given it a certain stamp. Thus, Son of man in Judaism is a product of foreign influence on pre-existing conception, making an eschatological figure out of a primeval. Cf. S. Mowinckel's criticism in 'Henokskikkelsen i senjødisk apokalyptikk. Innleg som 1ste ordinære opponent ved H. Ludin Jansens doctordisputats. Specimen: Die Henochgestalt. Eine vergleichende religionsgeschichtliche Untersuchung, 1939', *NTT* 41 (1940), pp. 206-36.

57. W.F. Albright, *From the Stone Age to Christianity: Monotheism and the Historical Process* (1940, 4th edn, 1946), pp. 219-20.

58. D. Völter, 'Der Menschensohn in Dan 7,13', *ZNW* 3 (1902), pp. 173-74. Later Völter abandoned this hypothesis.

In 1903, in Germany, two classic works appeared on the religion of Late Judaism. One of these was by the Tübingen Old Testament professor Paul Volz (1871–1941), titled *Jüdische Eschatologie von Daniel bis Akiba*,[59] the other by Wilhelm Bousset, titled *Die Religion des Judentums im neutestamentlichen Zeitalter*. While Volz is content with the statement that 'the meaning and function of the visional man is that of the sovereign-messiah (Bedeutung und Funktion des visionalen Menschen ist die des Herrschermessias)',[60] and only in a general way points to a concept of a Primeval Man (Urmensch) as a possible background, Bousset boldly ventures to enter the history of religion. The new, transcendent picture of the Messiah which turns up in *1 Enoch* and *4 Ezra* is unheard of 'in the world of ideas of Israel and something totally new (in den Gedankenwelt Israels unerhört und ein völliges Novum)'.[61] That this should be the result of a misunderstanding of the saying in Daniel, seems highly improbable to Bousset:

> That such an important and influential idea as the one of a heavenly preexistent Messiah should arise simply from a misunderstanding of a biblical saying, is simply incomprehensible... The assumption that Daniel in his prophecy artificially conceived the figure Son of man already known to him as a symbol of the people of Israel, would solve this difficulty. This invites the assumption that two figures are fused together in the preexistent Son of man: the Jewish Messiah and a preexistent heavenly being, whose origin and descent is still obscure. But of what sort this figure could be, is related in the new title of this composite figure: Son of man. It is somehow a form of the idea of the heavenly Man (Urmenschen) which has been united with the Jewish idea.[62]

Exactly this transcendent picture of the Messiah was also employed in the Gospels because its supernatural character better than the more politically coloured picture of the Messiah as Son of David expressed the messianic self-consciousness of Jesus, or the understanding of the first community. At any rate, with regard to the religio-historical background of the concept of the Son of man, Bousset had to admit: 'Up to the present, it is "counting with nothing but unknown quantities", the origin and original meaning of the Man until now being a great speculative religio-historical riddle'.[63] Bousset draws attention to a wide range of possible parallels: besides Philo, the Jewish and Christian Adam legend and the rabbinic speculation, there are also other figures of 'man': Primeval Man in Gnostic, Mandaic and Manichaean religion and in medieval kabbalistic speculation. Also in Persian religion, the Primeval Man (Gayomarth) played a certain role, and, among the Iranian believers, we hear of a sect calling themselves Gayomarthia after the Primeval Man. Hippolytus, in *Philosophumena* 5.7-8, relates how the Chaldeans—probably the followers of the Iranian religion—honored Adam. Finally, a

59. P. Volz, *Jüdische Eschatologie von Daniel bis Akiba* (2nd edn, 1934 = reprint 1966, with the new title, *Die Eschatologie der jüdischen Gemeinde im Neutestamentlichen Zeitalter*).

60. Volz, *Jüdische Eschatologie von Daniel bis Akiba*, p. 11. Cf. 2nd edn, 1934, p. 13, where Volz in a rewritten text maintains the same position.

61. Bousset, *Die Religion des Judentums*, p. 251.

62. Bousset, *Die Religion des Judentums*, pp. 253-54.

63. Bousset, *Die Religion des Judentums*, pp. 348-49.

newly detected Babylonian myth of Primeval Man (Adapa) deserves attention in this context.[64]

When the Iranian Primeval Man penetrated into Judaism, Bousset describes what happened in another place in the following way:

> The Primeval Man has become an eschatological figure and the character is essentially removed from the beginning of time to the end of time. Already in Persian religion...the Primeval Man Gayomarth played a special role at the resurrection... Likewise, the idea that the Man played a very special role at the end of time seems to have got a foothold in Judaism. In this way Daniel seems to have been confronted with the concept that the figure of a Man stood beside God at the final judgment and, in this way, he interpreted this idea symbolically. Very soon, then, this figure of Primeval Man grew together with the Jewish Messiah, and we should not be surprised, even in Jewish theology, to find something like a δεύτερος Θεός, a primordial being (uranfängliches Wesen), which appears just beside God the Almighty and nearly displaces him from the position of the judge of the world. In this way the idea penetrated further into New Testament literature, where its origin and original meaning, however, have become totally obscure and where they only remain as enigmatic hieroglyphs.[65]

Bousset seems to have been the first to propound the assumption so effective in the following decades of a 'pluralistic' background of the so-called Late Jewish (spätjüdischen) Son of man concept, which became one of several variants of an Oriental myth of Primeval Man. Thus the Achilles heel of this hypothesis, the synthetic viewing of many different witnesses from very different periods, is visible from the very beginning.

Among those following Bousset, directing attention to an Oriental myth of the Primeval Man as the background for the Son of man concept, although the accentuation could vary, is Hugo Gressmann (1877–1927), later teaching in Berlin. In *Der Ursprung der israelitisch-jüdischen Eschatologie* (1905), Gressmann warns against the misunderstanding springing from the identification of the first literary witness to an idea with its total and original extent. 'Because in Daniel 7, "the Man" turns up for the first time in literature, therefore one believes it necessary to seek the origin of this figure in this passage.'[66] To Gressmann, it is obvious that Son of man is not a Danielic creation, because *1 Enoch* and *4 Ezra* deliver a picture of this figure with details that did not originate in Daniel. Son of man is an eschatological figure, the pre-existent judge of the world and lord of the world, 'a parallel figure to the Messiah'. As the Messiah is an earthly, while the Son of man is a heavenly figure, they have nothing to do with each other originally and 'an internal

64. Bousset, *Die Religion des Judentums*, pp. 348-49. In the 1906 second edition, the paragraphs on Son of man are nearly identical with the first edition (see pp. 301-308, 404-407). However, the Naassenes for instance are added to the list of possible sources. In the third edition, *Die Religion des Judentums im späthellenistischen Zeitalter* (ed. H. Gressmann, 1926 [= reprint 1966]), only a few additions are found (see pp. 262-68, 352-54). Cf. also Bousset's review, 'R. Reitzenstein, Poimandres. Studien zur griech.-ägypt. und frühchristl. Literatur', *GGA* 167 (1905), pp. 692-712 (702-703).

65. W. Bousset, *Hauptprobleme der Gnosis* (1907), p. 219.

66. H. Gressmann, *Der Ursprung der israelitisch-jüdischen Eschatologie* (1905), p. 339. But cf. pp. 334-65.

Israelite development is impossible'.[67] With Bousset, Gressman does not want to stick to one specific religio-historical parallel, but contents himself with the conclusion: 'the Primeval Man is of non-Jewish origin'.[68]

At this juncture, we can observe a principal difference with regard to the basic methodological problem of religio-historical research. While Bousset is open to the possibility of Jewish apocalyptic giving mythological material its own stamp, Gressmann will not accept such a full absorption because of his apprehension of apocalyptic as an entity which does create new things.[69]

In his posthumously published *Der Messias* (1929), Gressmann once more returns to the Son of man problem: 'Ormuzd, Mithras, Primeval Man in the Iranian, Helios in the Hellenistic[70] and Son of man in the Jewish religion are certainly not entirely identical with each other, yet they can in any event often be mixed up with each other insofar as they exercise the same functions.'[71] He writes:

> In Daniel and *4 Ezra* the Hellenistic figure of the Saviour turns up for the first time on Jewish ground and combines itself with the old-Israelite figure of the Messiah. In *4 Ezra* 13, still clearly recognizable, the two stand beside each other: in the vision the 'Saviour' (σωτήρ); in the interpretation the 'Messiah'. The Messiah is the earthly ideal king who saves his people out of the power of its enemies and liberates Jerusalem and gives it sovereignty over the world and also adduces some ethical-religious goods. The Saviour, on the other hand, is a divine being coming down from heaven to the underworld to liberate men out of the force of death... In a word, the messianic ideal is mundane, the Saviour ideal is extra-mundane.[72]

Also to be mentioned in this context is one of the main figures in the History of Religions School, the Göttingen professor Richard Reitzenstein (1861–1931),[73] as well as

67. Gressmann, *Der Ursprung der israelitisch-jüdischen Eschatologie*, p. 361.

68. Gressmann, *Der Ursprung der israelitisch-jüdischen Eschatologie*, p. 364.

69. Cf. J.M. Schmidt, *Die jüdische Apokalyptik. Die Geschichte ihrer Erforschung von den Anfängen bis zu den Textfunden von Qumran* (1969), p. 229.

70. Already in Gressmann, 'Das religionsgeschichtliche Problem des Ursprungs der hellenistischen Erlösungsreligon. Eine kritische Auseinandersetzung mit Reitzenstein II', *ZKG* 41 NF 4 (1922), pp. 154-80 (177), Gressmann points to Mithras-Helios as a possible background for Son of man.

71. H. Gressmann, *Der Messias* (ed. H. Schmidt, 1929), pp. 357-58. But cf. pp. 341-414.

72. Gressmann, *Der Messias*, p. 372. In a separate chapter, Gressmann also points to Egyptian religion, uniting Son of man with the son-god Horus-Re-Atum. But cf. the remarks of J.M. Schmidt, *Die jüdische Apokalyptik*, pp. 230-31, on the sketchy and unfinished character of the material presented.

73. See *Poimandres. Studien zur griechisch-ägyptischen und frühchristlichen Literatur* (1904), where Reitzenstein speaks of 'the enigmatic word in the gospel ὁ υἱὸς τοῦ ἀνθρώπου, which somehow is connected with (the) God Ἄνθρωπος' (p. 81). In *Das mandäische Buch des Herrn der Größe und die Evangelienforschung* (1919), Reitzenstein returns to the problem, claiming that after the detection of the God Ἄνθρωπος in Iranian popular religion, it is no longer possible to isolate from it the designation 'the Man' or 'Son of man' of the Messiah or a messiah-like figure, or to consider the

Georg Hollmann,[74] the Bonn professor Carl Clemen (1865–1940),[75] Alfred Bertholet (1858–1951),[76] G.H. Box,[77] Eduard Meyer (1855–1930),[78] J.M. Creed,[79] the Giessen professor August Freiherr von Gall,[80] C.H. Kraeling, with his influential monograph *Anthropos and Son of Man: A Study in the Religious Syncretism of the Hellenistic Orient* (1927),[81] H. Schmidt (1877–1953),[82] Louise Troje,[83] the London professor W.O.E. Oesterley (1866–1950),[84] P. Volz,[85] Rudolf Otto,[86] the Copenhagen professor of Old

self-designation of Jesus as Son of man as without meaning (als bedeutungslos) (p. 45). Cf. finally also *Das iranische Erlösungsmysterium. Religionsgeschichtliche Untersuchungen* (1921), pp. 117-19.

74. G. Hollmann, *Welche Religion hatten die Juden, als Jesus auftrat?* (1905, 2nd edn, 1910), pp. 53-54.

75. C. Clemen, *Religionsgeschichtliche Erklärung des Neuen Testaments. Die Abhängigkeit des ältesten Christentums von nichtjüdischen Religionen und philosophischen Systemen* (1909), pp. 116-25.

76. A. Bertholet, 'I M(enschensohn) im AT und Judentum', *RGG*, IV (1913) cols. 296-97. Bertholet views Son of man as an angelic figure of the same type as the Urmensch returning in the last days as redeemer.

77. G.H. Box, 'IV Ezra', in Charles (ed.), *The Apocrypha and Pseudepigrapha of the Old Testament*, II, p. 616. Like Bertholet, Box sees an angelic figure, namely, Michael.

78. E. Meyer, *Ursprung und Anfänge des Christentums* (1921), II, p. 199, where Meyer with regard to Dan. 7 claims a direct borrowing from Parseeism. The man-like is the angel Sraosa, the genius of religion, slaying the wrath-demon Aesma, melted together with the savior Saosyant, the offspring of Zoroaster, the judge of the world, miraculously conceived and gifted with wonderful power, bringing about resurrection and Paradise. Cf. pp. 336-52.

79. J.M. Creed, 'The Heavenly Man', *JThS* 26 (1925), pp. 113-36 (135): 'It is conceivable, though it is certainly not established, that the Son of Man of Jewish Apocalyptic is another variant of the Persian Primal Man. If so, we have a further example of the complete transformation of the idea.'

80. A.F. von Gall, *ΒΑΣΙΛΕΙΑ ΘΟΥ ΘΕΟΥ. Eine religionsgeschichtliche Studie zur vorkirchlichen Eschatologie* (1926), p. 409: Son of man is nothing but Primeval Man coming from the eschatology of Parseeism 'where he is sometimes equated with Astvatereta, the victorious Saosyant'.

81. In this work, Kraeling points to the Iranian Gayomard as 'the ultimate origin of the Anthropos' (p. 94). However, 'in Daniel it is Marduk who most nearly but not completely approximates the Bar Nasha' (p. 147). Even if the thought of the Anthropos as redeemer is weak because 'the whole idea of the re-manifestation is a secondary element' (p. 123); 'our analysis of the Gnostic evidence serves us well, for it has shown conclusively that as he passed through Mesopotamia, the Iranian figure was identified with Marduk and consequently changed his character'. Thus Kraeling, like Gunkel, seeks the ultimate origin in Babylon.

82. H. Schmidt, 'Der Menschensohn: I. Im AT und Judentum', *RGG*, III (2nd edn, 1929), cols. 2117-18.

83. L. Troje, 'Urmensch', *RGG*, V (2nd edn, 1931), cols. 1416-17.

84. W.O.E. Oesterley, *II Esdras (The Ezra Apocalypse)* (1933), pp. 158-64. Oesterley, too, with regard to 'the Man' in *4 Ezra* 13, points to Iranian Shaoshyant, although in the vision as such he also sees influence from Marduk from the Babylonian creation myth.

Testament Aage Bentzen (1894–1953),[87] Walter Baumgartner[88] and William Manson (1882–1958).[89] It is proper to summarize here with the words of Baumgartner, who concludes his research report with a comment that even if it is not possible to answer all questions concerning the origin of 'the Man' and the other material in the vision in Daniel 7, it can be concluded from the whole discussion,

> that it is about an ad hoc figure, created on internal Jewish premises, but in the last resort a foreign figure, which to some degree has been adapted into the Jewish environment and thereby become a new sort of Messiah. Daniel has known but not accepted this concept...and has for this reason used 'the Man' only as a symbolical figure for the people of God, destined to have dominion. The other Son of man texts seem to have partially known this expectation as such; however, with regard to Daniel 7, they stick more to the role of 'the Man' in the vision than to its use in the interpretation. In this way our chapter [Daniel 7], without being messianic in itself, has become of greatest importance for the history of messianic expectation.[90]

A special phase of the discussion was initiated by Joachim Jeremias (1900–1979), on the one hand adhering to the hypothesis of a connection between Son of man and Primeval Man, but also claiming that

> the new Man (the designation of Jeremias for Son of man) of the esoteric theology of Late Judaism (spätjüdischen) is a Redeemer glorified through suffering (ein durch Leiden verherrlichter Erlöser). These facts were—even if not expressly testified—already secured through the religio-historical considerations with regard to the origin of the designation of the Redeemer as bar enasa; because the 'new Man' in the surrounding world generally is a redeemer redeemed by going through suffering (ein durch Leiden hindurchgegangener erlöster Erlöser).[91]

According to Jeremias, this form of soteriology can be dated to the second century BCE. He concludes:

85. P. Volz, *Die Eschatologie der jüdischen Gemeinde im neutestamentlichen Zeitalter* (2nd edn, 1934 [= reprint, 1966]), especially pp. 189-90.

86. See R. Otto, *Reich Gottes und Menschensohn* (1934, 3rd edn, 1954, here and below quoted according to the English translation: *The Kingdom of God and the Son of Man* [1938, 3rd edn, 1951]), especially 'Appendix IV: Son of Man and Primordial Man' (pp. 388-92; German edn, pp. 314-21) where among other things it is said: 'The Son of Man is not a primordial man. He is simply the "fravashi" of the righteous man taken as exemplar, viz. Enoch. In harmony with general Iranian conceptions, he is finally united with his "fravashi"' (p. 390, in the German edn, p. 319). For the exegetical consequences drawn by Otto, see below.

87. A. Bentzen, *Daniel* (1937), pp. 33-34 (cf. 2nd edn, 1952, pp. 62-63).

88. W. Baumgartner, 'Ein Vierteljahrhundert Danielforschung', *ThR* NF 11 (1939), pp. 59-83, 125-44, 201-28 (214-22).

89. W. Manson, *Jesus the Messiah* (1943, 2nd edn, 1948), pp. 174-90.

90. Baumgartner, 'Ein Vierteljahrhundert Danielforschung', p. 222.

91. J. Jeremias, 'Erlöser und Erlösung im Spätjudentum und Urchristentum', *Deutsche Theologie* 2 (1929), pp. 106-19 (109).

> The teaching of the Saviour glorified through suffering has been the deepest religious longing of the whole of the Old Orient: Tammuz, Bel-Marduk—one must think about his New Year Festival!—Osiris, Adonis-Esmun, Attis, Dionysos, Ormuzd and Enos are witnesses: Ezekiel 8 depicts the way the women weep for Tammuz in the temple. But it is first in the fifty-third chapter of Isaiah that the (until then) nature-oriented expectation has experienced its religious concentration and purification through the thought of substituting atonement for sins, a concentration which could only be surpassed by one thing: through its fulfilment in history.[92]

Consent to this hypothesis of Early Judaism, including the concept of a suffering Son of man, was in the following years given only by a few, among them Willy Staerk[93] and Nils Johansson,[94] but also by Ernst Lohmeyer. Most interpreters commenting on the hypothesis distanced themselves directly, even if a few, for instance Gerhard Kittel,[95] the Danish scholar Paul Seidelin (1906–1981)[96] and Y. Joutsi,[97] would admit that in *1 Enoch* 37–71 and *4 Ezra* the Danielic and the Isaianic pictures of the Messiah were connected. However, none of these writings draw the consequences of this— for the first time it is done by Jesus.[98]

92. Jeremias, 'Erlöser und Erlösung', pp. 118-19.

93. W. Staerk, *Soter. Die biblische Erlösererwartung als religionsgeschichtliches Problem. Eine biblisch-theologische Untersuchung* (1933), pp. 84-86.

94. Nils Johansson, *Parakletoi. Vorstellungen von Fürsprechern für die Menschen vor Gott in der alttestamentlichen Religion, im Spätjudentum und Urchristentum* (1940), pp. 113-19.

95. G. Kittel, 'Menschensohn: II. Im NT', *RGG*, III (2nd edn, 1929), cols. 2118-21.

96. P. Seidelin, 'Der Ebed Jahwe und die Messiasgestalt im Jesajatargum', *ZNW* 35 (1936), pp. 194-231 (230-31).

97. Y. Joutsi, 'Der Menschensohn' is the author's German summary of his *Ihmisen Poika* = Der Menschensohn. Untersuchung der im NT benutzten Benennung gegen ihrer spätjüdischen Hintergrund [1936]), *Theologia Fennica* 2 (1940), pp. 45-52 (48).

98. Cf. G. Kittel, 'Menschensohn: II Im NT', *RGG*, III (2nd edn, 1929), col. 2120. A thorough discussion of the hypothesis of Jeremias by E. Sjöberg, 'Känna 1 Henok och 4 Esra tanken på den lidande Människosonen?' ['Does *1 Enoch* and *4 Ezra* Know of the Thought of a Suffering Son of Man?'], *SEÅ* 5 (1940), pp. 163-83; *idem*, 'Frågan om den lidande Människosonen i 1 Henok' ['The Question about the Suffering Son of Man in 1 Enoch'], *SEÅ* 7 (1942), pp. 141-44 (against Johansson). Sjöberg repeats and expands his criticism in *Der Menschensohn im äthiopischen Henochbuch* (1946), pp. 116-39. That Sjöberg did not convince Jeremias is seen from Jeremias' review of Sjöberg's monograph, *ThLZ* 74 (1949), cols. 405-406, and from his article 'παῖς θεοῦ', in *ThWNT*, V (1954), pp. 676-713 (686-87). A detailed assessment in H. Riesenfeld, *Jésus transfiguré* (1947), pp. 314-17: Appendice II. 'Le Messie souffrant dans le Judaïme d'après les recherches recentes'; H.H. Rowley, 'The Suffering Servant and the Davidic Messiah', *OTS* 8 (1950 = reprint in *idem*, *The Servant of the Lord and Other Essays on the Old Testament* [1952], pp. 59-88); Martin Rese, 'Überprüfung einiger Thesen von Joachim Jeremias zum Thema des Gottesknechtes im Judentum', *ZThK* 60 (1963), pp. 21-41. In *Neutestamentliche Theologie. Erster Teil. Die Verkündigung Jesu* (1971), p. 259, Jeremias is on the defense when saying: 'When auch keine eindeutigen Leidensaussagen

***

Some of the interpreters mentioned in the preceding excursus offer more or less cautious opinions with regard to the connection between the historical Jesus and this concept of Son of man. Some reach the conclusion that any titular use of Son of man by Jesus in the Gospels is a product of community theology. In his classic history of earliest christology, *Kyrios Christos. Geschichte des Christusglaubens von den Anfängen des Christentums bis Irenäus* from 1913,[99] Wilhelm Bousset is convinced even more than before that Son of man in the Gospels expresses the dogmatic thinking of the earliest community:

> We shall have to assume a priori that the community of Jesus' disciples has deposited in the gospel tradition its faith and its view of the messianic meaning of the person of Jesus, even when it has frequently only repeated genuine material of its master's messianic self-expression and has not created something. For the gospel tradition is sketched from the first from the standpoint of a community of messianic faith and for the purpose of bearing witness to this messianic faith.[100]

The reason for the phrase only being found in the mouth of Jesus in the Gospel tradition is that the specific transcendent-eschatological content of the title, and perhaps also its enigmatic character, made it impossible in the community tradition to let others speak of the earthly Jesus as ὁ υἱὸς τοῦ ἀνθρώπου, while, as a self-designation of Jesus, it preserved the character of the subjective-proleptic and the enigmatic mystery. However, Bousset will not totally exclude the notion that Jesus may have used it himself, because such things cannot be proven beyond doubt. In the great majority of sayings, it is community tradition.[101] Bousset subscribes to the opinion that the Aramaic original simply meant 'man', but he also thinks that it 'is utterly beyond comprehension why a general term such as "the man" could not, under certain conditions, also have become a messianic term'.[102] Thus, it

über den Gottesknecht auf den "Menschen" übertragen werden, ist es doch in höchsten Mass bedeutsam, dass durch diese Verbindung von Menschensohn- und Gottesknecht-aussagen (it is in *1 Enoch* and *4 Ezra*) ein Einsatz geboten war, der von Jesus weitergeführt werden konnte'.

99. The quotations below are taken from the English translation, W. Bousset, *Kyrios Christos: A History of the Belief in Christ from the Beginnings of Christianity to Irenaeus* (1970).

100. Bousset, *Kyrios Christos*, p. 2; English translation, p. 33.

101. See Bousset, *Kyrios Christos*, p. 5; English translation, p. 36.

102. Bousset, *Kyrios Christos*, p. 12; English translation, p. 43. Of course, this has to be seen in connection with the result of his religio-historical analysis of the background of the expression.

stands as a reference to Dan. 7.13, interpreting the symbol there messianically, whereby the Messiah became a supernatural figure. In this way, the whole Jewish pre-formed Son of man dogmatic was imported into the theology of the early community together with this title. Only one thing was added from the point of view of the new belief; namely, the idea of the exaltation of the earthly Jesus from Nazareth to the glory of the Son of man, this being something that was not pre-figured in the Jewish Son of man dogmatic.[103] This taking over of the concept of the Son of man implied a refusal of the ideal of the Son of David. The development was swift:

> We may suspect that the Messiah-Son of Man idea was approximately as ancient in the primitive community as the belief in Christ itself. The messianic faith of the primitive community *could* be formed after the death of Jesus in no other form than that of the ideal of a transcendent Messiah. The hope that Jesus as an earthly man would take over the role on earth of the king from David's tribe was once and for all shattered. There remained only that heavenly figure which in the Jewish tradition was indissolubly joined with the picture from the prophet Daniel and the name of the Son of Man. Very soon, after the disciples of Jesus grasped the daring faith that in spite of his suffering and death Jesus was the promised Messiah, their messianic faith will have taken the form of expectation of the Son of Man.[104]

The source of this conviction in the disciples should be seen in 'the incomparable, powerful, and indestructible impression which Jesus' personality had left behind in the souls of his disciples and which was more powerful than public humiliation and death, agony and defeat'.[105] After the death of Jesus and the first despair and disappointment it thus provoked, came a feeling of defiance, which—according to psychological law—makes the impossible possible. It was of immeasurable importance that contemporary apocalyptic could offer a concept of the Messiah which was able to solve the enigma. The disciples could rescue their hopes which they may have had as early as the lifetime of Jesus and which they now elaborated in a more powerful way. 'The disciples of Jesus salvaged their hopes, which certainly had already been stimulated during the lifetime of Jesus, by reshaping them into a loftier and more powerful form'.[106] Thus the eschatology of the earliest Palestinian community concentrated on the expectation of the coming Son of man. It was first when this community had lost its influence that such an expectation did as well. From then on, it survived only in Jewish Christian sects, where it underwent various Gnostic colourings.[107]

103. See Bousset, *Kyrios Christos*, p. 14; English translation, p. 49.

104. Bousset, *Kyrios Christos*, p. 17; English translation, pp. 49-50.

105. Bousset, *Kyrios Christos*, p. 17; English translation, p. 50.

106. Bousset, *Kyrios Christos*, p. 18; English translation, p. 50.

107. Cf. also *idem*, *Jesus der Herr. Nachträge und Auseinandersetzungen zu Kyrios Christos* (1916), especially pp. 7-9.

In grandiose outline, Bousset finally describes the relation between historical fact and spiritual conviction and the indispensable role of community theology as follows:

> But in this connection we should first of all observe how only in this peculiar combination of the historical figure of Jesus and the proclamation of the community that picture of Jesus was created which became so tremendously influential for the history of Christian piety. Only in that behind the gospel of Jesus the community placed the figure of the heavenly Son of Man, the Lord and Judge of the world, and let his glory, half veiled and concealed by his history, shine through in transparent fashion; only in that it sketched the picture of the wandering Preacher in the gold background of the miraculous, wove around his life the cluster of fulfilled prophecy and surrounded it with the charm of the half-disclosed secret; only in that it placed him in a great divine salvation history and had him appear as its crown and completion; only thus did the community make this picture of Jesus of Nazareth influential. For the purely historical actually is never able to have an effect, but only the vitally contemporary symbol in which one's own religious conviction clarified is presented [*sic*].[108]

Rudolf Bultmann is typical of who handles the problem of Son of man inspired by the History of Religion School. Only the sayings about the future Son of man as distinct from the person speaking can be original (the interpretation initiated by D.F. Strauss). The other sayings may be the result either of an erroneous translation of an expression originally only meaning 'man',[109] or of the insertion of the messianic title.[110]

For Bultmann this understanding is combined with his dialectical theology, rejecting any attempt to give faith a historical foundation. Following the impulse of Karl Barth, the distinction of the conservative Martin Kähler (1835–1912), between the historical Jesus and the historic, biblical Christ,[111] was revived. The historical Jesus belongs to the realm of historians; the biblical Christ is alone accessible to faith through preaching. In this approach the historical Jesus is irrelevant for theology. The combination of this disinterest and the denial of the possibility of reconstructing the messianic self-understanding of Jesus called forth the accusation against Bultmann that he made a virtue of necessity by taking refuge in the paradox of revelation because of his radicalism. Bultmann's famous answer was that

108. Bousset, *Kyrios Christos*, pp. 74-75; English translation, p. 117.

109. See R. Bultmann, *Geschichte der synoptischen Tradition* (1921), pp. 7, 14, 19, 91.

110. See Bultmann, *Geschichte der synoptischen Tradition*, pp. 74, 75, 76, 94, 96.

111. Cf. M. Kähler, *Der sogenannte historische Jesus und der geschichtliche, biblische Christus* (1892, and later reprints).

> Until now I have never felt myself uncomfortable in my critical radicalism, but quite comfortable. However, I often have the impression that it is my conservative colleagues who feel themselves uncomfortable in the New Testament; because I can see that they are always engaged in rescue operations. I calmly let it burn; because I see that everything which is thereby burnt up, are the fantasy-images of the Life of Jesus theology, and that it is Christ himself according to the flesh. But Christ according to the flesh does not concern us. How it looked in the heart of Jesus I don't know, and I also don't want to know.[112]

Thus the attempt to reconcile faith and knowledge, foundational to liberal theology, was here abandoned, and the community theology was no more viewed as a derailment, but as the necessary interpretation of faith.

On the other hand, we find a number of interpreters of course who are equally vocal and see Jesus employing the title, aware of its supernatural implications. Some are more cautious than others. The liberal Jewish scholar Claude G. Montefiore (1858–1938) thinks that Daniel 7, *1 Enoch* 37–71, and *4 Ezra* 13 allow us to assume the existence of a specific Son of man as a heavenly Redeemer, although confused with the concept of the Messiah. 'And it is not impossible that Jesus might have fastened his attention upon the conception of the heavenly Man more than upon the conception of the Messiah', because of the political implications of the latter.[113] This identification has also helped him 'to believe that, somehow or other, he, after his death, would be invested with the office of the Man, and would reappear upon earth as "the Man", whom Daniel had foreseen'.[114] Behind the Son of man Montefiore sees Primeval Man as a Redeemer figure: 'He is a parallel figure to the Messiah, but of different origin'.[115] Admitting the highly hypothetical character of the whole enterprise, J.M. Creed finds it hard to say if Jesus himself used the term, but finds it 'an attractive theory that he used it with studied ambiguity'.[116] C.H. Kraeling is very restrictive in assuming that Anthropos was a redeemer figure, because 'the whole idea of the re-manifestation is a secondary element... Thus to connect the Christian Son of Man as saviour with the Anthropos directly seems foredoomed to failure because of the fact that in his soteriological manifestation the Anthropos is definitely a product of the second Christian century.'[117] According to

112. Bultmann, 'Zur Frage der Christologie', *Zwischen den Zeiten* 5 (1927), pp. 41-69; quoted according to the reprint in *idem*, *Glauben und Verstehen*, I (1933, 2nd edn, 1954), pp. 85-13 (101).

113. C.G. Montefiore, *The Synoptic Gospels Edited with an Introduction and a Commentary* (1909, 2nd edn, 1927), I, pp. 64-80 (note on the 'Son of Man', pp. 68-69).

114. Montefiore, *The Synoptic Gospels*, p. 69.

115. Montefiore, *The Synoptic Gospels*, p. 74.

116. Creed, 'The Heavenly Man', pp. 135-36.

117. C.H. Kraeling, *Anthropos and Son of Man: A Study in the Religious Syncretism of the Hellenistic Orient* (1927), pp. 123, 126-27.

Kraeling, influence from the Anthropos figure on the Son of man in the Gospels is not obvious at all. However, he is not totally unwilling to subscribe to R. Reitzenstein's reference to the Mandaic messengers. 'Inevitably they will raise the question whether Jesus, in referring to himself as "the man", did not at first employ this expression to designate himself as "the expected man" in the sense of messenger or forerunner', resulting in its messianic use.[118]

A major result of this religio-historical approach was that the idea from the nineteenth century of two different conceptions of Messiah inside Judaism obtained a new foundation. Now it was no longer only a question of a more spiritual interpretation but of one determined by another genealogy, embedding the Son of Man messianism in Near Eastern mythology with the result that a figure from primordial history became an eschatological agent. To quote C.H. Kraeling once again: 'Cosmogony is thus the substratum of eschatology, and the Anthropos of primordial history the necessary prototype of the eschatological Son of Man'.[119]

Karl Ludwig Schmidt (1891–1956) thinks that the expression Son of man, in Aramaic meaning nothing more than 'man', nevertheless comes from Dan. 7.13-14, speaking of the heavenly pre-existent Man. It is a possibility that Jesus himself made it the name of the Messiah. 'Essential for this title of glory (Würdetitel) is the fact that the Messiah comes from Heaven and that the coming glory is hidden in insignificance.' By employing this title, 'Jesus places himself on the same level as his brethren and, at the same time, as unique and above them'.[120]

Joachim Jeremias argues in a similar way that although the expression in itself means nothing more than 'man', Dan. 7.13 witnesses to small circles using it of the Messiah, combining Daniel's Son of man with the Suffering Servant of Isa. 52.13–53.12, and thus awaiting a Redeemer of the world, passing through suffering to obtain redemption not only for the people of Israel but for the whole world. In these circles, they called the Redeemer 'the Servant of God' (Gottesknecht) and the 'Man'.[121] This is confirmed by research in the history of religions, especially by Reitzenstein, who shows the connection with the concept of the Primeval Man as a redeemer figure. This is all the more clear in the Pauline concept of the first and the second Adam or Man in 1 Cor. 15.22, 45-47 and Rom. 5.12-21.[122] Thus:

> When Jesus uses this messianic designation of himself and identifies himself as the new Man, he rejects all national-political expectations combined with

118. Kraeling, *Anthropos and Son of Man*, pp. 185-86.
119. Kraeling, *Anthropos and Son of Man*, p. 150.
120. K.L. Schmidt, 'Jesus Christus', *RGG*, III (2nd edn, 1929), cols. 101-51 (150).
121. J. Jeremias, *Jesus als Weltvollender* (1930), pp. 53-57 (55).
122. Cf. further Jeremias, ''Αδάμ', in *ThWNT* (1933), I, pp. 141-43.

> the Son of David and presents himself as the re-newer of the world (Welterneuerer), who passes to glory through suffering and brings about the new aeon. Thus, we do not here have to do with a designation of Jesus in abasement, but in exaltation.[123]

Some balanced the results of the religio-historical investigations with the mind of Jesus in a way which made them more or less harmless. The Uppsala New Testament professor Anton Fridrichsen (1888–1953) could, without any problem, subscribe to the religio-historical analysis, seeing the origin of Son of man in Iran. However, he saw Jesus combining it with the deeper meaning of the expression itself. It was in the name 'Man' that he recovered the secret inherent in his being: that the divine redeemer and judge, one of the revealer of the new age, was a man and indeed one of the small ones, the poor. The secret found its significant expression and thereby also its higher elucidation in the Son of man of the apocalyptic tradition and the word of the holy prophet. However, we are not competent enough to detect the deepest foundations of Jesus' conviction of his high mission. One of the presuppositions is the self-consciousness in Judaism of being the elect people, of which martyrdom is also a part.[124]

The protestant New Testament professor in Paris, Maurice Goguel (1880–1955), in his *Jésus* (1932) also adheres to the thesis of the existence of a messianic apocalyptic Son of man with roots in the concepts of Primeval Man, adopted by Jesus with regard to his future role but perhaps also adapted 'by a totally natural anticipation' to describe his ministry in a way that was only intelligible to those adhering to his thought.[125]

Caution was sometimes abandoned in favour of bolder hypotheses. Thus the Jena professor Willy Staerk had earlier not allowed any 'Messiastum' for his historical Jesus. Now, in his two-volume monograph, *Soter. Die biblische Erlösererwartung als religionsgeschichtliches Problem. Eine biblisch-theologische Untersuchung* (1933–38),[126] he offers quite another opinion. From Daniel 7, *1 Enoch* 37–71 and *4 Ezra* 13, he concludes that 'the eschatological figure of the *barnas* in apocalyptic circles in the 2nd

123. Jeremias, *Jesus als Weltvollender*, p. 56.

124. A. Fridrichsen, *Vem ville Jesus vara? Kristustrons historiska grundval enligt nutida bibelforskning* (*Who Would Jesus Be? The Historical Foundation of the Christian Faith according to Contemporary Biblical Study*) (1931), especially pp. 47-48. Cf. *idem*, 'Människosonen och Israel' ('The Son of Man and Israel'), *Till Gustav Aulén* (1939), pp. 110-16.

125. M. Goguel, *Jésus*, pp. 557-63 (562). In the 1950 second edition, the discussion of the Son of man problem is placed in the middle of the presentation, pp. 244-50, the understanding being essentially the same.

126. *1. Theil: Der biblische Christus* (1933). *2. Theil. Die Erlösererwartung in den östlichen Religionen. Untersuchungen zu den Ausdrucksformen der biblischen Christologie* (Soter II) (1938).

century BC and earlier generations obtained a decisive role in creating expectations of the future'.[127] Staerk also finds a connection between this concept and the idea of the Suffering Servant from Isaiah 53, summarizing it as follows: 'the figure of the royal Messiah–Son of David appears with the features of the transcendent Messiah and this is adjusted to the figure of God's *ebed* through transference of the predicates of the *ebed* to the *barnas*'.[128] The way Son of man is employed in the Synoptic Gospels shows that in fact Jesus used the expression of himself:

> The name of dignity, 'man', as stamped in Jewish christology was the appropriate name for his person to express his consciousness of mission and role as Son, because it transcended the limited humanity (Menschtum) of the fallen creation in the most distinct way, in which he, of essence, had no part, because he belonged to the world of God.[129]

Later, under the heading 'The pre-Christian and the primitive Christian Son of Man dogmatic', Staerk concludes the first volume of his *Soter* with the words:

> The redemption through the 'man' Christ Jesus was essentially becoming 'man' ('Mensch'werdung), *restitutio ad integrum*, because according to his essence Christ is Adam, 'man', that is, Primordial Man (Urmensch), who brings the creation back to its original state (Urstande) by virtue of the ζωή, which he is and which he has.[130]

Even more optimistic about the possibilities of comparative religious studies as an efficient way to solve the question of how Jesus looked upon himself and his task, is the famous historian of religion Rudolf Otto (1869–1937), professor in Marburg. The results of his research are found in his widely read monograph *Reich Gottes und Menschensohn: Ein religionsgeschichtlicher Versuch*, which was originally published in 1934.[131] Being very confident regarding the use of the Gospels as reliable sources for the historical Jesus, Otto views them as reflecting how Jesus took over the Son of Man concept from the book of *Enoch*. Because of the influence of *Reich Gottes und Menschensohn*, we will go into some detail with it.

127. W. Staerk, *Soter*, I, p. 86. Cf. pp. 37-40 and pp. 72-77.

128. Staerk, *Soter*, I, p. 152. With regard to the question of the existence of a suffering Messiah in Judaism, see above.

129. Staerk, *Soter*, I, p. 95.

130. Staerk, *Soter*, I, p. 160. Cf. *Soter*, II, Chapter 7, 'Der "Menschensohn"', pp. 421-76.

131. R. Otto, *Reich Gottes und Menschensohn. Ein religionsgeschichtlicher Versuch* (1934, 3rd edn, 1954; below quoted according to the English translation, *The Kingdom of God and the Son of Man: A Study in the History of Religion* [1938]).

As is seen from the title, Otto puts Son of man and Kingdom of God together, this being admissible on the grounds of the implicit logic of the eschaton:

> For the Son of man belongs to the kingdom of God. The kingdom throws its shadows forward into the present; it is not yet here in power, but is already here secretly. Likewise: The Son of Man is not yet here in his power, but is already here 'before his power,' like his shadow cast before him, as the one who some day will be the Son of Man in his power. And all this belongs closely together and every part requires every other.[132]

On the question of if and, in case of a positive answer, which Christology Jesus had, Otto thinks that a positive answer is obvious because of Jesus' preaching of the coming Son of man and connecting himself with this figure. We are to look especially at the Enochian as 'it was genuinely his own, for it was poles apart from the Christology which soon arose, as was inevitable, in his church. His consciousness of mission was expressed in his Christology.'[133] Thus Otto is convinced of the necessity of a messianic conception. Then:

> Such a consciousness of mission (Sendungs-bewußtsein) did not arise and does not receive its true explanation from apocalyptic or other historical antecedents, although its forms may be determined by and contained in such antecedents. But for a person to apply them to himself and to think of himself as referred to in them, the first requirement would be an immediate sense of vocation which belonged to the person and his very nature because he was what he was, and which was immediately felt and comprehended by that person. If a consciousness of this vocation was present, it necessarily took on a concrete historical form. To one who was conscious of a mission of such loftiness, with these contents, in this situation, supported by ideas drawn from late Jewish apocalyptic, related to a kingdom which was coming and was already operative, indeed operative in him and through him, this form could be no other than that of a Messiah, and determined in particular by the idea of the apocalyptic Son of Man.[134]

However, because a man wandering and teaching in Galilee cannot already be 'the Messiah–Son of Man' (der Menschensohn-Messias), we have to console ourselves with the thought that with the expression he 'laid claim to be Son of Man' (Prätendent auf den Menschensohn). Jesus did not think of a pre-existence. Instead 'we might apply the term 'post-existential thinking' to a mode of thinking which places one in (paradoxical, anticipative) relation to

132. Otto, *Reich Gottes und Menschensohn*, p. 120; English translation, p. 161. The words 'before his power' are from *1 En.* 62.7.

133. Otto, *Reich Gottes und Menschensohn*, p. 126; English translation, p. 168.

134. Otto, *Reich Gottes und Menschensohn*, pp. 130-31; English translation, p. 174.

a being which has yet to come into existence'.[135] Exactly such a conception was to be found in Enoch's apocalyptic, reflecting the Iranian concept of the 'fravashi'—in Iranian religion a fravashi is the soul of the deceased which can perform as a guardian spirit—the righteous Enoch being finally united with his 'fravashi'. Thus:

> A strange tissue of mythical ideas and consequences rises before our view in this Son of Man. These ideas and consequences were originally distinct, and the object of religio-historical research is to discover the constitutive elements by analysis and derivation. On the one hand, there is a human yet supernatural intermediate being introduced between the highest deity who is situated at a distance from world and man; on the other side are the world and mankind... But the science of comparative religion would be a farce if it could do nothing more than carry on this analysing and see only the strangeness and not also the greatness and depth of the imagery. Syncretism? There is more here than syncretism. Here, arising from the living incentive synthesis, a religious conception has originated which is really a conception, a vital conceiving, not a dead agglomeration of ideas. It is not merely a strange, but a quite wonderful figure that arises, that of deity, highly exalted by 'sacrosanctitas', therefore untouchable, unapproachable, far from the sinful world; foreseeing from eternity and revealing in his own time the mediating figure of the Son... [It is] a saviour religion in the bud, and on the very point of bursting open; in fantastic apocalyptic dress, but more than fantastic apocalyptic; a stern message of looming judgment, and yet in essence good news, a vestment of conceptions, worthy and kingly, and fully ready for the Coming One who in his inmost nature knows himself called to wear it.[136]

Otto sums up that this Son of man conception in Late Judaism belongs 'to the loftiest conceptions (Erhabensten) that have ever appeared in the realm of religion'. But it is of even more interest to state

> that, long before Christ's appearance, a certain idea was fully developed in circles which had plainly been formed long before him and to which he himself plainly belonged. The idea was that of a powerful preacher alike of righteousness, the coming judgment, and the blessed new age, a prophet of the eschatological Son of Man, would be transported at the end of his earthly career to God; that he would be exalted to become the one whom he had proclaimed, in the literal sense that he himself would become the very one whom he had proclaimed. But that also meant that his activity even during his earthly life was nothing else than the proleptic activity of this very redeemer. ...We assert that if there is any such thing in history conceived as a complex of ideas, and if powerful traditions do offer moulds and settle outlines, then such a one not only could, but *must* have known himself as the one destined

135. Otto, *Reich Gottes und Menschensohn*, pp. 131-32; English translation, pp. 174-75.

136. Otto, *Reich Gottes und Menschensohn*, pp. 148-49; English translation, pp. 193-94.

> to be the Son of Man, and at work even now as representative of the Son of Man. This idea was the form which his consciousness of mission necessarily assumed under the conditions of his age.[137]

The question 'as to whether such a consciousness of mission could rise to the height of a transcendent conception of the Son of Man', Otto answers with the statement that Son of Man alone is a soteriological figure and not a cosmological one. There is no idea of pre-existent Enoch being exalted to something which he was not before. Otto explains the words of *1 En.* 71.14 as expressing anticipation. 'They are a simple explication of the Jewish ideas of divine election and predestination for redemptive purpose.' Otto reduces every more determinant apocalyptic element in Jesus' taking over of the concept of the Enochian Son of Man. According to Otto, Jesus 'can scarcely be called an apocalyptist. He completely lacks interest in the speculations and oddities of apocalyptic preaching. All his interest attaches to the eschatological redemptive counsel of God as such.'[138] It also has to be noticed that in the presentation of a redeemer not possessing such dignity, the Enochian Son of Man could and did take over traits from the 'Suffering Servant' of Deutero-Isaiah.

In this way we can witness a certain spiritualization. In taking over the concept, Jesus knew himself to be the future Son of man, but just as Enoch, Jesus did not proclaim himself Son of man. It was God who revealed him as such. As it is said later:

> Similarly Jesus knew himself to be the 'filius hominis praedestinatus'; therefore he summoned, worked and acted as the one upon whom the choice had fallen; he worked proleptically with the powers of the Son of Man, with divine commission and divine anointing; but he did not deliver teachings in regard to his being the Son of Man, any more than did Enoch.[139]
>
> That means Jesus was the agent of the Son of Man, he worked and spoke with his aim and in his name just as Enoch also preached as the agent alike of the Son of Man and of his righteousness, wisdom, and power of revelation.[140]

Thus Otto thinks that Jesus, after the episode at Caesarea Philippi and in the presence of his disciples, in fact employed the expression with regard to his suffering and coming exaltation.[141] From there it entered into sayings which originally had the pronoun 'I'. In those 'Urstellen' there is no insecurity or

137. Otto, *Reich Gottes und Menschensohn*, pp. 165-66; English translation, pp. 212-13.

138. Otto, *Reich Gottes und Menschensohn*, pp. 167-68; English translation, pp. 214-16.

139. Otto, *Reich Gottes und Menschensohn*, p. 171; English translation, p. 219.

140. Otto, *Reich Gottes und Menschensohn*, p. 178; English translation, p. 227.

141. The following summarizes Otto, *Reich Gottes und Menschesohn*, pp. 180-86; English translation, pp. 230-36.

change between 'I' and 'Son of Man'. Here the tradition is as hard as diamond (diamanten fest). According to this concept, Jesus imagined that his death would be followed immediately by his elevation. Death through suffering was inescapable. Otto sums up as follows the new in Jesus' use:

> Ancient popular Messianism (die alte Volks-messianik) and transcendent Messianism had long been synthesized. Now a new synthesis appeared, of which no one had thought or could think: the synthesis of the Christ with the suffering and dying servant of God from Deutero-Isaiah. It was not only unprecedented; it must have seemed blasphemous. This fact may still be reflected in Mt. xvi.22, where Peter dares to reproach Christ when, for the first time, he began to teach that the Son of Man must suffer and where Christ repulsed him with the unusually sharp words of Mt. xvi. 23.[142]

Rudolf Otto's *Reich Gottes und Menschensohn* has been summarized rather extensively to pass on an impression of this comprehensive attempt to give the Life of Jesus project a new religio-historical basis. Otto is singularly important for bringing his reconstruction of the religio-historical concept and the messianic self-consciousness of Jesus forward in such a tight connection. Its widespread popularity cannot conceal that it rested on textual presuppositions which take the reader back before both literary criticism (of, for instance, William Wrede) and form criticism (as it manifested itself in especially Martin Dibelius' and Rudolf Bultmann's investigations). Otto still shows the will to deem all those Jesus sayings original which fit his thesis. Because of his theory of the Enochian Son of Man concept coming from the Persian *fravashi* concept, he thinks it possible to define this concept as both independent from Jewish Messianism and mixed up with it—and to see Jesus as the religious genius applying it to himself in such a way that both the present and the coming time are included.

Rudolf Bultmann, in a lengthy review,[143] vehemently rejected this attempt to save a messianic consciousness in the historical Jesus. He evaluates Otto's reconstruction of the Son of Man concept in *1 Enoch* as a total illusion (eine völlige Illusion). Bultmann sees the explanation of *1 En.* 71.14 in the circumstance that Judaism took over from Iranian eschatology the figure of the pre-existent Son of Man who should come in the last days to judgment. On the other hand, Judaism knew of a pious one from the past; namely, Enoch, who because of his righteousness was taken to heaven. What takes place in *1 En.* 71.14 is a combination of both concepts through an identification of

142. Otto, *Reich Gottes und Menschensohn*, pp. 194-95; English translation, p. 246.

143. R. Bultmann, 'Reich Gottes und Menschensohn. Rudolf Otto: Reich Gottes und Menschensohn. Ein religionsgeschichtlicher Versuch, 1934', *ThR* NF 9 (1937), pp. 1-35 (reprint in *idem*, *Theologie als Kritik* [ed. M. Dreher and K.W. Müller [2002)], pp. 328-53).

Enoch with the Son of Man. In other words: The foreign Son of man tradition is judaized by answering the question of the identity of this enigmatic man who, already in primeval time, was taken to heaven to stay there until he returns in the last days. It could only be the Enoch who, in primeval time, was caught up into heaven and was the 'righteous'.[144]

How this religio-historical attempt resulted at the end of the day in an interpretation very much resembling the attempt in the *Life of Jesus-Forschung* and fantasy to replace the more political–national concept of Messiah by a more elevated universal–transcendent Son of man concept is also visible in the outline of Ernst Lohmeyer (1890–1946). Lohmeyer was one of the most influential German New Testament scholars of this period. In 1936 he was removed from Breslau to Greifswald because of his opposition to Nazism, and in 1939–1943 he was (again!) in military service. After the war he was appointed rector of Greifswald University, but was immediately imprisoned and afterwards executed by the Russians.

Lohmeyer distinguished between, on the one hand, a Galilean Son of man tradition originating in Jesus himself and the circle around him, and, on the other hand, a Messiah tradition rooted in the Jerusalem community. The 'nazoreischen' or Galilean branch of the primitive Church he finds documented in the answer of Jesus' relatives to Domitian (Eusebius, *Historia ecclesiastica* III 20.4), the description of James the brother of Jesus (II 23.8-18), the story of the rich young man (Mk 10.17-27) and a number of other passages. The messiahship of Jesus is described by Lohmeyer in the following way:

> In his lifetime, Jesus is Son of Man as a teacher in God's commission and power (in Gottes Auftrag und Macht), because of which it is the God-given duty of every Jew to 'follow' him. And this empowered teacher, who is present as Son of Man, but hidden, as the revealed will be seated 'at the right hand of the Great Power and coming with the clouds of heaven'.[145]

144. The treatment of the Son of man concept is on pp. 19-22. In another review article, the Norwegian L. Brun considers both the book of Otto and the review of Bultmann (see 'Guds rike og Menneskesønnen', *NTT* 38 [1937], pp. 105-25). What Otto thinks the loftiest idea ever to have appeared in the history of religions, Brun deems nothing more than a bold and spiritual fantasy in the head of Otto, and that Jesus should have been acquainted with the book of *Enoch* and its Son of Man concept, is totally improvable. In contrast to Bultmann, Brun is not refusing the possibility of a Son of man consciousness in the historical Jesus, as he sees a connection between this and the Suffering Servant of the Lord in Isa. 53 (cf. above).

145. See E. Lohmeyer, *Galiläa und Jerusalem* (1936), p. 71. This monograph was written together with Lohmeyer's famous commentary in the Meyer series, *Das Evangelium des Markus* (1937, with several reprints), where Son of man is treated in the introduction on pp. 4-7.

The determinative factor is the eschatological framing of the two concepts. These concepts are not far away from each other, even if their historical and factual roots are. Both deal with the figure of the eschatological fulfiller (Vollender) and the eschatological fulfilment (Vollendung), and both do it in relation to the people and the nations. They could melt completely (vollends) together, when the Jewish hope of the Coming One in the primitive Christian faith became 'the One who has come'. Even if Son of man and Messiah are dissimilar as regards origin and meaning, they are no longer separated, only different—just as Galilee and Jerusalem.

The background is seen in the Jewish apocalyptic teaching of the two aeons, which also penetrated the New Testament understanding of Son of Man. Thus the Son of man is the Lord and bringer of the new aeon, as in sayings like Mk 8.38; 13.26 and 14.62. These same sayings also show 'that the name Son of Man conceals what it originally and essentially meant. As with a parable, it alludes to the One, who in truth is "the Son of God".'[146] Following J. Jeremias and R. Otto, Lohmeyer finds that at least some circles in pre-Christian Judaism knew of a suffering Son of Man as the redeemer and fulfiller. This is confirmed in the apocalyptic δεῖ in Mk 8.31, the 'proof from Scripture' in Mk 9.12, as well as in the formulation 'the Son of man has come'. In a dualistic way, the old fights the new.[147]

According to Lohmeyer, it is difficult to ascertain when and where the ideas of Son of Man and Suffering Servant were combined. It is clear that both are related to the Jewish people, the community which belongs to God, and for that reason they are the poor and enslaved in this world. Thus occasioned by the Son of Man, eternal salvation is also liberation from oppression. This points to the *anawim*, the silent in the country, as those who believe in a Son of Man:

> The Son of Man belief seems connected to Galilee and gives this country of the *anawim* the consecration of the first eschatological fulfilment; Jesus with his brothers and other relatives, his nearer and more distant Galilean disciples seem to carry it jointly. The Messianic belief renews and strengthens the traditional holiness of Jerusalem. The Twelve especially seem to have cultivated it. How tightly both ranges of ideas are connected and how strongly the

146. Lohmeyer, *Das Evangelium des Markus*, p. 5.

147. Lohmeyer, *Das Evangelium des Markus*, p. 5. Later, in *Gottesknecht und Davidssohn* (1945, new edition, 1953), pp. 148-49, Lohmeyer again pleads for a connection between the Son of Man tradition and the concept of the Servant of the Lord: 'Von der ersten Zeit an, da die Urgemeinde sich nach dem Tode Jesu in Galiläa und Jerusalem bildete, leben und wirken diese drei christologischen Deutungen mit und neben einander, die vom Gottesknecht und Menschensohn stärker auf das Erbteil der Verkündigung Jesu gestützt und dadurch zwillingshaft verschwistert, die von dem Messias Jesus auf die Macht der Auferstehung gegründet und damit gleichsam jener ersten jüngere Schwester'.

> Son of Man belief dominates in this connection is shown finally in this. Primitive Christianity lives thanks to the one sure hope in the parousia of the Lord.[148]

There is, accordingly, a peculiar relationship between Son of Man and the community. 'Just as it is oppressed and persecuted, he is also persecuted and delivered to death, and just as once it will be transfigured, so he will be. The suffering and glory of the Son of Man are the eschatological means. He is the eschatological mediator, through whom God will lead the community out of suffering to glory.'[149] The relation between Servant and Son of Man makes the latter an earthly suffering human leading a historical life. This historical figure of the Son of Man is simply an eschatological secret and wonder to Lohmeyer:

> He who bears the name Son of Man is thus a transcendent form, a foreigner in this age and Lord of the coming aeon; with him the coming eschatological event is present. And at the same time he is a human form, a Jew among Jews, child of his land and his history; with him every present aspect of his work is directed to the coming aeon and every event of his life to the highest sign of the eschatological day. This double divine–human designation is not only the secret of his essence, but also of the decree of God through which the coming aeon is brought into the present and the present into the future. It holds these two in hiddenness, which is only the shell of revelation, so that both lead to a revelation in glory.[150]

Here, it is seen how the concept of Son of Man with its own origin and meaning is taken for granted but also how the mind of Jesus and the later theology of the community are perceived as creative factors. This understanding of the concept is employed in an attempt to attribute a transcendent consciousness to the historical Jesus as a historical point of departure for later christological thinking.[151]

148. Lohmeyer, *Galiläa und Jerusalem*, p. 94. Cf. *idem*, *Das Evangelium des Markus* (1937), pp. 4-6.

149. Lohmeyer, *Das Evangelium des Markus*, p. 6.

150. Lohmeyer, *Das Evangelium des Markus*, p. 6. I owe the translation of this passage to W. Baird, *History of New Testament Research*, II, p. 466.

151. A witness to the impact of Lohmeyer's interpretation is found in the Finnish professor of New Testament in Åbo, Rafael Gyllenberg (1893–1982), in the article 'Människosonen eller Messias' ('Son of Man or Messiah'), *TA-TT* 45 (1940), pp. 27-42. Gyllenberg claims that the time was then ripe to write an account of the Christology of the Primitive Church, corresponding to Bousset's *Kyrios Christos*, and this because of one name—Lohmeyer. Gyllenberg further detects the tension between the two different christologies effective through the whole later history of the Church. For a critical assessment of Lohmeyer's achievement, see M. Veit, *Die Auffassung von der Person Jesu im Urchristentum nach den neuesten Forschungen* (1946), pp. 1-54. Her conclusion

On quite the same track, we find Leonhard Goppelt (1911–1973). Goppelt also includes Son of man as a figure establishing a connection between the Primeval Man and the Perfect Man of the end of days in his monograph on typology, as especially seen in the sayings of the pre-existent Son of man in the Similitudes of the book of *Enoch*.[152] Jesus' personal contribution is the combination of the Suffering Servant of the Lord and the Son of man, which had not yet really been present in contemporary apocalyptic. Goppelt formulates it this way: 'The Son of man has now come to do the task of the Servant of the Lord, and the risen and exalted Servant of the Lord will return as Son of man'.[153]

The co-founder of Form Criticism, the Heidelberg New Testament professor Martin Dibelius (1883–1947), likewise belongs here. Unlike Lohmeyer, he stresses the hiddenness of the Son of man, not his sufferings. Although not as confident as Otto with regard to the possibilities of reaching the meaning of the words in the mouth of Jesus, Dibelius—and not the least because of Mt. 8.20—considers whether Jesus could have hinted in this way 'at the contrast between the hiddenness of his poor earthly existence and the glory of the "Man" from Heaven, marking the contrast and also the connection, because the destitute life belongs to the hiddenness of the Son of Man and points to the future'.[154]

With Lohmeyer, Goppelt, and Dibelius, we leave this period summarizing what the History of Religions School achieved—namely, to give new life to an old interpretation by offering a new foundation. The alternative was to accept a foreign origin for the concept of the Son of Man, or, if possible, to argue for a purely biblical and Jewish origin. This alternative was strongly determined by the degree of willingness to accept the thought of Jesus taking over concepts from pagan religions. As we have seen in the previous chapter, some exegetes came to the conclusion that Jesus could not have employed the concept because of its lofty content. However, some saw the cause of its intrusion in the Gospel tradition in the Aramaic idiom with *bar nash* being originally used as a circumlocution for the person speaking, or even only as an indefinite pronoun.

Thus the period up to the Second World War ended with a wide range of interpretations. Nearly all would agree about one thing. As the term turns up in the New Testament Gospels, it is a Messianic title and indicates a taking over of a more or less prefigured concept or, at least, a recognizable symbol from

is (p. 53): 'Worin besteht also der Fehler L[ohmeyer]'s? Zunächst fasst er jenen Mythus in den Namen "Menschensohn" zusammen, mit dem er nichts zu tun hat'.

152. L. Goppelt, *Typos. Die typologische Deutung des Alten Testaments im Neuen* (1939, reprint 1973), p. 37.

153. Goppelt, *Typos*, p. 115.

154. M. Dibelius, *Jesus* (1939, 3rd edn, 1960), pp. 73-85 (82).

the Old Testament. One way or the other the expression was taken as a key to the Christology, if not of Jesus' own, then, at least, that of the early community. A Son of man concept was taken for granted. 'Son of man' was the specific Jewish apocalyptic designation for a variant of the Primeval Man concept. For some interpreters, it was natural to find this concept present also in passages in the New Testament, where other designations were employed. The 'usual suspects' were 1 Cor. 15.22-23, 45-47; Rom. 5.12-21 and Phil. 2.6-8.

13. Interlude

Several trajectories connect the time before the Second World War with the last part of the twentieth century. Nevertheless, it is convenient to use this event in making a distinction in the history of the understanding of the expression Son of man. First, the more outward reason is that, with a few exceptions, we see an intermission in the stream of literature in these years. The second reason is that, new tendencies of a more profound sort begin to develop. At least among critical scholars, we can observe a noticeable decrease in the will to find the use of Son of man as a key to a messianic consciousness in the historical Jesus. This, however, also has to be seen as a result of the impact of dialectical theology, which renounced all interest in historical facts as a point of departure ('Anknüpfungspunkt') for faith. As we have seen, an outspoken representative of this attitude is Rudolf Bultmann. If 'Son of man' were a messianic title, and even if Jesus had employed it for himself, it would be of no use for faith. As it stands, it is to be seen as a product of a community theology. A 'historical' cause for its intrusion could be the Aramaic pronominal or generic use of *bar nash* by Jesus.

The second half of the twentieth century was also dominated to some degree by the redaction-historical or redaction-critical approach, especially to the Gospels. Increasing attention was focused on the authors behind the Gospels as theologically productive. This, of course, was not totally new. Roots went as far back as Ferdinand Christian Baur and his tendency criticism, while William Wrede also achieved insights of lasting value in this field. However, the loosening not the least of a theological interest in the historical Jesus and his supposed messianic self-consciousness, made it possible to investigate the Gospels in a new way: no longer only as possible sources for the historical Jesus, but as sources of the theology of each evangelist. Pioneers in this enterprise were Günther Bornkamm and Hans Conzelmann. It is only in this period that there is a common insight of the radical difference between the Son of man sayings in the Synoptic Gospels on the one hand and in the Gospel of John on the other.

Whereas the question of whether, and, in case of a positive answer, how Jesus himself employed the expression Son of man had earlier dominated the scene, we can now observe a strong interest in the tripartition Son of man sayings in the Gospels. If not directly initiated,[1] this tripartition became commonly accepted with Bultmann's seminal *Die Geschichte der synoptischen Tradition*.[2] Here, the Synoptic Son of man sayings were divided into those pertaining to the coming Son of man, those speaking of the suffering Son of man, and those concerning the Son of man's fate and mission on earth. Where an apocalyptic Son of man concept was assumed, it was seen, of course, as miles apart from the 'earthly' Son of man. The problem was how to overcome this gap.

The period is also characterized by an ever more sober handling of the religio-historical question. At first, it was recognized that the History of Religions School had been over-optimistic with regard to the source material pertaining to the concept of Primeval Man ('Urmensch') and its possible connection with the biblical concept of the Son of man. Secondly, interpreters became much more attentive to differences between the use of a concept or picture, and its possible original meaning. This, also, was nothing new, being already anticipated in the discussion referred to above between Hermann Gunkel and Julius Wellhausen. It is far more the actual context than an eventual original meaning that determines significance.

In the late 1960s, the old question was raised again as to the Aramaic origin of the expression and possible consequences for the understanding of the Son of man sayings in the Gospels. The 'first Aramaic stage' in Son of man research was neutralized—if not with philological reason, then with the hypothesis of the History of Religion School of a god 'Man' as possible prototype. However, the question was re-opened, and its basis was extended with new textual material. A few scholars had contributed to the discussion of the Aramaic background in the first decades after the Second World War. A pioneer of the field was Geza Vermes and his results were deepened and clarified in the works of Maurice Casey. There developed a growing awareness of the roots of the Gospel traditions in Aramaic layers and its consequences (cf. below, Chapter 15).

At nearly the same time, another important change came up in the Son of man interpretation. Where an *opinio communis* in scholarship had almost been established with regard to an apocalyptic Son of man concept as the

1. As shown by, for instance, Douglas R.A. Hare, *The Son of Man Tradition* (1990), p. 7 n. 23, pointing to both W. Baldensperger, 'Die neueste Forschung über den Menschensohn', *ThR* 3 (1900), p. 207, and Foakes J.F. Jackson and Kirsopp Lake (eds.), *The Beginnings of Christianity* (1920), I, p. 376, for a similar tripartition.

2. *Die Geschichte der synoptischen Tradition* (1921, 2nd edn, 1931), pp. 163-64 (English translation: *The History of the Synoptic Tradition* [revised edn, 1963], pp. 150-52), but clearer in *Theologie des Neuen Testaments* (5th edn, 1965), pp. 31-32 (English translation: *Theology of the New Testament* [1955], I, p. 30).

background of the occurrence of the expression in the Gospels—Dan. 7.13, *1 Enoch* 37–71, and *4 Ezra* 13 being the *loci classici* in this construction—a few scholars raised the question of whether it was at all possible to speak of a Son of man concept in Judaism at this time. Especially influential with respect to deconstructing the concept of the Son of man was Ragnar Leivestad, and a number of exegetes followed him.

Once again, the picture took on a staggering variety. This time, the variations were not, as earlier, dependent on the feelings of the interpreter or his boldness in reconstructing the mind of Jesus. Although this aspect cannot be totally excluded, the weight of argument was now placed rather on the question of the presuppositions of philological and historical hypotheses. The question has been raised again and again whether the problem of the Son of man is insoluble. At times one feels that such claimed insolubility and difficulty are part of a rhetorical scheme. The answer must be that it is soluble but ever according to the presuppositions assumed.

The relevant literature on the problem of the Son of man from the time before the Second World War was extensive and books and articles containing the expression have been relevant for the survey. The second half of the twentieth century, however, witnessed an explosion in secondary literature which makes it very difficult to get an overall view. Monographs, articles and commentaries have been published in such volume that the bibliographical work becomes immense. The scientific study of the Bible in these decades has also expanded from Western Europe and North America to Eastern Europe and the so-called third world. Some books and articles containing the expression Son of man or its equivalents are not relevant to our context,[3] or the language used, or the publication form (or non-publication) makes them inaccessible to the present author.[4] While almost all of the secondary

3. This pertains to (the order is chronological): Odilo Kaiser, 'Menschensohn, Menschensohnforschung und praktische Verkündigung. Überlegungen zur Dialektik von Autonomie und Finalisierung neutestamentlicher Wissenschaft', in Rudolf Pesch and Rudolf Schnackenburg (eds.), *Jesus und der Menschensohn* (FS Anton Vögtle, 1975), pp. 435-88; Ilse Tödt, 'Der "Menschensohn" und die Folgen', in Christoffer Frey and Wolfgang Huber (eds.), *Schöpferische Nachfolge* (FS Heinz Eduard Tödt, 1978), pp. 541-61.

4. For example (the order is chronological): C.W. Jones, 'The Use of the Title "Son of Man" in Mark' (unpublished dissertation, Southern Baptist Theological Seminary 1948; cf. *Bib* 32 [1951] Elenchus 626c); E. Haapa, *Ihmisen Pojan kuolema kolmessa ensimmäisessä evankeliumissa. Synoptisen tradition kristologiaa* (1949; cf. *TA-TT* 54 [1949], pp. 271-73); A. Rolla, 'Il giorno del Figlio dell' Uomo nei Vangeli: la fine di Gerusalemme e la Chiesa', *Pal. Clero* 33 (1954), pp. 83-89, 108-17 (cf. J. Coppens, *De Mensenzoon-logia* [1973], p. 32); A.K. Papageorgakopoulos, *Ὁ Υἱὸς τοῦ ἀνθρώπου. Συμβολὴ εἰς τὴν ἱστορίαν καὶ ἑρμηνείαν τοῦ ὅρου ὁ "Υἱὸς τοῦ ἀνθρώπου" κατὰ τὴν Καινὴν Διαθήκην* (*The Son of Man: Symbol in the History and Interpretation of the Title 'The Son of Man' according to the New Testament* [1958, 2nd edn, 1963]); J.R. Scheifler, 'El hijo del hombre en Daniel', *Estudios Ecclesiásticos* 34 (1960), pp. 789-804;

E. Nardoni, 'El Hijo del hombre viniendo sobre las nubes', *Revista Bíblica* 21 (1959), pp. 121-24; *idem*, *El Hijo del hombre viniendo sobre las nubes* (1961; cf. *Bib* 43 [1962] Elenchus 1986); J.L. Clark, 'A Re-Examination of the Problem of the Messianic Secret in Mark in its Relationship to the Synoptic Son of Man Sayings' (unpublished dissertation, New Haven, 1962; cf. J. Coppens, *De Mensenzoon-logia in het Markus-Evangelium* [1973], p. 34); J. Pezzana, *De filio hominis, Dan 7,13-14, atque de solutionibus recentioribus catholicorum inde ab anno 1953* (Diss. Antonianum, Rome, 1962; cf. *Bib* 44 [1963] Elenchus 1434); L.G. Arion, 'Invatatura despre "Fiul Omului" in Sfintele Evanghelii', *Studii Teologice* 18 (1966), pp. 470-88 (Rumanian); L.F. Rivera, 'El misterio del Hijo del Hombre en la transfiguración (Mr 9,2-3)', *Revista Bíblica* 28 (1966), pp. 19-34; 79-89; Alberto G. Salceda, *Bar-Nasha: El Hombre* (1969; cf. A. Ferch, *The Son of Man in Daniel 7* [1983], p. 232); Hsia Ch'i-Lung, 'Lun Jowang fuyin chung ti "jentzu"', *Collectanea Theologica Universitatis Fujen* (= Shensüeh Lunchi) 10 (1971) (cf. *Bib* 53 [1972] Elenchus 2860) (Chinese); H. Langkammer, 'Oczekiwanie przyjscia "Pana" i "Syna Czlowieczego" w najstarszych gminach chrzscijanskich [Adventus "Domini" et "Filius hominis" expectatus a christianis primis]', *Ateneum Kaplanskie* 77 (1971), pp. 92-104 (cf. *Bib* 53 [1972] Elenchus 5250) (Czech); *idem*, 'Syn czlowieczy w Ewangeliach synoptycznych [Le Fils de l'Homme dans les Évangiles synoptiques]', in *Colloquium Salutis, Wroclawskie Studia Teologiczne* 4 (1972), pp. 79-93 (cf. *IZBG* 21 [1974–75] 1154) (Czech); M.D. Wogstad, 'Recent NT Research and the "Son of Man" in Mk 14:62 (par)', *Shensüeh yü Chiaohui* 10.1 (1971–72), pp. XXII-XXXVII (in Chinese: Chintai hsinyüeh Shengching chih T'anchiu chi Mak'e fuyin 14:62 chung chih 'Jentzu', Op. cit. pp. 5-17 (*Bib* 53 [1972] Elenchus 2729); V. Mihoc, '"Fiul Omului" dupa NT. Filius Hom. sec. NT', *Studii Teologice* 25 (1973), pp. 33-44 (cf. *Bib* 55 [1974] Elenchus 3455) (Rumanian); Clyde G. Glazener, 'An Investigation of Jesus' Usage of the Term Son of Man: A Possible Interpretative Key to the Gospel of Matthew' (ThD dissertation, Southwestern Baptist Theological Seminary, 1974; cf. Ferch, *The Son of Man in Daniel 7* [1983], p. 218); B.E. Klakowicz, 'Il "Figlio dell'Uomo"', *Divinitas* 22 (1978), pp. 237-41; Alberto Ricciardi, 'El Elegido-Hijo del hombre, vindicador de los oprimidos', *Revista Bíblica* 44 (1982), pp. 207-32; Félix Asensio, 'El protagonismo del "Hombre-Hijo del Hombre" del Salmo 8', *Estudios Bíblicos* NS 41 (1983), pp. 17-51; Józef Homerski, 'Syn Czlowieczy w Wizji Proroka Daniela (Dn 7,13-14)' ('The Son of Man in the Vision of the Prophet Daniel [Dan. 7,13-14]'), *Roczniki Teol. Kanonicze* (Katolocki Universytet Lubelski, Poland) 32 (1985), pp. 47-62 (cf. *OTS* 14 [1991] 1082) (Polish); Matti Myllykoski, 'Jeesus ja Ihmisen Poika—ikuinen arvoitus?', *TAik* 92 (1987), pp. 498-502 (Finnish); W.L. Dols, Jr, 'Toward a Field Critical Hermeneutic of the Phrase "ho huios tou antropou" in the Narrative World of Mark: Interreadings from Literary Criticism, Analytical Psychology and Cultural Anthropology' (unpublished dissertation, Berkeley, Graduate Theological Union, 1987; cf. *EThL* 67 [1991] Elenchus 5177; *DissAbstr* 49 [1988–89], pp. 1847-48); A. Ternier, 'Een eeuw filologisch onderzoek naar de term "mensenzoon"' (unpublished licentiate thesis, Leuven, 1991; cf. Jean-Claude Loba Mkole, 'The Kiswahili mwana a mtu and the Greek ho huios tou anthrópou', in Gerald O. West and Musa W. Dube [eds.], *The Bible in Africa: Transactions, Trajectories and Trends* [2000], pp. 557-66 [566]); A.D. Hix, 'Comparative Analysis of the Christological Titles Son of Man and High Priest as Reflected in the Humiliation, Exaltation, and Redemptive Significance of Jesus' Mission' (unpublished dissertation, New Orleans Baptist Theological Seminary, 1990; cf. *EThL* 69 [1993] Elenchus 4686; *DissAbstr* 52

literature listed in the bibliography from before c. 1945 is treated in the present study,[5] this is no longer the case for the second half of the century.

[1991–92], pp. 567-68); B.J. Jones, 'A Study of the Son of Man in Revelation with Special Reference to the Suffering Servant Motif' (unpublished dissertation, New Orleans Baptist Theological Seminary, 1990; cf. *EThL* 68 [1992] Elenchus 6109; *DissAbstr* 52 [1991–92], pp. 185-86); S.D.E. Premawardhana, 'Parusia and the Son of Man: A Comparative Study of Mythology' (unpublished dissertation, Northwestern University, 1992; cf. *EThL* 70 [1994] Elenchus 5027; *DissAbstr* 53 [1992–93], p. 1956); Mutombo-Mukendi, 'L'apport théologique du Fils de l'Homme dans le deuxième évangile' (unpublished dissertation, Bruxelles: Theol. prot., 1992; cf. *EThL* 70 [1994] Elenchus 5441); H. Jagersma, 'Zoon des mensen', *Interpretatie* 93–98 (1993), pp. 26-27; Juan Mateos and F. Camacho, *El Hijo del hombre: Hacia la plenitud humana* (1995); Lucas Berk, 'Zoon van de mens', *Interpretatie* 4.4 (1996), pp. 16-17; Jean Galot, 'Il mistero del Figlio dell'uomo', *Civiltaà Cattolica* 147 (1996), pp. 130-42; *idem*, 'Il figlio dell'uomo', *Civiltaà Cattolica* 149 (1998), pp. 227-38; José Ornelas Carvalho, *Caminho de morte, destino de vida: O projecto do Filho do Homem e dos seus discípulos a luz de Mc 8,27–9,1* (1998); Filipe Fernández Ramos, 'El Hijo del hombre y el Reino', *Studium Legionense* 39 (1998), pp. 89-119; *idem*, 'La "figura" del hijo del hombre', *Naturaleza y Gracia* 45 (1998), pp. 107-35; *idem*, 'El hijo del hombre en el cuarto evangelio', *Studium Legionense* 40 (1999), pp. 45-92; *idem*, 'El Hijo del hombre: Las tres fases de su atuacíon', *Naturaleza y Gracia* 47 (2000), pp. 295-358; Leslie Walck, 'The Son of Man in Matthew and the "Similitudes of Enoch"' (unpublished PhD dissertation, University of Notre Dame, 1999); José Roberto Cristofani, 'A expressão "Filho do homem" em Daniel. Anotacõs preliminares sobre uma proposita metodológica', *Estudos de Religião* 19 (2000), pp. 25-44; Lok Young Hong, 'Jesus und der Menschensohn. Eine form- und religionsgeschichtliche Untersuchung zu den alttestamentlichen, jüdischen Menschensohntraditionen' (unpublished dissertation, Heidelberg, 2000); Alfonso Novo, 'El hijo del hombre en los evangelios sinóppticos', *Estudios ecclesiasticos* 75 (2000), pp. 23-78; Giovanni Bissoli, 'Il Figlio dell'uomo in Marco: problema insolubile?', and Giovanni Claudio Bottini, 'Luca 18,31-33: Il misterio del Figlio dell'uomo', in Ettore Franco (ed.), *Mysterium Regni—Ministerium Verbi (Mc 4,11, at 6,4)* (FS Vittorio Fusco, 2001), pp. 597-604 and 705-14, respectively; Markus Müller, *Jüngerschaft im Reich des Menschensohnes. Ein Beitrag zur Eschatologie des Matthäusevangeliums* (unpublished Diss. Hab. Erlangen 2001); G.C. Pagazzi and R. Vignolo, 'Su *"il Figlio dell'uomo"*, l'autoaffezione prediletta di Gesù. In margine ad uno studio recente', *Teologica* 29 (2004), pp. 180-200; L. Orlando, 'Il Figlio dell'uomo. Percorso teologico', *Antonianum* 80 (2005), pp. 207-44; Juan José Ayán Calvo, 'Jesucristo, Hijo del hombre e Hijo de dios según Gnacio de Antioquía', in Juan José Ayán Calvo, Patricio de Navascués Benlloch and Manuel Aroztegui Esnaoloa (eds.), *Filición—Cultura pagana, religión de Israel, origins del cristianismo: Actas de las I y II Jornadas de Estudio "La filiacion en los inicios de la reflexión cristiana"* (2005), pp. 303-35.

5. This is not the case with (the order is chronological): B. Oikonomidos, *῾Ο Υἱὸς τοῦ ἀνθρώπου. Κατὰ τὰς θεμελιώδεις ἀρχὰς τῆς᾽ Ορθοδόξου᾽ Ανατολικῆς᾽ Εκκλησίας ἔναντι τοῦ ὀρθολογισμοῦ* (1878) (*The Son of Man': According to the Fundamentals of the Ancient Eastern Orthodox Church*); Vogel, 'Der johanneische Menschensohn', *Deutsch-amerikanische Zeitschrift für Theologie und Kirche* (it has not been possible to identify the article, the reference to 1904 being wrong in F. Tillmann, *Der Menschensohn* [1907],

Nevertheless, all titles are included in the bibliographical notes to give an impression of the extent of this field of New Testament exegesis. The period before 1945 witnessed only a small number of overview articles concerning the interpretation of the expression Son of man.[6] This has changed remarkably with respect to the second half of the century. The review literature has also been abundant.[7] However, mostly these articles cover only a limited

p. 108); H. Offerman, 'The Son of Man and the Son of God', *The Lutheran Church Review* 29 (1910), pp. 710-20; 30 (1911), pp. 120-26 (the section on the Son of man is missing in my source, *NTTS* 6 [1966]); Thomas C. Allen, 'Jesus' Use of the Title, The Son of Man' (unpublished PhD dissertation, the Southern Baptist Theological Seminary, 1927; cf. A.J. Ferch, *The Son of Man in Daniel 7* [1983], p. 205); P.I. Mpratisotes, '"῾Ο Υἱὸς τοῦ Ανθρώπου", Συμβολὴ εἰς τὴν ἱστορίαν τοῦ ὅρου', *Θεολογία* 7 (1929), pp. 193-98 ('The Son of Man Symbol in the History of Research', *Theologia* 7).

6. Besides what is to be found in monographs, summarizing the debate in their introductions, the following articles could be mentioned (the order is chronological): W. Baldensperger, 'Die neueste Forschung über den Menschensohn', *ThR* 3 (1900), pp. 201-10, 243-55; W. Schmiedel, 'Die neuesten Auffassungen des Namens "Menschensohn"', *PrM* 5 (1901), pp. 333-51; J. Croskery, 'Recent Discussion on the Meaning of the Title "Son of Man"', *ET* 13 (1901–1902), pp. 351-55; N. Schmidt, 'Recent Study on the Term "Son of Man"', *JBL* 45 (1926), pp. 326-49.

7. Mostly overviews and critical assessments of other positions are (the order is chronological): C.C. McCown, 'Jesus, Son of Man: A Survey of Recent Discussion', *JR* 28 (1948), pp. 1-12; A.J.B. Higgins, 'Son of Man-*Forschung* Since "The Teaching of Jesus"', in *idem* (ed.), *New Testament Essays: Studies in Memory of Thomas Walter Manson* (1959), pp. 119-35; P.C. Hodgson, 'The Son of Man Problem and the Problem of Historical Knowledge', *JR* 41 (1961), pp. 91-108; M. Black, 'The Son of Man Problem in Recent Research and Debate', *BJRL* 45 (1962–63), pp. 305-18; I.H. Marshall, 'The Synoptic Son of Man Sayings in Recent Discussion', *NTS* 12 (1965–66), pp. 327-51 (reprint in *idem*, *Jesus as Saviour* [1990], pp. 73-100); J.C. Hindley, 'The Son of Man: A Recent Analysis', *The Indian Journal of Theology* 15 (1966), pp. 172-78 (including a reference to *idem*, 'Jesus as "Son of Man" in Light of Some Recent Discussions', *Bulletin of the Society of Biblical Studies* 1 [1964], which has not been accessible); R. Marlow, 'The *Son of Man* in Recent Journal Literature', *CBQ* 28 (1966), pp. 20-30; G. Haufe, 'Das Menschensohn-Problem in der gegenwärtigen wissenschaftlichen Diskussion', *EvTh* 26 (1966), pp. 130-41 (= 'Le problème du Fils de l'Homme', *EThR* 42 [1967], pp. 311-22); A.J.B. Higgins, 'Is the Son of Man Problem Insoluble?', in E.E. Ellis and M. Wilcox (eds.), *Neotestamentica et Semitica* (FS Matthew Black, 1969), pp. 70-87; J.N. Birdsall, 'Who is This Son of Man?', *EvQ* 42 (1970), pp. 7-17; I.H. Marshall, 'The Son of Man in Contemporary Debate', *EvQ* 42 (1970), pp. 67-87 (= reprint in *idem*, *Jesus as Saviour* [1990], pp. 100-20); J.-M. Cangh, 'Le Fils de l'homme dans la tradition synoptique', *Revue Théologique de Louvain* 1 (1970), pp. 411-19; R. Maddox, 'Methodenfragen in der Menschensohnforschung', *EvTh* 32 (1972), pp. 143-60 (= 'The Quest for Valid Methods in "Son of Man" Research', *ABR* 19 [1971], pp. 36-51); E. Ruckstuhl, 'Die johanneische Menschensohnforschung 1957–1969', *Theologische Berichte* 1 (1972), pp. 171-284; Hendrikus Boers, 'Where Christology is Real: A Survey of Recent Research on New Testament Christology', *Interpretation* 26 (1972), pp. 300-27; S. Légasse, 'Jésus historique et le Fils de l'homme aperçu sur les opinions contemporaines', in L. Monloubou

space of time or a special theme. Besides the few unpublished dissertations on this topic,[8] we only find the aforementioned monograph by Delbert

(ed.), *Apocalypses et théologie de l'espérance* (1977), pp. 271-98; M. Black, 'Jesus and the Son of Man', *JSNT* 1 (1978), pp. 4-18; G. Vermes, 'The "Son of Man" Debate', *JSNT* 1 (1978), pp. 19-32; *idem*, 'The Present State of the "Son of Man" Debate', *JJS* 29 (1978), pp. 123-34 (reprinted in *idem*, *Jesus and the World of Judaism* [1983], pp. 89-99, 175-80); M.D. Hooker, 'Is the Son of Man Problem Really Insoluble?', in E. Best and R.M. Wilson (eds.), *Text and Interpretation* (FS Matthew Black, 1979), pp. 155-68; W.G. Kümmel, 'Jesusforschung seit 1965. Der persönliche Anspruch Jesu', *ThR* 45 (1980), pp. 40-84 (reprinted in *idem*, *Dreissig Jahre Jesusforschung [1950–1980]* [ed. H. Merklein, 1985], pp. 330-74); J. Coppens, 'Où en est le problème de Jésus "Fils de l'homme"', *EThL* 56 (1980), pp. 282-302 (reprinted in *idem*, *Le Fils de l'homme néotestamentaire* [1981], pp. 1-21); F.J. Moloney, 'The End of the Son of Man?', *The Downside Review* 98 (1980), pp. 280-90; C. Colpe, 'Neue Untersuchungen zum Menschensohnproblem', *ThRv* 77 (1981), pp. 353-72; C. Tuckett, 'Recent Work on the Son of Man', *Scripture Bulletin* 12 (1981), pp. 14-18; W.G. Kümmel, 'Jesusforschung seit 1965: Nachträge 1975–1980. V. Der persönliche Anspruch Jesu', *ThR* 47 (1982), pp. 370-78 (reprinted in *idem*, *Dreissig Jahre Jesusforschung [1950–1980]* [ed. by H. Merklein, 1985], pp. 519-28); W.O. Walker, 'The Son of Man: Some Recent Developments', *CBQ* 45 (1983), pp. 584-607 (reprinted in W.R. Farmer [ed.], *New Synoptic Studies* [1983], pp. 261-301); Don Jackson, 'A Survey of the 1967–1981 Study of the Son of Man', *Restoration Quarterly* 28 (1985–86), pp. 67-78; J.R. Donahue, 'Recent Studies on the Origin of "Son of Man" in the Gospels', *CBQ* 48 (1986), pp. 484-98; W.G. Kümmel, 'Jesusforschung seit 1981. V. Der persönliche Anspruch sowie der Prozeß und Kreuzestod Jesu', *ThR* NF 56 (1991), pp. 391-420 (391-412) (reprinted in *idem*, *Vierzig Jahre Jesusforschung [1950–1990]* [ed. Helmut Merklein, 1994), pp. 661-90); P. Maurice Casey, 'Method in our Madness, and Madness in their Methods: Some Approaches to the Son of Man Problem in Recent Scholarship', *JSNT* 42 (1991), pp. 17-43; F.H. Borsch, 'Further Reflections on "The Son of Man": The Origins and Development of the Title', in James H. Charlesworth (ed.), *The Messiah: Developments in Earliest Judaism and Christianity* (1992), pp. 130-44; Walter E. Aufrecht, 'The Son of Man Problem as an Illustration of the *Techne* of New Testament Studies', in Bradley H. MacLean (ed.), *Origins and Method: Towards a New Understanding of Judaism and Christianity* (FS John Hurd, 1993), pp. 282-94; Delbert R. Burkett, 'The Non-Titular Son of Man: A History and Critique', *NTS* 40 (1994), pp. 504-21. Besides these articles we also find overviews of the Son of man interpretation in several monographs, for instance in Norman Perrin, *The Kingdom of God and the Teaching of Jesus* (1963), pp. 90-129; F.H. Borsch, *The Son of Man in Myth and History* (1967), pp. 15-64; A.J.B. Higgins, *The Son of Man in the Teaching of Jesus* (1980), pp. 3-53; Chrys C. Caragounis, *The Son of Man: Vision and Interpretation* (1986), pp. 9-33; Douglas R.A. Hare, *The Son of Man Tradition* (1990), pp. 29-45. Mainly overviews are: F. Neugebauer, *Jesus der Menschensohn. Ein Beitrag zur Klärung der Wege historischer Wahrheitsfindung im Bereich der Evangelien* (1972); W.G. Kümmel, *Jesus der Menschensohn?* (1984); and Anton Vögtle, *Die 'Gretchenfrage' des Menschensohnproblems. Bilanz und Perspektive* (1994).

8. Thus, besides the aforementioned dissertations of W. Bracht, *Der Menschensohn. Eine Untersuchung zum Bedeutungswandel und zur Geschichte der Auslegung und der Erforschung des neutestamentlichen Begriffs* (1971–72), and Ch. Weist, *Wer ist dieser*

Burkett, *The Son of Man Debate: A History and Evaluation* (1999), which, in its basic design, is not chronological. In consideration of the impact of the expression Son of man in the reconstruction of the mind of the historical Jesus and its central role in christological thinking, this absence is astonishing.

Menschensohn? Die Geschichte der Exegese zum Menschensohn-Begriff (1972): P. Leroueil, *Énigmes et certitudes de la recherche contemporaine sur the theme du 'Fils de l'homme' dans l'Apocalyptique juive et dans la tradition synoptique. État des questions* (1974, cf. *EThL* 51 [1975], p. *152).

14. Continuations

During the first decades after the Second World War, Son of man research was dominated primarily by continuation. Recent and older[1] positions were repeated and new tendencies took a foothold only slowly. Thus, in his huge *Die Kirchliche Dogmatik* (*Church Dogmatics*), Karl Barth (1886–1968) simply takes up the very old juxtaposition of Son of Man and Son of God, the former signifying the humanity of Christ. This happens in *Die Lehre von der Schöpfung* (*The Doctrine of Creation*) (III.2, 1948) in which Barth's theological anthropology is based on his Christology: the old way of doing Christology (moving from anthropology) is impossible because of human sin. Taking his point of departure from the sayings of Pilate in the Gospel of John (19.5, 'Behold the man [*Ecce homo*, ἰδοὺ ὁ ἄνθρωπος]', and 19.14, 'Look, your king!'), Barth argues that the term used in 19.5

> can be anything but equivalent to the phrase which occurs about seventy times in the Synoptists, twelve times in John and sporadically in the rest of the New Testament—the phrase υἱὸς τοῦ ἀνθρώπου in its relationship to υἱὸς τοῦ θεοῦ. Even these two are not mutually exclusive and opposed, but are different aspects of one and the same definition. Both are Messianic titles and describe Jesus as the embodiment of the coming kingdom of God. In the Gospels 'the Son of man' is always Jesus' description of Himself. Whether texts in which this name occurs refer to the humiliation of His passion and death or to the glory of His resurrection and future coming makes no difference to its essential meaning. The name as such means Son of God, namely, the Son of God who as such has become man, and who as man has acted as the Son of God and proved Himself to be such.[2]

1. Also very old 'solutions' are repeated in this period. Thus C.M. Henze, 'Quis sit genuinus sensus locutionis "ὁ υἱὸς τοῦ ἀνθρωπου"', *Divus Thomas. Commentarium de philosophia et theologia* 50 (1947), pp. 69-80, discusses the identity of the human being whose son Jesus is. Cf. *idem*, 'Der Sohn des Menschen', *ThPQ* 104 (1956), pp. 70-74. Similar in the conclusions is Jean Galot, 'L'enigme du "Fils de l'homme"', *Revue du Clergé Africain* 12 (1957), pp. 215-27, 338-52 (227 and 352); also pp. 347-49, where the Son of man is identified as Mary's son.

2. K. Barth, *Die Kirchliche Dogmatik* (1948), III.2, pp. 52-53, quoted according to the English translation, *Church Dogmatics*. III. *The Doctrine of Creation* Part 2 (1960), p. 45, but cf. pp. 44-46.

Barth then notes the use in Ezekiel, Dan. 7.13 and Ps. 8.5, but also includes other New Testament passages, which describe Christ as man (Phil. 2.7; 1 Cor. 15.21-22, 45-49; Rom. 5.12-21). Without further ado, the expression is taken as a messianic title and ascribed indiscriminately to Jesus. No distance is seen between his use and its meaning in the Gospels. Barth, of course, knows the religio-historical positions and the alternative between an individual and a collective interpretation, but is not the least distracted in his understanding of the two 'titles' as defining Christ's natures. The tone is even closer to what is found in the Church fathers when in the fourth part of his Church Dogmatics, vol. 2, *Die Lehre von der Versöhnung* (*The Doctrine of Reconciliation*) (IV,2, 1955), in §64 'Die Erhöhung des Menschensohnes (The Exaltation of the Son of Man)', Barth begins speaking of the covenant and of God not being alone. There also is a covenant people and the covenant man:

> The centre of this event is indeed that God was not content merely to be God, but that *propter nos homines*, and without ceasing to be God, He Himself became man in His Son. An Israelite, this Israelite, the Son of Abraham, David and Mary, and therefore the Son of Man, for the conversion of all men to Himself.[3]

Then, in §64.2, 'Die Heimkehr des Menschensohnes (The Homecoming of the Son of Man)', he repeatedly uses the term Son of Man in formulas such as 'The atonement as it took place in Jesus Christ is the one inclusive event of this going out of the Son of God and coming in of the Son of Man',[4] and 'What else can the Son of God, who humbled Himself as man, become and be but the Son of Man who is not divinised, but exalted at the side of God?'[5] One is also not surprised to find the term in connection with an inclusion of the teaching of a *communicatio idiomatum*: 'If the Word became flesh, this means that the Son of God also became Son of Man—a man, yet not any man, but *the* Son of Man, the bearer of human essence, who, as such, is also the bearer of divine essence'.[6] Thus, Barth concludes, 'The older Christology gave us the right answer that he is the Son of God and Son of Man who, as such, is of divine and human essence'.[7] In an astonishing way, there seems to be no friction between biblical scholarship and dogmatics.

Probably the most popular view at first was that the expression Son of man in the Gospels functions as a christological title—German: Hoheitstitel—

3. Barth, *Die Kirchliche Dogmatik*, IV.2, p. 4. Quoted according to the English translation in *Church Dogmatics*. IV. *The Doctrine of Reconciliation* Part 2 (1958), p. 6. The section runs pp. 1-422. I owe the references to this volume to D.R.A. Hare, *The Son of Man Tradition* (1990), pp. 29-30.

4. Barth, *Die Kirchliche Dogmatik*, IV.2, p. 21; English translation, p. 21.

5. Barth, *Die Kirchliche Dogmatik*, IV.2, pp. 29-30; English translation, p. 28.

6. Barth, *Die Kirchliche Dogmatik*, IV.2, p. 79; English translation, p. 73.

7. Barth, *Die Kirchliche Dogmatik*, IV.2, p. 120; English translation, p. 108.

adopting a special apocalyptic Son of man expectation, developed in Early Judaism in the centuries before the Common Era with Dan. 7.13 as its main basis, more or less in contrast to common Messianic expectation. All—or at least the great majority—of the Gospel Son of man sayings are interpreted as referring to this concept, the main question being whether this Son of man Christology had been introduced by the earthly Jesus himself, or had been the product of christological thinking on behalf of the early community. This period also sees other attempts with regard to the derivation of the expression or title. Some look for alternative Old Testament sayings; others for a more idiomatic use. Often, this attempt to consider the use of the expression as originating with Jesus and to see it as the very key to his self-understanding is connected with either liberal or conservative theology, both in their own way being bound up with the Jesus of history. The common denominator for the majority of the 'solutions' referred to in this chapter is that the Son of man sayings, as they now stand in the Gospels, represent a more or less coherent concept dominated by the implied reference to Dan. 7.13. The variations are due to different views concerning the question of how it was employed by the earthly Jesus and the eventual degree of Daniel's influence on his use.

1. *Jesus Expressed his Messianic Self-Consciousness through an Existing Apocalyptical Son of Man Expectation*

The list of supporters for the view that Jesus took over a more or less pre-existing Jewish apocalyptic Son of man concept representing an alternative to the more common Messianic expectation is long.[8] The variations are many, although, basically, the melody is the same. Some assume a development in Jesus' use of the term. There is also a discussion concerning the relation of the three categories of Son of man sayings to each other and, further, to what degree Jesus transformed the concept, for instance, by combining his use of Dan. 7.13 with one or other Old Testament saying.[9]

8. Because the Son of man literature in the period after the Second World War becomes more and more abundant, considerations of space forbid going into detail with every contribution. I will only mention a few of the more 'prominent' and influential contributions, confining the rest to footnotes.

9. The order in the following is chronological but in the case of multiple contributions by the same author, they are listed together: W. Manson, *Jesus the Messiah* (1943, 2nd edn, 1948), pp. 88-92; *idem*, 'The Son of Man and History', *SJTh* 5 (1958), pp. 113-22 (reprinted in *idem*, *Jesus and the Christian* [1967], pp. 67-76); T.A. Burkill, 'The Son of Man: A Brief General Statement', *ET* 56 (1944–45), pp. 305-306; J.W. Bowman, *The Intention of Jesus* (1945), pp. 106-36; *idem*, 'The Background of the Term "Son of Man"', *ET* 59 (1947–48), pp. 283-88; Nils Johansson, 'De urkristna föreställningarna om Människosonen och vår Kristustro', *STK* 21 (1945), pp. 1-13; M. Black,

'The "Son of Man" in the Teaching of Jesus', *ET* 60 (1948–49), pp. 32-36; *idem*, 'The Servant of the Lord and the Son of Man', *SJTh* 6 (1953), pp. 1-11 (who is undecided); *idem*, 'The "Son of Man" Passion Sayings in the Gospel Tradition', *ZNW* 60 (1969), pp. 1-8; C.C. McCown, 'Jesus, Son of Man: A Survey of Recent Discussion', *JR* 28 (1948), pp. 1-12; J.M. Vosté, 'The Title "Son of Man" in the Synoptic Gospels', *The American Ecclesiastical Review* 120 (1949), pp. 310-26; J. Munck, 'Menneskesønnen', *Illustreret Religionsleksikon*, II (1950), p. 572; H. Riesenfeld, 'Människosonen. 2. *N.T.*', *SBU*, II (1952), cols. 403-405 (= 2nd edn, 1963, cols. 232-34); Ernst Percy (1901–1968), *Die Botschaft Jesu. Eine traditionskritische und exegetische Untersuchung* (1953), pp. 225-307 (238-59); J. Delorme, *Le Fils de l'homme* (1954); R.H. Fuller, *The Mission and Achievement of Jesus: An Examination of the Presuppositions of New Testament Theology* (1954, 6th edn, 1970), pp. 95-108 (later Fuller changed his mind); Ch. De Beus, 'Achterground en enhoud van de uitdrukking "de Zoon des Mensen" in de synoptische Evangelien', *NedThT* 10 (1954–55), pp. 272-95; C.P. van Andel, *De structuur van de Henochtraditie en het Nieuwe Testament* (1955), pp. 102-103; A. Feuillet, 'Fils de l'homme', *Catholicisme* IV (1956), cols. 1295-302; P. Seethaler, 'Kleine Studie über den "Menschensohn"', *BuK* 11 (1956), pp. 85-87; M. Zalampis, 'The Relation of Echatology to the Son of Man and the Kingdom of God', *Review and Expositor* 53 (1956), pp. 326-31; M. Brändle, 'Der Menschensohn. Selbstbezeichnung Jesu oder Theologie der Urkirche?', *Orientierung. Katholische Blätter für weltanschauliche Information* 21 (1957), pp. 27-31; J.P. Lettinga, 'De uitdrukking "de Zoon des mensen"', *Almanak van het Corpus Studiosorum in Academi Campensi 'Fides Quadrat Intellectum' 1955–1957* (1957), pp. 141-49; I.L. Sanders, 'The Origin and Significance of the Title "The Son of Man" as Used in the Gospels', *Scripture* 10 (1958), pp. 49-56; B. Willaert, 'Jezus, de Mensenzoon', *Collationes Brugenses et Gandavenses* 5 (1959), pp. 515-36; E. Ashby, 'The Coming of the Son of Man', *ET* 72 (1960–61), pp. 360-63; J. Guillet, 'A propos des titres de Jésus: Christ, Fils de l'homme, Fils de Dieu', in M. Jourjon *et al.* (eds.), *A la recontre de Dieu.* Mémorial Albert Gelin (1961), pp. 309-17; much later this view is more or less reiterated in *idem*, 'Le Fils de l'homme: Titre eschatologique ou mission prophétique?', *RSR* 88 (2000), pp. 615-38; reprinted in Pierre Gibert and Christoph Theobald (eds.), *Le cas Jésus Christ: Exégètes, historiens et théologiens en confrontation* (2002), pp. 171-204 (cf. *NTA* 45 [2001], p. 242); F. Lang, 'Menschensohn', *Calwer Bibellexikon* (1961, 2nd edn, 1967), pp. 888-91; L. Paul, *Son of Man: The Life in Christ* (1961); G.H.P. Thompson, 'The Son of Man—Some Further Considerations', *JThS* NS 12 (1961), pp. 203-209; S.E. Johnson, 'Son of Man', *The Interpreter's Dictionary*, IV (1962), pp. 413-20; M. Cambe, 'Le Fils de l'homme dans les évangiles synoptiques', *LV* 12 (1963), pp. 32-64; L. Goppelt, 'Zum Problem des Menschensohns. Das Verhältnis von Leidens- und Parusieankündigung', in H. Sierig (ed.), *Mensch und Menschensohn* (FS Karl Witte, 1963), pp. 20-32 (reprinted in *idem*, *Christologie und Ethik* [1969], pp. 66-78); *idem*, *Theologie des Neuen Testaments* (ed. by J. Roloff, 1975), I, pp. 226-47; J. Bieneck, 'Menschensohn. Im NT', *Biblisch-Historisches Handwörterbuch*, II (1964), cols. 1192-93; J. Christensen, 'Menneskesøn', in *Gads danske Bibelleksikon*, II (1966), cols. 188-91 (= 2nd edn, 1982, II, cols. 552-55); C.J.L. Proudman, 'Remarks on the "Son of Man"', *Canadian Journal of Theology* 12 (1966), pp. 128-31; August Strobel, *Kerygma und Apokalyptik. Ein religionsgeschichtlicher und theologischer Beitrag zur Christusfrage* (1967), pp. 45-84; J. Jensen, 'Son of Man', *The New Catholic Encyclopaedia* (1967), XIII, pp. 431-33; H.H. Straton, 'The Son-of-man and the Messianic

One of the more 'prominent' representatives of this view is the Erlangen New Testament professor Ethelbert Stauffer (1902–1979). In *Die Theologie des Neuen Testaments* (1941), he declares that '"Son of Man" is just about the most pretentious piece of self-description that any man in the ancient East could possibly have used!'[10] He continues:

> Jesus claims for himself all the heavenly majesty of this Son of Man. Yet this celestial glory belongs to a man who, at the height of improbability, treads the way of suffering. The heavenly man in the form of a servant—that of the Son of Man of whom Jesus speaks. So on the lips of Jesus the old apocalyptic idea is given a deep paradoxical meaning, which is developed in three groups of sayings: about the hidden majesty, the *via dolorosa* and the revealed glory of the Son of Man.[11]

Although the expression is found predominantly in the Gospels, the idea of the Son of man idea is also present in the letters of Paul, the apostle using the concept 'man', which also better expresses the antithetic analogy between Christ and Adam. In a later article, Stauffer confronts every confusion of the Messianic concept with the Son of man concept:

> First of all, the titles of honour (Würdenamen), Messiah and Son of Man, in Early Judaism (Spätjudentum), are two basically different concepts, having a very different prehistory and belonging primarily to different circles. Anyway

Secret', *The Journal of Religious Thought* 24 (1967), pp. 31-49; R. Maddox, 'The Function of the Son of Man according to the Synoptic Gospels', *NTS* 15 (1968–69), pp. 45-74 (cf. *idem*, 'The Son of Man and Judgment' [Summary of his doctoral dissertation], *HThR* 57 [1964], pp. 387-88); J. Nelis, 'Menschensohn', *Bibel-Lexikon* (2nd edn, 1968), cols. 1128-34; D. Stanley, 'The Quest of the Son of Man', *The Way: A Quarterly Review of Christian Spirituality* 8 (1968), pp. 3-17; B. de Margerie, 'Le Fils de l'Homme, Rédempteur d'une Église corémptrice', *Communio. Commentarii Internationales de Ecclesia et Theologia* 3 (1970), pp. 227-73; F. Neugebauer, *Jesus der Menschensohn. Ein Beitrag zur Klärung historischer Wahrheitsfindung im Bereich der Evangelien* (1972); W. Stott, '"Son of man"—A Title of Abasement', *ET* 83 (1971–72), pp. 278-81; K.H. Schelkle, *Theologie des Neuen Testaments*. II. *Gott war in Christus* (1973), pp. 199-207; Marcel Bastin, 'La Passion du Fils de l'homme dans les dits de Jésus. Contribution à l'étude du Jésus de l'histoire' (dissertation, Strasbourg, 1973), especially pp. 211, 244; Rudolf Pesch, 'Die Passion des Menschensohnes. Eine Studie zu den Menschensohnworten der vormarkinischen Passionsgeschichte', in R. Pesch and R. Schnackenburg (eds.), *Jesus und der Menschensohn* (FS Anton Vögtle, 1975), pp. 166-95 (193-95). Because of the new situation created around 1970 by the impact of the revival of an Aramaic approach and the decline of the belief in the existence of a pre-formed Jewish apocalyptic-eschatological Son of man concept, the list stops here. Later representatives are to be found in Chapter 16.

10. E. Stauffer, *Die Theologie des Neuen Testaments* (1941, 4th edn, 1948), p. 88. Quoted according to the English translation, *New Testament Theology* (1955), p. 108.

11. Stauffer, *Die Theologie des Neuen Testaments*, p. 89; English translation, p. 109.

> they were concepts to which were attached totally different and often opposite concepts and expectations. Second is the tradition history of both concepts, also in the New Testament, as heterogeneous as possible...
>
> Jesus has not designated himself as the Messiah... The reason is obvious: The Messianic expectation was the foremost hope of the Jewish resistance movement, the hope for the future of a political religion. Jesus will have nothing to do with this Messianic hope. But also the Messianic concept of the disciples and the de-militarized and de-politicized Messianic concept of the silent in the land was not enough for him. It was too narrow for the apocalyptic mission claimed by Jesus, too pietistic, too spiritual. Therefore Jesus did not designate himself as the Messiah, but as the Son of Man.[12]

In 1951, the Norwegian Old Testament scholar Sigmund Mowinckel (1884–1965) published his influential monograph on 'the messianic expectation in the Old Testament and at the time of Jesus', which is, in fact, the subtitle of his *Hans som kommer: Messiasforventningen i Det gamle testament og på Jesu tid* (the 1956 English edition bore the shorter title *He that Cometh*). Programmatically, Mowinckel continues and summarizes the views and intentions of the History of Religions School with regard to Jesus' use of Son of man:

> The matter may summarily be expressed thus: Jesus came to be, not the Messiah, but the Son of Man. He wanted to be the Messiah only in so far as the idea of the Messiah had been modified by, and was compatible with, that of the Son of Man... By using the title 'Son of Man' and some of the conceptions which were then associated with it, Jesus may be said to have associated Himself with the varied history which had led up to the late Jewish idea of the Messiah, with its borrowings in form and content from Jewish and pagan sources. He laid all the emphasis on those aspects of that idea which were represented by the title 'the Son of Man'. In so doing He set His seal on that process of religious development, and acknowledged its validity as revelation history. He also hallowed those features in it which were of non-Jewish origin, and in fact attested that He was the saviour for both Jews and Gentiles, the fulfilment of the hope of all mankind, being 'Son of Man' in the more modern sense of the term, which is justified by the connexion with the idea of the Primordial Man.[13]

The Swedish scholar Erik Sjöberg (1907–1963), in his 1955 work, *Der verborgene Menschensohn*, assumes that Jesus has taken over the motive of the hiddenness of the pre-existent apocalyptic Son of man in heaven from *1 Enoch* and *4 Ezra*. But Jesus had not just taken it over. He also transformed

12. E. Stauffer, 'Messias und Menschensohn', *NT* 1 (1956), pp. 81-102. The quotations are from pp. 81 and 102. Cf. *idem*, *Jesus. Gestalt und Geschichte* (1957), pp. 122-24.

13. Sigmund Mowinckel, *He that Cometh* (1956), pp. 445-46 (= *Han som kommer* [1951], p. 289). Chapter 10, 'The Son of Man' (pp 346-450), is both the longest and the concluding chapter. Cf. also *idem*, 'Menneskesönnen', *Nordisk Teologisk Leksikon* II (1955), cols. 1006-1010.

it, according to his understanding of God and his own mission.[14] He understood the man-like of Dan. 7.13 as an individual messianic figure coming at the end of time as redeemer and judge, and he perceived himself as this Son of man. In the Synoptic Gospels, the thought of pre-existence has disappeared and it seems as if it had only played a secondary role in the thinking of Jesus. However, the aspect of the concept of pre-existence, indicating Jesus as representative of God, is present. Thus, Jesus did not only understand himself as a Messiah designatus. He, rather, perceived himself as the hidden Messiah. According to the Synoptic tradition, 'Jesus was already the Messiah during his earthly life. It was only therefore that it was possible to speak about the intrusion of the Kingdom of God through his ministry.'[15] The greatest difference in relation to the Jewish concept of the Son of man was the attitude of Jesus towards sinners. He did not come as judge but as the bringer of grace and redemption. This trait too is connected with his being the hidden Messiah, a task which was first fulfilled at his death. 'A suffering Son of Man was unknown in Judaism, but Jesus included death in his messianic task. He interpreted it according to Isaiah's promises of a suffering servant of God... *The hidden Son of man as the suffering servant of God*—was how the apprehension of Jesus of his messianic task was fulfilled.'[16] Sjöberg concludes:

> The revelation of the Son of man should not happen before the end of time. Before, he was and should be hidden: only known by those to whom God has revealed him. Apocalyptic knew of no earthly epiphany of the Son of man before the revelation at the end of time. But when the Son of man, as for example with Jesus, functioned on earth already before and in accordance with the existing Son of man concepts, he could only do so as hidden.[17]

Thus the concept of the Messianic secret is not a secondary construction. It is integrated in the earthly ministry of Jesus. This means that Son of man sayings placed in the public ministry of Jesus cannot be original.[18]

14. Cf. especially E. Sjöberg, *Der verborgene Menschensohn* (1955), pp. 241-46. Cf. the earlier and more popular 'Människosonen i judendom och urkristendom', *Tjugoåttonde svenska läroverksläramötet i Stockholm 2–5 januari i 1946 och dess förhandlinger* (1946), pp. 254-70.

15. Sjöberg, *Der verborgene Menschensohn*, p. 243.

16. Sjöberg, *Der verborgene Menschensohn*, pp. 244-45.

17. Sjöberg, *Der verborgene Menschensohn*, p. 245.

18. Cf. Sjöberg, *Der verborgene Menschensohn*, pp. 238-39, where Sjöberg enumerates the following Son of man sayings as sayings in which Son of man is secondary: Mk 2.10, 28; Mt. 8.20; 11.19; 12.32, 40; Lk. 19.10, all with parallels. With respect to the thought of a messianic secret, Sjöberg is followed by Rudolf Schnackenburg, *Gottes Herrschaft und Reich. Eine biblisch-theologische Studie* (1959, 4th edn, 1965), pp. 110-22, where (p. 116) it is said that: 'Wenn er nicht einfach "ich" sagt, so geschieht das

Another influential example is *Die Christologie des Neuen Testaments* from 1957 by the Basel professor of New Testament and Church History, Oscar Cullmann (1902–1999). Cullmann represents what could be called a pan-Son of man-ism, seeing the influence from the Son of man concept in places where the expression is not found. However, the influence from pagan mythology in the New Testament concept is channelled through Judaism. Thus it is declared that

> when Jesus designates himself the Son of Man, he establishes a direct contact with the particular view current in certain circles among his people. We must in fact even go beyond Judaism, because, as is the case with the Logos concept...this concept was widespread (in different forms of course) in other religions. This might seem to call for a special section devoted to the Son of Man in non-biblical religions. If we nevertheless deal with the question within the framework of our investigation of the Son of Man in Judaism, it is because the non-biblical idea of this figure did not *directly* influence Jesus and the early Church. The debate about the extra-Jewish figure of a 'heavenly man' took place within Judaism, so that the connection between Jesus the Son of Man and the non-biblical Son of Man passes through Judaism.
>
> We conclude that, apart from one or two passages in which the term may designate all men [it is Mk 2.27-28; Mt. 12.31-32 = Lk. 12.10], Jesus used the title Son of Man to express his consciousness of having to fulfil the work of the Heavenly Man in two ways: (1) In glory at the end of time—a thought familiar to the expectation of the Son of Man in certain Jewish circles. (2) In the humiliation of the incarnation among sinful men—a thought foreign to all earlier conceptions of the Son of Man.[19]

The next to be mentioned is Frederick Houk Borsch, professor of New Testament in Evanston, whose work, *The Son of Man in Myth and History* from 1967, represents the last comprehensive attempt to understand Jesus' use of the Son of man from the background of a broader spectrum of forerunners in the history of religion.[20] After a study of vast material reviving many of the results of the History of Religions School, but also adding evidence from the Dead Sea Scrolls, Borsch proposes the hypothesis that:

wegen seines "Messiasgeheimnisses": Er wollte die Identität des einmal in Herrlichkeit kommenden Menschensohnes mit seiner eigenen Person nicht unverhüllt, sondern nur andeutungsweise aussprechen'.

19. O. Cullmann, *Die Christologie des Neuen Testament* (1957), pp. 139, 167. The chapter 'Jesus der Menschensohn' covers pp. 138-98 (here quoted according to the English translation, *The Christology of the New Testament* [revised edn, 1963], pp. 137-38 and p. 164) and is the longest in the book (in the English version, pp. 137-92). Maria Furth Sulzbach, 'Who Was Jesus? The Theology of the Son of Man', *Religion in Life* 30 (1961), pp. 179-86, is a summary of Cullmann's interpretation.

20. Some years before Borsch published something approaching a summary of his later book: 'The Son of Man', *AThR* 45 (1963), pp. 174-90. Cf. also *idem*, 'Mark XIV.62 and I Enoch LXII.5', *NTS* 14 (1967–68), pp. 565-67.

> We hold that there are now many good reasons for believing that there were extant during the first century AD and probably for some time earlier a number of Jewish sects which practised forms of baptism as an ordination/coronation rite and which were likely open to at least a measure of *foreign* (or simply indigenous but non-Jewish) influences. Even our evidence from the second century or later points *consistently* back to this area and this time. It is also our contention that for a number of these groups, and often in connection with their baptismal rites, speculation about or belief in the Man (in one or more guises) had a significant role to play. In our opinion the sources of both many of these water rites and of the concern with the Man, as well as the interrelation between the two, reach back to the ancient kingship ideologies. Fragmented and varied though the practices are (or we see them), almost every group offers cause for seeking a background of thought and/or custom in the older king-Man rituals and mythologies.
>
> It is against this background and in this historical setting that we wish to examine what we regard as the earliest strains of Christian tradition, especially as they pertain directly to the Son of Man. We believe it quite likely that Jesus could have been influenced by the beliefs of one or more groups like these.[21]

The conclusion which Borsch reaches is found in the Old Testament and later exegetical speculations; after which he asks a surprising question:

> Yet what if one went to the Old Testament with the conviction that a number of its great heroes had been representatives or types of the Man? In other words, instead of picturing Jesus as a kind of super-exegete, we should perhaps see him as one influenced by this belief, this idea that the Adamite one, the Son of Man, could be manifested on earth at different times in history. Seen in these terms, it would be natural to view the earthly Adam himself and David and the royal servant and perhaps also Enoch, Moses, Elijah, Ezekiel, Jonah and maybe others, as earlier representatives of the Man. It would become natural for Jesus, believing himself to have been appointed to act as the Son of Man in this age, to have seen his own life and future foreshadowed in the lives of these great figures and types from the past.[22]

Borsch offers an attempt to see Jesus as epitomizing the different concepts of a mythical Man figure in such a way that he can also declare that 'on our view it would appear that the life of Jesus was not just mythically interpreted, but that is was first mythically inspired'.[23] According to Borsch

21. F.H. Borsch, *The Son of Man in Myth and History* (1967), pp. 218-19. In the 1963 article, 'The Son of Man', p. 183, Borsch directly proposes the Nazarenes as a possible candidate for the group from whom Jesus had become acquainted with the Man concept.

22. Borsch, *The Son of Man in Myth and History*, pp. 400-401. P. 407 Borsch quotes with approval the Danish Old Testament professor Aage Bentzen (*King and Messiah* [1955], p. 79): 'The result is that Jesus reunites all aspects of the idea of Primeval Man and Primeval King in his own person, and so the entire mythology of the Ancient East is reinstated'.

23. Borsch, *The Son of Man in Myth and History*, pp. 404-405, and also for the following quotations.

> we could even say that God had given him this myth. Jesus, however, was not content to preach about a myth; he had to discover how that myth related to the actualities of his own life and those of his disciples... Without the myth, Jesus might not have been able to accept the cross; without the cross we would never have known how much truth lay beyond even the revelatory powers of this myth.

This insight into the story helps us to see 'how Jesus could have been a full human being and yet possess a sense of supranatural commissioning'. According to Borsch, such supranatural features were integral to his life and 'issued from this belief that he had been chosen to act as the Son of Man'. This aspect, vital in the life of Jesus, was replaced later in the Church by the good news about Jesus himself. On the other hand, later 'gnostic usage of the Son of Man designation, in part, derives from forms of early Christian tradition, which developed differently from those which eventually reached the canonical gospels'.[24]

The last to be mentioned under this heading is Werner Bracht, whose dissertation, *Der Menschensohn* (1972), is not merely a history of interpretation.[25] To Bracht, the Son of man is a christological title with a pre-Christian background, 'because from the beginning the gospel texts presuppose the Son of man as a known entity, which can only be deduced from Jewish apocalypticism'.[26] What is seen in the Synoptic Gospels is the result of a christological re-interpretation (Umprägung), where the Son of man title everywhere retains its eschatological-transcendent meaning (Sinngehalt). What happens outside the New Testament is 'that in a remarkable way the apocalyptic background of the title sinks into total oblivion and thus, in its Hellenistic milieu, is interpreted literally to serve the theological argument for the true humanity of the Son of God'.[27]

If Jesus had really employed Son of man as *the* christological title which especially expressed his messianic self-consciousness, it is a mystery if it is not found in the New Testament outside the Gospels (*pace* Acts 7.56). Thus, a series of interpreters find the concept present even where the expression is absent.[28] Especially the 'man' (ἄνθρωπος) in 1 Cor. 15.21, 47 and Rom.

24. This is part of the conclusion in the later work of Borsch, *The Christian and Gnostic Son of Man* (1970), p. 114.

25. As is the case with the dissertation of Christoph Weist from the same year, 'Wer ist dieser Menschensohn? Die Geschichte der Exegese zum Menschensohn-Begriff', utilized in the exposition above.

26. Bracht, *Der Menschensohn*, p. 1.

27. Bracht, *Der Menschensohn*, p. 6.

28. For a few interpreters this even pertains to some Gospel sayings. Thus E. Schweizer, 'υἱός κτλ.', in *ThWNT*, VIII (1969), pp. 373-74—just as earlier 'Pseudo-Athanasius', *Sermo maior de fide*, Eustathius of Antioch and Ambrose—finds the Son of man behind the Son in Mk 13.32 (Mt. 24.36), and P. Stuhlmacher, 'Das Bekenntnis zur

5.15 has been taken as evidence of Paul's knowledge and use of the concept.[29] A few have included 'as a man' (ὡς ἄνθρωπος) in Phil. 2.7.[30] Moreover, to some, 1 Thess. 1.9-10 is an original Son of man saying.[31] An additional candidate has been the Maranatha prayer in 1 Cor. 16.22, where Marana is seen as a designation of Jesus when the Aramaic primitive community called upon him as the Son of man.[32] This has been combined with the hypothesis that the Son of man concept lies behind the expectation

Auferweckung Jesu von den Toten und die Biblische Theologie', *ZThK* 70, pp. 365-403; reprinted in *idem*, *Schriftauslegung auf dem Wege zur biblischen Theologie* (1975), pp. 128-66 (156-57), thinks that the Danielic Son of man hides himself behind ὡς ἄνθρωπος in Mk 4.26.

29. According to R.H. Fuller, *The Foundation of New Testament Christology* (1965), pp. 233-34, J. Weiss, *Earliest Christianity* (1959), I, pp. 485-86 (= *Das Urchristentum* [edited posthumously by R. Knopf, 1917], pp. 374-75), and W. Bousset, *Kyrios Christos* (2nd edn, 1921), pp. 140-45 and 203, appear to have formulated this thesis. Later representatives include: J. Jeremias, 'ἄνθρωπος κτλ.', in *ThWNT* (1933), I, pp. 365-67 (367); T.W. Manson, *The Teaching of Jesus* (2nd edn, 1935), p. 233; E. Stauffer, *Theologie des Neuen Testaments* (4th edn, 1948), pp. 91-92; L. Bouyer, 'La notion christologique du Fils de l'homme a-t-elle disparu dans la patristique greque?', *Mélanges bibliques* (FS A. Robert, 1957), pp. 519-30. O. Cullmann offers a whole section on 'Paulus und der Menschensohnbegriff' in his *Christologie* (pp. 169-86). See further, K. Smyth, 'Heavenly Man and Son of Man in St Paul', *Studiorum Paulinorum Congressus Internationalis Catholicus 1961* (1963), pp. 219-30, where it is said that 'it is hard to avoid the conclusion, from the parallels in vocabulary and imagery, that St Paul was steeped in the apocalyptic Son of Man tradition, and that he none the less eliminated the title' (p. 227) because 'the Heavenly Man' better expressed his mind. Also F.H. Borsch, *The Son of Man in Myth and History* (1967), offers a whole chapter to this theme (pp. 232-56). C. Colpe, 'ὁ υἱὸς τοῦ ἀνθρώπου', in *ThWNT*, VIII (1969), pp. 475-77, thinks that the relation is best expressed through 'das Stichwort "Umformung der Menschensohn-Christologie in Adam-Anthropos-Soteriologie"' (p. 476). That Paul in Jesus saw the Son of man of Dan. 7 is also claimed by H. Sahlin, 'Paulus och Danielsboken', *SEÅ* 46 (1981), pp. 95-111, and Pierre de Martin de Vivies, *Jésus et le Fils de l'homme* (1995), pp. 95-98.

30. E. Lohmeyer, *Kyrios Jesus. Eine Untersuchung zu Phil. 2,5-11* (1928, 2nd edn, 1961), p. 68; Cullmann, *Die Christologie des Neuen Testaments*, pp. 178-86. Also G.H. ter Schegget, *Het lied van de Mensenzoon. Studie over de Christuspsalm in Filippenzen 2:6-11* (1975), especially pp. 53-58, finding here a combination of the apocalyptic Son of man and the Adam speculation. See, further, H. Sahlin, 'Paulus och Danielsboken', *SEÅ* 46 (1981), pp. 96-97; Pierre de Martin de Vivies, *Jésus et le Fils de l'homme* (1995), pp. 98-100.

31. Thus G. Friedrich, 'Ein Taufied hellenistischer Judenchristen', *ThZ* 21 (1965), pp. 502-16 (513-14); E. Schweizer, 'υἱὸς κτλ.', in *ThWNT*, VIII (1969), p. 372 (cf. p. 384); cf. also C. Colpe, 'Gottessohn', *RAC* XII (1983), pp. 19-58 (45). Further H. Merklein's contribution mentioned below in n. 53.

32. Thus Werner Kramer, *Christos, Kyrios Gottessohn* (1963), p. 97.

of the Parousia.[33] Some argue that, though Paul was familiar with the Son of man concept, he had reasons for not using it.[34]

At least one scholar has taken 'by a man' (ἐν ἀνδρί) in Acts 17.31 as a piece of Son of man christology.[35] With regard to the indefinite Son of man in Heb. 2.6 (quoting Ps. 8.5), opinions diverge widely. Some find it designating the human nature of Christ and thus complementary to Son of God.[36] Others look at the inclusion of Ps. 8.5-7 as a result of an identification of its Son of man with the self-designation used by Jesus.[37]

33. Cf. Ulrich B. Müller, 'Parusie und Menschensohn', *ZNW* 92 (2001), pp. 1-19, refuting this, claiming (p. 16) with H.E. Tödt, *Der Menschensohn in der synoptischen Tradition* (1959), p. 45, 'Naherwartung ist Menschensohn-Erwartung *geworden*'. The italization is Müller's.

34. Thus, for instance, A. Vögtle, 'Die Adam-Christus-Typologie und "der Menschensohn"', *Trierer Theologische Zeitschrift* 60 (1951), pp. 309-28; *idem*, '"Der Menschensohn" und die paulinische Christologie', *Studiorum Paulinorum Congressus Internationalis Catholicus 1961* (1963), pp. 199-218; E. Brandenburger, *Adam und Christus. Exegetisch-religionsgeschichtliche Untersuchung zu Röm 5,12-21 (1 Kor. 15)* (1962), p. 154; U. Wilckens, 'Christus, der "letzte Adam", und der Menschensohn. Theologische Überlegungen zum überlieferungsgeschichtlichen Problem der paulinischen Adam-Christus-Antithese', in Pesch and Schnackenburg (eds.), *Jesus und der Menschensohn* (FS Anton Vögtle, 1975), pp. 387-403; J. Coppens, 'Le Fils de l'homme dans le dossier paulinien', *EThL* 52 (1976), pp. 309-330 (= *BEThL* 55 [1981], pp. 23-44), pp. 329-30 (= 43-44).

35. Thus Kirsopp Lake and H.J. Cadbury, *The Beginnings of Christianity* (1933), IV, p. 219, where it is claimed: 'This is pure "Son of Man" eschatology'.

36. Thus E. Grässer, 'Beobachtungen zum Menschensohn in Hebr 2,6', in Pesch and Schnackenburg (eds.), *Jesus und der Menschensohn* (FS Anton Vögtle, 1975), pp. 404-14. Grässer compares the indefinite occurrence with Jn 5.27; Barn. 12.10 and Ignatius' *Ephesians* 20.2, taking its meaning to be ἄνθρωπος ἐξ ἀνθρώπων (cf. Justin, *Dialogue* 48–49). It emphasizes the 'Menschlichkeit (das vere homo) im Unterschied zur Göttlichkeit (vere Deus) Jesu. Die Entwicklung der späteren Zeit läuft immer stärker darauf zu. Der Hebr. steht am Anfang dieser Entwicklung' (p. 410). 'Der Autor ad Hebraeos hat den im Urchristentum selten christologisch gedeuteten Ps 8 nicht in messianischer, sondern in eschatologischer Perspektive gelesen und interpretiert' (pp. 412-13). Cf. J. Coppens, 'Le Fils de l'homme dans le dossier paulinien', pp. 324-29 (pp. 38-43), mostly following Grässer.

37. Earlier E. Käsemann, *Das wandernde Gottesvolk. Eine Untersuchung zum Hebräerbrief* (1939); English translation: *The Wandering People of God: An Investigation of the Letter to the Hebrews* (1984), pp. 75-79, saw here 'the Son of Man speculation', and together with it 'the *Urmensch* doctrine' as the presupposition for the use of Ps. 8 in Heb. 2.6. A.J.B. Higgins, *Jesus and the Son of Man* (1964), pp. 146-47, thinks that 'the High Priest Christology is the fruit of reflection on the belief in the exaltation to the heavenly world of Jesus as Son of Man', the author interpreting 'the psalm Christologically as best suiting his purpose of contrasting Christ as Son of man with the angels, as in the first chapter he has contrasted him with them as Son of God'. Cf. also

Of course, the two occurrences of the indeterminate ὅμοιον υἱὸν ἀνθρώπου in Rev. 1.13 and 14.14 also have been included in this context. Two older classical commentaries on Revelation by, respectively, Wilhelm Bousset and R.H. Charles, are in agreement as to who this figure is: it is the apocalyptic Son of man Messiah from Dan. 7.13—although Bousset finds that this figure in 14.14 by the author of the Revelation has been changed into an angel.[38] Charles straightforwardly states: 'The Being whom the Seer sees is not "like the Son of Man," but is the Son of Man… This technical phraseology in Apocalyptic means that the Being so described is not a man.' It is thus 'the exact equivalent of ὁ υἱὸς τοῦ ἀνθρώπου in the Gospels and Acts vii.56.'[39] Interestingly, in the clearest example of the use of Dan. 7.13, namely, in Rev. 1.7, there is no trace of the expression. The period after 1945 experiences a continuation of the discussion of the meaning of Rev. 1.13 and 14.14. With regard to 1.13, there is no question as to who is meant. It is the exalted Christ. But whereas the wording is mostly taken as an allusion to Dan. 7.13,[40] some scholars find that the passage simply employs a visionary style.[41] When it comes to 14.14, the identity is more difficult to solve because of the reference to another angel (ἄλλος ἄγγελος) in v. 15.

P. Giles, 'The Son of Man in the Epistle to the Hebrews', *ET* 86 (1974–75), pp. 328-32. C. Colpe, 'ὁ υἱὸς τοῦ ἀνθρώπου', in *ThWNT*, VIII (1969), pp. 467-68, finds that the expression Son of man in Ps. 8.5 has inspired the author to a messianic interpretation. A 'titular' understanding is also found, for instance, in G.W. Buchanan, *To the Hebrews* (1972, 2nd edn, 1976), p. 27 (cf. pp. 38-40). Michael Goulder, 'Psalm 8 and the Son of Man', *NTS* 48 (2002), pp. 18-29, argues for the messianic interpretation of Ps. 8.5 by the *auctor ad Hebraeos* in 2.6 to be the missing link in the creation of the determined form of the expression first to turn up in the Markan reception, the Son of man in Mark and the other Gospels simply stemming from a creative use of Ps. 8 channelled through Heb. 2.

38. Wilhelm Bousset, *Die Offenbarung Johannis* (KEK XVI, 1906), pp. 193-94, 388.

39. R.H. Charles, *A Critical and Exegetical Commentary on the Revelation of St. John* (1920), I, p. 27. For 14.14, see II, pp. 19-20.

40. Thus, besides Bousset and Charles, for instance C. Colpe, 'ὁ υἱὸς τοῦ ἀνθρώπου', in *ThWNT*, VIII (1969), p. 467; Eduard Lohse, 'Den Menschensohn in der Johannesapokalypse', in Pesch and Schnackenburg (eds.), *Jesus und der Menschensohn*, pp. 415-20 (416-17). F. Sieg, '"Ὅμοιον υἱὸν ἀνθρώπου (Offb 1,13): Schlussfolgerungen aus der Untersuchung (Offb 1,13-16.17c.18, 2,1.8.12.18; 3,1.7.14)', *Filologia Neotestamentica* 7 (1994), pp. 3-15, assumes in Rev. 1.13 a hidden quotation from Dan. 7, but also that the description is based on the personal experience of the writer of Revelation (cf. *NTA* 39 [1995] 1012, p. 259). For more references also with regard to the points of view discussed in the following notes, see M. Müller, *Der Ausdruck 'Menschensohn' in den Evangelien* (1984), pp. 146-50.

41. Thus, for instance, earlier G. Dalman, *Die Worte Jesu I* (2nd edn 1930), p. 206, where the reference is not to Dan. 7.13 but to 10.5, 6. Also M. Casey, *Son of Man: The Interpretation and Influence of Daniel 7* (1979), pp. 144-45.

Not a few adhere to an angelic interpretation,[42] while others prefer a christological, messianic understanding.[43]

2. *Jesus Preached the Apocalyptic Coming Son of Man Implying Some Sort of Identity*

A group of influential scholars thinks that Jesus preached exclusively about the coming Son of man, in one way or another, presupposing an identification between himself and this figure. The non-apocalyptic Son of man sayings are considered products of a community theology, proleptically identifying the earthly Jesus with this apocalyptic Son of man. Among others,[44] the list of adherents to this solution includes Anton Vögtle,[45] A.J.B. Higgins, Joachim Jeremias and Carsten Colpe. Higgins, in *Jesus and the Son of Man* from 1964, finds that the only genuine Son of man sayings are found in Lk. 11.30; 12.8; 17.22, 24, 26 and parallels, because the 'distinction between Jesus and the Son of man...could not possibly have been invented by Christians, but must stem from Jesus himself'.[46] He continues:

42. Thus Ulrich B. Müller, *Messias und Menschensohn in jüdischen Apokalypsen und in der Offenbarung des Johannes* (1972), pp. 190-97; also the note of J. Coppens, 'La mention d'un Fils d'homme angélique en Ap 14,14', in J. Lambrecht (ed.), *L'Apocalypse johannique et l'Apocalyptique dans le Nouveau Testament* (1980), p. 229.

43. Thus C. Colpe, 'ὁ υἱὸς τοῦ ἀνθρώπου', in *ThWNT*, VIII (1969), p. 467. Further A.P. van Schaik, '"Ἄλλος ἄγγελος in Apk 14', in Lambrecht (ed.), *L'Apocalypse johannique*, pp. 217-28 (223), where it is emphazised that it is not about Christology but about christophany. Adela Yarbro Collins, 'The "Son of Man" Tradition and the Book of Revelation', in James H. Charlesworth (ed.), *The Messiah: Developments in Earliest Judaism and Christianity* (1992), pp. 536-68 (reprinted in *idem*, *Cosmology and Eschatology in Jewish and Christian Apocalypticism* [1996], pp. 159-97), likewise argues for an understanding in both sayings as speaking of the risen Christ and finds an analogy to the use of the expression by Jesus (cf. Chapter 16, below). Further Thomas B. Slater, '*Homoion huion anthropou* in Rev 1.13 and 14.14', *BT* 44 (1993), pp. 359-60, and the most recent monograph, Konrad Huber, *Einer gleich einem Menschensohn. Die Christusvision in Offb 1,9-20 und Offb 14,14-20 und die Christologie der Johannesoffenbarung* (2007).

44. A variant is found in D.Y. Archibald, 'The Son of Man', *ET* 62 (1950–51), pp. 348-49, like R. Otto, seeing the background in the Iranian *fravashi* and having Jesus employ a sort of indirect communication à la Søren Kierkegaard.

45. Thus in the article 'Menschensohn', *LThK*, VII (2nd edn, 1962), pp. 297-300. Later Vögtle changed his view.

46. A.J.B. Higgins, *Jesus and the Son of Man* (1964), p. 189. Cf. the other contributions on this topic by Higgins, 'Son of Man-*Forschung* since "The Teaching of Jesus"', in A.J.B. Higgins (ed.), *New Testament Essays: Studies in Memory of Thomas Walter Manson* (1959), pp. 119-35; 'The Sign of the Son of Man (Matt. XXIV.30)', *NTS* 9 (1962–63), pp. 380-82; *Menschensohn-Studien* (1961); 'The Son of Man Concept and the

> The conception in Jesus' teaching is characterized by the quite new idea that the attitude of the Son of man in the presence of God depends on man's acceptance or rejection of Jesus. Further, in Jesus' teaching the Son of man is as much an advocate as a judge... The upshot is that if Jesus was acquainted with a belief of this kind he could hardly have regarded himself, a man on earth, as the Son of man and have been sane. His references to the Son of man must have been directed as if to another than himself... Jesus said nothing whatever about himself as the Son of man. He referred to him as if to a future advocate, witness, or judge.[47]

However, Higgins seemingly contradicts himself when, in the following, he claims:

> I do not think that any of the attempts to demonstrate that Jesus thought of himself as the Son of man or as destined to become Son of man or to be identified with him in the future can be sustained. The problem can only be understood correctly when his *non-identification* with the Son of man is brought into the centre.[48]

Higgins also writes that: 'In Jesus' thought the Son of man is none other than the Son of God. The Son of man idea was adapted by Jesus to denote himself as the Son of God he already believed himself to be, reinstalled in his heavenly seat.'[49] Higgins, therefore, after all, seems to belong to this group and not to the adherents of the view that Jesus did not identify himself with the coming Son of man he preached.

Joachim Jeremias, arguing that only the logia transmitted without parallels not containing the 'title' can be genuine, likewise reaches the conclusion that only a series of predominantly future Son of man sayings go back to the

Historical Jesus', *SE* 5 = *TU* 103 (1968), pp. 14-20; 'Is the Son of Man Problem Insoluble?', in E.E. Ellis and M. Wilcox (eds.), *Neotestamentica et Semitica* (FS Matthew Black, 1969), pp. 70-87; '"Menschensohn" oder "ich" in Q: Lk 12,8-9/Mt 10,32-33?', in Pesch and Schnackenburg (eds.), *Jesus und der Menschensohn* (FS A Vögtle, 1975), pp. 117-23; *The Son of Man in the Teaching of Jesus* (1980).

47. Higgins, *Jesus and the Son of Man*, p. 199-200. Cf. *idem*, *The Son of Man in the Teaching of Jesus*, where Lk. 17.30 has replaced Lk. 17.22 among the 'the kernel sayings' (pp. 123-25; cf. pp. 59-65).

48. Higgins, *Jesus and the Son of Man*, p. 200.

49. Higgins, *Jesus and the Son of Man*, p. 202. Cf. the critical remarks in N. Birdsall, 'Who is the Son of Man?', *EvQ* 42 (1970), pp. 7-17 (12), who finds, that 'Higgins succumbs to the British tendency to demand a solid basis for belief in Jesus in Jesus' own beliefs'. His later *The Son of Man in the Teaching of Jesus*, p. 125, confirms the impression that he thinks of an identity, when he speaks of the significant absence of apocalyptic features from the kernel sayings, 'virtually the only item of apocalyptic imagery is the Son of man himself. But this is so interpreted that, for Jesus, the Son of man is not a personal figure, but a symbolical description of his own expected dignity, status and function as judge.'

earthly Jesus (Mk 13.26; 14.62; Mt. 8.20; 10.23; 24.27, 37; 25.31; Lk. 17.22, 30; 18.8; 21.36, and Jn 1.51, all with parallels).[50] Later, in *Neutestamentliche Theologie*, Jeremias removes Mt. 8.20 from the list and concludes that just as in Jewish apocalyptic, Son of man in the mouth of Jesus is a '*terminus gloriae*', by which he expressed the universalism of his dignity. The distinction Jesus makes between himself and the Son of man is not between two figures, but between his actual present state and his *status exaltationis*, the words in the third person bringing out this 'enigmatic relation'.[51]

Carsten Colpe, in the very influential Son of man article in *Theologisches Wörterbuch zum Neuen Testament* from 1969, reduces the number of genuine Son of man sayings to eight (namely, Mt. 10.23; 24.27, 30, 37; Lk. 17.30; 18.8; 21.36 and 22.69 [all with parallels]) and concludes:

> The apocalyptic Son of man is a symbol of Jesus' assurance of perfecting (Vollendungsgewissheit). With a shift from the assurance to the one who has it, the whole process may be interpreted as a dynamic and functional equating of Jesus and the coming Son of Man with the future perfecting of Jesus in view. On this view the primitive community then made of it a static personal identification accomplished already in the present Jesus.[52]

Other scholars belong to this group.[53] This category also includes the revival of the view of Rudolf Otto that Jesus perceived himself as *filius hominis praedestinatus*.[54]

50. 'Die älteste Schicht de Menschensohn-Logien', *ZNW* 58 (1967), pp. 159-72.

51. J. Jeremias, *Neutestamentliche Theologie. Erster Teil. Die Verkündigung Jesu* (1971), pp. 245-62, and especially pp. 259-63. The expression 'geheimnisvolle Relation' stems from E. Bammel, 'Erwägungen zur Eschatologie Jesu', *SE* 2.1 = *TU* 88 (1964), p. 23.

52. Colpe, 'ὁ υἱὸς τοῦ ἀνθρώπου', p. 443; cf. pp. 437-40, quoted according to English translation in *ThDNT*, VIII (1972), p. 441. Further *idem*, 'Traditions überschreitende Argumentationen zu Aussagen Jesu über sich selbst', in Gert Jeremias, Heinz-Wolfgang Kuhn and Hartmut Stegemann (eds.), *Tradition und Glaube* (FS K.G. Kuhn, 1971), pp. 230-45.

53. As for instance Helmut Merklein, 'Die Auferstehung Jesu und die Anfänge der Christologie (Messias bzw. Sohn Gottes und Menschensohn)', *ZNW* 72 (1981), pp. 1-26 (16-25), where it is argued among other things that Son of man is not a title. The apocalyptic functions of the Son of man were used to describe Jesus' messianic task, as is seen in 1 Thess. 1.10. It is Merklein's thesis that it is not the concept of the messianic task of Jesus at the Parousia which lead to the thought of an enthronization. It was the other way round: the messianic task that Jesus undertook because of the resurrection was also interpreted as including the function at the end of days.

54. Thus P. Ciholas, '"Son of Man" and Hellenistic Christology', *Review and Expositor* 79 (1982), pp. 487-501. In this form, it only survived in a small group of Hellenistic Christians around Stephen which may also have included a few of the first disciples of Jesus. At any rate, 'a Son of Man christology was never part of the early kerygma controlled by the disciples and particularly Peter. Paul chose not to adopt the christologi-

3. *Jesus Preached an Apocalyptic Son of Man without Identifying Himself with this Figure*[55]

The old idea of David Friedrich Strauss could still find notable adherents. Rudolf Bultmann repeats the position in his *Die Geschichte der synoptischen Tradition* (1921, 2nd edn, 1931) and in his *Theologie des Neuen Testaments* (1948–53). Once again, he points to Mk 8.38; Lk. 12.8-9 par.; Mt. 24.27, 37, 44 par., and Lk. 11.30, as genuine Jesus sayings where, however, Jesus is not identifying himself with the coming Son of man referred to. It is the later community which first identified the two, then created the other future Son of man sayings and the Passion predictions. Some of these Son of man sayings stemmed from Christian prophets.[56] The third category speaking of the Son of man on earth owes its existence to a mistranslation of an Aramaic expression, being not a messianic title but having rather the meaning of 'man' or 'I'.[57]

This is also the position adopted by Günther Bornkamm (1905–1990) in his influential *Jesus von Nazareth* (1956),[58] as well as by John Knox (1900–1990),[59] Ernst Fuchs (1903–1983)[60] and R.P. Casey, the latter thinking it likely 'that Jesus' own eschatology included a figure something like "the Man" of *Enoch* and *4 Ezra*, in that he regarded himself as "the Man's" representative on earth before the End'.[61]

cal position of the Hellenists of the Book of Acts. Thus it was dropped in its embryonic form. Possibly a rehabilitation of Stephen took place after 70 A.D. but too late to change the major christological trends. Whatever Son of Man sayings survived outside of Pauline traditions were projected back to the historical Jesus and entered the Gospel narratives without a clear understanding of their christological meaning' (p. 496). Cf. *idem*, 'Son of Man in the Synoptic Gospels', *BThB* 11 (1981), pp. 17-20.

55. Cf. Müller, *Der Ausdruck 'Menschensohn' in den Evangelien*, pp. 165-67, the last part of Excursus H. 'Die Hypothese, Jesus habe den "Menschensohn" als eschatologische Gestalt verkündigt, ohne sich mit dieser zu identifizieren'.

56. Cf., on this topic, M. Eugene Boring, *Sayings of the Risen Jesus: Christian Prophecy in the Synoptic Tradition* (1982).

57. R. Bultmann, *Theologie des Neuen Testaments* (5th edn, 1965), pp. 30-32. Cf. earlier *idem*, 'Die Frage nach der Echtheit von Mt 16,17-19', *ThBl* 20 (1941), quoted according to the reprint in *idem*, *Exegetica* (1967), pp. 255-77 (273-75).

58. G. Bornkamm, *Jesus von Nazareth* (1956, 7th edn, 1965), p. 208.

59. J. Knox, *The Death of Christ: The Cross in New Testament History and Faith* (1958, quoted according to paperback edition, 1967), pp. 77-80.

60. E. Fuchs, 'Jesus und der Glaube', *ZThK* 55 (1958), pp. 170-85; reprinted in *idem*, *Zur Frage nach dem historischen Jesus*. Gesammelte Aufsätze II (1960), pp. 238-57 (252).

61. R.P. Casey, 'The Earliest Christologies', *JThS* NS 9 (1958), pp. 253-77 (265). Casey leaves the 'normal' tripartition of the Son of man sayings when he continues: 'this is the most natural sense of the claim to forgive in Mark ii.10'.

The standard presentation of this interpretation is *Der Menschensohn in der synoptischen Überlieferung* (1959, 2nd edn, 1963 = 5th edn, 1984) by Heinz Eduard Tödt (1918–1991), where this hypothesis is worked out in detail. His conclusion with regard to the existence of a Jewish Son of man concept is that:

> With regard to the deep-rooted differences which separate the figure of the Son of Man in the sixth vision of IV Ezra on the one hand from the Man in I Enoch and Dan. 7 on the other hand, it may be doubted whether a definite set of concepts concerning the Son of Man was generally accepted in Jewish apocalyptic literature (ob man von jenem geschlossenen Menschensohnanschauungskreis in der spätjüdischen Apokalyptik sprechen darf). The spirit which lives in the visions issued from very different contexts. And yet it is possible that to the earliest Christian congregations these different figures of a Son of Man appeared to come together. Since they were seen in a fresh light, the differences could recede into the background in favour of the similarities in several of the specific traits of the visions.

> In Jesus' teaching the apocalyptic statements about the Son of Man are reduced to a minimum. In view of the scantiness of specific features we might be inclined to comment that in Jesus' sayings the figure of the Son of Man has again forfeited the distinction which it had laboriously achieved. And yet, the Son of Man here gains a soteriological function of highest importance. He is the guarantor before God that the fellowship of following Jesus on earth will be continued in a way which will mean salvation (Lk. 12.8ff.)

> It is supposed, for example, that the primitive community which expected Jesus to arrive as the transcendent Son of Man transferred the myth of an unreal heavenly Son of Man to the real historical person of Jesus. We have indeed seen that Mark and Matthew took over directly the Jewish concept of the Son of Man—they referred back to Dan. 7 and I Enoch; but we have seen as well that this transference was a secondary procedure. Christological understanding primarily referred to the sayings of Jesus, thus accepting the meaning of the name Son of Man which it had been given when this title was taken up to serve in Jesus' teaching. Jesus had assigned to the Son of Man the function of being the eschatological guarantor of attachment to Jesus on earth. This function remained the distinguishing mark of the title when the post-Easter community identified Jesus with the Son of Man. The content of the community's Christological understanding was determined by Jesus' soteriological word. In spite of the conflict with the whole tradition, the community designated Jesus as the one who acts on earth with full authority by the name Son of Man because Jesus himself had correlated the guarantee of the Son of Man with his own earthly activity.[62]

62. The three following quotations are from *Der Menschensohn in der synoptischen Überlieferung*, pp. 27, 208 and 266, and quoted according to English translation *The Son of Man in the Synoptic Tradition* (1965), pp. 30, 227 and 294-95. The confusion of Son of Man in *4 Ezra* (read 'Man') and Man in *1 Enoch* (read 'Son of Man') is also present in the German text.

Thus, the use of Son of Man in sayings about his activity on earth are to be characterized as proleptic.

This view was shared by Eberhard Jüngel in his seminal hermeneutical investigation, *Jesus und Paulus. Eine Untersuchung zur Präzisierung der Frage nach dem Ursprung der Christologie* (1962). Jüngel finds a testimony of an implicit christology in the historical Jesus' preaching of the coming Son of man. Not least, Lk. 12.8-9 offers reason to believe that

> the absoluteness with which Jesus' preaching and Jesus' attitude to men demands an attitude on behalf of these men to him which in turn will be confirmed through the attitude of the Son of man to these men, all the more implicates a christology, which allows Jesus to stand on the side of the near God, binding men to the future of the distant Son of man to the present, qualified by the proximity of the Kingdom of God (Die Absolutheit, mit der Jesu Verkündigung und Jesu Verhalten zu den Menschen ein Verhalten dieser Menschen zu ihm fordert, das durch das Verhalten des Menschensohnes zu diesen Menschen bestätigt werden wird, impliziert vielmehr eine Christologie, die Jesus als einen die Zukunft des fernen Menschensohnes an die durch die Nähe der Gottesherrschaft qualifizierte Gegenwart bindenden Menschen auf der Seite des *nahen Gottes* zu stehen kommen läßt).[63]

In later attempts to maintain this interpretation, Lk. 12.8-9 also plays a central role. In the impressive monograph, *Christologische Hoheitstitel. Ihre Geschichte im frühen Christentum* from 1963, Ferdinand Hahn declares that 'the special features of the saying in Lk. 12:8f., which refers to the function of the Son of man as judge, show that it may form a point of departure; its genuineness is not to be disputed'.[64] Immediately before, Hahn has summarized his view on the development of tradition in a representative way:[65]

> It must be established that of the three groups of Son of man words, those about the suffering and rising again of the Son of man can least of all lay claim to authenticity. The words about the earthly deeds may not in general be interpreted, as customary among older critics, as misunderstood statements about 'man', as also the reproduction of 'I' by 'Son of man' is not provable from contemporary Aramaic. The priority of the sayings about the earthly deeds cannot be supported by alleging that the concept of the suffering and

63. E. Jüngel, *Jesus und Paulus. Eine Untersuchung zur Präzisierung der Frage nach dem Ursprung der Christologie* (1962, 2nd edn, 1964), p. 262; cf. pp. 215-62. A similar position is taken by the Danish scholar Lone Fatum, 'Jesu "selvbevidsthed" og kristologien', *DTT* 30 (1967), pp. 147-82.

64. F. Hahn, *Christologische Hoheitstitel. Ihre Geschichte im frühen Christentum* (1963, 3rd edn, 1966), pp. 40-41 (cf. pp. 32-42), quoted according to English translation, *The Titles of Jesus in Christology* (1969), p. 33.

65. Hahn, *Christologische Hoheitstitel*, p. 32; English translation, p. 28. In a shorter form Hahn also has expressed his view in 'Menschensohn', *Exegetisches Wörterbuch zum Neuen Testament*, III (1983), cols. 927-35.

> exalted righteous one is implied. For it is only within the framework of apocalyptic that unequivocal presuppositions for an understanding of the Son of man idea are to be found, and for this reason the words about the coming Son of man stand necessarily at the beginning of the development. Only after the identification of the future Son of man with Jesus had been made could the Jesus who worked on earth in full power and authority be described likewise as the 'Son of man', and this description was finally extended to cover the statements about his suffering and rising again. If the priority of the words about the eschatological working of the Son of man is made clear, then further the origin of some of these words on the lips of Jesus cannot be denied. Neither the relative lack of connection with sayings about the Kingdom of God nor the peculiar features of the teaching of Jesus furnish essential arguments against authenticity.

The similarly influential *The Foundations of New Testament Christology* (1965) by Reginald Horace Fuller follows this path when it is said that 'the Son of man merely acts as a kind of rubber stamp at the End for the salvation which is already being imparted in Jesus. Despite the distinction between Jesus and the Son of man, the *ultimate import of this saying is therefore implicitly christological.*'[66] Günter Haufe, also adhering to this solution, directly addressed the question of the understanding of Lk. 12.8-9 to be 'die Gretchenfrage des Menschensohn-Problems'.[67] Walter Schmithals

66. R.H. Fuller, *The Foundations of New Testament Christology* (1965), p. 123. Cf. *idem*, 'The Clue to Jesus' Self-understanding', *SE* 2.1 = *TU* 88 (1964), pp. 58-66; 'The *Son of Man* Came to Serve', in Francis A. Eigo (ed.), *Ministering in a Servant Church* (1978), pp. 45-72; 'The Son of Man: A Reconsideration', in Dennis E. Groh and Robert Jewett (eds.), *The Living Text* (FS Ernest W. Saunders, 1985), pp. 207-17, where Fuller once again has changed his view and becomes an adherent to the circumlocutional understanding (cf. Chapter 16, below). Earlier, in *The Mission and Achievement of Jesus: An Examination of the Presuppositions of New Testament Theology* (1954, 6th edn, 1970), pp. 106-107, Fuller took a different stand, arguing that not only the future Son of man sayings could be genuine, claiming that 'he was *proleptically* exercising the functions of the coming Son of Man, just as in his proclamation and healings the powers of the Kingdom were already at work'.

67. G. Haufe, 'Das Menschensohn-Problem in der gegenwärtigen wissenschaftlichen Diskussion', *EvTh* 26 (1966), pp. 130-41 (140); French: 'Le problème du Fils de l'Homme', *EThR* 42 (1967), pp. 311-22. Of other adherents to this solution of the Son of man problem the following should be mentioned: Norbert Brox, 'Das messianische Selbstverständnis des historischen Jesus', in Kurt Schubert (ed.), *Vom Messias zum Christus* (1964), pp. 165-201 (178-80); R.E.C. Formesyn, 'Was there a Pronominal Connection for the "bar nasha" Selfdesignation?', *NT* 8 (1966), pp. 1-35 (19-21); H.R. Balz, *Methodische Probleme der neutestamentlichen Christologie* (1967), pp. 121-22; Herbert Braun (1903–1991), *Jesus. Der Mann aus Nazareth und seine Zeit* (1969), pp. 55-56; Harold A. Guy, 'Did Jesus Call Himself the Son of Man?', *The Modern Free Churchman* 91 (1970), pp. 30-34; W. Hendriks, 'De komende Mensenzoon', *Schrift. Populaire Bibeltijdschrift* 18 (1971), pp. 225-29; G. Rochais, 'Jésus et le Fils de l'Homme', *'Jesus' Héritage et projet* 9 (1974), pp. 83-122 (117-21).

takes up an old thread, going so far as to say that before Mark, that is, before c. 75 CE, there was not at all such a thing as a Son of man concept in the Church tradition. Mark got it from a precursor to Q, originating in Galilee. In these communities, adhering exclusively to the tradition about what Jesus had said and done and not taking any notice of an Easter faith, they preserved 'the lot of apocalyptic sayings about a coming, judging Son of man. These sayings in the mouth of Jesus—if authentic or not is in abeyance—speak without exception of the Son of man in the third person and identify him...*not* with the speaker: Lk. 6.22; 11.30 par.; 12.40 par.; 17.23 par., 30 par.; Mt. 10.23; 19.28.'[68]

4. *The Apocalyptic Son of Man Christology as Purely Community Theology*

Where Son of man in the Gospels was perceived as an apocalyptic messianic title, the consequence was for a number of exegetes that the Son of man christology had to be attributed to community theology.[69] A representative spokesman is Anton Vögtle (1910–1996), advocating this view in a series of contributions,[70] the last being *Die 'Gretchensfrage' des Menschensohn-problems. Bilanz und Perspektive* from 1994.[71]

68. Walter Schmithals, 'Die Worte vom leidenden Menschensohn. Ein Schlüssel zur Lösung des Menschensohn-Problems', in C. Andresen and G. Klein (eds.), *Theologia crucis—signum crucis* (FS Erich Dinkler, 1979), pp. 417-45 (439).

69. This pertains to, for instance, Gerhard Iber, *Überlieferungsgeschichtliche Untersuchungen zum Begriff des Menschensohnes im Neuen Testament* (1953), according to the summary in *ThLZ* 80 (1955), pp. 115-16; Ernst Käsemann, 'Das Problem des historischen Jesus', *ZThK* 51 (1954), pp. 125-53 (150) (reprinted in *idem*, *Exegetische Versuche und Besinnungen*, I [1960], pp. 187-214 [211]). Further *idem*, 'Neutestamentlicher Sammelbericht', *VF* 9 (*Theologischer Jahresbericht* 1958/59) (1960–62), pp. 97-108 (99-102) (review of H.E. Tödt); Hans Conzelmann, 'Gegenwart und Zukunft in der synoptischen Tradition', *ZThK* 54 (1957), pp. 277-96 (282); *idem*, 'Jesus Christus', in *RGG*, III (3rd edn, 1959), pp. 619-53 (603-604); *idem*, 'Jesu självmedvetande', *SEÅ* 28–29 (1963–64), pp. 49-53; in German, together with the first mentioned article, reprinted in *idem*, *Theologie als Schriftauslegung. Aufsätze zum Neuen Testament* (1974), respectively pp. 42-61 and pp. 30-41. Further *idem*, *Grundriss der Theologie des Neuen Testaments* (1967), pp. 151-56; James M. Robinson, *A New Quest of the Historical Jesus* (1959, 4th edn, 1966), pp. 101-104 (enlarged German edition, *Kerygma und historischer Jesus* [2nd edn, 1967], pp. 186-91); G. Ory, 'L'intrusion du Fils de l'Homme dans nos évangiles', *Bulletin de Cercle Ernest-Renan* 104 (1964), pp. 1-3; Eduard Lohse, *Grundriss der neutestamentlichen Theologie* (1974, 2nd edn, 1979), pp. 43-50 (48-49).

70. A. Vögtle, 'Bezeugt die Logienquelle die authentische Redeweise Jesu vom "Menschensohn"?', in J. Delobel (ed.), *Logia. Les paroles de Jésus—The Sayings of Jesus*. Mémorial Joseph Coppens (1982), pp. 77-99 (95-99) (reprinted in *idem*, *Offenbarungsgeschehen und Wirkungsgeschichte* [1985], pp. 50-69); 'Eine überholte "Menschensohn-

Philipp Vielhauer (1914–1977)[72] argues, as H.B. Sharman had earlier (cf. above, Chapter 12), that Jesus' concept of the Kingdom of God makes it impossible that he should also have expected, not to say identified himself with, the coming Son of man. The Son of man and Messiah are not melted together in Judaism. Vielhauer concludes: '1. No Son of man saying speaks of the Kingdom of God. 2. No saying about the coming Son of man with a probability amounting almost to certainty comes from the historical Jesus.'[73] Further, 'From the pure concept of the Kingdom of God it is impossible that Jesus had expected the coming Son of man or had moreover identified himself with him.'[74] The concept of the Son of man was highly suitable, making plain 'the identity of the earthly with the exalted together with his eschatological meaning, especially because the exaltation of a human to become Son of man was already preformed in the book of Enoch (ch. 71).'[75] It is first at the redactional level that the two concepts were connected. Willi Marxsen (1919–1993) likewise reaches the conclusion that the preaching of Jesus as Son of man is exclusively a community theology. According to Marxsen, there was a stage in the very early community 'where the proclaimed (der Verkündigte) still not expressis verbis and therefore not unambiguously appears as the one proclaimed (Verkündigter), but as the proclaimer (Verkündiger)'.[76] Through the preaching of the coming Son of man the community qualified the present relation to the word of Jesus on the basis of an eschatological expectation. This is the very beginning of christology. 'This relation is an eschatologically qualified one; and thus *the*

Hypothese"?', in Kurt Aland und Siegfried Meurer (eds.), *Wissenschaft und Kirche* (FS Eduard Lohse, 1989), pp. 70-95.

71. Alfons Weiser, *Theologie des Neuen Testaments*. II. *Die Theologie der Evangelien* (1993), pp. 222-23, ends up accepting the interpretation of Vögtle. Likewise P. Hoffmann, 'Menschensohn. II. Neues Testament', *LThK* VII (3rd edn, 1998), cols 131-32. Another catholic exegete, Joachim Gnilka, in his *Theologie des Neuen Testaments* (1994), surprisingly does not thematize the question.

72. P. Vielhauer, 'Gottesreich und Menschensohn in der Verkündigung Jesu', in W. Schneemelcher (ed.), *FS Günter Dehn* (1957), pp. 51-79 (reprinted in *idem*, *Aufsätze zum Neuen Testament* [1965], pp. 55-91). See, further, *idem*, 'Jesus und der Menschensohn. Zur Diskussion mit Heinz Eduard Tödt und Eduard Schweizer', *ZThK* 60 (1963), pp. 133-77 (reprinted in *idem*, *Aufsätze zum Neuen Testament*, pp. 92-140).

73. Vielhauer, 'Gottesreich und Menschensohn in der Verkündigung Jesu', p. 71 (= reprint p. 80).

74. Vielhauer, 'Gottesreich und Menschensohn in der Verkündigung Jesu', p. 88 (= reprint p. 78).

75. Vielhauer, 'Gottesreich und Menschensohn in der Verkündigung Jesu', p. 90 (= reprint p. 79).

76. W. Marxsen, *Anfangsprobleme der Christologie* (1960, 6th edn, 1969), p. 27. But see pp. 20-34.

eschatological moment is the Christological Urdatum (und so ist das eschatologische *Moment das christologische Urdatum*).'[77]

Other scholars come to the same conclusion, thinking, however, that the concept of the apocalyptic Son of man has entered into the Gospel tradition either through some of the sayings about the earthly Son of man, viewed as genuine,[78] or—in the wave of 'the second Aramaic stage' (cf. the next chapter)—stemming from a neutral Aramaic speech-mode employed by the earthly Jesus.[79]

H. Teeple tries to reconstruct the development his own way. Because all Son of man sayings in the Gospels presuppose it as a messianic title, none of them can be original sayings of Jesus. 'Jesus surely must not have identified himself with the Son of man, because the latter did not fit with his human career. If Jesus thought of himself as a human being born on earth, he could not have identified himself with the heavenly, pre-existent supernatural being.'[80] Accordingly, it had its origin in the belief in the exaltation and Parousia of Jesus. The Acts of the Apostles shows that Psalm 110 was the source of the belief in Jesus' exaltation from the beginning, because Stephen alone, 'the radical hellenistic convert', speaks of the Son of man, and that a standing Son of man. Teeple thinks that these two streams of tradition merged for the first time in the Gospel of Mark (14.62). The immediate source is seen in *1 Enoch* 46 and the following chapters. 'Probably the Son of man Christology entered Christianity first, and then the similarity of the phrase "one like a son of man" in Daniel to the title "Son of Man" in Enoch, together with the use of Daniel in Enoch and the Christian need for support for the Parousia faith caused the use of Dan 7,13 as a proof text.'[81] In the beginning, this new Christology was met with resistance. That is the reason why the Gospels let Jesus use the title again and again. 'This is a literary device to promote the acceptance of the concept through repetition and through the authority of Jesus himself.'[82] The Son of Man Christology

77. Marxsen, *Anfangsprobleme der Christologie*, p. 28. Here it is also said: 'Die ganze Relation ist Christologie. Dann wird aber auch deutlich, daß *diese* Christologie immer mehr aussagt als jede sogenannte explizite Christologie'.

78. Here we meet, for instance, Ernst Bammel, 'Erwägungen zur Eschatologie Jesu', *SE* 2.1 (= *TU* 88, 1964), pp. 3-32 (19-23); Thorleif Boman, *Die Jesus-Überlieferung in der neueren Volkskunde* (1967), pp. 148-83 (165-69); Karlheinz Müller, 'Menschensohn und Messias. Religionsgeschichtliche Vorüberlegungen zum Menschensohnproblem in den synoptischen Evangelien' *BZ* NF 16 (1972), pp. 161-87; 17 (1973), pp. 52-66 (66).

79. Cf. Chapter 15 below, 'The Second Aramaic Stage'.

80. H. Teeple, 'The Origin of the Son of Man Christology', *JBL* 84 (1965), pp. 213-50 (220).

81. Teeple, 'The Origin of the Son of Man Christology', p. 241.

82. Teeple, 'The Origin of the Son of Man Christology', p. 245.

emerges for the first time in Hellenistic Jewish Christianity, be it in the circle of Stephen or, and more plausibly, in Syria.

Also to be mentioned under this heading is the, in theological circles, notorious book *Jesus Menschensohn* (1972) by the editor of *Der Spiegel*, Rudolf Augstein, who rejects the idea that Jesus should have perceived himself as Son of man in any sense meaning Son of God.[83]

5. *The Corporate Interpretation*

The so-called corporate interpretation is inextricably connected with Daniel 7. In the shape it was given by T.W. Manson,[84] it met with approval by a number of primarily English exegetes.[85] One of the most influential British New Testament scholars, C.H. Dodd (1884–1973), turned to this interpretation of Son of man in his *According to the Scriptures* from 1952, writing:[86]

> To have brought together...the Son of Man who is the people of the saints of the Most High, the Man of God's right hand, who is also the wine of Israel, the Son of Man who after humiliation is crowned with glory and honour, and the victorious priestking at the right hand of God, is an achievement of interpretative imagination which results in the creation of an entirely new

83. Rudolf Augstein, *Jesus Menschensohn* (1972), especially pp. 73-78. The book is not a monograph on the Son of man, but takes Son of man into the title probably because of the 'attraction belonging to something foreign (anheimelnde Fremdzugehörigkeit)'. Reactions to Augstein's interpretation are: Eduard Schweizer, 'Jesus—Menschensohn', *Neue Zürcher Zeitung* 15.11.1972 (Mittagsausgabe) (reprinted in R. Pesch and G. Stachel [eds.], *Augstein's Jesus. Eine Dokumentation* [1972], pp. 55-64); F.J. Schierse, 'Jesus Menschensohn—Herausforderung des Glaubens', *Diakonia* 4 (1973), pp. 280-83; Martin Hengel, 'Ein Blick zurück im Zorn: Rudolf Augsteins "Jesus Menschensohn"', *Theologische Beiträge* 32 (2001), pp. 158-63.

84. See above, Chapter 12; cf. for the following the last part of Excursus G: Kollektive Deutung des Ausdrucks 'Menschensohn' in Jesu Mund und in den Evangelien, in Müller, *Der Ausdruck 'Menschensohn' in den Evangelien*, pp. 157-63 (160-63).

85. Cf. W.E. Wilson, 'The Coming of the Son of Man', *The Modern Churchman* 36 (1946), pp. 44-66; Vincent Taylor, 'The "Son of Man" Sayings Relating to the Parousia', *ET* 58 (1946–47), pp. 12-15; *idem*, *The Gospel according to St. Mark* (1952, 5th edn, 1959), *passim*; *idem*, *The Names of Jesus* (1953), pp. 25-35; Théo Preiss, 'Le Mystère du Fils de l'Homme', *Dieu Vivant* 8 (1947), pp. 15-36; *idem*, 'Le Fils de l'Homme. Fragments d'un cours sur la Christologie du Nouveau Testament', *ETR* 26 (1951), fasc. 3; *idem*, 'Le Fils de l'Homme' (Suite), *ETR* 28 (1953), pp. 1-75; W.D. Davies, *Paul and Rabbinic Judaism. Some Rabbinic Elements in Pauline Theology* (1948), p. 280 n. 1; W.D. Davies and Dale Allison, *The Gospel according to Saint Matthew*, II (1991), pp. 43-52 (50-51); E.G. Jay, *Son of Man, Son of God* (1965), pp. 32-43.

86. C.H. Dodd, *According to the Scriptures* (1952), pp. 109-10, 118. Cf. p. 117 where, as background for the understanding of the Son of man in the Gospels, Dodd points to both Pss 8 and 80, and Dan. 7.

> figure. It involves an original, and far-reaching, resolution of the tension between the individual and the single focus on the 'plot' of the Servant poems of II Isaiah, of the psalms of the righteous sufferer, and of the prophecies of the fall and recovery (death and resurrection) of the people of God, and finally offers a fresh understanding of the mysterious imagery of apocalyptic eschatology. This is a piece of creative thinking. Who was responsible for it? The early Church, we are accustomed to say, and perhaps we can safely say no more. But creative thinking is rarely done by committees... The Gospels offer us one. Are we compelled to reject this offer?... The New Testament use of the title 'Son of Man' for Christ results from the individuation of this corporate conception. 'In Christ', mankind is delivered and exalted by the visitation of God, and becomes the people of the saints of the Most High.

The title applied to the Messiah. It implies, for Dodd, that Jesus 'is identified with the people of God as their "inclusive representative"'.[87]

A similar attempt to reconstruct his self-understanding from Scripture, his mission, and his destiny is found in Charles Francis Digby Moule (1908–2007). However, Moule does not think it necessary to include Isaiah 53 as background for speaking of the suffering Son of Man. He thinks the question in Mk 9.12 rather points to Dan. 7.21, because when the holies are symbolized by the Son of man, 'then "the Son of Man" already means "the representative of God's chosen people, destined through suffering to be exalted"'.[88] For that reason

> the application of 'the Son of Man' to Jesus seems to mean that it at least represents his expectation of victory through suffering, vindication after defeat. But it means more than being vindicated: it means vindicating; for on any showing the term is to this extent a collective one that the person is representative, inclusive, incorporative; and therefore if his cause is vindicated, then with it he becomes *Vindex* of the body of the people whom he represents and sum up.[89]

Moule later returns to the question and deepens his understanding. That the Gospels determine the undetermined 'as a son of man' in Daniel makes it 'a reasonable conjecture that it represents a reference to the Danielic phrase', just as, in an independent way and with a different purpose, we see it in *1 Enoch* 37–71.[90] According to Moule, this is also the reason why it is only

87. Dodd, *According to the Scriptures*, p. 121.

88. C.F.D. Moule, 'From Defendant to Judge—and Deliverer: An Inquiry into the Use and Limitation of the Theme of Vindication in the New Testament', *BSNTS* 3 (1952), pp. 40-53; quoted according to the reprint in *The Phenomenon of the New Testament* (1967), pp. 82-99 (89) (italicized in Moule).

89. Moule, 'From Defendant to Judge—and Deliverer', p. 90.

90. C.F.D. Moule, 'Neglected Features in the Problem of "the Son of Man"', in Joachim Gnilka (ed.), *Neues Testament und Kirche* (FS Rudolf Schnackenburg, 1974), pp. 413-28 (421).

found in the mouth of Jesus in the Gospels. It is 'not a title so much as a description...of his martyr-ministry on earth in the past and for his heavenly vindication looked for in the future'. For his present position at the right hand of God, other titles such as Son of God, Lord or Christ were more appropriate.[91]

In *The Son of Man in Mark: A Study of the Background of the Term 'Son of Man' and its Use in St. Mark's Gospel* from 1967, Morna D. Hooker develops the interpretation of Moule in an attempt to show that all the Son of man sayings in the Gospel of Mark are open to an understanding from what is said about the Holies of the Most High in Daniel 7, namely, as an expression for the role Jesus took upon himself:

> It would have been meaningful for Jesus himself to claim authority, accept the necessity for suffering and confidently affirm ultimate vindication, on the basis that he was the Son of man, of whom these things were 'written', for 'the Son of man' denotes primarily one to whom authority belongs and who can confidently expect vindication. To the early Church, however, the term was inappropriate: Jesus had already been vindicated and exalted to God.[92]

The common denominator is seen in his authority. According to Hooker, the Markan use of Son of man also reflects an insight which deserves attention as a reliable representation of the use and understanding of Jesus himself. It is,

> as an expression of the basis and meaning of his person and destiny: it expresses his position in the world, a position founded upon his relationship with God, for it is his relationship with God (expressed in the terms of choice, obedience and 'Son of God') which expresses his relationship with men (expressed in terms of authority, rule and 'Son of man'); Jesus, like Israel, can be termed 'Son of man' only because his relationship with God is such that he can also be described as 'Son of God'. The authority, necessity for suffering, and confidence in final vindication, which are expressed in the Markan sayings, can all be traced to Dan. 7.[93]

In a later article, Hooker can affirm that, as in Daniel, 'Son of man' is better understood as a reference to a role than as a title, it is further only the context which makes it plain whether *bar nasha* is to be understood as 'I' rather than as 'man' in general. Thus: 'The Son of man sayings contain a

91. Moule, 'Neglected Features in the Problem of "the Son of Man"', p. 424. Cf. *idem*, *The Origin of Christology* (1977), pp. 11-22, where Moule summarizes his understanding, and *idem*, '"The Son of Man": Some Facts', *NTS* 41 (1995), pp. 277-79.

92. M.D. Hooker, *The Son of Man in Mark: A Study of the Background of the Term 'Son of Man' and its Use in St. Mark's Gospel* (1967), p. 191.

93. Hooker, *The Son of Man in Mark*, p. 192. Jane Schaberg, 'Daniel 7,12 and the New Testament Passion-Resurrection Predictions', *NTS* 31 (1985), pp. 208-22, likewise sees the Passion predictions unfolding a feature inherent in Dan. 7.13.

challenge to others to be included and to make a corporate interpretation a reality instead of a possibility.'[94]

Another extensive attempt to understand Son of man in the Gospels from the background of Daniel 7 was offered by Lloyd Gaston. Gaston admits that the Church consequently interpreted Daniel 7 in relation to Jesus in the terms of exaltation. But if the question is put as to why Son of man and the Kingdom of God are not related in the Synoptic tradition (cf. the thesis of Vielhauer referred to above) the answer according to Gaston is not that one of these items penetrated secondarily into the tradition. There is another possible conclusion; namely, that 'the two phrases are used by Jesus synonymously'. This conclusion is in accordance with Daniel, which leads Gaston to the thesis that 'Jesus used the phrase Son of Man to refer not to himself but to the community he came to call into existence, which was to undergo first suffering and then exaltation'.[95] The weakness in the interpretation of T.W. Manson lies in the assumption that from the Gospel of Mark it is possible to conclude why Son of man later assumed another content. According to Gaston, only one hypothesis is able to help: 'It will be this, that when the evangelists use the phrase Son of Man they use it nearly consistently as a designation of Jesus, but when Jesus used the phrase, he used it consistently as a designation of the community he came to found'.[96] In the use of Jesus, it is a 'collective term'.[97]

Further representatives of this understanding can be arrayed,[98] some of whom connect it with an idealistic interpretation (cf. below). The intention

94. M.D. Hooker, 'Is the Son of Man Problem Really Insoluble?', in Ernest Best and R.M. Wilson (eds.), *Text and Interpretation* (FS Matthew Black, 1979), pp. 155-68 (167-68). In the article, 'The Son of Man and Christian Discipleship', *Lutheran Theological Journal* 39 (2005), pp. 110-21, Francis J. Moloney practically repeats this position, and states: 'Applying this expression used to describe the holy ones in Daniel 7, Jesus saw that his lifestyle was leading him into suffering, persecution and death. The "one like a son of man" becomes "the Son of Man" in the person of Jesus' (p. 114). And this lifestyle the disciples were invited to imitate (cf. especially pp. 117-20).

95. L. Gaston, *No Stone on Another: Studies in the Significance of the Fall of Jerusalem in the Synoptic Gospels* (1970), p. 393; cf. p. 409.

96. Gaston, *No Stone on Another*, pp. 394-95.

97. Gaston, *No Stone on Another*, p. 408.

98. For instance Wendelin Kellner, *Der Traum vom Menschensohn. Die politisch-theologische Botschaft Jesu* (1985); Theodore W. Jennings, 'The Martyrdom of the Son of Man', in Theodore Jennings Jr. (ed.), *Text and Logos: The Humanistic Interpretation of the New Testament* (FS Hendrikus de Boers, 1990), pp. 229-43; C.B. Caird, *New Testament Theology* (completed and edited by L.D. Hurst, 1994), pp. 369-84; and Thomas Kazen, 'Son of Man as Kingdom Imagery: Jesus between Corporate Symbol and Individual Redeemer Figure', in Tom Holmén (ed.), *Jesus from Judaism to Christianity* (2007), pp. 87-108, claiming the corporate understanding for Jesus alone. 'This interpretation of the Son of Man *includes* Jesus, however, and thus makes the transmutation both possible and comprehensible' (p. 108).

behind these attempts to give the Son of man in the mouth of Jesus or in the Gospels a symbolic interpretation is to reach an understanding in line with the meaning given to the figure in Daniel 7. They are also connected with a denial of the hypothesis of the existence of an apocalyptic Son of man figure in ancient Judaism.[99] On the one hand, they see a connection between nearly all Son of man sayings and Daniel 7 when they let it express not a title but a role. On the other, they make their understanding dependent on a traditio-historical hypothesis with regard to the use of the expression by the historical Jesus in a way which necessitates a distinction between this use and its later content in the Gospels. Maurice Casey touches a tender spot when he states that 'the remarkable fact about the "corporate" Son of man sayings is that they do not show detectable signs of influence from Dan. 7.13, whereas the group of sayings that show clear signs of this influence do not show corporate characteristics'.[100]

6. *Son of Man as Expression for Jesus' Prophetic Consciousness or his Consciousness of Being in a Unique Way a Representative of Humanity*

Some few interpreters in this period restate the view that Son of man in the mouth of Jesus stems first of all from the divine way of addressing the prophet in the book of Ezekiel.[101] One of the more significant adherents is Allan Richardson, who writes in his *An Introduction to the Theology of the New Testament* from 1958 that: 'The choice of the actual term "Son of Man" is not hard to explain. Jesus, like Ezekiel, regarded himself (Ezek. 12.6; 24.24) as a sign to his generation.'[102] There are also other interpreters who adopt this perspective.[103]

99. Cf. for instance Moule, 'Neglected Features in the Problem of "the Son of Man"', p. 417; Hooker, 'Is the Son of Man Problem Really Insoluble?', p. 155; Gaston, *No Stone on Another*, p. 374.

100. Casey, *The Son of Man*, p. 211.

101. Following the series of representatives enumerated above in Chapter 11 are W.A. Curtis, *Jesus Christ the Teacher: A Study of His Method and Message Based Mainly on the Earlier* Gospels (1943, 2nd edn, 1945), pp. 127-43; G.S. Duncan, *Jesus, Son of Man: Studies Contributory to a Modern Portrait* (1948); J.Y. Campbell, 'Son of Man', in A. Richardson (ed.), *A Theological Wordbook of the Bible* (1950), pp. 230-32 (cf. *idem*, 'The Origin and Meaning of the Term Son of Man', *JThS* 48 [1947], pp. 145-55 [150 n. 1], where Campbell declares that he has omitted the use of the Son of man in Ezekiel owing to the necessarily limited scope of the paper).

102. A. Richardson, *An Introduction to the Theology of the New Testament* (1958), p. 145; cf. pp. 128-46. Richardson also includes the corporate aspect in his interpretation of the Son of man in the mouth of Jesus (pp. 136-41).

103. W. Eichrodt, 'Zum Problem des Menschensohnes', *EvTh* 19 (1959), pp. 1-3; E.J. Tinsley, 'The Way of the Son of Man: The "Imitation of Christ" in the Gospel

The understanding of the Son of man in the mouth of Jesus as an expression of his consciousness of representing humanity in a unique way still finds its adherents.[104] J.B. Cortés and F.M. Gatti even find that 'it is not improbable that Jesus himself may have pronounced the expression "Son of Man" in the Greek language'.[105] He meant thereby 'the Son *par excellence* of the Man *par excellence*, namely Adam, or, in a more extended sense, *the*

Tradition', *Interpretation* 7 (1953), pp. 418-25; *idem*, 'The Sign of the Son of Man', *SJTh* 8 (1955), pp. 297-306; J. Christensen, 'Le Fils de l'homme s'en va, ainsi qu'il est écrit de lui', *StTh* 10 (1956), pp. 83-92. Cf. *idem*, *Menneskesønnen* (1996), where it is discussed whether the use of the expression 'Son of man' in the book of Ezekiel together with the later perception of Ezekiel has not suggested that this expression in later literature became applicable as a designation of a figure brought forward to the throne of God in the heavenly world (see p. 23). According to Christensen, an analysis of Son of man in Mark results in the idea that 'where the expression "son of man" is used in connection with an eschatological figure in books later than the Book of Ezekiel, in principle this figure always appears in a visionary context' (p. 70). Further C. Hassell Bullock, 'Ezekiel, Bridge Between the Testaments', *JEThS* 25 (1982), pp. 23-31 (27-29), where Ezekiel's Son of man is seen as 'a simpler model and therefore a more wieldy one than the complex form that we find in Jewish apocalyptic' (p. 29). With special regard to John, B. Vawter, 'Ezekiel and John', *CBQ* 26 (1964), pp. 450-58. A.W. Blackwood, *The Other Son of Man: Ezekiel, Jesus* (1966) (which has not been accessible) and David N. Freedman, 'Son of Man, Can these Bones Live?', *Interpretation* 29 (1975), pp. 171-86; J. Burnier-Genton, 'Ézéchiel fils d'homme', *Essais bibliques* 5 (1982; cf. summary in *ZAW* 95 [1983], p. 300); William H. Brownlee, '*Son of Man* Set Your Face: Ezekiel the Refugee Prophet', *HUCA* 54 (1983), pp. 83-110; C.B. Houk, 'בן־אדם Patterns as Literary Criteria in Ezekiel', *JBL* 88 (1989), pp. 184-90, are of no relevance in our context.

104. In the first part of the period, we find J.Y. Campbell, 'The Origin and Meaning of the Term Son of Man', *JThS* 48 (1947), pp. 145-55 (155): 'a phrase which expressed and even emphasized His real humanity and His solidarity with mankind'. Also E. Pfenningsdorf, *Der Menschensohn. Wesen—Geheimnis—Wirken* (1948), *passim*; R.K. Harrison, 'The Son of Man', *EvQ* 23 (1951), pp. 46-50; L. Johnston, 'The Son of Man', *Scripture* 6 (1954), pp. 181-83; J. Galot, 'L'énigme du "Fils de l'homme"', *Revue de Clergé Africain* 12 (1957), pp. 215-27, 338-52; W.K. Grossouw, *De Zoon des Mensen. De bijbelse grondslag van het christelijk humanisme* (1957); O. Moe, 'Der Menschensohn und der Urmensch', *StTh* 14 (1960), pp. 119-29 (126-27): Jesus would, with this designation, 'als ein geborenes Glied des gegenwärtigen Menschengeschlechts hervortreten, schließlich als der Sohn des ersten Menschen, der als solcher Erbe und Schuld der gesamten Menschheit übernommen hat' (an abridged edition appeared in Norwegian, 'Menneskesønnen og Urmennesket', *TTK* 32 [1961], pp. 65-73). Further H.F. Davies, 'The Son of Man—I. The Image of the Father', *The Furrow* 12 (1961), pp. 39-48; Bernhard P. Pruzak, 'The Son of Man Came Eating and Drinking: An Overview of Christological Perspectives in the Incarnation', in F. Eigo (ed.), *Who do People Say I Am?* (1980), pp. 1-46 (35) (this article only treats the expression Son of man in passing).

105. B. Cortés and F.M. Gatti, 'The Son of Man or The Son of Adam', *Bib* 49 (1968), pp. 457-502 (465).

Descendent of Adam'.[106] They continue: 'He is at the same time *one* and *many*. He is "one" because he is an historical and individual person, Jesus of Nazareth; he is "many" because in a mysterious way he incorporated all mankind in himself.'[107] This interpretation has been renewed by Joel Marcus, in a revised form, claiming that ὁ υἱὸς τοῦ ἀνθρώπου in the Gospels means 'the son of Adam'. Adam is here not only perceived as the biblical protoplast but also as the figure appearing in the Adamic speculations in Judaism where he possesses a dominion and divine glory to be restored in the eschaton. Thus the conceptions gathered around this Adam are able to explain the use in all three categories of Son of man sayings. The conclusion is that Son of man does not designate Jesus as 'mere human, since Adam is a figure of great glory, even godliness, in some of the traditions upon which the Son of Man sayings draw. Jesus, as Son of Man, presents a glorified picture of human destiny, showing humanity eschatologically transformed to fulfil the destiny that God intended for it "in the beginning".'[108] The idealistic overtone is not easy to miss.

An idealistic interpretation is, by the way, also found in one of the fathers of modern psychiatry, Carl Gustav Jung and the Marxist philosopher Ernst Bloch. Jung (1875–1961) understands Jesus not least through an archetypal interpretation of the expression Son of man, that 'as the historical Son of Man and anthropos, he [Jesus] is the prototype of the individual inner man and at the same time the culmination, goal and totality of the empirical man'.[109] In *Atheismus im Christentum. Zur Religion des Exodus und des Reichs* (1968), Bloch (1885–1977) finds that 'only an atheist can be a good Christian, but also, in truth, only a Christ can be a good atheist. How else could the Son of Man call himself equal to God?'[110] This Bloch finds confirmed in a subversive line of thought in the Bible:

106. Cortés and Gatti, 'The Son of Man or The Son of Adam', p. 472.

107. Cortés and Gatti, 'The Son of Man or The Son of Adam', p. 477.

108. J. Marcus, 'Son of Man as Son of Adam', *RB* 110 (2003), pp. 38-61, 370-86. The quotation from the summary p. 370.

109. C.G. Jung, *Civilization in Transition*, in *Collected Works*, X (1974), p. 397 (I owe this reference to W. Wink, *The Human Being* [1992], p. 336 n. 10) (German: *Ein moderner Mythus von Dingen die am Himmel gesehen werden* [1958]; reprinted in *idem*, *Zivilisation im Übergang* [Gesammelte Werke Band 10, 1974], pp. 336-474 [433]). Other references are found scattered around in the works of Jung, for instance *Antwort auf Hiob* (1952/1961), reprinted in *Gesammelte Werke*, II (1963), pp. 385-506 (456-66).

110. Ernst Bloch, *Atheismus im Christentum. Zur Religion des Exodus und des Reichs* (1968), p. 24. The preface, from which this quotation comes, is not included in the English translation, *Atheism in Christianity: The Religion of Exodus and the Kingdom* (1972), from which the following quotations stem.

> It is clear that there is such an underground Bible, both *infra* and *contra* and *ultra* the heteronomous light of the theocratic firmament. Criticism has made investigation possible, though it has hardly yet begun. The *homo absconditus*, from *Eritis sicut deus* to the Son of man, who had no transcendent heavenly throne, but an eschatological Kingdom—that was the real *Biblia pauperum*.

This is the context in which Bloch understands the expression Son of Man. Thus, in a chapter with the title 'Christ's Secret Name is Son of Man, Not Son of God: The "Mystery of the Kingdom"',[111] he claims

> 'Son of Man' only appears modest or powerless when set alongside 'Son of God'. But in fact it is the highest title of all, and it means that man has got a very long way indeed; he has become a figure of final, all-conquering strength... In truth, then, as it is used in the Bible from Daniel 7.13 on, the title means, even in its Semitic form, something both unusual and very powerful. The Son of Man, *ben adam*, is in fact the son of the *Heavenly Man*, the divine Adam.[112]

Bloch refers to Paul's second man from heaven (1 Cor. 15.47). He also confronts the eschatological Son of man title with the later cultic Kyrios-Christos title: Jesus employed Son of man as a self-designation in a purely apocalyptic sense and it was only later in Hellenistic Christianity that the figure of Jesus changed into a cult-hero:

> When it happened, the Son of Man passed over to the poor: to those who inwardly, and above all outwardly, kicked against the realm of the On-high, where there was no room for man...
>
> It may have seemed that the future belonged entirely to this Kyrios; but the only future to do so was that which lay under the hand of Church and state authorities. The other future, the dawning of the 'better age', belonged to the early community and to its Son of Man. This future has, to put it mildly, been a constant stone of contradiction to Christianity with its Lord Jesus—a stone which Christian hypocrisy has always tried to hide. For even if the Lord-Jesus figure did set himself up as the official Son of God in the place left by the Son of Man, he did so, despite everything, despite the official myth of sonship, not as Kyrios, but once again as Son of Man. *Deus homo factus est*—this final twist to the biblical Exodus, making it an exodus from Yahweh, too, transformed his triumphant Day at the end of days into the unveiling of quite a different face: The face of man, and of Son of Man. And this was true even for Paul (2 Cor. 3.18).
>
> Or again, if earlier eschatology had foretold the coming of God, Christian eschatology foretold the Parousia of Christ. That is the Bible's last and greatest word on the *topos* Son of Man—a *topos* which is not even anti-theocratic any more, but just untheocratic. And one whose inner depths

111. Bloch, *Atheismus im Christentum*, pp. 190-201; English translation, pp. 145-56.
112. Bloch, *Atheismus im Christentum*, pp. 191-92; English translation, p. 146.

> remain in profound disharmony with the haze of titles cast over Jesus by the court of theologians—notably the pagan, cultic title *Kyrios*, and its ultimate development, the Byzantine Pantocrator.[113]

To Bloch, Jesus is the Son of Man as representative of the true human, without any alienation—neither from within nor from without.[114] A similar understanding can be found with the Tübingen systematician, Jürgen Moltmann.[115]

Exegetes too, adhering to the view that there was no such thing as an expectation of an apocalyptic Son of man, reach an understanding belonging to this group. Ragnar Leivestad claims particularly that in those Son of man sayings, which, in his

> opinion are most likely to be authentic...the Son of man is not a pretentious designation but a humble one, denoting solidarity and identification with the sons of men. The Son of man is he who is a friend of sinners. The Son of man is he who came to serve and give his life. The self-designation is evidence of his self-dedication to men.[116]

113. Bloch, *Atheismus im Christentum*, pp. 212; English translation, pp. 164-65.

114. The interpretation of Bloch has called for a commentary: Claude Geffré, 'L'herméneutique athée du titre de fils de l'homme chez Ernst Bloch', in Marco M. Olivetti (ed.), *Religion et politique* (1978), pp. 203-17 (German: 'Die Hermenutik des Titels "Menschensohn" bei Ernst Bloch', in Franz Theunis [ed.], *Glaube und Politik* [1979], pp. 144-53 [153]: 'Der Menschensohn ist die Chiffre der Unfertigkeit des auf eine unbekannte Verwirklichung seiner selbst zustrebenden Menschen'). A similar understanding is dominant in Lucio Lombardo-Radice, 'Sohn des Menschen', in Iring Fetscher and Milan Machoved (eds.), *Marxisten und die Sache Jesu* (1974), pp. 17-21. Further, Raimundo Panikkar, 'Sécularisation de l'herméneutique: le cas du Christ: fils de l'homme et fils de Dieu', in Enrico Castelli (ed.), *Herméneutique de la sécularisation* (1976), pp. 213-48 (German: 'Die Säkularisierung der Hermeneutik: der Fall Christus: Menschensohn und Gottessohn', in Franz Theunis [ed.], 'Zum Problem der Säkularisierung', Kerygma und Mythos VI = *ThF* 60 [1977], pp. 141-64).

115. J. Moltmann, 'Man and Son of Man', in J.R. Nelson (ed.), *No Man is Alien: Essays on the Unity of Mankind* (FS W.A. Visser' Hooft, 1971), pp. 203-24. Also to be mentioned in this context is the contribution of Huey P. Newton, 'Son of Man', *Radical Religion* 2 (1975), 68-72, which was written in 1973 as a sort of manifesto by the founder and chief theoretician of the Black Panther Party. According to the introduction, it is fundamental to understand Newton's 'Son of man' in connection with this concept of Revolutionary Suicide. To him, Son of Man is a revolutionary title.

116. R. Leivestad, 'Exit the Apocalyptic Son of Man', *NTS* 18 (1971–72), pp. 243-67 (267). This article is an abridged version of Leivestad's first contribution to this question, 'Der apokalyptische Menschensohn ein theologisches Phantom', *ASThI* 6 (1968), pp. 49-105, where the conclusion is found on p. 103. Cf., however, also *idem*, 'Jesus—Messias—Menschensohn. Die jüdischen Heilandserwartungen zur Zeit der ersten römischen Kaiser und die Frage nach dem messianischen Selbstbewußtsein Jesu', in *ANRW* II.25.1 (1982), pp. 220-64 (246-55), where Leivestad himself calls the thought that Son of man denotes solidarity and identification with the sons of men 'wishful

Thus, an 'idealistic' interpretation has experienced a certain revival.[117]

Another branch of interpretation is initiated by Eduard Schweizer (1913–2006). Assuming that while none of the sayings about the coming Son of man go back to Jesus and not a few of the sayings about the earthly Jesus seems to be genuine (this may also apply to Mk 14.62, originally a saying about exaltation), Schweizer claims that 'he thereby has intentionally taken up a designation which in no way was firmly outlined dogmatically... The term could just as well be understood as a somewhat unusual circumlocution for the I of a normal man as an expression of the original in Jesus' way.'[118] In relation to Early Jewish apocalyptic, where Son of man figures in connection with the thought of exaltation, what is new and original with Jesus is

> that he also took up the ambiguous expression 'Son of man' for the way of the righteous on earth through rejection, suffering and death, which aimed at the enigma of his mission without speaking it aloud... The Son of man is thus originally not the coming bringer of salvation, but an earthly being waiting for his exaltation from shame and suffering.[119]

However, according to Schweizer, this understanding was not maintained in later tradition.[120]

The Tübingen New Testament professor Otto Michel (1903–1993) similarly thinks that Jesus has used the expression Son of man in sayings indicating his way and fate. Michel calls it 'idiomatic'. However, he will not

thinking' (p. 251). Further *idem*, *Jesus in His Own Perspective* (1987; Norwegian original, *Hvem ville Jesus være?* [1982]), pp. 160-61. Thus in the last two contributions this interpretation is moderated (as to Leivestad's main contribution to the Son of man question, see below, Chapter 16). Also W. Kellner, *Der Traum vom Menschensohn* (1985), who otherwise represents a corporate understanding (cf. above).

117. Thus also Fritz Neugebauer, 'Die Davidssohnfrage (Mark xii,35-37 par) und der Menschensohn', *NTS* 21 (1974–75), pp. 81-108; J.M. Ross, 'The Son of Man', *Irish Biblical Studies* 13 (1991), pp. 186-98; A.P. Dominic, 'Learning from Jesus, the Son of Man', *Review for Religious* 62 (2003), pp. 63-71.

118. E. Schweizer, 'Der Menschensohn (Zur eschatologischen Erwartung Jesu)', *ZNW* 50 (1959), pp. 185-209; quoted according to the reprint in *idem*, *Neotestamentica* (1963), pp. 56-84 (74-75).

119. Schweizer, 'Der Menschensohn', pp. 79-80.

120. Cf. also the other contributions of Schweizer to the Son of man problem: 'The Son of Man', *JBL* 79 (1960), pp. 119-29; *Erniedrigung und Erhöhung bei Jesus und seinen Nachfolgern* (2nd edn, 1962); 'The Son of Man Again', *NTS* 9 (1962–63), pp. 256-61 (reprinted in *idem*, *Neotestamentica* [1963], pp. 85-92); 'Menschensohn', *Die Zeichen der Zeit* 22 (1963), pp. 361-63; *Jesus Christus im vielfältigen Zeugnis des Neuen Testaments* (1968), pp. 22-26; 'Menschensohn und eschatologischer Mensch im Frühjudentum', in Pesch and Schnackenburg (eds.), *Jesus und der Menschensohn* (FS A. Vögtle, 1975), pp. 100-16 (reprinted in *idem*, *Neues Testament und Christologie* [1982], pp. 104-20); 'Jesus Christus I', *TRE* 16 (1987), pp. 670-726 (713-15).

exclude the possibility that, among the Son of man sayings, we also find different categories, each with its special origin in the teaching of Jesus. Besides the idiomatic, he also assumes 'functional' Son of man sayings in the mouth of the earthly Jesus, functioning as apocalyptic teaching and being 'until today, a reference to the eschatological aspect in the teaching and story (Geschichte) of Jesus that is not to be overlooked'.[121]

Two further interpretations belong here. The Swedish scholar, Gösta Lindeskog (1904–1984), declares that Son of man in the Synoptic Gospels stems from quite another concept than Jewish apocalyptic. It has only the name in common. At the time of Jesus, it was a known designation, but the Son of man Christology in the Synoptic Gospels is nonetheless an original and independent creation and—according to Lindeskog—goes back to Jesus himself: 'Jesus is here the occasion (Anstoß), the prima causa, and he is that through his life and activity'.[122] 'However, he has not interpreted his word and it remains a genuine Jesuanic enigma (ein echt jesuanisches Rätselswort), "like a sign and ambiguous (zeichenhaft und doppeldeutig)", like so many other words of Jesus.'[123] The community later identified Jesus with the apocalyptic coming Son of man. This identification also became valid for the sayings about the fate of the present and, not least, the suffering Son of man. The community knew of no discontinuity. The apocalyptic concept underwent, thereby, a renewal in a manner that it is of no use in our understanding of its use in the Gospels. 'No description of the life of Jesus is clearer, more unambiguous, more human and more comprehensive than the circumlocution of Jesus: "the Son of Man".'[124]

121. Otto Michel, 'Der Menschensohn in der Jesus-Überlieferung', *Theologische Beiträge* 2 (1971), pp. 119-28 (128); also *idem*, 'Der Menschensohn. Die eschatologische Hinweisung. Die apokalyptische Aussage. Bemerkungen zum Menschensohn-Verständnis des N.T.', *ThZ* 27 (1971), pp. 81-104; *idem*, 'Der Umbruch: Messianität = Menschensohn. Fragen zur Markus 8,31', in Gert Jeremias *et al.* (eds.), *Tradition und Glaube. Das frühe Christentum in seiner Umwelt* (FS K.G. Kuhn, 1971), pp. 310-16; *idem*, 'ὁ υἱὸς τοῦ ἀνθρώπου', in *ThBNT*, III (2nd edn, 1972), pp. 1153-66 (revised by W. Grimm in *Neubearbeitete Ausgabe*, II [2000], pp. 205-24). Earlier, Michel contributed with 'Menschensohn und Völkerwelt', *Evangelische Missions-Zeitschrift* 2 (1941), pp. 257-67, primarily an exegesis of Mt. 28.16-20.

122. Gösta Lindeskog, 'Das Rätsel des Menschensohnes', *StTh* 22 (1968), pp. 149-76 (171).

123. Lindeskog, 'Das Rätsel des Menschensohnes', p. 173. The quotation is from E. Stauffer, *Jesus. Gestalt und Geschichte* (1957), p. 24. The translation of Stauffer is mine.

124. Lindeskog, 'Das Rätsel des Menschensohnes', p. 174. A shorter Swedish edition is 'Människosonens gåta', *Religion och Bibel* 26 (1967), pp. 3-13. A similar conclusion is reached by Wilhelm Resenhöfft, *Der Tag des Menschensohnes. Die Geschichte Jesu im Wortlaut der Urquellen* (1975), especially pp. 211-12, where it is also claimed to be 'ein Rätselwort' and contested that it should be a circumlocution for the title of the Messiah: 'So löst sich das Rätselwort: in der zeitweiligen Verhüllung verbirgt sich das

The other interpretation is that of Joan Massyngberd Ford, who takes Son of man in the mouth of Jesus to be a euphemism for Son of God, referring especially to Mt. 26.63-65. That is also to be understood of the accusation against Jesus of making himself like God (Jn 5.18), although, according to the Gospels, he never used this title for himself. Thus 'the explanation for the absence of evidence that Jesus called himself "Son of God" may lie in the fact that the title, whereby he did designate himself, "Son of man", might be a euphemism for "Son of God"'.[125] Ford 'very tentatively' puts forward the hypothesis 'that the writers of the NT were still influenced by Semitic practices and that they still observed the practice of *qere* and *kethib*'.[126]

R.G. Hamerton-Kelly follows E. Schweizer in only accepting sayings concerning the Son of man on earth as genuine sayings of Jesus. Looking to the Wisdom tradition he even pleads for an understanding of Jesus' use of Son of man, which implies the concept of pre-existence. 'Although the Son of Man was not a well-defined figure or "concept" in Jewish apocalyptic, there was a relatively stable group of ideas associated with the term," one of them being pre-existence.'[127] Thus Hamerton-Kelly thinks it possible to conclude[128]

> that Jesus referred to himself as the Son of Man in contexts in which his authority was challenged, or his person rejected. He implied by the title that he would appear as the heavenly advocate in the future, and then men would see, who he really is. Even on earth he was the Son of Man, but rejected and humiliated. It is not difficult to see how the sayings concerning his 'coming' and his 'suffering' grew out of these authentic sayings. They might be said to have been implied in the authentic teaching of Jesus concerning the Son of Man...
>
> It is possible that Jesus, in teaching in the style of a sage, and referring to himself as the 'Son of Man', consciously took up this tradition [where the Messiah was called 'Man' and was understood as a wise man], and by using the term 'Son of Man'—which had certain connotations of transcendence—

wahre Wesen des Menschensohnes; dieses gleicht dem strahlenden Licht, wenn es unvermutet hervorbricht'. Jesus may have chosen it 'wegen des Klanges echter Demut' (p. 258). Further A.-M. Besnard in the more popular article, 'Au dire des gens qu'est le Fils de l'homme', *La vie spirituelle* 56 (1974), No. 602, Part 128, pp. 410-14. Later representatives of the 'riddle'-understanding will be mentioned below in Chapter 16.

125. Joan Massyngberd Ford, '"The Son of Man"—A Euphemism?', *JBL* 87 (1968), pp. 257-66 (257).

126. Ford, '"The Son of Man"—A Euphemism?', p. 263. Cf. *idem*, 'The Epithet 'Man' for God', *IThQ* 38 (1971), pp. 72-76.

127. R.G. Hamerton-Kelly, *Pre-existence, Wisdom, and the Son of Man: A Study of the Idea of Pre-existence in the New Testament* (1973), p. 41.

128. Hamerton-Kelly, *Pre-existence, Wisdom, and the Son of Man*, pp. 96, 100.

> rather than 'Man', interpreted the tradition to make it express the heavenly nature and pre-existence of the Messiah... In using this self-designation, Jesus implied his own pre-existence.

So Hamerton-Kelly focuses on another aspect of Daniel's Son of man, also accentuated in *1 Enoch* 37–71 and *4 Ezra* 13.

More heavy-handed is Seyoon Kim, in *The 'Son of Man' as the Son of God* (1983), who argues in a fundamentalistic way that already in the time before Christ, Judaism understood Son of man in Dan. 7.13 as the Son of God. However, Jesus used it in this meaning to point to himself as the divine figure, who acted as the inclusive representative of the eschatological people of God. The background is foremost to be found 'in Jesus' creative combination of Dan 7 and Isa 42–53'.[129]

Finally, an advocate is also found in this period for the understanding of Jesus' use of Son of man in the sense 'man per se', as 'the man exemplary in his insignificance',[130] while a few think it contains both the meaning of abasement and exaltation, thus combining the content normally present in the Old Testament expression and the one in Daniel 7.[131]

All these interpretations have the Son of man go back to a special non-apocalyptic use by the earthly Jesus, although some of them accept that it later changed its content in its reuse by the community. Most are confident in their abilities to rediscover the original meaning.

This chapter cannot be concluded without mentioning that there are examples in this period of book-titles including Son of man in an almost programmatic way as a mere synthesis of their authors' view of Jesus mostly representing an idealistic or speculative understanding.[132] There are also

129. Seyoon Kim, *The 'Son of Man' as the Son of God* (1983), p. 71. Cf. *idem*, 'Jesus—The Son of God, the Stone, the Son of Man, the Servant: The Role of Zechariah in the Self-Identification of Jesus', in Gerald Hawthorne with Otto Betz (eds.), *Tradition and Interpretation in the New Testament* (FS E. Earle Ellis, 1987), pp. 134-48.

130. S. Ben-Chorin, *Bruder Jesus: Der Nazarener in jüdischer Sicht* (1967), pp. 132-35.

131. Thus Wilfrid Stott, '"Son of Man"—A Title of Abasement', *ET* 83 (1971–72), pp. 278-81; John Bowker, 'The Son of Man', *JThS* NS 28 (1977), pp. 19-48; John L. MacKenzie, 'The Son of Man Must Suffer', *The Way* 7 (1967), pp. 6-17 (reprinted in Michael J. Taylor [ed.], *The Mystery of Suffering and Death* [1973], pp. 31-44 [32]), remarks only that 'Jesus himself preferred a title [Son of Man] which emphasized his common humanity'.

132. Thus Heinz Flügel, *Mensch und Menschensohn* (1947; published earlier in a shorter edition as *Ein Feuer auf Erden* [1941]); Wilhelm Kelber, *Der Menschensohn* (1967), includes results from exegetical research but reaches conclusions clearly inspired by the anthroposophy of the school of Rudolf Steiner; Ralph G. Turnbull, *The Profile of the Son of Man* (1969), belongs to the devotional genre; John C. Dwyer, *Son of Man and Son of God: New Language for Faith* (1983), which, although a book on Christology,

articles with the Son of man in the title, but without thematizing the expression.[133] Finally, it can be mentioned that when the Danish Bible Society published a cartoon in 1995 on the life of Jesus, drawn and narrated by a famous cartoonist, Peter Madsen, it bore the title *Menneskesønnen* (*The Son of Man*).

practically only has 'Son of man' in its title; J. Drane, *Son of Man: A New Life of Christ* (1993); Andrew Harvey, *Son of Man: The Mythical Path to Christ* (1998), where the author is described among other things as 'a mystical scholar' and the goal of the book to offer 'a comprehensive vision of Christ as a total mystical and social revolutionary, the incendiary pioneer of a wholly new form of human life' (p. xiv), not being a monograph on the Son of man. Clint Willis (ed.), *Son of Man: Great Writing about Jesus Christ* (2002), is an anthology of 21 texts by novel authors, philosophers and exegetes, not focusing especially on the problem of the Son of man. In this context, Tore Ahlbäck also belongs, *Människosonen—en självgjord messias i Tyskland efter första världskriget* (1983), which is about Oskar Ernst Bernhardt (1875–1941), a representative of the so-called 'Gralsbewegung', proclaiming himself as the Son of man.

133. This applies to George R. Beasley-Murray, 'Resurrection and Parousia of the Son of Man', *Tyndale Bulletin* 42 (1991), pp. 296-309.

15. The Second Aramaic Stage

1. *Preludes*

After the first Aramaic stage of the Son of Man research, James Stalker thought it could be reckoned among the ghosts appearing for an hour on the stage of learning, attracting attention and admiration, but having no permanent connection with reality. This turned out to be wishful thinking. Ghosts walk.[1] Some ideas demand time to show their connection with reality. This seems to be the case with the Aramaic approach. After having left but a relatively few traces after its first blossoming, it emerged with renewed force in the years after Geza Vermes published his seminal excursus in 1967. The question was raised again whether an Aramaic antecedent of the Gospel Son of man could after all have functioned as a messianic title.

Before this, sporadic attempts were made to revive the Aramaic approach. In 1947, J.Y. Campbell pointed to the Aramaic manner of speaking of oneself in the third person as the background of Son of man in the Gospels, presupposing a demonstrative adjective so that the expression came to mean 'this man', similar to Paul's way of speaking in 2 Cor. 12.2.[2] In the following year, John Bowman introduced new material to the discussion, namely, the Palestinian Pentateuch-Targum discovered in the Cairo geniza where 'in Gn 4.14, *Bar-Nash* is used for "anyone" while in Gn 9.5-6 *Bar-Nasha* (thrice) and *Bar-Nasha* (twice) alike translate *Ha-Adam*, man'.[3]

1. Cf. the quotation of James Stalker from *The International Standard Bible Encyclopaedia*, V (1915, 2nd edn, 1925), col. 2828 (above, Chapter 9 n. 53). For the following, cf. the last part of the Excursus I: Die Versuche, den Ausdruck 'Menschensohn' in den Evangelien vom hebräischen und aramäischen Sprachgebrauch her zu verstehen, in Müller, *Der Ausdruck 'Menschensohn' in den Evangelien*, pp. 228-32.

2. J.Y. Campbell, 'The Origin and Meaning of the Term Son of Man', *JThS* 48 (1947), pp. 145-55 (152-55). In the dictionary article, 'Son of Man', in A. Richardson (ed.), *A Theological Dictionary of the Bible* (1950), pp. 230-32, Campbell, however, points to the use of Son of man in Ezekiel as the background for Jesus' use.

3. John Bowman, 'The Background of the Term "Son of Man"', *ET* 59 (1947–48), pp. 283-88 (286). Later, John Bowman revised his view. Compare J. Jeremias' comment on Bowman's article in a review of M. Black's book mentioned below, 'Die aramäische

Matthew Black (1908–1994) rejects the assumption of a prefixed demonstrative adjective and is sympathetic to the thought that sayings such as Mt. 11.19 = Lk. 7.34 seem to reflect a Palestinian-Aramaic use of *bar nash*, referring to the person speaking. Black is also the first to point to an Aramaic example of such a way of speaking, namely, *Genesis Rabbah* 7.[4] Finally, Erik Sjöberg discusses the meaning of בן אדם and בר אנש in Hebrew and Aramaic, respectively, rejecting Dalman's suggestion that בר אנש should be a poetic and elevated expression. In contrast, it is considered mostly a daily word with an almost pronominal meaning. Sjöberg adheres to the thesis of Fiebig (although on other presuppositions) that the expression was common in the time of Jesus, not at the time when the book of Daniel was written. That it was a religious term at that time is suggested by the prefixed ב. However, from such presuppositions it is not clear whether the expression had a solemn ring in daily speech.[5]

While Eduard Schweizer took up the circumlocutional understanding to defend the present Son of man sayings as authentic,[6] Samuel Sandmel pleaded for the meaning 'I' in some Markan Son of man sayings, claiming the author of Mark to have invented it as a title.[7] The Gordian knot is cut too elegantly by R.E.C. Formesyn, in an article from 1966.[8] Formesyn offers two hypotheses, namely, first, that Jesus used the expression Son of man of a figure not identical with himself and second, that he used it pronominally about himself:

> As to the main part of the objection, *why* the title *only* appears on the lips of Jesus, we would like to suggest a solution which, although very simple, explains the whole problem completely. It would seem to us that the Son of

Vorgeschichte unserer Evangelien', *ThLZ* 74 (1949), pp. 527-32 (528-29): 'Dalmans (auf dem Targum Onkelos fussende, von ihm selbst aber später erheblich modifizierte) These, dass בר נשא nicht der palästinischen Umgangssprache angehört habe, ja in der älteren jüdisch-aramäischen Literatur vollständig unerhört sei, ist danach definitiv ad acta zu legen'.

4. Matthew Black, 'The "Son of Man" in the Teaching of Jesus', *ET* 60 (1948–49), pp. 32-36. Cf. *idem*, *An Aramaic Approach to the Gospels and Acts* (1946, 2nd edn, 1954), pp. 246-47.

5. Erik Sjöberg, 'Die Bedeutung von בן אדם und בר אנש im Hebräischen und Aramäischen', *AcOr* 21 (1953), pp. 57-65, 91-107.

6. Eduard Schweizer, 'Der Menschensohn (Zur eschatologischen Erwartung Jesu)', *ZNW* 50 (1959), pp. 185-209 (198); reprinted in *Neotestamentica* (1963), pp. 56-84 (70). Cf. Chapter 14, above.

7. Samuel Sandmel, 'Son of Man', in Daniel Jeremy Silver (ed.), *In the Time of Harvest* (FS A.H. Silver, 1963), pp. 355-67; reprinted as '"The Son of Man" in Mark', in *idem*, *Living Traditions* (1972), pp. 166-77. Cf. further below, Chapter 17.

8. R.E.C. Formesyn, 'Was there a Pronominal Connection for the Bar Nasha Selfdesignation?', *NT* 8 (1966), pp. 1-35.

> Man title always occurs in the mouth of Jesus because of its interchangeability in Aramaic with the first person of the pronominal pronoun. In both the earthly and suffering Son of Man sayings this interchangeability gave rise to a messianic re-reading, or *messianisation* of the pronoun. So Son of Man always occurs in the mouth of Jesus because it is a messianisation of a pronominal form of the first person. In the future Son of Man sayings however there is of course no question of a messianisation of an original personal pronoun... Here it is our opinion that they occur only in the mouth of Jesus because of the same interchangeability, here in case the *potential pronominalisation* of the Son of Man title gave perhaps the first push to the process of identification of Jesus with the future Son of Man whom he predicted.[9]

That Jesus should have used the same expression with two such different meanings was not found convincing.

Besides Dan. 7.13, which in earlier times was the only instance of the use of Aramaic בר נשׁ(א) to be dated securely to the time before Jesus, four new witnesses are available. Three are from the Dead Sea Scrolls: *Genesis Apocryphon* 21.13,[10] together with 11QtgJob 9.9 and 26.3, where it substitutes for the Hebrew בן אדם. The fourth is from the far older inscription on the third stele from *Sefire* (3.14-17), dating to c. 750 BCE.[11] All instances point to a generic or circumlocutional meaning.

9. Formesyn, 'Was there a Pronominal Connection?', pp. 25-26; cf. the conclusion, p. 34.

10. For the sake of convenience, I offer it in the translation of M. Casey, 'Aramaic Idiom and the Son of Man Problem', *JSNT* 25 (2002), pp. 3-32 (29): 'And I will multiply your seed like the dust of the earth which no son of man (בר אנושׁ) can count'. Yochanan Thorion, 'אדם und בן אדם in den Qumrantexten', *RdQ* 10 (1980), pp. 305-308, confirms the Hebrew to have the same meaning.

11. F. Vattioni, 'La prima menzione aramaica di "figlio dell' uomo"', *Biblos-Press* 6 (1965), pp. 6-7, is a short notice about this example. It stems from a treaty. In the translation of Casey (see note above), it runs: 'And if you think of killing me and you put forward such a plan, and if your son's son thinks of killing my son's son and puts forward such a plan, or if your descendents think of killing my descendents and put forward such a plan, and if the king of Arpad think of it, in any case a son of man (בר אנשׁ) dies, you have been false to all the gods of the treaty which is in this inscription.' Cf. the remarks of Casey, pp. 28-29. Through an analysis in *Vorfragen zur Christologie*, I (1978), pp. 113-15, Kearns seeks to show that the expression means more than 'human being' (cf. below Chapter 16). Also to be mentioned here is Mark S. Smith, 'The "Son of Man" in Ugarit', *CBQ* 45 (1983), pp. 59-60, pointing to a place in an incantation text found at Ras Ibn Hani, where the phrase *bn adm* obviously bears the same meaning as in the Old Testament, 'human being'. H. Haag, 'בן־אדם', *ThWAT* (1973), I, col. 684, also mentions a later instance, an Aramean–Greek bilingual edition from Georgia (*JNES* 15 [1956], pp. 20-24) from the second century CE.

2. *Geza Vermes's Contribution*

In 1965, the Jewish scholar Geza Vermes gave a lecture entitled 'The Use of בר נשא/בר נש in Jewish Aramaic', which, after its publication in 1967,[12] initiated a new era in the discussion that deserves to be labelled the second Aramaic stage in Son of Man research. Based on material from the Jerusalem Talmud, the Aramaic parts of *Genesis Rabbah*, the *Genesis Apocryphon* from Qumran and parts of the material from the Palestinian Targum, including the geniza fragments and the Neophiti-codex, Vermes succeeds not only in substantiating the thesis that the expression can be used with the meanings 'a man', 'the man', 'one', 'someone', but also in showing that בר נש(א) did have a 'circumlocutional use', which in more respects was similar to the use of the Hebrew *hahû gabra*, 'this man'. 'In most instances, the sentence contains an allusion to humiliation, danger, or death, but there are also examples where reference to the self in the third person is dictated by humility or modesty.' In contrast to *hahû gabra*, which can mean both 'I' and 'you', *bar nasha* always relates to 'I'. It is also to be maintained that 'the idiom is Palestinian-Galilean', and with regard to any assumed messianic content, Vermes concludes 'that not one among the hundreds of examples scrutinized by me suggests that *bar nash(a)* was ever employed as a messianic designation'.[13]

In his *Jesus the Jew: A Historian's Reading of the Gospels* (1973), Vermes also treats the Son of man sayings of the Synoptic Gospels. He differentiates sayings that are without any connection with Dan. 7.13 from those directly or indirectly alluding to it. While sayings in the first group 'echo a peculiar speech-form that is genuinely Aramaic, and fit so well into the Gospels...that there is no reasonable doubt why Jesus should not have uttered them' the second group carries the stamp of dogmatic speculation based on Scripture, while the third—sayings only indirectly connected with Dan. 7.13—is a secondary development of it. Of the possibly genuine Son of man sayings, it is claimed that 'if only half these sayings are authentic, it would still be justifiable to infer that the *son of man* circumlocution belonged to the stylistic idiosyncrasies of Jesus himself'.[14] The speech-form is characterized 'in accordance with Aramaic usage. The speaker refers to himself as the *son of man* out of awe, reserve or humility... [I]t is this

12. As Appendix E in the third edition of Matthew Black's *An Aramaic Approach to the Gospels and Acts* (1967), pp. 310-28. Cf. the notice 'The Theological Implications of Dr. Vermes' Observations', pp. 328-30, where Black sticks to his understanding from 1948.

13. Vermes, 'The Use of בר נשא/בר נש in Jewish Aramaic', p. 327.

14. Vermes, *Jesus the Jew*, p. 182. Of sayings with no reference to Dan. 7 and therefore possibly genuine, Vermes enumerates 20 different instances in a scheme, p. 179.

neutral speech-form that apocalyptically-minded disciples of Jesus appear to have "eschatologized" by means of a midrash based on Daniel 7:13.'[15] Finally, Vermes remarks, that:

> Since 'the *son of man*' is not a Greek phrase, but Aramaic, if it is to make sense at all it must be Aramaic sense. It would be a caricature of scholarship first to admit these premises, then to decide, on unhistorical and non-linguistic grounds, what the New Testament expression means, and finally to assert that this must also be the import of the Aramaic idiom: and a fig for the absence of any evidence of such use in the extant corpus of Aramaic literature.[16]

Of scholars subscribing to the circumlocutional understanding, we find, among others,[17] Charles Harold Dodd. In *The Founder of Christianity* (1971), Dodd realizes that Son of Man was not a current title in Jewish circles at the time of Jesus and declares that 'the indirect form might often be understood if Jesus wished to suggest, without saying it in so many words, that he was fulfilling a role which could be recognized by those sensitive to his message, while others would be left asking (as John says they did ask), "What son-of-man is this?"'[18]

Not surprisingly, Vermes' understanding also met with criticism, not least because it made it impossible in certain cases to understand Son of man messianically in the mouth of Jesus. Philologically, two objections arose. While admitting that בר נשׁ(א) in a certain speech-form can include the person speaking, it is maintained that the expression had a generic meaning. It is accordingly contested that it can function exclusively as a circumlocution for 'I'. This objection was put forward, for instance, by J. Jeremias,[19] Roger Le Déaut,[20] C. Colpe,[21] J. Bowker[22] and a number of scholars

15. Vermes, *Jesus the Jew*, p. 186.

16. Vermes, *Jesus the Jew*, p. 177.

17. Thus, for instance, I.H. Marshall, 'The Synoptic Son of Man Sayings in Recent Discussion', *NTS* 12 (1965–66), pp. 327-52 (328) (Marshall later changed his view); J.C. O'Neill, 'The Silence of Jesus', *NTS* 15 (1968–69), pp. 153-67; H. Wansbrough, 'Jesus of Galilee: Who Did He Think He Was?', *Clergy Review* 60 (1975), pp. 647-57, 760-66; 61 (1976), pp. 136-42; especially 60 (1975), pp. 760-66.

18. Dodd, *The Founder of Christianity*, p. 112, cf. pp. 110-13, also in a note referring to the work of Vermes.

19. J. Jeremias, 'Die älteste Schicht der Menschensohn-Logien', *ZNW* 58 (1967), pp. 159-72 (165 n. 9); idem, *Neutestamentliche Theologie* (1971), I, pp. 248-49 n. 21.

20. Roger Le Déaut, 'Le substrat araméen des Évangiles: Scolies en margie de l'*Aramaic Approach* de Matthew Black', *Bib* 49 (1968), pp. 388-99.

21. C. Colpe, 'ὁ υἱὸς τοῦ ἀνθρώπου', *ThWNT*, VIII (1969), p. 406.

22. J. Bowker, 'The Son of Man', *JThS* NS 28 (1977), pp. 19-48. From the Targums to Psalms and Job Bowker thinks to be able to see 'a strong tendency to choose *bar nash*...in those contexts where the meaning suggests "man born to die", "man in contrast to God"' (p. 37). Comparing this with Dan. 7, where it is said about the Son of man that

mentioned below.[23] The other comes from Joseph A. Fitzmyer, who admits the expression can function as 'a surrogate for "I"', but thinks this speech-mode was non-existent at the time of Jesus.[24]

3. *Maurice Casey's Stabilization of the Second Aramaic Stage*

One name is especially connected with the further attempt to stabilize an understanding of the Gospel Son of man on the basis of an Aramaic speech mode: Maurice Casey. In a considerable number of contributions, Casey corrects and refines the insights of Vermes. After a few preliminary studies, his understanding was first presented in *Son of Man: The Interpretation and Influence of Daniel 7* from 1979. Taking his point of departure in the messianic interpretation in *1 En.* 37–71 and *4 Ezra* 13 of the originally symbolic man-like in Dan. 7.13, Casey considers the influence of this verse in the New Testament a result of community theology rather than as originating in the earthly Jesus. However, according to Casey, 'that the Church should have attributed its exegesis to Jesus himself accords with normal practice.'[25] Instead, Casey points out twelve Son of man sayings as authentic because, in

he will be vindicated, Bowker concludes: 'To some extent, the two senses are not entirely separated, since the vindicated figure in Dan. vii is involved (or associated with) suffering and death. But one Biblical sense emphasizes death (without reference to vindication), the other emphasizes vindication' (p. 44). On the basis of the Markan Son of man sayings, Bowker finds that both meanings have been present in Jesus' use: 'Obviously, the argument attributes an originality of mind to Jesus, in the sense that he seems to have been unique in linking the two major Biblical senses of the phrase' (p. 47). P. Garnet, 'The Baptism of Jesus and the Son of Man Idea', *JNTS* 9 (1980), pp. 49-65, subscribes to this understanding.

23. To be mentioned are, however, those primarily arguing against the equation of בר נש(א) with the first person pronoun 'I': Jens Christensen (arguing against my adoption of this interpretation in my thesis; cf. below) in *Menneskesønnen. En bibelteologisk studie* (1996), esp. pp. 43-52; B. Barry Levi, 'Why *Bar-nash* Does Not Mean "I"', in Barry Walfish (ed.), *Frank Talmage Memorial Volume* (1992), pp. 85-101.

24. Joseph A. Fitzmyer, 'Matthew Black, An Aramaic Approach to the Gospels and Acts (1967). Third Edition. Appendix on the Son of Man by Geza Vermes', *CBQ* 30 (1968), pp. 417-28 (424-28); *idem*, 'Another View on the "Son of Man" Debate', *JNTS* 4 (1979), pp. 58-68; *idem*, 'The New Testament Title "Son of Man" Philologically Considered', in *idem*, *A Wandering Aramean: Collected Essays* (1979), pp. 143-60; the quotation is from p. 154. J. Coppens, 'Le dossier non biblique de l'expression araméenne *br ᵓns*', *EThL* 56 (1980), pp. 122-24, is a review of Fitzmyer's book.

25. Maurice Casey, *Son of Man: The Interpretation and Influence of Daniel 7* (1979), p. 215. But cf. all of Chapter 8: 'The Gospels and Acts', pp. 157-223. Preliminary works to the monograph are the articles of *idem*, 'The Use of the Term "Son of Man" in the Similitudes of Enoch', *JSJ* 7 (1976), pp. 11-29; 'The Corporate Interpretation of "One like a Son of Man" (Dan. VII 13) at the Time of Jesus', *NT* 18 (1976), pp. 167-80, and the article mentioned in the following note.

them, Son of man functions in a way similar to the Aramaic *bar nash* in rabbinic sayings, that is, in generalizing statements. Accepting the results of Vermes, Casey refines them to claim that the Aramaic expression belongs in statements which are general statements. Against the objection of Fitzmyer that it was not yet so at the time of Jesus, Casey finds that the New Testament evidence gives 'good reason to conjecture that in the time of Jesus the absolute and emphatic states of בר נש(א) were in use without any difference in meaning'.[26] Going on to treat Son of man sayings in the Gospels, Casey concludes that it appears that: 'Each example has two levels of meaning. The first level is that of the general statement, which will be unfamiliar in many cases. The second level is that in which the speaker says something about himself.' The genuine are to be sought, where 'the fact that a general statement is being used results in these sayings being understood of Jesus in the sense that they were believed by him to be true of other people as well as of himself'. According to Casey, this pertains to the original utterance behind twelve Gospel Son of man sayings; namely, Mk 2.10 par.; Mk 2.28 par.; Mt. 8.20 par.; Mt. 11.19 par.; Mt. 12.32 par.; Lk. 22.48; Mk 10.45; Mk 14.21a and b also with parallels, and the three Passion predictions Mk 8.31 par.; 9.31 par. and 10.33-34 par.[27] Casey imagines that what has happened

> [is that] With these examples in mind, we can consider the process of translation of these Aramaic sayings into Greek. Apart from the articles, the use of the literalistic υἱὸς ἀνθρώπου rather than the more idiomatic Greek ἄνθρωπος is probably due simply to the difficulties in translating an exclusively Aramaic idiom. I know of no genuinely equivalent idiom in Greek, and translators of the period tend to be literalistic when they cannot see how to translate an idiom idiomatically. The articles have caused more trouble. Here the random variation between בר אנש and בר אנשא in this idiom set a problem for the translator, because it meant that the emphatic state of אנש(א) did not tell him whether he should use the Greek articles or not. Therefore he had to use other criteria, and the obvious criterion to a Greek speaker would be normal Greek usage. In Greek the definite article is used to indicate a particular, previously known entity. To any early Christian Jesus was a particular, previously known entity. Thus a translator of a saying which employs this idiom, selecting the most important level of meaning of such a saying, that at which Jesus is saying something about himself, would use the articles on the ground that the entity represented by בר נש(א) was a particular, previously known entity. Knowing that the saying was on another level a general statement, he

26. Casey, *Son of Man*, p. 228. The concluding Chapter 9: 'The Son of Man Problem', pp. 224-40, consists of a revised edition of an article with the same title in *ZNW* 68 (1976), pp. 147-54.

27. Cf. Casey, *Son of Man*, pp. 228-30, and the table on p. 236 where Casey ascribes the Matthean and Lukan sayings—with Lk. 22.48 as the only exception—to Q. Mark 9.12 is the only Son of man saying not ascribed to Jesus, which, nevertheless, is thought to be a general statement; cf. p. 233.

> would find his decision to use the articles perfectly in order because of the so-called 'generic' use of the definite article in Greek... This hypothesis accounts for the origin of the Gospel term ὁ υἱὸς τοῦ ἀνθρώπου. Once this term had got into Gospel traditions which circulated in Greek, it is only to be expected that it should be used in the development of these traditions where there was no occurrence of it in any underlying Aramaic. It is here that the group of Son of man sayings which have been the primary concern of this book should probably be fitted in. It was probably exegetes who already knew of the term 'Son of man' as a term used by Jesus to refer to himself who found his second coming in the text of Dan. 7.13.[28]

Casey later argues that the Greek rendering with two articles by the Gospel translators was 'wholly in accordance with the known habits of translation in their culture'.[29] 'The first article is accordingly as near as possible to the Aramaic idiom, in which a general statement is used with particular reference to an individual, and the second article, always τοῦ, is simply generic.'[30] The rendering with both articles

> first of all enabled bilingual translators to perceive the original idiom which Jesus used, and then made reference to a known figure in sayings which had sufficient contextual indicators to make clear a reference to Dan 7.13... By this process, it emerged as an unusual title referring to the man who was the centre of salvation.[31]

This solution of the Son of man problem Casey defended and developed further on several occasions,[32] particularly against Paul Owen and David Shepherd, who tried to revive Gustaf Dalman's position, claiming, on the basis of Qumran evidence, that the emphatic state had not yet lost its determinative force in the Palestinian Galilean dialect of Western Aramaic at the time of Jesus.[33]

28. Casey, *Son of Man*, p. 230 and pp. 234-35.

29. Maurice Casey, 'Idiom and Translation: Some Aspects of the Son of Man Problem', *NTS* 41 (1995), pp. 164-82 (172).

30. Casey, 'Idiom and Translation', p. 173.

31. Casey, 'Idiom and Translation', p. 181.

32. Cf. Maurice Casey, 'Aramaic Idiom and the Son of Man Sayings', *ET* 96 (1984–85), pp. 233-36; 'The Jackals and the Son of Man (Matt. 8.20//Luke 9.58)', *JSNT* 23 (1985), pp. 3-22; 'General, Generic and Indefinite: The Use of the Term "Son of Man" in Aramaic Sources and in the Teaching of Jesus', *JSNT* 29 (1987), pp. 21-56; *From Jewish Prophet to Gentile God: The Origins and Development of New Testament Christology* (1991), esp. pp. 46-54; 'Method in Our Madness, and Madness in their Methods: Some Approaches to the Son of Man Problem in Recent Scholarship', *JSNT* 42 (1991), pp. 17-43; 'The Use of the Term בר (א)נש(א) in the Aramaic Translations of the Hebrew Bible', *JSNT* 54 (1994), pp. 87-118; *Aramaic Sources of Mark's Gospel* (1998), *passim*.

33. Paul Owen and David Shepherd, 'Speaking Up for Qumran, Dalman and the Son of Man: Was *bar enasha* a Common Term for "Man" in the Time of Jesus?', *JSNT* 81 (2001), pp. 81-122 (104); the following two quotations are from the conclusions 3 and 5 on p. 121.

> The proposed idiom, by which a speaker might use the Aramaic expression for 'son of man' as a means of idiomatic self-reference, whether exclusively (Vermes), or inclusively as part of a generic statement (Lindars [cf. below], Casey), is not attested in Middle Aramaic, nor in any phase of Aramaic pre-dating the time of Jesus... There is very little evidence that the Aramaic expression (א)בר אנש was a common term for "man" in the time of Jesus.

In answering, Casey reiterates the view that: 'Aramaic was a relatively stable language for centuries before and after the time of Jesus... [T]here were no firm barriers between the Aramaic of the time of Jesus and later Aramaic, or between East and West', wherefore careful use can be made also of later sources. 'Aramaic sources from before the time of Jesus provide clear evidence of the optional use of the emphatic state in generic and some other uses'.[34] In 2007, Maurice Casey summarized his investigations and nuanced his results in the monograph *The Solution to the 'Son of Man' Problem*. He adds that Mark 2.27-28, for instance, ensured

> that ὁ υἱὸς τοῦ ἀνθρώπου would effectively be interpreted as 'the son of humankind', so the most important person of earth, appropriately described also as ὁ υἱὸς τοῦ θεοῦ (Mk 3.11; Mt 16.16; Lk 4.41 etc). This fit almost all Son of man sayings perfectly, since they generally refer to Jesus himself, and the early church regarded him as the most important person who had been on earth.[35]

A harmonizing solution is advocated by Shizuka Uemura who finds a generic use by the earthly Jesus, for instance in Mk 2.10, 28, the source for introducing the non-messianic ברנשׁא in the meaning 'this man, that man' in sayings about the coming son of man, which are later translated into the Greek ὁ υἱὸς τοῦ ἀνθρώπου because of a misunderstanding and which became a christological title.[36]

4. *The Outcome*

A great number of scholars accepted the results of the Second Aramaic Stage, taking the Greek 'title' ὁ υἱὸς τοῦ ἀνθρώπου to originate in a

34. Maurice Casey, 'Aramaic Idiom and the Son of Man Problem: A Response to Owen and Shepherd', *JSNT* 25 (2002), pp. 3-32 (31-32).

35. *The Solution to the 'Son of Man' Problem*, p. 263. Cf. M. Müller, 'Er løsningen på "menneskesøn"-problemet fundet? I anledning af Maurice Caseys nye "menneske-søn"-bog', *DTT* 71 (2008), pp. 42-49.

36. Shizuka Uemura, 'The Origin of the "Son of Man" as a Messianic Title: A Philological and Tradition-Historical Study', *Annual of the Japanese Biblical Institute* 28 (2002), pp. 3-32 (24-32), where Uemura claims that (p. 32): 'Mark (or his church) created the "suffering and resurrecting Son of man" traditions to serve his unique Christology in his crucifixion theology', while Matthew and Luke regarded it as a messianic self-designation of Jesus and also employed it in their redactorial works. 'Thus, the messianic "Son of Man" was formed in the Gospels.'

non-titular Aramaic mode of speech practiced by the earthly Jesus. The divide here was between scholars accepting the understanding of Vermes (the Aramaic idiom being employed as a circumlocution for the person speaking), on the one hand, and scholars adhering to the line of Casey, on the other, arguing that only Son of man sayings reflecting a general statement could be authentic. In both cases, the Son of man sayings, which directly or indirectly referred to Dan. 7.13, were assumed to be secondary creations of the later community. The understanding of the Gospel Son of man from an Aramaic background was often combined with a conviction about the non-existence of an apocalyptic Son of man figure. On the other hand, the great majority of adherents to the Aramaic 'solution' find that Son of man has become a title in the Gospel tradition, not least because of the inclusion of the reference to Dan. 7.13. It is assumed either that a link was thereby established to a certain concept or image or that the reference created a special community Christology, without antecedent in Judaism. One way or the other, it became a title. The question remains, however, whether this 'title' is not simply observing the Christology in the Gospels without any special contours of its own.

A mediation between these positions is attempted by Barnabas Lindars (1923–1991), who was 'converted' from his earlier view about an apocalyptic Son of man.[37] After accepting 'The New Look on the Son of Man' in an article with this title in 1980–81,[38] he published *Jesus Son of Man: A Fresh Examination of the Son of Man Sayings in the Gospels in the Light of Recent Research* in 1983. Accepting the results of Vermes, he is, like Casey, now convinced that Aramaic *bar nash* could not function as a messianic title, but must belong to a special mode of speech, having a generic meaning as found in rabbinic examples. Lindars thinks that there were three ways of referring to oneself by means of the third person: (1) a general statement in which the speaker includes himself, (2) an exclusive self-reference and (3) 'the idiomatic use of the generic article, in which the speaker refers to a class of persons, with whom he identifies himself'. That the first should be intended in the Gospel Son of man sayings was Casey's mistake, while the second was advocated possibly mistakenly by Vermes. However, the third possibility, 'properly requiring *bar (e)nasha* rather than *bar (e)nash*, provides the best guidance for the use of the Son of Man in the sayings of Jesus'.[39]

37. Cf. Barnabas Lindars, 'Re-Enter the Apocalyptic Son of Man', *NTS* 22 (1975–76), pp. 52-72, arguing mainly against the conclusions of Leivestad. Cf. M. Müller, 'Über den Ausdruck "Menschensohn" in den Evangelien', *StTh* 31 (1977), pp. 65-82 (71-76).

38. Published in *BJRL* 63 (1980–81), pp. 437-62. The 'new look' was partly anticipated in *idem*, 'Jesus as Advocate: A Contribution to the Christology Debate', *BJRL* 62 (1979–80), pp. 476-97.

39. B. Lindars, *Jesus Son of Man: A Fresh Examination of the Son of Man Sayings in the Gospels in the Light of Recent Research* (1983), pp. 23-24.

Lindars also finds that he can re-detect this in a series of Son of man sayings in Mark and Q—namely, Mt. 8.20 par.; Mt. 11.19 par.; Mt. 12.32 par.; Lk. 11.30; Mt. 9.6 par.; Mt. 10.32-33 par., the original sayings behind the Passion predictions in Mk 8.31; 9.31; 10.33-34, and Mk 14.21a with parallels and Mk 10.45. Already in Q and the Gospel of Mark, Son of man is interpreted eschatologically from Dan. 7.13-14, as also in the Gospel of Matthew. In Luke, it turns up in new connections, appealing to the feelings of the reader and in the Gospel of John, where Lindars considers Jn 3.14 to be the bridge between the Synoptic Passion predictions and the Johannine Son of man sayings, it being employed about Jesus as the bearer of the revelation. Because of the connection with Dan. 7.13-14 in the Gospels, it stands as a designation for the Messiah, the Greek translation with the two articles having removed any ambiguity. Lindars thinks the 'advocate' saying in Mt. 10.32-33 par. has played a decisive role in the identification of Jesus with the man-like in Dan. 7.13. Thus the Gospel Son of man is the result of a misunderstanding of the Aramaic speech mode employed by the earthly Jesus.[40]

Richard Bauckham critiques Lindars' proposal for speaking of the 'idiomatic use of the generic article' with respect to a whole class, as the rabbinic examples do not allow the conclusions drawn.[41] Instead, Bauckham proposes 'that Jesus used *bar enash* (rather than *bar nasha*) in the indefinite sense ("a man", "someone", which is itself a very common usage), but used it as a form of deliberately oblique or ambiguous self-reference'.[42]

40. Lindars reiterates his view in 'Son of Man', in R.J. Coggins and J.L. Houlden (eds.), *A Dictionary of Biblical Interpretation* (1990), pp. 639-42. M. Black, 'Aramaic Barnasha and the "Son of Man"', *ET* 95 (1983–84), pp. 200-206, is mainly a discussion of Lindars' results which maintain the view that (p. 202): 'It is a capital error to assume that *barnasha*/*bar ᵉnasha* in the Old Aramaic (or Hebrew *ben adam*), "the son of Man", cannot be used as a designation or with titular force for a particular individual, especially for one of a class "where usage has elevated into distinctive prominence a particular individual of the class"'. The quotation from A.B. Davidson, *Hebrew Syntax*, p. 25. A critique of this critique is found in M. Casey, 'Aramaic Idiom and the Son of Man Sayings', *ET* 96 (1984–85), pp. 233-36.

41. Richard Bauckham, 'The Son of Man: "A Man in My Position" or "Someone"', *JSNT* 23 (1985), pp. 23-33. In 'Response to Richard Bauckham: The Idiomatic Use of Bar Nasha', *JSNT* 23 (1985), pp. 35-41, Lindars defends himself while admitting that Bauckham 'correctly sees that we are dealing with indefinite statements, but because he has not grasped the idiom of the generic article he denies the force of the article, and even suggests that anarthrous *bar enash* lies behind the Greek. But this is inconceivable, as *bar enash* is always translated *huios anthropou* in the few places where we have both Aramaic and Greek versions' (p. 40).

42. Bauckham, 'The Son of Man', p. 29. Bauckham enumerates 16 sayings, mostly those also accepted by Vermes and Casey, as possibly genuine.

Although accepting an Aramaic background for the Greek translation, some interpreters give the expression another content. The Swedish Semitist Christopher Toll thinks it possible that the term, as it now stands, bears the meaning 'a foreigner' (Fremder) or 'another' (ein Anderer), rather than 'I', though that is what was meant.[43]

In my doctoral thesis, *Der Ausdruck 'Menschensohn' in den Evangelien. Voraussetzungen und Bedeutung* from 1984, I took the position, in extension of an argument for the non-existence of a specific apocalyptic Son of man concept in Judaism (cf. Chapter 16, below), that the expression in the Gospels is not to be understood as a christological title. Although in the process of translation any ambiguity was removed, Son of man is an unmistakable reference to Jesus and originates in an Aramaic circumlocutional mode of speech. Not least in the Synoptic Gospels, it achieved a near-monopoly in sayings in which the Gospels' Jesus speaks about his task, fate, destiny or future, using the expression out of 'awe, reserve, or humility' (Vermes). Its seemingly christological content is ascribed to the fact that the expression always occurs in christological contexts. This is also clearly the case in the Gospel of John.[44] Even the reference to Dan. 7.13 is to be understood in a non-titular way. I summarized my view in an article appearing at the same time:

> As the expression stands in our Gospels today, it should be understood both as a self-reference used by Jesus and as a way of emphasizing who it is that speaks. Consequently it is always found in significant statements. The expression in itself provides no clue to the problems how Jesus understood himself and his mission, as if this could be answered by 'I am "the son of man"', but neither does it give us any reason to deny that the historical Jesus used it as a self-reference...
>
> In any case, those 'son of man' sayings which may be supposed to be authentic Jesus-sayings convert Jesus from being *only* a proclaimer of the Word to being anything but an *accidental* proclaimer. It is here we have the seed that developed into an explicit christology in the 'son of man' sayings and other Jesus sayings in the Gospel of John. Jesus' use of the expression may thus be described as one clue among others to his understanding of himself. Certainly the expression 'son of man' does not in itself denote Messiah. But there are many testimonies, also when the stress in these

43. Christopher Toll, 'Zur Bedeutung des aramäischen Ausdruckes *bar nas*', in Tryggve Kronholm and Eva Riad (eds.), *On the Dignity of Man* (FS Fridhiof Rundgren, 1986), pp. 421-28.

44. Cf., besides *Der Ausdruck 'Menschensohn' in den Evangelien*, Mogens Müller, '"Have You Faith in the Son of Man?" (John 9.35)', *NTS* 37 (1991), pp. 291-94. An earlier contribution is: 'Über den Ausdruck "Menschensohn" in den Evangelien', *StTh* 31 (1977), pp. 1-17 ('Om udtrykket "menneskesønnen" i evangelierne', *DTT* 40 [1977], pp. 1-17).

> sayings is alone on what they say *about* 'the son of man', of the unbreakable relationship between the message and life of the historical Jesus and the kingdom of God, which he proclaimed.
>
> In such a context, if anywhere, the Aramaic phrase using *bar nash(a)* as a substitute for the speaker in statements about himself becomes comprehensible. It cannot be a mere coincidence that nearly all 'son of man' sayings in the Gospels seem to presuppose an 'I believe'.[45]

The innovation in this conclusion was that Son of man need not be understood as a title even in the Gospels.[46] This point of view was reiterated shortly afterwards by Günther Schwarz in *Jesus 'der Menschensohn'. Aramaistische Untersuchungen zu den synoptischen Evangelien* from 1986. He also accepted the circumlocutional understanding of the Aramaic, *bar nasha*, as had been proposed by Vermes. According to Schwarz, it cannot have been a title in the mouth of Jesus, and had not become so in the Gospels.[47]

45. M. Müller, 'The Expression "the Son of Man" as Used by Jesus', *StTh* 38 (1984), pp. 47-64 (= 'Jesu brug af udtrykket "menneskesønnen"', *DTT* 46 [1983], pp. 201-20): pp. 57-58. Cf. *Der Ausdruck 'Menschensohn' In den Evangelien*, pp. 258-60. I later reiterated this view in 'Son of Man', in Bruce Metzger and Michael D. Coogan (eds.), *The Oxford Companion to the Bible* (1993), pp. 711-13; 'Menneskesøn', in *Gads Bibelleksikon* (1998), II, pp. 66-67; 'Menschensohn im Neuen Testament', in *RGG*, V (4th edn, 2002), cols. 1098-100. Cf. also '"Son of Man" in the Gospels: Quotation, Concept, Or?', in *idem*, *Skriften i Skriften. Mellem tradition og reception. Fjorten afhandlinger* (2007), pp. 181-89.

46. So, for example, Reginald H. Fuller, 'The Son of Man: A Reconsideration', in Dennis E. Groh and Robert Jewett (eds.), *The Living Text* (FS Ernest W. Saunders, 1985), pp. 207-17, changing his mind once again, now denies the existence of a pre-Christian apocalyptic Son of man and proposes that Son of man is not a title even in the Gospels, but a self-reference of Jesus, which could be translated 'a man', 'a fellow' or 'a guy'. Fuller sees a special problem in the future Son of man sayings in Q, but saves them as authentic by replacing Son of man in these sayings with the 'Kingdom of God' (p. 215). Further, G. Svedlund, 'Notes on *bar nash* and the Detrimental Effects of Its Transformation into the Title "The Son of Man"', in Tryggve Kronholm and Eva Riad (eds.), *On the Dignity of Man* (FS Frithiof Rundgren, 1986), pp. 401-13; Jean-Claude Loba Mkole, 'The Kiswahili *mwana wa mtu* and *ho huios tou anthropou*', in Gerald O. West and Musa W. Dube (eds.), *The Bible in Africa: Transactions, Trajectories and Trends* (2000), pp. 557-66, however, ending up seeing the expression designating Jesus' human nature; cf. *idem*, '"Son of Man" and Exegetical Myths', *Hervormde Teologiese Studies* 59 (2003), pp. 837-58 (840-42, 847, 853).

47. In a Foreword, Schwarz announces he will present evidence for 'daß das "Menschensohnproblem" nichts weiter ist als ein christologisches Scheinproblem'. The main object of Schwarz's investigation is to reconstruct the Aramaic wording of the original sayings of Jesus, of which he finds 25 in the Synoptic Gospels, while 12 are secondary. For a description and critique of Schwarz's whole enterprise in an earlier work with the same goal, cf. M. Casey, *Aramaic Sources of Mark's Gospel* (1998), pp. 44-50.

The same conclusion was drawn in Douglas R.A. Hare's more influential work, *The Son of Man Tradition*, from 1990. Inspired by Vermes' results in regard to the Aramaic and especially by Ragnar Leivestad's thesis that there existed no apocalyptic Son of Man expectation in contemporary Judaism (cf. below, Chapter 16), Hare analyzes the whole of the New Testament material anew. In doing so he employs a 'backward approach' working from Luke–Acts by way of John, Matthew and Mark and the pre-Gospel tradition to Jesus. Distinguishing between the denotations and connotations of the expression—namely, what it could designate and what it meant by itself throughout—Hare arrives at the conclusion that Son of man is employed in christological connections. The christological moment, however, does not derive from the expression but from the context in which it functions. That is entirely so in the Lukan writings, while in John the 'term refers to the incarnational existence of the Logos. It points to the unique humanity of the Incarnate One.'[48] In Matthew, which is treated in the longest chapter of the book (70 pages), the conclusion is that 'it is not a revelatory expression. It communicates nothing of importance regarding Jesus' nature, function and destiny', though 'it is found primarily in passages where Jesus does speak of his vocation and destiny'.[49] For the most part, the same can be said of Mark and the pre-Gospel traditions.

Hare recapitulates the six possibilities of function for the expression, which had been suggested on the basis of the same Aramaic form, *bar enasha*. Of the six, the first three are easily excluded; namely,

1. It was a well-known apocalyptic title.
2. It was easily perceived as a title, even by those who may have been ignorant of its meaning.
3. It was genuinely ambiguous, so that hearers/readers would not be immediately certain whether it was titular or nontitular.

A discussion of the three last, namely:

4. It was a special idiom that was used only for general statements in which a speaker could refer to himself indirectly but not exclusively.

48. Douglas R.A. Hare, *The Son of Man Tradition* (1990), p. 111, where it is also said: 'There is thus good reason to believe that John stands in close proximity to the Christian writers of the second and succeeding centuries, who employ *huios anthropou* as a way of speaking of the genuine humanity of Jesus in their battle against the docetists'. Some of these conclusions, among them the value of working 'backwards to the unknown', were already announced in *idem*, 'The Quest of the Son of Man: A Progress Report', in P. Sigal (ed.), *Proceedings of the Eastern Great Lakes and Midwest Bible Society* 4 (1984), pp. 166-80 (176).

49. Hare, *The Son of Man Tradition*, p. 181.

5. It was an everyday expression meaning 'a man', or 'someone'.
6. It was an easily recognizable circumlocution for 'I',[50]

not surprisingly leads Hare to the conclusion that, 'Whatever its spelling and pronunciation, the Aramaic underlying *ho huios tou anthropou* was understood as referring exclusively to Jesus'.[51] Hare sides with Vermes (no. 6) against the positions of Casey and—with little variation—Lindars (no. 4) and Bauckham (no. 5). Competing for recognition as genuine Jesus sayings are Mt. 11.19 par.; Lk. 12.10 par.; Lk. 12.8-9 (cf. Mt. 10.32-33); Mt. 8.20 par.; Lk. 11.30 (cf. Mt. 12.40); Mk 2.10, and some sayings that are antecedent to the Passion predictions. The apocalyptic sayings all seem to be inauthentic. Hare goes on to say:

> In those few Son of man sayings that raise the fewest doubts concerning authenticity, Jesus refers to his own vocation and destiny in third-person language, employing *bar nasha* as a modest self-reference. As far as we can tell from the way these sayings were transmitted in the early church, the linguistic power of the phrase was denotative only; it pointed to the speaker without conveying anything about his self-estimate. That is, Jesus' use of *bar nasha* communicates nothing to us about 'Jesus' own Christology', except that he regarded modesty in speech as an appropriate form of behaviour.[52]

While some assume that *bar enash(a)* included a clear self-reference as used by Jesus,[53] a number of scholars follow Maurice Casey in accepting that Son of man reflects an Aramaic idiom in the authentic stock of sayings in the Synoptic Gospels, where *bar (e)nash* is used in general statements in which the speaker includes himself, but which becomes in the Greek translation a clear reference to the person speaking.[54] Others restrict themselves to the claim that, philologically, the background is the Aramaic *bar (e)nash(a)*, which 'can have a triple meaning: generic, indefinite and circumlocutional'

50. Hare, *The Son of Man Tradition*, p. 235.
51. Hare, *The Son of Man Tradition*, p. 246. Cf. p. 256.
52. Hare, *The Son of Man Tradition*, p. 280.
53. For instance, Otfried Hofius, 'Ist Jesus der Messias? Thesen', *JBTh* 8 (1993), pp. 103-29 (119), claiming that the oldest determined titular use of 'Son of man' is the Son of man sayings in the Gospels and that, if Jesus did not employ the expression about himself in a titular way, this first emerged with the translation from Aramaic into Greek.
54. For instance, Chris Mearns, 'The Son of Man Trajectory and the Eschatological Development', *ET* 97 (1985–86), pp. 8-12; R. Kearns, *Die Entchristologisierung des Menschensohnes* (1988), pp. 57-126; Yolanda Dreyer, 'The Institutionalization of Jesus' Charismatic Authority: "Son of Man" as Case Study', *Hervormde Teologiese Studies* 56 (2000), pp. 1057-78; Robert M. Price, *The Incredible Shrinking Son of Man: How Reliable is the Gospel Tradition?* (2004), pp. 278-80—as the subtitle indicates, it is not a monograph on the Son of man.

and 'refers indistinctively to a human being and...does not automatically endow a messianic statute'.[55]

Some scholars go one step further, claiming that Jesus both employed the Aramaic expression as a circumlocutional way of speaking about himself and coined an individual interpretation of Dan. 7.13 in speaking of himself. Hans Bietenhard, in a substantial contribution in the colossal and not yet completed project *Aufstieg und Niedergang der römischen Welt* from 1982,[56] finds that it was the very remarkable way Jesus used *bar enasha* to draw attention to his particularity and to say something special about himself which lead to the conspicuous Greek rendering. In sayings with Son of man, compared with those containing an 'I', we are confronted with the 'bedrock of tradition' (Urgestein der Überlieferung).[57] This also explains its disappearance apart from the Gospels. Since there was no Son of man expectation in contemporary Judaism (cf. next chapter), Bietenhard concludes that 'it was Jesus, who first interpreted Dan 7.13f. in an individual way and no longer connected this figure with "the people of the Most High" but with himself'.[58]

In a judicious article, 'To Judge the Son of Man' (1991), Mahlon H. Smith reviews the linguistic arguments and concludes that the gospel evidence invites an understanding of 'the Son of man' in the mouth of Jesus as a circumlocution for the first person. Smith then proposes that

> [t]wo principles that may help identify sayings that can reasonably be traced back to Jesus are dialectical difficulty and ambiguity. The less explicit the saying, the more likely it originated in a pre-crucifixion context. And the more problematic its formulation from the perspective of the post-resurrection community, the less likely it is to have been produced by a mind other than that of Jesus.[59]

Analyzing the Synoptic Son of man sayings, Smith arrives at the 'verdict' that it is possible to 'isolate eleven sayings whose perspective antedates those of the post-crucifixion kerygma and eschatological expectations'. Five are from Mark: 2.10, 28; 10.45a; 14.21a and 9.35b (all with parallels), and the others are Mt. 8.20; 11.18-19; Lk. 17.22, 24, 26 and 12.10 (again with

55. For instance J.-C. Loba Mkole, 'Une synthèse d'opinions philologiques sur le Fils de l'homme', *Journal of Nothwest Semitic Languages* 22 (1996), pp. 107-23 (107).

56. Hans Bietenhard, '"Der Menschensohn"—ὁ υἱός τοῦ ἀνθρώπου. Sprachliche und religionsgeschichtliche Untersuchungen zu einem Begriff der synoptischen Evangelien I. Sprachlicher und religionsgeschichtlicher Teil', *ANRW* II 25,1 (1982), pp. 265-350. The announced continuation in *ANRW* II 26,2, 'Exegetischer Teil. Auslegung der Menschensohnworte der synoptischen Evangelien', has never appeared.

57. Bietenhard, '"Der Menschensohn"', p. 307.

58. Bietenhard, '"Der Menschensohn"', p. 345.

59. Mahlon H. Smith, 'To Judge the Son of Man', *Forum* 7 (1991), pp. 207-42 (220).

parallels).[60] Smith arrives at much the same result as his predecessors, regarding which Son of man sayings are to be taken as authentic.

On the other hand, Bruce D. Chilton[61] has argued that 'Jesus was smart enough to use the phrase in both ways (as generic and as angelic)'. 'Because Jesus, a son of man on earth, saw himself as paired with the Danielic Son of Man in heaven, there is a sliding scale of reference.'[62] James D.G. Dunn also denied the existence of any Son of man concept in contemporary Judaism and, therefore, excluded a titular understanding. Similarly, he found that it is Jesus himself who has introduced Dan. 7.13 to express his hope for vindication. This 'can also explain a threefold development of the Son of Man motif from the beginning: the post-Easter identification of Jesus himself with this Son of Man...the expansion of the motif in terms of Jesus, the Son of Man's role in judgment; and the transformation of the "coming" into the idea of a return to earth.'[63] Dunn continues:

> In addition to which, Jesus was, arguably, one of the most creative Jewish interpreters of scripture of his day, worthy of comparison (at the very least) with the Teacher of Righteousness and Hillel. So it is hardly implausible to argue that it was Jesus himself who linked his own idiomatic בר אנשא usage to the Danielic בר אנש figure... But it would mean that the Danielic influence on the Jesus/Son of Man tradition in the Gospels began before Easter, and that it began with Jesus himself.[64]

The Aramaic approach has implications for the translation of the Gospel expression only if it is not understood as a messianic title. The ambivalence inherent in Aramaic, however, should not be maintained as the Gospel term exclusively refers to Jesus.[65] A single scholar has claimed the rendering to be

60. Smith, 'To Judge the Son of Man', pp. 237-38. Cf. the earlier contribution of *idem*, 'No Place for a Son of Man', *Forum* 4 (1988), pp. 83-107.

61. An earlier study is Bruce D. Chilton, 'The Son of Man: Human and Heavenly', in F. van Segbroeck, C.M. Tuckett, G. van Belle and J. Verheyden (eds.), *The Four Gospels* (FS Frans Neirynck, 1992), I, pp. 203-18. Reprinted in Jacob Neusner (ed.), *Religious and Theological Studies* (1993), pp. 97-114, and in *idem*, *Judaic Approaches to the Gospels* (1994), pp. 75-104.

62. Bruce D. Chilton, 'The Son of Man: Who Was He?', *Bible Review* 12 (1996), pp. 35-39, 45-47; quotations from p. 45 and p. 46; also *idem*, '(The) Son of (the) Man, and Jesus', in Bruce Chilton and Craig A. Evans (eds.), *Authenticating the Words of Jesus* (1999), pp. 259-87 (284).

63. J.D.G. Dunn, 'The Danielic Son of Man in the New Testament', in John J. Collins and Peter W. Flint (eds.), *The Book of Daniel: Composition and Reception* (2001), pp. 228-44 (243).

64. Dunn, 'The Danielic Son of Man in the New Testament', p. 547. Cf. also *idem*, *Jesus Remembered* (2003), pp. 724-62.

65. Thus Ralph Hill, 'Further Considerations on Translating "The Son of Man"', *Notes on Translation* 93 (1983), pp. 35-51 (Hill here refers to two earlier contributions:

analogous to a tendency in the Targums to replace the first personal pronoun with a third person pronoun, thus changing the perspective from the text's speaking person to the writer's reference to the speaker.[66]

Of course, the gender problem also has been raised, especially in English speaking contexts, where 'man' in Son of man is not as gender neutral as Greek ἄνθρωπος and German 'Mensch'.[67]

The permanent outcome of the second Aramaic stage is that every serious attempt to trace the Gospel expression Son of man back to the earthly Jesus has to reckon with the possible presuppositions of the Aramaic spoken in Galilee and Judea in the centuries around the beginning of the Common Era. Because the expression in the New Testament Gospels does not allow any doubt as to whom is meant, the essential question is whether this is the result of a semantic change in the Greek rendering, or whether it reflects the speech mode of the earthly Jesus.

John Beekman, 'The Son of Man', *Notes on Translation with Drills* [1965], and John Austin, 'Translating "Son of Man" into Aboriginal Languages', *Notes on Translation* 75 [1979]); John Ellington, '"Son of Man" and Contextual Translation', *BiTr* 40 (1989), pp. 201-208, pleads for a translation adapted to the context, except in the Gospels and Acts, where he considers it a title, and the same applies to Dan Davis, 'The Semantic Content of 'Son of Man', *Notes on Translation* (Dallas) 4 (1990), pp. 9-23. Jean Claude Loba Mkole, 'The Kiswahili *mwana wa mtu* and *ho huios tou anthropou*', in Gerald O. West and Musa W. Dube (eds.), *The Bible in Africa: Transactions, Trajectories and Trends* (2000), pp. 557-66, argues for the Kiswahili translation being not titular. Jean Galot, 'L'énigme du "Fils de l'homme"', *Revue du Clergé Africain* 13 (1958), pp. 355-62, discusses the meaning of the expression in different African languages.

66. Thus A. Díez Macho, 'L'usage de la troisième personne au lieu de la première dans le Targum', in P. Casetti *et al.* (eds.), *Mélanges Dominique Barthélemy* (1981), pp. 61-89; *idem*, 'La Cristologia del Hijo del Hombre y el uso de la tercera persona en vez de la primera', *Scripta theologica* 14 (1982), pp. 189-201, according to *NTA* 27 (1983), p. 23, exemplifying it at Mk 8.38 and Lk. 12.8.

67. Cf. the discussion in Adela Yarbro Collins, 'The Origin of the Designation of Jesus as "Son of Man"', *HThR* 80 (1987), pp. 391-407 (391-92). Further Joan E. Taylor, '*ho huios tou anthropou*, "The Son of Man": Some Remarks on an Androcentric Convention of Translation', *BiTr* 48 (1997), pp. 101-109, argues from the Hebrew and Aramaic for replacing the androcentric 'son of man' with 'a human being' or the like. Paul Ellingworth, 'Translating "The Son of Man": A Response', *BiTr* 48 (1997), pp. 109-13, is open to these considerations—but also to the strength of the traditional translation. David J.A. Clines, '*Ecce vir*, or Gendering the Son of Man', in Paul Ellingworth and Philip R. Davies (eds.), *Biblical Studies/Cultural Studies: The Third Sheffield Colloquium* (1998), pp. 352-75, does not contribute anything to our issue as it is solely a discussion of the impact of the maleness of Jesus. This also applies to Tat-siong Benny Liew, 'Re-Mark-able Masculinities: Jesus, the Son of Man, and the (Sad) Sum of Manhood?', in Stephen D. Moore and Janice Capel Anderson (eds.), *New Testament Masculinities* (2003), pp. 93-135.

16. Exit the Apocalyptic Son of Man?

1. *The Presuppositions*

The period following the Second World War saw the zenith and the decline of the hypothesis concerning the existence of the concept of a distinct Jewish apocalyptic Son of man. Only a year after the beginning of the Second Aramaic Stage, another severe attack was launched against the dominant assumption of the existence of an apocalyptic Son of man expectation in pre-Christian Judaism.

The discussion of the sources and tradition-history of Daniel 7 and of the relation between this chapter and *1 Enoch* 37–71 and *4 Ezra* 13 became more and more intense. The New Testament evidence was now taken into consideration as a possible source.

Excursus III: *The Interpretation of Daniel 7.13,* 1 Enoch *37–71, and* 4 Ezra *13 from the Second World War Until Today*

a. *The Messianic Interpretation of Daniel 7.13*

In this period, a number of exegetes defended a messianic interpretation of 'the one like a Son of man' in Dan. 7.13.[1] The Uppsala Old Testament professor Ivan Engnell (1906–1964) totally rejected a symbolical understanding:

> It is clear that this interpretation is incredible; or to put it more exactly, impossible, because the 'Son of man' is described in very personal terms in vv. 13 f.; it is an ancient, individual messianic term associated with the savior-king or Messiah...and in Jewish apocalypticism in the period after Daniel, the 'Son of Man' appears as an individual messianic figure, the savior and judge of the last time.[2]

1. For the first sections, cf. Müller, *Der Ausdruck 'Menschensohn' in den Evangelien*, pp. 36-38.

2. Ivan Engnell, 'Människosonen', *SBU*, II (1952), cols. 399-403 (401) (2nd edn, 1963, cols. 229-32 [230-31]); quoted according to English translation in *idem*, 'The Son of Man', in *Critical Essays on the Old Testament* (1970), pp. 237-41 (239).

The Frenchman André Feuillet (1909–1998), thinking the background of Dan. 7.13 is to be found in Wisdom literature, similarly understands the one like a Son of man as a messianic figure. However, he is of the opinion that, compared with the traditional concept of the Messiah, a significant change is to be seen with respect to transcendence and universalism.[3] The fundamentalistically minded Edward J. Young did not find an 'actual interpretation of the one like a Son of man' in Dan. 7.13 for which reason, the identification of this figure is to be supposed from vv. 13-14 alone. 'The actual description...in verses 13 and 14 is such that it leads one to believe that the writer is speaking of an individual, namely, the Messiah'.[4] From totally other presuppositions; namely, because of an acceptance of the results of the History of Religions School, Heinz Eduard Tödt claimed a messianic understanding, seeing in Dan. 7.13-14 'the figure of a transcendent redeemer (transzendenten Vollenders)'.[5]

James Muilenberg also prefers a messianic understanding, which, according to him, does not exclude 'the collective interpretation'.[6] Julian Morgenstern earlier (1961, cf. below, p. 352) assumed the Tyrian national god Melcart behind the figure in Dan. 7.13, finding these verses as either a fragment of an original story in the book of Daniel, which was then lost, or a later interpolation; only five years later, he reached quite another conclusion. Assuming that vv. 13-14 should be placed after v. 28, because the reason for Daniel's distress is that he finds something missing, and as vv. 13-14 'bring the vision to a meaningful conclusion', Morgenstern now maintained:

> that vv. 13f imply that this 'one like a son of man', this 'son of man', is the king, divinely destined from old, of this restored and eternal, world dominating kingdom of Israel. And as king of Israel he must be of the Davidic line, and accordingly of divine descent, as Ps. 89.27f states, in the line of the first-born of the divine Father. Consequently, despite his human, earthly form, he is still in a very positive sense a being of superhuman, heavenly character, and therefore quite properly he comes upon the clouds of heaven and into the very presence of the Ancient of Days and His heavenly court. And from there he descends, by divine will, to earth, here to fulfill the mission entrusted to him by the Deity. Such was this 'son of man' of Dan. 7.13 f.[7]

3. André Feuillet, 'Le Fils de l'Homme de Daniel et la tradition biblique', *RB* 60 (1953), pp. 170-202 and pp. 321-46 (191-96).

4. Edward J. Young, *Daniel's Vision of the Son of Man* (1958); quoted according to reprint in J.H. Skilton (ed.), *The Law and the Prophets* (FS Oswald Thompson, 1974), pp. 425-51 (432, 450). On p. 451 one reads: 'Our Lord did not alter or modify an already existing interpretation of the Son of man which the writer of Daniel had made'.

5. Heinz Eduard Tödt, *Der Menschensohn in der synoptischen Überlieferung* (2nd edn, 1963), p. 19; English translation, *The Son of Man in the Synoptic Tradition* (1965), p. 22. R.B.Y. Scott, '"Behold He Cometh with the Clouds"', *NTS* 5 (1958–59), pp. 127-32, likewise emphasizes the transcendence of the scene, referring especially to the clouds.

6. James Muilenberg, 'The Son of Man in Daniel and the Ethiopic Apocalypse of Enoch', *JBL* 80 (1961), pp. 197-209 (201).

7. Cf. Julian Morgenstern, *Some Significant Antecedents of Christianity* (1966), pp. 64, 67.

Frederic Houk Borsch, who produced one of the last larger attempts to find a solution for the Son of man problem on the basis of a more comprehensive inclusion of the history of religion, concludes his investigations of the Son of man in Dan. 7.13 as follows:

> Is he the Messiah? The best answer is both yes and no. He is the messianic king in the sense that he is the royal figure, derived ultimately from kingship ideology, who will do all that is expected of the Messiah. There would be no room both for a Messiah and for one such as Daniel describes him. Yet he is not the Messiah in so far as others would be thinking of an earthly hero who would establish his glorious reign on earth. Seen in this way, the two conceptions are mutually exclusive even though they spring from the same soil.[8]

Not everyone subscribes to the view that such foreign influence on Daniel's Son of man. There was no hindrance, however, to giving it a messianic interpretation.[9] An attempt at a messianic interpretation of Dan. 7.13 is offered on the basis of a Davidic messianology by the Tübingen Old Testament professor Hartmut Gese, who considers the Son of man expectation as the last decisive development of messianism. Thus Gese claims:

> We are bound to encounter in it a transformation of the traditional Davidic messianology; for if, in Dan. 7, a human being is installed in the position of a royal ruler over the world as representative of God's kingship, then this concurs so precisely with the Davidic conception of kingship on Zion and its messianology that we have to assume in this confluence an internal connection, and not merely an additional tradition.[10]

8. Cf. Frederic Houk Borsch, *The Son of Man in Myth and History* (1967), p. 143.

9. The list of scholars adhering to a messianic understanding continues with Kurt Schubert, 'Die Entwicklung der eschatologischen Naherwartung im Frühjudentum', in *idem* (ed.), *Vom Messias zum Christus. Die Fülle der Zeit in religionsgeschichtlicher und theologischer Sicht* (1964), pp. 1-54 (38); F. Dexinger, *Das Buch Daniel und seine Probleme* (1969), pp. 55-67; A. Lacocque, *Le Livre de Daniel* (1976), p. 111; F.M. Wilson, 'The Son of Man in Jewish Apocalyptic Literature', *Studia Biblica et Theologica* 8 (1978), pp. 28-52 (33); Helge Kvanvig, 'Struktur und Geschichte in Dan. 7,1-14', *StTh* 32 (1978), pp. 95-117; Arthur J. Ferch, 'The Apocalyptic "Son of Man" in Daniel 7' (dissertation 1979), later published as *The Son of Man in Daniel 7* (1983); Robert D. Rowe, 'Is Daniel's "Son of Man" Messianic?', in Harold H. Rowden (ed.), *Christ the Lord* (FS Donald Guthrie, 1982), pp. 71-96 (94-96); Jens Christensen, *Menneskesønnen. En bibelteologisk studie* (1996), pp. 27-36. It is a misunderstanding when K. Koch, *Das Buch Daniel* (1980), p. 218, lists my *Messias og 'menneskesøn'* (1972), as representing a messianic interpretation of Dan. 7.13. On the basis of Koch, Marc Girard, 'Le semblant de fils d'homme de Daniel 7, un personage du monde d'en haut: approche structurelle', *Science et Esprit* 35 (1983), pp. 265-96 (288 n. 34), reiterates the mistake. Obviously, the title of the book is open to this misunderstanding. Magne Sæbø, 'Messias—Herrens tjener og menneskesønn', in Thorleiv Austad and Øyvind M. Wee (eds.), *Hvem er Jesus?* (1984), pp. 19-30 (26-30), finding the Messiah in Dan. 7.13, and the Jewish people in the interpretation of the vision and speaks about a 'democratisation' where focus has moved from an individual mediator of redemption to the Jewish people and its role as ruler.

10. Hartmut Gese, 'Die Weisheit, der Menschensohn und die Ursprünge der Christologie als konsequente Entfaltung der biblischen Theologie', *SEÅ* 44 (1979), pp. 77-114

This is confirmed by *1 Enoch* 37–71 and *4 Ezra* 13, which bring different motives from Davidic messianology into connection with the Son of man.

Another—more conservative—attempt to support a tradition-history coming mainly from within Judaism is that of Wolfgang Bittner, who points to influence from Ezekiel 1.26. According to Bittner, Daniel's Son of man is to be connected with the epiphany of the glory of God's throne in the shape of a human. It is God himself, in his revelation as the glory of his throne who will appear as Son of man in the eschaton. The messianic interpretation begins already in Daniel 7, God in this way interpreting and proclaiming the Son of man as the eschatological Davidic Messiah and representative of the eschatological purified people of God.[11]

A variant of the messianic interpretation is the understanding that the Messiah is not mentioned but nonetheless implied, because a messianic kingdom without a king is inconceivable.[12] That scholars, accepting a conception of the Primordial Man or the like behind the Son of man, would think of a re-interpretation of Dan. 7.13, accentuating the collective aspect, is understandable.[13] Also to be listed here are interpreters seeing behind the Son of man in Daniel 7 the sacred king pointing to Pss 8.5 and 80.18, and sometimes also to Ps. 146.3, as witnesses to *ben-adam* as a kingly messianic title. This is done by both Aage Bentzen and Ivan Engnell, who assume influence from the royal ideology of the ancient Near East on the Israelite, an ideology which presents the king as Primordial Man and reincarnation of the First King. This is also understood as the source for the use of Son of man in Dan. 7.13 and the Gospels.[14]

(94). Quoted according to the English translation, 'Wisdom, Son of Man, and the Origins of Christology: The Consistent Development of Biblical Theology', *Horizons in Biblical Theology* 3 (1981), pp. 23-57 (38).

11. Wolfgang Bittner, 'Gott—Menschensohn—Davidssohn. Eine Untersuchung zur Traditionsgeschichte von Daniel 7,13f.', *Freiburger Zeitschrift für Philosophie und Theologie* 32 (1985), pp. 343-72 (370-71). A similar conclusion was reached by G.R. Beasley-Murray, 'The Interpretation of Daniel 7', *CBQ* 45 (1983), pp. 44-58.

12. Above, in Excursus II in Chapter 12, we met some representatives of this understanding. To be added are: J.T. Nelis, 'De mysterieuze mensenzoonfiguur van het boek Daniël', *Het Heilig Land* 9 (1956), pp. 185-87; A.B. Rhodes, 'The Kingdom of Men and the Kingdom of God: A Study of Daniel 7:1-14', *Interpretation* 15 (1961), pp. 411-30 (428); E. Dhanis, 'De Filio hominis in Vetere Testamento et in iudaismo', *Gregorianum* 45 (1964), pp. 5-59 (15); J. Jensen, 'Son of Man', *The New Catholic Encyclopaedia*, XIII (1967), pp. 431-33.

13. Cf. below, the discussion of the religio-historical background. As a prominent representative, we here mention only Mowinckel, *He That Cometh*, p. 352.

14. See A. Bentzen, *Det sakrale Kongedømme. Bemærkninger i en løbende Diskussion om de gammeltestamentlige Salmer* (*The Sacral Kingship: Observations in a Continous Discussion about the Old Testament Psalms*) (1945), pp. 76-77, 95, 117, 118 n. 3; *idem*, 'Kan ordet "Messiansk" anvendes om Salmernes kongeforestillinger?' ('Is the Word "Messianic" to be Employed about the Concept of the King in the Psalms?'), *SEÅ* 12 (1947), pp. 36-50; *idem*, *Messias—Moses redivivus—Menschensohn* (1948), esp. pp. 12-13, 37-42 (in the English edition, *King and Messiah* [1955, 2nd edn, 1970], pp. 17-18, 39-47); *idem*, 'King Ideology—"Urmensch"—Troonbestijgingsfeest', *StTh* 3 (1950–51), pp. 143-57 (148-50); *idem*, *Daniel* (2nd edn, 1952), p. 63. I. Engnell, 'Adam. 1. *G.T.*', in *SBU*, I (1948), cols. 13-15 (= 2nd edn, 1962, cols. 18-21); *idem*, 'Människosonen. 1.

A single scholar assumed that '[t]here is much internal and external evidence to support and clarify a high priestly identification of the "one like a son of man"' in Dan. 7.13.[15] Thus, Crispin H.T. Fletcher-Louis assumes a temple setting and Day of Atonement focus for Daniel 7, where 'the High Priest plays the role of Baal to Yahweh's El in the *Chaoskampf* complex'.[16]

In a similar way, a few scholars point to *ben-adam* in the Psalms as at least one of the factors leading to or confirming a messianic interpretation of Dan. 7.13.[17] The book of Ezekiel has also received attention as part of the background.[18]

G.T.', *SBU*, II (1952), cols. 399-403 (= 2nd edn, 1963, cols 229-32). While Bentzen detects influence from the concept both of the Primordial Man and first created man from the Anthropos Myth, Engnell accepts a connection with the first mentioned only. See Engnell, 'Die Urmenschvorstellung und das Alte Testament', *SEÅ* 22–23 (1957–58), pp. 265-89. Cf. S. Mowinckel, 'Urmensch und "Königsideologie"', *StTh* 2 (1949–50), pp. 71-89 (71-75). For a rejection of the hypothesis that *ben-adam* should be a title in the Old Testament, cf. E. Sjöberg, 'Uttrycket "Människosonen" i Gamla Testamentet', *STK* 26 (1950), pp. 35-44. A more detailed discussion in M. Müller, *Messias og 'menneskesøn'* (1972), pp. 20-27. One of the few to follow Bentzen in this respect is F.H. Borsch (cf. above in Chapter 14).

15. Thus Crispin H.T. Fletcher-Louis, 'The High Priest as Divine Mediator in the Hebrew Bible: Dan 7:13 as a Test Case', *SBL 1997 Seminar Papers* (1997), pp. 161-93; *idem*, 'The Revelation of the Sacral Son of Man: The Genre, History of Religious Context and the Meaning of the Transfiguration', in Friedrich Avemarie and Hermann Lichtenberger (eds.), *Auferstehung—Resurrection* (2001), pp. 247-98 (257-61).

16. As formulated in the hypothesis to be proven in Fletcher-Louis, 'The High Priest as Divine', p. 168.

17. Thus, for instance, A. Gelston, 'A Sidelight on the "Son of Man"', *SJTh* 22 (1969), pp. 189-96, pointing to Ps. 80.18—for some reasons unknown to me it is v. 17 in English Bibles—claiming 'that its use in Ps. 80.17 of the king, later understood as the Messiah, paved the way for the later interpretation of Dan. 7,13 in messianic terms alike by Jesus and the Jews' (p. 196). David Hill, '"Son of Man" in Psalm 80 v. 17', *NT* 15 (1973), pp. 261-69, takes one step forward suggesting 'that what Ps. lxxx says of the king may itself contain, or could have been interpreted justifiably as containing, messianic overtones, apart altogether from the explicit targumic identification of the "son" (בן)' (p. 265). Cf. also B. McNeil, 'The Son of Man and the Messias: A Footnote', *NTS* 26 (1979–80), pp. 419-21. F.J.Moloney, 'The Re-Interpretation of Psalm VIII and the Son of Man Debate', *NTS* 27 (1980–81), pp. 656-72 (revised version of 'The Targum on Ps. 8 and the New Testament', *Salesianum* 37 [1975], pp. 326-36), proposes that the possible rendering of *enosh* and *ben-adam* in early targums was *bar nash* and 'that Ps. viii was, very early in the history of the reading of the Psalms in Aramaic, as later reflected in our Targum on the Psalms, interpreted in an individual, messianic direction' (p. 667). There may have existed Aramaic sources, 'which give us background for a messianic use of the term "Son of Man"' (p. 657). Lending weight to the possibility of influence from *ben-adam* in the Psalms is R.D. Rowe, 'Is Daniel's "Son of Man" Messianic?', in Harold H. Rowden (ed.), *Christ the Lord* (FS Donald Guthrie, 1982), pp. 71-96, and K. Koch, 'Das Reich der Heiligen und des Menschensohns. Ein Kapitel politischer Theologie', in *idem*, *Die Reiche der Welt und der kommende Menschensohn. Studien zum Danielbuch.* Gesammelte Aufsätze 2 (ed. Martin Rösel, 1995), pp. 140-72 (170), directly referring to Moloney.

A very sophisticated way of arguing for a messianic interpretation of Dan. 7.13 is found in a work in five volumes by Rollin Kearns, consisting of no fewer than ten different studies. The first six are published as *Vorfragen zur Christologie* I–III (1978–1982).[19] Through a morphological, semasiological, transmission-historical, reception-historical, religio-historical and traditio-historical study, Kearns attempts to show that Aramaic *brns* is not an equivalent of Hebrew *bn ᶜdm*, but became an epithet 'in the framework of an apocalyptic coloured structure of tradition for an eschatological exalted figure becoming epiphanious, an apocalyptic exalted figure (im Rahmen eines apokalyptisch geprägten Traditionsgefüges zum Epitheton eines eschatologisch epiphan werdenden Hoheitswesen, eines apokalyptischen Hoheitswesens geprägt [wurde])'.[20] The immediate background is a Palestinian pagan Hadad mythology, where *brns* could function as a predicate to Hadad in the meaning 'Lord of the world'. The Aramaic *brns* also could be equal to the indefinite pronoun, but not in an apocalyptic context like Dan. 7.13. In *1 En.* 46.1-3, it is also seen how it could be a title to be transferred to the elect, and in *4 Ezra* 13, this figure simply replaces Yahweh. What developed later is investigated in two studies on, respectively, the original shape of the Son of man tradition and the earliest changes within it.[21] Kearns finds the presupposition for the Gospel Son of man sayings partly in a non-titular use of the Aramaic *brns*, in the meaning of 'divinely empowered' and partly in a special apocalyptic tradition, where Son of man is a title (reflected in Mk 9.31; 13.26, and Mt. 24.27/Lk 17.24) with its background in the pagan Hadad mythology. Because of a false etymology, also implied in the Greek rendering ὁ υἱὸς τοῦ ἀνθρώπου, it ended up not only as a concept of transcendental-eschatological epiphany, but also as an epiphany to the world, where Son of man expressed the manifestation of the eschatological being, becoming eventually a human. The original Son of man tradition underwent a change, where, in Egyptian Judaism, it was identified with either the returning Elijah or a coming ruler, intervening for the Jews. This is the background of the aforementioned Son of man

18. Thus Jens Christensen, *Menneskesønnen* (1996), esp. pp. 40-42.

19. The full titles are: *Vorfragen zur Christologie I. Morphologische und Semasiologische Studie zur Vorgeschichte eines christologischen Hoheitstitels* (1978); *Vorfragen zur Christologie II. Überlieferungsgeschichtliche und Rezeptionsgeschichtliche Studie zur Vorgeschichte eines christologischen Hoheitstitels* (1980); *Vorfragen zur Christologie III. Religionsgeschichtliche und Traditionsgeschichtliche Studie zur Vorgeschichte eines christologischen Hoheitstitels* (1982). For a fuller exposition of Kearns argument, cf. Müller, *Der Ausdruck 'Menschensohn' in den Evangelien*, pp. 27-32: Excursus A: Rollin Kearns' Versuch nachzuweisen, daß es sich bei *bar nasch* in Dan. 7,13 um einen Beinamen für ein apokalyptisches Hoheitswesen handelt; *idem*, 'Betydningen af בר אנש i Dan. 7,13. En anmeldelsesartikel', *DTT* 47 (1984), pp. 177-86. An interesting discussion between Kearns and Carsten Colpe, reviewing *Vorfragen* I, is found in *ThRv* 77 (1981), cols. 373-78. In recent years, Kearns himself has published a series called *Mutmaßungen zur Christologie*, which reiterates his conclusions of the aforementioned 5 volume work; cf. esp. No. 2 (2003): *Ὁ υἱὸς τοῦ ἀνθρώπου als hoheitstitulares Wortgebilde* and No. 3 (2003): *Die Epiphanie des Menschensohnes in der Welt. Die transzendent-eschatologische Epiphanie des Menschensohnes*, and No. 5 (2006): *Die Historisierung des Traditionsgefüges um den Weltenherrn.*

20. Kearns, *Vorfragen* II, p. 3.

21. Kearns, *Das Traditionsgefüge um den Menschensohn. Ursprünglicher Gehalt und älteste veränderung im Urchristentum* (1986).

sayings and not the dependence on Daniel 7. Of the two last studies,[22] the first concentrates on how the Son of man tradition was connected with Jesus through the concepts of the innocent suffering a violent death, afterwards to be exalted, and the revelation of God's punishing dominion, the ruler of which appears as the Son of man. The second and longer one shows how these traditions separately were connected respectively with the fate of Jesus and his message, only secondarily to be combined in a unified picture of Jesus as the Son of man both acting on earth and appearing in the last days. This caused confusion where the original structures in the Son of man tradition faded away, the expression being used in sayings which had nothing to do with them. In this process, Son of man was changed into a prophetological title of honour (einen prophetologischen Würdetitel). All of the original meaning was lost in the actual Son of man sayings, as they function and are to be understood in the canonical Gospels. It is what Kearns himself calls 'a de-christologizising of the Son of man (eine Entchristologisierung des Menschensohnes)'.[23]

Another 'solution' based on—false—etymology also needs to be mentioned here: namely, the Swedish Old Testament scholar, Gillis Gerleman's attempt to prove that the Greek ὁ υἱὸς τοῦ ἀνθρώπου is not only a clumsy but a false translation of the Aramaic expression in Dan. 7.13 where *bar* in reality means something like 'separated from'.[24] Thus the meaning of *bar nasha* is 'separated from what is human', an understanding Gerleman sees confirmed in the New Testament in the names Barjesus (Acts 13.6) and Barjona (Mt. 16.17) respectively, which are to be understood as 'separated from salvation'[25] and 'separated from a (silly) dove'. The candidate for the meaning 'separated from what is human' is no other than King David. The meaning behind the expression is accordingly to depict Jesus as the *David redivivus*, a meaning also present in Dan. 7.13, which, therefore, is to be interpreted messianically.[26] Were such an interpretation true, this originally intended meaning must have disappeared nearly immediately the moment the text was written down, as it has left no trace whatsoever, only to be detected by a scholar c. 1900 years later.[27]

b. *The Symbolic Interpretation of Daniel 7.13*

In this period, a number of interpreters adhere to the symbolic understanding of the one like a Son of man in Dan. 7.13, even if some see it as an interpretation of a Son of man

22. Kearns, *Die Entchristologisierung des Menschensohnes. Die Übertragung des Traditionsgefüges um den Menschensohn auf Jesus* (1988).

23. I have offered a relatively large amount of space to this exposition since it is difficult to convey a fair impression of Kearns' complicated hypothesis with fewer words.

24. Gillis Gerleman, *Der Menschensohn* (1984).

25. Gerhard Svedlund, 'Notes on *bar nash* and the Detrimental Effects of Its Transformation into the Title "The Son of Man"', in Tryggve Kronholm and Eva Riad (eds.), *On the Dignity of Man* (FS Fridhiof Rundgren, 1986), pp. 401-13 (402), correctly notes that I have given a mistaken translation of *Barjesus* in M. Müller, 'Betydningen af בר אנש i Dan. 7,13', p. 184.

26. A more detailed description is found in M. Müller, 'Betydningen af בר אנש i Dan. 7,13', pp. 184-86.

27. Zdravko Stefanovic, 'The Use of the Aramaic Word *bar* ("son") as a Noun of Relation in the Book of Daniel', *Asia Advent Seminary Studies* 6 (2003), pp. 77-81, according to *OTA* 28 (2005), p. 341, points to the generalizing function of Aramaic *bar*, allowing Dan. 7.13 to mean 'like a member of the human family'.

concept.[28] Mowinckel claims that 'in the present form of Daniel's visions of the beasts, the Son of Man is a pictorial symbol of the people of Israel, not an individual figure, and not a personal Messiah of any kind'.[29] Erik Sjöberg thinks that it is too simple to say that Son of man is a symbol for the people of Israel or that the righteous are going to inherit the kingdom. Interpreted is not the Son of man himself, but his assumption of power. Thus, he represents the people in the moment of triumph.[30]

Matthew Black moves in the same direction in his interpretation of Dan. 7.13, when, without denying any connection between the Son of man and Iranian concepts, he asserts that 'Daniel's Son of Man is not mythology, but symbolic eschatology', where 'the Son of Man is the glorified Israel in the coming eschatological Israel'.[31] Later, Black proceeds one step further and speaks of the Son of man as the 'apotheosis of Israel'. Making use of a traditio-historical analysis of the Danielic vision from 1 Kgs 22.19-22; Isa. 6.1-6, and Ezek. 1.26-28; 2.1, he concludes that Daniel 7 knows of two manifestations of the godhead: the 'Ancient of Days' and the 'Son of Man'. A form-critical analysis of this pericope also confirms this understanding in regard to the throne-vision: Daniel 7 is not only reliant on Isaiah 6 (cf. *1 En.* 14) and Ezekiel 1 as theophanies, it also is an important development from these towards a theology that is virtually ditheistic. Compared with the interpretation of the vision where Daniel has undoubtedly understood the Son of Man as a symbol of the saints of the Most High, it is redeemed Israel, and it is correct that what Daniel has beheld is the apotheosis of Israel in the last days, a 'deification' of 'the saints of the Most High'.[32]

Other representatives in this period of symbolic understanding speak of the man-like in Dan. 7.13 in terms of 'a corporate personality'[33] or a 'representative figure'[34] or as a

28. Cf. the last part of Excursus C. Die symbolische Auslegung von Dan. 7.13 in Müller, *Der Ausdruck 'Menschensohn' in den Evangelien*, pp. 43-44.

29. Sigmund Mowinckel, *He That Cometh* (1956), p. 350 (= *Han som kommer* [1951], p. 229). Cf. also 'Ophavet til den senjødiske forestilling om Menneskesønnen', *NTT* 45 (1944), pp. 189-244 (189).

30. Erik Sjöberg, 'Människosonen och Israel', *Religion och Bibel* 7 (1948), pp. 1-16 (13).

31. Matthew Black, 'Unsolved New Testament Problems: The "Son of Man" in Old Biblical Literature', *ET* 60 (1948–49), pp. 11-15 (12 and 11).

32. Matthew Black, 'Die Apotheose Israels: eine neue Interpretation des danielischen "Menschensohns"', in R. Pesch and R. Schnackenburg (eds.), *Jesus und der Menschensohn* (FS Anton Vögtle, 1975), pp. 92-99 (98-99). Further *idem*, 'The Throne-Theophany Prophetic Commission and the "Son of Man": A Study in Tradition-History', in Robert Hamerton-Kelly and Robin Scroggs (eds.), *Jews, Greeks and Christians: Religious Cultures in Late Antiquity* (FS William David Davies, 1976), pp. 57-73. A similar view is represented by William Moulder, 'The Son of Man in the Old Testament and the Gospel Tradition' (typewritten thesis, St Andrews, 1973–74).

33. Thus, for instance, Norman Porteous, *Das Danielbuch* (1962), p. 91; D.S. Russell, *Method and Message of Jewish Apocalyptic* (1964), p. 327; Jean Burnier-Genton, *Le Rêve subversive d'un sage. Daniel 7* (1993), esp. Chapter 4, pp. 219-310.

34. Thus for instance Otto Plöger (1910–1999), *Das Buch Daniel* (1965), p. 113; M.D. Hooker, *The Son of Man in Mark* (1967), pp. 28-29; Otto Michel, 'ὁ υἱὸς τοῦ ἀνθρώπου', in *ThBNT*, III (2nd edn, 1972), pp. 1153-66 (1154) (revised by W. Grimm in a new edition [2000], pp. 1061-76 [1062-63]).

symbol of theocratic Israel.[35] One scholar contributing continuously to the debate, the Leuven Old Testament professor Joseph Coppens, finds 'the symbol of the Son of man in Dan. 7.13 to be an allusion at one and the same time to the coming of the kingdom of the angelic hosts and to the Jewish people regenerated through persecution'.[36] A 'simple' symbolical understanding also continues to have its adherents.[37]

c. *Other Interpretations of the Man-Like in Daniel 7.13*

The attempt to identify the man-like with a historical figure or an angel[38] was mentioned above,[39] where it was noted that Paul Haupt pleaded for an identity with Judas the Maccabean, while Moses Gaster found it to be with Moses. While the latter did not find any followers, the first suggestion was taken up again by Harald Sahlin[40] and G. Wesley

35. Thus, for instance, L.-M. Orrieux, 'Le problème du fils de l'homme dans la litterature apocalyptique', *LV* 12 (1963), pp. 9-31 (12-14); Norman Perrin, 'The Son of Man in Ancient Judaism and Primitive Christianity: A Suggestion', *BR* 11 (1966), pp. 17-28; quoted according to reprint in *idem*, *A Modern Pilgrimage to New Testament Christology* (1974), pp. 23-40 (27-28) ('That the figure is "one like the Son of Man" is probably a pure accident; any other cryptically designated figure would have served as well'); H. Haag, 'בן־אדם', in *ThWANT*, I (1973), cols. 682-89 (688); P. Grelot, 'L'intronisation du fils d'homme. Dn 7,13-14', *Assemblées du Seigneur* 65 (1973), pp. 30-55 (33); A. Deissler, 'Der "Menschensohn" und "das Volk der Heiligen des Höchsten" in Dan. 7', in R. Pesch and R. Schnackenburg (eds.), *Jesus und der Menschensohn* (FS Anton Vögtle, 1975), pp. 81-91 (91); A.A. Di Lella, 'The One in Human Likeness and the Holy Ones of the Most High in Daniel 7', *CBQ* 39 (1977), pp. 1-19 (practically identical with L.F. Hartman and A.A. Di Lella, *The Book of Daniel* [1978], pp. 85-102; cf. p. 218); M. Casey, *Son of Man in Daniel 7* (1979), pp. 7-50; Hans Bietenhard, ' "Der Menschensohn"—ὁ υἱὸς τοῦ ἀνθρώπου. Sprachliche und religionsgeschichtliche Untersuchungen zu einem Begriff der synoptischen Evangelien I. Sprachlicher und religionsgeschichtlicher Teil', in *ANRW* II 25.1 (1982), pp. 265-350 (313-17).

36. Joseph Coppens, *Le Fils d'homme vétéro- et intertestamentaire* (1983), p. 112.

37. For instance: W.O. Walker, 'Daniel 7:13-14', *Int* 39 (1985), pp. 176-81. Further Johannes Lubsczyk, 'Gott offenbart das Geheimnis seines Reiches im Kommen des Menschensohnes', in W. Ernst and F. Feiereis (eds.), *Denkender Glaube im Geschichte und Gegenwart* (FS aus Anlaß der Gründung der Universität Erfurt vor 600 Jahren und aus der Anlaß des 40jährigen Bestehens des Philosophisch-Theologischen Studiums Erfurt, 1992), pp. 216-46 (226-27); Othmar Keel, 'Die Tiere und der Mensch in Daniel 7', in Othmar Keel and Urs Staub, *Hellenismus und Judentum. Vier Studien zu Daniel 7 und zur Religionsnot unter Antiochus IV* (2000), pp. 1-35 (28-29). Keel, however, emphasizes that it is the contrast between animal and man which is the decisive moment in this and previous chapters, here taking over a concept from the otherwise despised Hellenism.

38. 'Excursus D. Versuche einer Identifizierung des Menschenähnlichen in Dan. 7,13 mit einer historischen Gestalt oder einem Engel', in M. Müller, *Der Ausdruck 'Menschensohn' in den Evangelien*, pp. 44-46.

39. Cf. Excursus II in Chapter 12.

40. Harald Sahlin, 'Antiochus IV. Epiphanes and Judas Mackabäus', *StTh* 23 (1969), pp. 41-68 (40). Later Sahlin, 'Wie wurde urspünglich die Benennung "Der Menschensohn" verstanden?', *StTh* 37 (1983), pp. 147-79, pleads for an identity with the archangel Michael, pointing to all the places in the Old and New Testament where angels are

Buchanan.[41] H. Schmid looks in another direction and points to the pseudonymous Daniel as a candidate.[42]

A great many scholars have attempted an identification of Daniel's Son of man with a heavenly being or an angel.[43] While a few have been precise in choosing the archangel Michael,[44] a sole interpreter, Ziony Zevit, has voted for Gabriel.[45]

depicted as men. He also assumes this meaning with respect to both *1 Enoch* and other Jewish and Christian literature as well as Jesus himself (cf. above Chapter 14).

41. G. Wesley Buchanan, *To the Hebrews* (1976), pp. 42-48.

42. H. Schmid, 'Daniel, der Menschensohn', *Judaica* 27 (1971), pp. 192-220 (219). In fact, Schmid seems to have a forerunner in Otto Plöger, *Theokratie und Eschatologie* (1959), p. 32. Plöger does not repeat this in his *Das Buch Daniel* (1965). Morna D. Hooker, *The Son of Man in Mark* (1967), p. 47, argues that when the author of the Similitudes in *1 Enoch* identifies the seer there with the Son of man, he 'was helped to this interpretation by his reading of the text of Daniel where Daniel in 8.17 is addressed as "son of man"'.

43. Earlier representatives of this understanding were H. Gressmann, *Der Ursprung der israelitisch-jüdische Eschatologie* (1905), p. 348, and F. Stier, *Gott und Engel im Alten Testament* (1934), p. 129. In our period we have: J. Coppens, *Le Fils de l'homme et les Saints du Très-Haut en Daniel* (1961), pp. 5-51 (12) = J. Coppens and L. Dequeker, *Le Fils de l'homme et les Saints du Très-Haut en Daniel, VII, dans les Apocryphes et dans le Nouveau Testament* (1961), pp. 55-101 (61); L. Dequeker, 'Wie is de mensenzoon?', *Collectanea Mechliniensia* 46 (= NS 31) (1961), pp. 407-17; *idem*, 'The "Saints of the Most High" in Qumran and Daniel', *OTS* 18 (1973), pp. 108-87; Bo Reicke, 'Menschensohn', *Biblisch-Historisches Wörterbuch*, II (1964), cols. 1191-92 (1192); C. Colpe, 'ὁ υἱὸς τοῦ ἀνθρώπου', in *ThWNT*, VIII (1969), p. 424; K. Müller, 'Beobachtungen zur Entwicklung der Menschensohnvorstellung in den Bilderreden des Henoch und im Buche Daniel', in Ch. Suttner and C. Patock (eds.), *Wegzeichen* (FS H.M. Biedermann, 1971), pp. 253-61 (259) (speaking about 'himmlischen Doppelgänger'); *idem*, 'Menschensohn und Messias', *BZ* NF 16 (1972), pp. 161-87; 17 (1973), pp. 52-66: 16 (1972), p. 177; *idem*, 'Der Menschensohn im Danielzyklus', in R. Pesch and R. Schnackenburg (eds.), *Jesus und der Menschensohn* (FS Anton Vögtle, 1975), pp. 37-80 (78); M. Müller, *Messias og 'menneskesøn'* (1972), p. 32 n. 58; M.-G. Bulteau, 'Le Fils de l'homme dans la littérature apocalyptique', *'Jésus'. Heritage et projet* 9 (1974), pp. 69-81 (73); D.R. Catchpole, 'The Angelic Son of Man in Luke 12:8', *NT* 24 (1982), pp. 255-25; Marc Girard, 'Le semblant de fils d'homme de Daniel 7, un personage du monde d'en haut: approche structurelle', *Science et Esprit* 35 (1983), pp. 265-96 (287-92); Johannes P. Floss, 'Menschensohn—Reich Gottes—Auferstehung im Buch Daniel', in Sigurd Martin Daecke and Peter R. Sahm (eds.), *Jesus von Nazareth und das Christentum* (2000), pp. 153-70 (161-62), where, however, the Son of man is only hinted at; Stefan Beyerle, 'Der mit den Wolken des Himmels kommt', in D. Sänger (ed.), *Gottessohn und Menschensohn* (2004), pp. 1-52 (51-52); *idem*, '"One Like a Son of Man": Innuendoes of a Heavenly Individual', in Gabriele Boccaccini (ed.), *Enoch and Qumran Origins: New Light on a Forgotten Connection* (2005), pp. 54-58.

44. An earlier representative was A. Bertholet, 'M[enschensohn] im AT und Judentum', *RGG*, IV (2nd edn, 1913), cols. 296-97. More recent spokesmen are H. Kruse, 'Compositio Libri Danielis et idea Filii Hominis', *Verbum Domini* 37 (1959), pp. 147-61, 193-211 (210); U.B. Müller, *Messias und Menschensohn in jüdischen*

A related question is the identity of the 'saints of the Most High' (Dan. 7.18, 22, 25) or 'the people of the saints of the Most High' (Dan. 7.27).[46] While the majority of interpreters think that the '(people of the saints) of the Most High' signifies God's people, Israel,[47] some have proposed that these saints indeed are heavenly beings.[48] A few have

Apokalypsen und in der Offenbarung des Johannes (1972), pp. 27-30; John J. Collins, 'The Son of Man and the Saints of the Most High in the Book of Daniel', *JBL* 93 (1974), pp. 50-66 (53); A. Lacocque, *Le Livre de Daniel* (1976), p. 103; John J. Collins, *The Apocalyptic Vision of the Book of Daniel* (1977), pp. 144-47; later *idem*, *Daniel* (1993), pp. 304-10 (Excursus: 'One Like a Human Being'); John Day, *God's Conflict with the Dragon and the Sea: Echoes of a Canaanite Myth in the Old Testament* (1985), pp. 167-77; Klaus Koch, 'Das Reich der Heiligen und des Menschensohns. Ein Kapitel politischer Theologie', in *idem*, *Die Reiche der Welt und der kommende Menschensohn. Studien zum Danielbuch* (ed. Martin Rösel, 1995), pp. 140-72 (162-64); Bruce Chilton, '(The) Son of (the) Man, and Jesus', in Bruce Chilton and Craig A. Evans (eds.), *Authenticating the Word of Jesus* (1999), pp. 259-87 (276); Matthias Albani, 'Der Menschensohn in Dan 7,13 und die Israelitische Königstheologie', *Leqach* 5 (2004), pp. 5-14; English version, 'The "One Like a Son of Man" (Dan 7:13) and the Royal Ideology', in Gabriele Boccaccini (ed.), *Enoch and Qumran Origins: New Light on a Forgotten Connection* (2005), pp. 47-53.

45. Z. Zevit, 'The Structure and Elements of Daniel 7', *ZAW* 80 (1968), pp. 385-96 (396), arguing from the identity with Gabriel in Dan. 9.21.

46. Cf. Excursus F. Die Diskussion über die Bezeichnung 'die Heiligen des Höchsten' in Dan. 7, in M. Müller, *Der Ausdruck 'Menschensohn' in den Evangelien*, pp. 63-65.

47. Thus, for instance, N.W. Porteous, *Das Danielbuch* (1962), p. 96; D.S. Russell, *The Method and Message of Jewish Apocalyptic 200 BC—AD 100* (1964), pp. 324-27; O. Plöger, *Das Buch Daniel* (1965), p. 113; C.H.W. Brekelmans, 'The Saints of the Most High and their Kingdom', *OTS* 14 (1965), pp. 305-29 (325-26, 329); M.D. Hooker, *The Son of Man in Mark* (1967), pp. 13-17; A. Caquot, 'Le quatre bêtes et le "Fils d'homme" (Daniel, 7)', *Semitica* 17 (1967), pp. 37-71 (60-62); M. Delcor, 'Les sources dy chapitre VII de Daniel', *VT* 18 (1968), pp. 290-312 (305); O. Michel, 'ὁ υἱὸς τοῦ ἀνθρώπου', in *ThBNT*, III (3rd edn, 1972), col. 1154; P. Grelot, 'L'intronisation du fils d'homme. Dn 7,13-14', *Assemblées du Seigneur* 65 (1973), pp. 30-35 (33); W.J. Dumbrell, 'Daniel 7 and the Function of Old Testament Apocalyptic', *RThR* 34 (1975), pp. 16-23 (21-22); G.F. Hasel, 'The Identity of "The Saints of the Most High" in Daniel 7', *Bib* 56 (1975), pp. 173-92 (190-92); A. Deissler, 'Der "Menschensohn" und "das Volk des Heiligen des Höchsten" in Dan 7', in R. Pesch and R. Schnackenburg (eds.), *Jesus und der Menschensohn* (FS Anton Vögtle, 1975), pp. 81-91 (91); V.S. Poytress, 'The Holy Ones of the Most High in Daniel VII', *VT* 26 (1976), pp. 208-13; A.A. di Lella, 'The One in Human Likeness and the Holy Ones of the Most High in Daniel', *CBQ* 39 (1977), pp. 1-19 (= L.F. Hartman and A.A. di Lella, *The Book of Daniel* [1978], pp. 85-102); M. Casey, *Son of Man* (1979), pp. 40-48.

48. This understanding is already present in H. Venema, *Dissertationes ad vaticinia Danielis emblematica Cp. II, VII, et VIII* (1745), p. 550. In various forms it is advocated by for instance by: O. Procksch, 'Der Menschensohn als Gottessohn', *Christentum und Wissenschaft* 3 (1927), pp. 425-43, 473-81 (429); *idem*, 'Christus im Alten Testament', *NKZ* 44 (1933), pp. 57-83 (80); R.H. Charles, *A Critical and Exegetical Commentary on*

assumed that the saints of the Most High designates both heavenly beings and the Jewish people: 'It is as civitas mundi already civitas dei'.[49]

d. *The Significance of* 1 Enoch 37–71 *and* 4 Ezra 13

The Son of man in *1 Enoch* 37–71 also attracted much interest during this period as a possible source or parallel to the Son of man sayings in the Gospels.[50] Three main possibilities prevailed. Either Son of man in the Parables[51] reflected a concept lying behind Dan. 7.13 as an independent witness, or the figure is drawn directly from Daniel's saying and, thus, was secondary to it. A third possibility is that the Enochic Son of man is dependent on the occurrence in the New Testament, either being the result of Christian interpolation or the expression of a Jewish counterpoint to the use of the expression Son of man about Jesus in the Gospels.

Of course there has been a parallel discussion about the date and provenience of the Parables. This discussion was animated by the fact that, whereas the other four books of *Enoch* were found among the Dead Sea Scrolls fragments, the Parables were conspicuous by their absence.[52] Thus we see attempts at a very late dating of the Parables, the latest

the Book of Daniel (1929), p. 187; M. Noth, '"Die Heiligen des Höchsten"', in *Interpretationes ad Vetus Testamentum* (FS Sigmund Mowinckel, 1955), pp. 146-61 (= *NTT* 56 [1955], pp. 146-61); reprint in *idem*, *Gesammelte Studien zum Alten Testament* (1957), pp. 274-90; J. Coppens, 'Le messianisme sapiental et les origins du Fils de l'homme danièlique', in M. Noth and Winton Thomas (eds.), *Wisdom in Israel and in the Ancient Near East* (FS H.H. Rowley, 1955), pp. 33-41; *idem*, *Le Fils de l'homme et les Saints du Très-Haut en Daniel* (1961), pp. 5-51 = J. Coppens and L. Dequeker, *Le Fils de l'homme et les Saints du Très-Haut en Daniel, VII, dans les Apocryphes et dans le Nouveau Testament* (1961), pp. 55-101; Coppens has reiterated this view in a series of contributions (cf. the bibliography), some of which were reprinted in *idem*, *le Fils d'homme vétéro- et intertestamentaire* (1983); H. Haag, 'בֶּן־אדם', in *ThWAT*, I (1973), pp. 682-89 (687-88); M.-G. Bulteau, 'Le Fils de l'homme dans la literature apocalyptique', *'Jesus'. Héritage et projet* 9 (1974), pp. 69-81 (75); P. Weimar, 'Daniel 7. Eine Textanalyse', in R. Pesch and R. Schnackenburg (eds.), *Jesus und der Menschensohn* (FS Anton Vögtle, 1975), pp. 11-36 (36); K. Koch, *Das Buch Daniel* (1980), pp. 234-39; *idem*, 'Das Reich der Heiligen und des Menschensohns. Ein Kapitel politischer Theologie', in *idem*, *Die Reiche der Welt und der kommende Menschensohn. Studien zum Danielbuch.* Gesammelte Aufsätze 2 (ed. Martin Rösel, 1995), pp. 140-72 (147-55); Marc Girard, 'Le semblant de fils d'homme de Daniel 7, un personage du monde d'en haut: approche structurelle', *Science et Esprit* 35 (1983), pp. 265-96 (284-87); J.J. Collins, *Daniel* (1993), pp. 313-18 (with the Excursus: 'Holy Ones').

49. R. Hanhart, 'Die Heiligen des Höchsten', in B. Hartmann (ed.), *Hebräische Wortforschung* (FS Walter Baumgartner, 1967), pp. 90-101 (100); J.J. Collins, 'The Son of Man and the Saints of the Most High in the Book of Daniel', *JBL* 93 (1974), pp. 50-66 (63); A. Lacocque, *le Livre de Daniel* (1976), p. 102.

50. Cf. Müller, *Der Ausdruck 'Menschensohn' in den Evangelien*, pp. 67-80.

51. For consistency, I use the designation 'Parables', not 'Similitudes'.

52. If *1 En.* 56.5-8 is seen as reflecting the Parthian intrusion in c. 40 BCE and the Parables are thus to be dated to the last decades of the first century BCE, their absence in the Qumran findings is easily explained if the hiding of the scrolls was, in fact, carried out during the unrest around 40 BCE as at least some scholars now think again.

being in the second half of the third century CE.[53] Others have suggested the first century CE[54] or the beginning of the second,[55] but more and more the *opinio communis* is the first century BCE[56] or, less precisely, the centuries around the beginning of Common Era,[57]

53. Thus J.T. Milik, 'Problèmes de la littérature Hénochique à la lumière des fragments araméens de Qumran', *HThR* 64 (1971), pp. 333-78; *idem*, *The Books of Enoch: Aramaic Fragments of Qumrân Cave 4* (with the collaboration of M. Black, 1976). The crucial question is the exact identity of the Parthian enemy in *1 En.* 56.5-8. Milik points to the victory of Sapur 1 over Valerian in 260 CE. Cf. the comment of Ch. Böttrich, 'Konturen des "Menschensohnes" in äthHen 37–71', in D. Sänger (ed.), *Gottessohn und Menschensohn* (2004), pp. 53-90 (57 n. 15): 'wieder einmal favorisiert Milik die am weitesten entfernte und unwahrscheinlichste Lösung'. In 'The "Parables" of Enoch (1 En 37-71) and the ‚Son of Man', *ET* 88 (1976–77), pp. 5-8, Black seems to be of the same opinion as Milik, but a little later, as 'a pleasant surprise', claimed a date 'from around A.D. 100'. Cf. J.H. Charlesworth, 'Seminar Report. The SNTS Pseudepigrapha seminars at Tübingen and Paris on the Books of Enoch', *NTS* 25 (1979), pp. 315-23 (321).

54. Ch.L. Mearns, 'The Parables of Enoch—Origin and Date', *ET* 89 (1977–78), pp. 118-19; *idem*, 'Dating the Similitudes of Enoch', *NTS* 25 (1979), pp. 360-69 (c. 40 CE); M.A. Knibb, 'The Date of the Parables of Enoch: A Critical Review', *NTS* 25 (1979), pp. 345-59 (end of first century CE); M. Jas, 'Henoch et le fils de l'homme. Datation du livre des paraboles pour une situation de l'origine du Gnosticisme', *La Revue Réformée* 30 (1979), pp. 105-19, prefers the first half of the first century CE, seeing Son of man in the Parables as an expression of Jewish polemic against Jesus as the Son of man.

55. Thus J.C. Hindley, 'Towards a Date of the Similitudes of Enoch', *NTS* 14 (1967–68), pp. 551-65 (around 115–117 CE).

56. Such is the case if *1 En.* 56.5-8 is seen as reflecting the Parthian intrusion c. 40 BCE: E. Hammershaimb, 'Første Enoksbog', in E. Hammershaimb *et al.* (eds.), *De gammeltestamentlige Pseudepigrafer*, I (1953–63), pp. 69-174 (74); G.H.P. Thompson, 'The Son of Man: The Evidence from the Dead Sea Scrolls', *ET* 72 (1960–61), p. 125 (first century BCE or earlier!); G. Bampfylde, 'The Similitudes of Enoch: Historical Allusions', *JSJ* 15 (1984), pp. 9-31 (c. 50 BCE); Ch. Böttrich, 'Konturen des "Menschensohnes"' (2004), p. 55-71 (around the beginning of the Common Era).

57. Thus Erik Sjöberg, *Der Menschensohn im äthiopischen Henochbuch* (1946), pp. 35-39, points to the times of Herod the Great, or Archelaos, but will not exclude the time of the first procurators. M. Casey, *Son of Man* (1979), p. 99: 'it should probably be dated *c.* 100 B.C.—A.D. 70, since its ideas can be made intelligible against the background of this period'. David Winston Suter, *Tradition and Composition in the Parables of Enoch* (1979), p. 32: 'between the last quarter of the first century B.C. and the fall of Jerusalem in A.D. 70'. Cf. *idem*, 'Weighed in the Balance: The Similitudes of Enoch in Recent Discussion', *Religious Studies Review* 7 (1981), pp. 217-21. Siegbert Uhlig, 'Das Äthiopische Henochbuch', *JSHRZ* 6 (1984), p 494: partly the end of first century BCE but with essential parts from the first decades CE; M. Black, 'The Messianism of the Parables of Enoch: Their Date and Contribution to Christological Origins', in James H. Charlesworth (ed.), *The Messiah: Developments in Earliest Christianity* (1992), pp. 145-68 (161-68), now pleads for the centuries around the turn of the millennia and for the Parables to contain pre-Christian Jewish traditions, although he will not rule out a Christian 'editing' of some of the Son of Man visions altogether; Ch. Böttrich, 'Konturen des "Menschensohnes" in äthHen 37–71', pp. 55-71 (58): the end of the first century BCE.

even if a few put it earlier.[58] The chronological argument speaks for dependence on Dan. 7.13, for which reason Son of man in the Parables should not be taken as an independent witness to a concept, lying behind the man-like in Daniel. Because the content of the Parables, with regard to the Son of man, can be made intelligible within Judaism in the centuries around the beginning of the Common Era, there is no reason for postulating Christian interpolations,[59] not to say a Jewish polemic against Jesus' or the Christian's use of the designation.[60] This is also in regard to *1 Enoch* 70–71, which is taken by some scholars to be a later addition. There is no compelling reason for this, as these chapters are very well understood when a structure is seen in the Parables that builds up to the identification of the Son of man as Enoch at the end of the Parables.[61]

The prevailing view is that the Son of man in the Parables represents a messianic interpretation of the man-like figure in Dan. 7.13 within Early Judaism.[62] Influential here

58. Thus Marco Treves, 'Le Fils de l'homme et le pontificat de Judas', *Cahiers du Cercle Ernest Renan* 112 (1979), pp. 147-51, identifying the Enochian Son of man with Judas the Maccabean.

59. Thus earlier (cf. Chapter 8 and Excursus II in Chapter 12, above) B. Bauer, A. Hilgenfeld, J. Drummond, W. Bousset (in 1892), J. Wellhausen, F. Buhl, E.G. Hirsch, D. Völter, N. Messel, G. Dupont. To this list now can be added: J.Y. Campbell, 'The Origin and Meaning of the Term of Son of Man', *JThS* 48 (1947), pp. 145-55 (147-48).

60. Thus Jas, 'Henoch et le fils de l'homme', p. 112. The Parables claim that not Jesus, but Enoch, is he Son of man. Also J.J. Collins, 'The Similitudes of Enoch', in *idem*, *The Apocalyptic Imagination: An Introduction to Jewish Apocalyptic Literature* (2nd edn, 1998), pp. 177-93 (191). The chapter is partly a reworking of the earlier article: 'The Heavenly Representative: The "Son of Man" in the Similitudes of Enoch', in J.J. Collins and G. Nickelsburg (eds.), *Ideal Figures in Ancient Judaism* (1980), pp. 111-33 (126). To be mentioned here also is S. Schreiber, 'Henoch als Menschensohn. Zur problematischen Schlußidentifikation in den Bilderreden des äthiopischen Henochbuches (äthHen 71,14)', *ZNW* 91 (2000), pp. 1-17 (11-14), however, only with regard to a late, anti-Christian redaction, altering a 'man' in 71.14 to Son of man and thus identifying Henoch with the Son of man.

61. As done conclusively by Morna D. Hooker, in her *The Son of Man in Mark* (1967), and confirmed by M. Casey, 'The Use of the Term "Son of Man" in the Similitudes of Enoch', *JSJ* 7 (1976), pp. 11-29 (19): 'M.D. Hooker, in a fine discussion of the problem, has at last enabled us to see the structure, with identification of the son of man figure as Enoch at the end'. Further, James C. VanderKam, 'Righteous One, Messiah, Chosen One, and Son of Man in *1 Enoch* 37–71', in James H. Charlesworth (ed.), *The Messiah. Developments in Earliest Christianity* (1992), pp. 169-91 (177-85).

62. Thus, besides U.B. Müller (cf. below), for instance—and for most of the scholars mentioned the same understanding is valid with regard to *4 Ezra* 13—J. Bowman, 'The Background of the Term "Son of Man" in the Old Biblical Literature', *ET* 60 (1948–49), pp. 11-15 (13-15); Pierre Grelot, 'Le Messie dans les Apocryphes de l'Ancien Testament. État de la question', in Édourd Massaux (ed.), *La Venue du Messie. Messianisme et Eschatologie* (1962), pp. 19-50; E. Dhanis, 'De Filio hominis in Vetere Testamento et in iudaismo', *Gregorianum* 45 (1964), pp. 5-59 (16-27); M.-G. Bulteau, 'Le Fils de l'homme dans la littérature apocalyptique', *'Jesus'. Héritage et projet* 9 (1974), pp. 69-81 (75-77); Johannes Theisohn, *Der auserwählte Richter* (1975), pp. 5-30; F.M. Wilson, 'The Son of Man in Jewish Apocalyptic Literature', *Studia Biblica et Theologica* 8 (1978), pp. 28-52

was Ulrich B. Müller's *Messias und Menschensohn in jüdischen Apokalypsen und in der Offenbarung des Johannes* from 1972. Müller finds that a Son of man concept first emerges in *1 Enoch* through the personification of God's intervention in the last days in the figure of 'the Elected' being connected with the man-like of Dan. 7.13. *1 Enoch* 48.10 and 52.4, where the designation 'the Anointed' was introduced, are isolated as secondary just as *1 Enoch* 71.[63] The same concept is found again in *4 Ezra* and *2 Baruch*, although there it is contaminated with messianic expectations.[64] It is also found in the Revelation of John, where ch. 12 is seen as a parallel to *1 Enoch* 71.[65] According to U.B. Müller, *1 Enoch* remains the only true witness to a special Son of man concept.

It has also been argued that just as the man-like in Daniel is interpreted as a collective, 'the saints of the Most High', the Enochic Son of man, being expressly connected with righteousness (46.3; cf. 38.2; 53.6), could be said to function not so much as a personification of the righteous community but 'as its heavenly *Doppelgänger*'. 'While the Son of Man is conceived as a real being, he symbolizes the destiny of the righteous community both in its present hiddenness and its future manifestation.'[66]

Of course the proclamation in *1 En.* 71.14 of Enoch to be the Son of man has caused keen interest. There is no need to understand the exaltation as identification with an already existing redeemer figure, as if the two here melted together into one.[67] The description does not mean that Enoch is exalted to a place near to the Messiah Redeemer as a reward for his righteousness,[68] because the address in 71.14 is an appellative and Son

(38-49); Barnabas Lindars, 'Enoch and Christology', *ET* 92 (1980–81), pp. 295-99; C.K. Beale, *The Use of Daniel in Jewish Apocalyptic Literature and in the Revelation of John* (1984), pp. 108-12; James C. VanderKam, 'Daniel 7 in the Similitudes of Enoch (*1 Enoch* 37–71)', in Charlotte Hempel and Judith Lieu (eds.), *Biblical Traditions in Transmission* (FS Michael A. Knibb, 2006), pp. 291-307.

63. Müller, *Messias und Menschensohn*, esp. pp. 38-43.

64. Müller, *Messias und Menschensohn*, pp. 107-55.

65. Müller, *Messias und Menschensohn*, pp. 157-216.

66. J.J. Collins, 'The Similitudes of Enoch', p. 187 (1980 version, p. 116). Referred to with sympathy by Ch. Böttrich, 'Konturen des "Menschensohnes" in äthHen 37–71', p. 84; also Collins, *Daniel* (1993), pp. 80-82. Cf. further M. Black, 'The Messianism of the Parables of Enoch: Their Date and Contribution to Christological Origins', esp. pp. 150-56, extends his thesis about Daniel's Son of man as an apotheosis of Israel also to pertain to Enoch's Son of man, seeing *1 En.* 71 likewise as a Throne-vision.

67. This view was earlier held by G. Beer, 'Das Buch Henoch', in E. Kautzsch (ed.), *Die Apokryphen und Pseudepigraphen des Alten Testaments*, II (1900), pp. 217-310 (277), seeing Enoch as the incarnated Son of man, and W. Bousset, *Die Religion des Judentums im späthellenistischen Zeitalter* (3rd edn, 1926), pp. 155-57, reckoning with mythical fusion. For R. Otto, see Chapter 12 above. Other earlier representatives are P. Volz, *Die Eschatologie der jüdischen Gemeinde im neutestamentlichen Zeitalter* (1934), p. 25; H. Ludin Jansen, *Die Henochgestalt* (1939), pp. 124-27. From the period after 1945 could be mentioned: E. Sjöberg, *Der Menschensohn im äthiopischen Henochbuch* (1946), pp. 147-89; C.P. van Andel, *De structuur van de Henoch-traditie en het Nieuwe Testament* (1955), *passim*; E. Hammershaimb, 'Første Enoksbog', pp. 127-29.

68. As assumed by S. Mowinckel, 'Henokskikkelsen i senjødisk apokalyptikk. Innlegg som 1ste ordinære opponent ved H. Ludin Jansens doktordsiputas. Specimen: Die Henochgetalt. Eine vergleichende religionsgeschichtliche Untersuchung, 1939', *NTT*

of man does not point back to the first occurrence in 46.1 as in all the other places in *Enoch*. Nor is it convincing that Son of man should be understood at precisely this place in the meaning 'man'; as a man, he is elevated to community with the Son of man.[69] It does seem as if Enoch (in 71.14) is proclaimed to be the Son of man he has seen in 46.1.[70] Whether this chapter has to be seen as primary to chs. 37–69 or whether the description of Enoch's journey to heaven is dependant on *1 En.* 14.8,[71] is of secondary

41 (1940), pp. 206-36 (209, 228-30); *idem*, 'Henok og "Menneskesønnen"', *NTT* 45 (1944), pp. 57-69; *idem, He That Cometh* (1956), pp. 437-44 (= *Han som kommer* (1951), pp. 284-88). Also J. Torris, 'Le Fils de l'Homme dans le Livre d'Henoch', *Bulletin de Cercle Ernest Renan* 91 and 92 (1962); M. Müller, *Messias og 'menneskesøn' i Daniels Bog, Første Enoksbog og Fjerde Ezrabog* (1972), pp. 55-57. I changed my mind in *Der Ausdruck 'Menschensohn' in den Evangelien* (1984), pp. 74-76, but in the process of translation into German, the meaning has become unclear (cf. n. 70 below). R.H. Charles, 'Book of Enoch', in *idem* (ed.), *The Apocrypha and Pseudepigrapha of the Old Testament* (1913), II, p. 237, supposes that a passage has been lost between 71.13 and 71.14 'wherein the Son of Man was described as accompanying the Head of Days and Enoch asked one of the angels (as in xlvi.3) concerning the Son of Man as to who he was' and translates v. 14 accordingly: 'and he (*i.e.* the angel) came to me and greeted me with his voice, and said unto me: "This is the Son of Man"...' It is easy to follow T.W. Manson, when he says: 'Here we abandon *Charles*, who has rewritten the rest of the passage in accordance with his view of what Enoch ought to have said.' See 'The Son of Man in Daniel, Enoch and the Gospels', *BJRL* 32 (1949–50), pp. 171-93; quoted according to reprint in *idem*, *Studies in the Gospels and Epistles* (1962), pp. 123-45 (139 n. 1).

69. Thus Mowinckel, *He that Cometh* (1956), p. 443 (= *Han som kommer* [1951], pp. 286-87); E. Isaac, '1 (Ethiopic Apocalypse of) Enoch', in J. Charlesworth (ed.), *The Old Testament Pseudepigrapha* (1983), I, pp. 5-89 (50); J.J. Collins, 'The Son of Man in First Century Judaism', *NTS* 38 (1992), pp. 448-66 (456); S. Schreiber, 'Henoch als Menschensohn', pp. 11-14, thinks this is the meaning in the original text, which, however, later has been altered in an attempt to wrest the Son of man from the Christians, whereas K. Luke, 'Enoch and the Son of Man', *Indian Theological Studies* 37 (2000), pp. 46-64 (62-64), concludes that this is also the meaning in the present text.

70. For instance, J.J. Collins, 'The Son of Man Who Has Righteousness', *SBLSP* 18 (1979), II, pp. 1-13 (5-8); *idem*, 'The Similitudes of Enoch', pp. 187-91 (1980 version, p. 116). Collins evaluates it as a secondary development; further, M. Müller, *Der Ausdruck 'Menschensohn' in den Evangelien*, pp. 72-76. Unfortunately, the meaning has been blurred in the German translation not least as a result of following Beer, 'Das Buch Henoch', in E. Kautzsch (ed.), *Die Apokryphen und Pseudepigraphen des Alten Testaments* (1900), II, p. 277, who renders the beginning of *1 En.* 71.14: 'Du bist der Mannessohn'. It should have been 'Menschensohn'. Also S. Uhlig, 'Das Äthiopische Henochbuch', p. 634; J.C. VanderKam, 'Righteous One, Messiah, Chosen One, and Son of Man in 1 Enoch 37–71', pp. 182-85; Daniel C. Olson, 'Enoch and the Son of Man in the Epilogue of the Parables', *JSP* 18 (1998), pp. 27-38.

71. This is the opinion, for instance, of M. Black, 'The Eschatology of the Similitudes of Enoch', *JThS* NS 3 (1952), pp. 1-10 (8-10); N. Perrin, 'The Son of Man in Ancient Judaism and Primitive Christianity: A Suggestion', *BR* 11 (1966), pp. 17-28, quoted according to reprint in *idem*, *A Modern Pilgrimage*, pp. 23-40 (28-30); *idem*, *Rediscovering the Teaching of Jesus* (1967), pp. 167-70.

interest compared with the fact that it is possible to view its content in an organic way, continuing and completing the three previous 'parables'.

The view that Son of man in *1 Enoch* 37–71 witnesses to a messianic interpretation of Dan. 7.13 within Judaism gains more and more ground. The assumption that it is a result of Christian influence[72] or interpolation is proportionately weakened.[73] The dependence on Daniel is Johannes Theisohn's conclusion in *Der auserwählte Richter. Untersuchungen zum traditionsgeschichtlichen Ort der Menschensohngetalt der Bilderreden des äthiopischen Henoch* (1975), in which it is claimed that the Parables reinterpret the man-like of the book of Daniel, identifying him with the elected and filling the Son of Man title with a concept that is new to the degree that the Parables begin their own Son of man tradition. Besides Daniel 7, traditions have come in especially from Ps. 110.1; Isa. 11, and 49 and Prov. 8.23-36, while the Judge-aspect has come to dominate.[74] 'By the reception of Daniel's son of man-tradition, the author has penetrated Daniel's interpretation and, with the identification of the man-like with the elected Judge, he has established a link to the pre-Danielic concept of Son of man as single eschatological figure. Through this identification, the Parables establish a new beginning for a particular Son of man-tradition.'[75]

The same view prevails with regard to *4 Ezra* 13, where the 'Man' is normally taken to be the result of a messianic interpretation of Dan. 7.13.[76] The thought that it should be a conscious reaction to a Christian use of Dan. 7.13 has found at least one adherent.[77] The earlier assumption that *4 Ezra* gave witness to two messianic conceptions with principally different origins, where, however, the interpretation identifies the Son of Man with the national Messiah, is decreasing in popularity.[78] The thesis that these texts, or one

72. The possibility that *1 En.* 71.14 reflects a Jewish reaction on the Christian employment of the 'title' Son of man for Jesus is evaluated positively by J.J. Collins, 'The Similitudes of Enoch', pp. 190-91 (1980 version, p. 126), and Bietenhard, '"Der Menschensohn"—ὁ υἱὸς τοῦ ἀνθρώπου' (cf. n. 35 above), pp. 317-27.

73. Cf. to he following the last part of Excursus E, 'Der Versuch der religionsgeschichtlichen Schule, die Grundlage des Menschenähnlichen in Dan. 7,13 in den Mythen von einem Urmenschen zu finden, sowie andere religionsgeschichtliche Deutungsversuche', in Müller, *Der Ausdruck 'Menschensohn' in den Evangelien*, pp. 54-58.

74. Theisohn, *Der auserwählte Richter*, esp. p. 51.

75. Theisohn, *Der auserwählte Richter*, p. 99. Part of Theisohn's thesis is that in the New Testament the author of Matthew is the first to introduce this Enochian Son of man tradition in the Gospel tradition (esp. Mt. 19.28; 25.31).

76. Thus, for instance, Howard C. Kee, '"The Man" in Fourth Ezra: Growth of a Tradition', *SBLSP* 20 (1981), pp. 199-208; C.K. Beale, 'The Problem of the Man from the Sea in IV Ezra 13 and its Relations to the Messianic Concept in John's Apocalypse', *NT* 25 (1983), pp. 182-88; cf. *idem*, *The Use of Daniel in Jewish Apocalyptic Literature and in the Revelation of John* (1984), pp. 139-44.

77. H. Bietenhard, '"Der Menschensohn"—ὁ υἱὸς τοῦ ἀνθρώπου' (cf. n. 35 above), pp. 327-32.

78. It is still advocated by Bent Noack, 'Fjerde Ezrabog', in E. Hammershaimb *et al.* (eds.), *De gammeltestamentlige Pseudepigrafer*, I (1953–63), pp. 1-68 (60-64); Michael Stone, 'The Concept of the Messiah in IV Ezra', in Jacob Neusner (ed.), *Religions in Antiquity: Essays in Memory of E.R. Goodenough* (1968), pp. 295-312; *idem*, *Fourth Ezra: A Commentary on the Book of Fourth Ezra* (1990), pp. 209-12, 382-84; Ulrich B.

of them, should be independent witnesses to a special Son of man expectation, widely represented in the beginning of the period, was gradually abandoned in the 1960s, thereafter, the hypothesis of the History of Religions School of a pre-Christian Gnostic redeemer-myth being found as untenable. This opened the field for other hypotheses about the origin of the imagery in Daniel 7.

The recognition of the Son of man—or as *4 Ezra* has it, 'the Man'—sayings in the Jewish apocalypses as the result of an interpretation of the man-like in Dan. 7.13 and especially the identification of an originally human being with a transcendent messianic redeemer was not impossible in Judaism, as can be confirmed through the Qumran-fragment 11QMelchizedek, where the legendary King Melchizedek is ascribed a role similar to Enoch's.[79]

e. *Other Sources?*

Besides the interpretation of Dan. 7.13 in the two pseudepigraphic apocalypses, other texts have been considered as possible sources for a Son of man expectation. Some have pointed to *Wisdom of Solomon* 1–6 and *2 Baruch*,[80] but attention has also been given to the *Testament of Abraham* 13, where Abel functions as judge. Some have seen this as a misunderstanding of an original Hebrew *ben adam*, which eventually could have been rendered Son of man, with regard to the man-like in Dan. 7.13.[81] Of course, the Dead Sea

Müller, *Messias und Menschensohn in jüdischen Apokalypsen und in der Offenbarung des Johannes* (1972), pp. 107-34; Josef Schreiner, 'Das 4. Buch Esra', in *JSHRZ* 4 (1981), p. 393. Bruce M. Metzger, 'The Fourth Book of Ezra', in James Charlesworth (ed.), *The Old Testament Pseudepigrapha* (1983), I, pp. 517-59, do not touch upon the problem.

79. Cf. A.S. van der Woude, 'Melchisedek als himmlische Erlösergestalt in den neugefundenen eschatologischen Midraschim aus Höhle XI', *OTS* 14 (1965), pp. 354-73; David Flusser (1917–2000), 'Melchizedek and the Son of Man (A Preliminary Note on a New Fragment from Qumran)', *Christian News from Israel* 17 (1966), pp. 23-29; reprint in *idem*, *Judaism and the Origins of Christianity* (1988), pp. 186-92: Flusser finds an influence from the Son of man concept on the Melchizedek-concept. See further M. de Jonge and A.S. de Woude, '11Q Melchizedek and the New Testament', *NTS* 12 (1965–66), pp. 301-26; J.A. Fitzmyer, 'Further Light on Melchizedek from Qumran Cave 11', *JBL* 86 (1967), pp. 25-41; F.L. Horton, *The Melchizedek Tradition* (1976), pp. 64-82; M.A. Knibb, 'The Date of the Parables of Enoch: A Critical Review', *NTS* 25 (1978–79), pp. 345-59 (352). Also S. Agourides, 'The Son of Man in Enoch', *Bulletin of Biblical Studies* 2 (1973), pp. 130-47, finds the Enochian Son of Man understandable inside Judaism (cf. report in *ZAW* 86 [1974], p. 357). Adela Yarbro Collins, 'The Origins of the Designation of Jesus as "The Son of Man"', *HThR* 80 (1987), pp. 391-407 (405), adds the picture of Moses in Ezekiel the Tragedian from about 200 BCE and in Philo's *De Sacrificiis Abelis et Caini* 9–10 (called *On the Birth of Abel* by Collins).

80. For instance G.W. Nickelsburg, 'Son of Man', in *ABD*, VI (1992), pp. 139-41.

81. Cf., for instance, R. Steve Notley, 'Abel, Jesus, and the Son of Man', *AAR/SBL Abstracts 2001* (2001), p. 37. Earlier Wolfgang Roth, 'Jesus as the Son of Man: The Scriptural Identity of a Johannine Image', in Dennis E. Groh and Robert Jewett (eds.), *The Living Text* (FS Ernest W. Saunders, 1985), pp. 11-26, arrived at a similar understanding with respect to the Gospel of John, although understanding *ben adam* as literally referring to Abel, the son of Adam (cf. also below Chapter 17).

Scrolls have also been scoured in this connection. John J. Collins has pointed to 4Q246 as evidence of an individual messianic interpretation of the man-like figure in Dan. 7.13.[82] This hypothesis has been met with both approval and disapproval.[83]

To be mentioned also is the reading of some Septuagint versions (Papyrus 967, Miniscule 88 and the Syro-Hexapla) in Dan. 7.13, which replace the ἕως before παλαιὸς ἡμερῶν παρῆν with ὡς with the apparent effect that Son of man is identified with the Ancient of Days.[84] This has caused some interpreters to postulate that this translation witnesses to a supernatural Son of man[85] or even Son of God.[86] Otfried Hofius has sought to dismantle this construction, connecting ὡς to παλαιὸς ἡμερῶν and claiming the meaning to be 'one like an ancient of days', 'one who looked like an ancient of days' and translating: 'and he who looked like an ancient of days was present'.[87] In this case, the

82. John J. Collins, 'The *Son of God* Text from Qumran', in M. de Boer (ed.), *From Jesus to John: Essays on Jesus and New Testament Christology* (FS M. de Jonge, 1993), pp. 65-82; a later version in *idem*, *The Scepter and the Star: The Messiahs of the Dead Sea Scrolls and Other Ancient Literature* (1995), pp. 154-72; *idem*, 'Jesus and the Messiahs of Israel', in Hubert Cancik, Hermann Lichtenberger and Peter Schäffer (eds.), *Geschichte—Tradition—Reflexion III. Frühes Christentum* (FS Martin Hengel, 1996), pp. 287-302 (292-96).

83. Thus J.D.G. Dunn, '"Son of God" as "Son of Man" in the Dead Sea Scrolls? A Response to John Collins on 4Q426', in S.E. Porter *et al.* (eds.), *The Scrolls and the Scriptures* (1997), pp. 198-210, contests the idea, while Géza Xeravitz, 'Does the Figure of the "Son of Man" have a Place in the Eschatological Thinking of the Qumran Community?', *Louvain Studies* 26 (2001), pp. 334-45, is positive in his conclusion (p. 345): '4Q246 is an important text, since it can reveal the transitional phase of a tradition. In this transition, the collective views of Daniel's "Son of Man" was interpreted individually as the eschatological ruler of the chosen people. The author of 4Q246 avoided the use of the title itself. Its meaning may have been well known in the Judaism of his time. But this author made a very important step towards forming the "Son of Man" figure present in 1Enoch, 4Ezra, and the New Testament.' Cf. further Karl A. Kuhn, 'The "One like a Son of Man" Becomes "the Son of God"', *CBQ* 69 (2007), pp. 22-42, arguing that the author of the Gospel of Luke (1.32-35) took over this interpretation in his account of Jesus' birth.

84. For a detailed analysis of all textual and interpretational aspects, see Otfried Hofius, 'Der Septuaginta-Text von Daniel 7,13-14. Erwägungen zu seiner Gestalt und Aussage', *ZAW* 117 (2005), pp. 73-90 (for a refutation, see Klaus Koch, 'Der "Menschensohn" in Daniel', *ZAW* 119 [2007], pp. 369-85).

85. Thus earlier W. Bousset and H. Gressmann, *Die Religion des Judentums im späthellenistischen Zeitalter* (3rd edn, 1926 = 4th edn, 1966), pp. 264-65: 'Spuren von der Annahme eines präexistenten Messias'. Later, for instance, F.F. Bruce, 'The Oldest Greek Version of Daniel', in H.A. Brongers *et al.* (eds.), *Instruction and Interpretation* (1977), pp. 22-40 (25-26); M. Hengel, '"Setze dich zu meiner Rechten!" Die Inthronisation Christi zur Rechten Gottes und Psalm 110,1', in M. Philonenko (ed.), *Le Trône de Dieu* (1993), pp. 108-94 (159-60).

86. Thus Seyoon Kim, *The 'Son of Man' as the Son of God* (1983), pp. 22-25.

87. Hofius, 'Der Septuaginta-Text von Daniel 7,13-14', pp. 85-86. As examples of a misunderstood rendering, Hofius (p. 84 n. 56) mentions my *Der Ausdruck 'Menschensohn' in den Evangelien*, p. 19, and L.T. Stuckenbruck, '"One like a Son of Man as the Ancient of Days" in the Old Greek Recension of Daniel 7,13: Scribal Error or

Septuagint version of Dan. 7.13 is not a preformation of what is found in the New Testament christological interpretation.[88]

f. *The Quest for the Religio-Historical Background of the Son of Man*[89]

(1) *The hypothesis of a connection with the myth of Primordial Man, and/or the Gnostic 'redeemed Redeemer'.* Representative of much critical scholarship immediately following the Second World War is the work of the Norwegian Old Testament professor Sigmund Mowinckel (1884–1965). In an article from 1944, his contribution characteristically consists of a summary and screening of the research hitherto.[90] Mowinckel's article is, in fact, a prepatory work to his influential monograph of 1951, *Han som kommer*, which appeared in 1956 in the English edition, *He that Cometh*. (For the sake of convenience, I quote from the English translation.) Mowinckel's point of departure is that 'the Messiah and the Son of Man have no common origin, not even in the royal ideology of the ancient east'.[91] In the discussions, 'thought has concentrated more and more on the widespread oriental conceptions of the divine, Primordial Man, "the god Anthropos", a figure of varying importance in a number of Hellenistic religions and religio-philosophical systems'.[92] A detailed description of the most important features in the figure of

Theological Translation', *ZAW* 86 (1995), pp. 268-76, although in a Greek translation of this article in *DBM* 15 (1996), pp. 8-14.

88. The conclusion in Aileen Guilding, 'The Son of Man and the Ancient of Days', *EvQ* 23 (1951), pp. 210-12, that the answer of Jesus in Mk 14.62, in accordance with the Septuagint reading of Dan. 7.13, concurs with 'a claim to be one with God' (p. 211), therefore, seems without basis. For further discussion, see J. Lust, 'Daniel 7,13 and the Septuagint', *EThL* 54 (1978), pp. 62-69, Casey, *Son of Man*, p. 132. The case for influence from the Septuagint reading is stronger in Rev. 1.13-14. However, in 'The Textual History of the Septuagint-Daniel and Theodotion-Daniel', in John J. Collins and Peter W. Flint (eds.), *The Book of Daniel* (2001), pp. 586-607 (591), Alexander A. Di Lella argues that the Septuagint reading should not be dismissed too easily as a deliberate corruption of ἕως τοῦ παλαιοῦ. Not included by Di Lella is the article of Stuckenbruck mentioned in the previous note, '"One like a Son of Man as the Ancient of Days" in the Old Greek Recension of Daniel 7,13', which also hesitates to dismiss the Septuagint reading as being merely a scribal error and raises 'the question of whether the theological activity, coordinating the "ancient of days" with "one like a son of man", cannot be observed on the level of translation itself' (p. 276). With Hofius' reading, a dismissal is not even needed.

89. Cf. again Jürg Eggler, *Influences and Traditions Underlying the Vision of Daniel 7:2-14: The Research History from the End of the 19th Century to the Present* (2000), esp. pp. 55-110.

90. Sigmund Mowinckel, 'Ophavet til den senjødiske forestilling om Mennesкesønnen', *NTT* 45 (1944), pp. 189-244. Already in his *Thronbesteigungsfest Jahwäs und der Ursprung der Eschatologie. Psalmenstudien II* (1922), p. 305, Mowinckel had touched upon the Son of man problem declaring that it was of mythological origin and originally had nothing directly to do with a Messiah, but was only related to him.

91. Mowinckel, *He that Cometh*, p. 421 (= *Han som kommer*, p. 273). Cf. for the whole section, 'The Origin of the Conception of the Son of Man', pp. 420-37 (= *Han som* kommer, pp. 273-84), the article 'Ophavet til den senjødiske forestilling om Menneskesønnen', which provides a short summary of the research appearing in the later book.

92. Mowinckel, *He that Cometh*, p. 422 (= *Han som kommer*, p. 273).

Anthropos and in the Son of Man and a comparison between them 'put it beyond doubt that they are akin to each other or, more precisely, that they have common roots. Anthropos and the Son of Man both go back to the myths about the Primordial Man.'[93] Thus, according to Mowinckel,

> the figure of the Son of Man in later Judaism may be regarded as a new, specifically Jewish variant of a widespread, oriental, Hellenistic type, which readily combines in itself features from the 'god Anthropos' and the Primordial Man as found in the most diverse religions and systems, and which may also reflect the influence of other divine or mythical figures alongside features from the Old Testament and from genuine Jewish tradition.[94]

The conclusion of this analysis was that there was an essential difference between Messiah and Son of Man, which was never quite eliminated. This made it possible that the expression Son of Man pointed to a heavenly universal redeemer figure, which basically differed from the earthly national expectation of a Messiah. Mowinckel shared a common interest with a lot of interpreters when he saw a deliberate dissociation from the political-national Messiah behind the occurrence of the expression in the mouth of Jesus.

The list of adherents to the hypothesis that Dan. 7.13 witnesses to the influence of the concept of the Primordial Man in Early Judaism, no matter whether Daniel's saying is seen as a direct or indirect testimony to a Son of man expectation differing from the common messianic expectation, is long and includes Erik Sjöberg,[95] R. Bultmann, Johannes Munck,[96] Walter Schmithals, Oscar Cullmann,[97] Heinz Eduard Tödt,[98] Hans-Friedrich Weiss,[99] Ferdinand Hahn[100] and F.H. Borsch.[101]

Here I will concentrate on Bultmann as a representative of the History of Religions School and Walter Schmithals as an extreme spokesman for the same trend, allowing Borsch, who has produced the most recent comprehensive effort to understand the Son of man problem from the background of the history of religions, summarize what he understood as the result of such an analysis. In *Das Urchristentum im Rahmen der antiken Religionen* from 1949, Bultmann claims that instead of the Messiah as the national king in Late Judaism

93. Mowinckel, *He that Cometh*, p. 431 (= *Han som kommer*, pp. 279-80).

94. Mowinckel, *He that Cometh*, pp. 431-32 (= *Han som kommer*, p. 280).

95. Erik Sjöberg, *Der Menschensohn im äthiopischen Henochbuch* (1946), esp. p. 192.

96. Johannes Munck, 'Menneskesønnen', *Illustreret Religionsleksikon*, II (1950), p. 572.

97. Oscar Cullmann, *Die Christologie des Neuen Testaments* (1957, 2nd edn, 1963), pp. 139-54 = *The Christology of the New Testament* (1959), pp. 137-52.

98. Heinz Eduard Tödt, *Der Menschensohn in der synoptischen Überlieferung* (1959, 2nd edn, 1963), pp. 19-28 = *The Son of Man in the Synoptic Tradition*, pp. 22-31.

99. Hans-Friedrich Weiss, 'Menschensohn', *RGG*, IV (3rd edn, 1960), cols. 874-76.

100. Ferdinand Hahn, *Christologische Hoheitstitel. Ihre Geschichte im frühen Christentum* (1963, 2nd edn, 1966), pp. 20-23 = *The Titles of Jesus in Christology* (1969), pp. 19-21.

101. F.H. Borsch, see below, n. 105.

> there emerges a new figure, the supernatural agent of redemption who is to appear at the end of the days to inaugurate the new age. This figure bears the enigmatic title, 'Man'. He is a figure of cosmic eschatology, the archetypal man as the head of a new humanity (der Urmensch als Inaugurant einer neuen Menschheit), entering first into Judaism from the East, and thence penetrating westwards until he is found eventually in the Fourth (Messianic) Eclogue of Vergil. It is possible that the same conception underlies the picture of the Man coming on the clouds of heaven in Dan. 7.13, though there it is transformed into the embodiment of the people of Israel. In later Jewish apocalyptic writings the 'Man' combined the functions of Judge and agent of redemption, thus becoming a rival of God himself. Hence we may easily understand how the figures of the Messiah and the 'Man' coalesced in the Synoptic Gospels.[102]

Walter Schmithals follows the same line of thought when he writes in his controversial *Die Gnosis in Korinth* (1956) that the hymn lying behind Dan. 7.13 obviously concerns the Messiah, but the designation '*barenash*' for the Messiah points to Gnostic influence. This allows for the inference that

> the messianic views of our text are alone understandable, when there exists in the background a myth in which the expected eschatological Saviour in Judaism was identified with the Gnostic Primordial Man, with a Babylonian stamp; that is, with the Primordial Man already residing in heaven. At the latest, at the end of the third pre-Christian century, the Jewish form of the Gnostic redeemed Redeemer is to be demonstrated. It must have been widespread as it also influenced orthodox Judaism.[103]

Both *1 Enoch* 37–71 and *4 Ezra* 13 presuppose, according to Schmithals, 'a Jewish Gnosticism with Messiah–Son of man speculation'. This does not suggest a direct Gnostic influence. 'But the figure of a Man turning up at the Judgment, interpreted as pre-existent Son of God, must be traced to a Jewish-gnostic Son of Man–Messiah; that is, to a Redeemer that also possessed anthropogonic significance.'[104]

F.H. Borsch, in *The Son of Man in Myth and History* from 1967, the last to propose a comprehensive religio-historically grounded solution to the Son of man problem, concludes with regard to Dan. 7.13 that

> there is no need to trace all this to any one source, be it Babylonian, Iranian, Israelite, Ugaritic, Tyrian or Canaanite. Daniel was probably influenced by one source more than others, but the reference is too brief to permit exactitude. Our point is this: around the year 176 BCE there was known to the

102. Bultmann, *Das Urchristentum*, pp. 95-96. Quoted according to the English translation, *Primitive Christianity in its Contemporary Setting* (1956, 2nd edn, 1960), p. 102. In *Die religionsgeschichtliche Schule* (1961), p. 57, Carsten Colpe says of Bultmann: 'Er zog die Summe aus der komplizierten Forschungen der Schule verständlicher, als ihre Vertreter es vermocht hatten'.

103. Walter Schmithals, *Die Gnosis in Korinth* (1956), Excursus II: Der erlöste Erlöser, pp. 82-134 (100-104). The quotation is from p. 101.

104. Schmithals, *Die Gnosis in Korinth*, p. 103. In the 2nd edn of 1965 (= 3rd edn, 1969), this whole Excursus has disappeared.

> author of Daniel (and very likely to many of his readers) a kind of ideogram of an idealized, semi-divine, royal figure who would rule in the great age to come. He could be described as being 'like a son of man'. This manner of speaking may well have had at least a quasitechnical background, but Daniel himself may only be thinking of a grand conception, of a Man-like hero, a heavenly king who would rule over all the earth.[105]

In 1961, Carsten Colpe, in his seminal *Die religionsgeschichtliche Schule. Darstellung und Kritik ihres Bildes vom gnostischen Erlösermythus*, contested the whole attempt to understand the Son of man figure as a result of an adaption of a known Oriental myth of Primordial Man. According to Colpe, it is simply building on sand when synthetic conclusions are drawn on the basis of analogies. As he formulates it:

> Not every analogy contains a genealogy (Nicht jede Analogie enthält eine Genealogie). Older research was inclined to place as much as possible on genealogies, but this research did not suppress the differences between conceptions which should hang together, but offered material and opinions together with their theses, with the help of which the intended religio-historical evidence of continuity could be refuted. A critical view of the material offered by researchers invites doubt by itself; for instance, the connections between Gayomard and the Manichaean Primordial Man, between Son of Man and the soul of the World, Son of Man and Primordial Man, 'Arian cosmogony' and 'Gnostic Redeemer-myth'. We should be on guard against every equivocation which in older research has caused comparisons to be mixed and manifold overlapping genetic connections to be identified. We should not bring together all text-witnesses as if they were modifications of the same already existing, but often only tacitly presupposed, 'Oriental Myth of Primordial Man' and explain the differences as the result of a shorter or longer lapse of time in the history of the myth or of the peculiarity of the actual religious community employing it. In this way, one can explain everything.[106]

Later, in his similarly influential article, 'ὁ υἱὸς τοῦ ἀνθρώπου', in the *Theologisches Wörterbuch zum Neuen Testament*, VIII (1969), Colpe summarizes as follows:

> The historical findings (Der religionsgeschichtliche Befund) warn us against putting too much stress on the human form of the figure at issue. This applies also to the crystallisation of the concept in the description 'as a man' in Da(niel), where the angels are also presented in human form... [O]ne may assume, not that traditions of a cosmic heavenly macroanthropos, a protoplast put in the end-time, or an archetypal primal man was adopted, but rather that Jewish apocalyptic itself had been fruitful in developing the figure of the Son of Man.[107]

105. F.H. Borsch, *The Son of Man in Myth and History* (1967), p. 143.

106. Colpe, *Die religionsgeschichtliche Schule*, pp. 195-96. Cf. esp. Chapter 4: 'Richtiges und Problematisches am Modell "gnostischer Erlösermythus" und an den Formel "Urmensch-Erlöser" und 'Erlöster Erlöser', pp. 171-93. Cf. *idem*, 'New Testament and Gnostic Christology', in Jacob Neusner (ed.), *Religions in Antiquity: Essays in Memory of E.R. Goodenough* (1968), pp. 227-43.

107. *ThWNT*, VIII (1969), p. 422. Quoted according to the English translation in *ThDNT*, VIII (1972), pp. 419-20. Further *idem*, 'Der Begriff "Menschensohn" und die

The effect of Colpe's *Die religionsgeschichtliche Schule* is felt, for example, in *Der Gott 'Mensch' in der Gnosis* from 1962 by Hans-Martin Schenke. He states that the myth of the 'redeemed Redeemer' did not exist before Manichaeism, and for this reason it cannot serve to explain the Son of man.[108] Instead, Schenke sees the background of the concept in a certain version of the myth of the Primordial Man. This myth of Primordial Man and Paradisic King had already influenced common messianology and eschatology in Israel. According to the thought-scheme of 'beginning of time and end of time (Urzeit-Endzeit)' the picture of the time of salvation was painted with the colours of Paradise. In a period where the Danielic king no longer meant anything and where God was removed from contact with this world, the thought arose that the time of salvation did not only mean the return to Paradise, but also of its king, the first man, as representative of God. 'One could now understand the eschatological figure either as returning Adam or as the first manifestation of the prototype of exactly this Adam, which would explain the concept of pre-existence combined with the Son of man figure.'[109]

A similar reticence towards the Gnostic myth is seen in the work of Egon Brandenburger, who contends that Son of man has nothing to do with the first man, Adam or Primordial Man, but points instead to the heavenly man known for instance in Philo.[110] Kurt Rudolph declares that 'a unified so-called "oriental myth of Primordial Man" (orientalischer U[rmensch]mythos), as postulated by R. Reitzenstein, among others, does not exist'.[111]

(2) *The attempt to understand Daniel 7.13 as the result of a process inside Israel.* Besides the hypothesis of a connection between the Son of man and an oriental myth of Primordial Man or Gnostic Redeemer, this period sees scholars trying to explain the figure in Dan. 7.13 primarily from Old Testament presuppositions. Thus, T.F. Glasson finds Daniel fully understandable because of the implication of *1 Enoch* 14, which, in his conviction, stems from pre-Maccabean times.[112] Ivan Engnell will not deny a connection

Methode der Erforschung messianischer Prototypen', *Kairos* NF 11 (1969), pp. 241-63; 12 (1970), pp. 81-112; 13 (1971), pp. 1-17; 14 (1972), pp. 141-257, esp. 11 (1969), pp. 241-63.

108. Cf. Hans-Martin Schenke, *Der Gott 'Mensch' in der Gnosis* (1962), p. 148.

109. Schenke, *Der Gott 'Mensch' in der Gnosis*, pp. 151-52.

110. Egon Brandenburger, *Adam und Christus. Exegetisch-religionsgeschichtliche Untersuchung zu Röm. 5,12-21 (1. Kor. 15)* (1962), pp. 131-39.

111. Kurt Rudolph, 'Urmensch', *RGG*, VI (3rd edn, 1962), cols. 1195-97 (1195). Later the same reluctance to claim Gnostic influence earlier is also seen in A.J.N. Wedderburn, 'Philo's "Heavenly Man"', *NT* 15 (1973), pp. 310-26; Charles H. Talbert, 'The Myth of a Descending-Ascending Redeemer in Mediterranean Antiquity', *NTS* 22 (1976), pp. 418-39.

112. Cf. T.F. Glasson, *The Second Advent: The Origin of the New Testament Doctrine* (1945, 2nd edn, 1947), p. 14; cf. pp. 16-17, where it is also said: 'It does not follow from this that the writer of Daniel vii identified the one like unto a son of man with Enoch; he merely drew upon the imagery of the earlier work in depicting this symbolic figure, which in his vision represents "the people of the saints of the Most High"'. Further *idem*, 'The Son of Man Imagery: Enoch xiv and Daniel vii', *NTS* 23 (1976–77), pp. 82-90, where Glasson sees his conclusion confirmed through the findings from Qumran. A critical evaluation of this can be found in J. Coppens, 'La Vision de Très-haut en

between the Son of man and Primordial Man, but understands the latter as the first created man, otherwise presuming that the influence from this concept of Primordial Man is channelled through the ideology of so-called sacral kingship. According to Engnell, the only thing distinguishing the perceived sacral royal figure from the Son of Man is emphasis on an eschatological aspect.[113]

André Feuillet follows another path and sees the background of the man-like in Dan. 7.13 primarily in Ezek. 1.26-27, Daniel's Son of man being a sort of visible manifestation of the invisible God. For this reason, clouds in the Bible normally accompany theophanies. Indeed, they are reserved for theophanies. When angels appear, clouds are absent.[114] Feuillet sees Ezekiel as a counterpart to Gen. 1.26-27, where man is created in the image of God, while in Ezek. 1.26-27, the divine glory takes the shape of a human being. As the first world had as its point of departure humanity bearing divine resemblance, the new world will in principle see the divine glory carrying the form of a human, the connection to Genesis also offering a universal perspective.[115] The question of how this transformation of the traditional messianic expectation came about, Feuillet answers by pointing to the conceptions found in Jewish speculations about wisdom.[116] This last reference is

Dan., VII et Hén.éthiop. XIV', *EThL* 53 (1977), pp. 187-89, pointing to Ezek. 1.4-28 as a possible background.

113. See the references given above (n. 14). Further 'Människosonen', *SBU*, II (1952), pp. 399-403 (= 2nd edn, 1963), pp. 229-32. English in *idem*, *Critical Essays on the Old Testament* (1970), pp. 237-41, where it is also said (p. 241, in the original, respectively p. 402 and p. 232): 'Although the sources available to us are sporadic and weak, they are sufficient to let us see that the origin of the idea of the Son of Man came from within Israel and was ancient, and to let us hypothetically reconstruct its development. At first, the emphasis was predominantly positive, but with a minor negative aspect. As time went on, this negative feature with its emphasis on suffering became more and more prominent. Later, the nationalistic aspect again came to prevail, along with the emphasis on eschatology and the development of the heavenly aspect of the Son of Man (which was present from the very beginning) into the concept of transcendence.' A similar derivation from an internally Jewish source is advocated by H. Riesenfeld, *Jésus transfiguré* (1947), pp. 63-65; *idem* 'The Mythological Background of New Testament Christology', in W.D. Davies and D. Daube (eds.), *The Background of the New Testament and its Eschatology* (FS Charles Harold Dodd, 1954, 2nd edn, 1964), pp. 81-95. Later also W. Wifall, 'Son of Man—A Pre-Davidic Social Class?', *CBQ* 37 (1975), pp. 331-40, sees a connection between Son of man and king ideology. Thus Wifall thinks he is able to substantiate (p. 332) 'that the expression "Son of Man" had been associated with royal traditions in Palestine even prior to the Davidic monarchy in Jerusalem', and 'although the term has followed a long trajectory from 2d millennium B.C. to the NT, it consistently reflected its "messianic" origins in both the OT and late Jewish apocalyptic'. With regard to H. Gese's attempt to establish a connection between Son of Man and Davidic kingship ideology, see above in this Excursus, Section A: 'The Messianic Interpretation of Daniel 7.13'.

114. André Feuillet, 'Le Fils de l'homme de Daniel et la tradition biblique', *RB* 60 (1953), pp. 170-202, 321-46 (187).

115. Cf. Feuillet, 'Le Fils de l'homme de Daniel et la tradition biblique', p. 190.

116. Cf. Feuillet, 'Le Fils de l'homme de Daniel et la tradition biblique', pp. 321-41; *idem*, 'Fils de l'homme', *Catholicisme*, IV (1956), cols. 1295-302.

followed up by James Muilenberg in regard to Daniel's Son of man, asking whether we may 'not be dealing here with an apocalypticized and mythologized wisdom?'[117]

Somewhat in the same understanding as Feuillet, H.R. Balz wants to compare the description of the theophany in Ezek. 1.26-27 and the traditions building therefrom with the thinking of hypostases so characteristic in Late Judaism. We see a splitting up of the gods (Götterspaltungen), where the scattered functions of God often become independent personifications.[118] What the apocalypticist has done in Daniel 7 was then to combine the transcendent elements of the speculation about the elevated reign of God in heaven with eschatological elements in the prophetic-apocalyptic expectation of salvation.[119] On this basis, Balz does not wish to speak of a Son of man title nor of a contoured concept. Although he sees a conjoining of the Son of man tradition with the messianic concept, he, nonetheless, assumes the existence of a special eschatological 'Man' in Jewish apocalyptic performing as 'a hypostasized expression, turned into a figure of the eschatological action of God himself (ein hypostasierter und ins Bildhafte gewendeter Ausdruck für das endzeitliche Handeln Gottes selbst)'.[120]

Before leaving this sub-section,[121] it should be mentioned that some find Son of man in Daniel to be understood in analogy with other Old Testament sayings containing the (Hebrew) expression, especially Ps. 80.18-20,[122] but also Ps. 8.5 and Job 25.4-6 (15.14-16).[123]

(3) *The Canaanite hypothesis.* In 1958, two scholars independently pointed to Canaanite mythology as it had become known through findings from Ras Shamra (Ugarit) as the possible background of the figurative language in Daniel 7. Earlier parallels had been assumed, but Leonhard Rost was the first to introduce them in connection to the Son of man scene in Dan. 7.9-10, 13-14, comparing it with the mythological Ras Shamra texts which describe how an older god gave power over to a younger deity. The books mentioned in Dan. 7.10, in analogy to Est. 6.1-3 (with its books of memorable deeds and

117. James Muilenberg, 'The Son of Man in Daniel and the Ethiopic Apocalypse of Enoch', *JBL* 79 (1960), pp. 197-209 (209). In opposition to Feuillet, Muilenberg has great sympathy for the various attempts to find the background of the 'Son of man' in the neighbouring religions. After all, it was a syncretistic age.

118. Cf. H.R. Balz, *Methodische Probleme der neutestamentlichen Christologie* (1967), p. 87.

119. Cf. Balz, *Methodische Probleme der neutestamentlichen Christologie*, p. 95.

120. Balz, *Methodische Probleme der neutestamentlichen Christologie*, p. 111.

121. With regard to the attempt of Chrys C. Caragounis in *The Son of Man: Vision and Interpretation* (1986) to see Daniel's Son of Man as the result of a process inside Israel, cf. below in this chapter.

122. For instance, Glasson, *The Second Advent*, p. 38; C.H. Dodd, *According to the Scriptures: The Substructure of New Testament Theology* (1952), p. 117: 'There is a clear analogy with the "Son of Man" of Ps. lxxx and Dan. vii, which speak of Israel, under the similitude of a human figure, humiliated into insignificance until visited by God and raised to glory'. The connection between Dan. 7 and Ps. 80 is conceived in quite another way than by Bentzen and Engnell (cf. above, n. 14).

123. For instance, A.A. Di Lella, 'The One in Human Likeness and the Holy Ones of the Most High in Daniel 7', *CBQ* 39 (1977), pp. 1-19 (14-18) (practically identical with L.F. Hartman and A.A. Di Lella, *The Book of Daniel* [1978], pp. 98-102).

chronicles), could indicate that it concerned an official reward. The old god, El, designates his successor, Baal, in the same way as David installs Solomon.[124] However, there is no reason not to suppose that the author of the book of Daniel here made foreign material serve his purpose, much as he has done in other places of his book. John A. Emerton looks in the same direction for the source of the pictures of Daniel 7, but arrives at more far-reaching conclusions. Inspired by A. Bentzen's utilization of S. Mowinckel's ritual of enthronement as a background for Daniel 7, he considered the chapter 'an eschatological form of the situation at that festival'.[125] Taking up a suggestion from Feuillet regarding the clouds, he concludes that the coming of the Son of man is a theophany of Yahweh, the Son of man having taken over Yahweh's role at the enthronement festival. 'There are good grounds for believing that the enthronement of the Son of man by the aged deity goes back to Canaanite myth and ritual and that behind this figure of the Son of man lies Yahweh, and ultimately Baal.'[126]

Julian Morgenstern is also to be mentioned in this context, although he thinks 'that the immediate antecedent of the divine figure, the "one like a human being", was the Tyrian god, Melcart, while the antecedent of "the Ancient of Days" was the other major Tyrian deity, the reciprocal form of this one, composite Tyrian national god, Ba'al Shamem'.[127] However, not even Morgenstern was able to maintain this fantastic hypothesis, not to mention the even more fantastic consequences which he drew from it.[128]

In the following period the Canaanite hypothesis, formulated by Rost and Emerton gained a hearing, not least by C. Colpe,[129] M. Müller[130] and Rollin Kearns,[131] although others might also be mentioned.[132] For various reasons, it was contested by A.J. Ferch,

124. Leonhard Rost, 'Zur Deutung des Menschensohnes in Daniel 7', in *Gott und die Götter* (FS Erich Fascher, 1958), pp. 41-43; reprint in *idem*, *Studien zum Alten Testament* (1974), pp. 72-75.

125. John A. Emerton, 'The Origin of the Son of Man Imagery', *JThS* NS 9 (1958), pp. 225-42 (231) (reprint in Austin Farrer [ed.], *The Communication of the Gospel in New Testament Times: Some Recent Studies* [1961], pp. 35-56).

126. Emerton, 'The Origin of the Son of Man Imagery', p. 242.

127. Julian Morgenstern, 'The "Son of Man" of Daniel 7,13 f: A New Interpretation', *JBL* 80 (1961), pp. 65-77 (75).

128. Cf. Morgenstern, *Some Significant Antecedents of Christianity*, pp. 61-80 (64), where Morgenstern totally abandons his earlier interpretation—however, only to propose a new and, if possible, even more fantastic one. Cf. above, p. 327.

129. Colpe, 'ὁ υἱὸς τοῦ ἀνθρώπου', pp. 418-22, where it is called 'eine tragfähige Hypothese'; cf. *idem*, 'Der Begriff "Menschensohn" und die Methode der Erforschung messianischer Prototypen', *Kairos* NF 12 (1970), pp. 110-12.

130. Müller, *Messias og 'menneskesøn'*, pp. 34-41, and *Der Ausdruck 'Menschensohn' in den Evangelien*, pp. 60-63

131. Kearns, *Vorfragen zur Christologie III* (1982), pp. 3-82.

132. As, for instance, K. Schubert, 'Die Entwicklung der eschatologischen Naherwartung im Frühjudentum', in *idem* (ed.), *Vom Messias zum Christus* (1964), pp. 1-54 (37-38); Norman Perrin, 'The Son of Man in Ancient Judaism and Primitive Christianity: A Suggestion', *BR* 11 (1966), pp. 17-28. Quoted according to reprint in *idem*, *A Modern Pilgrimage*, pp. 23-40 (27). Further *idem*, *Rediscovering the Teaching of Jesus* (1967), p. 166, where Perrin had had the opportunity to see Colpe's manuscript of the *ThWNT* article; Frank M. Cross, *Canaanite Myth and Hebrew Epic* (1973), p. 17 (according to

who thinks that it is far-fetched to see parallels between Daniel 7 and the mythological concepts of the Ras Shamra texts. He follows the suggestion of Claus Westermann that particularistic comparison never produces parallels, because parallels are only possible where on both sides of the parallel connections can be shown. Even if 'the apocalyptic S(on of) M(an) and Ancient of Days may share some rather remote resemblances with Baal and El...and the visionary scene of judgment succeeds that of the beasts, these incidental correspondences are outweighed by significant differences'.[133] This is not due to 'creative freedom' on behalf of the author of Daniel 7, 'for so many modifications have to be assumed that there would be no difference between proposing an extremely fertile creativity of the apocalyptist and a discontinuity between Ugarit and Daniel 7... Once the single parallel term is studied in its total context a discontinuity between Ugarit and Daniel 7 suggests itself.'[134] Perhaps the sharp alternative demanded between parallel and non-parallel is misleading. What is rather at stake is a certain use of a metaphor more or less loosened from its original setting and content. As C. Colpe remarks:

> it was exclusively the process of taking over dominion (Herrschaftsübernahme), in whatever way it was described in the mythological fragment employed in Dan. 7.9-10, 13-14, which made this text suitable to the author of the first Daniel-vision as a conclusion of the exaltation (Überhöhung) of the realms of earthly governments. His motivation to do so did not come from the content of this tradition. This was prevented already by the incongruence of the Canaanite gods and Israelite God, but from the apocalyptic understanding of history, the beginning of which...had other causes.[135]

Ferch [see below], p. 76); J.J. Collins, *The Apocalyptic Vision of the Book of Daniel* (1977), pp. 99-104; later *idem*, *Daniel* (1993), after a longer discussion of 'The Religio-historical Background', pp. 280-94, again reaches this understanding. See further Day, *God's Conflict with the Dragon and the Sea* (1985), pp. 157-67; Bernhard Lang, 'Der monarchische Monotheismus und die Konstellation zweier Götter im Frühjudentum: Ein neuer Versuch über Menschensohn, Sophia und Christologie', in W. Dietrich and M.A. Klopfenstein, *Ein Gott allein? JHWH-Verehrung und biblischer Monotheismus im Kontext der israelitischen und altorientalischen Religionsgeschichte* (1994), pp. 559-64, however, primarily interested in the tradition of two gods.

133. A.J. Ferch, 'Daniel 7 and Ugarit: A Reconsideration', *JBL* 99 (1980), pp. 75-86 (85-86). The reference is to C. Westermann, 'Sinn und Grenze religionsgeschichtlicher Parallelen', *ThLZ* 90 (1965), cols. 490-96 (490-91).

134. Ferch, 'Daniel 7 and Ugarit: A Reconsideration', p. 86.

135. C. Colpe, 'Der Begriff "Menschensohn" und die Methode der Erforschung messianischer Prototypen', *Kairos* NS 12 (1970), p. 111. Cf. p. 82 where it is claimed that 'paradoxer Weise ein Weg zur Aufstellung neuer Bezüge dann frei wird, wenn man den horizontalen Zusammenschluß der Motive, der wegen seiner Direktheit verführerisch, aber ein methodologischer Kurzschluß ist, vermeidet und einen Rückbezug des jeweiligen Überlieferungskomplex auf die historische Situation an seine Stelle setzt. Divergenzen stören dann nicht mehr die intendierte Verwandtschaftstheorie, und Übereinstimmungen bekommen ein anderes Gewicht: als ihr Hintergrund steht dann nicht mehr ihre literarische oder traditionsgeschichtliche Fixiertheit da, sondern ein anthropologisches und vielleicht sozialpsychologisches Referenzsystem, das seinerseits zu untersuchen wäre'. Cf. the debate between Wellhausen and Gunkel referred to above in Excursus II.

Paul G. Mosca believes he has found the missing link between Canaanite mythology and Daniel 7; namely, the adoption of that myth in Psalm 89, where the reign is given to David, while in Psalm 8 we find the 'Son of man' as king. It was here that the author of Daniel found it ready-made for his use. The interpretations in Psalm 89 and Psalm 8 of the mythic pattern reaching back to Bronze Age Canaan serve 'as a sort of *praeparatio danielica*'.[136]

This also pertains to the next attempt to detect the background of Daniel's vision in ancient mythology; namely, that of Helge Kvanvig, looking to an old Akkadian vision, which presumably 'opens up a completely new horizon for understanding Dan 7 and the "son of man"'.[137] The most recent larger investigation by Andrew R. Angel finds the Hebrew *Chaoskampf* tradition, existing between 515 B.C. and 200 C.E., integral to the development of Jewish and Christian apocalyptic, forming an important part of the background for the development of the apocalyptic Son of man figure.[138]

***

The deconstruction of a specific mythological background for the man-like in Daniel and the Son of man/Man in *1 Enoch* 37–71 and *4 Ezra* 13 respectively, became, as a natural consequence, the 'exit of the apocalyptic Son of man' as a figure significantly different from the Messiah. A last attempt to save a specific Son of man concept can be seen in C. Colpe's effort, when, with respect to the meagre Jewish apocalyptic material, he admits:

> In view of this, we are driven to the conclusion that Jewish apocalyptic material does not provide an answer to the crucial question as to the incipient shape of the NT Son of Man concept in Judaism between 50 B.C. and 50 A.D. Even allowing, then, for the circular argument of exegesis and history, one must conclude that the oldest stratum of the Synoptic tradition suggests a Jewish Son of Man tradition which provisionally constitutes a fourth source alongside those already mentioned.[139]

136. Paul G. Mosca, 'Ugarit and Daniel 7: A Missing Link', *Bib* 67 (1986), pp. 496-517 (517).

137. Announced in the 'preliminary report' of 'a forthcoming study' in 'An Akkadian Vision as Background for Dan 7?', *StTh* 35 (1981), pp. 85-89. This study appeared in 1988 as *Roots of Apocalyptic. The Mesopotamian Background of the Enoch Figure and the Son of Man*. Amar Annus, 'Ninurta and the Son of Man', in R.M. Whiting (ed.), *Mythology and Mythologies: The Neo-Assyrian Text Corpus Project* (2001), pp. 7-17, also looks for the roots of the Son of man in Mesopotamian sources, especially in the figure of Ninurta becoming king of the universe with the victory over the forces of chaos. This understanding also pertains to Son of man used about David in the psalms. '[I]n the New Testament the Son of Man is explicitly equated with the Messiah (Mk 8:29-31)' (p. 13).

138. *Chaos and the Son of Man. The Hebrew Chaoskampf Tradition in the Period 515 BCE to 200 CE* (2007). Cf. *NTA* 51 (2007), pp. 413-14.

139. Colpe, 'ὁ υἱὸς τοῦ ἀνθρώπου', pp. 431-32; quoted according to the English translation in *ThDNT*, VIII (1972), p. 429.

In the years to follow, some scholars still adhere to the notion of the existence of a Jewish Son of man taken over by Jesus, though it is only the later community which identifies Jesus himself with this figure with the help of sayings, where Son of man is used with the meaning 'man'.[140]

2. *Exit the Apocalyptic Son of Man*

Norman Perrin (1920–1976) was among the first to question what had nearly become a consensus concerning the existence of an apocalyptic Son of man. He arrived at the conclusion that Son of man Christology has its origin exclusively in early Christianity. In an article from 1966, Perrin claims that 'there is no "Son of man concept", but rather a variety of uses of Son of Man imagery'. It 'is not restricted to Jewish apocalyptic and the New Testament, but continues on into the midrashic traditions'. The result of a brief examination of the Jewish material led Perrin to the conclusion that

> What we have is not the conception of the coming of a transcendent, sovereign figure, the heavenly redeemer, the Son of Man. There is no sufficient relationship between the use of the Son of Man in 1 Enoch and 4 Ezra for us to suppose that they are both reflections of a common conception. What we have is the imagery of Dan 7:13 being used freely and creatively by subsequent seers and scribes. These uses are independent of one another. The common dependence is upon Dan 7:13, on the one hand, and upon the general world of apocalyptic concepts, on the other.[141]

Perrin sees the beginning in an interpretation of the resurrection belief taking its point of departure from Ps. 110.1. This resulted in the preaching of the risen as 'Lord' (Aramaic *mar*; cf. 1 Cor. 16.22) and in an interpretation attached to Dan. 7.13, resulting in an understanding of the resurrection as exaltation to God.[142] Alongside this, another exegetical tradition turned up,

140. Thus for instance Georg Strecker, *Theologie des Neuen Testaments* (ed. F.W. Horn, 1996), pp. 273-75; cf. pp. 296-98, where it is stated (p. 298) that: 'Der Menschensohnbegriff ist...die zentrale christologische Prädikation der Urgemeinde; ihre Christologie ist eigentlich eine Menschensohnchristologie'.

141. Norman Perrin, 'The Son of Man in Ancient Judaism and the Primitive Christianity: A Suggestion', *BR* 11 (1966), pp. 17-28 (26). Quoted according to reprint in *idem*, *A Modern Pilgrimage*, pp. 23-40 (33). Cf. also the earlier work of Perrin, *The Kingdom of God in the Teaching of Jesus* (1963). This view is then unfolded by Perrin in *Rediscovering the Teaching of Jesus* (1967), pp. 164-73, and in a series of subsequent articles: 'Mark XIV.62: The End Product of Christian Pesher Tradition?', *NTS* 12 (1965–66), pp. 150-55; 'The Son of Man in the Synoptic Tradition', *BR* 13 (1968), pp. 3-25; 'The Creative Use of the Son of Man Tradition by Mark', *USQR* 23 (1968), pp. 357-65; all four articles are reprinted in *idem*, *A Modern Pilgrimage*, respectively pp. 23-40, 10-22, 57-83, 84-93; further *idem*, 'Son of Man', in *IDBSup* (1976), pp. 833-36.

142. The idea of an interaction between Ps. 110.1 and Dan. 7.13 in the interpretation and description of the resurrection and elevation of Jesus is developed further by, for

interpreting the crucifixion from the background of Zech. 12.10-12, and, through another use of Dan. 7.13, added the expectation of a Parousia. It is this 'particular form of the *maranatha* expectation which we call the apocalyptic Son of Man expectation',[143] the reminiscences of which are to be found in the New Testament which was developed by the author of the Gospel of Mark into what we today in the New Testament Gospels meet as Son of man Christology. This understanding of the Son of man in the Gospels, which sees it as the outcome of the exegetical work of earliest Christianity, interpreting the resurrection of Jesus in the light of the Old Testament, is taken up in the following years by a number of scholars.[144] Paul Winter, in oft-quoted words from a review of Perrin's *Rediscovering the Teaching of Jesus* (1967), states: 'If P(errins)'s interpretation of the Son of Man sayings in the Synoptic Gospels is right—and it is supported by Vermes'...study of the linguistic use of the word "bar-nash(a)" in Jewish Aramaic—then the place of origin of the myth must be sought neither in Iran nor in Judea, nor even in Ugarit, but in German universities'.[145]

J.C. O'Neill also supposes an interplay between a non-terminological use of the expression by Jesus himself and its use as a christological title in connection with Dan. 7.13, in the preaching of the community to create 'an explicit dominical teaching about the enthronement and Second Coming'.[146] O'Neill sees Son of man Christology as the result of a Christian exegetical tradition and not as the adoption of an existing concept.

instance, Terrence Callan, 'Psalm 110:1 and the Origin of the Expectation that Jesus Will Come Again', *CBQ* 44 (1982), pp. 624-26, but not least in Donald Juel, *Messianic Exegesis: Christological Interpretation of the Old Testament in Early Christianity* (1988), esp. pp. 135-79.

143. Perrin, *A Modern Pilgrimage*, p. 59.

144. For instance R.A. Edwards, 'The Eschatological Correlative as a Gattung in the New Testament', *ZNW* 60 (1969), pp. 9-20; Hendrikus de Boers, 'Where Christology is Real: A Survey of Recent Research on New Testament Christology', *Interpretation* 26 (1972), pp. 300-27 (310-15); William O. Walker, 'The Origin of the Son of Man Concept as Applied to Jesus', *JBL* 91 (1972), pp 482-90; further *idem*, 'The Son of Man Question and the Synoptic Problem', *NTS* 28 (1982), pp. 374-88, where Walker makes use of the evidence to 'prove' the Griesbach hypothesis. Morna D. Hooker, 'The Son of Man and the Synoptic Problem', in F. van Segbroeck, C.M. Tuckett, G. van Belle and J. Verheyden (eds.), *The Four Gospels 1992* (FS Frans Neirynck, 1992), I, pp. 189-201, is a rebuttal of this (Walker's earlier 'The Kingdom of the Son of Man and the Kingdom of the Father in Matthew: An Exercise in *Redaktionsgeschichte*', *CBQ* 30 [1968], pp. 573-79, is not relevant in this context); O.F.J. Seitz, 'The Future Coming of the Son of Man: Three Midrashic Formulations in the Gospel of Mark', *SE* 6 (= *TU* 112, 1973), pp. 478-94.

145. Paul Winter, Review of Perrin's *Rediscovering the Teaching of Jesus* (1967), *Deutsche Literaturzeitung* 89 (1968), cols. 783-85 (784).

146. J.C. O'Neill, 'The Silence of Jesus', *NTS* 15 (1968–69), pp. 153-67 (161).

Independently of Perrin, but no less effective in initiating the new understanding, was the Norwegian scholar Ragnar Leivestad (1916–2002), who published two seminal articles 1968 and 1971/2, the first of which carries the title 'Der apokalyptische Menschensohn ein theologisches Phantom',[147] the second being a sort of summary of the first, 'Exit the Apocalyptic Son of Man'.[148] Leivestad contested the possibility of speaking of a distinct Son of man concept in Judaism which Jesus or the early community could have employed. Originally a pupil of Mowinckel, Leivestad was brought up with the idea of a heavenly Son of man having taken over the role of Messiah in certain circles inside Judaism.[149] He now arrives at the conclusion that 'the Son of man title is a modern invention. A Jewish Son of man title was completely unknown to Jesus and the primitive Church'.[150] Leivestad formulates his main thesis as follows: 'The designation Son of man in its original use by Jesus and the primitive Christian tradition, was never intended or understood as an independent "messianic" title'. Leivestad himself concentrates his arguments in nine points, the order here being chiefly a matter of coincidence:

1. A titular application of the term Son of man has not been established in contemporary Jewish literature.
2. The Son of man has no place in Christian confessions of faith; the term is not used as a predicate.
3. There is no christological application of the term *ben adam* or its Greek equivalent in quotations from the Old Testament.
4. The designation is almost exclusively used by Jesus.
5. The designation is irrelevant to 'the messianic secret'.
6. There does not exist a single saying that makes sense solely on the supposition that the 'Son of man' was a Jewish title.
7. There are several sayings that only make sense on the supposition that 'Son of man' was *not* a title.
8. In cases where it is formally possible to take 'Son of man' as a designation of someone different from Jesus, such a possibility has apparently never occurred to anyone. No precautions have been taken to prevent misunderstanding.

147. Published in *ASThI* 6 (1968), pp. 49-105. A short Norwegian version is 'Er den apokalyptiske menneskesønn en moderne teologisk opfinnelse?', *NTT* 70 (1969), pp. 221-35.

148. Published in *NTS* 18 (1971–72), pp. 243-67.

149. Thus in his doctoral thesis, published as *Christ the Conqueror: Ideas of Conflict and Victory in the New Testament* (1954), pp. 9-11.

150. Ragnar Leivestad, 'Exit the Apocalyptic Son of Man', pp. 244-45, from which the following thesis and nine points are also quoted. The reference in 'Der apokalyptische Menschensohn' is to pp. 96-97. In Leivestad's text, the text of the thesis is italicized.

9. Although the postulated apocalyptic Son of man is meant to be a heavenly figure connected with supernatural power and glory, the Son of man in the Gospels is often connected with earthly lowliness, with suffering and death, without any emphasis on the newness and paradoxicality of this application.

Leivestad will not deny that Dan. 7.13-14 exercised 'a profound influence on the messianic expectations before the Christian era', though he does not believe 'that it gave rise to a messianic Son of man designation.' Thus 'the meaning of the term Son of man can only be defined from within the New Testament, and the Son of man problem is merely one aspect of the quest for the historical Jesus'. The historical Jesus, when making 'a statement or a prediction about himself, his vocation, his destiny and fate, is inclined to use a periphrasis'.[151] However—as seen above in Chapter 14—according to Leivestad, Son of man in the mouth of Jesus was not merely a circumlocution. In those sayings which are most likely to be authentic, 'the Son of man is not a pretentious designation but a humble one, denoting solidarity and identification with the sons of men... The self-designation is an evidence of his self-dedication to men.'[152]

The situation now changed and two alternatives prevailed. The first was between claiming the existence of a pre-Christian Son of man concept or accepting Leivestad's position denying this possibility. The other was between accepting a circumlocutional meaning of the expression even in the New Testament Gospels or seeing it constituting there a specific Christian Son of man title.

In the years to follow, a number of scholars consented to the position of Leivestad, accepting the 'exit of the apocalyptic Son of man'—often combined with the acceptance of the evidence of the second Aramaic stage. Thus some of the same names turn up once again.[153] Leivestad's thesis, with

151. Leivestad, 'Exit the Apocalyptic Son of Man', pp. 264-65; cf. 'Der apokalyptische Menschensohn', p. 99.

152. Leivestad, 'Exit the Apocalyptic Son of Man', p. 267; cf. 'Der apokalyptische Menschensohn', p. 102-103.

153. In addition, see L. Gaston, *No Stone on Another* (1970), p. 335; B. Lindars, 'The Re-Enter of the Apocalyptic Son of Man', *NTS* 22 (1975–76), pp. 52-54, but clearer in his later contributions, among them also 'Jesus as Advocate: A Contribution to the Christology Debate', *BJRL* 62 (1979–80), pp. 476-97; M. Casey, *Son of Man* (1979), p. 139; J.D.G. Dunn, *Christology in the Making: An Inquiry into the Origins of the Doctrine of Incarnation* (1980, 2nd edn, 1985), pp. 82-97; *idem*, 'Messianic Ideas and Their Influence on the Jesus of History', in James H. Charlesworth (ed.), *The Messiah: Developments in Earliest Judaism and Christianity* (1992), pp. 365-81 (369-70); 'The Danielic Son of Man in the New Testament', in John J. Collins and Peter W. Flint (eds.), *The Book of Daniel: Composition and Reception* (2001), pp. 228-44; Bietenhard, '"Der Menschensohn"—ὁ υἱὸς τοῦ ἀνθρώπου' (cf. n. 35, above), pp. 337-38; Donald Juel, *Messi-*

regard to the Jewish material, was substantiated through my investigations of the three so-called *loci classici* of the apocalyptic Son of man concept, first in *Messias og 'menneskesøn' i Daniels Bog, Første Enoksbog og Fjerde Ezrabog* from 1972, then in *Der Ausdruck 'Menschensohn' in den Evangelien* from 1984, in which the first chapters analyze these texts.[154] Whole-hearted consent is also to be found in Douglas R.A. Hare's *The Son of Man Tradition* (1990), claiming outright that Leivestad's 'Exit the Apocalyptic Son of Man' article was 'the decisive turning point in modern study of "the Son of man"'.[155]

While Klaus Berger, for instance, shares the presupposition that the Gospel Son of man is the result of a community interpretation,[156] John Pairman Brown reaches an almost identical understanding through quite another way. He follows Perrin in the denial of the existence of any Son of man concept in Late Judaism. Even in *1 Enoch* 37–71 and *4 Ezra* 13, the language is perhaps influenced by the Christian Church, which has transmitted these writings and 'the Gospels provide the oldest relatively datable development of an apocalyptic concept of the Son of man'. When an un-terminological use of the expression is unthinkable because it would be meaningless, '[t]he only remaining possibility is that "Son of man" is the name that other men gave to Jesus'.[157] This distancing speech-mode (Brown thus renders son of man with 'this fellow') is adapted by Jesus when he speaks of himself. Later, the disciples do the same when they create sayings of Jesus about

anic Exegesis: Christological Interpretation of the Old Testament in Early Christianity (1988), esp. pp. 151-79; W.D. Davies and D. Allison, *The Gospel According to Saint Matthew* (1991), II, pp. 45-46; Marcus Borg, *Jesus in Contemporary Scholarship* (1994), pp. 51-53; Jacques Buchhold, 'Jésus ou l'énigme du Fils de l'homme', *Théologie Évangélique* 1 (2002) No. 1, pp. 21-46, No. 2, pp. 3-24.

154. The following articles are two revised formal oppositions to the thesis and a review from the third member of the committee: Ragnar Leivestad, 'Betydningen av uttrykket "menneskesønnen". Mogens Müller. Der Ausdruck "Menschensohn" in den Evangelien. Voraussetzungen und Bedeutung. AThD 17 (1984)', *DTT* 48 (1985), pp. 172-94; Niels Hyldahl, 'Mogens Müllers disputats om "menneskesønnen"', *Fønix* 10 (1986), pp. 175-83; Hejne Simonsen, 'Dansk disputats om udtrykket "menneskesønnen"', *SEÅ* 51–52 (1986–87), pp. 219-28 (practically identical with *Præsteforeningens Blad* 74 [1984], pp. 717-22). Cf. further M. Müller, 'Messias og "menneskesønnen" i den intertestamentale periode', in Sten Hidal *et al.* (eds.), *Judendom och kristendom under de första århundradena* (1986), I, pp. 98-111.

155. Douglas R.A. Hare, *The Son of Man Tradition* (1990), p. x.

156. Klaus Berger, *Die Auferstehung des Propheten und die Erhöhung des Menschensohnes. Traditionsgeschichtliche Untersuchungen zur Deutung des Geschickes Jesu in frühchristlichen Texten* (1976), esp. pp. 132-38 and the notes, pp. 411-20.

157. John Pairman Brown, 'The Son of Man: "This Fellow"', *Bib* 58 (1977), pp. 361-87 (367). In this and other quotations I have not reproduced Brown's italics.

himself. Thus, 'the "theology of the Son of man" is the first stage in the Church's reworking of Jesus' ironical self-description'.[158] The next stage was 'the paradoxical shift when "Son of man" came to be seen as a title of honor and combined with the exalted figure of Dn 7,13'.[159] Brown, accordingly, totally ignores the Aramaic approach.

A few adhere to the old thesis that the Gospel expression goes back to Jesus using 'Son of Adam' about himself. For instance, John Bowman 'thinks one should not rule out the possibility that Jesus in his use of the title Son of Man as describing himself was referring to himself as Son of Adam'.[160] In the mouth of Jesus, it was meant as a messianic designation—as, for instance, in Mk 2.25, 26 where Son of Man is over and above David—because in Jewish thought the spirit of Adam before the fall would also be in the Messiah. The inclusion of Adam in the Lukan genealogy (Lk 3.38) and the Pauline teaching on the second Adam points, for example, in this direction:

> The heavenly Son of Man or Eschatological Son of Man (one and the same) = Paul's second Adam can present the basic connection between the Synoptic and the Pauline Christology. Both have distanced themselves from the man Jesus though the son of man description of himself was intended as a claim of true humanity.[161]

Bowman arrives at his conclusions suggesting that we should seek the key for understanding in Rabbinic sources.[162]

Two German contributions also belong here. Martin Karrer, in *Jesus Christus im Neuen Testament* (1998), accepts a non-titular understanding. In non-Christian sources 'man' belongs to epiphany terminology and it is possible that Jesus has employed it. Karrer points to sayings like Lk 17.24, 26-27, but also Lk 12.8 and Mk 8.38. He concludes that the New Testament Son of man 'is not a preformed predicate. For this reason, it is *first of all*

158. Brown, 'The Son of Man: "This Fellow"', p. 384.

159. Brown, 'The Son of Man: "This Fellow"', p. 385. Cf. further *idem*, 'The Son of Man and Jesus' Irony', *AAR/SBL Abstracts 2001* (2001), pp. 37-38. This understanding is very similar to the one of Wolfgang Schenk, *Das biographische Ich-Idiom 'Menschensohn' in den frühen Jesus-Biographien* (1997), pp. 66 and 226 (cf. Chapter 17). Earlier representatives are Ch.A. Heumann (cf. Chapter 5, Section 3, above), D. Smith (Chapter 11, Section 3, above).

160. John Bowman, 'David, Jesus Son of David and Son of Man', *Abr-Nahrain* 27 (1989), pp. 1-22 (9, 12), pointing to a similar understanding in E.A. Abbott.

161. Bowman, 'David, Jesus Son of David and Son of Man', p. 17.

162. A little later, Robert Funk advocates a similar interpretation in *Honest to Jesus: Jesus for the Millennium* (1996), pp. 89-94. Joel Marcus, 'Son of Man as Son of Adam', *RB* 110 (2003), pp. 38-61, 370-86 (summarized above, Chapter 14, Section 6) could also have been treated here.

a paraphrase of the speech of Jesus. It attains its meaning through its *contexts*.'[163] There is some similarity between this interpretation and the one seeing Jesus, in preaching a future Son of man and somehow identifying himself with this figure. The other contribution is Matthias Kreplin, *Das Selbstverständnis Jesu* (2001). He held that there was no Son of man concept in Jewish apocalyptic, nor in the New Testament gospels. Son of man functions as an expression created by Jesus himself as an indirect designation of himself in sayings about his mission on earth and perhaps also his suffering. Those alluding to Dan. 7.13-14, on the other hand, belong to the time after Easter when the term became a title.[164] After an analysis of the possibilities of detecting a messianic self-consciousness in the historical Jesus, with respect to Son of man, Kreplin concluded that this way of speaking, as it is often presumed, has its origin in an Aramaic speech-mode, which, however, Jesus did not employ in a generic but in an individual way. Kreplin goes further, seeing two sets of associations connected with it; namely, first, as in the book of Ezekiel, where Son of man designates the representative of God towards men, and, second, the claim to be the true man. None of these connotations was explicitly pronounced by Jesus, in accordance with the reticence characteristic of him. Nonetheless, they may have played a role.[165]

Taking into account the decline of the belief in a relatively stable apocalyptic Son of man expectation in Early Judaism and being sceptical towards the conclusions of 'the second Aramaic stage' (cf. ch. 14 above), Delbert R. Burkett reaches, however, a similar conclusion in his *The Son of Man Debate* (1999). Burkett finds it difficult to 'speak of a unified "Son of Man" tradition in ancient Judaism' from the existing interpretation of Dan. 7.13 in Jewish texts, seeing instead 'a shared set of messianic and messianically interpreted scriptural texts that the exegetes combined and interpreted in various ways to produce a variety of portraits of the Messiah'.[166] Rejecting the hypothesis that the background for the titular use in the Gospels should be Jesus' use of a non-titular idiom,[167] Burkett, therefore, thinks 'the likeliest solution to be that the third-person speech represents the voice of the church rather than of Jesus'.[168]

163. Martin Karrer, *Jesus Christus im Neuen Testament* (1998), p. 303. Cf. the section on the Son of man, pp. 287-306.

164. Cf. the thorough analysis in Keplin, *Das Selbsverständnis Jesu*, pp. 88-197.

165. Cf. Kreplin, *Das Selbstverständnis Jesu*, pp. 305-308.

166. Delbert R. Burkett, *The Son of Man Debate* (1999), p. 120.

167. Cf. Burkett, *The Son of Man Debate*, pp. 82-96: Chapter 8, 'The Idiomatic/ Nontitular Son of Man', is a revised version of *idem*, 'The Nontitular Son of Man: A History and Critique', *NTS* 40 (1994), pp. 504-21.

168. Burkett, *The Son of Man Debate*, p. 123. Thus Burkett denounces his earlier conclusions in *The Son of Man in the Gospel of John* (1991). Cf. below, Chapter 17.

A comprehensive alternative attempt to understand Son of man in the mouth of Jesus without recurrence to an apocalyptic Danielic Son of man is Walter Wink's *The Human Being: Jesus and the Enigma of the Son of the Man* (2002). Wink will not deny that the post-Easter Son of man sayings introduce apocalyptic into the interpretation of Jesus' afterlife as both the ascended and the one to come. The pre-Easter Son of man sayings, however, most of which go back to Jesus, reflect his self-understanding as the archetypal Human Being. It is for this reason that Wink also renders the expression 'the son of the man' as 'the Wisdom's Child':

> It is this study's judgment that Jesus did indeed utter a number of the pre-Easter son-of-the-man sayings in the Gospels; that he expresses the core of the suffering sayings, in that he did anticipate his execution; and that he looked forward to the transformation of human beings into the fuller humanity exemplified and made possible by Jesus as the Human Being. That churches developed additional sayings is only to be expected. That they were not always true to his meaning goes without saying. Scholars have erred, however, by applying exclusively rational categories to what are essentially archetypal images. These images were precipitated involuntarily from the unconscious, as indications from the psychic depths about the significance of Jesus' life. Their truth lies not in their historicity but in their faithful rendering of the intrapsychic transformation taking place in believers after the ascension, that is, after Jesus entered the archetype of the Human Being. That is the real miracle of Easter.
>
> Put in another way: As bearer of the archetype of the Human Being, Jesus activates the numinous power that is capable of healing, transforming, or rebirthing those who surrender themselves to it. As such, Jesus knew himself to be in the grip of a power greater than he. A problem arises at just this point, however. When Jesus is worshiped as the sole bearer of the archetype of humanness, he is made a supernatural being. As such, he loses his connection to the struggle to be human, and becomes a cult figure in a religion focused on his person rather than on the reality that he bore.[169]

The ultimate source of this 'Human Being' tradition is Ezekiel's vision.[170] Wink claims that this archetypal explanation is not based in modernism as similar thoughts are found not only in Plato but Philo as well. As it is seen from 'Psalm 80 and Daniel 7, the Gospels and the post-Christian Similitudes of Enoch and *4 Ezra* 13:52, there is a collective dimension':

169. Walter Wink, *The Human Being: Jesus and the Enigma of the Son of the Man* (2002), p. 256. Wink argues for a similar understanding of the Johannine Son of man in '"The Son of the Man" in the Gospel of John', in Robert T. Fortna and Tom Thatcher (eds.), *Jesus in Johannine Tradition* (2001), pp. 117-23.

170. Cf. Wink, *The Human Being*, pp. 267-69: 'Appendix 3: Ezekiel's Influence on Jesus', where Wink declares that he believes 'that Ezekiel is the best clue for understanding Jesus' use of the term'.

> If Jesus alone is Sophia's Child, if he alone assumes archetypal dimensionality, if he alone is at the heart of reality, then Christianity does indeed possess monopoly on truth. But if he is an elder brother within a large family (Rom. 8:29), then we can interpret Jesus' ascension as a mutation of the archetype of wholeness. The Human Being has the capacity to make humans humane, whatever their religion or lack thereof.[171]

That Wink is heavily inspired by both Ludwig Feuerbach and Carl Gustav Jung will not come as a surprise; unsurprising too is that he does not find an insurmountable gap between the usage of Jesus and the meaning of the expression in the Gnostic sources—with Paul's speaking of Christ as 'the Man' as a proportional mean.[172] God is absorbed in the idea of the true Human Being. Thus 'son-of-the-man' is not a messianic title, but 'Jesus' way of eschewing *all* titles'.[173] Wink's interpretation is probably the most consequential attempt by a New Testament scholar to see Jesus' employment of the expression in the light of archetypal thinking.

3. *Re-enter an Apocalyptic Son of Man?*[174]

As was to be expected, this attack on the belief in a pre-formed apocalyptic Son of man expectation in Judaism certainly did not carry the day entirely. However, the situation was altered after the contributions of Leivestad and others, just as interpreters after the revival of the 'Aramaic solution' had to argue once again for the possibility of seeing Son of man as a meaningful messianic title. It did not hinder at all a number of scholars from continually arguing for the hypotheses of the existence of a more or less Jewish-contoured Son of man expectation. A representative is George W. Nickelsburg's 'Son of Man' article in the influential *Anchor Bible Dictionary* (1992), in which the thought of a concept is still present, but not necessarily connected with the designation Son of man. On the basis of Daniel 7, *1 Enoch* 37–71, Wisdom of Solomon 1–6, *4 Ezra* 11–13 and *2 Baruch*, however, Nickelsburg finds evidence indicating

171. Wink, *The Human Being*, p. 252.

172. Cf. Wink, *The Human Being*, pp. 207-11.

173. Wink, *The Human Being*, p. 251. Wink quotes Kathlene Peterson Nicol's unpublished B.D. thesis, '"Son of Man": Its Background and New Testament Usage' (1970), Epilogue. Wink goes on to quote the likewise unpublished Ph.D. dissertation by William L. Dols, 'Toward a Field Hermeneutic of the Phrase *ho huios tou antropou* in the Narrative World of Mark' (1987), p. iii: '*ho huios tou antropou* is the one description of Jesus that the church from the very beginning had been unable to define and thus own. It thereby retains an element of the numinous. It bears witness to the mysterious transforming power of God enfleshed in Jesus and longing to be born in each of us.'

174. Cf. the title of an article by B. Lindars from just before he was fully 'converted' to 'the new look': 'Re-Enter the Apocalyptic Son of Man', *NTS* 22 (1975–76), pp. 52-72.

> that the idea of a transcendental judge and deliverer was a known element in Jewish eschatology by the latter part of the 1st century C.E. The texts in question attest a common model that was composed of elements from Israelite traditions about the Davidic king, the Deutero-Isaianic servant/chosen one, and the Danielic 'Son of man'. The model surely existed apart from these texts, and, in order to posit belief in such a transcendent savior figure in any given case, we need not presume that any one of the texts was known and used as a literary source. For a modern critic, however, the texts serve as extant testimonies and expressions of the belief… The tradition was fluid and its components interacted with one another in different ways. The transcendent deliverer was often identified with Daniel's one like a son of man, although he was not always called 'son of man'.[175]

Similar (and not always minimizing) models for accepting a Son of man concept are surely present in scholarship at the end of the twentieth century.[176] So is the thought that the use of Son of man in the mouth of Jesus or the inclusion of it by the authors of the Gospels would call forth the picture of an apocalyptic-eschatological figure, at least to some contemporaries. Others—mostly conservative interpreters—contended that Jesus

175. Georg W. Nickelsburg, 'Son of Man', in *ABD*, VI (1992), pp. 137-50 (141); cf. *idem*, 'Son of Man', in *DDD*, pp. 800-804; *idem*, *Resurrection, Immortality, and Eternal Life in Intertestamental Judaism and Early Christianity* (expanded edn, 2006), pp. 281-314.

176. Thus Frederick M. Wilson, 'The Son of Man in Jewish Apocalyptic Literature', *Studia biblica et theologica* 8 (1978), pp. 28-52 (33); William Horbury, 'The Messianic Associations of "The Son of Man"', *JTS* NS 36 (1985), pp. 34-55; revised reprint in *idem*, *Messianism among Jews and Christians: Biblical and Historical Studies* (2003), pp. 125-55; Horbury is not arguing for a Son of man expectation different from the 'normal' Messianic expectation; John J. Collins, 'The Son of Man in First Century Judaism', *NTS* 38 (1992), pp. 448-66; reprint in a revised form as 'The Danielic Son of Man', in *idem*, *The Scepter and the Star. The Messiahs of the Dead Sea Scrolls and Other Ancient Literature* (1995), pp. 173-94; Klaus Koch, 'Messias und Menschensohn. Die zweistufige Messianologie der jüngeren Apokalyptik', in *Der Messias* (JBTh 8, 1993), pp. 73-102, here also including the *Apocalypse of Baruch* (*Syrian Baruch*) and working with a two step messianism; *idem*, 'Das Reich der Heiligen und des Menschensohns. Ein Kapitel politischer Theologie', in *idem*, *Die Reiche der Welt und der kommende Menschensohn. Studien zum Danielbuch.* Gesammelte Aufsätze 2 (ed. Martin Rösel, 1995), pp. 140-72 (170); *idem*, 'Der "Menschensohn" in Daniel', *ZAW* 119 (2007), pp. 369-385 (a refutation of O. Hofius; n. 84 above); Raymond E. Brown, *An Introduction to New Testament Christology* (1994), pp. 89-100 (92-96); Thomas B. Slater, 'One Like a Son of Man in First-Century CE Judaism', *NTS* 41 (1995), pp. 183-98 (Slater also introduces *The Apocalypse of Abraham* 10.1-4 as a related text). Further, Pierre de Martin de Vivies, *Jésus et le Fils de l'homme* (1995), pp. 8-37; Gottfried Nebe, 'The Son of Man and the Angels: Reflections on the Formation of Christology in the Context of Eschatology', in Henning Graf Reventlow (ed.), *Eschatology in the Bible and in Jewish and Christian Tradition* (1997), pp. 111-31 (117-24); Martin E. Sheldon, 'The Eschatological Son of Man in Jewish and Christian Literature', *Evangelical Journal* 17 (1999), pp. 60-75.

himself created a Son of man christology through his inclusion of Dan. 7.13 in his preaching about himself. This attempt to insist on the relevance of an apocalyptic Son of man concept in the mapping of Jesus' self-understanding is to be held apart from the interpretation described above in Chapter 14, letting the apocalyptic Son of man enter into christology through the community's identification of Jesus with this figure, not least because of his use of the circumlocutional way of speaking which includes the Aramaic *bar (e)nash*.

The successor of Rudolf Bultmann in Marburg, Werner Georg Kümmel (1905–1995), is still convinced that Jesus employed the Jewish apocalyptic expectation of an eschatological 'Man' and combined it with his preaching of the Kingdom of God. He connects it with the thought that Jesus also transcended the Jewish world of conceptions by combining it in a new way with his person also at the same time seizing it with regard to actual activity. However, Kümmel did not accept the authenticity of the Passion predictions.[177] Not all share his reservations in this regard.

I. Howard Marshall claimed the possibility 'that Jesus made it His self-designation in a quasi-titular manner, taking over the use of the term from the Old Testament and especially from Daniel'. Although he had a consciousness of divine Sonship, he did not want to 'reveal it openly. The phrase "Son of man", referring in Dan. 7 to a heavenly, messianic being, could be used as a veil for His true title and at the same time as a means of expressing His solidarity with the people of Israel'.[178] Joachim Jeremias is in no doubt in his *Neutestamentliche Theologie. Erster Teil. Die Verkündigung Jesu* (1971) that, as in Jewish apocalyptic, 'so in the sayings of Jesus, Son of man is a *terminus gloriae*'.[179] Jesus employs it to reject political Messianic expectations, letting Son of man express the universality of his highness. He

177. Cf. Werner Georg Kümmel, *Die Theologie des Neuen Testaments nach seinen Hauptzeugen* (1969), pp. 68-76. Further *idem*, 'Das Verhalten Jesus gegenüber und das Verhalten des Menschensohnes. Markus 8,38 par und Lukas 12,8f par Matthäus 10,32f', in R. Pesch and R. Schnackenburg (eds.), *Jesus und der Menschensohn* (FS Anton Vögtle, 1975), pp. 210-24 (reprinted in *idem*, *Heilsgeschehen und Geschichte* Band 2. Gesammelte Aufsätze 1965–77 [1978], pp. 201-14); *idem*, *Jesus der Menschensohn?* (1984), pp. 1-46.

178. I. Howard Marshall, 'The Son of Man in Contemporary Debate', *EvQ* 42 (1970), pp. 67-87 (81); cf. *idem*, *The Origins of New Testament Christology* (1976), pp. 63-82; 'The Son of Man and the Incarnation', *Ex Auditu* 7 (1991), pp. 29-43; 'Son of Man', in J.B. Green and S. McKnight (eds.), *Dictionary of Christ and the Gospels* (1992), pp. 775-81; 'The Synoptic "Son of Man" Sayings in the Light of Linguistic Study', in T. Schmidt and M. Silva (eds.), *To Tell the Mystery* (FS Robert H. Gundry, 1994), pp. 72-94.

179. Joachim Jeremias, *Neutestamentliche Theologie*. I. *Die Verkündigung Jesu* (1971), pp. 245-63 (259).

brings salvation to the whole world. When Jesus distinguishes between himself and the Son of man, speaking in the third person, 'he distinguishes not between two figures, but between his present position and the *status exaltationis*. The third person expresses the "mysterious relation" existing between Jesus and the Son of man: he is not yet the Son of man, but he will be exalted to Son of man.'[180]

That Daniel 7 reflects the twofold pattern, where one of suffering is followed by vindication opens up the possibility for some interpreters to see this double motif as the background for the so-called present Son of man sayings. Christopher Tuckett finds that Mk 2.1–3.6 presents a Son of man whose authority is rejected, pointing to the future suffering, which fits into the pattern of suffering and vindication. To Tuckett, this means that the Son of man as a suffering figure appears also in Q, which is no proof, but which removes the argument against the authenticity of the Son of man Passion sayings lacking in Q.[181] In a series of contributions,[182] Tuckett later deepens his views, putting the Son of man concept in connection with other examples of the idea in contemporary Jewish thinking 'that in the final judgment God would be assisted by another figure'. Tuckett believes that this understanding can go back to the earthly Jesus:

> The possibility...that Jesus used the Aramaic phrase *bar nash*, or *bar nasha*, to refer to himself *and* to evoke the context of the Danielic scene is thus not impossible given the way that language and verbal shorthands function with all groups within human society. In doing so he may then have been giving expression to his conviction that he, like others before him, were destined to suffer rejection, hostility and violence because of his commitment to God, but that he would be subsequently vindicated in the heavenly court. As S(on of) M(an) too he invited others to share with him this route.[183]

180. Jeremias, *Neutestamentliche Theologie*, p. 263. L. Sabourin, 'The Son of Man', *BThB* 2 (1972), pp. 78-80, is a review and an appraisal of Jeremias's understanding. Further *idem*, 'About Jesus' Self-Understanding', *Religious Studies Bulletin* 3 (1983), pp. 129-34 (130-31).

181. Christopher Tuckett, 'The Present Son of Man', *JSNT* 14 (1982), pp. 58-81 (70). Tuckett picks up the ideas of Moule and Hooker, finding the motif of suffering in Dan. 7 through their corporate interpretation. Cf. above, Chapter 14.

182. Apart from the studies particularly devoted to the Son of man in Q (cf. Chapter 17, below): Christopher Tuckett, 'The Son of Man and Daniel 7: Q and Jesus', in Andreas Lindemann (ed.), *The Sayings Source Q and the Historical Jesus* (2001), pp. 371-94 (389-94), where Tuckett also pleads for understanding the bare Aramaic expression as a possible allusion to Daniel 7 in certain contexts. Tuckett's 'The Son of Man and Daniel 7: Inclusive Aspects of Early Christologies', in Kieran J. O'Mahony (ed.), *Christian Origins: Worship, Belief and Society* (2003), pp. 164-90, is a later, reworked version of the article from 2001. Cf. also *idem*, *Q and the History of Early Christianity* (1996), pp. 239-82, where also the question of background is investigated (pp. 266-76).

183. Christopher Tuckett, 'The Son of Man and Daniel 7: Inclusive Aspects of Early Christologies', p. 184. Cf. 'The Son of Man and Daniel 7: Q and Jesus', p. 394.

Some contributions deserve a fuller treatment because of their impact on the discussion. The first is *The Son of Man: Vision and Interpretation* (1986) by the conservative (if not fundamentalist) New Testament professor in Lund, Chrys C. Caragounis. Caragounis not only denies a Maccabean date for the book of Daniel,[184] he welcomes developments 'taking place in recent Gospel research, whereby the synoptics have come to be regarded as independent parallel sources,'[185] which, of course, in this case would strengthen their worth as sources for the life of the earthly Jesus.

It is first declared that '[t]he circumlocutional theory in all versions in which it has appeared, has failed to provide the answer to the Son of Man problem in the Gospels'.[186] With regard to '[t]he "Son of Man" in the Old Testament in general and in Daniel in particular',[187] the 'various Near Eastern reconstructions of possible backgrounds are shown to be unsuccessful and lacking in credibility', as is both the Israelite and the angelic interpretation.[188] '[A] careful exegesis of Dan 7 reveals that the "SM" is portrayed as a heavenly being with honors and powers normally predicated of God.' The key to this interpretation of Son of man in Dan. 7.13, Caragounis finds partly in an understanding of the preposition כ signalling that '[h]ere the son of man is no actual human being, but a figure in human form symbolizing a non-human reality'[189] and partly in assuming the Son of man interpreted in the expression *'Elyônîn* in Dan. 7.18, 22, 25, 27 (in the last passage he prefers the reading of Theodotion, which reads without 'people'), where he arbitrarily claims 'that the author distinguishes the "Most High" spoken of in connection with the saints from the Most High as referring to God'.[190] This figure is not to be identified with the Messiah, but is a 'Transcendental Figure', perhaps 'developed from the imagery of Ez 1' and 'dictated by Daniel's dynamic conception of history and the human situation (so-called apocalyptic)', where the Messiah is 'superseded by a new conception of the Agent of God's Kingdom and the Vindicator and Leader of God's people'.[191]

184. Caragounis, *The Son of Man*, p. 86 n. 18.

185. Caragounis, *The Son of Man*, pp. 161-62. The main argument, that 'the recognition that the Gospel statements ought to be taken seriously and be tested objectively by scientific research has as a corollary the laying of the burden of proof upon the claim to inauthenticity' (p. 162).

186. Caragounis, *The Son of Man*, p. 33, but see the whole Chapter 1, pp. 9-33. Main targets in the more recent discussion are Vermes, Casey, and Lindars. Casey's generic reference version is simply described as 'too flat to make much sense of the Gospel logia.'

187. Caragounis, the heading of Chapter 2, pp. 35-81.

188. Caragounis, *The Son of Man*, p. 80.

189. Caragounis, *The Son of Man*, p. 61.

190. Caragounis, *The Son of Man*, p. 75.

191. Caragounis, *The Son of Man*, pp. 80-81.

This interpretation is confirmed through an analysis of '[t]he "Son of Man" in "Some Strands of Jewish and Rabbinic Thought"',[192] offering evidence for such a new concept in some parts of Judaism at the time of Jesus. With reference to such passages as Jn 8.28; 9.35; 12.34; Mk 14.60-62 par., and Acts 7.56, it is further claimed that '[i]t has often been overlooked that the NT ought to be reckoned among the possible sources for the existence of a pre-Christian Son of Man concept in Judaism'.[193] On this basis, it is no surprise that the analysis of the Son of man in the New Testament and its relation to Daniel's Son of Man leads to the conclusion that Jesus employed the expression about himself, to signify that he was Daniel's Son of Man (to Caragounis practically all Son of man sayings in the Gospels are authentic):

> Thus, what in Daniel's vision is only an unidentified entity spoken of in terms of a simile, in the Gospels, standing at the end of the process of concretization and identification, the 'like' is dropped and the 'son of man' is identified with Jesus and thus becomes '*the* Son of Man'![194]

Caragounis takes the occurrences of the sentence ἅ (ὅσα) δεῖ γενέσθαι in the Septuagint and Theodotion versions of Nebuchadnezzar's dream in Daniel 2 (2.28, 29 [*bis*] and, Theodotion alone, 2.45) as identifying the will of God and covering the remainder of human history; that is, the events which lead up to 'SM's appearance and his investment with absolute power' for Jesus, letting it become

> the inexorable *must* of divine necessity in reference to his own role and place as Son of Man in that divine purpose. Here we reach the bedrock. By means of this innovation, the traditional nature and function of the SM is widened to include that which according to Jesus' conviction is God's call to humiliation and suffering as the necessary preliminary to exaltation and glory. In this Danielic δεῖ, we have the key to Jesus' view of his mission expressed in the phrase δεῖ γὰρ τὸν υἱὸν τοῦ ἀνθρώπου...[195]

Another moment in the influence from Daniel is 'that the Son of Man and the Kingdom of God are connected with each other in Jesus' teaching'.[196] In this way, Caragounis tries to establish a new basis for reintroducing an apocalyptic Son of man and to let it be the key to Jesus' self-understanding. This apocalyptic Son of man rests on feet of clay.[197]

192. Caragounis, the heading of Chapter 3, pp. 83-144.

193. Caragounis, *The Son of Man*, pp. 136-37.

194. Caragounis, *The Son of Man*, p. 173.

195. Caragounis, *The Son of Man*, pp. 198-99.

196. Caragounis, *The Son of Man*, p. 243; cf. pp. 232-42. Further *idem*, 'Kingdom of God, Son of Man and Jesus' Self-Understanding', I-II. *Tyndale Bulletin* 40 (1989), pp. 3-23, 223-38, exemplifying the same understanding with regard to Mt. 12.25-32par.

197. For a thorough criticism, see M. Casey, 'Method in Our Madness, and Madness in Their Methods. Some Approaches to the Son of Man Problem in Recent Scholarship', *JSNT* 42 (1991), pp. 17-43 (33-41).

Even after the attempt to bring an effective end to the Jewish apocalyptic Son of man, a number of scholars continue to employ the concept as a key in their interpretation of Jesus' self-understanding. The list includes scholars who assume a pre-Christian Son of man concept as the background for Jesus' employment of Son of man.[198]

On the other hand, a few interpreters consider the apocalyptic Son of man in the Gospels as a creation of Jesus himself, often including other Old Testament concepts as well. Thus, a conservative scholar like R.T. France, in *Jesus and the Old Testament: His Application of Old Testament Passages to Himself and His Mission* (1971), can claim that Jesus essentially created the Son of man concept himself, including also the Suffering Servant of Deutero-Isaiah. Although Jesus' use of Son of man was derived from Daniel, it was not a current title 'in contemporary Judaism as a recognized name for the figure of Daniel 7:13'. 'This may well have been Jesus' intention in using the title; its source made it a suitable one around which to gather his ideas of Messiahship, which...were sharply opposed to current ideas of a political deliverer.' However: 'The attempt to trace the contents of all Son of man sayings to a source in Daniel 7 would result in a ludicrous example of "eisegesis"'.[199] It is only where the content of a saying invites it that a connection to Daniel 7 should be recognized. Of such allusions, France finds seven (Mk 8.38 par.; Mt. 10.23; Mk 13.26 par.; Mk 14.62 par.; Mt. 28.18; Mt. 19.28, and Mt. 25.31), seeing that: 'The keynote of Daniel 7 is that of vindication and exaltation to an everlasting and universal dominion'

198. R.G. Hamerton-Kelly, *Pre-existence, Wisdom, and the Son of Man* (1973), pp. 241-42; Richard Kugelman, 'Son of Man Theology: Some Questions', *CBQ* 35 (1973), pp. 494-95; Paul T. Coke, 'Los Angeles del Hijo del Hombre', *Estudios Bíblicos* 32 (1973), pp. 283-89 (English: 'The Angels of the Son of Man', in A. Fuchs [ed.], *Probleme der Forschung* [1978], pp. 91-98) where the main theme is the disciples as the angels of the resurrected Christ; Margaret Barker, *The Lost Prophet: The Book of Enoch and Its Influence on Christianity* (1988), pp. 91-104 (103-104); J.H. Charlesworth, *Jesus Within Judaism* (1988), pp. 39-42, 139; Ben Witherington, III, *The Christology of Jesus* (1990), pp. 233-62 (261-62); E.A. Obeng, 'The "Son of Man" Motif and the Intercession of Jesus', *Africa Theological Journal* 19 (1990), pp. 155-67; George W.E. Nickelsburg, 'Son of Man', in *ABD*, VI (1992), pp. 137-50 (149) (very tentatively); Raymond E. Brown, *An Introduction to New Testament Christology* (1994), pp. 89-100 (96); André Paul, 'L'*évangélion*: Synthèse de l'*oïkouménè* et de l'*apokalypsis*: De Jésus de Méditerranéen à Jésus le Fils de l'Homme', in J.-L. Schlegel *et al.* (eds.), *Temps, histoire, espérance: De la vigilance chrétienne en temps de crise* (1994), pp. 45-63 (56-60); Pierre de Martin de Vivies, *Jésus et le Fils de l'homme* (1995), esp. pp. 153-62; Pierre Grelot, 'Jésus, Fils de l'homme', *Revue Thomiste* 105 (2005), pp. 89-102 (96-99); M.B. Shepherd, 'Daniel 7:13 and the New Testament Son of Man', *WThJ* 68 (2006), pp. 99-111 (cf. *NTA* 50 [2006], No. 1871).

199. R.T. France, *Jesus and the Old Testament: His Application of Old Testament Passages to Himself and His Mission* (1971), p. 138.

in Jesus' use of that chapter. France imagines this fulfilment happening in three stages:

> (a) Immediately after the resurrection, Jesus, vindicated over those who rejected and judged him, receives the dominion of the Son of man (Mt. 28:18; Mk. 14:62). (b) This dominion is to be manifested in a specific historical act of judgement, which is imminent, and is probably to be identified with the destruction of Jerusalem (Mk. 8:38; Mt. 10:23; Mk. 13:26, and probably a secondary element in Mk 14:62). (c) The final manifestation of this dominion will be in the judgment of all nations (Mt. 19:28; 25:31)... The application of Daniel is therefore consistently to the period after the resurrection. There is no allusion to Daniel 7 by Jesus with reference to his earthly life and death.[200]

France is exceptional in not relating Mk 13.26 par. to the Parousia[201] and he considers Mt. 28.18 to confirm his interpretation of Mk 14.62, 'as referring to a state of exaltation shortly to begin. Daniel 7:13-14 is explicitly so applied here.'[202]

Another interpretation implies that Jesus used the expression in an enigmatic way. This is true, for instance, of Martin Hengel, who is convinced that the conspicuous Greek expression renders Jesus' use of it as a riddle, on the one hand as a reference to Dan. 7.13 designating himself as a *Messias designatus* and on the other as a man exposed to debasement, suffering and death. The origin is probably to be sought among the Hellenists, the circle to which Stephen belonged (cf. Acts 7.56).[203] An influential monograph working practically along the same lines, is that of Volker Hampel, *Menschensohn und historischer Jesus. Ein Rätselswort als Schlüssel zum messianischen Selbstverständnis Jesu* (1990). As is evident from the title, Hampel resumes the old idea of Son of man as a riddle in the mouth of Jesus. Hampel admits that 'an explicit Son of man dogmatic (Menschensohndogmatik) as an independent (eigenständige) conception is deeply foreign to Jewish theology. After all, one can only speak about a Son of man exegesis supported by Daniel 7.13f.'[204]

200. France, *Jesus and the Old Testament*, p. 145.

201. Cf. France, *Jesus and the Old Testament*, pp. 235-36.

202. France, *Jesus and the Old Testament*, p. 143. Cf. 'Excursus 3 "The Son of man in Daniel 7"', pp. 169-71.

203. Cf. Martin Hengel, 'Zwischen Jesus und Paulus. Die "Hellenisten", die "Sieben" und Stephanus (Apg 6,1-5; 7.54–8.3)', *ZThK* 72 (1975), pp. 151-206 (202-203) (English: 'Between Jesus and Paul. The "Hellenists", the "Seven" and Stephen [Acts 6.1-15; 7.54–8.3]', in *idem*, *Between Jesus and Paul. Studies in Earliest History of Christianity* [1983], pp. 1-29). Cf. also *idem*, 'Jesus der Messias Israels', in Martin Hengel and Anna Maria Schwemer, *Der messianische Anspruch Jesu und die Anfänge der Christologie* (2001), pp. 1-80 (65-69).

204. V. Hampel, *Menschensohn und historischer Jesus*, p. 48.

> It is only too understandable why Jesus returned to בר אנשא as a circumlocution for his messianic 'I' and his not yet revealed Messiahship. The term presented itself because of its polysemy and indefinitness (Vieldeutigkeit und Unbestimmtheit) as the best means of concealing but also declaring his demand on mission, without thereby openly dissolving its secret (in verhüllender und doch deklaratorischer Weise auf seinen Sendungsanspruch hinzuweisen, ohne dabei dessen Geheimnis offen preiszugeben). This is because one could hear everything possible from בר אנשא: the everyday generic or an indefinite meaning, a designation for Israel, a mere 'I', apocalyptic associations, a predicate of a king or Messiah.
>
> In the mouth of Jesus, בר אנשא, for the outsider, is an enigma which immediately invites the question: Who is this? For his own, on the other hand, בר אנשא is a reference to the messianic mission of Jesus. It is a cipher for his function as Messiah designatus.
>
> According to this specific use, בר אנשא is a consciously enigmatic mode of speech of the historical Jesus (Im Sinne dieses spezifischen Gebrauchs ist בר אנשא eine bewußt geheimnisvolle Redeweise des historischen Jesus).[205]

Even in the form of a riddle,[206] Son of man is seen as Jesus' means of expressing his messianic self-consciousness. Other scholars see it as a more direct indication.[207] For instance, Joseph Coppens belongs here,[208] as does

205. Hampel, *Menschensohn und historischer Jesus*, p. 164.

206. Also John P. Meier, *A Marginal Jew: Rethinking the Historical Jesus*. III. *Companions and Competitors* (2001), p. 646, assumes an 'enigmatic riddle speech not unlike the parables'. Further Jacques Buchhold, 'Jésus ou l'énigme du Fils de l'homme', *Théologie Évangélique* 1 (2002) No. 1, pp. 21-46, No. 2, pp. 3-24 (21-24). A little earlier, John Nolland, 'The Son of Man in the Synoptic Gospels: The Man of Destiny', in David Petersen and John Pryor (eds.), *In the Fullness of Time* (FS Donald Robinson, 1992), pp. 17-28, speaks of a mysterious use in need of explication, first provided by Jesus 'in terms of the eschatological role identified in the link to Dan. 7, but not in the sense that "Son of Man" is now recognized to have been a cryptic reference to Daniel 7:13' (p. 26).

207. R.N. Longenecker, '"Son of Man" as a Self-Designation of Jesus', *JEThS* 12 (1969), pp. 151-58; *idem*, *The Christology of Early Jewish Christianity* (1970), pp. 82-93); *idem*, '"Son of Man" Imagery: Some Implications for Theology and Discipleship', *JEThS* 18 (1975), pp. 3-16; L. Sabourin, 'The Son of Man', *BThB* 2 (1972), pp. 78-80; *idem*, 'About Jesus' Self-Understanding', *Religious Studies Bulletin* 3 (1983), pp. 129-34; Graham Stanton, *Jesus of Nazareth in New Testament Preaching* (1974), pp. 156-67; F. Zehrer, 'Jesus, der Menschensohn', *Bibel und Liturgie* 47 (1974), pp. 165-76; R.O. Zorn, 'The Significance of Jesus' Selfdesignation "the Son of Man"', *Vox Reformata* 34 (1980), pp. 1-21; F.F. Bruce, 'The Background of the Son of Man Sayings', in Harold H. Rowden (ed.), *Christ the Lord* (FS Donald Guthrie, 1982), pp. 50-70; David R. Jackson, 'The priority of the Son of Man Sayings', *WThJ* 47 (1985), pp. 83-96; Donald M. MacKinnon, 'Son of Man: A Comment', *The Scottish Journal of Religious Studies* 11 (1990), pp. 89-92; Craig A. Evans, 'Jesus' Self-designation "the *Son of Man*" and the Recognition of his Divinity', in Stephen T. Davis (ed.), *The Trinity: An Interdisciplinary Symposium on the Trinity* (1999), pp. 29-47 (32-40); *idem*, 'Defeating Satan and Liberating Israel: Jesus and Daniel's Visions', *Journal for the Study of the Historical Jesus* 1 (2003), pp. 161-70.

Otto Betz, having Jesus combine Dan. 7.13-14 with Psalm 103 and Isa. 56.2. Betz also sees in Mt. 10.23 an allusion to Gen. 49.10, the word 'shiloh' being on the same level with Son of man in Dan. 7.13.[209]

Randall Buth reaches a similar conclusion by other means. Buth argues for the possibility of Jesus having spoken Hebrew. When Jesus suddenly introduced an Aramaic *bar-enasha* in a saying like Mk 2.10, '[i]t would have the effect of putting the phrase in quotation marks'. It clearly points to the only place in Scripture containing Dan. 7.13. Buth call this 'the three-dimensional approach' where Hebrew functions as the third language, besides Aramaic and Greek. This remarkable use is then preserved in the unnatural Greek title which did not convey in itself the contextual signal and, therefore, went out of use.[210]

While the view that Jesus preached a coming Son of man, identifying himself with this eschatological figure, continues to find adherents,[211] a few advocate a revised form of the view that Jesus preached an apocalyptic Son of man as another than himself.[212] One of the more outspoken is Adela Yarbro Collins, who claimed that although no such concept existed beforehand, Jesus interpreted Son of man in Dan. 7.13 as referring to a heavenly figure soon to come, turning the indefinite form into a definite to point to that figure. However, the later community identified Jesus with this Son of man, the only genuine sayings being Mt. 24.27, 37-39, 44.[213] But she is not alone.[214]

208. Cf. especially the articles edited in Coppens, *Le Fils de l'homme néotestamentaire* (1981).

209. Otto Betz, 'Die Menschensohnworte Jesu und die Zukunftserwartung des Paulus (Daniel 7.13-14)', *Jesus und das Danielbuch*, Band II (1985), pp. 73-102. According to Betz (p. 101) 'auch schon Johannes der Täufer lebte nach der von Gen 49,10, Dan 7,13f. geprägten Erlösererwartung'.

210. Randall Buth, 'A More Complete Semitic Background for בר־אנשא, "Son of Man"', in C. Evans and James A. Sanders (eds.), *The Function of Scripture in Early Jewish and Christian Tradition* (1998), pp. 176-89 (187).

211. Gerd Theissen and Annette Merz, *Der historische Jesus. Ein Lehrbuch* (1996), pp. 470-80 (479); Gottfried Nebe, 'The Son of Man and the Angels: Reflections on the Formation of Christology in the Context of Eschatology', in Henning Graf Reventlow (ed.), *Eschatology in the Bible and in Jewish and Christian Tradition* (1997), pp. 111-31 (125-31); Klaus Beyer, 'Der Menschensohn als Gott der Welt: Der Ursprung der hohen Christologie bei Jesus selbst', in Sophia G. Vashalomidze and Lutz Greisiger (eds.), *Der christliche Orient und seine Umwelt* (FS Jürgen Tubachs, 2007), pp. 11-19.

212. For instance, Hans Hübner, *Biblische Theologie des Neuen Testaments*. III. *Hebräerbrief, Evangelien und Offenbarung. Epilegomena* (1995), pp. 272-74, where Hübner, p. 274 n. 78, concludes: 'Mir scheint diese Hypothese immer noch am plausibelsten'.

213. Cf. the following contributions of Adela Yarbro Collins: 'The Origin of the Designation of Jesus as "Son of Man"', *HThR* 80 (1987), pp. 391-407; reprint in *idem*, *Cosmology and Eschatology in Jewish and Christian Apocalypticism* (1996), pp. 139-58;

Interpreters who accept the idea that the expression Son of man in the mouth of Jesus has its origin in an Aramaic way of speaking without any titular content, often think that it nevertheless becomes a christological title in the Gospels. Opinions differ on the question of how this came about. Assuming it to stem from Q, some think Lk 9.58 the crucial saying for understanding what Jesus meant. They seize on it for a generic meaning in the context of subversive wisdom, while his followers identified him with the apocalyptic Son of man.[215]

Ulrich B. Müller assumes that it has happened through the transference of the concept of the Day of Yahweh to Jesus upon his return.[216] Of special importance in this regard, Müller finds the sayings about 'the day of the Son of man' in Lk 17.24, 26-27, 30 to originate not with the historical Jesus but in the time after Easter. Thus, there are sayings about the future Son of man, which are not influenced by Dan. 7.13-14; for instance, Mt. 10.23 and Lk 12.40, showing how the circumlocutional way of speaking caused the early

'The Son of Man Sayings in the Sayings Source', in M.P. Horgan and P.J. Kobelski (eds.), *To Touch the Text* (FS Joseph Fitzmyer, 1989), pp. 369-89; 'Daniel 7 and Jesus', *Journal of Theology* 93 (1989), pp. 5-19; 'Daniel 7 and the Historical Jesus', in H.W. Attridge, J.J. Collins and T.H. Tobin (eds.), *Of Scribes and Scrolls* (FS John Strugnell, 1990), pp. 181-93; 'The Apocalyptic Son of Man Sayings', in Birger A. Pearson (ed.), *The Future of Early Christianity* (1991), pp. 220-28; *idem*, 'The Influence of Daniel on the New Testament', in J.J. Collins, *Daniel* (1993), pp. 90-123 (90-105); 'The "Son of Man" Tradition and the Book of Revelation', in James H. Charlesworth (ed.), *The Messiah: Developments in Earliest Judaism and Christianity* (1992), pp. 536-68 (reprinted in *idem*, *Cosmology and Eschatology in Jewish and Christian Apocalypticism* [1996], pp. 159-97).

214. Thus, Dale C. Allison, *Jesus of Nazareth: Millenarian Prophet* (1998), pp. 115-20; Michael Cahill, 'Did Jesus Refer to Himself in the Third Person? A Contribution to the Son of Man Debate', *Proceedings of the Irish Biblical Association* 25 (2002), pp. 58-68 (65-68).

215. Andries Van Aarde, 'Jesus and the Son of Man: A Shift from the "Little Tradition" to the "Great Tradition"', *EThL* 80 (2004), pp. 423-38, reworked edition of the version in Afrikaans, 'De uitdrukking "seun van die mens" in die Jesus-tradisie: 'n Ontwikkeling vanaf 'n landbou-omgewing na die wêreld van skrifgeleerdes', *Hervormde Teologiese Studies* 58 (2002), pp. 1625-53. A similar conclusion is reached by Yolanda Dreyer, 'The Institutionalization of Jesus' Charismatic Authority: "Son of Man" as Case Study', *Hervormde Teologiese Studies* 56 (2000), pp. 1057-78.

216. Ulrich B. Müller, 'Jesus als "der Menschensohn"', in D. Sänger (ed.), *Gottessohn und Menschensohn* (2004), pp. 91-129 (114-29). The conclusion is: 'Ursprünglich war "der Menschensohn" nur eine Selbstbezeichnung Jesu, die in besonderen Fällen um bewusster Zurückhaltung willen die Rede in der 3. Pers. dem ausdrücklichen "Ich" vorzog. Die frühe Gemeinde übernahm seine Redeweise, wobei diese nun wie ein Titel Verwendung fand.' Thus in this contribution U.B. Müller has changed his earlier view that there existed an apocalyptical Son of man concept in Early Judaism (see his p. 98 n. 11).

community to resume the expression, it now becoming a title. The last stage of development within the Gospel tradition involves the implication of Dan. 7.13-14.

A variant is represented by Crispin H.T. Fletcher-Louis's understanding of Jesus' employment of Son of man as a way of claiming to be the true High Priest, an interpretation which also pertains to Dan. 7.13:

> Whilst Jesus does not deny the glorious form of the Son of Man as the Jewish populace would have understood the figure, he does insist throughout this section [The Caesarea Philippi-Transfiguration Cycle in Matthew] that the Son of Man's glory is manifest through suffering. What little evidence there is in contemporary Jewish sources for the expectation that the end-time redeemer would suffer to the point of death unanimously speaks for the priestly figure and/or the Day of Atonement.[217]

With the reduction of the background of Daniel 7 to imagery and the breakdown of the hypothesis of the existence of a special apocalyptic Son of man concept in Early Judaism, which neither Jesus nor the early community could have taken over, interest naturally focused ever more on the creative interpretation of Daniel's saying by Jesus or the early community. The attempt to make the 'exit [of] the apocalyptic Son of man' effective was followed up by some scholars with a counter movement, which attempted to save some sort of Jewish concept as the presupposition of the Gospel sayings or—as in conservative-fundamentalistic scholarship—by letting Jesus be the initiator of it. The variable factor was the different understandings of the possibility of the Aramaic approach to solve the problem, eventually producing the common denominator between a circumlocutional mode of speech and the saying in Dan. 7.13. As we observed, solutions varied from seeing Jesus as 'smart enough' to use the expression in two ways, a circumlocutional way of speaking by the earthly Jesus having caused the introduction of Dan. 7.13 to be the key to its meaning. The fact that the Son of man in the gospels, in spite of it being third person, is obviously exclusively referring to Jesus naturally invites christological interpretations. Even in the sayings alluding to Dan. 7.13, it is foremost the motive of exaltation or second coming that is in focus. All this invites us to see the Gospel Son of man sayings as getting their meaning primarily from their gospel context. That is, the efforts of the evangelists to produce a story of the earthly Jesus illuminated by the faith in him as the risen Lord.

217. Crispin H.T. Fletcher-Louis, 'The Revelation of the Sacral Son of Man: The Genre, History of Religious Context and the Meaning of the Transfiguration', in Friedrich Avemarie and Hermann Lichtenberger (eds.), *Auferstehung—Resurrection* (2001), pp. 247-98 (286). Also hinted at in *idem*, 'The High Priest as Divine Mediator in the Hebrew Bible: Dan 7:13 as a Test Case', *SBL 1997 Seminar Papers* (1997), pp. 161-93 (192-93).

17. Son of Man as a Product of the Gospel Tradition

Interpreters accepting the conclusions summarized in the previous chapters have had to look for new ways of understanding Son of man in the Gospels. If the most likely Aramaic idiom behind the Greek ὁ υἱὸς τοῦ ἀνθρώπου did not carry any content in itself but functioned mostly (be it as a substitute for 'I' or generic) within a category of sayings in which the speaker spoke of himself in the third person, and if, secondly, there was no specific apocalyptic Son of man expectation in Early Judaism to which Jesus or the first Christians could have referred by using the 'title', and if, thirdly, it is not possible to verify another content going back to the usage of the earthly Jesus, the most obvious place to look for the creation of the expression is the Gospel tradition itself. As the interpreter now meets Son of man in the Gospels, it is in a Greek form where any possible *double entendre* has been removed by both the striking double determination and the context making the exclusive reference to Jesus unmistakable.

It is conspicuous that this development coincides with a christological trend, considering Christology a product of the interpretative efforts of the first community. With the timely remark about New Testament christology that 'Probably no other factor has contributed more to the current aridity of the discipline than this fascination with the palaeontology of christological titles', Leander E. Keck put his finger on a vulnerable issue.[1] This fascination with titles became an obsession that produced hindrances on the way to interpreting the independent theological thinking of the authors of the Gospels in their construction of Christology through narrative. For this, Martin Karrer coined the expression 'lived christology' (gelebte Christologie).[2]

1. Leander E. Keck, 'Toward the Renewal of New Testament Christology', *NTS* 32 (1986), pp. 362-77 (368).

2. Martin Karrer, *Jesus Christus im Neuen Testament* (1998), p. 278. Italicized in Karrer's text. Cf. Karrer's instructive reflections on the meaning of the designation 'title', pp. 18-21.

This need not mean that the interpreter should think of Jesus as being without a messianic self-understanding. He probably had one, but the Christology of the earliest believers not only directly took over any eventual self-understanding, but Christology is best understood as a largely independent effort to comprehend the impact of Jesus' teaching, preaching, suffering and death. This was done first of all in light of the belief in his resurrection, in itself an interpretation of experiences of his first followers. The earliest written sources of this christological enterprise are found in the letters of Paul from between 51 and 54 CE. Probably for the first time, the Gospel of Mark attempts to model the christological thinking in a narrative sequence, using the stories of his baptism and death of Jesus as two extremes. The later Gospels prolonged the story by adding both a birth story and stories about meeting with the risen Lord. They created a framework for Jesus' teaching and preaching and his interpretation of his task and fate in life and death, and after death, through a series of sayings. In these christologically loaded sayings we find the expression Son of man. Their christological context is, in fact, their only common denominator. Thus the meaning of the expression is to be sought in their function within the individual Gospels.

Wolfgang Schenk, in *Das biographische Ich-Idiom 'Menschensohn' in den frühen Jesus-Biographien. Der Ausdruck, seine Codes und seine Rezeption in ihren Kotexten* (1997), became a significant spokesman for this new attitude and is paradigmatic.[3] Working along the lines of what he names a 'Copernican watershed in semiotics', Schenk gives all weight to the present text, claiming above all a synchronic understanding. Schenk abandons the usual 'tradition history' with its binary determination of tradition and interpretation. With regard to the gospels, this means that he deals primarily with a narrative or rhetorical Jesus, the central figure of the individual holy antique biography of the other Gospel authors. The so-called historical Jesus is regarded as a construct of the ideals of bourgeois liberalism in the eighteenth and nineteenth centuries, only to be resumed in its renaissance in the form of the 'new quest' in the second half of the twentieth century. The historical Jesus is an archaeological datum:

> Instead of 'a historical Jesus', it would be more sensible to speak about an 'archaeological Jesus' (unlike any 'literary/rhetorical Jesus'). Too much effort has been invested in showing Son of man to be a Jesuanic idiom, while questions about the different semantic contents in the present texts has been strongly underexposed.[4]

3. *The Son of Man Tradition* (1990) by D.R.A. Hare, could also have been used. Somewhat inconsequently, the work of Hare is taken up in connection with the individual Gospels.

4. Schenk, *Das biographische Ich-Idiom*, p. 17.

The basic question is not how the 'proclaimer' became the 'proclaimed', but—turned upside down—how the one who was proclaimed after Easter was later made the 'proclaimer' by the Synoptics. Thus Schenk will not take recourse to the meaning of a supposed Aramaic substratum, which he thinks is impossible, nor to any literal meaning of the components of the Greek expression, but seeks its content on a synchronic basis in the actual use it had in the different Gospels.[5]

Another presupposition is that there is no need to look for an Aramaic antecedent, all the less so because Greek was not an unknown language in Galilee.[6]

Taking the so-called Q to be 'The First Gospel', Schenk finds the saying Q 7.34 (= Lk. 7.34: 'The Son of man has come eating and drinking...') to be the sensible starting point for the use of the 'I-idiom' of Son of man, as this saying answers the basic question regarding who the Jesus of Q is. In this way he assumes that the Gospel Son of man originates in an inter-textual quotation of an adversarial designation: 'a common man'. 'The definite article had the specific deictic (and precisely intertextual) function of reference and would point back to this adversary's depreciating assertion: "*he whom they call a common man* (*der, den sie einem gewöhnlichen Mensch nennen*)"'.[7]

Schenk, consequently, detects a development in the use of the 'I-idiom' in the Jesus biographies of the Gospels. In the eight sayings ascribed to Q (7.[33-]34 [Mt. 11.19]; 9.[57-]58 [Mt. 8.19-20]; 11.30 [Mt. 12.38-39]; 12.10 [Mt. 12.32]; 12.40 [Mt. 24.44]; 17.24 [Mt. 24.37]; 17.26, 30 [Mt. 24.37, 39]), he finds the biography of a philosopher. The first five sayings describe his rejection and the last three his Parousia. All these sayings are provocatively enhanced I-sayings of Jesus.[8] In the Gospel of Mark, the idiom is taken over in 'the teacher/pupil-biography about the Son who was rejected as man,

5. This paragraph paraphrases more or less the points of departure sketched in the initial chapter, 'Das Vorfeld der Ausgangsfragen', of Schenk's *Das biographische Ich-Idiom*, pp. 16-17. Schenk refers several times to Bruce Chilton, 'The Son of Man: Human and Heavenly', in F. van Segbroeck, C.M. Tuckett, G. van Belle and J. Verheyden (eds.), *The Four Gospels* (FS Frans Neirynck, 1992) I, pp. 203-18.

6. Schenk, *Das biographische Ich-Idiom*, p. 21. Thus the whole discussion about translation is eliminated.

7. Schenk, *Das biographische Ich-Idiom*, p. 66; cf. 'Peroratio', pp. 226-31 (227) (where Schenk offers a summary of his results). This understanding reminds one of John Pairman Brown, 'The Son of Man: "This Fellow"', *Bib* 58 (1977), pp. 361-87 (cf. Chapter 16, Section 2 and the older precursors mentioned there).

8. The chapter on Q has the heading: 'Die Redensammlung Q ("The First Gospel") als urchristliche Primärquelle für die biographische Jesuanisierung des MS-Idioms' (p. 55).

whom God rehabilitated and who in the future will rehabilitate his rejected pupils'.[9] In the Gospel of Matthew, the enhanced 'I-idiom' is employed of the one rejected by Israel but legitimated at Easter, calling the whole of humanity into obedience under his realm in opposition to the realm of Satan. At his Parousia, before his throne and with his angels, he will execute a universal judgment rewarding obedience to his religious law and destroying those rejecting him.[10] Adhering to the trend which assumes that the Gospel of Luke is dependent among others on the Gospel of John, Schenk takes the latter as the fourth stage. In this, Son of man is the one seen by the witnesses to the revelation, the Son of God who descended from the pre-existent community in life eternal with the God-Father and, until his re-ascending in a revelatory way, has spoken the word of life which he himself had heard from the God-Father, the founding myth collecting the whole of the heavenly fraternity.[11] The last stage is the two-volume Lukan work, the oldest Gospel harmony, where Jesus is the true ruler, acting in the name of God.[12] In this Gospel Schenk also assumes that the anaphoric element in the definite article points back to the designation in the genealogical table, Lk. 3.38, where Jesus is declared Son of Adam as well as Son of God, the last definition being totally unheard of in Jewish genealogies.[13]

In this way, loosening the expression Son of man from any connection with the 'archaeological Jesus', Schenk achieves freedom to interpret it in a totally synchronic reading of the individual gospel. The first paragraph of his Conclusion runs:

9. Heading to the chapter on Mark; Schenk, *Das biographische Ich-Idiom*, p. 84. The German text runs: 'Die Lehrer/Schüler-Biographie über den als Menschen verworfenen Sohn, den Gott rehabilitiert hat und der künftig seine verworfenen Schüler rehabilitieren wird'.

10. Heading to the chapter on Matthew; Schenk, *Das biographische Ich-Idiom*, p. 125. In the German original: 'Der von Israel verworfene und österlich legitimierte, die ganze Menschheit als seinen Herrschaftsbereich im Widerstreit mit der Satansherrschaft im verstärkenden Ich-Idiom zum Gehorsam Rufende, wird bald als Parusierichter im universalen Weltgericht von seinem Thron her mit seinen Engeln den Gehorsam gegen sein Religionsgesetz lohnen, aber seine Verwerfer vernichten'.

11. In Schenk, *Das biographische Ich-Idiom*, p. 151, the German reads: 'Der vom Offenbarungszeugen gesehene, aus der präexistenten Gemeinschaft ewigen Lebens mit dem Vater-Gott abgestiegene Sohn-Gott, der bis zu seinem Wiederaufstieg das vom Vater-Gott selbst gehörte Lebens-Wort offenbarend geredet hat, als Gründungsmythos für die Sammlung der ganzen himmlischen Brüdergemeinschaft'.

12. In Schenk, *Das biographische Ich-Idiom*, p. 175, the German reads: 'Das "lukanische" Doppelwerk, die älteste "Evangelien-Harmonie": Jesus ist der wahre, im Namen Gottes handelnde Regent über Gottes Volk'.

13. Schenk, *Das biographische Ich-Idiom*, p. 184; cf. pp. 230-31.

In the Jesus-biographies, the determined I-idiom, 'Son of man', has its primary place in the sayings of the hero about himself as indexicalization (purely referring) enhanced renominalisation of the pure (and therefore weaker) biographic governing I-pronoun.[14]

In what follows, we will see how the interpretation of the Son of man in the four Gospels moves from having been dominated by tradition history; that is, the adaptation of an existing concept, to be an expression more or less in freefall, the foremost meaning due to its role in the individual gospel. Of course, this development coheres to the growing tendency among scholars to exclude the existence of a distinct Son of man concept in Early Judaism.

Son of man in the Gospel of John was the first to be found differing from the presumably more 'original' usage in the Synoptic Gospels. For this reason (although it is against the 'chronology'), we will start looking at issues of development in the understanding of the Son of Man in this Gospel.[15]

1. *Son of Man in the Gospel of John*[16]

The content of the expression Son of man in the Gospel of John has seldom been made the object of special investigation.[17] Usually, Son of man sayings

14. In Schenk, *Das biographische Ich-Idiom*, p. 226, the German reads: 'Das determinierte Ich-Idiom "MS" hat in den Jesus-Biographien seinen primären Platz in den Selbstaussagen des Heros als indexikalisierend (bloß verweisend) verstärkende Renominalisierung des bloßen (und damit schwächeren) biographisch leitenden Ich-Pronomens'.

15. Studies comparing the christologies of the four Gospels, such as, for instance, R. Schnackenburg, *Die Person Jesu Christi im Spiegel der vier Evangelien* (1993), do not try to describe a development in the use of Son of man.

16. The following studies, mainly dealing with only one Johannine Son of man saying or pericope, are only exceptionally taken up below: **1.51**: Joachim Jeremias, 'Die Berufung des Nathanaels', *Angelos* 3 (1928), pp. 2-5; Hans Windisch, 'Angelophanien um den Menschensohn auf Erden. Ein Kommentar zu Joh 1,51', *ZNW* 30 (1931), pp. 215-33; Gilles Quispel, 'Nathanael und der Menschensohn (Joh 1,51)', *ZNW* 47 (1956), pp. 281-83; I. Fritsch, '"et videbitis ... angelos Dei ascendentes et descendentes super Filium hominis" (Io. 1,51)', *Verbum Domini* 37 (1959), pp. 3-11; Wilhelm Michaelis, 'Joh. 1,51, Gen. 28,12 und das Menschensohn-Problem', *ThLZ* 85 (1960), cols. 561-78; Stephen S. Smalley, 'Johannes 1,51 und die Einleitung zum vierten Evangelium', in R. Pesch and R. Schnackenburg (eds.), *Jesus und der Menschensohn* (FS Anton Vögtle, 1975), pp. 300-13; Jerome H. Neyrey, 'The Jacob Allusion in John 1:51', *CBQ* 44 (1982), pp. 586-605; Christopher Rowland, 'John 1.51, Jewish Apocalyptic and Targumic Tradition', *NTS* 30 (1984), pp. 498-507; Willy Rordorf, 'Gen 28,10ff und Joh 1,51 in der patristischen Exegese', in Martin Rose (ed.), *Johannes-Studien: Interdisziplinäre Zugänge zum Johannes-Evangelium* (FS Jean Zumstein, 1990), pp. 39-46; William O. Walker, 'John 1:43-51 and "The Son of Man" in the Fourth Gospel', *JSNT* 56 (1994), pp. 1-42; J.C. O'Neill, 'Son of Man, Stone of Blood (John 1:51)', *NT* 45 (2003), pp. 374-81; Yves-Marie Blanchard, 'Le fils de l'homme et l'échelle de Jacob: Refléxion

sur l'intertextualité scriptuaire et relecture de Jean 1,51, à la lumière de Bible juive', in C. Focant and A. Wénin (eds.), *Analyse narrative et bible* (2005), pp. 181-95; J. Harold Ellens, 'Exegesis of Second Temple Texts in a Fourth Gospel Son of Man Logion', in Isaac Kalimi and Peter J. Haas (eds.), *Biblical Interpretation in Judaism and Christianity* (2006), pp. 131-49. **3.13-14**: E.M. Sidebottom, 'The Ascent and the Descent of the Son of Man in the Gospel of St. John', *AThR* 39 (1957), pp. 115-22; J.P. Haspels, 'De koperen slang en de Zoon des mensen', *Ministerium. Tijdschrift voor praktische theologie* 3 (1969), pp. 41-46; Eugen Ruckstuhl, 'Abstieg und Erhöhung des johanneischen Menschensohns', in R. Pesch and R. Schnackenburg (eds.), *Jesus und der Menschensohn* (FS Anton Vögtle, 1975), pp. 314-41 (reprinted in *idem*, *Jesus im Horizont der Evangelien* [1988], pp. 277-307 [Nachtrag, pp. 307-10]); Peder Borgen, 'Some Jewish Exegetical Traditions as Background for Son of Man Sayings in John's Gospel (Jn 3,13-14 and context)', in M. de Jonge (ed.), *L'Evangile de Jean* (1977), pp. 243-58 (reprinted in *idem*, *Logos was the true Light and other Essays on the Gospel of John* [1983], pp. 133-48); John W. Pryor, 'The Johannine Son of Man and the Descent-Ascent Motif', *JEThS* 34 (1991), pp. 341-51; Pierre Létourneau, *Jésus, Fils de l'homme et Fils de Dieu. Jean 2,23–3,36 et la double christologie johannique* (1993); Michèle Morgen, 'Le Fils de l'homme élevé en vue de la vie éternelle (Jn 3,14-15 éclaré par diverses traditions juives)', *RSR* 68 (1994), pp. 5-17; John F. Brug, 'Exegetical Brief: The *Son of Man* Who Is in Heaven', *Wisconsin Lutheran Quarterly* 93 (1996), pp. 140-41 (arguing for the longer text of John 3.13); John W. Romanowsky, '"When the Son of Man is Lifted Up": The Redemptive Power of the Crucifixion in the Gospel of John', *Horizons* 32 (2005), pp. 100-116 (also discussing 8.28 and 12.32); Martinus de Boer, 'Johannine History and Johannine Theology: The Death of Jesus as the Exaltation and the Glorification of the Son of Man', in G. Van Belle (ed.), *The Death of Jesus in the Fourth Gospel* (2007), pp. 293-326 (likewise also discussing 8.28 and 12.3. **6.53**: Charles Kingsley Barrett, 'Das Fleisch des Menschensohnes (Joh 6,53)', in R. Pesch and R. Schnackenburg (eds.), *Jesus und der Menschensohn* (FS Anton Vögtle, 1975), pp. 342-54; David A. Dorman, 'The Son of Man in John: A Fresh Approach through Chapter 6', *Studia Biblica et Theologica* 13 (1983), pp. 121-42; R. Zuurmond, 'Vlees en bloed van de Mensenzoon: Opmerkingen bij Johannes 6:53', *Amsterdamse Cahiers* 13 (1994), pp. 88-96. **8.28**: Johannes Riedl, 'Wenn Ihr den Menschensohn erhöht habt, werdet ihr erkennen (Joh 8,28)', in R. Pesch and R. Schnackenburg (eds.), *Jesus und der Menschensohn* (FS Anton Vögtle, 1975), pp. 355-70. **9.35**: Mogens Müller, '"Have You Faith in the Son of Man" (John 9.35)?', *NTS* 37 (1991), pp. 291-94; (= '"Tror du på menneskesønnen?" (Joh 9,35)', in M. Müller, *Skriften i Skriften* [2007], pp. 190-94). **12.23**: Andreas Leinhäupl-Wilke, '"Die Stunde des Menschensohnes" (Joh 12,23): Anmerkungen zur "heimlichen Mitte" des Johannesevangeliums', in Martin Fussnacht, A. Leinhäupl-Wilke and Stefan Lücking (eds.), *Die Weisheit—Ursprünge und Rezeption* (FS Karl Löning, 2003), pp. 185-210. **12.32, 34**: I. de la Potterie, 'L'exaltation du Fils de l'homme (Jn 12,31-36)', *Gregorianum* 49 (1968), pp. 460-78; R.L. Sturch, 'The Replacement of "Son of Man" by a Pronoun', *ET* 94 (1982–83), p. 333 (finds that Jn 12.32 originally must have been a Son of man saying because of the question in 12.34); George R. Beasley-Murray, 'John 12,31-32: The Eschatological Significance of the Lifting up of the Son of Man', in W. Schrage (ed.), *Studien zum Text und zur Ethik des Neuen Testaments* (FS Heinrich Greeven, 1986), pp. 70-81; John Dennis, 'The "Lifting Up of the Son of Man" and the Dethroning of the "Ruler of This World": Jesus' Death as the Defeat of the Devil in John 12,31-32', in of this Gospel were found to be a Johannine version of the same concept as in the Synoptics. Thus, Vincent Hartl[18] does not touch on this question, while F.W. Grosheide,[19] H. Dieckmann[20] and J.H. Bernard[21] content themselves with stating that there is no real difference in usage. This could be expected if it is assumed that in both cases we are confronted with sayings going back to the historical Jesus.

With the rise of the History of Religions School the picture changed. Wilhelm Bousset, in his *Kyrios Christos*, declares it a paradox 'that the Fourth Gospel has retained the old title of Jewish messianology which stands at the centre of the dogmatics of the Palestinian primitive community, the title ὁ υἱὸς τοῦ ἀνθρώπου'.[22] According to Bousset, the evangelist John,

> while he took over the concept with its entire contents and all its individual consequences, yet spiritualized and reinterpreted it in a grandiose fashion. He completely separated the Son of Man from Jewish eschatology and apocalypticism and from the ardent expectation of his return in popular Christianity. In the same moment in which he faithfully explains the ancient meaning of the title, that God has given the judgment to Jesus because he is the Son of Man, he spiritualizes and makes contemporary the great 'works' of the resurrection of the dead and the judgment in such a way that he falls into the danger of completely eliminating the primitive Christian eschatology. In this manner the title 'Son of Man' becomes for him the comprehensive designation of the pre-existent and eternal glory of Jesus which surpasses everything earthly, in comparison with which the earthly sojourn of Jesus is only an episode.[23]

G. Van Belle (ed.), *The Death of Jesus in the Fourth Gospel* (2007), pp. 677-91. **19.5**: Rudolf Schnackenburg, 'Die Ecce-homo-Szene und der Menschensohn', in R. Pesch and R. Schnackenburg (eds.), *Jesus und der Menschensohn* (FS Anton Vögtle, 1975), pp. 371-86, discusses but dismisses the thought that Son of man stands behind ὁ ἀνθρώπος in Pilate's exclamation.

17. For the first part of this section, cf. Müller, *Der Ausdruck 'Menschensohn' in den Evangelien*, pp. 233-37: Excursus J. Das Verständnis der Beziehung zwischen der Anwendung des Ausdrucks 'Menschensohn' in den synoptischen Evangelien und im Johannesevangelium in der bisherigen Forschung. The period 1957–69 is given a detailed analysis by E. Ruckstuhl, 'Die johanneische Menschensohnforschung 1957–1969', *Theologische Berichte* 1 (1972), pp. 171-284.

18. Vincent Hartl, 'Anfang und Ende des Titels "Menschensohn", Ein Beitrag zur johanneischen Frage', *BZ* 7 (1909), pp. 342-54.

19. 'Υἱὸς τοῦ ἀνθρώπου in het Evangelium naar Johannes', *Theologische Studiën* 35 (1917), pp. 242-48.

20. '"Der Sohn des Menschen" im Johannesevangelium', *Scholastik* 2 (1927), pp. 229-47.

21. *A Critical and Exegetical Commentary on the Gospel According to St. John* (1928), pp. cxii-cxxxiii.

22. Wilhelm Bousset, *Kyrios Christos* (1913, 2nd edn, 1921), p. 155. Quoted according to the English translation, *Kyrios Christos* (1970), p. 212.

23. Bousset, *Kyrios Christos*, p. 156; English translation, p. 213.

Rudolf Bultmann follows the same track, maintaining that 'while the Son of man figure in the Synoptic Gospels obviously stems from Jewish apocalypticism, where it has lost its essential features, the Son of man sayings in the Gospel of John show precisely these essential features of the "Ανθρωπος-myth in a complete way'.[24]

That the Gospel of John not only spiritualizes the Jewish apocalyptic concept in its Son of man sayings but goes behind it by resuming its very basis, the myth of Primeval Man, in a gnostic edition, is assumed by G. Iber,[25] C.H. Dodd[26] and Y.-B. Tremel.[27] Others, like E.M. Sidebottom[28] and R.G. Hamerton-Kelly,[29] point instead to the concept of a heavenly man in Early Judaism as the basis of the Johannine Son of man sayings. In both cases, interpreters have reckoned with concepts which are essentially different from those assumed behind the Synoptic Son of man sayings. In an influential article, 'The Man from Heaven in Johannine Sectarianism', from 1972, Wayne A. Meeks turns this upside down by having the Gospel of John create the presupposition for the later Gnostic Son of man. Claiming that the Gospel of John 'functions for its readers in precisely the same way that the epiphany of its hero functions within its narratives and dialogues'[30] and calling it 'an etiology of the Johannine group', Meeks writes:

24. Rudolf Bultmann, 'Die Bedeutung der neuerschlossenen mandäischen und manichäischen Quellen für das Verständnis des Johannesevangeliums', *ZNW* 24 (1925), pp. 100-46; quoted according to reprint in *idem*, *Exegetica* (1967), pp. 55-104 (97). This is of course also Bultmann's understanding in *Das Evangelium des Johannes* (1941), passim.

25. G. Iber, *Überlieferungsgeschichtliche Untersuchungen zum Begriff des Menschensohns im Neuen Testament* (typewritten dissertation 1953). Here according to the summary of the author in *ThLZ* 80 (1955), cols. 115-16.

26. C.H. Dodd, *The Interpretation of the Fourth Gospel* (1953, 7th edn, 1965), pp. 241-49 (243).

27. Y.-B. Tremel, 'Le Fils de l'homme selon saint Jean', *LV* 12 (1963), pp. 65-92 (91-92).

28. E.M. Sidebottom, 'The Ascent and the Descent of the Son of Man in the Gospel of John', *AThR* 39 (1957), pp. 115-22 (117). In *idem*, 'The Son of Man in the Fourth Gospel', *ET* 68 (1956–57), pp. 231-35, 280-83, Sidebottom especially points to the influence from Ezekiel (p. 233): 'it is hard to see why writers so constantly ignore or minimize the influence of the Son of Man in Ezekiel on the New Testament usage. Only here in pre-Christian literature is the expression certainly a title.' Another scholar to emphasize the influence from Ezekiel is B. Vawter, 'Ezekiel and John', *CBQ* 26 (1964), pp. 450-58 (451).

29. R.G. Hamerton-Kelly, *Pre-existence, Wisdom, and the Son of Man* (1973), pp. 241-42.

30. Wayne A. Meeks, 'The Man from Heaven in Johannine Sectarianism', *JBL* 91 (1972), pp. 44-72 (69). The sentence is italicized in the original.

> In telling the story of the Son of Man who came down from heaven and re-ascended after choosing a few of his own out of the world, the book defines and vindicates the existence of the community that evidently sees itself as unique, alien from its world, under attack, misunderstood, but living in unity with Christ and through him with God.[31]

The Fourth Gospel transformed the Christ-Wisdom into the masculine Logos, the Son of Man, 'and once the social dynamics of the anti-worldly sect were in motion, all the forces were present for the production of the Valentine type'.[32]

We also meet the assumption that the Johannine use of Son of man, following the special eschatology of this Gospel, is a transformation and development of speech patterns as found in the Synoptics. Sigfried Schulz, in the first real monograph on the topic, *Untersuchungen zur Menschensohn-Christologie im Johannesevangelium. Zugleich ein Beitrag zur Methodengeschichte der Auslegung des 4. Evangeliums* (1957), also assumes an essential difference between the Son of man christology of the Synoptic Gospels and the Son of man theme in the Gospel of John. Also the last mentioned is a Son of man Christology: 'Jesus at the same time is the wandering one, the enthroned and the future eschatological Son of man'.[33] In this Gospel, the originally apocalyptic Son of man sayings are subjected to a re-interpretation, coloured by Christian, Old Testament and non-Jewish ideas, although the basic Jewish character is maintained in God being the one conferring authority to and glorification of the Son of man. Schulz summarizes his view in the following way:

> The apocalyptic expectations of Late Judaism are partly fulfilled insofar as the transcendent heavenly Son of man has appeared in Jesus receiving the authority to complete the judgment of the world and claiming the divine doxa. On the other hand, the revealing of the judgment of humanity (5,28-29) and the glorification of the Son of man through God, still stand out as expectations of the near eschaton (13,31-32).[34]

In the following years, several scholars adhere to this view of the Johannine Son of man as an independent reworking of the Synoptic Son of man christology primarily and indirectly influenced by thoughts of Jewish or non-Jewish origin.[35] This also applies to Francis J. Moloney, writing the next

31. Meeks, 'The Man from Heaven in Johannine Sectarianism', pp. 69-70.
32. Meeks, 'The Man From Heaven in Johannine Sectarianism', p. 72.
33. Sigfried Schulz, *Untersuchungen zur Menschensohn-Christologie im Johannesevangelium. Zugleich ein Beitrag zur Methodengeschichte der Auslegung des 4. Evangeliums* (1957), p. 123.
34. Schulz, *Untersuchungen zur Menschensohn-Christologie*, p. 123.
35. Thus W. Michaelis, 'Joh. 1,51, Gen. 28,12 und das Menschensohn-Problem', *ThLZ* 85 (1960), cols. 561-78; A.J.B. Higgins, *Jesus and the Son of Man* (1964),

extensive monograph on the topic, *The Johannine Son of Man* (1976). With regard to the possible background of the Johannine Son of man Christology, Moloney reaches the conclusion that 'there appears to be little necessity to look beyond early Christian traditions to find the source for the Johannine use of "the Son of Man"'.[36] A few interpreters present the opinion that the difference between the Synoptic and Johannine Son of man should not be exaggerated.[37] Robert Maddox finds that 'in spite of considerable differences of vocabulary and imagery, the fundamental significance of the title "the Son of Man" in John is not different from that which it has in the Synoptic Gospels. Already in the *Similitudes of 1 Enoch*, the Son of Man is the eschatological judge who stands in intimate relationship to those who look to him for vindication and salvation and who will save them at the end.'[38]

pp. 153-84 (183-84) (more or less identical with *idem*, *Menschensohn-Studien* [1965], pp. 21-51); R. Schnackenburg, 'Der Menschensohn im Johannesevangelium', *NTS* 11 (1964–65), pp. 123-37; *idem*, *Das Johannesevangelium* 1 (1965, 2nd edn, 1967), pp. 411-23: Excursus 5: 'Der Menschensohn im Johannesevangelium', a reworked version of the German article; C. Colpe, 'ὁ υἱὸς τοῦ ἀνθρώπου', in *ThWNT*, VIII (1969), pp. 468-74; E. Ruckstuhl, 'Die johanneische Menschensohnforschung 1957–1969', *Theologische Berichte* 1 (1972), pp. 171-84 (193, 282); B. Lindars, 'The Son of Man in Johannine Christology', in B. Lindars and Stephen S. Smalley (eds.), *Christ and the Spirit in the New Testament* (FS Charles Digby Moule, 1973), pp. 43-60; according to Lindars, Son of man in John is not a genuine title, but a reference to the picture in Dan. 7. Further J. Coppens, 'Le Fils de l'homme dans l'évangile johannique', *EThL* 52 (1976), pp. 28-81 (reprinted in *idem*, *BEThL* 55 [1981], pp. 45-103); 'Logia johannique du Fils de l'Homme', in M. de Jonge (ed.), *L'Evangile de Jean: sources, rédaction* (1977), pp. 311-15 (reprinted in *idem*, *BEThL* 55 [1981], pp. 98-103); 'Le Fils de l'homme johannique', *EThL* 54 (1978), pp. 126-30. Peder Borgen, 'Some Jewish Exegetical Traditions as Background for Son of Man Sayings in John's Gospel (Jn 3,13-14 and Context)', in M. de Jonge (ed.), *L'Évangile de Jean* (1977), pp. 243-58, sees (p. 253) '[t]he use of the phrase 'the Son of Man' in Jn 3,13...to be due to a fusion of ideas from the Sinaitic ascent and Dan 7,13-14'.

36. Francis J. Moloney, *The Johannine Son of Man* (1976), p. 16. Cf. Moloney's own summary, 'The Johannine Son of Man', *BThB* 6 (1976), pp. 177-89, and *idem*, 'A Johannine Son of Man Discussion?', *Salesianum* 39 (1977), pp. 93-102. Repeated and nuanced in *idem*, 'The Johannine Son of Man Revisited', in Gilbert Van Belle, Jan G. van der Watt and Petrus Maritz (eds.), *Theology and Christology in the Fourth Gospel: Essays by the Members of the SNTS Johannine Writings Seminar* (2005), pp. 177-202.

37. Thus also Th. Preiss, 'Le Fils de l'Homme (Suite)', *EThR* 28 (1953), pp. 1-75; W.J. Moulder, *The Son of Man in the Old Testament and the Gospel Traditions* (typewritten thesis, 1973–74), pp. 203-302. With regard to R. Maddox, see next note.

38. Robert Maddox, 'The Function of the Son of Man in the Gospel of John', in R. Banks (ed.), *Reconciliation and Hope: Essays on Atonement and Eschatology* (FS L.L. Morris, 1974), pp. 186-204 (203).

Similar conclusions are suggested by F.H. Borsch[39] and Stephen S. Smalley,[40] who assume that the Johannine Son of man sayings are not secondary to the Synoptics but reflect the use of the expression used by the earthly Jesus to the same extent as these. Borsch maintains that the differences and similarities are best explained through the hypothesis 'that the Johannine traditions and those inherited by the Synoptic evangelists became, for all practical purposes, separated at a relatively early date. Each of them have preserved and developed authentic elements from the primitive strata in their own way.'[41]

Others, for example F.-M. Braun, see not only influence from Dan 7.13 in the Johannine Son of man concept, but also from the personification of Lady Wisdom in Wisdom literature. Braun finds that the Johannine Son of man functions in such a way that the figure 'is nearer to the Wisdom than to the apocalyptic figure',[42] and that 'The identification of Messiah with the Wisdom is probably the result of an effort on the mystery of the Son of man'.[43]

A few, however, think that the difference is to be interpreted as if there were no longer a distinct Son of man concept to be found in the Gospel of John. Ch. de Beus concludes that, in contrast to the Synoptic Gospels, where it is an eschatological messianic designation rooted in Daniel, in the Gospel of John, Jesus as Son of man is identified with the Son of God in line with the special preaching of this gospel.[44] According to his hypothesis, only Son of man sayings which lack competing parallels without the expression, can be counted as original. Joachim Jeremias finds this to be the case only in John 1.51. For this reason, he doubts that the expression is original to the other twelve Johannine Son of man sayings.[45] The conclusion is no different

39. F.H. Borsch, *The Son of Man in Myth and History* (1967), pp. 257-313.

40. Stephen S. Smalley, 'The Johannine Son of Man Sayings', *NTS* 15 (1968–69), pp. 278-301.

41. Borsch, *The Son of Man in Myth and History*, pp. 264-65.

42. F.-M. Braun, 'Messie, Logos et Fils de l'Homme', in E. Massaux (ed.), *La Venue du Messie. Messianisme et Eschatologie* (1962), pp. 133-47 (146).

43. Braun, 'Messie, Logos et Fils de l'Homme', p. 147. A similar view is taken by H.-M. Dion, 'Quelques traits originaux de la conception johannique du Fils de l'Homme', *Sciences Eccclésiastiques* 19 (1967), pp. 49-65 (64-65).

44. Ch. de Beus, 'Achterground en inhoud van de uitdrukking "de Zoon des Mensen" in de synoptische evangeliën', *NedThT* 9 (1954–55), pp. 272-95, as well as *idem*, 'Het gebruik en de betekenis van de uitdrukking "de Zoon des Mensen" in het Evangelie van Johannes', *NedThT* 10 (1955–56), pp. 237-51 (250-51).

45. Joachim Jeremias, 'Die älteste Schicht der Menschensohn-Logien', *ZNW* 58 (1967), pp. 159-72 (170). Earlier, in 'Die Berufung des Nathanael', *Angelos* 3 (1928), pp. 2-5, Jeremias suggested that Son of man is to be identified with the Bethel stone as the symbol of the gateway to heaven (Gen. 28.17). This interpretation later was taken up with

when E.D. Freed thinks that the employment of Son of man in the Gospel of John is the result of its author's 'zeal for variation', because 'all the evidence indicates that there is no separate Son of man christology in the fourth gospel apart from that of the earthly Jesus who for the writer was also the Christ, the Son of God, the Son of man, etc. The various titles are all used as variations for each other and for the name of Jesus.'[46]

That it is the Johannine Jesus who decides the content of the expression, is also defended by Elisabeth Kinniburgh, who claims 'that the term "Son of Man" has meaning for John only in the context of what he tells us of Jesus of Nazareth in his actions among men or in his death'.[47] She continues:

> The term may still represent an eschatological figure, but now one who has been known, who has spoken to men and given them gifts, and whose glory is to be seen, not in the coming on the clouds of heaven, but in the death of a particular man at a particular time. It is therefore a term of realized eschatology and the historicity of the language is reinforced. Since all other titles belong to this man (chapter 1), this is where God's dealings with man take place. The Son of man term is therefore taken up indirectly into mediatorial terms in John.

Thus:

> For John, what the Son of man is, is the total story of Jesus; and the problem of history is crucial.[48]

Margaret Pamment assumes that the Gospel of John in its use of Son of man 'seems to be drawing especially on the speculation in Dan. vii. 13f., which can be read to mean that "one like a Son of man" is the representative of "the saints of the Most High"'. Her thesis is that the expression 'draws particular attention to his representative humanity; that is, Jesus is pictured as representing not what everyman is, but what man could and should be'.[49] This line of thought is later intensified by Walter Wink, who sees in the Gospel of John an independent witness to the same '[f]aith in the Earthly Archetypal Human Being' as is found in the Synoptic Gospels.[50]

approval by J.C. O'Neill, 'Son of Man, Stone of Blood (John 1:51)', *NT* 45 (2003), pp. 374-81, finding the reason for Son of man in this saying in a wordplay between בן אדם and אבן דם, 'stone of blood',

46. E.D. Freed, 'The Son of Man in the Fourth Gospel', *JBL* 86 (1967), pp. 402-409 (409).

47. Elisabeth Kinniburgh, 'The Johannine "Son of Man"', *SE* 4 = *TU* 102 (1968), pp. 64-71 (64).

48. Kinniburgh, 'The Johannine "Son of Man"', pp. 70-71.

49. Margaret Pamment, 'The Son of Man in the Fourth Gospel', *JThS* NS 36 (1985), pp. 55-66 (58).

50. Walter Wink, '"The Son of the Man" in the Gospel of John', in Robert T. Fortna and Tom Thatcher (eds.), *Jesus in Johannine Tradition* (2001), pp. 117-23. The quotation

Following another line of argument, David A. Dorman sees Son of man in the Gospel of John as an expression parallel with Son of God. In John 6, '[t]he use of the title is a test of faith rather than a profession of faith' and 'that "Son of Man" has no character as such, but is only a function, a role'. So, 'for John the Son of Man is the Son before humanity (in the context of the problem of humanity) and the Son of God is the Son before God (the Son in context of the answer of God)'.[51]

Others, in the same decade, suggest that the Johannine Son of man has a specific reference. Wolfgang Roth thinks the relevant background is the Genesis story about Adam and his sons, the Greek expression originating in a *ben adam* as pointing to Abel. Taken together, the Johannine Son of man sayings portray Jesus as 'Abel-Re-Incarnate', an understanding Roth also finds confirmed in *The Testament of Abraham* A 12-13.[52]

Two shorter monographs likewise deny that, in John, Son of man is an apocalyptic title. Robert Rhea opines that Son of man in the Gospel of John functions as a messianic title, but that it should be seen in the light of poetic usage in the Psalms, in the addressing of Ezekiel and in *The Testament of Abraham*. 'It is, therefore, highly probable that the term Son of Man was a somewhat obscure yet significant phrase which provided a means of referring to prophetic office. It served to indicate the divine presence which made itself manifest to the human prophet.'[53] Delbert Royce Burkett, on the other hand, is more precise. The descent motive, especially in Jn 3.13, and the assumption that the Greek expression is to be translated literally 'the son of the man' leads Burkett to see the background in Prov. 30.1-4. Thus 'the man' in Prov. 30.1 is taken as an enigmatic designation for God, and 'his son' in v. 4 to be the son of this man, that is, the Son of God, to the effect that the expression is to be understood 'as a veiled synonym for "the Son of God"'.[54]

is the heading on p. 120. Cf. for the same author's *The Human Being: Jesus and the Enigma of the Son of the Man* (2002), discussed in Chapter 16, above.

51. David A. Dorman, 'The Son of Man in John: A Fresh Approach through Chapter 6', *Studia Biblica et Theologica* 13 (1983), pp. 121-42 (134, 138, 141).

52. Wolfgang Roth, 'Jesus as the Son of Man: The Scriptural Identity of a Johannine Image', in Dennis E. Groh and Robert Jewett (eds.), *The Living Text* (FS Ernest W. Saunders, 1985), pp. 11-26 (20-24). For the later attempt by R. Steven Notley in the same direction, cf. Chapter 16 above.

53. Robert Rhea, *The Johannine Son of Man* (1990), p. 70. The conclusion rests mainly on an analysis of 5.27; 6.62; 9.35, and 6.53, and the author thinks it not impossible that the sayings offer a door to the self-understanding of Jesus.

54. Delbert Royce Burkett, *The Son of Man in the Gospel of John* (1991), p. 74. The assumption that this derivation is also relevant to the Synoptic Gospels and the self-understanding of the earthly Jesus, is abandoned in Burkett's later book, *The Son of Man Debate* (1999), pp. 66-67, where the conclusions are declared valid only for the Fourth Gospel.

Some scholars continue to assume the apocalyptic concept of a messianic Son of man as the background of the Johannine Son of man. This understanding is found in the monograph by Kanika Pabayim Mided Kuzenzama.[55] John Painter likewise presupposes that 'there was in first century Judaism a tradition of the Son of Man as a heavenly messianic figure'. 'The initial reference to the Son of Man identifies him as an enthroned heavenly figure, [and] only in the subsequent references does it become apparent that he is enthroned by way of the cross'.[56] This means 'that there is no Son or Son of Man christology in John but that motifs from these traditions contributed to John's christology'.[57]

The latest significant monograph, *Der Menschensohn im Evangelium nach Johannes* (2000) by Markus Sasse, likewise sees the Johannine Son of man functioning as an interpretation of the title 'Son' in a community bewildered by the break with the synagogue and fighting to maintain monotheistic belief. Sasse sees the key to the interpretation of the Johannine Son of man in Jn 3.13, which describes the descent and ascent of the Son of man.[58] The employment of the Son of man is conditioned by two moments in tradition, the possibility of participation in the Son of man, and that he is

55. Kanika Pabayim Mided Kuzenzama, *Le titre johannique du fils de l'homme. Essai lexicographique* (1990), esp. pp. 15-22, and p. 75.

56. John Painter, 'The Enigmatic Johannine Son of Man', in F. van Segbroeck, C. M. Tuckett, G. van Belle, and J. Verheyden (eds.), *The Four Gospels 1992* (FS Frans Neirynck, 1992), III, pp. 1869-88 (1877, 1876).

57. Painter, 'The Enigmatic Johannine Son of Man', p. 1887. A somewhat similar understanding is found in Bertold Klappert, 'The Coming Son of Man Became Flesh: High Christology and Anti-Judaism in the Gospel of John', in R. Bieringer, D. Pollefeyt and F. Vandecasteele-Vanneuville (eds.), *Anti-Judaism and the Fourth Gospel* (2001), pp. 159-86. As seen from the subtitle, the aim of the article is not really to detect the meaning of the Son of man in John, which is presupposed to be a messianic title given a specific role in the Johannine christology and used of the one becoming flesh: 'The Johannine Son of Man logia are to be understood from the proleptic eschatology characteristic of the Gospel of John' (p. 168). Ype Bekker, *Zoon van God, Messias, Mensenzoon. De structuur van het Evangelie naar Johannes* (1997), does not discuss the meaning of Son of man in John, but presupposes the correctness of Karl Barth's understanding of the expression as signifying his human nature (cf. for this, the beginning of Chapter 14, above). See especially pp. 26-27 where Bekker brings a lengthy quotation from Barth's *Kirchliche Dogmatik* forward as an argument. C. Ham, 'The Title "Son of Man" in the Gospel of John', *Stone Campbell Journal* 1 (1998), pp. 67-84, finds that the Johannine Son of Man reflects the imagery found in Dan. 7.13-14 and *1 En.* 37–71. It also looks back to Adam through Ezekiel (and Ps. 8).

58. Accordingly, Jn 3.13 receives the most extensive treatment of all the Johannine Son of man sayings. See Markus Sasse, *Der Menschensohn im Evangelium nach Johannes* (2000), pp. 79-156, which also includes an analysis of the background of the expression (pp. 140-49).

known as a pre-existent individual figure belonging to the divine sphere. Thus the expression is suitable for a person whose true home is the heavenly sphere. The point of departure for the Jewish Son of man tradition is Daniel 7 and *1 Enoch* 37–71. Later, *4 Ezra* 13 shows how this tradition could be developed. It is, however, not possible to speak about a 'firm fixed pre-Christian-Jewish Son of man concept (von einem fest fixierten vorchristlich-jüdischen Menschensohn-Konzept)', only of a special Son of man exegesis building on Daniel 7.[59] In the Gospel of John, Son of man is used in a post-Easter perspective and reflects the already concluded life of the earthly Jesus. Thus 'the 13 Son of man sayings convey a unified picture of the Johannine Son of man'.[60] According to Sasse,

> The Son of man is an empty expression with regard to its content. Nothing really is said about the Son of man. He is totally subsumed in a way. The Son of man proclaims nothing. He descends from heaven, is exalted through being crucified and returns back to his point of departure. The Son of man goes, so to say, through the Gospel.[61]

Later, Sasse states:

> The Son of man functions as a christological corrective. As a christological designation, it corrects christological expectations which are deficient from John's point of view (1.51, 3.13 ff., 6.27, 9.35), respectively supplementing and interpreting another christological designation. The Son of man, however, is nowhere clarified by another designation. Therein lies its special meaning.[62]

According to Sasse, the Johannine Son of man is used about Jesus as the one descended from heaven, the redeemer whose fate on earth his believers are going to share. The Son of man is representative of God's dominion (cf. Dan. 7). He is brought as near as possible to God. At the same time, only Son of man christology offers a theological interpretation of the death of Jesus. 'All texts, which are about the death of Jesus, are dependent on the program advanced in 3.13-15. Here appears the meaning of the notion of the Son of man (Menschensohnbegriff) for the Johannine christology, which is not to be abandoned.'[63]

There is a only a weak tendency to view the content of the expression in the Gospel of John as deriving from its role inside Johannine Christology. Among the few who read the expression in this way is Mary Margaret Pazdan. Inspired not least by Paul Ricoeur's thoughts about metaphorical

59. Sasse, *Der Menschensohn im Evangelium nach Johannes*, pp. 140-41.
60. Sasse, *Der Menschensohn im Evangelium nach Johannes*, p. 237.
61. Sasse, *Der Menschensohn im Evangelium nach Johannes*, p. 245.
62. Sasse, *Der Menschensohn im Evangelium nach Johannes*, p. 247.
63. Sasse, *Der Menschensohn im Evangelium nach Johannes*, p. 264.

interpretation, she finds that the study should not be limited to the designation Son of man alone, but also to Son. According to Pazdan,

> The result is a recognition of the integral connection of Son and Son of man as two metaphors which invite the reader to reconsider the importance of the images and names used to describe Jesus as well as what they reveal about him as the incarnate Logos... The Significance of the Son of man, then, is located within what is revealed about Jesus throughout the Fourth Gospel as well as what the reader discovers, which may extend beyond the understanding of the first-century community.[64]

Douglas R.A. Hare finds the Johannine Son of man 'in close proximity to the Christian writers of the second and succeeding centuries, who employ *huios anthropou* as a way of speaking of the genuine humanity of Jesus in their battle against the docetists'. Thus: 'The term refers to the incarnational existence of the Logos. It points to the unique humanity of the Incarnate One.'[65]

Where an apocalyptic Son of man concept or a Gnostic Anthropos-myth is no longer presupposed as the background, the interpretation of Son of man in the Gospel of John tends more and more to see the meaning of the expression as a creation from inside the Johannine tradition. It is difficult not to assume some dependence on one or both of the older of the Synoptic Gospels (Mark and Matthew), but, obviously, the expression has not offered much resistance to being integrated in Johannine Christology where it seemingly receives all its content from its context. The study of the Johannine Son of man opened a perspective of the use of Son of man in the different Gospels, each on its own merits. We will now look at the development in research on the Synoptic Gospels (including the hypothetical Q).

2. *The Markan Son of Man*[66]

The ice broken by studies on the Johannine Son of man, growing attention to the peculiarities of the Synoptic Gospels in later years gradually resulted in viewing the use of Son of man in these three Gospels as more or less a deliberate utilization of the expression in the construction of individual

64. Mary Margaret Pazdan, *The Son of Man: A Metaphor for Jesus in the Fourth Gospel* (1991), p. 85.

65. Douglas R.A. Hare, *The Son of Man Tradition* (1990), p. 111.

66. The following studies, mainly dealing with only one Markan Son of man saying or pericope, are only exceptionally mentioned below: **2.10, 28**: T.W. Manson, 'Mark ii.27f.', in *Coniectanea Neotestamentica*, XI (FS Anton Fridrichsen, 1947), pp. 138-46; A. Feuillet, 'L'ἐξουσία du Fils de l'Homme (d'après *Mc*. II,10-28 et parr.)', *RSR* 42 (1954), pp. 161-92; J. Duplacy, 'Marc, 2,10, Note de syntaxe', in *Mélanges bibliques* (FS

christologies, not least in connection to the loss of confidence in the existence of an apocalyptic Son of man concept within contemporary Judaism.[67]

A. Robert, 1957), pp. 420-27; H. Troadec, 'Le Fils de l'homme est maître même du sabbat (Marc 2,23-3,6)', *BVC* 21 (1958), pp. 73-83; C.P. Ceroke, 'Is Mk 2,10 a Saying of Jesus?', *CBQ* 22 (1960), pp. 369-90; Lewis S. Hay, 'The Son of Man in Mark 2,10 and 2,28', *JBL* 89 (1970), pp. 69-75; Karl Kertelge, 'Die Vollmacht des Menschensohnes zur Sündenvergebung (Mk 2,10)', in Paul Hoffmann *et al.* (eds.), *Orientierung an Jesus. Zur Theologie der Synoptiker* (FS Josef Schmid, 1973), pp. 205-13; J. Gnilka, 'Das Elend vor dem Menschensohn (Mk 2,1-12)', in R. Pesch and R. Schnackenburg (eds.), *Jesus und der Menschensohn* (FS Anton Vögtle, 1975), pp. 196-209; Darell J. Doughty, 'The Authority of the Son of Man (Mk 2,1-3,6)', *ZNW* 74 (1983), pp. 161-81; M. Casey, 'Culture and Historicity: The Plucking of the Grain (Mark 2.23-28)', *NTS* 34 (1988), pp. 1-23. **3.28**: C. Colpe, 'Der Spruch von der Lästerung des Geistes', in Eduard Lohse (ed.), *Der Ruf Jesu und die Antwort der Gemeinde* (FS Joachim Jeremias, 1970), pp. 63-79; Evald Lövestam, *Spiritus blasphemia. Eine Studie zu Mk 3,28f par Mt 12,31f, Lk 12,10* (1968). **8.31**: Otto Michel, 'Der Umbruch: Messianität = Menschensohn. Fragen zur Markus 8,31', in Gert Jeremias *et al.* (eds.), *Tradition und Glaube. Das frühe Christentum in seiner Umwelt* (FS K.G. Kuhn, 1971), pp. 310-16; W.J. Bennett (Jr), '"The son of man must..."', *NT* 17 (1975), pp. 113-29; René Kieffer, 'Det synoptiska problemet i de tre förutsägelserna om Människosonens lidande', *SEÅ* 69 (2004), pp. 191-98; **8.38**: O.J.F. Seitz, 'The Future Coming of the Son of Man: Three Midrashic Formulations in the Gospel of Mark', *SE* 4 (= *TU* 112, 1973), pp. 478-94 (treating also 13.26; 14.62); Werner Georg Kümmel, 'Das Verhalten Jesus gegenüber und das Verhalten des Menschensohnes. Markus 8,38 par und Lukas 12,8f par Matthäus 10,32f', in R. Pesch and R. Schnackenburg (eds.), *Jesus und der Menschensohn* (FS Anton Vögtle, 1975), pp. 210-24 (reprinted in *idem*, *Heilsgeschehen und Geschichte* Band 2. Gesammelte Aufsätze 1965–77 [1978], pp. 201-14; Barnabas Lindars, 'Jesus as Advocate: A Contribution to the Christology Debate', *BJRL* 62 (1979–80), pp. 476-97; Ragnar Leivestad, 'Wer ist der Vater des Menschensohns? Einige Reflexionen über den Ausdruck "in der Herrlichkeit seines Vaters" in Mk 8,38', in Jarmo Kiilunen, Vilho Riekkinen and Heikki Räisänen (eds.), *Glaube und Gerechtigkeit. Rafael Gyllenberg in memoriam* (1983), pp. 95-108; E. Adams, 'The Coming of the Son of Man in Mark's Gospel', *Tyndale Bulletin* 56 (2005), pp. 39-61 (treating also 13.26; 14.62). **10.45**: Theodor Preiss, 'The Son of Man Came to Minister: Mark 10:35-45', *Interpretation* 4 (1950), pp. 189-92; Charles Kingsley Barrett, 'The Background of Mark 10:45', in A.J.B. Higgins (ed.), *New Testament Essays: Studies in Memory of T.W. Manson* (1959), pp. 1-18; Karl Kertelge, 'Der dienende Menschensohn (Mk 10,45)', in R. Pesch and R. Schnackenburg (eds.), *Jesus und der Menschensohn* (FS Anton Vögtle, 1975), pp. 225-39; W.J. Moulder, 'The Old Testament Background and the Interpretation of Mark X.45', *NTS* 24 (1977–78), pp. 120-27; Peter Stuhlmacher, 'Existenzvertretung für die Vielen: Mk 10,45 (Mt 20,28)', in Rainer Albertz, Hans Peter Müller, H.H. Wolff and Walter Zimmerli (eds.), *Werden und Wirken des Alten Testaments* (FS Claus Westermann, 1980), pp. 412-27; reprint in *idem*, *Versöhnung, Gesetz und Gerechtigkeit. Aufsätze zur biblischen Theologie* (1981), pp. 27-42; Adrian Schenker, 'Substitution du chatiment ou prix de la paix: don la vie du fils de l'homme en Mk 10:45 et par à lumière de l'Ancien Testament', in Martin Benzerath, Aloyse Schmid and Jacques Guillet (eds.), *La pâque du Christ mystère de salut: Melanges offerts au Francois-Xavier Durrwell* (1982), pp. 75-90. **13.26**: C.H. Valentine, 'The Son

For the great majority of scholars working on the basis of the Markan hypothesis, the Gospel of Mark became the centre of attention as the oldest accessible use of Son of man. The question regarding what the transition from Aramaic to Greek meant became significant. Whatever its meaning was in Aramaic, the Greek ὁ υἱὸς τοῦ ἀνθρώπου, if not a title, seemed to function as an unambiguous reference to Jesus. In research, the Markan

of Man Coming in the Clouds. Mark xiii.26; Matthew xxiv.30; Luke xxi.27', *Theology* 23 (1931), pp. 14-21; T.F. Glasson, 'Mark xiii and the Greek Old Testament', *ET* 69 (1957–58), pp. 213-15; Franz Mussner, 'Die Wiederkunft des Menschensohnes nach Markus 13,24-27 und 14,61-62', *BuK* 16 (1961), pp. 105-107; Lars Hartman, 'La Parousie du Fils de l'homme. Mc 13,24-32', *Assemblées du Seigneur* 64 (1969), pp. 47-57; Ferdinand Hahn, 'Die Rede von der Parusie des Menschensohnes Markus 13', in R. Pesch and R. Schnackenburg (eds.), *Jesus und der Menschensohn* (FS Anton Vögtle, 1975), pp. 240-66; Martin Stowasser, 'Mk 13,26f und die urchristliche Rezeption des Menschensohns: Eine Anfrage an Anton Vögtle', *BZ* NS 39 (1995), pp. 246-52. **14.21**: Jens Christensen, 'Menneskesønnen gaar bort, som der staar skrevet om ham', *DTT* 19 (1956), pp. 83-92 (reprinted in *idem*, *Menneskesønnen* [1996], pp. 71-80; French: 'Le fils de l'homme s'en va, ainsi qu'il est écrit de lui', *StTh* 10 [1956], pp. 28-39). **14.41**: Werner Kelber, 'The Hour of the Son of Man and the Temptation of the Disciples (Mark 14:32-42)', in *idem* (ed.), *The Passion in Mark* (1976), pp. 41-60; Pierre Chamard-Bois, 'L'heure du Fils de l'homme: Marc 14,32-42', *Sémiotique and Bible* 91 (1998), pp. 53-57. **14.62**: John A.T. Robinson, 'The Second Coming—Mark xiv.62', *ET* 67 (1955–56), pp. 336-40; H.K. McArthur, 'Mark XIV.62', *NTS* 4 (1957–58), pp. 156-58; T.F. Glasson, 'The Reply to Caiaphas (Mark XIV.62)', *NTS* 7 (1960–61), pp. 88-93; André Feuillet, 'La Triomphe du Fils de l'homme d'après la déclaration du Christ aux Sanhédrites (Mc., XIV,62; Mt., XXVI,64; Lc., XX,69)', in Édourd Massaux (ed.), *La Venue du Messie. Messianisme et Eschatologie* (1962), pp. 149-71; Norman Perrin, 'Mark XIV.62: The End Product of a Christian Pesher Tradition?' *NTS* 12 (1965–66), pp. 150-55 (reprinted with Postscript in *idem*, *A Modern Pilgrimage in New Testament Christology* [1974], pp. 10-22); D.R. Catchpole, 'The Answer of Jesus to Caiaphas', *NTS* 17 (1970–71), pp. 213-26; P.J. Maartens, 'The Son of Man as Compound Metaphor in Mk 14.62', in J.H. Petzer and P.J. Hartin (eds.), *A South African Perspective on the New Testament* (1986), pp. 76-98; Timothy Radcliffe, 'The Coming of the Son of Man: Mark's Gospel and the Subversion of 'the Apocalyptic Imagination', in Brian Davies (ed.), *Language, Meaning, and God* (FS Herbert McCabe, 1987), pp. 176-89; this article offers only an interpretation of Mk 14.62 as describing Jesus' enthronement at the crucifixion, not the Parousia, and thus inaugurating the subversion of the apocalyptic imagination presupposing a new age to come in the near future, a hope being given up when the Temple in Jerusalem was destroyed without anything happening.

67. One remarkable exception here is Bruce A. Stevens, 'Why "Must" the Son of Man Suffer? The Divine Warrior in the Gospel of Mark', *BZ* NF 31 (1987), pp. 101-10, seeing behind the Markan Son of man the Divine Warrior originating in Canaanite mythology and being 'like a tapestry with many threads: Suffering, redemption, death and resurrection. His role merged with that of the faithful remnant—the goal of God's action. What was loosely woven, was soon to be bound tightly in the Marcan community' (p. 107).

hypothesis is mostly combined with the Two Source Theory or the Two Document Hypothesis, which postulates a now-lost written source. This source, generally named Q, or—in German—'Logienquelle', should have been constituted nearly exclusively by sayings of Jesus. It is sometimes compared with the *Gospel of Thomas* from Nag Hammadi. Allegedly contemporary with or even older than the Gospel of Mark, this source later should also have been exploited by the authors of Matthew and Luke.[68] Although many would place Q before Mark, it is placed here in the second place as it is a highly hypothetical source.

One of the first to characterize the special Markan use of Son of man is Heinz Eduard Tödt in *Der Menschensohn in der synoptischen Überlieferung* (1959). Tödt finds that it is the interest in old apocalyptic prophecy which has caused the reception of traditional elements of the concept of the Son of man:

> The reason for the community's linking up with this particular concept was probably their recollection of Jesus' teaching in which the Son of Man was spoken of, although without any reference to Dan. 7...
>
> Consequently we do not see in the Son of Man sayings in Mark a primary channeling of the Son of Man concept into the synoptic tradition. Ready-formed sayings using this name have been extended and supplemented here by bringing scriptural passages and traditional apocalyptic literature into play.[69]

The first[70] significant contribution with regard to the peculiarity of the use of the Son of man in Mark is by Samuel Sandmel from 1963.[71] Anticipating later interpretations, Sandmel claims:

68. A notable exception is William O. Walker, 'The Son of Man Question and the Synoptic Problem', *NTS* 28 (1982), pp. 374-88, who, adhering to the Griesbach hypothesis, thinks that Mark is later than both Matthew and Luke and using both them and their source, 'Q'.

69. Heinz Eduard Tödt, *Der Menschensohn in der synoptischen Tradition* (1959), p. 205. Quoted according to English translation, *The Son of Man in the Synoptic Tradition* (1965), p. 223.

70. T.A. Burkill, 'The Hidden Son of Man in St. Mark's Gospel', *ZNW* 52 (1961), pp. 189-213 (reprinted, in a slightly expanded form, in *idem*, *New Light on the Earliest Gospel: Seven Markan Studies* [1972], pp. 1-38), is not interesting in our context as it attempts to show that the messianic secret motif originates with Jesus. There also exist two earlier unpublished dissertations, C.W. Jones, 'The Use of the Title "Son of Man" in Mark' (Southern Baptist Theological Seminary, 1948), and J.L. Clark, 'A Re-examination of the Problem of the Messianic Secret in Mark in its Relationship to the Synoptic Son of Man Sayings' (Yale University, 1962). It was not possible to procure Francois P. Viljoen, 'Mark, the Gospel of the Suffering Son of Man: An Encouragement Directed to a Despondent Religious Minority in the City of Rome', *Die Skriftlig* 36 (2002), pp. 455-74.

71. Samuel Sandmel, 'Son of Man', in Daniel Jeremy Silver (ed.), *In the Time of Harvest* (FS A.H. Silver, 1963), pp. 355-67 (reprinted as '"Son of Man" in Mark', in

> Son of Man as a title is a literary device of Mark. While conceivably the Jesus of history in his lifetime may have been associated or identified either in his own mind or in that of his disciples with the Son of Man in Daniel, we are in the realm of conjecture. What we can be sure of is that Mark's use of the phrase as a title is a literary device, and not primarily an echo of the Jesus of history. In Mark, Son of Man has only the dimmest echoes of the antecedent Jewish use. Mark is far from being a document faithful to the Jewish scene; it is a tendentious, highly theological document, coming from a Gentile Christian environment.[72]

With regard to the original meaning of the expression, Sandmel subscribes to Lietzmann's 'valid distinction between Son of Man as a phrase, and its use in the Gospels as a title', which 'implies that before the term became a title, it had some good currency as merely a phrase'.[73]

This rather radical interpretation for that time did not immediately gain a hearing. In the years to follow it was still either—as for instance in the contributions of Morna D. Hooker[74] and Joseph Coppens[75]—tradition-history in general which dominated the interpretation or—as in the contributions of Norman Perrin—more specifically a particular exegetical tradition implicating a number of Old Testament sayings in the interpretation of the person of Jesus.[76] Viewing 2.10, 28; 8.31, 38; 9.9, 31; 10.33, 45 as the result of Markan redaction, Perrin sees here:

> A threefold purpose: the necessity for combating a false understanding of Jesus as Son of God and replacing it by one which emphasized the necessity for suffering; the development of the theme that the necessity for suffering is laid also upon the disciples, and the understanding of that necessary suffering as the way to salvation of mankind when accepted by Jesus and the way to glory for the believer when accepted by him.[77]

idem, *Two Living Traditions. Essays on Religion and the Bible* [1972], pp. 166-77), quoted according to the original printing.

72. Sandmel, 'Son of Man', p. 367.

73. Sandmel, 'Son of Man', p. 357.

74. Morna D. Hooker, *The Son of Man in Mark: A Study of the Background of the Term 'Son of Man' and its Use in St Mark's Gospel* (1967). Cf. above, Chapter 14, for more details.

75. Joseph Coppens, *De Mensenzoon-logia in het Markus-Evangelie. Avec un résumé, des notes et une bibliographie en francais* (1973). French: 'Les logia du Fils de l'homme dans l'évangile de Marc', in M. Sabbe (ed.), *L'évangile selon Marc. Tradition et rédaction* (1974), pp. 487-528 (reprint in *idem*, *Le Fils de l'homme néotestamentaire* [1981], pp. 109-49).

76. Norman Perrin, 'The Creative Use of the Son of Man Tradition by Mark', *USQR* 23 (1968), pp. 357-65. Quoted according to reprint in *idem*, *A Modern Pilgrimage in New Testament Christology* (1974), pp. 84-93. Cf. above, Chapter 16, for more details.

77. Perrin, 'The Creative Use of the Son of Man Tradition by Mark', pp. 92-93. Cf. *idem*, 'Mark 14:62. The End Product of a Christian Pesher Tradition?', *NTS* 12

That Son of man as a christological title is a Markan creation is also postulated by John H. Elliott, pointing to the circumstance that, in nine out of the fourteen Son of man sayings in this Gospel, the title is juxtaposed with either 'man' or 'men'. On this basis, Elliott concludes that 'through this redactional device of juxtaposition Mark subtly indicated the relation between christology and anthropology, their similarities and contrasts and the manner in which the former can give substance, direction and hope to the latter'.[78] Son of man also becomes an expression of the humanity of Jesus, as when he says that

> as Son of God Jesus is in solidarity with God. As Son of Man Jesus is Son of God in solidarity with man. Through Jesus as both Son of God and Son of Man the God–man relationship is established and affirmed. God/Son of God/Son of man/man is the implicit fundamental juxtaposition of the Markan Gospel.[79]

According to Walter Schmithals, it is the author behind the Gospel of Mark who introduced Son of man to the Gospel tradition. The expectation of a coming Son of man had until then (c. 75 CE), only existed in circles exclusively adhering to the words and deeds of Jesus, knowing nothing of any Easter faith. Thus, only Mk 8.38 and 13.26 are not Markan creations.[80]

In his *The Son of Man Tradition* (1990), Douglas R.A. Hare contests the attribution to Mark of any 'Son of Man Christology', preferring instead to speak of a 'Jesus Christology'. 'If we rephrase them [the statements that Jesus makes about himself using Son of man], substituting "Jesus" for "the Son of man" in each case, we would have a good summary of the Markan view of Jesus' self-understanding, without being distracted by the self-designation itself.'[81] The Danish scholar, Ole Davidsen, on the basis of 'A Semiotic Reading of Mark's Gospel', in effect reaches a similar conclusion. Expressly consenting to the results of my *Der Ausdruck 'Menschensohn' in den Evangelien* (1984), Ole Davidsen declares: 'what the expression "the

(1965–66), pp. 150-55; *idem*, 'The Christology of Mark: A Study of Methodology', *JR* 51 (1971), pp. 173-87; both reprinted in *idem*, *A Modern Pilgrimage*, pp. 10-11 and pp. 84-93, respectively. An in some respects similar understanding is found in the more popular contribution of R.G. Rank, 'Who is this Man? The Son of Man According to Mark', *BiTod* 63 (1972), pp. 959-65.

78. John H. Elliott, 'Man and Son of Man in the Gospel According to Mark', in Trutz Rendtorff and Arthur Rich (eds.), *Humane Gesellschaft. Beiträge zu ihrer sozialen Gestaltung* (FS H.-D. Wendland, 1970), pp. 47-59 (51).

79. Elliott, 'Man and Son of Man in the Gospel According to Mark', p. 58.

80. Walter Schmithals, 'Die Worte vom leidenden Menschensohn. Ein Schlüssel zur Lösung des Menschensohn-Problems', in C. Andresen and G. Klein (eds.), *Theologia crucis—signum crucis* (FS Erich Dinkler, 1979), pp. 417-45 (424). Cf. for further details Chapter 16, above.

81. Hare, *The Son of Man Tradition*, pp. 183-211 (211).

Son of Man" means must be determined on the basis of the information (both discursive and narrative) that the gospel narrative itself provides'.[82]

Other scholars operate with a Son of man christology which is more or less a Markan creation. The phrase is treated as a title or concept, but not necessarily a preformed one. Accordingly, Michael Theobald finds that the Markan employment of Son of man is in accordance with an early Christian remembrance of the fact that this title did not belong to the vocabulary of Jesus' language. In Mark, it functions as a circumlocution for Jesus when he wishes to hide his dignity as Christ or Son of God (messianic secret). In the presence of the crowds, the Markan Jesus only once speaks of the Son of man and that is about his coming (8.38). It means that the Son of man sayings are keywords in the christology of this author.[83] The Danish scholar Jens Christensen is inclined to accept that it is not possible to speak of the designation 'Son of man' as a messianic title in pre-Christian Judaism.[84] However, he is certain that it is the case in the Gospels and thinks it likely that this innovation is due to the creation of the Gospels, or to their Hebrew/Aramaic presuppositions, if not to Jesus himself. In fact, Jens Christensen sees *4 Ezra* 13 and *1 Enoch* 37–71 as reactions to this. The common denominator for the use of Son of man in Mark (but also in the other Gospels and Acts 7.56) Christensen finds in visionary contexts. It is employed by Jesus as a titular self-designation in a way which also allows the messianic figure to appear as the visionary prophet.

Ulrich Kmiecik, in his monograph, *Der Menschensohn im Markusevangelium* (1997), sees the author of the Gospel of Mark as adjusting an expectation of the coming Son of man, presupposing an identification of the figure in Dan. 7.13-14 with the risen Christ. Kmiecik does not note a titular use in Mark, 'much more Son of man is used as Jesus' self-designation with a quasi-titular meaning'.[85] A text-pragmatic analysis of Mk 13.1-37 shows

82. Ole Davidsen, *The Narrative Jesus: A Semiotic Reading of Mark's Gospel* (1993), pp. 194-204 (198).

83. Michael Theobald, 'Gottessohn und Menschensohn. Zur polaren Struktur der Christologie im Markusevangelium', *SNTU*/A 13 (1988), pp. 37-79 (42-45).

84. Jens Christensen, 'Menneskesønnen i Markusevangeliet', in *idem*, *Menneskesønnen. En bibelteologisk studie* (1996), pp. 53-70. As noted above in Chapter 14, Jens Christensen finds a main presupposition for the use of Son of man in the Gospels in the book of Ezekiel.

85. Ulrich Kmiecik, *Der Menschensohn im Markusevangelium*, p. 11 n. 2. Cf. pp. 12-13, where it is said that the investigation presupposes, 'daß im Markusevangelium wichtigen Titel nicht aufgrund ihrer religionsgeschichtlichen und historischen "Präformierungen" geeignet sind, zum Verständnis der Christologie des Markustexts hinzuführen. Die Christologie hängt nicht so sehr an den überkommenen Inhalten einzelner Begriffe, sondern "sie hängt an ganzen Texten". Die Person Jesu, wie sie vom Autor des Markusevangeliums in diesen Texten dargestellt ist, in ihrer Verkündigung und in ihrem Wirken, prägt im entscheidenden Maß die Bedeutung der jeweiligen Titel.'

the expectation of the Son of man coming after a cosmic catastrophe and introducing the new aeon. For the addressees of the Gospel of Mark, the incidents in connection with the Jewish revolt 66–70 awakened the expectation that this event was about to be realized.[86] In this situation, the author wanted to stress both that the coming of the Son of man is not connected with historical events—which were partly foretold by Jesus—and, at the same time, to add nuance to the picture of the Son of man. Where the addressees are supposed to think of Jesus as the one who is the justified because of his resurrection, the exalted and present one for God as the Son of man to come in the future, the author seeks to supplement this Son of man concept. This Son of man is the very same one who was condemned and had to suffer. Suffering and being handed over for execution also belong to the picture. Precisely his suffering and death revealed the eschatological glory of the Son of man. In this way the author draws a picture of the fate of the Son of man as analogous not only to the fate of the suffering righteous, but to what could happen to the addressees on account of Jesus.[87] According to Kmiecik,

> Son of man becomes the key to understanding of the titles for the addressees, expressing the dignity of Jesus, Christ and the Son of God. Through Jesus' self designation as Son of man, it is finally made clear what the content of Son of God and Messiahship is (Durch Jesu Selbstbezeichnung Menschensohn ist letztlich inhaltlich ausgefüllt, was seine Gottessohnschaft und Messianität ausmacht). Jesus is the Christ and the Son of God, who, as Son of man, must suffer, die and rise and, only as such, will he come again at the end of this aeon.[88]

Jens Schröter thinks it possible to show with regard to both Mark and Q 'that the decisive designation with which the claim that Jesus is the representative of the βασιλεία is expressed in ὁ υἱὸς τοῦ ἀνθρώπου.'[89] As the exclusive self-designation of Jesus, it has peculiar weight, and the use in both Mark and Q makes clear that it has gained another meaning than in Aramaic, where it is not understood exclusively as a personal pronoun since the Son of man sayings stress the peculiarity of Jesus:

86. See Kmiecik, *Der Menschensohn im Markusevangelium*, pp. 76-78; cf. 230-31.
87. See Kmiecik, *Der Menschensohn im Markusevangelium*, pp. 231-32.
88. Kmiecik, *Der Menschensohn im Markusevangelium*, p. 233.
89. Jens Schröter, 'Jesus, der Menschensohn. Zum Ansatz der Christologie in Markus und Q', in *idem*, *Jesus und die Anfänge der Christologie. Methodologische und exegetische Studien zu den Ursprüngen des christlichen Glaubens* (2001), pp. 140-79. Quoted according to the English version: 'The Son of Man as the Representative of God's Kingdom: On the Interpretation of Jesus in Mark and Q', in Michael Labahn and Andreas Schmidt (eds.), *Jesus, Mark and Q: The Teaching of Jesus and its Earliest Records* (2001), pp. 34-69 (54).

> An interpretation of the expression 'Son of Man' in Mark and Q has, therefore, to take its starting point from the sayings in the Gospels themselves. Here the expression 'Son of Man' explains the particular claim of Jesus, describes his rejection linked to that claim, and finally expresses his power to the future. In this way, the expression Son of Man in Mark and Q becomes a title of honour, by means of which the reign of God and the person of Jesus are linked with one another in one concept... In view of what was said above about the Son of Man sayings it becomes clear that a fixed concept was not transferred to him. Rather the expression was interpreted anew in view of his activity and destiny.[90]

Schröter, somehow, tries both to have his cake and eat it. While persisting on a prefixed, if not concept, then background, he depends on a creative interpretation in Mark and Q in order to integrate the different aspects of Jesus' activity and destiny in the Son of man sayings. Finally Schröter claims 'that the combination of the proclamation of the Kingdom with the Son of Man concept, presents an independent model of early Christian thinking about Jesus, which was linked to the Antiochene model of the pre-Pauline tradition by Mark'.[91] Peter Müller, although unlike Schröter in seeing Son of man as superior to other titles, arrives at a similar understanding. Working at both the intertextual (Old Testament passages) and the intratextual level (cross-references inside the Gospel of Mark), he finds a 'tension in the employment of Son of man sayings between "attachment and outdistancing (Anknüpfung und Distanznahme)", a dialogue begun, in which it simultaneously applies to foreknowledge and new accentuation (Vorwissen und Neuakzentuirung)'.[92] It is not superior to titles like Christ and Son of God, but, in Son of man sayings, these are supplemented and interpreted. To Peter Müller, a reception of Dan. 7.13 is basically the background for the use of Son of man in Mark, hinted at in the sayings about the ἐξουσία of the Son of man in Mk 2.10, 28 and more explicitly stated in the allusions in 13.26 and 14.62. The Passion story belonged to the category of a 'new accentuation'.[93] Peter Müller's balanced analysis of the Markan Son of man sayings and their intratextual interrelation shows how difficult it is to distinguish between what could be inclusion of a new accentuated concept

90. Schröter, 'The Son of Man as the Representative of God's Kingdom', p. 61, where it, however, also is said that this use could build on a background of the one being visible in Dan. 7; *1 En*. 37–71 and *4 Ezra* 13.

91. Schröter, 'The Son of Man as the Representative of God's Kingdom', p. 68.

92. 'Zwischen dem Gekommenen und dem Kommenden. Intertextuelle Aspekte der Menschensohnaussagen im Markusevangelium', in Dieter Sänger (ed.), *Gottessohn und Menschensohn* (2004), pp. 130-57 (157).

93. Peter Müller, 'Zwischen dem Gekommenen und dem Kommenden', p. 155: 'Es ist vielmehr zu erkennen, dass auf einen von Dan 7 beeinflussten Motiv- und Argumentationskomplex zurückgegriffen wird'.

or tradition of understanding on the one hand, and what could be outright Markan christology on the other.

Simon Gathercole also argues for seeing Daniel 7 as the primary source of the imagery in the Markan Son of man sayings. He wants to broaden the assessment of Morna D. Hooker (as especially referred to above in Chapter 14, Section 5: The Corporate Interpretation). The conclusion is that 'the narrative pattern which holds the Son of Man sayings together is: *the authoritative Son of Man revealed—the authority of the Son of Man rejected—the authority of the Son of Man vindicated*. Each of these elements...is derived primarily, though not exclusively, from Daniel 7.'[94]

A more unusual interpretation is offered by George Aichele in his article 'The Son of Man and the Sons of Men' from 2002. His point of departure is taken from the plural form 'sons of men' in Mk 3.28, a saying which the author wants to count among Markan Son of man sayings. In this expression, Aichele sees an explanation for the otherwise inexplicable tension between the 'human' son of man in some sayings and the marvellous, supernatural in other. He finds that the Markan 'son of man is *any person whatsoever*: it is the plural being, the sons of men, all of humanity'.[95] The key to understanding is thus the *Gospel of Thomas* 106 and 3, which, taken together with Markan sayings such as 8.33; 11.23, but also 5.34 and 7.29, leads to the 'suggestion that Mark's Jesus' son of man story, including the saying at 3:28, teaches that any human woman or man can realize that they are supernatural sons of men'. According to Aichele,

> If the troublesome sons of men sayings in 3:28 is a son of man saying like the others in Mark, then Jesus' son of man story implies a 'new age' christology, an anthroposophy of gnostic or perhaps Buddhistic enlightenment available to *any* human being 'who has ears to hear'.[96]

Among the latest attempts (not surprisingly), a rhetorical reading of the Markan Son of man sayings turns up. Thus Paul Danove finds that:

> Formulation of a coherent portrait of a character, such as the Son of Man, presumes an integrative framework that makes available to interpreters a synthetic organization of the vast array of information about the Son of Man,

94. Simon Gathercole, 'The Son of Man in Mark's Gospel', *ET* 115 (2003–2004), pp. 366-72 (372). Also Isa. 53 is seen as a part of the background (p. 369).

95. George Aichele, 'The Son of Man and the Sons of Men', in Gary A. Phillips and Nicole Wilkinson Duran (eds.), *Reading Communities, Reading Scripture* (FS Daniel Patte, 2002), pp. 311-23 (318).

96. Aichele, 'The Son of Man and the Sons of Men', p. 319. The reference to E. Lohmeyer's remark in his *Das Evangelium des Markus* (1937, 17th edn, 1967), p. 80, channelled through Tödt's *The Son of Man in the Synoptic Tradition*, p. 120 n. 3, is artificial if not directly misleading because of a shift in the subject to the predicative.

> that identifies this character with Jesus and relates this character to other characters in specific ways, evaluates this character positively, and presents expectations for his characterization along specific lines.[97]

Although he does not contest pre-existing beliefs about the Son of man, Paul Danove thinks that what is said both presumes that Jesus is the Son of man and establishes a deconstructive rhetorical strategy, introducing elements not cohering with these beliefs 'that emphasize the Son of Man's present exercise of divine prerogatives and parousaic identity and activity. In contrast, repetition ensures that this contradictory content is central to the narrative audience's cultivated beliefs about the Son of Man.'[98] 'This repeated structure simultaneously cultivates beliefs concerning the relationship between the Son of Man and those who would be disciples of Jesus'.[99] Danove states:

> Thus, the characterization of the Son of Man functions to encourage the rejection of the authorial (and real) audience's pre-existing beliefs about the Son of Man, which are deficient from the perspective of the narrative audience, and acceptance of the narrative audience's cultivated beliefs, which alone offer the prospect of seeing the reign of God come in power, of not destroying one's reward, and of being among the many for whom the Son of Man gives his life.[100]

Working with narrative criticism, Elizabeth Struthers Malbon introduces the term 'refracted christology', taking the image 'from the way a prism refracts "white" light and thus shows its spectral colors'. Turned and looked at from another angle, something appears different. That is what happens when 'the Markan Jesus bends the "christologies" of others by his statements about the "Son of Man", especially in juxtaposition with "christological titles" offered by other characters'.[101] Noting further that in the employment of Son of man by the Markan Jesus, the 'self-reference is implicit and never explicit, needing its completion by the implied audience,'[102] Malbon sees Peter's confession in Mk 8.29 and the High Priest's question in Mk 14.61 as especially calling for 'refraction'. Mark 10.45, which concludes the Passion predictions, also becomes important. In 14.62, 'Jesus adds a Danielic "Son of Man", as if to refract both "Christ" and "Son of God", to bend the traditional "titles" to which he gives reticent assent

97. Paul Danove, 'The Rhetoric of the Characterization of Jesus as Son of Man and Christ in Mark', *Bib* 84 (2003), pp. 16-34 (118).

98. Danove, 'The Rhetoric of the Characterization of Jesus', p. 25.

99. Danove, 'The Rhetoric of the Characterization of Jesus', p. 27.

100. Danove, 'The Rhetoric of the Characterization of Jesus', p. 33; cf. p. 34.

101. Elizabeth Struthers Malbon, 'Narrative Christology and the Son of Man: What the Markan Jesus Says Instead', *Biblical Interpretation* 11 (2003), pp. 373-85 (374).

102. Malbon, 'Narrative Christology and the Son of Man', p. 374.

only in order to lose his life in order to save it'. The tension called forth by 'the multi-dimensional narrative and its multi-layered "christology"' is not solved but 'the implied author of Mark sets up this tension to draw in the implied audience—not to resolve the tension but to enable hearing of the story of Jesus in its full complexity and mystery'.[103]

Harry L. Chronis also tries to detect the narrative logic in Mark's use of the Son of man. He finds the expression where, logically, the title Son of God would be expected. 'That is, to belabor the obvious, what Jesus says of "the Son of Man" he appears to say of "the Son of God" and all the predicates of "the Son of Man" appear to be, assuming the narrative logic, predicates of "the Son of God"'.[104] Thus Chronis understands it as a part of the 'secrecy motif':

> That is, by revealing the term's potential as a transparent and purposeful contradiction, employed by Jesus himself, these clues hint at its connection to a larger set of 'containment' strategies by which Jesus resists the premature disclosure of his identity as 'the Son of God'. They suggest that Jesus is using 'the Son of Man' to talk about himself as 'the Son of God', to fill this 'title' of majesty, which belongs exclusively to him, with its requisite christological content, without at the same time violating his own injunction to secrecy. As a systematic theologian might put it, referring to himself as 'the Son of Man' ostensibly allows Jesus, in the story-world of Mark, to conceal his *person*, under an apparent contradiction of his divine identity, while he openly reveals his *work*. But this would apply only in the story-world and to all human characters there, prior to 15.39.[105]

That is also the reason why 'the Son of Man' could easily be replaced by the personal pronoun 'I', if not by 'the Son of God'. The 'term never tells who Jesus is, it never identifies him, in the technical sense and with a view toward confession'.[106] This points to a background in the Old Testament for υἱὸς ἀνθρώπου in, for instance, Pss 8.5; 79.16, 18; an understanding confirmed by the introduction of the plural form in Mk 3.28. Chronis thinks it

103. Malbon, 'Narrative Christology and the Son of Man', p. 384. Edwin K. Broadhead, 'Reconfiguring Jesus: The Son of Man in Markan Perspective', in Thomas R. Hatina (ed.), *Biblical Interpretation in Early Christian Gospels*. I. *The Gospel of Mark* (2006), pp. 18-30, is a bit more positive about the impact of the included texts. Showing that not least Mk 14.62 'draws the Son of Man title into a web of character traits' (p. 26), Broadhead concludes: 'This end result is not a unilinear correction which extinguishes the prior texts and traditions. The engagement of texts against text in the Gospel of Mark creates a patter of reciprocity which realigns all traditions about Jesus. This intratextual strategy is clearly at work in the Son of Man title' (p. 27).

104. Harry L. Chronis, 'To Reveal and to Conceal: A Literary-Critical Perspective on the "Son of Man" in Mark', *NTS* 51 (2005), pp. 459-81 (463).

105. Chronis, 'To Reveal and to Conceal', p. 465.

106. Chronis, 'To Reveal and to Conceal', p. 475.

possible to conclude that the narrative function 'as a paradoxically ambiguous incognito for Jesus' identity as "the Son of God"—corresponds to what Mark believes was its function in Jesus' own usage'.[107] This means that what Jesus meant, has to be found in Old Testament passages describing the Son of God![108]

As can be seen, there is a strong tendency in the study of the Markan Son of man passages at present to abandon an understanding built on tradition history and in favour of interpreting the expression on its own merits within the text of Mark. Among other things, this means that any connection with Old Testament sayings are secondary and not the reason for the introduction of the expression. This suggests that the Gospel of Mark marks the beginning of the application of Son of man to Jesus.

3. *The Son of Man in Q*[109]

Even if one does not accept the hypothesis of the existence of a (at least in principle reconstructable) written source containing the material common to Matthew and Luke and not stemming from Mark—it seems more plausible that one of the later Gospels knew the other. For instance, the author of Luke knew the Gospel of Matthew[110]—in a survey of Son of man research, one has to treat the Son of man in Q, because a significant quantity of literature is devoted to this source. This literature—as Q research altogether—is determined by a confidence in the possibility of not only reconstructing this source and its tradition history in their main trajectories, but also in the viability of writing its theology. Of course, if such a source existed and has been used by the authors of the later Gospels, it has impact on a judgment

107. Chronis, 'To Reveal and to Conceal', p. 480.

108. 'Innovative' is also Gordon D. Kirchhevel, 'The "Son of Man" Passages in Mark', *BBR* 9 (1999), pp. 181-87, claiming (p. 187) that 'the earliest readers of Mark could have understood the "Son of Man" passages principally in terms of *three* OT scriptures': Ps. 8 (Mk 2.10, 28); Isa. 52.13–53.12 (Mk 8.31; 9.9, 12, 31; 10.32b-34, 45; 14.21, 41) and Isa. 5 (Mk 8.38; 13.26; 14.62).

109. For an outline of the beginning of the discussion, starting with H.E. Tödt and also including a few more participants than below, cf. John S. Kloppenborg, 'The Sayings Gospel Q and the Quest of the Historical Jesus', *HThR* 89 (1996), pp. 307-44 (315-19). Daniel Kosch, *Die eschatologische Tora des Menschensohnes. Untersuchungen zur Rezeption der Stellung Jesu zur Tora in Q* (1989), is of no relevance in our context, and the same pertains to G. Dautzenberg, 'Tora des Menschensohnes? Kritische Überlegungen zu Daniel Kosch', *BZ* 36 (1992), pp. 93-103. Joachim Kügler, 'Die Botschaft der Menschensohn zählt', *Orientierung* 67 (2003), pp. 180-82, is a survey of the problems and 'results' concerning Q and its christology.

110. Cf. the various contributions of Michael Goulder, especially *Midrash and Lection in Matthew* (1974).

regarding their creativity and independence. The discussion of the meaning of Son of man in sayings ascribed to Q concentrates partly on the possible distribution of the sayings to different layers in the production of the final edition of Q, partly—in connection with the first—on the question as to whether apocalyptic sayings belong to the oldest stratum, or are only added at a later redactional stage.

In his *Der Menschensohn in der synoptischen Überlieferung* (1959), Heinz Eduard Tödt offers relatively considerable space to an analysis of Son of man sayings attributed to Q. The sayings are the following twelve (or eight): Lk. 6.22 (Q?); Lk. 7.34 = Mt. 11.19; Lk. 9.58 = Mt. 8.20; Lk. 11.30 = Mt. 12.40; Lk. 12.8-9 = Mt. 10.32-33; Lk. 12.10 = Mt. 12.32; Lk. 12.40 = Mt. 24.44; Lk. 17.23-24 = Mt. 24.26-27; Lk. 17.26-27 = Mt. 24.37-39; Lk. 17.28-30 (Q?); Mt. 10.23 (Q?); Mt. 19.28 (Q?). Accepting the tripartition of the Synoptic Son of man sayings and the assumption that Q did not contain any Passion sayings, Tödt divides the Q Son of man sayings between those concerning the coming Son of man and those about his activity on earth. The analysis of the first group leads to the picture of a heavenly transcendent figure whose coming signals the end of this world and is identical with the coming of the Kingdom of God. In Lk. 12.8-9, supposed to be a genuine Jesus saying, those being on earth in Jesus' community are promised a future community with this Son of man. A soteriological link is established between Jesus and the heavenly transcendent Son of man and it is—according to Tödt—thus possible to speak of a Son of man Christology in Q. Remarkably, there is no explicit allusion to Daniel 7 in Q. 'This concept shed the features of apocalyptic elaboration and theology.'[111] For the sayings concerning his activity on earth, it seems that, 'by the name Son of Man a unique sovereignty is ascribed to Jesus. It may be called a Christological dignity in a wider sense. What this dignity conveys is not determined by the traditional concepts of the transcendent Son of Man.' Unlike the sayings in the first group, those in this second group are not authentic Jesus sayings. An interpretation assuming both categories to be authentic 'would face insurmountable difficulty'.[112]

In the (to my knowledge) first large monograph on the theology of Q, Paul Hoffmann's *Studien zur Theologie der Logienquelle* (1972), nearly half of the 334 pages are devoted to 'Jesus, der Menschensohn'.[113] Hoffmann

111. Heinz Eduard Tödt, *Der Menschensohn in der synoptischen Überlieferung*, pp. 44-62 (61). In the English translation, *The Son of Man in the Synoptic Tradition*, pp. 47-67; the quotation is from p. 66.

112. Tödt, *Der Menschensohn in der synoptischen Überlieferung*, pp. 106-16, in the English translation, pp. 114-25; the quotations are from pp. 124 and 125.

113. Originally a Habilitationsschrift from 1968, the same year as the Habilitationsschrift by A. Polag's *Die Christologie der Logienquelle* appeared, which, however, was

shares the view of Tödt that the origin of the expression Son of man in the Synoptic tradition is the preaching about this figure by Jesus without identifying himself with it.[114] He also presupposes the existence of a Son of man expectation in contemporary Judaism. On the basis of Lk. 10.21-22/Mt. 11.25-27, Hoffmann first concludes, under the heading 'the revelation of the Son', that the Easter experience for the Q community resulted in the identification of Jesus with the coming Son of man. Hoffmann discovers a parallel to the exaltation of Enoch in *1 En.* 71.14-17. This also leads to the insertion of Son of man in other sayings concerning the earthly life of Jesus (Lk. 9.58/Mt. 8.20; Mt. 11.19/Lk. 7.34; Lk. 12.10/Mt. 12.32; Lk. 6.22/[Mt. 5.11]). The identification of Jesus with the Son of man did not mean that the Q people gave up preaching the earthly Jesus, but that they stressed the eschatological meaning of this preaching. 'Were these sayings once legitimated through the authority of the earthly Jesus, they are now legitimated through the authority of the Son of man, on whom eternal salvation or perdition depends.'[115] This also implied a re-interpretation of Jesus as prophet, because the identification of Jesus as Son of man included the eschatological Son of man. Those rejecting the earthly Son of man in this way anticipated the judgment belonging to the coming Son of man. This motif of rejection, which is assumed to go back to the earliest Jewish-Christian community, later, in continuation of Paul's interpretation of the sufferings as atonement (Rom. 3.25; 2 Cor. 5.18-19), resulted in the 'Passion kerygma', which was unknown to Q. Finally, the confession to Jesus as Son of man resulted in the interpretation of the coming one in John the Baptist's preaching as Jesus, thereby making John the Baptist the forerunner.

first published in 1977. Thus Hoffmann had the possibility of incorporating Polag's results in his book. The part on the Son of man occupies pp. 81-233. I am only too well aware that I have left out a series of important contributions to Q research, but I think those included are representative for the discussion of the Son of man in Q. Some of the later contributions are discussed in Hoffmann, 'QR und der Menschensohn' [QR in this title stands for *Q-Redaktion*], in F. van Segbroeck, C. M. Tuckett, G. van Belle and J. Verheyden (eds.), *The Four Gospels 1992* (FS Frans Neirynck, 1992), I, pp. 421-56 (English: 'The Redaction of Q and the Son of Man: A Preliminary Sketch', in Ronald A. Piper [ed.], *The Gospel Behind the Gospels* [1995], pp. 159-98).

114. In two later articles, Hoffmann argues that the expression Son of man is not removed from the Jesus-saying in Mt. 10.32-33. Nor is it original in Lk. 12.8: 'Jesus versus Menschensohn. Mt 10,32f. und die synoptische Menschensohnüberlieferung', in L. Oberlinner and P. Fiedler (eds.), *Salz der Erde—Licht derWelt. Exegetische Studien zum Matthäusevangelium* (FS Anton Vögtle, 1991), pp. 165-202, and: 'Der Menschensohn in Lukas 12.8', *NTS* 44 (1998), pp. 357-79. Thus this saying, without 'Son of man', could be a genuine Jesus saying.

115. Paul Hoffmann, *Studien zur Theologie der Logienquelle* (1972), pp. 157-58.

Heinz Schürmann, in the earliest article explicitly devoted to the theme, finds that Son of man in Q appears only in introductory and concluding sayings and did not belong to the final redaction.[116] Schürmann distinguishes between four strata in Q where Son of man sayings belong to the second, (being 'Kommentarworte' to sayings in the first). The third are smaller collections and the fourth, finally, larger speech complexes. Schürmann also contested the view of Q as an eschatological or apocalyptic document.

Athanasius Polag finds in the earliest Aramaic layers in Q (Primärtradition) the expression as a circumlocution for a function of Jesus, which then secondarily is given an apocalyptic interpretation and becomes an honorific title (Hoheitstitel); that is, before translation into Greek and inclusion in the main collection (Hauptsammlung) of Q.[117] Hence the christologically most relevant Son of man sayings, connecting Jesus with a future Son of man, are not likely to go back to the earthly Jesus.[118]

Adela Yarbro Collins, in dialogue primarily with Heinz Schürmann's contribution, concludes that 'apocalyptic Son of Man sayings are found at the earliest (Matt 24:26-27/Luke 17:23-24) and at the latest stages (Matt 24:37-39/Luke 17:26-27 and Luke 11:30; cf. Matt 12:40)',[119] so that Son of man in Q is not a title but remains an abstract figure. The apocalyptic Son of man was not only of interest at the beginning, but also to the final editor of Q.

Leif E. Vaage ascribes only Q (= Luke) 7.34 and 9.58 to the earliest stratum, seeing the other, according to his numbering, seven sayings as additions from a later redaction. He starts with a picture of the Son of man very much like the Cynic Diogenes, noting,

116. Heinz Schürmann, 'Beobachtungen zum Menschensohn-Titel in der Redequelle. Sein Vorkommen in Abschluß- und Einleitungswendungen', in R. Pesch and R. Schnackenburg (eds.), *Jesus und der Menschensohn* (FS Anton Vögtle, 1975), pp. 124-47 (reprinted in *idem*, *Gottes Reich—Jesu Geschick: Jesu ureigener Tod im Licht seiner Basileia-Verkündigung* [1983], pp. 153-82) (English: 'Observations on the Son of Man Title in the Speech Source: Its Occurrence in Closing and Introductory Expressions', in J. Kloppenborg (ed.), *The Shape of Q* [1994], pp. 74-97).

117. Athanasius Polag, *Die Christologie der Logienquelle* (1977), esp. pp. 182-83, but see also pp. 102-17 for a sketch of the Son of man problem.

118. Anton Vögtle, 'Bezeugt die Logienquelle die authentische Redeweise Jesu vom "Menschensohn"?', in Joël Delobel (ed.), *Logia. Les paroles de Jésus—The Sayings of Jesus. Mémorial Joseph Coppens* (1982), pp. 77-99 (reprinted in *idem*, *Offenbarungsgeschehen und Wirkungsgeschichte* [1985], pp. 50-69), is foremost an appreciation of Polag's analysis, confirming the assumption of Vögtle himself that the apocalyptic expectation of a coming Son of man first arose in the time after Easter. Cf. above, Chapter 14.

119. Heinz Schürmann, 'The Son of Man Sayings in the Sayings Source', in M.P. Horgan and P.J. Kobelski (eds.), *To Touch the Text* (FS Joseph Fitzmyer, 1989), pp. 369-89 (373-82, the quotation is from p. 382).

> The figure's contribution to the saying itself is quite abstract: we would even say mathematical... Logically, in every case we could replace the 'son of man' with an x and still grasp whatever is at stake. The only thing added by the actual words 'son of man' in the text of Q's redaction is semantic contact with a certain intertextual (apocalyptic) field of play. The name allows a set of associations to be made, giving the interested imagination (e.g. that of New Testament scholars) a range to fill the blank.[120]

Christopher Tuckett is not inclined to such 'minimalism'.[121] More in line with Adela Yarbro Collins, Tuckett finds the Son of man in Q representing an example of the idea that God would be assisted by another figure at the final judgment—Tuckett thereby assumes a scenario common to much Jewish thinking of the period. He is not interested in distinguishing between different layers, but works with Q as the final product, a Greek text which also had been available to the authors of Matthew and Luke. Tuckett wants to argue that it is the same whoever is the earthly Son of man and the subject of the eschatological sayings. An analysis leads Tuckett to the conclusion that a common feature in the Q sayings about the present Son of man is that they are primarily concerned with hostility, suffering and rejection.[122] The eschatological sayings add the trait of vindication and judgment after suffering. Although some of these features 'started to take on overtones of meaning from Dan 7', it may be 'that exclusive concentration on Dan 7 alone is misleading and unhelpful',[123] because the context is far wider. The conclusion, however, is that 'the S[on of]M[an] sayings in Q *in toto* represents a remarkable homogeneity and consistency'.[124]

James M. Robinson finds in Q 'a rather impressive list of instances, where son of man refers indefinitely to a human and by implication to Jesus

120. Leif E.Vaage, 'The Son of Man Sayings in Q', in John S. Kloppenborg and Leif E. Vaage (eds.), *Early Christianity, Q and Jesus* (1992), pp. 103-29 (124).

121. Christopher Tuckett, 'The Son of Man in Q', in Marinus C. de Boer (ed.), *From Jesus to John: Essays on Jesus and New Testament Christology* (FS Marinus de Jonge, 1993), pp. 196-215. This article, in a reworked and enlarged version, functions as Chapter 8 of Tuckett's *Q and the History of Early Christianity. Studies on Q* (1996), pp. 239-82. Cf. further *idem*, 'Q 12,8: Once again "Son of Man" or "I"?', in Jon A. Asgeirsson, Kristin de Troyer and Marvin W. Meyer (eds.), *From Quest to Q* (FS James M. Robinson, 2000), pp. 171-88.

122. Cf. the earlier article of Tuckett, 'The Present Son of Man', *JSNT* 14 (1982), pp. 58-81, referred to above, Chapter 16.

123. Tuckett, *Q and the History of Early Christianity*, p. 267. Cf. further the later article of *idem*, 'The Son of Man and Daniel 7: Q and Jesus', in A. Lindemann (ed.), *The Sayings source Q and the Historical Jesus* (2001), pp. 371-94, and the reworked version of it, 'The Son of Man and Daniel 7: Inclusive Aspects of Early Christologies', in Kieran J. O'Mahony (ed.), *Christian Origins: Worship, Belief and Society* (2003), pp. 164-90. Cf. the treatment Chapter 16, above.

124. Tuckett, *Q and the History of Early Christianity*, p. 276.

himself'. Some of them seem to be genuine sayings of Jesus.[125] Robinson also asserts that the basic apocalyptic instances of what is called 'eschatological correlatives' are found precisely in the Q-apocalypse (Lk. 17.24, 26, 27, 30/Mt. 24.38-39 (where Lk. 17.28-29 refers instead to Lot). 'The Q community would perhaps qualify as the otherwise unattested 'fourth tradition' within Judaism, as a context, a *Sitz im Leben*, for the apocalyptic son of man'. Robinson alludes to the claim of Carsten Colpe (to whom the article is dedicated), that the Synoptic tradition, besides Daniel 7, *1 Enoch* 37–71 and *4 Ezra* 13, may be seen as a fourth witness to a Son of man tradition in Early Judaism. According to Robinson, Q attests the change from a non-titular meaning to a titular:

> When the Q community...ascribed to him [Jesus] a decisive role at the judgment, the idiom characteristic of his speech was put on his tongue in apocalyptic sayings. This then led to the appropriation of other Jewish apocalyptic traditions where the idiom also occurred, resulting in the Danielic apocalypticism attested in the canonical Gospels, on the way to the Apostle's Creed: '...come to judge the quick and the dead'.[126]

Arto Järvinen, in a narrative analysis wishes

> to argue that the 'Son of man' functions as an important symbol that helped the Q community to interpret the rejection and failure of its mission to Israel. Jesus' role as the scorned Son of man and his glorious parousia—two quite contradictory phenomena—provided the Q community with applicable analogues to their own situation.[127]

In the literary planning of Q, Son of man sayings 'function as an (interpretative) link between the "deuteronomistic" material and what has most appropriately been termed "wisdom-language"'.[128] This last mentioned use is the most surprising, because 'the title is certainly more easily associated with the apocalyptic thought-world'. Järvinen detects a development in the employment of the term. From being at first a comforting figure whose fate foreshadows the rejection of his followers (Q 6.22; 7.34; 9.58 [12.10]), Son of man receives 'judgmental aspects that any Christian was likely to perceive in the title (Q 11.30; 12.8-9, [10])'. In the end, these aspects take over with the aim of seeking to 'warn the followers not to fall under God's wrath (Q 12.40; 17.24, 26, 30)'.[129]

125. James M. Robinson, 'The Son of Man in the Sayings Gospel Q', in Christoph Elsas *et al.* (eds.), *Tradition und Translation* (FS Carsten Colpe, 1994), pp. 315-35 (325).

126. Robinson, 'The Son of Man in the Sayings Gospel Q', p. 335.

127. Arto Järvinen, 'The Son of Man and His Followers: A Q Portrait of Jesus', in David Rhoads and Kari Syreeni (eds.), *Characterization in the Gospels* (1999), pp. 180-222 (182).

128. Järvinen, 'The Son of Man and His Followers: A Q Portrait of Jesus', p. 220.

129. Järvinen, 'The Son of Man and His Followers: A Q Portrait of Jesus', p. 222.

4. *The Matthean Son of Man*[130]

The interest in the specific Matthean understanding of Son of man awakened only relatively late.[131] The first to analyze it extensively was Heinz Eduard

130. The following studies, mainly dealing with only one Matthean Son of man saying or pericope, are not included below: **8.20**: M. Casey, 'The Jackals and the Son of Man (Matt. 8.20//Luke 9.58)', *JSNT* 23 (1985), pp. 3-22; Mahlon H. Smith, 'No Place for a Son of Man', *Forum* 4 (1988), pp. 83-107; L. Löning, 'Die Füchse, die Vögel und der Menschensohn (Mt 8,19f par Lk 9,57f)', in H. Frankemölle and K. Kertelge (eds.), *Vom Urchristentum zu Jesus* (FS Joachim Gnilka, 1989), pp. 82-102. **10.23**: W.D. Chamberlain, 'Till the Son of Man Be Come', *Interpretation* 7 (1953), pp. 3-13; Jacques Dupont, '"Vous n'aurez pas achevé les villes d'Israël avant que le Fils de l'homme ne vienne" (Mat. X 23)', *NT* 2 (1958), pp. 228-44; Heinz Schürmann, 'Zur Traditions- und Redaktionsgeschichte von Mt 10,23', *BZ* NF 3 (1959), pp. 82-88; Ernst Bammel, 'Matthäus 10,23', *StTh* 15 (1961), pp. 79-92; A. Feuillet, 'Les origines et la signification de Mt 10,23b. Contribution à l'étude du problème eschatologique', *CBQ* 23 (1961), pp. 182-98; Hans Martin Künzi, *Das Naheerwartungslogion Matthäus 10,23. Geschichte seiner Auslegung* (1970); Leopold Sabourin, '"You will not have gone through all the towns of Israel, before the Son of Man comes" (Mat 10:23b)', *BThB* 7 (1977), pp. 5-10; John M. McDermott, 'Mt. 10:23 in Context', *BZ* NF 28 (1984), pp. 230-40; Volker Hampel, '"Ihr werdet mit den Städten Israels nicht zu Ende kommen". Eine exegetische Studie über Matthäus 10,23', *ThZ* 45 (1989), pp. 1-31. **10.32-33**: Paul Hoffmann, 'Jesus versus Menschensohn. Mt 10,32f. und die synoptische Menschensohnüberlieferung', in L. Oberlinner and P. Fiedler (eds.), *Salz der Erde—Licht der Welt. Exegetische Studien zum Matthäusevangelium* (FS Anton Vögtle, 1991), pp. 165-202. **11.19**: Olof Linton, 'The Parable of the Children's Game: Baptist and the Son of Man (Matt. XI.16-19 = Luke VII.31-5): A Synoptic Text-Critical, Structural and Exegetical Investigation', *NTS* 22 (1976), pp. 159-79; **12.32**: R. Schippers, 'De Zoon des mensen in Mt. 12,32 – Lk. 12,10, vergeleken met Mk. 3,28', in *Ex Auditu Verbi* (FS G.C. Berkouwer, 1965), pp. 233-57 (abridged English version: 'The Son of Man in Matt. xii.32 = Lk. xii.10, compared with Mk. iii.28', *SE* 4 [= *TU* 102, 1968], pp. 231-35). **16.13**: Joseph Gnilka, '"Für wen halten die Leute des Menschen Sohn?" (Mt 16,13)', *BuK* 17 (1962), pp. 38-41; F. Sieg, 'The Son of Man, the Messiah, the Son of God and Simon Peter (Mt 16,13-20)', *Bobolanum* 6 (1995), pp. 27-47. **16.28**: Jürgen Roloff, 'Das Reich des Menschensohnes: ein Beitrag zur Eschatologie des Matthäus', in M. Evang *et al.* (eds.), *Eschatologie und Schöpfung* (FS Erich Grässer, 1997), pp. 275-92. **19.28**: Jacques Dupont, 'Le logion des douze trones (Mt 19,28: Lc 22,28-30)', *Bib* 45 (1964), pp. 355-92. **24.30**: J.B. Bauer, 'Das Zeichen des Menschensohnes', *Klerus-Blatt* 88 (1955), pp. 222-23; E.J. Tinsley, 'The Sign of the Son of Man', *SJTh* 8 (1955), pp. 297-306; A.J.B. Higgins, 'The Sign of the Son of Man (Matt. XXIV.30)', *NTS* 9 (1962–63), pp. 380-82; T.F. Glasson, 'The Enseign of the Son of Man (Matt. XXIV,30)', *JThS* NS 15 (1964), pp. 299-300; F. Martin, 'Le signe du Fils de l'homme', *LV* 31 (1982), pp. 61-77; Jonathan A. Draper, 'The Development of "the Sign of the Son of Man" in the Jesus Tradition', *NTS* 39 (1993), pp. 1-21. **25.31**: P.S. Minear, 'The Coming of the Son of Man (An Exegesis of Matthew 25:31-46)', *Theology Today* 9 (1952–53), pp. 489-93; Ingo Broer, 'Das Gericht des Menschensohnes über die Völker. Auslegung von Mt 25,31-46', *Bibel und Leben* 11 (1970), pp. 273-95; D.R. Catchpole, 'The Poor on Earth and the Son of Man in Heaven: A Re-Appraisal of Matthew

Tödt who, as in Mark, found in Matthew the use of the designation Son of man as the result of a secondary channelling:

> Whilst the authentic sayings of Jesus keep strictly away from apocalyptic description, Matthew introduces a great number of traditional motifs; with regard to this, we may speak of a renaissance of apocalyptic elements within the synoptic Son of Man sayings (Matt. 13.41; 25.31; 24.30f.; 16.27; 19.28). Mark refers chiefly to the one biblical passage Dan. 7.13; Matthew, on his part, refers to broader streams of tradition. Some sayings formed by him are closely related to statements from the book of Enoch...[132]

Jack Dean Kingsbury, on the other hand, wants to 'establish the thesis that, for Matthew, the title Son of Man is "public" in nature and is meant to complement the title Son of God, which is "confessional" in nature'.[133] Thus Kingsbury declares that

> It is rather fruitless to attempt to determine the relationship Matthew establishes between the titles Son of Man and Son of God solely on the basis of the association of ideas surrounding each one (the 'content'). Proceeding in this manner, we can draw only one or two conclusions: either that there is much similarity of 'content' between the two and that the principle of discrimination is largely contextual or simply not discernible; or that the distinction Matthew draws between them is primarily not material in nature but formal...[134]
>
> At the point of the parousia and the Last Judgment...the secret of the person of Jesus will be disclosed to every eye, and what the church has

xxv.31-46', *BJRL* 61 (1978–79), pp. 355-97; Louis Panier, 'Le Fils de l'homme et les nations. Lecture de Mt 25,31-46', *SémiotBib* 69 (1993), pp. 39-52. **26.64**: D.A. Frøvig, 'Jesu ord til ypperstepræsten om sit komme paa himmelens skyer. (Mt 26,64). Til belysning av de synoptiske utsagn om Menneskesønnens snarlige komme', *Teologisk Tidsskrift for den danske Folkekirke*, 4. Række 1 (1920), pp. 257-79. **28.18**: Günter Bornkamm, 'Der Auferstandene und der Irdische. Mt 28,16-20', in E. Dinkler (ed.), *Zeit und Geschichte* (FS Rudolf Bultmann, 1964), pp. 171-91; Anton Vögtle, 'Das christologische und ekklesiologische Anliegen von Mt. 28,18-20', *SE* 2 = *TU* 87 (1964), pp. 266-94; Joachim Lange, *Das Erscheinen des Auferstandenen im Evangelium nach Mattäus. Eine traditions- und redaktionsgeschichtliche Untersuchung zu Mt 28,16-20* (1973). 28.18 is included because it is often reckoned to reflect a Son of man tradition.

131. The first study, J. Mouson, 'De locutione "filius hominis" apud Matthaeum', *Collectanea Mechliniensia* 37 (= NS 22) (1952), pp. 627-31, is not especially innovative, regarding all Matthean Son of man sayings as original sayings of Jesus, thereby identifying himself with Daniel's Son of man.

132. Tödt, *Der Menschensohn in der synoptischen Überlieferung*, p. 205; quoted according to English translation, *The Son of Man in the Synoptic Tradition*, p. 223.

133. Jack Dean Kingsbury, 'The Title "Son of Man" in Matthew's Gospel', *CBQ* 37 (1975), pp. 193-202; quoted according to reprint in *idem*, *Matthew: Structure, Christology, Kingdom* (1976), pp. 113-22 (113; cf. p. 122).

134. Kingsbury, 'The Title "Son of Man" in Matthew's Gospel', p. 114.

> hitherto known by revelation of God the world, too, is given to perceive. In christological categories, what the latter signifies is that the titles Son of God and Son of Man have coalesced.[135]

The division between 'public' and 'confessional' sayings cannot conceal that the first category has Jesus as subject, while the latter has other people, the point of coordination being the person concerned. The interpretation of Kingsbury thus leaves Son of man a christological title, and in spite of the titles being 'of paramount importance in the first Gospel', nevertheless 'the title "Son of God" is superior to that of the Son of Man throughout this age'.[136]

Barnabas Lindars, having abandoned the view of Son of man as a christological title, sees no new contribution of authentic sayings by Matthew besides those incorporated from Mark and Q. But, according to Lindars, Matthew

> seized the phrase as a characteristic feature of the sayings tradition. He understands it as an exclusive self-reference. He is particularly delighted to find that Jesus is represented as referring to himself in this way in contexts which deal with the parousia... The proliferation of sayings in which Jesus speaks of himself as the apocalyptic Son of Man is thus due to Matthew's interest in apocalyptic, not to general currency of a Son of Man title.[137]

Margaret Pamment, on the other hand, finds that 'a consistent picture emerges' from a study of the Matthean Son of man sayings:

> Only Jesus uses the term 'the Son of man' and he does so to define his destiny and to call the disciples to participate in it. The Son of man is a representative and exemplary figure. Jesus as the Son of man exemplifies the meaning of righteousness and mercy and leads the way dictated by righteousness and mercy, through suffering and death. The disciples are to follow his example... As the representative of the righteous man, the Son of man calls all men to follow his example, but also stands in judgment against the unrighteous and unmerciful.[138]

Heinz Geist, in the one and only monograph on the Matthean Son of man up to this point, *Menschensohn und Gemeinde* (1986), accepts the hypothesis of the existence of an apocalyptic Son of man concept in Early Judaism and held that Jesus himself employed it with a titular meaning even though he was aware of its multiplicity of meanings.[139] He finds, however, a

135. Kingsbury, 'The Title "Son of Man" in Matthew's Gospel', p. 121.
136. Kingsbury, 'The Title "Son of Man" in Matthew's Gospel', p. 122.
137. Barnabas Lindars, *Jesus Son of Man* (1983), p. 130.
138. 'The Son of Man in the First Gospel', *NTS* 29 (1983), pp. 116-29 (126-27).
139. *Menschensohn und Gemeinde. Eine redaktionskritische Untersuchung zur Menschensohnprädikation im Matthäusevangelium* (1986), pp. 33-71, esp. pp. 50-51.

correlation to ecclesiology in the specific Matthean interpretation, which makes it 'a signal of an "ecclesiastical" christology (zum Signal einer "ekklesialen" Christologie)'.[140] In a summary of his analyses of the Matthean Son of man sayings, Geist writes among other things that:

> Of particular relevance is the Matthean interpretation of the parable of darnel among the wheat (13.36-43). It shows the removal of spatial, time-related and personal borders in the Matthean Son of man concept. The field of action of the Son of man not only embraces his earthly activity in Israel and his eschatological function. Far more, it embraces the whole of the cosmos, including both Israel and the pagans and extends itself to the time both before and after Easter until the parousia. The redactional combination of the basileia concept and the Son of man concept is especially conspicuous in the syntagma βασιλεία τοῦ υἱοῦ τοῦ ἀνθρώπου. The Matthean epilogue 28.16-20 which, with a high degree of probability, is also marked by the Matthean Son of man concept and defined as a commandment to the disciples, is to be seen in correlation to this Son of man conception, which is also hinted at in 13.36-43. A narrow connection between christological saying and ecclesiological dimension is thus already outlined here.[141]

Douglas R.A. Hare, not accepting the existence of any Son of man concept in Early Judaism, claims that although Son of man in Matthew '*denotes* Jesus' in all his christological aspects, 'it cannot be demonstrated from Matthew's use, however, that the phrase *connotes* any of this'. The conclusion is, 'that for Matthew it is not a revelatory expression. It communicates nothing of importance regarding Jesus' nature, functions, and destiny.'[142] Although inclined to 'think that the earliest Christians and even Jesus himself, shared the conviction of some Jewish apocalyptic circles that a messianic heavenly judge called "the son of the man" would appear and that they believed that Jesus was that son of the man',[143] Ulrich Luz does not find that Matthew drew on this expectation:

> There is no indication whatsoever that Matthew presupposed an apocalyptic meaning of 'the son of the man' among his readers, because there is no indication whatsoever that he himself was conscious of such a meaning besides his own Christian traditions about Jesus the son of the man.[144]

Thus Luz concludes: 'It is not possible to interpret ὁ υἱὸς τοῦ ἀνθρώπου as a christological title, because it never states who Jesus is'. Further,

140. *Menschensohn und Gemeinde*, p. 436; cf. pp. 410-11.

141. *Menschensohn und Gemeinde*, p. 368.

142. *The Son of Man Tradition* (1990), p. 181.

143. Ulrich Luz, 'The Son of Man in Matthew: Heavenly Judge or Human Christ', *JSNT* 48 (1992), pp. 3-21 (3-4) (reprinted in *idem*, *Studies in Matthew* [2005], pp. 97-112).

144. Luz, 'The Son of Man in Matthew', p. 8.

> It is, unlike other christological titles, a typical expression of the Jesus language, and its content is entirely filled by the history of Jesus. It is not the title 'son of the man' which makes clear who Jesus is; rather the history of Jesus makes clear who Jesus the son of man is. It is not the title 'son of the man' which adds to Matthew's Christology an apocalyptic dimension, but because Jesus the son of man will exact the future judgment, the expression 'son of the man' has also an apocalyptic dimension. The history of Jesus, narrated by Matthew, determines the significance of the expression 'son of the man' entirely anew.[145]

This 'freedom' in the use of the expression continues in later centuries:

> Just as Matthew's use of 'son of the man' was entirely determined by *his* story of Jesus (and that means also by his Christology), and not by the apocalyptic tradition, in the same way in the second century the expression again was entirely determined by *their* new Christologies and not by the Gospels. The main bridge is the *newness* of the concepts, the way in which the traditional word-shell 'son of the man' was filled with new Christologies.[146]

Luz' assumption of the existence of a Jewish son of man expectation turns out to have no consequence whatsoever for his interpretation of the Son of man in Matthew, the Matthean christology being here the one and only decisive factor.

The tendency we discovered in the Markan Son of man is also visible in the understanding of the Matthean Son of man. The employment of the expression seems foremost due to the introduction of it from Mark.

5. *The Lukan Son of Man*[147]

The 'chronological' place of the Gospel of Luke is disputed. In accordance with the two-sources hypothesis, the overwhelming majority still assume that it is dependant on Mark and Q. Others—such as the present writer—are inclined to see the Gospel of Matthew among its sources. In recent years, a few have found that it is more plausible to count on the dependence of Luke on John than the contrary. This of course also indicates a relatively late origin, thus making the Gospel of Luke the 'real' Fourth Gospel. Besides the

145. Luz, 'The Son of Man in Matthew', pp. 18-19.

146. Luz, 'The Son of Man in Matthew', p. 20. For the innovative usage in the second century, Luz especially (p. 4) points to Ignatius and some Nag Hammadi texts.

147. The following studies, mainly dealing with alone one Lukan Son of man saying or pericope, are not taken up below: **11.30**: D. Zeller, 'Entrückung zur Ankunft als Menschensohn (Lk 13,34f; 11,29f)', in *A cause de l'Evangile* (FS Jacques Dupont, 1985), pp. 513-30. **12.8-9**: A.J.B. Higgins, '"Menschensohn" oder "ich" in Q: Lk 12,8-9/Mt 10,32-33?', in R. Pesch and R. Schnackenburg (eds.), *Jesus und der Menschensohn* (FS Anton

question whether the hypothesis of the existence of an apocalyptic Son of man expectation in Early Judaism is correct or not, these different points of view are reflected in the different understanding of the meaning of Son of man in Luke. The main alternatives are between the interpretation of the Lukan Son of man as reflecting an apocalyptic Son of man expectation, on the one hand—that is, it functions as a christological title—and the notion that the author behind the Gospel of Luke does not connect any specific content with the expression on the other. A third possibility is that this author, taking the expression over from tradition, gives it some new content, discernible from an analysis of the Son of man sayings particular to Luke. As with the other Gospels, an analysis is made more difficult by the fact that Son of man turns up in this Gospel only in christological contexts. This often leads us to take it as a christological title.

Among scholars assuming the existence of an apocalyptic Son of man, Heinz Eduard Tödt arrives at the conclusion that

> Luke conceives of the Son of Man in a specific way... Luke does not reach back to the Jewish tradition. He obviously refers only to the Son of Man sayings transmitted to him by Christian traditions. It is the concept in these sayings which Luke develops by associating it with Christian Hellenistic terms and fitting it into his specific concept of Christology.[148]

Vögtle, 1975), pp. 117-23; John M. McDermott, 'Luke, XII,8-9: Stone of Scandal', *RB* 84 (1977), pp. 523-37; *idem*, 'Luc. XII,8-9: Pierre angulaire', *RB* 85 (1978), pp. 381-401; Rudolf Pesch, 'Über die Autorität Jesu. Eine Rückfrage anhand des Bekenner- und Verleugner-Spruchs Lk 12,8f par.', in Rudolf Schnackenburg, Josef Ernst and Joachim Wanke (eds.), *Die Kirche des Anfangs* (FS Heinz Schürmann, 1978), pp. 25-55; D.R. Catchpole, 'The Angelic Son of Man in Luke 12:8', *NT* 24 (1982), pp. 255-65; Paul Hoffmann, 'Der Menschensohn in Lukas 12.8', *NTS* 44 (1998), pp. 357-79; Ch. Tuckett, 'Q 12,8: Once again "Son of Man" or "I"?', in Jon A. Asgeirsson, Kristin de Troyer and Marvin W. Meyer (eds.), *From Quest to Q* (FS James M. Robinson, 2000), pp. 171-88. **12.10**: H.-Th. Wrege, 'Zur Rolle des Geisteswortes in frühchristlichen Traditionen (LC 12,10 parr.)', in Joël Delobel (ed.), *Logia. Les paroles de Jésus—The Sayings of Jesus: Mémorial Joseph Coppens* (1982), pp. 373-77. **17.22, 24, 26**: A.R.C. Leaney, 'The Days of the Son of Man (Luke xvii.22)', *ET* 67 (1955–56), pp. 28-29; Eric Ashby, 'The Days of the Son of Man', *ET* 67 (1955–56), pp. 124-25; W. Powell, 'The Days of the Son of Man', *ET* 67 (1955–56), p. 219; E.A. McDowell, 'The Kingdom of God and the Day of the Son of Man: A Study of Luke 17:20-37', *Review and Expositor* 39 (1962), pp. 54-64; Alain Dagron, *Aux Jours de Fils de l'Homme. Essai sur le service de la parole: Luc XVII,1 à XVIII,8; lecture sémiotique et propositions théologiques* (1990). **18.8**: André Feuillet, 'La Venue du Regne de Dieu et du Fils de l'Homme (d'après Luc, XVII,20 a XVIII,8)', *RSR* 35 (1948), pp. 544-65; Frederick C. Grant, 'Can Faith Survive: Luke 18:8: "When the *Son of Man* Comes, will he find Faith on Earth"?', *USQR* 8 (1953), pp. 29-35; D.R. Catchpole, 'The Son of Man's Search for Faith (Luke XVIII 8b)', *NT* 19 (1977), pp. 81-104; Franz Mussner, 'Die Skepsis des Menschensohnes. Zu Lk 18,8b', in Christoph Niemand (ed.), *Forschungen zum Neuen Testament und seiner Umwelt* (FS

Carsten Colpe, on the other hand, evaluating the question of sources in a different way, concludes that the author of the Gospel of Luke is faithful to his sources and that it is not possible to discern any peculiar Lukan Son of man christology.[149] Georg Schneider, in the first study dedicated to this specific theme, follows Tödt, convinced that the author connected a special content with his Son of man sayings.[150]

Barnabas Lindars, after becoming an adherent of the Aramaic approach, concludes his analysis of Luke by noting:

> the Son of Man is a self-designation which Jesus used when speaking of his ministry to the outcast and the tax-collectors as well as in apocalyptic contexts. He thinks of it as a special feature of Jesus' style—as indeed it was,

Albert Fuchs, 2002), pp. 271-75. **21.27, 36**: A. George, 'La venue du Fils de l'homme. Lc 21,25-28.34-36', *Assemblées du Seigneur* 5 (1969), pp. 71-78. **22.69**: Joseph Plevnik, 'Son of Man Seated at the Right Hand of God: Luke 22:69 in Lucan Christology', *Bib* 72 (1991), pp. 331-47; Darrell L. Bock, 'The Son of Man Sitting at God's Right Hand and the Debate over Jesus' Blasphemy', in J.B. Green and M. Turner (eds.), *Jesus of Nazareth* (1994), pp. 181-91; C. Focant, 'Du Fils de l'homme assis (Lc 22,69) au Fils de l'homme debout (Ac 7,56). Enjeux théologique et littéraire d'un changement sémantique', in J. Verheyden (ed.), *The Unity of Luke–Acts* (1999), pp. 563-74. **Acts**: H.P. Owen, 'Stephen's Vision in Acts VII.55-6', *NTS* 1 (1954–55), pp. 224-26; Charles Kingsley Barrett, 'Stephen and the Son of Man', in Walter Eltester and Franz H. Ketteler (eds.), *Apophoreta* (FS Ernst Haenchen, 1964), pp. 32-38; G.D. Kilpatrick, 'Acts vii.56: Son of Man?', *ThZ* 21 (1965) p. 209 (reprinted in *idem*, *The Principles and Practice of New Testament Textual Criticism: Collected Essays* (ed. J.K. Elliott, 1990), pp. 415-16; Rudolf Pesch, *Die Vision des Stephanus. Apg 7,55-56 im Rahmen der Apostelgeschichte* (1966); Viktor Hasler, 'Jesu Selbstzeugnis und das Bekenntnis des Stephanus vor dem hohem Rat. Beobachtungen zur Christologie des Lukas', *SThU* 36 (1969), pp. 36-47; G.D. Kilpatrick, 'Again Acts vii.56: Son of Man?', *ThZ* 34 (1978) p. 232 (reprinted in *idem*, *Principles*, pp. 417-18); Franz Mussner, 'Wohnung Gottes und Menschensohn nach der Stephanusperikope (Apg 6,2-8,2)', in R. Pesch and R. Schnackenburg (eds.), *Jesus und der Menschensohn* (FS Anton Vögtle, 1975), pp. 283-99; M. Sabbe, 'The Son of Man Saying in Acts 7,56', in J. Kremer (ed.), *Les Actes des Apôtres. Traditions, rédaction, théologie* (1979), pp. 241-79 (reprinted in *idem*, *Studia Neotestamentica: Collected Essays* [1991], pp. 389-95 [additional note, pp. 396-97]); P. Doble, 'The Son of Man Saying in Stephen's Witnessing: Acts 6.8–8.2', *NTS* 31 (1985), pp. 68-84; J. Duncan M. Derrett, 'The *Son of Man* Standing (Acts 7:55-56)', *Bibbia e Oriente* 30 (1988), pp. 71-84; Nicole Chibici-Revneanu, 'Ein himmlischer Stehplatz: Die Haltung Jesu in der Stephanusvision (Apg 7.55-56) und ihre Bedeutung', *NTS* 53 (2007), pp. 459-88.

148. Tödt, *Der Menschensohn in der synoptischen Überlieferung*, p. 101. Quoted according to English translation, *The Son of Man in the Synoptic Tradition*, pp. 108-109.

149. Cf. Colpe, 'ὁ υἱὸς τοῦ ἀνθρώπου', in *ThWNT*, VIII (1969), p. 462.

150. Georg Schneider, '"Der Menschensohn" in der lukanischen Christologie', in R. Pesch and R. Schnackenburg (eds.), *Jesus und der Menschensohn* (FS Anton Vögtle, 1975), pp. 267-82 (281).

> though not quite in the way Luke thought. He thus employs it in comments which are designed to appeal to the reader's emotions. This is true of most sayings peculiar to this gospel.[151]

Christopher Tuckett, further, thinks that Son of man in Luke belongs within a certain set of contexts, finding that the 'picture that seems to emerge is one of Luke as what might be described as a "conservative redactor", with perhaps care needed to stress both halves of the description'.[152] As, for instance, Lk. 22.69 shows where the emphasis has shifted from the Parousia to the present exalted state of the resurrected, 'Luke has pressed the SM traditions to a certain extent into the service of his own ideas', but he 'does *not* introduce SM terminology into other contexts for which there is no justification in his sources'.[153]

Jack Dean Kingsbury is much less inclined to see the author of Luke as only taking over a special Son of man tradition. Not accepting Son of man as a christological title in Luke, Kingsbury simply thinks that the meaning is 'this man' or 'the man':

> Once one recognizes that 'the Son of man' in Luke's Gospel means 'the man,' or 'the human being' (dynamic equivalent: 'this man,' or 'this human being'), one can easily make sense of the striking phenomenon we noted above: that Jesus can openly designate himself as 'the Son of man' before the religious authorities, the people, and the disciples, and yet no one—neither supernatural being or human being—ever asks him whether, or declares that, he is 'the Son of man'.[154]

According to Kingsbury, it 'does not function as a title of majesty but as a technical term',[155] bearing a precise meaning within the world of Luke's Gospel by referring exclusively to 'Jesus'. Douglas R.A. Hare is even more 'minimalistic': 'In Luke's use, the phrase shines like the moon with no light of its own but only the reflection of its various contexts... Like the proper name "Jesus", the phrase for Luke is completely denotative in function. It points to Jesus without saying anything specific about him.'[156] As noted above, Wolfgang Schenk even asserts a new beginning for the understanding of the Lukan Son of man, seeing its presupposition in naming Jesus 'Son of Adam' in Lk. 3.38.[157]

151. Barnabas Lindars, *Jesus Son of Man* (1983), p. 143.

152. Christopher Tuckett, 'The Lukan Son of Man', in *idem* (ed.), *Luke's Literary Achievement* (1995), pp. 198-217 (211).

153. Tuckett, 'The Lukan Son of Man', p. 211 and p. 212.

154. Jack Dean Kingsbury, 'Observations on "the Son of Man" in the Gospel According to Luke', *Currents in Theology and Mission* 17 (1990), pp. 283-90 (289).

155. Kingsbury, 'Observations on "the Son of Man"', p. 290.

156. Hare, *The Son of Man Tradition*, pp. 77-78.

157. Wolfgang Schenk, *Das biographische Ich-Idiom*, pp. 230-31. Cf. the introductory section of the present chapter.

Although the study of the Lukan Son of man is still in its beginning stages, it seems clear that the author behind this Gospel has his own understanding of the expression. That this is the case also seems to be evident from the special Lukan employment of Son of man in sayings such as Lk. 6.22; 22.48; 24.7, and Acts 7.56, which otherwise would be exceptions when compared with the usage of the other Gospels.

18. Conclusion

The history of the interpretation of the Gospel expression Son of man has shown that whatever its meaning may have been in the Gospels, it almost immediately received its significance outside the New Testament from the actual christological thinking of each epoch. We have witnessed an impressive variety of meanings from being synonymous with the Highest God to an expression of humility, from being a designation for a man representing all the nobility of true humanity to a degrading nickname, even hinting at familial impropriety.

Through next to a thousand years, Son of man was understood nearly exclusively on the basis of its wording, which also allowed for a good many variations. A special chapter, however, was that dealing with the Gnostic use where 'man' was interpreted of the god Man. In the wave of renewed biblical studies at the time of the Reformation, there developed a trend to interpret it from the background of the Old Testament. The clear allusions to Dan. 7.13 came to be seen as an indication that it might be a title for the Messiah. Later, with a growing historical consciousness, it was no longer mainly understood so much as a description, as a term originating in the mind of the earthly Jesus to express his self-understanding. Again, it allowed for a wide range of meanings. All the while, we observe that the understanding steadily reflects the various interpreters' christological thinking.

This also pertains to what happens around the middle of the nineteenth century when pseudepigraphic Jewish writings were consulted for possible concepts of the Messiah in the centuries around the beginning of the Common Era. It is no longer the mind of Jesus alone which is seen as the possible source of the meaning of the expression. Scholars also counted which concepts of the Messiah could have made an impression on the mind of Jesus. Mostly, however, the mind of Jesus is understood to be the deciding moment for meaning, because of the transformation the expression experienced through his use of it. The impact of apocalyptic was in most cases counterbalanced by the interpreter's christology, transferred to the thoughts of the earthly Jesus.

A decisive step in the history of interpretation was the so-called first Aramaic stage in the decade around 1900, when linguistic possibilities of the language most probably spoken by Jesus were taken into consideration. The result was that the Aramaic expression, *bar (e)nash*—in the Old Testament only known from Dan. 7.13—was impossible as a messianic title, since it was also known from later rabbinic sources as a circumlocution for 'man', 'someone', if not more exclusively as a synonym for 'I'.

This understanding of the expression as a colourless circumlocution was soon counterbalanced by the influence from the History of Religions School, introducing the mythological concept of a Primeval Man and the Gnostic concept of a Redeemed Redeemer as the possible background for Son of man in Daniel, in Jewish pseudepigrapha (especially *1 Enoch* 37–71) and in the Gospels. It became nearly an *opinio communis* that Early Judaism knew of a specific apocalyptic expectation of a heavenly and universal Son of Man in the centuries around the beginning of the Common Era as a sort of alternative to the more nationalistic and particularistic Messiah.

The main alternative was whether it was Jesus himself who introduced this 'title', be it about himself or about a figure which he had expected to come, or whether it was the result of a 'community theology' identifying Jesus with this apocalyptic figure in regard not only to his second coming, but to his deeds and fate during his earthly ministry. It came as a blow when it was pointed out that the sources did not permit such a construction. The three *loci classici* for the supposed Jewish apocalyptic expectation of the Son of man—besides Dan. 7.13 and *1 Enoch* 37–71, also *4 Ezra* 13—could not be 'saved' by a fourth source in the New Testament Gospels. A little earlier, the hypothesis proposed by the History of Religions School concerning the existence of a pre-Christian Gnostic Redeemed Redeemer as a precursor of an apocalyptic Son of man, was made impossible by the fact that the oldest adduced evidence stemmed from the second century CE. What the evidence allowed was to speak of an exegetical tradition, interpreting Daniel's man-like of the Messiah, transferring exaltation and empowerment to a historical person (Enoch, Jesus).

This was confirmed by the second Aramaic stage, just a few years before, re-introducing the circumlocutional understanding of the Aramaic expression lying behind the Gospel Son of man. However, it also became clear that the conspicuous Greek expression, even if it had gone back to an Aramaic circumlocutional way of speaking, has lost every possible ambiguity in the Gospels. In the Gospels it is employed by the Jesus figure as a clear self-reference. Its only apparent messianic content does not come from the expression itself as if it were a title, but from what is said about the Son of man exposing the christology of the individual gospels.

The boundary has also moved in the last decade as a result of the impact partly of the second Aramaic stage, and partly of the break-down of the hypothesis of the expectation of a special Jewish apocalyptic Son of man. A possible meaning of the expression in the mouth of Jesus in the Gospels has by now begun to be seen as the result of the interpretation of the individual evangelists. Although a more or less colourless circumlocution in its origin, in the Gospels it gained a certain content through its placement in the construction of the story of the earthly Jesus as the Messiah. It is interesting to observe that once again the expression takes its meaning from contemporary christological thinking. What has happened in interpretation since the last decade of the twentieth century is that Christology is no longer primarily constructed as an extension of a supposedly messianic self-understanding—or lack of it—on the part of the historical Jesus. It is, first and foremost, the outcome of the interpretative efforts of the community. Not that it is impossible that the earthly Jesus could have understood himself as a messianic figure, whether he had proclaimed it expressly or only implicitly. Some sort of continuity is certainly a possibility. However, the main factor in the rise of New Testament christology is the interpretation on behalf of the community concerning the meaning and impact of Jesus' proclamation, teaching and fate, epitomized above all in the preaching of the one crucified as the risen Lord.

This fits in with the new development in the understanding of New Testament christology; namely, not primarily as an effort to go after different 'titles' as if they convey the meaning of Jesus as God's salvific intervention. This becomes ever more visible in what is said of Jesus, his preaching, teaching, wonders and other deeds bringing the Kingdom of God near. In this theological context, titles are understood primarily as pointers to the understanding which appears from the story. What the Gospels' Jesus is doing constitutes the content of christology.

We cannot trace the expression Son of man back before its emergence in the Gospel of Mark. Even if it has its roots in an Aramaic circumlocution, it has been transformed (perhaps also, through translation) with new meaning. The authors of the later Gospels took it over, either directly from the Gospel of Mark, or—what can only be a hypothesis—from sources behind Mark. Its inclusion in exclusively christologically weighted sayings alone is a remarkable fact. However, that it has *not* been changed into a christological title appears from the inevitable fact that it never turns up in the Gospels in confessional sayings, much as it is never employed in a predicative way.

The interpretation of the Son of man in the New Testament Gospels is in free fall until it is recognized that the expression does not have any special meaning before it receives it through its concrete context in the respective Gospels.

Bibliography

A. *Text-editions and Translations*

With a few exceptions, the Greek and Latin text normally is quoted according to Migne's *Patrologia*, the Greek (*MPG*) and the Latin Series (*MPL*), respectively.

With regard to the Church fathers, where possible, the translation in *The Ante-Nicene Fathers* (*ANF*) and *The Nicene- and Post-Nicene Fathers* (*NPNF*) has been used, normally only with the indication of the volume number.

Other text-editions and translations

Acta Apostolorum Apocrypha, I-II,1-2. Edited by R.A. Lipsius and M. Bonnet (Leipzig: Hermann Mendelsohn, 1891, 1898, 1903 = reprint Darmstadt: Wissenschaftliche Buchgesellschaft, 1959).

The Apocryphal New Testament translated by M.R. James (Oxford: Clarendon Press, 1924, reprint 1960).

The Apostolic Fathers. The Loeb Classical Library (LCL) (London: Heineman, 1912–13, reprint 1965 and 1959).

Didache in Armenian: G. Peradse, 'Die "Lehre der zwölf Apostel" in der georgischen Überlieferung'. *ZNW* 31 (1932), pp. 111-16.

The Nag Hammadi Library. Edited by James M. Robinson. *The Nag Hammadi Library in English* (Leiden: Brill, 1977).

Pseudo-Philo, *Les Antiquités Bibliques* I-II. Introduction et texte critiques par Daniel J. Harrington. Traduction par Jacques Cazeaux. Introduction littéraire, commentaire et index par Charles Perrot et Pierre-Maurice Bogaert. Sources Chrétiennes 229-30 (Paris: Éditions du Cerf, 1976).

Reuss, Josef, *Matthäus-Kommentare aus der griechischen Kirche*. TU 61 (Berlin: Akademie-Verlag, 1957).

—, *Johannes-Kommentare aus der griechischen Kirche*. TU 89 (Berlin: Akademie-Verlag, 1966).

"Adamantius", *Der Dialog des Adamantius*. Hrsg. von W.H. van de Sande Bakhuyzen. GCS (Leipzig: Hinrichs'sche Buchhandlung, 1901).

Apollinaris of Laodicea: Hans Lietzmann, *Apollinaris von Laodicea und seine Schule. Texte und Untersuchungen* (Tübingen: J.C.B. Mohr 1904 = reprint Hildesheim: Georg Olms Verlag, 1970).

Augustine, *Epistolae*: *Saint Augustine Letters* V (204-270). The Fathers of the Church 32 (Washington: The Catholic University of America Press, 1956).

—, *Enarratio in Psalmum*: *St. Augustine On the Psalms*. Psalm 30–37. Ancient Christian Writers 30 (London: Longmans, Green & Co., 1961).
—, *Sermones ad populum*: *The Works of Saint Augustine* III/4 (New York: New City Press, 1992).
—, *Contra sermonem arianorum* and *Contra Maximinum Arianum episcopum*: *The Works of Saint Augustine*. A Translation for the 21st Century I/18 (New York: New City Press, 1995).
Bonaventura, *Commentaria in quatuor libros sententiarum magistri Petri Lombardi. Opera Omnia* III (Florentia: Quaracchi, 1887).
—, *Vitis mystica seu tractatus de passione Domini. Opera Omnia* VIII (Florentia: Quaracchi, 1898).
Clement of Alexandria, Excerpta ex Theodoto: R.P. Pierce, *The Excerpta ex Theodoto of Clement of Alexandria: Edited with Translation, Introduction and Notes*. Studies and Documents 1 (London, 1934).
Didymus the Blind, Didymos der Blinde, *Psalmenkommentar* III. *Kommentar zu Psalm 29–34*. Edited by Michael Gronewald. Papyrologische Texte und Abhandlungen 8 (Bonn: Rudolf Habelt Verlag, 1969).
Epiphany, *Panarion*: *The Panarion of Epiphanius of Salamis*. Books II and III (Sects 47-80, *De Fide*). Translated by Frank Williams. Nag Hammadi and Manichaean Studies 36 (Leiden: Brill, 1994).
Eusebius of Caesarea, *Theophania*: Hugo Gressmann, *Eusebius Werke* III 2. GCS (Leipzig: Hinrichs'sche Buchhandlung, 1904).
—, *Contra Marcellum, De ecclesiastica theologia:* Erich Klostermann, *Eusebius Werke. Vierter Band. Gegen Marcell, Über die kirchliche Theologie, Die Fragmente Marcells*. GCS (Leipzig: Hinrichs'sche Buchhandlung, 1906).
—, *Demonstratio evangelica*: *The Proof of the Gospel being Demonstratio Evangelica of Eusebius of Cæsarea* I-II, by W.J. Ferrar. Translations of Christian Literature. Series 1. Greek Texts (London: SCM Press, 1920).
Heracleon: *Fragments from his Commentary on the Gospel of John*. The Gnostic Society Library. Gnostic Scriptures and Fragments. http://www.gnosis.org/library/fragh.htm.
Hippolytus, *Kommentar zum Buche Daniel und die Fragmente des Kommentars zum Hohenliede*: G.N. Bonwetsch, *Hippolyts Werke* I. GCS 1 (Leipzig: Hinrichs'sche Buchhandlung, 1897).
—, *Refutatio omnium haeresium*: Paul Wendland, *Hippolytus Werke* III. GCS 26 (Leipzig: Hinrichs'sche Buchhandlung, 1916).
Irenaeus, *Adversus haereses*: W. Wigand Harvey, *Sancti Irenæi episcopi Lugdunensis Libros quinque adversus Haereses* I-II (Cambridge: Cambridge University Press 1857).
—, *Epideixis*: Karapet Ter-Mekerttschian and Erwand Ter-Minassiantz, *Des heiligen Irenäus Schrift zum Erweise der apostolischen Verkündigung*. TU 31/1 (Leipzig: Hinrichs'sche Buchhandlung, 1931).
Isho'dad of Merw: Margaret Dunlop Gibson, *The Commentaries of Isho'dad of Merv*, in Syriac and English I-III. *Horae Semiticae* V, vol. I Translation (Cambridge: Cambridge University Press, 1911).
John Chrysostom, *Saint John Chrysostom, Commentary on Saint John the Apostle and Evangelist*. Homilies 1-47. The Fathers of the Church 33 (New York: Fathers of the Church, 1957).

Justin, *Apologia* and *Dialogue with Trypho*: Edgar J. Goodspeed, *Die ältesten Apologeten. Texte mit kurzen Einleitungen* (Göttingen: Vandenhoeck & Ruprecht. 1914, reprint 1984).

Marcellus of Ancyra, Die Fragmente Marcells, in Erich Klostermann, *Eusebius Werke. Vierter Band. Gegen Marcell, Über die kirchliche Theologie, Die Fragmente Marcells*. GCS (Leipzig: Hinrichs'sche Buchhandlung, 1906), pp. 185-215.

Nicolaus of Lyra, *Postillæ perpetuæ sive commentaria brevia in universa Biblia* IV (1472).

Origen, *In Johannem*: *Origenes' Johanneskommentar*. Hrsg von Erwin Preuschen. GCS 10 (Leipzig: Hinrichs'sche Buchhandlung, 1903).

Peter of Laodicea: C.F.G. Heinrici, *Des Petrus von Laodicea Erklärung des Matthäus-evangeliums*. Beiträge zur Geschichte und Erklärung des Neuen Testaments V (Leipzig: Deichert, 1908).

Pseudo-Athanasius, *Sermo maior de fide*: Robert P. Casey, *The Armenian Version of the Pseudo-Athanasian Letter to the Antiochenes and of the Expositio Fidei*. Studies and Documents 15 (London: Christophers; Philadelphia: University of Pennsylvania Press, 1947).

Thomas of Aquin, Commentary on the Gospel of John: *Sancti Thomae Aquinatis Opera Omnia*. Tomus 10 (Parma: Petrus Fiaccadori, 1860; reprint New York: Musurgia Publishers, 1949).

—, *Summa theologiae*: St Thomas Aquinas *Summa theologiæ*. Latin text and English translation 1-61 (Blackfriars, 1964–81).

— , Commentaries on the Gospel of Matthew and the Gospel of Mark: *S. Thomae Aquinatis Opera omnia* V (Stuttgart-Bad Cannstatt: Frommann & Holzboog, 1980).

B. *Monographs and Articles Containing 'Son of Man' or the Like in the Title*[1]

1. To the best of my knowledge, this part of the bibliography includes every book or article containing in its title the expression 'Son of man' or its equivalents. I have profited from the aid of bibliographies such as *Biblica Elenchus bibliographicus biblicus* (Rome, 1920ff.), *Ephemerides theologicae Lovaniensis. Elenchus Bibliographicus* (Leuven, 1924ff.), and *Internationale Zeitschriftenschau für Bibelwissenschaft und Grenzgebiete* (Düsseldorf, 1951ff.). Son of Man bibliographies also can be found, for instance, in B.M. Metzger (ed.), *Index to Periodical Literature on Christ and the Gospels*. New Testament Tools and Studies 6 (Leiden: Brill, 1966), pp. 437-42, its continuation in Watson E. Mills, *Index to Periodical Literature on Christ and the Gospels*. NTTS 27 (Leiden: Brill, 1998), pp. 689-700 (containing bad misplacement with a lengthy repetition as consequence), and Arland J. Hultgren, *New Testament Christology. A Critical Assessment and Annotated Bibliography*. Bibliographies and Indexes in Religious Studies 12 (New York: Greenwood Press, 1988), pp. 174-200. Also usefull were *Old Testament Abstracts* (Washington, 1978ff.) and *New Testament Abstracts* (Cambridge, MA, 1956ff.). Many titles, especially the older ones, have been picked up from references in the literature where the treatment of the Son of Man problem very often is introduced with a survey of the solutions until then. Some of the titles are obviously not of any scholarly interest. In a few cases reviews have been included. With regard to books or articles that were not been available, the bibliographical source is normally indicated. Because of the

Aarde, A.G. van, 'Die uitdrukking "seun van die mens" in die Jesus-tradisie: 'n Ontwikkeling vanaf 'n lanbou-omgewing na die wêreld van skriftgeleerdes (The Expression "Son of Man" in the Jesus Tradition: A Development from Agrarian Culture to a Scribal Context)'. *Hervormde Teologiese Studies* 58 (2002), pp. 1625-53. This article in Afrikaans is a reworked version of:

—, 'Jesus and the Son of Man: A Shift from the "Little Tradition" to the "Great Tradition"'. *EThL*80 (2004), pp. 423-38.

Abbott, Edwin A., *The Message of the Son of Man* (London: Black, 1909).

—, *'The Son of Man' or Contributions to the Study of the Thoughts of Jesus*. Diatessarica VIII (Cambridge: Cambridge University Press, 1910).

Adams, E., 'The Coming of the Son of Man in Mark's Gospel'. *Tyndale Bulletin* 56 (2005), pp. 39-61.

Adler, Adolf Peter, *Om Begrebet Menneskens Søn. En Afhandling* (København: C.A. Reitzel, 1858).

Agourides, S., 'The Son of Man in Enoch', *Bulletin of Biblical Studies* 2 (1973), pp. 130-47. Cf. *ZAW* 86 (1974), p. 357.

Ahlbäck, Tore, *Människosonen—en självgjord messias i Tyskland efter första världskriget*. Meddelanden från stiftelsen för Åbo Akademi Forskningsinstitut 81 (Åbo Akademi, 1983).

Aichele, George, 'The Son of Man and the sons of men'. In Gary A. Phillips and Nicole Wilkinson Duran (eds.), *Reading Communities, Reading Scripture*. FS Daniel Patte (Harrisburg, PA: Trinity Press International, 2002), pp. 311-23.

Albani, Matthias, 'Der Menschensohn in Dan 7,13 und die israelitische Königstheologie.' *Leqach* 5 (2004), pp. 5-14. English version, 'The "One Like a Son of Man" (Dan 7:13) and the Royal Ideology'. In Gabriele Boccaccini (ed.), *Enoch and Qumran Origins. New Light on a Forgotten Connection* (Grand Rapids: Eerdmans, 2005), pp. 47-53.

Alexander, Gross, *The Son of Man: Studies in His Life and Teachings* (Nashville/Dallas: Publishing House of the M.E. Church, South, 1900).

Allen, Thomas C., *Jesus' Use of the Title, The Son of Man*. Unpublished PhD dissertation (The Southern Baptist Theological Seminary, 1927). Cf. A.J. Ferch, *The Son of Man in Daniel 7* (1983), p. 205.

Andersen, Anders, *Menneskets Søn. Evangelieopfattelsernes Enhed fremstillet i Grundtræk* (København: Schønberg, 1894).

Angel, Andrew, *Chaos and the Son of Man. The Hebrew* Chaoskampf *Tradition in the Period 515 BCE to 200 CE*. The Library of Second Temple Studies 60 (London: T. & T. Clark/Continuum, 2007).

Annus, Amar, 'Ninurta and the Son of Man'. In R.M. Whiting (ed.), *Mythology and Mythologies*. The Neo-Assyrian Text Corpus Project. Melammu Symposia 2. University of Helsinki (Helsinki, 2001), pp. 7-17.

Appel, Heinrich, *Die Selbstbezeichnung Jesu: Der Sohn des Menschen. Eine biblisch-theologische Untersuchung* (Stavenhagen: Beholtz, 1896).

Archibald, D.Y., 'The Son of Man'. *ET* 62 (1950–51), pp. 348-49.

fortuitousness concerning the presence of the expression Son of man in the title of a book or an article of relevance, this part of the bibliography has to be compared with the list of books and articles listed under the heading 'C. Other Secondary Literature'.

Arion, L.G., 'Invatatura despre "Fiul Omului" in Sfintele Evanghelii'. *Studii Teologice* 18 (1966), pp. 470-88. (Romanian)

Asensio, Félix, 'El protagonismo del "Hombre-Hijo del Hombre" del Salmo 8'. *Estudios Bíblicos* NS 41 (1983), pp. 17-51.

Ashby, Eric, 'The Days of the Son of Man'. *ET* 67 (1955–56), pp. 124-25.

—, 'The Coming of the Son of Man'. *ET* 72 (1960–61), pp. 360-63.

Aufrecht, Walter E., 'The Son of Man Problem as an Illustration of the *Techne* of New Testament Studies'. In Bradley H. MacLean (ed.), *Origins and Method: Towards a New Understanding of Judaism and Christianity*. FS John C. Hurd. JSNTSup 86 (Sheffield: Sheffield Academic Press, 1993), pp. 282-94.

Augstein, Rudolf, *Jesus Menschensohn* (München: C. Bertelsmann, 1972).

Austin, 'Translating "Son of Man" into Aboriginal Languages'. *Notes on Translation* 75 (1979). Cf. Ralph Hill, 'Further Considerations on Translating "The Son of Man". *Notes on Translation* 93 (1983), p. 50.

Ayán Calvo, Juan José, 'Jesucristo, Hijo del hombre e Hijo de dios según gnacio de Antioquía'. In Juan José Ayán Calvo, Patricio de Navascués Benlloch, and Manuel Aroztegui Esnaoloa (eds.), *Filición—Cultura pagana, religión de Israel, origins del cristianismo: Actas de las I y II Jornadas de Estudio 'La filiacion en los inicios de la reflexión cristiana'.* Colección Estruturas y Procesas: Seie Religión (Madrid: Trotta, 2005), pp. 303-35.

Bacon, Benjamin W., 'Jesus as Son of Man'. *HThR* 3 (1910), pp. 325-40.

—, 'The "Son of Man" in the Usage of Jesus'. *JBL* 41 (1922), pp. 143-82.

Badham, F.P., 'The Title "Son of Man"'. *ThT* 45 (1911), pp. 395-448.

Baeck, Leo, 'Der "Menschensohn"'. *MGWJ* 81 (1937), pp. 12-24 = idem, *Aus drei Jahrtausenden.* Wissenschaftliche Untersuchungen und Abhandlungen zur Geschichte des jüdischen Glaubens (1938, 2nd ed. Tübingen, 1958), pp. 187-98.

Bakel, H.A. van, 'Ezechiel's Menschenzoon'. *NThT* 4 (1915), pp. 36-42.

Baldensperger, W., 'Die neueste Forschung über den Menschensohn'. *ThR* 3 (1900), pp. 201-10, 243-55.

—, '"Le fils de l'homme". Essai historique et critique par Georges Dupont'. *RHPR* 5 (1925), pp. 262-73.

Bard, Friedrich, *Der Sohn des Menschen. Eine Untersuchung über Begriff und Inhalt und Absicht solcher Jesusbezeichnung* (Gütersloh: Bertelsmann, 1908, 2nd ed. 1915).

Barrett, Charles Kingsley, 'Stephen and the Son of Man'. In Walter Eltester and Franz H. Ketteler (eds.), *Apophoreta.* FS Ernst Haenchen. BZNW 30 (Berlin: De Gruyter, 1964), pp. 32-38.

—, 'Das Fleisch des Menschensohnes (Joh 6,53)'. In R. Pesch and R. Schnackenburg (eds.), *Jesus und der Menschensohn.* FS Anton Vögtle (Freiburg: Herder, 1975), pp. 342-54.

Bartlet, Vernon, 'Christ's Use of the Term "The Son of Man"'. *Exp* 4/6 (1892), pp. 427-43.

—, 'Christ's Use of "the Son of Man"'. *ET* 4 (1892–93), p. 403.

—, '"The Son of Man": A Rejoinder'. *ET* 5 (1893–94), pp. 41-42.

Bastin, Marcel, *La Passion du Fils de l'homme dans les dits de Jésus. Contribution à l'étude du Jésus de l'histoire.* Typewritten dissertation (Strasbourg, 1973).

Bauckham, Richard, 'The Son of Man: "A Man in my Position" or "Someone"?' *JSNT* 23 (1985), pp. 23-33.

Bauer, J.B., 'Das Zeichen des Menschensohnes'. *Klerus-Blatt* 88 (1955), pp. 222-23.

Baur, Ferdinand Christian, 'Die Bedeutung des Ausdrucks: ὁ υἱὸς τοῦ ἀνθρώπου'. *ZwTh* 3 (1860), pp. 274-92.

Beale, Gregory K., 'The Problem of the Man from the Sea in IV Ezra 13 and its Relation to the Messianic Concept in John's Apocalypse'. *NT* 25 (1983), pp. 182-88.

Beasley-Murray, George R., 'John 12,31-32: The Eschatological Significance of the Lifting up of the Son of Man'. In W. Schrage (ed.), *Studien zum Text und zur Ethik des Neuen Testaments*. FS Heinrich Greeven. BZNW 47 (Berlin: De Gruyter, 1986), pp. 70-81.

—, 'Resurrection and Parousia of the *Son of Man*'. *Tyndale Bulletin* 42 (1991), pp. 296-309.

Beekman, John, 'The Son of Man'. In *Notes on Translation with Drills* (Santa Ana: Summer Institute of Linguistics, 1965). Cf. Ralph Hill, 'Further Considerations on Translating "The Son of Man"'. *Notes on Translation* 93 (1983), p. 50.

Bekker, Ype, *Zoon van God, Messias, Mensenzoon. De structuur van het Evangelie naar Johannes*. Unpublished dissertation (Kampen: Uitgeverij Kok, 1997).

Bennett, W.R., Jr., ' "The son of man must..." ' *NT* 17 (1975), pp. 113-29.

Bentzen, Aage, *Messias—Moses Redivivus—Menschensohn. Skizzen zum Thema Weissagung und Erfüllung*. AThANT 17 (Zürich: Zwingli Verlag, 1948). English: *King and Messiah*. Edited by G.W. Anderson (London: Lutterworth, 1955; 2nd ed. Oxford: Blackwell, 1970).

Berger, Klaus, *Die Auferstehung des Propheten und die Erhöhung des Menschensohnes. Traditionsgeschichtliche Untersuchungen zur Deutung des Geschickes Jesu in frühchristlichen Texten*. SUNT 13 (Göttingen: Vandenhoeck & Ruprecht, 1976).

Berk, Lucas, 'Zoon van de mens'. *Interpretatie* 4/4 (1996), pp. 16-17.

Bertholet, Alfred, 'I M(enschensohn) im AT und Judentum'. In *RGG*, IV (1913), pp. 296-97.

Besnard, A.-M., 'Au dire des gens qu'est le Fils de l'homme'. *La vie spirituelle* 56 (1974) No. 602. Tome 128, pp. 410-14.

Betz, Otto, *Die Menschensohnworte Jesu und die Zukunfterwartung des Paulus (Daniel 7,13-14)*. Jesus und das Danielbuch, Band II. ANTI 6 (II) (Bern: Verlag Peter Lang, 1985).

Beus, Ch. de, 'Achtergrond en inhoud van de uitdrukking "de Zoon des Mensen" in de synoptische evangelien'. *NedThT* 9 (1954–55), pp. 272-95.

— , 'Het gebruik en de betekenis van de uitdrukking "de Zoon des Mensen" in het Evangelie van Johannes'. *NedThT* 10 (1955–56), pp. 237-51.

Beyer, Klaus, 'Der Menschensohn als Gott der Welt: Der Ursprung der hohen Christologie bei Jesus selbst'. In Sophia G. Vashalomidze and Lutz Greisiger, *Der christliche Orient und seine Umwelt*. FS Jürgen Tubachs anlässlich seines 60. Geburtstags (Wiesbaden: Harrasowitz Verlag, 2007), pp. 11-19.

Beyerle, Stefan, '"Der mit den Wolken des Himmels kommt". Untersuchungen zum Traditionsgefüge "Menschensohn"'. In D. Sänger (ed.), *Gottessohn und Menschensohn*. BThS 67 (Neukirchen–Vluyn: Neukirchener Verlag, 2004), pp. 1-52.

— , '"One Like a Son of Man": Innuendoes of a Heavenly Individual'. In Gabriele Boccaccini (ed.), *Enoch and Qumran Origins: New Light on a Forgotten Connection* (Grand Rapids: Eerdmans, 2005), pp. 54-58.

Bieneck, J., 'Menschensohn. Im *NT*'. *BHH* 2 (1964), pp. 1192-93.

Bietenhard, Hans: '"Der Menschensohn"—ὁ υἱὸς τοῦ ἀνθρώπου. Sprachliche und religionsgeschichtliche Untersuchungen zu einem Begriff der synoptischen Evangelien I. Sprachlicher und religionsgeschichtlicher Teil'. *ANRW*, II 25,1 (Berlin: De Gruyter, 1982), pp. 265-350.

Billing, Einar, '"Människosonen" och "Gudsriket" i Jesu förkunnelse'. In *För Tanke och Tro*. FS Oscar Ekman (1923), pp. 241-83. Reprint in idem, *De etiska tankarna i urkristendommen* (Stockholm: Sveriges Kristliga Studentrörelsens Bokförlag, 2. opl. 1936), pp. 396-440.

Birdsall, J. Neville, 'Who is This Son of Man?' *EvQ* 42 (1970), pp. 7-17.

Bissoli, Giovanni, 'Il Figlio dell'uomo in Marco: problema insolubile?' In Ettore Franco (ed.), *Mysterium Regni—Ministerium Verbi (Mc 4,11, at 6,4)*. FS Vittorio Fusco. Supplementa alla Rivista Biblica 38 (Bologna: Dehoniane, 2001), pp. 597-604.

Bittner, Wolfgang, 'Gott—Menschensohn—Davidssohn. Eine Untersuchung zur Traditionsgeschichte von Daniel 7,13f.'. *Freiburger Zeitschrift für Philosophie und Theologie* 32 (1985), pp. 343-72.

Black, Matthew, 'Unsolved New Testament Problems. The "Son of Man" in Old Biblical Literature'. *ET* 60 (1948–49), pp. 11-15.

—, 'Unsolved New Testament Problems. The "Son of Man" in the Teaching of Jesus'. *ET* 60 (1948–49), pp. 32-36.

—, 'Servant of the Lord and Son of Man'. *SJTh* 6 (1953), pp. 1-11.

—, 'The Son of Man Problem in Recent Research and Debate'. *BJRL* 45 (1962–63), pp. 305-18.

—, 'The "Son of Man" Passion Sayings in the Gospel Tradition'. *ZNW* 60 (1969), pp. 1-8.

—, 'Die Apotheose Israels: eine neue Interpretation des danielischen "Menschensohnes"'. In R. Pesch and R. Schnackenburg (eds.), *Jesus und der Menschensohn*. FS Anton Vögtle (Freiburg: Herder, 1975), pp. 92-99.

—, 'The Throne-Theophany Prophetic Commission and the "Son of Man": A Study in Tradition-History'. In Robert Hamerton-Kelly and Robin Scroggs (eds.), *Jews, Greeks and Christians: Religious Cultures in Late Antiquity*. FS William David Davies. SJLA 21 (Leiden: Brill, 1976), pp. 57-73.

—, 'The "Parables" of Enoch (1 En 37–71) and the "Son of Man"'. *ET* 88 (1976–77), pp. 5-8.

—, 'Jesus and the Son of Man'. *JSNT* 1 (1978), pp. 4-18

—, 'Aramaic Barnasha and the 'Son of Man". *ET* 95 (1983–84), pp. 200-206.

Blackwood, Andrew W., *The Other Son of Man: Ezekiel, Jesus* (Grand Rapids: Baker, 1966).

Blanchard, Yves-Marie, 'Le fils de l'homme et l'échelle de Jacob: Refléxion sur l'intertextualité scriptuaire et relecture de Jean 1,51, à la lumière de Bible juive'. In C. Focant and A. Wénin (eds.), *Analyse narrative et bible. Deuxième colloque international du RRENAB, Louvain-la-Neuve, avril 2004*. BEThL 191 (Leuven: Peeters, 2005), pp. 181-95.

Bleibtreu, Walther, 'Jesu Selbstbenennung als der Menschensohn'. *ThStKr* 98/99 (1926), pp. 164-211.

Bock, Darrell L., 'The Son of Man Sitting at God's Right Hand and the Debate over Jesus' Blasphemy'. In J.B. Green and M. Turner (eds.), *Jesus of Nazareth* (Grand Rapids: Eerdmans, 1994), pp. 181-91.

Böhme, Christian Friedrich, 'Wie konnte sich Jesus zugleich Menschensohn und Gottessohn nennen?' *Theologische Monatsschrift für das Jahr 1802* (ed. von J.C.W. Augusti) 2 (1802), pp. 393-411.

—, *Versuch, das Geheimnis des Menschensohnes zu enthüllen* (Neustadt: Orla, 1839).

Boehmer, J., *Reich Gottes und Menschensohn im Buche Daniel. Ein Beitrag zum Verständnis seines Grundgedankens* (Leipzig: Deichert, 1899).

Boehmer, R., 'Zum Verständnis des "enschensohnes"'. *Die Studierstube* 3 (1905), pp. 411-18.

Boer, Martinus de, 'Johannine History and Johannine Theology: The Death of Jesus as the Exaltation and the Glorification of the Son of Man'. In G. Van Belle (ed.), *The Death of Jesus in the Fourth Gospel*. BEThL 200 (Leuven: Peeters, 2007), pp. 293-326.

Böttrich, Christfried, 'onturen des "Menschensohnes" in äthHen 37–71'. In D. Sänger (ed.), *Gottessohn und Menschensohn*. BThS 67 (Neukirchen–Vluyn: Neukirchener Verlag, 2004), pp. 53-90.

Bokum, L. ten, 'De Zoon des Menschen'. *Nederlandsche Katholieke Stemmen* 9 (1909), pp. 2-10.

Borgen, Peder, 'Some Jewish Exegetical Traditions as Background for Son of Man Sayings in John's Gospel (Jn 3,13-14 and Context)'. In M. de Jonge (ed.), *L'Évangile de Jean*. BEThL 44 (Gembloux: Duculot/Leuven University Press, 1977), pp. 243-58. Reprint in idem, *Logos was the true Light and other Essays on the Gospel of John*. Relieff 9 (Trondhejm: Tapir, 1983), pp. 133-48.

Borsch, Frederick Houk, 'The Son of Man'. *AThR* 45 (1963), pp. 174-90.

—, *The Son of Man in Myth and History*. The New Testament Library (London: SCM Press, 1967).

—, *The Christian and Gnostic Son of Man*. SBTh SS 14 (London: SCM Press, 1970).

—, 'Further Reflections on "The Son of Man": The Origins and Development of the Title'. In James H. Charlesworth (ed.), *The Messiah: Developments in Earliest Judaism and Christianity*. The First Princeton Symposium on Judaism and Christian Origins (Minneapolis: Fortress Press, 1992), pp. 130-44.

Bottini, Giovanni Claudio, 'Luca 18,31-33: Il misterio del Figlio dell'uomo'. In Ettore Franco (ed.), *Mysterium Regni – Ministerium Verbi (Mc 4,11, at 6,4)*. FS Vittorio Fusco. Supplementa alla Rivista Biblica 38 (Bologna: Dehoniane, 2001), pp. 705-14.

Bouyer, Louis, 'La notion christologique du Fils de l'homme a-t-elle disparu dans la patristique greque?' *Melanges Bibliques*. FS A. Robert. Travaux de l'Institut Catholique de Paris 4 (1957), pp. 519-30.

Bowker, John, 'The Son of Man'. *JThS* NS 28 (1977), pp. 19-48.

Bowman, John Wick, 'The Background of the Term "Son of Man"'. *ET* 59 (1947–48), pp. 283-88.

—, 'David, Jesus Son of David and Son of Man', *Abr-Nahrain* 27 (1989), pp. 1-22.

Bracht, Werner, *Der Menschensohn. Eine Untersuchung zum Bedeutungswandel und zur Geschichte der Auslegung und der Erforschung des neutestamentlichen Begriffs*. Typewritten dissertation (München, 1972). Preface (Vorbemerkung) dated 1986.

Brändle, M., 'Der Menschensohn. Selbstbezeichnung Jesu oder Theologie der Urkirche?' *Orientierung* 21 (1957), pp. 27-31.

Braun, F.-M., 'Messie, Logos et Fils de l'Homme', in E. Massaux (ed.), *La Venue du Messie. Messianisme et Eschatologie*. Recherches Bibliques 6 (Bruxelles: Desclée de Brouwer, 1962), pp. 133-47.

Broadhead, Edwin K., 'Reconfiguring Jesus: The Son of Man in Markan Perspective'. In Thomas R. Hatina, *Biblical Interpretation in Early Christian Gospels*. Vol. 1. *The Gospel of Mark*. Library of New Testament Studies 304 (London: T. & T. Clark, 2006), pp. 18-30.

Broer, Ingo, 'Das Gericht des Menschensohnes über die Völker. Auslegung von Mt 25,31-46'. *Bibel und Leben* 11 (1970), pp. 273-95.

Brown, John Pairman, 'The Son of Man: "This Fellow"'. *Bib.* 58 (1977), pp. 361-87.

—, 'The Son of Man and Jesus' Irony'. *AAR/SBL Abstracts 2001* (2001), pp. 37-38.

Brownlee, William H., '*Son of Man* Set your Face: Ezekiel the Refugee Prophet'. *HUCA* 54 (1983), pp. 83-110.

Bruce, Alexander Balmain, 'The Kingdom of God: The Son of Man and the Son of God'. *The Monthly Interpreter* 3 (1886), pp. 278-93.

Bruce, Frederick F., 'The Background to the Son of Man Sayings'. In Harold H. Rowden (ed.), *Christ the Lord.* FS Donald Guthrie (Leicester: Inter-Varsity Press, 1982), pp. 50-70.

Brückner, Wilhelm, 'Jesus "des Menschen Sohn"'. *JPTh* 12 (1886), pp. 254-78.

Brug, John F., 'Exegetical Brief: The *Son of Man* Who Is in Heaven'. *Wisconsin Lutheran Quarterly* 93 (1996), pp. 140-41.

Brun, Lyder, 'Guds rike og Menneskesønnen. Rudolf Otto, Reich Gottes und Menschensohn. Ein relgionsgeschichtlicher Versuch (1934).

Buchhold, Jaques, 'Jésus ou l'énigme du Fils de l'homme'. *Théologie Évangélique* 1 (2002), No. 2, pp. 21-46; No. 3, pp. 3-24.

Bulcock, H. 'Was the Double Use of "Son of Man" a Factor in the Deification of Jesus?' *The Congregational Quarterly* 17 (1939), pp. 44-55.

Bulteau, M.-G., 'Le Fils de l'homme dans la littérature apocalyptique'. In *Jesus. Héritage et projet* 9 (1974), pp. 69-81.

Bultmann, Rudolf, 'Reich Gottes und Menschensohn. Theologische Rundschau IX,1 (s. 1-35). 1937'. *NTT* 38 (1937), pp. 105-25.

Bultmann, Rudolf, 'Reich Gottes und Menschensohn. Rudolf Otto: Reich Gottes und Menschensohn. Ein religionsgeschichtlicher Versuch, 1934'. *ThR* NF 9 (1937), pp. 1-35. Reprint in idem, *Theologie als Kritik*. Edited by Matthias Dreher and Klaus W. Müller (Tübingen: Mohr Siebeck, 2002), pp. 328-53.

Burkett, Delbert Royce, *The Son of Man in the Gospel of John*. JSNTSup 56 (Sheffield: Sheffield Academic Press, 1991).

—, 'The Nontitular Son of Man: A History and Critique'. *NTS* 40 (1994), pp. 504-21.

—, *The Son of Man Debate: A History and Evaluation*. SNTSMS 107 (Cambridge: Cambridge University Press, 1999).

Burkill, T.A., 'The Son of Man: A Brief General Statement'. *ET* 56 (1944–45), pp. 305-306.

—, 'The Hidden Son of Man in St. Mark's Gospel'. *ZNW* 52 (1961), pp. 189-213. Reprint, slightly expanded, in idem, *New Light on the Earliest Gospel: Seven Markan Studies* (Ithaca: Cornell University Press, 1972), pp. 1-38.

Burnier-Genton, J., 'Ézéchiel fils d'homme'. *Essais bibliques* 5 (1982). Cf. *ZAW* 95 (1983), p. 300.

Burton, H., 'The Son of Man'. *Exp* 5, 4 (1896), pp. 388-400.

Buth, Randall, 'A More Complete Semitic Background for בר אנשא, "son of man"'. In C. Evans and James A. Sanders (eds.), *The Function of Scripture in Early Jewish and Christian Tradition*. JSNTSup 154. Studies in Scripture in Early Judaism and Christianity 6 (Sheffield: Sheffield Academic Press, 1998), pp. 176-89.

Cadoux, A.T., 'The Son of Man'. *Interp.* 18 (1920), pp. 202-14.
Cahill, Michael, 'Did Jesus Refer to Himself in the Third Person? A Contribution to the Son of Man Debate'. *Proceedings of the Irish Biblical Association* 25 (2002), pp. 58-68.
Camacho, F., see Mateos, J.
Cambe, M., 'Le Fils de l'homme dans les évangiles synoptiques'. *LV* 12 (1963), pp. 32-64.
Campbell, J.Y., 'Son of Man'. In Alan Richardson (ed.), *A Theological Word Book of the Bible* (London: SCM Press, 1950), pp. 230-32.
—, 'The Origin and Meaning of the Term Son of Man'. *JThS* 48 (1947), pp. 145-55. Reprint in idem, *Three New Testament Studies* (Leiden: Brill, 1965), pp. 29-40.
Cangh, Jean-Marie van, 'Le Fils de l'homme dans la tradition synoptique'. *Revue théologique de Louvain* 1 (1970), pp. 411-19.
Caquot, A., 'Les quatre bêtes et le "Fils d'homme" (*Daniel*, 7)'. *Semitica* 17 (1967), pp. 37-71.
Caragounis, Chrys C., *The Son of Man: Vision and Interpretation*. WUNT 38 (Tübingen: J.C.B. Mohr [P. Siebeck], 1986).
—, 'Kingdom of God, Son of Man and Jesus' Self-Understanding' I-II. *Tyndale Bulletin* 40 (1989), pp. 3-23, 223-38.
Carpzov, Johann Benedikt, *Dissertatio de Filio Hominis ad antiquum dierum delato, ad Daniel. VII: 13, 14* (1679). Reprint in Godefried Menthen (ed.), *Thesaurus theologico-philologicus, sive Sylloge dissertationum elegantiorum ad selectiora et illustriore Veteris et Novi Testamenti loca* I (Amsterdam, 1701), pp. 887-901.
Carr, A., 'The Son of Man as the Light of the World'. *Exp* 7/1 (1906), pp. 115-23.
Carrairon, Emile, *Essai historique et critique sur le titre de Fils de l'homme* (Nimes: Chastanier, 1886).
Carvalho, José Ornelas, *Caminho de morte, destino de vida: O projecto do Filho do Homem e dos seus discípulos a luz de Mc 8,27–9,1*. Fundamenta 18 (Lisboa: Edicoes Didaskalia, 1998).
Casey, P. Maurice, 'The Corporate Interpretation of "One like a Son of Man" (Dan. VII 13) at the Time of Jesus'. *NT* 18 (1976), pp. 167-80.
—, 'The Son of Man Problem'. *ZNW* 67 (1976), pp. 147-54.
—, 'The Use of the Term "Son of Man" in the Similitudes of Henoch'. *JSJ* 7 (1976), pp. 11-29.
—, *Son of Man: The Interpretation and Influence of Daniel 7* (London: SPCK, 1979).
—, 'Aramaic Idiom and the Son of Man Sayings', *ET* 96 (1984–85), pp. 233-36.
—, 'The Jackals and the Son of Man (Matt. 8.20//Luke 9.58)', *JSNT* 23 (1985), pp. 3-22.
—, 'General, Generic and Indefinite: The Use of the Term 'Son of Man' in Aramaic Sources and in the Teaching of Jesus'. *JSNT* 29 (1987), pp. 21-56.
—, 'Method in our Madness, and Madness in their Methods. Some Approaches to the Son of Man Problem in Recent Scholarship'. *JSNT* 42 (1991), pp. 17-43.
—, 'The Use of the Term בר (א)נש(א) in the Aramaic Translations of the Hebrew Bible'. *JSNT* 54 (1994), pp. 87-118.

—, 'Idiom and Translation: Some Aspects of the Son of Man Problem'. *NTS* 41 (1995), pp. 164-82.

—, 'Aramaic Idiom and the Son of Man Problem: A Response to Owen and Shepherd'. *JSNT* 25 (2002), pp. 3-32.

—, *The Solution to the 'Son of Man' Problem*. The Library of the New Testament Studies 343 (London: T. & T. Clark/Continuum, 2007).

Catchpole, D.R., 'The Son of Man's Search for Faith (Luke XVIII 8b)'. *NT* 19 (1977), pp. 81-104.

—, 'The Poor on Earth and the Son of Man in Heaven: A Re-Appraisal of Matthew xxv.31-46'. *BJRL* 61 (1978–79), pp. 355-97.

—, 'The Angelic Son of Man in Luke 12:8'. *NT* 24 (1982), pp. 255-65.

Cavalier, H.O., 'The Gospel of the Son of Man'. *Theology* 6 (1923), pp. 218-21.

Chamard-Bois, Pierre, 'L'heure du Fils de l'homme: Marc 14,32-42'. *Sémiotique & Bible* 91 (1998), pp. 53-57.

Chamberlain, W.D., 'Till the Son of Man Be Come'. *Interp.* 7 (1953), pp. 3-13.

Charles, R.H., 'The Son of Man'. *ET* 4 (1892–93), pp. 504-506.

Chilton, Bruce D., 'The Son of Man: Human and Heavenly'. In F. van Segbroeck, C. M. Tuckett, G. van Belle and J. Verheyden (eds.), *The Four Gospels*. FS Frans Neirynck. BEThL 100 (Leuven: Peeters Publishers, 1992) I, pp. 203-18. Reprint in Jacob Neusner (ed.), *Religious and Theological Studies*. Approaches to Ancient Judaism NS 4 = South Florida Studies in the History of Judaism 81 (Atlanta, GA: Scholar's Press, 1993), pp. 97-114, and in B.D. Chilton, *Judaic Approaches to the Gospels*. University of Florida International Studies on Christianity and Formative Judaism 2 (Atlanta, GA: Scholar's Press, 1994), pp. 75-104.

—, 'The Son of Man: Who Was He?' *Bible Review* 12 (1996), pp. 35-39, 45-47.

—, '(The) Son of (the) Man, and Jesus'. In Bruce Chilton and Craig A. Evans (eds.), *Authenticating the Words of Jesus*. NTTS 28,1 (Leiden: Brill, 1999), pp. 259-87.

Cho, T.Y., *The Son of Man Came Eating and Drinking (Matt 11:19): A Study of the Table Fellowship in Qumran and Q*. Unpublished dissertation (Drew University, 1992) (EThL 70 [1994] 5261; DissAbstr 53 [1992–93], p. 1958).

Christensen, Jens, 'Menneskesønnen gaar bort, som der staar skrevet om ham'. *DTT* 19 (1956), pp. 83-92. French: 'Le fils de l'homme s'en va, ainsi qu'il est écrit de lui'. *StTh* 10 (1956), pp. 28-39. Reprint in idem, *Menneskesønnen. En bibelteologisk studie* (1996), pp. 71-80.

—, 'Menneskesønnen'. *Gads Danske Bibelleksikon* II (København: Gad, 1966), pp. 188-91.

—, *Menneskesønnen. En bibelteologisk studie*. Bibel og historie 19 (Århus: Aarhus Universitetsforlag, 1996).

Chronis, Harry L., 'To Reveal and to Conceal: A Literary-Critical Perspective on the "Son of Man" in Mark'. *NTS* 51 (2005), pp. 459-81.

Ciholas, Paul, 'Son of Man in the Synoptic Gospels'. *BThB* 11 (1981), pp. 17-20.

—, '"Son of Man" and Hellenistic Christology'. *Review and Expositor* 79 (1982), pp. 487-501.

Clark, J.L., *A Re-Examination of the Problem of the Messianic Secret in Mark in its Relationship to the Synoptic Son of Man Sayings*. Unpublished dissertation (New Haven, 1962). Cf. J. Coppens, *De Mensenzoon-logia in het Markus-Evangelium* (1973), p. 34.

Clines, David J.A., 'Ecce vir, or, gendering the *Son of Man*'. In J. Cheryl Exum and Stephen D. Moore (eds.), *Biblical Studies/Cultural Studies*. JSOTSup 266 (Sheffield: Sheffield Academic Press, 1998), pp. 352-75.

Coke, Paul T., 'Los Angeles del Hijo del Hombre'. *Estudios Bíblicos* 32 (1973), pp. 283-89. English: 'The Angels of the Son of Man'. In A. Fuchs (ed.), *Probleme der Forschung*. SUNT Serie A Band 3 (1978), pp. 91-98.

Collins, Adela Yarbro, 'The Origin of the Designation of Jesus as "Son of Man"'. *HThR* 80 (1987), pp. 391-407. Reprint in idem, *Cosmology and Eschatology in Jewish and Christian Apocalypticism*. JSJSup 50 (1996), pp. 139-58.

—, 'The Son of Man Sayings in the Sayings Source'. In M.P. Horgan and P.J. Kobelski (eds.), *To Touch the Text*. FS Joseph Fitzmyer (New York: Crossroad, 1989), pp. 369-89.

—, 'The Apocalyptic Son of Man Sayings'. In Birger A. Pearson (ed.), *The Future of Early Christianity* (Minneapolis: Fortress Press, 1991), pp. 220-28.

—, 'The "Son of Man" Tradition and the Book of Revelation'. In James H. Charlesworth (ed.), *The Messiah: Developments in Earliest Judaism and Christianity* (Minneapolis: Fortress Press, 1992), pp. 536-68. Reprint in idem, *Cosmology and Eschatology in Jewish and Christian Apocalypticism*. JSJSup 50 (1996), pp. 159-97.

Collins, John J., 'The Son of Man and the Saints of the Most High in the Book of Daniel'. *JBL* 93 (1974), pp. 50-66.

—, 'The Son of Man who has Righteousness'. In *Society of Biblical Literature, Annual Meetings Seminar Papers 1979* (1979), II, pp. 1-13.

—, 'The Heavenly Representative: The "Son of Man" in the Similitudes of Enoch'. In J. Collins and G. Nickelsburg (eds.), *Ideal Figures in Ancient Judaism*. SCSt 12 (1980), pp. 111-33.

—, 'The Son of Man in First Century Judaism'. *NTS* 38 (1992), pp. 448-66. Reprint in a revised form as:

—, 'The Danielic Son of Man', in idem, *The Scepter and the Star: The Messiahs of the Dead Sea Scrolls and other Ancient Literature*. The Anchor Bible Reference Library (New York: Doubleday, 1995), pp. 173-94.

Colpe, Carsten, 'ὁ υἱὸς τοῦ ἀνθρώπου'. In *ThWNT*, VIII (1969), pp. 403-81. Photographic reprint in idem, *Kleine Schriften*. Dritter Band. Abteilung E. Menschensohn und Gottessohn. Edited by Christoph Elsas and Christiane Nasse (Berlin: Universitätsbibliothek der Freien Universität, 1996), pp. 17-95. English translation by Geoffrey W. Bromiley in *ThDNT* VIII (Grand Rapids: Eerdmans, 1972), pp. 400-477.

—, 'Der Begriff "Menschensohn" und die Methode der Erforschung messianischer Prototypen'. *Kairos* NF 11 (1969), pp. 241-63; 12 (1970), pp. 81-112; 13 (1971), pp. 1-17; 14 (1972), pp. 241-57. Photographic reprint in idem, *Kleine Schriften*. Dritter Band, pp. 96-183.

—, 'Neue Untersuchungen zum Menschensohn-Problem'. *ThRv* 77 (1981), cols. 353-72. Photographic reprint in idem, *Kleine Schriften*. Dritter Band, pp. 217-36.

—, 'Kearns, Rollin: Vorfragen zur Christologie I'. *ThRv* 77 (1981), cols. 373-78. Photographic reprint in idem, *Kleine Schriften*. Dritter Band, pp. 237-42.

Coppens, Joseph, 'Le messianisme sapiental et les origines littéraires du Fils de l'homme Daniélique'. In Martin Noth and D. Winton Thomas (eds.), *Wisdom in Israel and in the Ancient Near East*. FS Harold Henry Rowley. VTSup 3 (Leiden: Brill, 1955), pp. 33-41.

—, 'Le Fils d'homme danielique et les relectures de Daniel, VII, 13, dans les Apocryphes et les écrits du Nouveau Testament'. *EThL* 37 (1961), pp. 5-51 = J. Coppens and L. Dequeker, *Le Fils de l'homme et les Saints du Trés-Haut en Daniel, VII, dans les Apocryphes et dans le Nouveau Testament*. Analecta Lovaniensia Biblica et Orientalia III, 23 (1961), pp. 55-101.

—, 'L'origine du symbole "Fils d'homme"'. *EThL* 39 (1963), pp. 100-104.

—, 'Le serviteur de Yahvé et le fils d'homme danielique sont-ils des figures messianiques?' *EThL* 39 (1963), pp. 104-13.

—, 'Le fils d'homme danielique, vizir céleste?' *EThL* 40 (1964), pp. 72-80.

—, 'Les origines du symbole du Fils d'homme en Dan., VII'. *EThL* 44 (1968), pp. 497-502.

—, 'La vision danielique du Fils d'homme'. *VT* 19 (1969), pp. 171-82.

—, *De Mensenzoon-logia in het Markus-Evangelie. Avec un résumé, des notes et une bibliographie en francais*. Medelingen van de koninlijke Academie voor Wetenshappen, Letteren en schone Kunsten van België. Klasse der Letteren. Jaargang 35/3 (1973). French:

—, 'Les logia du Fils de l'homme dans l'évangile de Marc'. In M. Sabbe (ed.), *L'évangile selon Marc. Tradition et rédaction*. BEThL 34 (Leuven: University Press: Gembloux: Duculot, 1974), pp. 487-528. Reprint in idem, BEThL 55 (1981), pp. 109-49.

—, 'Le Fils de l'Homme dans la tradition évangélique'. *EThL* 50 (1974), pp. 260-63.

—, 'Le Fils d'homme dans le judaïsme de l'époque néotestamentaire.' *Orientalia Lovaniensia Periodica* 6–7 (1975–76), pp. 59-73.

—, 'Le Fils de l'homme dans l'évangile johannique'. *EThL* 52 (1976), pp. 28-81. Reprint in idem, BEThL 55 (1981), pp. 45-103

—, 'Le Fils de l'homme dans le dossier paulinien'. *EThL* 52 (1976), pp. 309-30. Reprint in idem, BEThL 55 (1981), pp. 23-44.

—, 'L'interpretation collective du Fils d'homme danielique'. *EThL* 53 (1977), pp. 189-91.

—, 'Logia johannique du Fils de l'Homme'. In M. de Jonge (ed.), *L'Evangile de Jean: sources, rédaction*. BEThL 44 (Leuven: University Press; Gembloux: Duculot, 1977), pp. 311-15. Reprint in idem, BEThL 55 (1981), pp. 98-103.

—, 'Le Fils de l'homme johannique'. *EThL* 54 (1978), pp. 126-30.

—, 'Le dossier non biblique de l'expression araméenne *br 'nš*. *EThL* 56 (1980), pp. 122-24. Reprint in idem, BEThL 61 (1983), pp. 108-11.

—, 'La mention d'un Fils d'homme angélique en Ap 14,14'. In J. Lambrecht (ed.), *L'Apocalypse johannique et l'Apocalyptique dans le Nouveau Testament*. BEThL 53 (Gembloux: Duculot; Leuven: University Press, 1980), p. 229.

—, 'Où en est le problème de Jésus "Fils de l'homme"'. *EThL* 56 (1980), pp. 282-302. Reprint in idem, BEThL 55 (1981), pp. 1-21.

—, 'Le Fils d'homme dans les traditions juives postbibliques hormis le Livre des Paraboles l'Hénoch éthiopien'. *EThL* 57 (1981), pp. 58-82. Reprint in idem, BEThL 61 (1983), pp. 159-83.

—, *Le Fils de l'homme néotestamentaire*. La relève apocalyptique du messianisme royal III. BEThL 55 (Leuven: Peeters, 1981).

—, *Le Fils d'homme vétéroet intertestamentaire* (La relève apocalyptique du messianisme royal II). Edited by J. Lust, BEThL 61 (Leuven: Peeters/Leuven University Press, 1983).

Cortés, Juan B., and Florence M. Gatti, 'The Son of Man or The Son of Adam'. *Bib.* 49 (1968), pp. 457-502.
Coulin, Franck, *Le Fils de l'homme* (Geneve, 1866).
Cristofani, José Roberto, 'A expressão "Filho do homem" em Daniel. Anotacõs preliminares sobre uma proposita metodológica'. *Estudos de Religião* 19 (2000), pp. 25-44.
Croskery, J., 'Recent Discussion on the Meaning of the Title "Son of Man"'. *ET* 13 (1901–1902), pp. 351-55.
Cruvellier, Jean, 'La notion de "Fils de l'Homme" dans les Evangiles'. *Études Évangéliques* 15 (1955), pp. 31-50.

Dagron, Alain, *Aux Jours de Fils de l'Homme. Essai sur le service de la parole: Luc XVII,1 à XVIII,8; lecture sémiotique et propositions théologiques*. Profac Biblique 3 (Lyon: Cadir, 1990).
Danove, Paul, 'The Rhetoric of the Characterization of Jesus as Son of Man and Christ in Mark'. *Bib.* 84 (2003), pp. 16-34.
D'Aquino, Pietro, 'Cristo figlio di dio e figlio dell'Uomo (Col 1,15-20)'. *Studia hierosolymitana* 2 (1976), pp. 135-45.
Dautzenberg, G., 'Tora des Menschensohnes? Kritische Überlegungen zu Daniel Kosch'. *BZ* 36 (1992), pp. 93-103.
Davis, Dan, 'The Semantic Content of 'Son of Man''. *Notes on Translation* (Dallas) 4 (1990), pp. 9-23.
Davis, H. Francis, 'The Son of Man—I. The Image of the Father'. *The Furrow* 12 (1961), pp. 39-48.
Deissler, A., 'Der "Menschensohn" und "das Volk der Heiligen des Höchsten" in Dan 7'. In R. Pesch and R. Schnackenburg (eds.), *Jesus und der Menschensohn*. FS Anton Vögtle (Freiburg: Herder, 1975), pp. 81-91.
Delorme, Jean, *Le Fils de l'homme*. 'Evangile' 35 NS 16 (Paris: Tournon, 1964).
Dennis, John, 'The "Lifting Up of the Son of Man" and the Dethroning of the "Ruler of This World": Jesus' Death as the Defeat of the Devil in John 12,31-32'. In G. Van Belle (ed.), *The Death of Jesus in the Fourth Gospel*. BEThL 200 (Leuven: Peeters, 2007), pp. 677-91.
Dequeker, L., 'Wie is de mensenzoon?'. *Collectanea Mechliniensia* 46 (= NS 31) (1961), pp. 407-17.
Derambure, Jean, 'Le "Fils de l'homme" dans les Évangiles'. *Revue Augustinienne* 13 (1908), pp. 708-20; 14 (1909), pp. 319-40.
de Rosa, Guiseppe, 'Gesù, "Figlio di Dio" e "Figlio dellu'omo": I ritratto di Gesù nel Vangelio di Marco'. *Civiltaà Cattolica* 155 (2004), pp. 143-55.
Derrett, J. Duncan M., 'The *Son of Man* Standing (Acts 7:55-56)'. *Bibbia e Oriente* 30 (1988), pp. 71-84.
Dhanis, Edouard, 'De Filio hominis in Vetere Testamento et in iudaismo'. *Gregorianum* 45 (1964), pp. 5-59.
Dieckmann, Hermann, 'Ὁ υἱὸς τοῦ ἀνθρώπου'. *Bib.* 2 (1921), pp. 69-71.
—, '"Der Sohn des Menschen" im Johannesevangelium'. *Scholastik* 2 (1927), pp. 229-47.
—, 'De Iesu Christi messianitate et divinitate quaestiones selectae. 1. De nomine "Filii hominis"'. *Verbum Domini* 8 (1928), pp. 295-301.

Díez Macho, A., 'La Cristologia del Hijo del Hombre y el uso de la tercera persona en vez de la primera'. *Scripta theologica* 14 (1982), pp. 189-201.
Dion, H.-M., 'Quelques trais originaux de la conception johannique du Fils de l'homme'. *Sciences Ecclésiastiques* 19 (1967), pp. 49-65.
Doble, P., 'The Son of Man Saying in Stephen's Witnessing: Acts 6.8–8.2'. *NTS* 31 (1985), pp. 68-84.
Dols, W.L., Jr., *Toward a Field Critical Hermeneutic of the Phrase 'ho huios tou antropou' in the Narrative World of Mark: Interreadings from Literary Criticism, Analytical Psychology and Cultural Anthropology*. Unpublished dissertation (Berkeley Graduate Theological Union, 1987). Cf. *EThL* 67 (1991) Elenchus 5177; DissAbstr 49 (1988–89), pp. 1847-48.
Dominic, A.P., 'Learning from Jesus, the Son of Man'. *Review for Religious* 62 (2003), pp. 63-71.
Donahue, John R., 'Recent Studies on the Origin of "Son of Man" in the Gospels'. In *A Wise and Discerning Heart.* FS Joseph A. Fitzmyer. *CBQ* 48 (1986), pp. 484-98.
Dorman, David A., 'The Son of Man in John: A fresh Approach through Chapter 6'. *Studia Biblica et Theologica* 13 (1983), pp. 121-42.
Doughty, Darrell J., 'The Authority of the Son of Man (Mk 2,1–3,6)'. *ZNW* 74 (1983), pp. 161-81.
Drane, J., *Son of Man: A New Life of Christ* (Grand Rapids: Eerdmans, 1993).
Draper, Jonathan A., 'The Development of "the Sign of the Son of Man" in the Jesus Tradition'. *NTS* 39 (1993), pp. 1-21.
Dreyer, Yolanda, 'The Institutionalization of Jesus' Charismatic Authority: "Son of Man" as Case Study'. *Hervormde Teologiese Studies* 56 (2000), pp. 1057-78.
Driver, Samuel Rolles, 'Son of Man'. In James Hastings (ed.), *A Dictionary of the Bible* IV (Edinburgh: T. & T. Clark, 1902), pp. 579-89.
Drummond, James, 'The Use and the Meaning of the Phrase "The Son of Man" in the Synoptic Gospels'. *JThS* 2 (1901), pp. 350-58, 539-71.
Duncan, G.S., *Jesus, Son of Man: Studies Contributory to a Modern Portrait* (London: Nisbet, 1948).
Dunn, James D.G., '"Son of God" as "Son of Man" in the Dead Sea Scrolls?: A Response to John Collins on 4Q246'. In S.E. Porter et al. (eds.), *The Scrolls and the Scriptures*. JSPSup 26 = Roehampton Institute London Papers 3 (Sheffield: Sheffield Academic Press, 1997), pp. 198-210.
—, 'The Danielic Son of Man in the New Testament'. In John J. Collins and Peter W. Flint (eds.), *The Book of Daniel: Composition and Reception*. VTSup 83/2 (Leiden: Brill, 2001), pp. 528-49.
Dupont, G., *Le Fils de l'homme. Essai historique et critique* (Paris: Fischbacher, 1924).
Dupont, Jaques, '"Vous n'aurez pas achevé les villes d'Israël avant que le Fils de l'homme ne vienne" (Mat. X 23)'. *NT* 2 (1958), pp. 228-44.
Dwyer, John C., *Son of Man and Son of God* (New York: Paulist Press, 1983).

Early, P.D., *The Conception of the Son of Man in the Fourth Gospel*. Unpublished dissertation (Southern Baptist Seminary, 1952). Cf. F.J. Moloney, *The Johannine Son of Man* (1976), p. 229.
Eaton, David, 'Prof. Dalman on "The Son of Man"'. *ET* 10 (1898–99), pp. 438-43.
Eerdmans, Bernardus Dirks, 'De oorsprong van de uitdrukking "Zoon des menschen" als Evangelische Messiastitel'. *ThT* 28 (1894), pp. 153-76.

—, 'De uitdrukking "Zoon des menschen" en het boek "Henoch"'. *ThT* 29 (1895), pp. 48-71.

Eichrodt, Walther, 'Zum Problem des Menschensohnes'. *EvTh* 19 (1959), pp. 1-3.

Ellens, J. Harold, 'Exegesis of Second Temple Texts in a Fourth Gospel Son of Man Logion'. In Isaac Kalimi and Peter J. Haas (eds.), *Biblical Interpretation in Judaism and Christianity*. Library of Hebrew Bible/Old Testament Studies 439 (London: T. & T. Clark, 2006), pp. 131-49.

Ellington, John, '"Son of Man" and Contextual Translation'. *The BiTr* 40 (1989), pp. 201-208.

Ellingworth, Paul, 'Translating "The Son of Man": A Response'. *The BiTr* 48 (1997), pp. 109-13.

Elliot, John H., 'Man and Son of Man in the Gospel According to Mark'. In Trutz Rendtorff and Arthur Rich (eds.), *Humane Gesellschaft. Beiträge zu ihrer sozialen Gestaltung*. FS H.-D. Wendland (Zürich: Zwingli, 1970), pp. 47-59.

Ellwein, Eduard, *Der Menschensohn*. Bekennende Kirche 10 (München: Kaiser, 1934).

Emerton, John A., 'The Origins of the Son of Man Imagery'. *JThS* NS 9 (1958), pp. 225-42. Reprint in Austin Farrer (ed.), *The Communication of the Gospel in New Testament Times: Some Recent Studies* (London: SPCK, 1961), pp. 35-56.

Engnell, Ivan, 'E. Sjöberg, *Der Menschensohn im äthiopischen Henochbuch* (1946)'. *Bibliotheca Orientalis* 8 (1951), pp. 187-92.

—, 'Människosonen. 1. *G.T.*'. *SBU* II (Gävle: Skolförlaget, 1952), pp. 399-403; 2nd ed. Stockholm: Nordiska Uppslagsböcker, 1963), pp. 229-32. English: 'The Son of Man'. In idem, *Critical Essays on the Old Testament* (London: SPCK, 1970), pp. 237-41.

Evans, Craig A., 'Jesus' Self-designation "the *Son of Man*" and the Recognition of his Divinity'. In Stephen T. Davis (ed.), *The Trinity: An Interdisciplinary Symposium on the Trinity* (Oxford: Oxford University Press, 1999), pp. 29-47.

Evans, Milton G., 'The Title "the Son of Man"'. *BS* 57 (1900), pp. 680-95.

Ferch, Arthur J., *The Son of Man in Daniel 7*. Andrew University Seminary Doctoral Dissertation Series 6 (1983). Cf. *The Apocalyptic 'Son of Man' in Daniel 7*. Unpublished ThD dissertation (Andrew University, 1979). Cf. *ZAW* 92 (1980), p. 154.

Fernández Ramos, Felipe, 'El Hijo del hombre y el Reino'. *Studium Legionense* 39 (1998), pp. 89-119.

—, 'La "figura" del hijo del hombre'. *Naturaleza y Gracia* 45 (1998), pp. 107-35.

—, 'El hijo del hombre en el cuarto evangelio'. *Studium Legionense* 40 (1999), pp. 45-92.

Feuillet, André, 'La Venue du Regne de Dieu et du Fils de l'Homme (d'après Luc, XVII,20 a XVIII,8)'. *RSR* 35 (1948), pp. 544-65.

—, 'Le Fils de l'homme de Daniel et la tradition biblique'. *RB* 60 (1953), pp. 170-202; 321-46. Reprint in idem, *Études d'exegése et de théologie biblique* (Paris: Gabalda, 1975), pp. 413-93.

—, 'L' ἐξουσία du Fils de l'Homme (d'après *Mc*. II,10-28 et parr.)'. *RSR* 42 (1954), pp. 161-92.

—, 'Fils de l'homme'. *Catholicisme* 4 (1956), pp. 1295-302.

—, 'La Triomphe du Fils de l'homme d'après la déclaration du Christ aux Sanhédrites (Mc., XIV,62; Mt., XXVI,64; Lc., XX,69)'. In Édourd Massaux (ed.), *La Venue du Messie. Messianisme et Eschatologie*. RechBib 6 (Bruges, 1962), pp. 149-71.

Fiebig, Paul, *Der Menschensohn*. Jesu Selbstbezeichnung mit besonderer Berücksichtigung des aramäischen Sprachgebrauches für "Mensch" (Tübingen/Leipzig: Mohr [Siebeck], 1901).

—, 'Der "Menschensohn" als Geheimname'. *PrM* 6 (1902), pp. 431-37.

—, 'Der Menschensohn und Wellhausen'. *PrM* 8 (1904), pp. 12-26.

Fitzmyer, Joseph, 'Matthew Black, An Aramaic Approach to the Gospels and Acts (1967). Third Edition. Appendix on the Son of Man by Geza Vermes'. *CBQ* 30 (1968), pp. 417-28.

—, 'Another View of the "Son of Man" Debate'. *JSNT* 4 (1979), pp. 58-68.

—, 'The New Testament Title "Son of Man" Philologically Considered'. In idem, *A Wandering Aramean*. Collected Aramaic Essays. SBLMS 25 (Missoula, MT: Scholars Press, 1979), pp. 143-60.

Fletcher-Louis, Crispin H.T., 'The Revelation of the Sacral Son of Man: The Genre, History of Religious Context and the Meaning of the Transfiguration'. In Friedrich Avemarie and Hermann Lichtenberger (eds.), *Auferstehung—Resurrection*. The Fourth Durham-Tübingen Research Symposium (Tübingen, 1999). WUNT 135 (Tübingen: Siebeck [Mohr], 2001), pp. 247-98.

Floß, Johannes P., 'Menschensohn—Reich Gottes—Auferstehung im Buch Daniel'. In Sigurd Martin Daecke and Peter R. Sahm (eds.), *Jesus von Nazareth und das Christentum* (Neukirchen–Vluyn: Neukirchener Verlag, 2000), pp. 153-70.

Flügel, Heinz, *Mensch und Menschensohn* (München: Kösel, 1947; published earlier, in 1941, in a shorter edition as *Ein Feuer auf Erden*).

Flusser, David, 'Melchizedek and the Son of Man (A preliminary note on a new fragment from Qumran)'. *Christian News from Israel* 17 (1966), pp. 23-29. Reprint in idem, *Judaism and the Origins of Christianity* (Jerusalem: Magnes Press, 1988), pp. 186-92.

Focant, C., 'Du Fils de l'homme assis (Lc 22,69) au Fils de l'homme debout (Ac 7,56). Enjeux théologique et littéraire d'un changement sémantique'. In J. Verheyden (ed.), *The Unity of Luke-Acts*. BEThL 142 (Leuven: Peeters Publishers, 1999), pp. 563-74.

Ford, Joan Massingberd, '"The Son of Man"—A Euphemism?' *JBL* 87 (1968), pp. 257-66.

Formesyn, R.E.C., 'Was there a Pronominal Connection for the "bar nasha" Self-Designation?' *NT* 8 (1966), pp. 1-35.

Fox, K.A., 'The Son of Man: A Criticism of Dr. Manson's Exposition in "The Teaching of Jesus"'. *ET* 57 (1945–46), p. 328.

Freed, E.D., 'The Son of Man in the Fourth Gospel'. *JBL* 86 (1967), pp. 402-409.

Freedman, David N., '*Son of man*, can these bones live?' *Interp.* 29 (1975), pp. 171-86.

Fridrichsen, Anton, 'Människosonen och Israel'. In *Till Gustaf Aulén* (Stockholm: Svenska Kyrkans Diakonistyrelses Bokförlag, 1939), pp. 100-16.

Fritsch, I., '"et videbitis...angelos Dei ascendentes et descendentes super Filium hominis" (Io. 1,51)'. *Verbum Domini* 37 (1959), pp. 3-11.

Frøvig, D.A., 'Jesu ord til ypperstepræsten om sit komme paa himmelens skyer (Mt 26,64). Til belysning av de synoptiske utsagn om Menneskesønnens snarlige komme'. *Teologisk Tidsskrift for den danske Folkekirke* 4/1 (1920), pp. 257-79.

Fuller, Reginald H., 'The *Son of Man* Came to Serve'. In Francis A. Eigo (ed.), *Ministering in a Servant Church* (Villanova, PA: University Press, 1978), pp. 45-72.
—, 'The Son of Man: A Reconsideration'. In Dennis E. Groh and Robert Jewett (eds.), *The Living Text*. FS Ernest W. Saunders (Lanham, MD: University Press of America, 1985), pp. 207-17.

Gaillard, Jaques, *Specimen questionum in novum instrumentum de filio hominis* (Lugduni-Batavorum, 1684). Cf. W. Scholten, *De appellatione τοῦ υἱοῦ τοῦ ἀνθρώπου* (1809), p. 59
Galot, Jean, 'L'énigme du "Fils de l'homme"'. *Revue du Clergé Africain* 12 (1957), pp. 215-27; pp. 338-52.
— (ed.), 'L'expression "Fils de l'Homme"'. *Revue du Clergé Africain* 13 (1958), pp. 355-62.
—, 'Il mistero del Figlio dell'uomo'. *Civiltaà Cattolica* 147 (1996), pp. 130-42.
—, 'Il figlio dell'uomo'. *Civiltaà Cattolica* 149 (1998), pp. 227-38.
Garnet, P., 'The Baptism of Jesus and the Son of Man'. *JSNT* 9 (1980), pp. 49-65.
Gass, Fr. Wilhelm, *De utroque Jesu Christi nomine in Novo Testamentum obvio Dei filii et hominis* I-II (Vratislavia: Friedländer, 1839–40).
Gaster, Moses, 'The Son of Man and the Theophany in Daniel, Ch. VII.: A New Interpretation'. *The Search* 1 (1931), pp. 15-30.
Gathercole, Simon, 'The Son of Man in Mark's Gospel'. *ET* 115 (2003–2004), pp. 366-72.
Gatti, Florence M., see Cortés, Juan B.
Gebhardt, H., 'Die Zukunft des Menschensohnes nach den Synoptikern'. *Zeitschrift für kirchliche Wissenschaft und kirchliches Leben* 6 (1885), pp. 449-61, 505-22.
Geffré, Claude, 'L'herméneutique athée du titre de fils de l'homme chez Ernst Bloch'. In Marco M. Olivetti (ed.), *Religion et politique* (Rome: Aubier, 1978), pp. 203-17. German: 'Die Hermenutik des Titels "Menschensohn" bei Ernst Bloch'. In Franz Theunis (ed.), *Glaube und Politik*. Kerygma und Mythos, VII.1 = ThF 63 (Hamburg-Bergstedt: Herbert Reich Evangelischer Verlag, 1979), pp. 144-53.
Geist, Heinz, *Menschensohn und Gemeinde. Eine redaktionskritische Untersuchung zur Menschensohnprädikation im Matthäusevangelium*. FzB 57 (Würzburg: Echter Verlag, 1986).
Gelston, A., 'A Sidelight on the „Son of Man"'. *SJTh* 22 (1969), pp. 189-96.
George, A., 'La venue du Fils de l'homme. Lc 21,25–28.34-36'. *Assemblées du Seigneur* 5 (1969), pp. 71-78.
Gerleman, Gillis, *Der Menschensohn*. Studia Biblica 1 (Leiden: Brill, 1983).
Gese, Hartmut, 'Die Weisheit, der Menschensohn und die Ursprünge der Christologie als konsequente Entfaltung der biblischen Theologie'. *SEÅ* 44 (1979), pp. 77-114. English: 'Wisdom, Son of Man, and the Origins of Christology: The Consistent Development of Biblical Theology'. *HBTh* 3 (1981), pp. 23-57.
Gibran, Kahlil, *Jesus the Son of Man: His Words and His Deeds as Told and Recorded by Those Who Knew Him* (New York, 1928).
Giles, Pauline, 'The Son of Man in the Epistle to the Hebrews'. *ET* 86 (1974–75), pp. 328-32.
Girard, Marc, 'Le semblant de fils d'homme de Daniel 7, un personnage du monde d'en haut: approche structurelle'. *Science et Esprit* 35 (1983), pp. 265-96.

Glasson, T.F., 'The Enseign of the Son of Man (Matt. XXIV,30)'. *JThS* NS 15 (1964), pp. 299-300.

—, 'The Son of man Imagery: Enoch xiv and Daniel vii'. *NTS* 23 (1976–77), pp. 82-90.

Glazener, Clyde G., *An Investigation of Jesus' Usage of the Term Son of Man: A Possible Interpretative Key to the Gospel of Matthew*. Unpublished ThD dissertation (Southwestern Baptist Theological Seminary, 1974). Cf. Ferch, *The Son of Man in Daniel 7* (1983), p. 218.

Gnilka, Joseph, '"Für wen halten die Leute des Menschen Sohn?" (Mt 16,13)'. *BuK* 17 (1962), pp. 38-41.

—, 'Das Elend vor dem Menschensohn (Mk 2,1-12)'. In R. Pesch and R. Schnackenburg (eds.), *Jesus und der Menschensohn*. FS Anton Vögtle (Freiburg: Herder, 1975), pp. 196-209.

Goppelt, Leonhard, 'Zum Problem des Menschensohnes. Das Verhältnis von Leidensund Parusieankündigung'. In Hartmut Sierig (ed.), *Mensch und Menschensohn*. FS Karl Witte (Hamburg: Friedrich Wittig Verlag, 1963), pp. 20-32. Reprint in idem, *Christologie und Ethik*: Aufsätze zum Neuen Testament (Göttingen: Vandenhoeck & Ruprecht, 1969), pp. 66-78.

Gottsched, H., *Der Menschensohn* (Gütersloh: Bertelsmann, 1908).

Gould, E.P., 'Son of Man'. In *A Dictionary on Christ and the Gospels* II (1909), pp. 659-65.

Goulder, Michael, 'Psalm 8 and the Son of Man'. *NTS* 48 (2002), pp. 18-29.

Grässer, Erich, 'Beobachtungen zum Menschensohn in Heb 2,6'. In R. Pesch and R. Schnackenburg (eds.), *Jesus und der Menschensohn*. FS Anton Vögtle (Freiburg: Herder, 1975), pp. 404-14.

Graham, John W., 'The Mind of the Son of Man'. *Interp.* 8 (1911–12), pp. 289-302.

Grant, Frederick C., 'Can Faith Survive: Luke 18:8: "When the *Son of Man* Comes, will he find Faith on Earth"?' *USQR* 8 (1953), pp. 29-35.

Grelot, Pierre, 'L'intronisation du fils d'homme. Dn 7,13-14'. *Assemblées du Seigneur* 65 (1973), pp. 30-35.

—, 'Jésus, Fils de l'homme'. *Revue Thomiste* 105 (2005), pp. 89-102.

Grønbech, Vilhelm, *Jesus Menneskesønnen* (København: P. Branner, 1935).

Grosheide, F.W., ''Ο υἱὸς τοῦ ἀνθρώπου in het Ev. naar Johannes'. *Theologische Studiën* 35 (1917), pp. 242-48.

Grossow, W.K., *De Zoon des Mensen. De bijbelse grondslag van het christelijk humanisme* (1957).

Gry, Léon, 'La dénomination messianisme "Fils de l'Homme" dans la Bible et les Apocryphes éthiopiens'. *XENIA*. Hommage international a l'Université nationale de Grèce à l'occasion du soixante-quinzième anniversaire de sa fondation (Athens: Meissner & Kargadouris, 1912), pp. i-xii.

Guilding, Aileen, 'The Son of Man and the Ancient of Days'. *EvQ* 23 (1951), pp. 210-12.

Guillet, Jaques, 'A propos des titres de Jésus: Christ, Fils de l'homme, Fils de Dieu'. In M. Jourjon et al. (eds.), *A la rencontre de Dieu*. Mémorial Albert Gelin. Bibliothèque de la Faculté catholique de theologie de Lyon 8 (Le Puy: Mappus, 1961), pp. 309-17.

—, 'Le fils de l'homme: Titre eschatologique ou mission prophétique?'. *RSR* 88 (2000), pp. 615-38. Reprint in Pierre Gibert and Christoph Theobald (eds.), *Le cas Jésus Christ: Exégètes, historiens et théologiens en confrontation* (Paris: Bayard, 2002), pp. 171-204.

Guy, Harold A., 'Did Jesus Call Himself the Son of Man?' *The Modern Free Churchman* 91 (1970), pp. 30-34.
Gyllenberg, Rafael, 'Människosonen eller Messias'. *TA-TT* 45 (1940), pp. 27-42.

Haag, Ernst, 'בן־אדם'. In *ThWAT*, I (1973), cols. 682-89.
—, 'Der Menschensohn und die Heiligen des Höchsten. Eine Literar-, Form-, und Traditionsgeschichtliche Untersuchung zu Daniel 7'. In A.S. van der Woude (ed.), *The Book of Daniel in the Light of New Findings*. BEThL 106 (Leuven: Peeters, 1993), pp. 137-85.
—, 'Menschensohn. I. Altes Testament u. Frühjudentum'. In *LThK*, VII (3rd ed. 1998), cols. 129-30.
Haapa, E., *Ihmisen Pojan kuolema kolmessa ensimmäisessä evankeliumissa. Synoptisen tradition kristologiaa* (Helsinki, 1949). Cf. *TA-TT* 54 (1949), pp. 271-73. Finnish.
Hahn, Ferdinand, 'Die Rede von der Parusie des Menschensohnes Markus 13'. In R. Pesch and R. Schnackenburg (eds.), *Jesus und der Menschensohn*. FS Anton Vögtle (Freiburg: Herder, 1975), pp. 240-66.
—, 'Menschensohn'. *Exegetisches Wörterbuch zum Neuen Testament* 3 (1983), cols. 927-35.
Ham, C., 'The Title "Son of Man" in the Gospel of John', *Stone Campbell Journal* 1 (1998), pp. 67-84.
Hamerton-Kelly, R.G., *Pre-existence, Wisdom, and the Son of Man: A Study of the Idea of Pre-existence in the New Testament*. SNTSMS 21 (Cambridge: Cambridge University Press, 1973).
Hampel, Volker, *Menschensohn und historischer Jesus. Ein Rätselwort als Schlüssel zum messianischen Selbstverständnis Jesu* (Neukirchen–Vluyn: Neukirchener Verlag, 1990).
Hare, Douglas R.A., 'The Quest of the *Son of Man*: A Progress Report'. In P. Sigal, *Proceedings*, Estn Gt Lakes and Midwest Bibl Soc. 4 (1984), pp. 166-80.
—, *The Son of Man Tradition* (Minneapolis: Fortress Press, 1990).
Harrison, R.K., 'The Son of Man'. *EvQ* 23 (1951), pp. 46-50.
Hartl, Vinzenz, 'Anfang und Ende des Titels "Menschensohn". Ein Beitrag zur Lösung der johanneischen Frage'. *BZ* 7 (1909), pp. 342-54.
Hartman, Lars, 'La Parousie du Fils de l'homme. Mc 13,24-32'. *Assemblées du Seigneur* 64 (1969), pp. 47-57.
Harvey, Andrew, *Son of Man: The Mythical Path to Christ* (New York: Tarcher, 1998).
Haspels, J.P., 'De koperen slang en de Zoon des mensen'. *Ministerium. Tijdschrift voor praktische theologie* 3 (1969), pp. 41-46.
Haufe, Günter, 'Das Menschensohn-Problem in der gegenwärtigen wissenschaftlichen Diskussion'. *EvTh* 26 (1966), pp. 130-41. French: 'Le problème du Fils de l'homme'. *EThR* 42 (1967), pp. 311-22.
Haupt, Paul, 'The Son of Man'. *The Monist* 29 (1919), pp. 125-33.
—, 'Hidalgo and Filius Hominis'. *JBL* 40 (1921), pp. 167-70.
—, 'The Son of Man = hic homo = ego'. *JBL* 40 (1921), p. 183.
Hay, Lewis S., 'The Son of Man in Mark 2,10 and 2,28'. *JBL* 89 (1970), pp. 69-75.
Hebel, Johann Peter, 'Bar Enasch oder des Menschen Sohn'. In idem, *Sämmtliche Werke* IV (Carlsruhe: Müller, 1838), pp. 287-95.
Heitmüller, Wilhelm, 'II Menschensohn im NT'. In *RGG*, III (2nd ed. 1929), cols. 297-300.

Hendriks, W., 'De komende Mensenzoon'. *Schrift. Populaire Bibeltijdschrift* 18 (1971), pp. 225-29.

Hengel, Martin, 'Ein Blick zurück im Zorn: Rudolf Augsteins "Jesus Menschensohn"'. *Theologische Beiträge* 32 (2001), pp. 158-63.

Henze, Clemens M., 'Quis sit genuinus sensus locutionis "ὁ υἱὸς τοῦ ἀνθρώπου"'. *Divus Thomas. Commentarium de philosophia et theologia* 50 (1947), pp. 69-80.

—, 'Der Sohn des Menschen'. *Theologisch-praktische Quartalschrift* 104 (1956), pp. 70-74.

Hertlein, Eduard, *Die Menschensohnfrage im letzten Stadium. Ein Versuch zur Einsicht in das Wesen altchristlichen Schrifttums* (Berlin-Stuttgart-Leipzig: Kohlhammer, 1911 [Dissertation Tübingen, 1915]).

—, 'Die Wolken des "Menschensohns" (Dan 7,13)'. *ZAW* 37 (1917–18), pp. 134-36.

—, 'Ὁ υἱὸς τοῦ ἀνθρώπου'. *ZNW* 19 (1920), pp. 46-48.

Heumann, Christoph August, *Solutio quaestionis huius: Cur Filius Dei perfrequenter seappellarit Filium Hominis* (Göttingen, 1740). Reprint in *Dissertationum Sylloge diligenter recognitarum novisqve illustratarum accessionibus* I (Göttingen, 1743), pp. 848-76.

Higgins, A.J.B., 'Son of Man-*Forschung* since 'The Teaching of Jesus". In A.J.B. Higgins (ed.), *New Testament Essays*. Studies in Memory of Thomas Walter Manson (Manchester: Manchester University Press, 1959), pp. 119-35.

—, 'The Sign of the Son of Man (Matt. XXIV.30)'. *NTS* 9 (1962–63), pp. 380-82.

—, *Jesus and the Son of Man* (London: Lutterworth, 1964).

—, *Menschensohn-Studien*. Franz Delitzsch-Vorlesungen 1961 (Stuttgart: Kohlhammer, 1965).

—, 'The Son of Man Concept and the Historical Jesus'. *SE* 5 (= TU 103 [1968]), pp. 14-20.

—, 'Is the Son of Man Problem Insoluble?' In E. Earle Ellis and Max Wilcox (eds.) *Neotestamentica et Semitica*. FS Matthew Black (Edinburgh: T. & T. Clark, 1969), pp. 70-87.

—, '"Menschensohn" oder "ich" in Q: Lk 12,8-9/Mt 10,32-33?'. In R. Pesch and R. Schnackenburg (eds.), *Jesus und der Menschensohn*. FS Anton Vögtle (Freiburg: Herder, 1975), pp. 117-23.

—, *The Son of Man in the Teaching of Jesus*. SNTSMS 39 (Cambridge: Cambridge University Press, 1980).

Hilgenfeld, Adolf, 'Der Menschensohn-Messias'. *ZWTh* 35 (1892), pp. 445-64.

—, 'Noch ein Wort über den Menschensohn'. *ZWTh* 42 (1899), pp. 149-51.

Hill, David, '"Son of Man" in Psalm 80 v. 17'. *NT* 15 (1973), pp. 261-69.

Hill, Ralph, 'Further Considerations on Translating "The Son of Man"'. *Notes on Translation* 93 (1983), pp. 35-51.

Hindley, J.C., 'The Son of Man: A Recent Analysis'. *The Indian Journal of Theology* 15 (1966), pp. 172-78.

—, 'Jesus as "Son of Man" in the light of some recent discussions'. Bulletin of the Society for Biblical Studies 1 (Bangalore, 1964; not accessible).

Hirsch, Emil G., 'Son of Man'. *Jewish Encyclopedia* XI (1905), pp. 461-63.

Hix, A.D., *Comparative Analysis of the Christological Titles Son of Man and High Priest as Reflected in the Humiliation, Exaltation, and Redemptive Significance of Jesus' Mission*. Unpublished dissertation (New Orleans Baptist Theological Seminary, 1990). Cf. *EThL* 69 (1993) Elenchus 4686, DissAbstr 52 (1991–92), pp. 567-68.

Hodgson, Peter C., 'The Son of Man and the Problem of Historical Knowledge'. *JR* 41 (1961), pp. 91-108.

Hoekstra, Sytse, *De benaming 'de Zoon des menschen.' Een historisch-kritisch onderzoek* (Amsterdam: van Kampen 1866).

Hoffmann, Paul, 'Jesus versus Menschensohn. Mt 10,32f. und die synoptische Menschensohnüberlieferung'. In L. Oberlinner and P. Fiedler (eds.), *Salz der Erde—Licht der Welt. Exegetische Studien zum Matthäusevangelium*. FS Anton Vögtle (Stuttgart: Katholisches Bibelwerk, 1991), pp. 165-202.

—, 'QR und der Menschensohn'. In F. van Segbroeck, C. M. Tuckett, G. van Belle and J. Verheyden (eds.), *The Four Gospels 1992*. FS Frans Neirynck. BEThL 100 (Leuven: Peeters, 1992), I, pp. 421-56. English: 'The Redaction of Q and the Son of Man: A Preliminary Sketch'. In Ronald A. Piper (ed.), *The Gospel Behind the Gospels*. NT.S 75 (Leiden: Brill, 1995), pp. 159-98.

—, 'Der Menschensohn in Lukas 12.8'. *NTS* 44 (1998), pp. 357-79.

—, 'Menschensohn. II. Neues Testament'. In *LThK*, VII (3rd ed. 1998), cols. 131-32.

Holsten, Carl, 'Biblisch-theologische Studien III. Die Bedeutung der Ausdrucksform ὁ υἱὸς τοῦ ἀνθρώπου im Bewusstsein Jesu'. *ZWTh* 34 (1891), pp. 1-79.

Holtzmann, Heinrich Julius, 'Ueber den NTlichen Ausdruck "Menschensohn"'. *ZWTh* 8 (1865), pp. 212-37.

Holzinger, Heinrich, 'Zur Menschensohnfrage'. In Karl Marti (ed.), *Beiträge zur alttestamentlichen Wissenschaft*. FS Karl Budde. BZAW 34 (Gießen: Töpelmann, 1920), pp. 102-106.

Homerski, Józef, 'Syn Czlowieczy w Wizji Proroka Daniela (Dn 7,13-14)' [The Son of Man in the Vision of the Prophet Daniel (Dan. 7,13-14)]. *Roczniki Teol.Kanonicze* (Katolocki Universytet Lubelski, Poland) 32 (1985), pp. 47-62. Cf. OTS 14 (1991) 1082. (Polish)

Hommel, Fritz, 'The Apocalyptic Origin of the Expression "Son of Man"'. *ET* 11 (1899–1900), pp. 341-45.

Hong, Lok Young, *Jesus und der Menschensohn. Eine form- und religionsgeschichliche Untersuchung zu den alttestamentlichen, jüdischen Menschensohntraditionen* . Unpublished dissertation (Heidelberg, 2000 [dir. K. Berger]).

Hooker, Morna D., *The Son of Man in Mark: A Study of the Background of the Term 'Son of Man' and its Use in St Mark's Gospel* (London: SPCK, 1967).

—, 'Is the Son of Man Problem really insoluble?' In Ernest Best and R.M. Wilson (eds.), *Text and Interpretation*. FS Matthew Black (Cambridge: Cambridge University Press, 1979), pp. 155-68.

—, 'The Son of Man and the Synoptic Problem'. In F. van Segbroeck, C. M. Tuckett, G. van Belle and J. Verheyden (eds.), *The Four Gospels 1992*. FS Frans Neirynck. BEThL 100 (Leuven: Peeters, 1992), I, pp. 189-201.

Hopkins, Martin A., 'The Son of Man'. *Union Seminary Review* 39 (1927–28), pp. 145-57.

Horbury, William, 'The Messianic Associations of "The Son of Man"'. *JThS* NS 36 (1985), pp. 34-55. Revised reprint in idem, *Messianism among Jews and Christians. Biblical and Historical Studies* (Edinburgh: T. & T. Clark, 2003), pp. 125-55.

Houk, C.B., 'בן־אדם Patterns as Literary Criteria in Ezekiel'. *JBL* 88 (1969), pp. 184-90.

Hsia Ch'i-Lung, 'Lun Jowang fuyin chung ti "jentzu": The "Son of Man" in John's Gospel'. *Collectanea Theologica Universitatis Fujen* (= Shensüeh Lunchi) 10 (1971). Cf. *Bib.* 53 (1972) Elenchus 2860 (Chinese)

Huber, Konrad, *Einer gleich einem Menschensohn. Die Christusvision in Offb 1,9-20 und Offb 14,14-20 und die Christologie der Johannesoffenbarung*. NTA 51 (Münster: Aschendorff Verlag, 2007).

Hyldahl, Niels, 'Mogens Müllers disputats om "menneskesønnen"'. *Fønix* 10 (1986), pp. 175-83.

Iber, Gerhard, *Überlieferungsgeschichtliche Untersuchungen zum Begriff des Menschensohns im Neuen Testament*. Typewritten dissertation (Heidelberg, 1953). Cf. Summary in *ThLZ* 80 (1955), cols. 115-16.

Ilmar, Lot, 'Bescheidene Vorstellung über die Heumännische Gedancken von dem Namen Christi, da er des Menschen Sohn heisset'. *Heßisches Heb-Opfer*. Theologischer und Philologischer Anmerckungen. 4. Band, 39. Stück (Gießen: Johann Philipp Krieger, 1747), pp. 834-46. ["Unter diesem Nahmen liegt ein auswärtiger gelehrter und alter Theologus verborgen." According to note in *Heßisches Heb-Opfer*, 4. Band, 37. Stück (1745), p. 616].

Jackson, David R., 'The Priority of the Son of Man Sayings'. *WThJ* 47 (1985), pp. 83-96.

Jackson, Don, 'A Survey of the 1967–1981 Study of the Son of Man'. *Restoration Quarterly* (Abilene, Texas) 28 (1985–86), pp. 67-78.

Jacobsen, Howard, 'The "Son of Man" in Ps.-Philo *Liber antiquitatum biblicarum*', *JThS* NS 34 (1983), pp. 531-33.

Järvinen, Arto, 'The Son of Man and His Followers: A Q Portrait of Jesus'. In David Rhoads and Kari Syreeni (eds.), *Characterization in the Gospels*. JSNTSup 184 (Sheffield: Sheffield Academic Press, 1999), pp. 180-222.

Jagersma, H., 'Zoon des mensen'. *Interpretatie* 93/8 (1993), pp. 26-27.

James, J. Courtenay, 'The Son of Man: Origin and Uses of the Title'. *ET* 36 (1924–25), pp. 309-14.

Jas, Michael, 'Hénoch et le fils de l'homme. Datation du livre des paraboles pour une situation de l'origine du Gnosticisme'. *La Revue Réformée* 30 (1979), pp. 105-19.

Jay, E.G., *Son of Man, Son of God* (Montreal: McGill University Press, 1965).

Jennings, Theodore W., 'The Martyrdom of the Son of Man'. In Theodore W. Jennings, Jr. (ed.), *Text and Logos: The Humanistic Interpretation of the New Testament*. FS Hendrikus Boers (Atlanta, GA: Shcolars Press, 1990), pp. 229-43.

Jensen, J., 'Son of Man'. *The New Catholic Encyclopaedia* XIII (1967), pp. 431-33.

Jeremias, Joachim, 'Die älteste Schicht der Menschensohn-Logien'. *ZNW* 58 (1967), pp. 159-72.

Johansson, Nils, 'De urkristna föreställningarna om Människosonen och vår Kristustro'. *STK* 21 (1945), pp. 1-13.

Johnson, Sherman E., 'Son of Man'. In *The Interpreter's Dictionary of the Bible* IV (Nashville: Abingdon Press, 1962), pp. 413-20.

Johnston, L., 'The Son of Man'. *Scripture* 6 (1954), pp. 181-83.

Jones, B.J., *A Study of the Son of Man in Revelation with Special Reference to the Suffering Servant Motif.* Unpublished dissertation (New Orleans Baptist Theological Seminary, 1990). Cf. *EThL* 68 (1992) Elenchus 6109; DissAbstr 52 (1991–92), pp. 185-86.

Jones, C.W., *The Use of the Title 'Son of Man' in Mark*. Unpublished PhD dissertation (Southern Baptist Theological Seminary, 1948). Cf. *Bib.* 32 (1951) Elenchus 626c.

Jonker, A.J. Th., 'De Zoon des Menschen. De uitdrukking ὁ υἱὸς τοῦ ἀνθρώπου in het Nieuwe Testament'. Academisch proefschrift, door H.L. Oort, 1893. *Theologische Studiën* 13 (1895), pp. 228-60.

Joutsi, Y., 'Der Menschensohn'. Summary of Y. Joutsi, *Ihmisen Poika*. Finnish = 'Der Menschensohn. Untersuchung der im NT benutzten Benennung gegen ihrer spätjüdischen Hintergrund' (Helsinki 1936). *Teologia Fennica* II (1940), pp. 45-52.

Kähler, Martin, *Der Menschensohn und seine Sendung an die Menschheit* (1893). Reprint in idem, *Schriften zur Christologie und Mission*. ThB 42 (München: Kaiser, 1971), pp. 3-43.

Kaiser, Otto, 'Menschensohn, Menschensohnforschung und praktische Verkündigung. Überlegungen zur Dialektik von Autonomie und Finalisierung neutestamentlicher Wissenschaft'. In R. Pesch and R. Schnackenburg (eds.), *Jesus und der Menschensohn*. FS Anton Vögtle (Freiburg: Herder, 1975), pp. 435-88.

Kazen, Thomas, 'Son of Man as Kingdom Imagery: Jesus between Corporate symbol and Individual Redeemer Figure'. In Tom Holmén (ed.), *Jesus from Judaism to Christianity*. Library of New Testament Studies 352 (London: T. & T. Clark, 2007), pp. 87-108.

Kearns, Rollin, *Vorfragen zur Christologie I. Morphologische und Semasiologische Studie zur Vorgeschichte eines christologischen Hoheitstitels* (Tübingen: Mohr [Siebeck], 1978).

—, *Vorfragen zur Christologie II. Überlieferungsgeschichtliche und Rezeptionsgeschichtliche Studie zur Vorgeschichte eines christologischen Hoheitstitels* (Tübingen: Mohr [Siebeck], 1980).

—, *Vorfragen zur Christologie III. Religionsgeschichtliche und Traditionsgeschichtliche Studie zur Vorgeschichte eines christologischen Hoheitstitels* (Tübingen: Mohr [Siebeck], 1982).

—, *Das Traditionsgefüge um den Menschensohn. Ursprünglicher Gehalt und älteste veränderung im Urchristentum* (Tübingen: Mohr [Siebeck], 1986).

—, *Die Entchristologisierung des Menschensohnes. Die Übertragung des Traditionsgefüges um den Menschensohn auf Jesus* (Tübingen: Mohr [Siebeck], 1988).

—, 'Ὁ υἱὸς τοῦ ἀνθρώπου als hoheitstitulares Wortgebilde'. *Mutmaßungen zur Christologie*. Heft 2 (Tübingen: Privatdruck, 2003).

—, 'Die Epiphanie des Menschensohnes in der Welt. Die tranzendent-eschatologische Epiphanie des Menschensohnes. *Mutmaßungen zur Christologie*. Heft 3 (Tübingen: Privatdruck, 2003).

—, 'Menschensohn' 1-7 (8 is by Werner Grimm). In Otto Betz, Beate Ego und Werner Grimm (eds.), *Calwer Bibellexikon* II (Stuttgart: Calwer Verlag, 2003), pp. 900-902.

Kee, Howard C., '"The Man" in Fourth Ezra: Growth of a Tradition'. In *Society of Biblical Literature, Seminar Papers 1981* (1981), pp. 199-208.

Keel, Otmar, 'Die Tiere und der Mensch in Daniel 7'. In O. Keel and U. Staub, *Hellenismus und Judentum. Vier Studien zu Daniel 7 und zur Religionsnot unter Antiochus IV*. OBO 178 (Freiburg, Schweiz)-Göttingen: Universitätsverlag, 2000), pp. 87-121.

Kelber, Werner, 'The Hour of the Son of Man and the Temptation of the Disciples (Mark 14:32-42)', in idem (ed.), *The Passion in Mark* (Philadelphia, 1976), pp. 41-60.

Kelber, Wilhelm, *Der Menschensohn* (Stuttgart: Verlag Urachhaus, 1967).

Kellner, Wendelin, *Der Traum vom Menschensohn. Die politisch-theologische Botschaft Jesu* (München: Kösel, 1985).

Kertelge, Karl, 'Die Vollmacht des Menschensohnes zur Sündenvergebung (Mk 2,10)'. In Paul Hoffmann et al. (eds.), *Orientierung an Jesus. Zur Theologie der Synoptiker*. FS Josef Schmid (Freiburg: Herder, 1973), pp. 205-13.

—, 'Der dienende Menschensohn (Mk 10,45)'. In Rudolf Pesch and Rudolf Schnackenburg (eds.), *Jesus und der Menschensohn*. FS Anton Vögtle (Freiburg: Herder, 1975), pp. 225-39.

Kieffer, René, 'Det synoptiska problemet i de tre förutsägelserna om Människosonens lidande'. *SEÅ* 69 (2004), pp. 191-98.

Kilpatrick, G.D., 'Acts vii.56: Son of Man?' *ThZ* 21 (1965), p. 209. Reprint in idem, *The Principles and Practice of New Testament Textual Criticism*. Collected Essays. Edited by J.K. Elliott. BEThL 96 (Leuven: Peeters/Leuven University Press, 1990), pp. 415-16.

—, 'Again Acts vii.56: Son of Man?' *ThZ* 34 (1978), p. 232. Reprint in idem, *Principles*, pp. 417-18.

Kim, Seyoon, *The 'Son of Man' as the Son of God*. WUNT 30 (Tübingen: Mohr [Siebeck], 1983).

—, 'Jesus—The Son of God, the Stone, the Son of Man, and the Servant: The Role of Zechariah in the Self-Identification of Jesus'. In Gerald Hawthorne with Otto Betz (eds.), *Tradition and Interpretation in the New Testament*. FS E. Earle Ellis (Grand Rapids: Eerdmans, Tübingen: Mohr [Siebeck], 1987), pp. 134-48.

Kingsbury, Jack Dean, 'The Title "Son of Man" in Matthew's Gospel'. *CBQ* 37 (1975), pp. 193-202. Cf. idem, *Matthew: Structure, Christology, Kingdom* (London: SPCK, 1976), pp. 113-22.

—, 'Observations on "The Son of Man" in the Gospel According to Luke'. *Currents in Theology and Mission* 17 (1990), pp. 283-90.

Kinniburgh, Elisabeth, 'The Johannine "Son of Man"'. *SE* 4 (= TU 102 [Berlin: Akademie-Verlag, 1968], pp. 64-71).

Kipp, J., '"Des Menschen Sohn"'. *Evangelische Kirchenzeitung* 1904 (1904), pp. 437-45, 459-63.

Kirchhevel, Gordon D., 'The "Son of Man" Passages in Mark'. *BBR* 9 (1999), pp. 181-87.

Kittel, Gerhard, 'Menschensohn: II Im NT'. In *RGG*, III (2nd ed. 1929), cols. 2118-21.

Klakowicz, B.E., 'Il 'Figlio dell'Uomo". *Divinitas* 22 (1978), pp. 237-41.

Klappert, Bertold, 'The Coming Son of Man Became Flesh: High Christology and Anti-Judaism in the Gospel of John'. In R. Bieringer, D. Pollefeyt and F. Vandecasteele-Vanneuville (eds.), *Anti-Judaism and the Fourth Gospel*. Papers of the Leuven Colloquium, 2000 (Assen: Royal van Gorcum, 2001), pp. 159-86.

Klöpper, A., 'Der Sohn des Menschen in den synoptischen Evangelien. Ein Beitrag zur Deutung dieser Selbstbezeichnung Jesu'. *ZWTh* 42 (1899), pp. 161-86.

Kmiecik, Ulrich, *Der Menschensohn im Markusevangelium*. FzB 81 (Würzburg: Echter Verlag, 1997).

Koch, Klaus, 'Messias und Menschensohn. Die zweistufige Messianologie des jüngeren Apokalyptik'. In *Der Messias*. JBTh 8 (1993), pp. 73-102. Reprint in idem, *Vor der Wende der Zeiten. Beiträge zur apokalyptischen Literatur*. Gesammelte Aufsätze 3, ed. by U. Gleßmer et al. (Neukirchen–Vluyn: Neukirchener Verlag, 1996), pp. 235-66.

—, 'Das Reich der Heiligen und des Menschensohns. Ein Kapitel politischer Theologie'. In idem, *Die Reiche der Welt und der kommende Menschensohn. Studien zum Danielbuch*. Gesammelte Aufsätze 2, ed. by Martin Rösel (Neukirchen–Vluyn: Neukirchener Verlag, 1995), pp. 140-72.

—, 'Der "Menschensohn" in Daniel'. *ZAW* 119 (2007), pp. 369-85.

König, Eduard, 'Der Menschensohn im Danielbuche'. *NKZ* 16 (1905), pp. 904-28.

Kolmodin, A., 'Jesus—människosonen'. *Kyrklig Tidskrift* 11 (1905), pp. 289-311.

Kosch, Daniel, *Die eschatologische Tora des Menschensohnes. Untersuchungen zur Rezeption der Stellung Jesu zur Tora in Q*. Novum testamentum et orbis antiquus 12 (Freiburg, Schweiz-Göttingen: Universitätsverlag, 1989).

Kraeling, Carl H., *Anthropos and Son of Man: A Study in the Religious Syncretism of the Hellenistic Orient*. Columbia University Oriental Studies 25 (Columbia University Press, 1927; reprint New York: AMS Press, 1966).

Krawutzcky, Adam, 'Ueber die Bedeutung des neutestamentlichen Ausdrucks Menschensohn und sein Verhältniss zur paulinischen Bezeichnung Christi als des zweiten Menschens'. *ThQ* 51 (1869), pp. 600-57.

Kristensen, William Brede, 'De term "Zoon des Menschen", toegelicht uit de anthropologie der ouden'. *ThT* 45 (1911), pp. 1-38.

Krop, Frédéric J., *La pensée de Jésus sur le Royaume de Dieu d'après les évangiles synoptiques avec un appendice sur la question du 'Fils de l'Homme'* (Paris: Fischbacher, 1897).

—, 'Jezus, de "Zoon van David?" – De Zoon des menschen. – De Zoon van God'. *Geloof en Vrijheid* 37 (1903), pp. 434-45.

Kruse, H., 'Compositio Libri Danielis et idea Filii Hominis'. *Verbum Domini* 37 (1959), pp. 147-61, 193-211.

Kügler, Joachim, 'Die Botschaft der Menschensohn zählt'. *Orientierung* 67 (2003), pp. 180-82.

Kümmel, Werner Georg, 'Das Verhalten Jesus gegenüber und das Verhalten des Menschensohnes. Markus 8,38 par und Lukas 12,8f par Matthäus 10,32f'. In R. Pesch and R. Schnackenburg (eds.), *Jesus und der Menschensohn*. FS Anton Vögtle (Freiburg: Herder, 1975), pp. 210-24. Reprint in idem, *Heilsgeschehen und Geschichte* Band 2. Gesammelte Aufsätze 1965–77, Marburger Theologische Studien 16 (Marburg: Elwert, 1978), pp. 201-14.

—, *Jesus der Menschensohn?* Sitzungsberichte der wissenschaftlichen Gesellschaft an der Johann Wolfgang Goethe-Universität Frankfurt am Main, Band 20/3 (Stuttgart: Steiner, 1984), pp. 143-88.

Kugelman, Richard, 'Son of Man Theology: Some Questions'. *CBQ* 35 (1973), pp. 494-95.

Kuhn, Karl A., 'The "One like a Son of Man" Becomes "the Son of God"'. *CBQ* 69 (2007), pp. 22-42.

Kuhnert, E., ''Ο υἱὸς τοῦ ἀνθρώπου'. *ZNW* 18 (1918), pp. 165-76.

Kuzenzama, Kanika Pabayim Mided, *Le titre johannique du fils de l'homme. Essai lexicographique*. Recherches africaines de théologie 11 (Kinhasa: Facultés catholiques de Kinhasa, 1990).

Kvanvig, Helge S., 'Henoch und der Menschensohn. Das Verhältnis von Hen 14 zu Dan 7'. *StTh* 38 (1984), pp. 101-33.

—, *Roots of Apocalyptic: The Mesopotamian Background of the Enoch Figure and the Son of Man*. WMANT 61 (Neukirchen–Vluyn: Neukirchener Verlag, 1988).

Lagrange, Marie-Joseph, 'L'Avénement du Fils de l'Homme', *RB* NS 3 (1906), pp. 382-411, 561-74.

Lang, Bernhard, 'Der monarchische Monotheismus und die Konstellation zweier Götter im Frühjudentum: Ein neuer Versuch über Menschensohn, Sophia und Christologie'. In W. Dietrich and M.A. Klopfenstein (eds.), *Ein Gott allein? JHWH-Verehrung und biblischer Monotheismus im Kontext der israelitischen und altorientalischen Religionsgeschichte*. OBO 139 (Freiburg, Schweiz: Universitätsverlag; Göttingen: Vandenhoeck & Ruprecht, 1994), pp. 559-64.

Lang, Friedrich, 'Menschensohn'. *Calwer Bibellexikon*. In fünfter Bearbeitung (1961, 2. Aufl 1967), pp. 889-91.

Langkammer, H., 'Oczekiwanie przyjscia "Pana" i "Syna Czlowieczego" w najstarszych gminach chrzscijanskich [Adventus "Domini" et "Filius hominis" expectatus a christianis primis]'. *Ateneum Kaplanskie* 77 (1971), pp. 92-104. Cf. *Bib.* 53 (1972) Elenchus 5250. (Czech)

— , 'Syn czlowieczy w Ewangeliach synoptycznych [Le Fils de l'Homme dans les Évangiles synoptiques]'. In *Colloquium Salutis, Wroclawskie Studia Teologiczne* 4 (1972), pp. 79-93. Cf. IZBG 21 (1974–75) 1154. (Czech)

Larsen, A.C., *Om Menneskesønnen* (København 1902); reprint in idem, *Gennem mange Aar* II (København: Gyldendal, 1905), pp. 170-94.

Leaney, A.R.C., 'The Days of the Son of Man (Luke xvii.22)'. *ET* 67 (1955–56), pp. 28-29.

Légasse, Simon, 'Jésus historique et le Fils de l'homme apercu sur les opinions contemporaines'. In L. Monloubou (ed.), *Apocalypses et théologie de l'espérance*. Lectio Divina 95 (Paris: Cerf, 1977), pp. 271-98.

Leinhäupl-Wilke, Andreas, '"Die Stunde des Menschensohnes" (Joh 12,23): Anmerkungen zur "heimlichen Mitte" des Johannesevangeliums'. In Martin Fußnacht, Andreas Leinhäupl-Wilke and Stefan Lücking (eds.), *Die Weisheit—Ursprünge und Rezeption*. FS Karl Löning. NTA NF 44 (Münster: Aschendorff, 2003), pp. 185-210.

Leivestad, Ragnar, 'Der apokalyptische Menschensohn ein theologisches Phantom'. *ASThI* 6 (1968), pp. 49-105. Abridged Norwegian edition:

— , 'Er den apokalyptiske menneskesønn en moderne teologisk opfinnelse?' *NTT* 70 (1969), pp. 221-35.

— , 'Exit the Apocalyptic Son of Man'. *NTS* 18 (1971–72), pp. 243-67.

— , 'Jesus—Messias—Menschensohn. Die jüdische Heilandserwartungen zur Zeit der ersten römischen Kaiser und die Frage nach dem messianischen Selbstbewußtsein Jesu'. *ANRW* II, 25,1 (1982), pp. 220-64.

— , 'Wer ist der Vater des Menschensohns? Einige Reflexionen über den Ausdruck "in der Herrlichkeit seines Vaters" in Mk 8,38'. In Jarmo Kiilunen, Vilho Riekkinen and Heikki Räisänen (eds.), *Glaube und Gerechtigkeit*. Rafael Gyllenberg in memoriam. Schriften der Finnischen Exegetischen Gesellschaft 38 (Helsinki, 1983), pp. 95-108.

— , 'Betydningen av uttrykket "menneskesønnen". Mogens Müller: Der Ausdruck "Menschensohn" in den Evangelien. Voraussetzungen und Bedeutung. AThD 17 (1984)'. *DTT* 48 (1985), pp. 172-94.

Lella, Alexander A. Di, 'The One in Human Likeness and the Holy Ones of the Most High in Daniel 7'. *CBQ* 39 (1977), pp. 1-19.

Leroueil, P., *Énigme et certitudes de la recherche contemporaine sur le theme du 'Fils de l'homme' dans l'Apocalyptique juive et dans la tradition synoptique. État des questions*. Unpublished dissertation (Strasbourg, 1974). Cf. *EThL* 51 (1975), *152.

Less, Gottfried, *Nonnulla de* Filio Hominis *praefatus* (Göttingen: Rosenbusch, 1776). Reprint in idem, *Opvscvla theologici exegetici atqve homiletici argvmenti* I-II (Göttingen: Rosenbusch, 1780–81), pp. 411-38.

Létourneau, Pierre, *Jésus, Fils de l'homme et Fils de Dieu. Jean 2,23–3,36 et la double christologie johannique*. Recherches NS 27 (Montreal: Bellarmin; Paris: Cerf, 1993).

Lettinga, J.P., 'De uitdrukking "de Zoon des mensen"'. *Almanak van het Corpus Studiosorum in Academia Campensi 'Fides Quadrat Intellectum' 1955–1957* (1957), pp. 141-49.

Levy, B. Barry, 'Why Bar-nash does not mean 'I''. In Barry Walfish (ed.), *Frank Talmage Memorial Volume* (Haifa: University Press, 1992), pp. 85-101.

Lietzmann, Hans, *Der Menschensohn. Ein Beitrag zur neutestamentlichen Theologie* (Freiburg im Breisgau und Leipzig: Mohr [Siebeck], 1896).

—, 'Zur Menschensohnfrage'. *Theologische Arbeiten aus dem rheinischen wissenschaftlichen Prediger-Verein*. NF 2. Heft (1898), pp. 1-14.

Liew, Tat-siong Benny, 'Re-Mark-able Masculinities: Jesus, the Son of Man, and the (Sad) Sum of Manhood?' In Stephen D. Moore and Janice Capel Anderson (eds.), *New Testament Masculinities*. Semeia Studies 45 (Atlanta, GA: SBL, 2003), pp. 93-135.

Lindars, Barnabas, 'The Son of Man in the Johannine Christology'. In Barnabas Lindars and Stephen S. Smalley (eds.), *Christ and the Spirit in the New Testament*. FS Charles Francis Digby Moule (Cambridge: Cambridge University Press, 1973), pp. 43-60. Reprint in idem, *Essays in John*. Edited by C.M. Tuckett. Studiorum Novi Testamenti Auxilia XVII (Leuven: Peters, 1992), pp. 33-50

—, 'Re-Enter the Apocalyptic Son of Man'. *NTS* 22 (1975–76), pp. 52-72.

—, 'The new Look on the Son of Man'. *BJRL* 63 (1980–81), pp. 437-62.

—, *Jesus Son of Man: A Fresh Examination of the Son of Man Sayings in the Gospels in the Light of Recent Research* (London: SPCK, 1983). Reprint of ch. 9: 'The Son of Man in the Theology of John', in idem, *Essays in John* (1992), pp. 153-66.

—, 'Response to Richard Bauckham: The Idiomatic Use of Bar Enasha'. *JSNT* 23 (1985), pp. 35-41.

—, 'Son of Man'. In R.J. Coggins and J.L. Houlden (eds.), *A Dictionary of Biblical Interpretation* (London: SCM/Philadelphia: Trinity Press International, 1990), pp. 639-42.

Lindeskog, Gösta, 'Människosonens gåta'. *Religion och Bibel* 26 (1967), pp. 3-13. Enlarged German edition:

—, 'Das Rätsel des Menschensohnes'. *StTh* 22 (1968), pp. 149-76.

Linton, Olof, 'The Parable of the Children's Game. Baptist and the Son of Man (Matt. XI.16-19 = Luke VII.31-5): A Synoptic Text-Critical, Structural and Exegetical Investigation'. *NTS* 22 (1976), pp. 159-79.

Loba Mkole, see Mkole.

Lønborg, Sven, *Jesus Menneskesønnen* (København: C.A. Reitzel, 1932). Danish translation from of Swedish: *Jesu från Nazara*. Translated by Otto Larsen (2nd ed. Uppsala, 1931).

Löning, K., 'Die Füchse, die Vögel und der Menschensohn (Mt 8,19f par Lk 9,57f)'. In H. Frankemölle and K. Kertelge (eds.), *Vom Urchristentum zu Jesus*. FS Joachim Gnilka (Freiburg: Herder, 1989), pp. 82-102.

Lohse, Eduard, 'Der Menschensohn in der Johannesapokalypse'. In R. Pesch and R. Schnackenburg (eds.), *Jesus und der Menschensohn*. FS Anton Vögtle (Freiburg: Herder, 1975), pp. 415-20.

Lombardo-Radice, Lucio, 'Sohn des Menschen'. In Iring Fetscher (ed.), *Marxisten und die Sache Jesu* (München: Kaiser; Mainz: Matthias Grünewald-Verlag, 1974), pp. 17-21.

Longenecker, Richard N., '"Son of Man" as a Self-Designation of Jesus'. *JEThS* 12 (1969), pp. 151-58.

—, '"Son of Man" Imagery: Some Implications for Theology and Discipleship'. *JEThS* 18 (1975), pp. 3-16.

Lubsczyk, Johannes, 'Gott offenbart das Geheimnis seines Reiches im Kommen des Menschensohnes'. In W. Ernst and K. Feiereis (eds.), *Denkender Glaube im Geschichte und Gegenwart*. Festschrift aus Anlaß der Gründing der Universität Erfurt vor 600 Jahren und aus der Anlaß des 40jähringen Bestehens des Philosophisch-Theologischen Studiums Erfurt. Erfurter Theologische Studien 63 (Leipzig: Benno, 1992), pp. 216-43.

Ludwig, Emil, *Der Menschensohn* (Berlin: Rowolt, 1928). Danish: *Menneskesønnen* (København: Jespersen & Pios Forlag 1928).

Luke, K., 'Enoch and the Son of Man'. *Indian Theological Studies* 37 (2000), pp. 46-64.

Luz, Ulrich, 'The Son of Man in Matthew: Heavenly Judge or Human Christ', *JSNT* 48 (1992), pp. 3-21. Reprint in idem, *Studies in Matthew* (Grand Rapids: Eerdmans, 2005), pp. 97-112.

Maanen, W.C. van, 'Naschrift (op Dr. Eerdmans' verhandeling over de uitdrukking "Zoon des Menschen")'. *ThT* 28 (1894), pp. 177-87.

—, 'De "Zoon des Menschen" bij Henoch'. *ThT* 29 (1895), pp. 263-67.

Maartens, P.J., 'The Son of Man as Compound Metaphor in Mk 14.62'. In J.H. Petzer and P.J. Hartin (eds.), *A South African Perspective on the New Testament* (Leiden: Brill, 1986), pp. 76-98.

Macgregor, W.M., 'Il Figlio dell' Uomo, Studio sugli Evangeli. By P. Vannutelli. The Messiah and the Son of Man. By A.S. Peake'. *Exp* 9/2 (1924), pp. 229-31.

MacKinnon, Donald M., '*Son of Man*: A Comment'. *Scottish Journal of Religious Studies* 11 (1990), pp. 89-92.

MacRory, J., '"The Son of Man"'. *IThQ* 10 (1915), pp. 50-63.

Maddox, R.J., 'The Son of Man and Judgment'. Summary of Doctoral dissertation. *HThR* 57 (1964), pp. 387-88.

—, 'The Function of the Son of Man according to the Synoptic Gospels'. *NTS* 15 (1968–69), pp. 45-74.

—, 'The Quest for Valid Methods in "Son of Man" Research'. *ABR* 19 (1971), pp. 36-51. German edition:

—, 'Methodenfragen in der Menschensohnforschung'. *EvTh* 32 (1972), pp. 143-60.

—, 'The Function of the Son of Man in the Gospel of John'. In R. Banks (ed.), *Reconciliation and Hope: Essays on Atonement and Eschatology*. FS L.L. Morris (Grand Rapids: Eerdmans, 1974), pp. 186-204.

Madsen, Peder, 'Menneskens Søn'. In *Kirke-Leksikon for Norden* III (København: Hagerup, 1911), pp. 228-29.

Madsen, Peter, *Menneskesønnen. En tegneserie om Jesus* (København: Det Danske Bibelselskab, 1995).

Malbon, Elizabeth Struthers, 'Narrative Christology and the Son of Man: What the Markan Jesus Says Instead'. *Biblical Interpretation* 11 (2003), pp. 373-85.

Maldonado, J., *De exaltatione Filii Hominis apud S. Joannem*. Unpublished dissertation (Studii Biblici Fransciscani, Jerusalem, 1964). Cf. *Bib.* 47 (1966) Elenchus 2633.

Mangold, Wilhelm Julius, 'Ueber die Bedeutung des Ausdrucks: 'ὁ υἱὸς τοῦ ἀνθρώπου'. *Theologische Arbeiten aus dem rheinischen wissenschaftlichen Prediger-Verein* 3 (1877), pp. 1-25.

Manson, Thomas Walter, 'The Son of Man: Some Observations on Mr. Fox's Criticism in the September Number'. *ET* 58 (1946–47), p. 83.

—, 'The Son of man in Daniel, Enoch and the Gospels'. *BJRL* 32 (1949–50), pp. 171-93. Reprint in idem, *Studies in the Gospels and Epistles*. Edited by Matthew Black (Manchester: Manchester University Press, 1962), pp. 123-45.

Manson, William, 'The Son of Man and History'. *SJTh* 5 (1958), pp. 113-22. Reprint in idem, *Jesus and the Christian* (London: James Clarke, 1967), pp. 67-76.

Marcus, Joel, 'Son of Man as Son of Adam'. *RB* 110 (2003), pp. 38-61, 370-86.

Margerie, D. de, 'Le Fils de l'Homme, Rédempteur d'une Église corédemptrice'. *Communio. Commentarii Internationales de Ecclesia et Theologia* 3 (1970), pp. 227-73.

Marlow, Ransom, 'The *Son of Man* in Recent Journal Literature'. *CBQ* 28 (1966), pp. 20-30.

Marshall, I. Howard, 'The Synoptic Son of Man Sayings in Recent Discussion'. *NTS* 12 (1965–66), pp. 327-51. Reprint in idem, *Jesus the Saviour: Studies in New Testament Theology* (London: SPCK, 1990), pp. 73-100.

—, 'The Son of Man in Contemporary Debate'. *EvQ* 42 (1970), pp. 67-87. Reprint in idem, *Jesus the Saviour* (1990), pp. 100-120.

—, 'The Son of Man and the Incarnation'. *Ex Auditu* 7 (1991), pp. 29-43.

—, 'Son of Man'. In J.B. Green and S. McKnight (eds.), *Dictionary of Christ and the Gospels* (Downers Grove, IL: InterVarsity Press, 1992), pp. 775-81.

—, 'The Synoptic "Son of Man" Sayings in the Light of Linguistic Study'. In T. Schmidt and M. Silva (eds.), *To Tell the Mystery*. FS Robert H. Gundry. JSNTSup (Sheffield: Sheffield Academic Press, 1994), pp. 72-94.

Martin, F., 'Le signe du Fils de l'homme', *LV* 31 (1982), pp. 61-77.

Martin de Vivies, Pierre de, *Jésus et le fils de l'homme, emplois et significations de l'expression 'Fils de l'homme' dans les évangiles* (Lyon: Profac, 1995).

Mateos, Juan, and Camacho, F., *El Hijo del hombre: Hacia la plenitud humana*. En los orígines del cristianismo 9 (Córdoba: El Almendro—Fundacíon Épsilon, 1995).

McCaig, A., 'The Title "Son of Man" in its Lofty Associations'. *Biblical Review* 12 (1927), pp. 44-56.

McCown, C.C., 'Jesus, Son of Man. A Survey of Recent Discussion'. *JR* 28 (1948), pp. 1-12.

McDowell, E.A., *Son of Man and Suffering Servant: A Historical and Exegetical Study of Synoptic Narratives Revealing the Consciousness of Jesus Concerning His Person and Mission* (Nashville: Broadman Press, 1944, 3rd ed. 1946).

—, 'The Kingdom of God and the Day of the Son of Man: A Study of Luke 17:20-37'. *Review and Expositor* 39 (1962), pp. 54-64.

McKenzie, J.L., 'The Son of Man Must Suffer'. *The Way*. A Quarterly Review of Christian Spirituality 7 (1967), pp. 6-17. Reprint in Michael J. Taylor (ed.), *The Mystery of Suffering and Death* (New York: Alba House, 1973), pp. 31-44.

McNaugher, 'The Son of Man'. *BS* 88 (1931), pp. 90-104.

McNeil, Brian, 'The Son of Man and the Messiah: A Footnote'. *NTS* 26 (1979–80), pp. 419-21.

Mearns, Chris, 'The Son of Man Trajectory and Eschatological Development'. *ET* 97 (1985–86), pp. 8-12.

Meeks, Wayne A., 'The Man from Heaven in Johannine Sectarianism'. *JBL* 91 (1972), pp. 44-72.

Meloni, G., 'Filius Hominis'. *Saggi di Filologia Semitica* (1913), pp. 315-19.

Merklein, Helmut, 'Die Auferweckung Jesu und die Anfänge der Christologie (Messias bzw. Sohn Gottes und Menschensohn)'. *ZNW* 72 (1981), pp. 1-26. Reprint in idem, *Studien zu Jesus und Paulus*. WUNT 43 (Tübingen: Mohr [Siebeck], 1987), pp. 231-46.

Messel, Nils, *Der Menschensohn in den Bilderreden des Henoch*. BZAW 35 (1922).

Messerschmid, Joannes Henricus, *Commentatio philologica de sacra forma et dictione* Ο ΥΙΟΣ ΤΟΥ ΑΝΘΡΩΠΟΥ *qva simvl sermonis graeci qvo N.F. est constriptvm castitatem adserit* (Leipzig, 1739).

Meulenbelt, H.H., 'De Zoon des menschen, de Zoon, de Zoon Gods'. *Theologische Studiën* 29 (1911), pp. 388-438.

Michaelis, Christian Benedikt, משיח בן אדם *sive Dissertatio philologica ex antiqvitate ivdaica, de nominibvs Christi, hvmanam ipsivs natvram designantibvs* (Halle, 1714).

—, *Tractatio philologico-theologica de Christo filio hominis* (Halle, 1736).

Michaelis, Wilhelm, 'Joh. 1,51, Gen. 28,12 und das Menschensohn-Problem'. *ThLZ* 85 (1960), cols. 561-78.

Michel, Otto, 'Menschensohn und Völkerwelt'. *Evangelische Missions-Zeitschrift* 2 (1941), pp. 257-67.

—, 'Der Menschensohn in der Jesusüberlieferung'. *Theologische Beiträge* 2 (1971), pp. 119-28.

—, 'Der Menschensohn. Die eschatologische Hinweisung. Die apokalyptische Aussage. Bemerkungen zum Menschensohn-Verständnis des N.T.' *ThZ* 27 (1971), pp. 81-104.

—, 'Der Umbruch: Messianität = Menschensohn. Fragen zur Markus 8,31'. In Gert Jeremias et al. (eds.), *Tradition und Glaube. Das frühe Christentum in seiner Umwelt*. FS K.G. Kuhn (Göttingen: Vandenhoeck & Ruprecht, 1971), pp. 310-16.

—, 'ὁ υἱὸς τοῦ ἀνθρώπου'. *Theologisches Begriffslexikon zum Neuen Testament* III (Wuppertal: Brockhaus, 2. Aufl., 1972), pp. 1153-66. Revised by W. Grimm in Neubearbeitete Ausgabe II (Wuppertal: Brockhaus, 2000), pp. 1061-76.

Micklem, N., 'The Son of Man'. *Queen's Quarterly* 36 (1929), pp. 205-24.

Mihoc, V., '"Fiul Omului" dupa NT. Filius Hom. sec. NT'. *Studii Teologice* 25 (1973), pp. 33-44. Cf. *Bib.* 55 (1974) Elenchus 3455. (Romanian)

Minear, P.S., 'The Coming of the Son of Man (An Exegesis of Matthew 25:31-46)'. *Theology Today* 9 (1952–53), pp. 489-93.

Mkole, Jean-Claude Loba, 'Une synthèse d'opinions philologiques sur le Fils de l'homme'. *Journal of Northwest Semitic Languages* 22 (1996), pp. 107-23.

—, 'The Kiswahili mwana wa mtu and the Greek ho huios tou anthrópou'. In Gerald O. West and Musa W. Dube (eds.), *The Bible in Africa: Transactions, Trajectories and Trends* (Leiden: Brill, 2000), pp. 557-66.

—, '"Son of Man" and Exegetical Myths'. *Hervormde Teologiese Studies* 59 (2003), pp. 837-58.

Moe, Olaf, 'Der Menschensohn und der Urmensch'. *StTh* 14 (1960), pp. 119-29. Abridged Norwegian edition:

—, 'Menneskeønnen og Urmennesket'. *TTK* 32 (1961), pp. 65-73.

Moloney, Francis J., *The Johannine Son of Man*. Bibliotheca di Scienze Religiose 14 (Rome: LAS, 1976, 2nd ed. 1978).

—, 'The Johannine Son of Man'. *BThB* 6 (1976), pp. 177-89.

—, 'A Johannine Son of Man Discussion?' *Salesianum* 39 (1977), pp. 93-102.

—, 'The End of the Son of Man?' *The Downside Review* 98 (1980), pp. 280-90.

—, 'The Re-interpretation of Psalm VIII and the Son of Man Debate'. *NTS* 27 (1980–81), pp. 656-72 (revised version of 'The Targum on Ps. 8 and the New Testament'. *Salesianum* 37 [1975], pp. 326-36).

—, 'The Son of Man and Christian Discipleship'. *Lutheran Theological Journal* 39 (2005), pp. 110-21.

—, 'The Johannine Son of Man Revisited'. In Gilbert Van Belle, Jan G. van der Watt and Petrus Maritz (eds.), *Theology and Christology in the Fourth Gospel: Essays by the Members of the SNTS Johannine Writings Seminar*. BEThL 184 (Leuven: Peeters, 2005), pp. 177-202.

Moltmann, Jürgen, 'Man and Son of Man'. In J.R. Nelson (ed.), *No Man is Alien: Essays on the Unity of Mankind*. FS W.A. Visser' Hooft (Leiden: Brill, 1971), pp. 203-24.

Morgen, Michèle, 'Le Fils de l'homme élevé en vue de la vie éternelle (Jn 3,14-15 éclaré par diverses traditions juives)'. *RSR* 68 (1994), pp. 5-17.

Morgenstern, Julian, 'The "Son of Man" of Daniel 7,13f. A New Interpretation'. *JBL* 80 (1961), pp. 65-77.

Moulder, William, *The Son of Man in the Old Testament and the Gospel Tradition*. Typewritten thesis (St. Andrews, 1973–74).

Moule, Charles Francis Digby, 'Neglected Features in the Problem of "the Son of Man"'. In Joachim Gnilka (ed.), *Neues Testament und Kirche*. FS Rudolf Schnackenburg (Freiburg: Herder, 1974), pp. 413-28. Reprint (slightly altered) in idem, *Essays in New Testament Interpretation* (Cambridge: Cambridge University Press, 1982), pp. 75-90.

—, '"The Son of Man': Some of the Facts'. *NTS* 41 (1995), pp. 277-79. Reprint in idem, *Forgiveness and Reconciliation: Biblical and Theological Essays* (London: SPCK, 1998), pp. 205-207.

Mouren, J., *Le Fils de l'homme, étude historique sur ce titre de Jésus, d'après les évangiles synoptiques* (Lyon: Paquet, 1903).

Mouson, J., 'De locutione "filius hominis" apud Matthaeum'. *Collectanea Mechliniensia* 37 (= NS 22) (1952), pp. 627-31.

Mowinckel, Sigmund, 'Henok og "menneskesønnen"'. *NTT* 45 (1944), pp. 57-69.

—, 'Ophavet til den senjødiske forestilling om Menneskesønnen'. *NTT* 45 (1944), pp. 189-244.

—, 'Menneskesönnen'. *Nordisk Teologisk Leksikon* II (1955), cols. 1006-1010.

Mprasiotes, P.I., '"῾Ο Υἱὸς τοῦ ᾿Ανθρώπου", Συμβολὴ εἰς τὴν ἱστορίαν τοῦ ὅρου'. *Θεολογία* 7 (1929), pp. 193-98.

Müller, Karlheinz, 'Beobachtungen zur Entwicklung der Menschensohnvorstellung in den Bilderreden des Henoch und im Buche Daniel'. In Chr. Suttner and C. Patock (eds.), *Wegzeichen.* FS H.M. Biedermann. Das östliche Christentum. NF, Heft 25 (Würzburg, Augustinus-Verlag, 1971), pp. 253-61.

—, 'Menschensohn und Messias. Religionsgeschichtliche Vorüberlegungen zum Menschensohnproblem in den synoptischen Evangelien'. *BZ* NF 16 (1972), pp. 161-87; 17 (1973), pp. 52-66. Reprint in idem, *Studien zur frühjüdischen Apokalyptik.* SBAB 11 (Stuttgart: Katholisches Bibelwerk, 1991), pp. 279-322.

—, 'Der Menschensohn im Danielzyklus'. In R. Pesch and R. Schnackenburg (eds.), *Jesus und der Menschensohn.* FS Anton Vögtle (Freiburg: Herder, 1975), pp. 37-80. Reprint in idem, *Studien zur frühjüdischen Apokalyptik*, pp. 229-78.

Müller, Markus, *Jüngerschaft im Reich des Menschensohnes. Ein Beitrag zur Eschatologie des Matthäusevangeliums.* Unpublished dissertation (Erlangen, 2001).

Müller, Mogens, *Messias og 'menneskesøn' i Daniels Bog, Første Enoksbog og Fjerde Ezrabog.* Tekst & Tolkning 3 (København: Gad, 1972).

—, 'Om udtrykket "menneskesønnen" i evangelierne'. *DTT* 40 (1977), pp. 1-17. German: 'Über den Ausdruck "Menschensohn" in den Evangelien'. *StTh* 31 (1977), pp. 65-82.

—, 'Jesu brug af udtrykket "menneskesønnen"'. *DTT* 46 (1983), pp. 201-20. English: 'The Expression "The Son of Man" as Used by Jesus'. *StTh* 38 (1984), pp. 47-64.

—, *Der Ausdruck 'Menschensohn' in den Evangelien. Voraussetzungen und Bedeutung.* AThD 17 (Leiden: Brill, 1984).

—, 'Betydningen af בר אנש i Dan. 7,13. En anmeldelsesartikel'. *DTT* 47 (1984), pp. 177-86.

—, 'Messias og "menneskesønnen" i den intertestamentale periode'. In Sten Hidal et al. (eds.), *Judendom och kristendom under de första århundradena.* Nordiskt patristikerprojekt 1982–85, vol. 1 (Oslo: University Press, 1986), pp. 98-111.

—, '"Have You Faith in the Son of Man" (John 9.35)'. *NTS* 37 (1991), pp. 291-94 Danish: '"Tror du på menneskesønnen?" (Joh 9,35)'. In Mogens Müller, *Skriften i Skriften . Mellem Tradition og reception. Fjorten Afhandlinger.* Afhandlinger ved Det Teologiske Fakultet. Afdeling for Bibelsk Eksegese, afhandling 2007/1 (København, 2007), pp. 190-94.

—, 'Son of Man'. In Bruce M. Metzger and Michael D. Coogan (eds.), *The Oxford Companion to the Bible* (New York/Oxford: Oxford University Press, 1993), pp. 711-13.

—, 'Schleiermacher und der Ausdruck Menschensohn. Ein typisches Beispiel und ein Ausblick'. In Dietz Lange und Peter Widmann (eds.), *Kirche zwischen Heilsbotschaft und Lebenswirklichkeit.* FS Theodor Jørgensen (Frankfurt am Main: Peter Lang, 1996), pp. 69-80. Danish: 'Schleiermacher og udtrykket menneskesønnen.Et typisk eksempel og et udblik'. In idem, *Skriften i Skriften* (2007), pp. 195-205.

—, 'Menneskesøn'. *Gads Bibelleksikon* II (København: Gad, 1998), pp. 66-67.

—, 'Menneskesønnen og teologihistorien. En kristologisk titels opståen og fald'. *Collegium Biblicum Årsskrift 2001* (2001), pp. 31-48.

—, 'Menschensohn im Neuen Testament'. In *RGG*, V (4th ed. Tübingen: Mohr [Siebeck], 2002), cols. 1098-100.

—, '"Son of Man" in the Gospels: Quotation, Concept, Or?' In idem, *Skriften i Skriften* (2007), pp. 181-89.

—, 'Er løsningen på "menneskesøn"-problemet fundet? I anledning af Maurice Caseys nye "menneskesøn"-bog'. *DTT* 71 (2008), pp. 42-49.

Müller, Peter, 'Zwischen dem Gekommenen und dem Kommenden. Intertextuelle Aspekte der Menschensohnaussagen im Markusevangelium'. In Dieter Sänger (ed.), *Gottessohn und Menschensohn*. Biblisch-theologischer Studien 67 (Neukirchen–Vluyn: Neukirchener Verlag, 2004), pp. 130-57.

Müller, Ulrich B., *Messias und Menschensohn in jüdischen Apokalypsen und in der Offenbarung des Johannes*. SNT 6 (Gütersloher Verlagshaus: Gerd Mohn, 1972).

—, 'Parusie und Menschensohn'. *ZNW* 92 (2001), pp. 1-19. Reprint in idem, *Christologie und Apokalyptik*. Gesammelte Aufsätze. Arbeiten zur Bibel und ihrer Geschichte 12 (Leipzig: Evangelischer Verlagsanstalt, 2003), pp. 124-43.

—, 'Jesus als "der Menschensohn"'. In Dieter Sänger (ed.), *Gottessohn und Menschensohn*. Biblisch-theologischer Studien 67 (Neukirchen–Vluyn: Neukirchener Verlag, 2004), pp. 91-129.

Muilenberg, James, 'The Son of Man in Daniel and the Ethiopic Apocalypse of Enoch'. *JBL* 79 (1960), pp. 197-209.

Muirhead, Lewis A., 'The Name "Son of Man" and the Messianic Consciousness of Jesus'. *ET* 11 (1899–1900), pp. 62-65.

—, 'Schmiedel on the Name "Son of Man"'. *ET* 11 (1899–1900), p. 124.

Munck, Johannes, 'Menneskesønnen'. *Illustreret Religionsleksikon* II (København: Skandinavisk Bogforlag, 1950), s. 572.

Mussner, Franz, 'Die Wiederkunft des Menschensohnes nach Markus 13,24-27 und 14,61-62'. *BuK* 16 (1961), pp. 105-107.

—, 'Wohnung Gottes und Menschensohn nach der Stephanusperikope (Apg 6,2–8,2)'. In R. Pesch and R. Schnackenburg (eds.), *Jesus und der Menschensohn*. FS Anton Vögtle (Freiburg: Herder, 1975), pp. 283-99.

—, 'Die Skepsis des Menschensohnes. Zu Lk 18,8b'. In Christoph Niemand (ed.), *Forschungen zum Neuen Testament und seiner Umwelt*. FS Albert Fuchs. Linzer Philosophisch-Theologische Beiträge 7 (Frankfurt am Main: Lang, 2002), pp. 271-75.

Mutombo-Mukendi, *L'apport théologique du Fils de l'Homme dans le deuxième évangile*. Diss (Bruxelles: Theol. prot., 1992) (*EThL* 70 [1994] Elenchus 5441).

Myllykoski, Matti, 'Jeesus ja Ihmisen Poika—ikuinen arvoitus?' *TAik* 92 (1987), pp. 498-502. (Finnish)

Nandrès, J.-J., *Jésus-Christ le Fils de l'homme* (Niort: Robin et Favre, 1867).

Nardoni, E., 'El Hijo del hombre viniendo sobre las nubes'. *Revista Bíblica* 21 (1959), pp. 121-24.

—, *El Hijo del hombre viniendo sobre las nubes*. Temas Bíblicos (1961). Cf. *Bib.* 43 (1962) Elenchus 1986.

Nebe, A., 'Ueber den Begriff des Namens ὁ υἱὸς τοῦ ἀνθρώπου'. *Denkschrift des herzoglich Nassauischen evangelisch-theologischen Seminars zu Herborn für das Jahr 1860* (1860), pp. 3-56.

Nebe, Gottfried, 'The Son of Man and the Angels: Reflections on the Formation of Christology in the Context of Eschatology'. In H. Graf Reventlow (ed.), *Eschatology in the Bible and in Jewish and Christian Tradition*. JSOTSup 243 (Sheffield: Sheffield Academic Press, 1997), pp. 111-31.

Nelis, J.T., 'De mysterieuze mensenzoonfiguur van het boek Daniël'. *Het Heilig Land* 9 (1956), pp. 185-87.

—, 'Menschensohn'. *Bibel-Lexikon* (2. Aufl., 1968), cols. 1128-34.

Nestle, Eberhard, 'The "Son of Man" in the Old Testament'. *ET* 11 (1899–1900), p. 238.

Neugebauer, Fritz, *Jesus der Menschensohn. Ein Beitrag zur Klärung der Wege historischer Wahrheitsfindung im Bereich der Evangelien.* Arbeiten zur Theologie 1. Rh. 50 Heft 1 (Stuttgart: Calwer, 1972).

—, 'Die Davidsssohnfrage (Mark xii,35-37 parr.) und der Menschensohn'. *NTS* 21 (1974–75), pp. 81-108.

Newman, Barclay M., 'Towards a Translation of "the Son of Man" in the Gospels'. *The BiTr* 21 (1970), pp. 141-46.

Newton, Huey P., 'Son of Man'. *Radical Religion* 2 (1975), pp. 68-72.

Nickelsburg, George W.E., 'Son of Man'. In *ABD*, VI (1992), pp. 137-50.

—, 'Son of Man'. In *DDD*, pp. 800-804.

Nicol, Kathlene Peterson, *'Son of Man': Its Background and New Testament Usage.* Unpublished BD thesis (Union Theological Seminary, New York, 1970). Cf. Walter Wink, *The Human Being* (2002), p. 336 n. 8.

Nösgen, Karl Friedrich, *Christus der Menschen- und Gottessohn. Eine Erörterung der Selbstbezeichnungen Jesu Christi in ihrer grundleglichen Bedeutung für die Christolologie* (Gotha: Perthes, 1869).

Nolland, John, 'The Son of Man in the Synoptic Gospels: The Man of Destiny'. In David Petersen and John Pryor (eds.), *In the Fullness of Time.* FS Donald Robinson (Homebush West, NSW: Lancer, 1992), pp. 17-28.

Non quis, sed quid!, 'Versuch über die Stellen im N.T. die vom Sohne Gottes, vom Sohne des Menschen, Christus uä. reden'. *Magazin für Religionsphilosophie, Exegese und Kirchengeschichte* (ed. von H.Ph.C. Henke) 1 (1794), pp. 129-208.

Notley, R. Steve, 'Abel, Jesus, and the Son of Man'. *AAR/SBL Abstracts 2001* (2001), p. 37.

Novo, Alfonso, 'El hijo del hombre en los evangelios sinóppticos'. *Estudios ecclesiasticos* 75 (2000), pp. 23-78.

Obeng, E.A., '"The Son of Man" Motif and the Intercession of Jesus'. *African Theological Journal* 19 (1990), pp. 155-67.

Offerman, H., 'The Son of Man and the Son of God'. *The Lutheran Church Review* 29 (1910), pp. 710-20; 30 (1911), pp. 120-26 (The part about "Son of Man" is missing in my source, NTTS 6 [1966] 8030).

Oikonomidos, B., *῾Ο Υἱὸς τοῦ ἀνθρώπου. Κατὰ τὰς θεμελιώδεις ἀρχὰς τῆς ᾿Ορθοδόξου ᾿Ανατολικῆς ᾿Εκκλησίας ἔναντι τοῦ ὀρθολογισμοῦ* (1878).

Olson, Daniel C., 'Enoch and the *Son of Man* in the Epilogue of the Parables'. *Journal for the Study of the Pseudepigrapha* 18 (1998), pp. 27-38.

O'Neill, J.C., 'Son of Man, Stone of Blood (John 1:51)'. *NT* 45 (2003), pp. 374-81.

Oort, Henricus Lucas, *De uitdrukking* Ο ΥΙΟΣ ΤΟΥ ΑΝΘΡΩΠΟΥ *in het Nieuwe Testament* (Leiden: Brill, 1893).

Orlando, L., 'Il Figlio dell'uomo. Percorso teologico'. *Antonianum* 80 (2005), pp. 207-44.

Orrieux, L.-M., 'Le problème du fils de l'homme dans la littérature apocalyptique'. *Lumière et Vie* 12 (1963), pp. 9-31.

Ory, Georges, 'L'intrusion du Fils de l'Homme dans nos évangiles'. *Bulletin de Cercle Ernest-Renan* 104 (1964), pp. 1-3.

Otto, Rudolf, *Reich Gottes und Menschensohn. Ein religionsgeschichtlicher Vergleich* (München: Beck, 1934, 3. Aufl. 1954). English: *The Kingdom of God and the Son of Man: A Study in the History of Religion* (1938). New and revised translation by Floyd V. Filson and Bertram Lee-Woolf (London: Lutterworth, 1943).

Owen, Paul, and Shepherd, David, 'Speaking up for Qumran, Dalman, and the Son of Man: Was *Bar Enasha* a Common Term for "Man" in the Time of Jesus?' *JSNT* 81 (2002), pp. 81-122.

Pagazzi, G.C., and Vignolo, R., 'Su *'il Figlio dell'uomo'*, l'autoaffezione prediletta di Gesù. In margine ad uno studio recente'. *Teologica* 29 (2004), pp. 180-200.

Painter, J., 'The Enigmatic Johannine Son of Man'. In F. van Segbroeck, C. M. Tuckett, G. van Belle and J. Verheyden (eds.), *The Four Gospels 1992*. FS Frans Neirynck. BEThL 100 (Leuven: Peeters, 1992), III, pp. 1869-88.

Pamment, Margaret, 'The Son of Man in the First Gospel'. *NTS* 29 (1983), pp. 116-29.

—, 'The Son of Man in the Fourth Gospel'. *JThS* NS 36 (1985), pp. 56-66.

Panier, Louis, 'Le Fils de l'Homme et les nations. Lecture de Mt 25,31-46', *SémiotBib* 69 (1993), pp. 39-52.

Panikkar, Raimundo, 'Sécularisation de l'herméneutique: le cas du Christ: fils de l'homme et fils de Dieu'. In Enrico Castelli (ed.), *Herméneutique de la sécularisation* (Paris: Aubier Montaigne, 1976), pp. 213-48. German: 'Die Säkularisierung der Hermeneutik: der Fall Christus: Menschensohn und Gottessohn'. In Franz Theunis (ed.), *Zum Problem der Säkularisierung*. Kerygma und Mythos VI = ThF 60 (Hamburg-Bergstedt: H. Reich, Evangelischer Verlag, 1977), pp. 141-64.

Papageorgakopoulos, A.K., *Ὁ Υἱος τοῦ ἀνθρώπου. Συμβολὴ εἰς τὴν ἱστορίαν καὶ ἑρμηνείαν τοῦ ὅρου ὁ 'Υἱὸς τοῦ ἀνθρώπου' κατὰ τὴν Καινὴν Διαθήκην* (Athens, 1958, 2nd ed. 1963).

Parker, Pierson, 'The Meaning of "Son of Man"'. *JBL* 60 (1941), pp. 151-57.

Patton, Carl S., 'Did Jesus Call Himself the Son of Man?' *JR* 2 (1922), pp. 501-11.

Paul, André, 'L'*évangélion*: Synthèse de l'*oïkouménè* et de l'*apokalypsis*: De Jésus de Méditerranéen à Jésus le Fils de l'Homme'. In J.-L. Schlegel et al. (eds.), *Temps, histoire, espérance: De la vigilance chrétienne en temps de crise*. Publications des Facultés universitaires Saint-Louis 60 (Bruxelles: Facultés universitaires Saint-Louis, 1994), pp. 45-63.

Paul, Leslie, *Son of Man: The Life of Christ* (London: Hodder & Stoughton, 1961).

Pazdan, Mary Margaret, *The Son of Man: A Metaphor for Jesus in the Fourth Gospel* (Collegeville, MN: Liturgical Press, 1991).

Peake, Arthur Samuel, 'The Messiah and the Son of Man'. *BJRL* 8 (1924), pp. 52-81. Reprint in idem, *The Servant of Yahweh* (Manchester: Manchester University Press, 1931), pp. 220-37.

Peloux, G., *Valeur et contenu du terme: le Fils de l'homme dans la bouche de Jésus. Essay de théologique biblique* (1906).

Perrin, Norman, 'The Son of Man in Ancient Judaism and Primitive Christianity: A Suggestion'. *BR* 11 (1966), pp. 17-28. Reprint with Postscript in idem, *A Modern Pilgrimage in New Testament Christology* (Philadelphia: Fortress Press, 1974), pp. 23-40.

—, 'The Creative Use of the Son of Man Tradition by Mark'. *USQR* 23 (1968), pp. 357-65. Reprint in idem, *A Modern Pilgrimage in New Testament Christology* (1974), pp. 84-93.

—, 'The Son of Man in the Synoptic Tradition'. *BR* 13 (1968), pp. 3-25. Reprint in idem, *A Modern Pilgrimage in New Testament Christology* (1974), pp. 57-83.

—, 'Son of Man'. In *The Interpreter's Dictionary of the Bible*. Supplementary Volume (Nashville: Abingdon Press, 1976), pp. 833-36.

Pesch, Rudolf, and Rudolf Schnackenburg (eds.), *Jesus und der Menschensohn*. FS Anton Vögtle (Freiburg: Herder, 1975).

—, 'Die Passion des Menschensohnes. Eine Studie zu den Menschensohnworten der vormarkinischen Passionsgeschichte'. In R. Pesch and R. Schnackenburg (eds.), *Jesus und der Menschensohn*. FS Anton Vögtle (Freiburg: Herder, 1975), pp. 166-95.

Pezzana, J., *De filio hominis, Dan 7,13-14, atque de solutionibus recentioribus catholicorum inde ab anno 1953*. Unpublished dissertation (Rome, 1962). Cf. *Bib.* 44 (1963) Elenchus 1434.

Pfenningsdorf, Emil, *Der Menschensohn. Wesen—Geheimnis—Wirken* (München: Erasmus-Verlag, 1948).

Phillips, Harold Cooke, 'Jesus, Son of Man'. *Religion in Life* 5 (1936), pp. 207-15.

Plevnik, Joseph, 'Son of Man Seated at the Right Hand of God: Luke 22:69 in Lucan Christology'. *Bib.* 72 (1991), pp. 331-47.

Pot, C.W. van der, 'Jets over den Zin en de Kracht der Benaming, De Zoon des Menschen'. *Waarheid in Liefde, een godgeleerde Tijdsschrift, voor beschaafde Christenen* (1846), pp. 74-99.

Potterie, I. de la, 'L'exaltation du Fils de l'homme (Jn 12,31-36)'. *Gregorianum* 49 (1968), pp. 460-78.

Powell, W., 'The Days of the Son of Man'. *ET* 67 (1955–56), p. 219.

Preiss, Theodor, 'Le Mystère du Fils de l'Homme'. *Dieu Vivant* 8 (1947), pp. 15-36.

—, 'The Son of Man Came to Minister: Mark 10:35-45'. *Interp.* 4 (1950), pp. 189-92.

—, 'Le Fils de l'Homme. Fragments d'un cours sur la Christologie du Nouveau Testament'. *ETR* 26 (Montpellier, 1951).

—, 'Le Fils de l'Homme' (Suite). *ETR* 28 (1953), pp. 1-75.

Premawardhana, S.D.E., *Parusia and the Son of Man: A Comparative Study of Mythology*. Diss (Northwestern University, 1992). Cf. *EThL* 70 (1994) 5027; DissAbstr 53 (1992–93) 1956.

Price, Robert M., *The Incredible Shrinking Son of Man: How Reliable is the Gospel Tradition?* (Amherst, MA: Prometheus Books, 2003).

Procksch, Otto, 'Der Menschensohn als Gottessohn'. *Christentum und Wissenschaft* 3 (1927), pp. 425-43, 473-81.

Proudman, C.L.J., 'Remarks on the "Son of Man"'. *Canadian Journal of Theology* 12 (1966), pp. 128-31.

Pruzak, Bernard P., 'The Son of Man Came Eating and Drinking: An Overview of Christological Perspectives in the Incarnation'. In Francis A. Eigo (ed.), *Who Do People Say I Am* (Villanova, PA: University Press, 1980), pp. 1-46.

Pryor, John W., 'The Johannine Son of Man and the Descent–Ascent Motif'. *JEThS* 34 (1991), pp. 341-51.

Quack, C.G.M., 'Warom gaf Jezus de voorkeur aan den naam: 'Zoon des Menschen', en niet aan den naam "Zoon van God"?' *Geloof en Vrijheid* 36 (1902), pp. 356-72.

Quispel, Gilles, 'Nathanael und der Menschensohn (Joh 1,51)'. *ZNW* 47 (1956), pp. 281-83.

Radcliffe, Timothy, 'The Coming of the Son of Man: Mark's Gospel and the Subversion of "the Apocalyptic Imagination"'. In Brian Davies (ed.), *Language, Meaning, and God.* FS Herbert McCabe (London: Chapman, 1987), pp. 176-89.

Ramos, Felipe Fernandez., 'La "figura" del Hijo del hombre'. *Naturaleza y Gracia* 45 (1998), pp. 107-35.

—, 'El Hijo del homre y el reino'. *Studium Legionense* 39 (1998), pp. 89-119.

—, 'El hijo del hombre en el cuarto evangelio', *Studium Legionense* 40 (1999), pp. 45-92.

—, 'El Hijo del hombre: Las tres fases de su atuacíon'. *Naturaleza y Gracia* 47 (2000), pp. 295-358.

Rank, R.G., 'Who is this man? The Son of Man According to Mark'. *BiTod* 63 (1972), pp. 959-65.

Reicke, Bo, 'Menschensohn (im *AT*)'. *BHH* II (1964), cols. 1191-92.

Resenhöfft, Wilhelm, *Der Tag des Menschensohnes. Die Geschichte Jesu im Wortlaut der Urquellen.* Europäische Hochschulschriften. Rh 23 Theologie. Band 40 (Bern: P. Lang, 1975).

Rhea, Robert, *The Johannine Son of Man.* AThANT 76 (Zürich: Theologischer Verlag, 1990).

Ricciardi, Alberto, 'El Elegido-Hijo del hombre, vindicador de los oprimidos'. *Revista Bíblica* 44 (1982), pp. 207-32.

Riedl, Johannes, 'Wenn Ihr den Menschensohn erhöht habt, werdet ihr erkennen (Joh 8,28)'. In R. Pesch and R. Schnackenburg (eds.), *Jesus und der Menschensohn.* FS Anton Vögtle (Freiburg: Herder, 1975), pp. 355-70.

Riesenfeld, Harald, 'Människosonen. 2. *N.T.*' *SBU* II (Gävle: Skolförlaget, 1952), cols. 403-405; (2nd ed. Stockholm: Nordiska Uppslagsböcker, 1963), cols. 232-34.

Rivera, L.F., 'El misterio del Hijo del Hombre en la transfiguración (Mr 9,2-3)'. *Revista Bíblica* 28 (1966), pp. 19-34, 79-89.

Robinson, James M., 'The Son of Man in the Sayings Gospel Q'. In Christoph Elsas et al. (eds.), *Tradition und Translation.* FS Carsten Colpe (Berlin: De Gruyter, 1994), pp. 315-35.

Rochais, G., 'Jésus et le Fils de l'homme'. "Jesus"'. *Héritage et projet* 9 (1974), pp. 83-122.

Rolla, A., 'Il giorno del Figlio dell' Uomo nei Vangeli: la fine di Gerusalemme e la Chiesa'. *Pal. Clero* 33 (1954), pp. 83-89, 108-17. Cf. J. Coppens, *De Mensenzoon-logia* (1973), p. 32.

Roloff, Jürgen, 'Das Reich des Menschensohnes: ein Beitrag zur Eschatologie des Matthäus'. In M. Evang et al. (eds.), *Eschatologie und Schöpfung.* FS Erich Gräßer. BZNW 89 (Berlin: De Gruyter 1997), pp. 275-92.

Romanowsky, John W., '"When the Son of Man is Lifted Up": The Redemptive Power of the Crucifixion in the Gospel of John'. *Horizons* 32 (2005), pp. 100-16.

Rongy, H., 'Le Fils d'homme dans Daniel VII,13'. *Revue Ecclésiastique de Liége* 14 (1922–23), pp. 96-100.

Rose, Vincent, 'Études évangélique III, Fils de l'homme et Fils de Dieu'. *Revue Biblique Internationale* 9 (1900), pp. 169-99. Reprint in idem, *Etudes sur les Evangiles* (Paris: Welter, 1902), pp. 157-82.

Roslaniec, Franciszek, *Sensus genuinus et plenus locutionis 'Filius Hominis', a Christo Domine adhibitae* (Rome: Typis Polyglottis Vaticanis, 1920).

Ross, A., 'The Title "Son of Man"'. *EvQ* 6 (1934), pp. 36-49.

Ross, J.M., 'The Son of Man'. *Irish Biblical Studies* 13 (1991), pp. 186-98.

Rost, Leonhard, 'Zur Deutung des Menschensohnes in Daniel 7'. In *Gott und die Götter*. FS Erich Fascher (Berlin: Evangelische Verlagsanstalt, 1958), pp. 41-43. Reprint in idem, *Studien zum Alten Testament*. BWANT 51 (Stuttgart: Kohlhammer, 1974), pp. 72-75.

Roth, Wolfgang, 'Jesus as the Son of Man: The Scriptural Identity of a Johannine Image'. In Dennis E. Groh and Robert Jewett (eds.), *The Living Text*. FS Ernest W. Saunders (New York: University Press of America, 1985), pp. 11-26.

Rowe, Robert D., 'Is Daniel's "Son of Man" Messianic?' In Harold H. Rowden (ed.), *Christ the Lord*. FS Donald Guthrie (Leicester: Inter-Varsity Press, 1982), pp. 71-96.

Ruckstuhl, Eugen, 'Die johanneische Menschensohnforschung 1957–1969'. In J. Pfammatter and F. Fuger (eds.), *Theologische Berichte* 1 (1972), pp. 171-284.

—, 'Abstieg und Erhöhung des johanneischen Menschensohns'. In R. Pesch and R. Schnackenburg (eds.), *Jesus und der Menschensohn*. FS Anton Vögtle (Freiburg: Herder, 1975), pp. 314-41. Reprint in idem, *Jesus im Horizont der Evangelien*. Stuttgarter Biblische Aufsatzbände 3 (Stuttgart: Katholisches Bibelwerk, 1988), pp. 277-307 (Nachtrag, pp. 307-10).

Rullmann, M. Georg Wilhelm, 'In welchem Sinne nennt sich Jesus des Menschen Sohn?' (Rinteln, 1785). Reprint in Johann Georg Schellenberg (ed.) *Selecta historico-philosophico-theologica* I (Leipzig: Bueschel, 1787), pp. 272-85.

Runze, G., *Das Zeichen des Menschensohnes und der Doppelsinn des Jonâzeichens. Glossen und Materialien zur Erklärung der Herrensprüche vom 'Zeichen'*. Studien zur vergleichende Religionswissenschaft 3 (Berlin: Gaertner, 1897).

—, 'Das Zeichen des Menschensohnes und der Doppelsinn des Jonâzeichens'. *ZWTh* 41 (1898), pp. 171-85.

Sabbe, M., 'The Son of Man Saying in Acts 7,56'. In J. Kremer (ed.), *Les Actes des Apôtres. Traditions, rédaction, théologie*. BEThL 48 (Gembloux: Duculot; Leuven: University Press, 1979), pp. 241-79. Reprint in idem, *Studia Neotestamentica: Collected Essays*. BEThL 98 (Leuven: Peeters/Leuven University Press, 1991), pp. 389-95 (additional note, pp. 396-97).

Sabourin, Leopold, 'The Son of Man'. *BThB* 2 (1972), pp. 78-80.

—, '"You will not have gone through all the towns of Israel, before the Son of Man comes" (Mat 10:23b)'. *BThB* 7 (1977), pp. 5-10.

Sänger, Dieter (ed.), *Gottessohn und Menschensohn. Exegetische Studien zu zwei Paradigmen biblischer Intertextualität*. BThS 67 (Neukirchen–Vluyn: Neukirchener Verlag, 2004).

Sahlin, Harald, 'Wie wurde ursprünglich die Benennung "Der Menschensohn" verstanden?' *StTh* 37 (1983), pp. 147-79.

Salceda, Alberto G., *Bar-Nasha: El Hombre* (Mexico, D.F.: Costa-Amic, 1969). Cf. A. Ferch, *The Son of Man in Daniel 7* (1983), p. 232.

Sanday, William, 'On the Title, "Son of Man."' *Exp* 4/3 (1891), pp. 18-32. Reprint in idem, *Essays in Biblical Criticism and Exegesis*. Edited by Craig A. Evans and Stanley E. Porter. JSNTSup 225 = Classics in Biblical and Theological Studies Supplement 2 (Sheffield: Sheffield Academic Press, 2001), pp. 155-66.

Sanders, Ian L., 'The Origin and Significance of the Title "The Son of Man" as Used in the Gospels'. *Scripture* 10 (1958), pp. 49-56.

Sandmel, Samuel, 'Son of Man'. In Daniel Jeremy Silver (ed.), *In the Time of Harvest*. FS A.H. Silver (New York: Macmillan 1963), pp. 355-67. Reprint with the title '"Son of Man" in Mark', in idem, *Two Living Traditions: Essays on Religion and the Bible* (Detroit, MI: Wayne State University Press, 1972), pp. 166-77.

Sanford, A.M., 'Did Jesus Call Himself the Son of Man? Another Point of View'. *JR* 3 (1923), pp. 308-13.

Sardi, M., 'Il "Figlio dell' Uomo"'. *Riv. Stor. Critica* 5 (1909), pp. 12-19. Cf. Coppens, *De Mensenzoon-logia in het Markus-Evangelium* (1973), p. 30.

Sasse, Markus, *Der Menschensohn im Evangelium nach Johannes*. TANZ 35 (Tübingen-Basel: Francke, 2000).

Schegget, G.H. ter, *Het Lied van de Mensenzoon. Studie over de Christuspsalm in Filippenzen 2:6-11* (Baarn. Wereldvenster, 1975).

Scheifler, J.R., 'El hijo del hombre en Daniel'. *Estudios Ecclesiásticos* 34 (1960), pp. 789-804.

Schenk, Wolfgang, *Das biographische Ich-Idiom 'Menschensohn' in den frühen Jesus-Biographien. Der Ausdruck, seine Codex und seine Rezeption in ihren Kontexten*. FRLANT 177 (Göttingen: Vandenhoeck & Ruprecht, 1997).

Schenkel, Daniel, 'Menschensohn'. In idem, *Bibel-Lexicon: Realwörterbuch zum Handgebrauch für Geistliche und Gemeindeglieder*, Band 4 (Leipzig: Brockhaus, 1872), pp. 170-75.

Schenker, Adrian, 'Substitution du chatiment ou prix de la paix: don la vie du fils de l'homme en Mk 10:45 et par a lumiere de l'Ancien Testament'. In Martin Benzerath, Aloyse Schmid and Jaques Guillet (eds.), *La pâque du Christ mystère de salut*: melanges offerts au Francois-Xavier Durrwell. Lectio Divina 112 (Paris: Éditions du Cerf, 1982), pp. 75-90.

Schierse, F.J., 'Jesus Menschensohn—Herausforderung des Glaubens'. *Diakonia* 4 (1973), pp. 280-83 (review of R. Augstein's book).

Schippers, R., 'De Zoon des mensen in Mt. 12,32—Lk. 12,10, vergeleken met Mk. 3,28'. In *Ex Auditu Verbi*. FS G.C. Berkouwer (Kampen: Kok, 1965), pp. 233-57. Abridged English: 'The Son of Man in Matt. xii.32 = Lk. xii.10, compared with Mk. iii.28'. *SE* 4 (= TU 102, 1968), pp. 231-35.

Schmid, H., 'Daniel, der Menschensohn'. *Judaica* 27 (1971), pp. 192-220.

Schmidt, Hans, 'Menschensohn: I. Im AT und Judentum'. In *RGG*, III (2nd ed. 1929), cols. 2117-18.

Schmidt, Karl Christian Ludwig, 'Ueber den Ausdruck "ὁ υἱὸς τοῦ ἀνθρώπου" im Neuen Testamente'. *(Neues) Magazin für Religionsphilosophie, Exegese und Kirchengeschichte* (ed. H.Ph.C. Henke) 2 (1798), pp. 507-26.

Schmidt, Nathaniel, 'Was בר נשׁא a Messianic Title?' *JBL* 16 (1896), pp. 36-53.

—, 'The "Son of Man" in the Book of Daniel'. *JBL* 19 (1900), pp. 22-28.

—, 'Son of Man'. *Encyclopædia Biblica* IV (1903, 2nd ed. 1907), cols. 4705-40.

—, 'Recent Study on the Term "Son of Man"'. *JBL* 45 (1926), pp. 326-49.

Schmiedel, Paul Wilhelm, 'Der Name "Menschensohn" und das Messiasbewusstsein Jesu'. *PrM* 2 (1898), pp. 252-67.

—, 'Bezeichnet Jesus den Menschen als solchen durch "Menschensohn"? Zugleich ein Beitrag zur Verständigung über einige Grundsätze der Evangelienkritik und der Erforschung des Lebens Jesu'. *PrM* 2 (1898), pp. 291-308.

—, 'Die neuesten Auffassungen des Namens "Menschensohn"'. *PrM* 5 (1901), pp. 333-51.

Schmithals, Walter, 'Die Worte vom leidenden Menschensohn. Ein Schlüssel zur Lösung des Menschensohn-Problems'. In C. Andresen and G. Klein (eds.), *Theologia crucis—signum crucis*. FS Erich Dinkler (Tübingen: Mohr [Siebeck], 1979), pp. 417-45.

Schnackenburg, Rudolf, 'Der Menschensohn im Johannesevangelium'. *NTS* 11 (1964–65), pp. 123-37.

—, 'Die Ecce-homo-Szene und der Menschensohn'. In R. Pesch and R. Schnackenburg (eds.), *Jesus und der Menschensohn*. FS Anton Vögtle (Freiburg: Herder, 1975), pp. 371-86.

Schneider, Gerhard, '"Der Menschensohn" in der lukanischen Christologie'. In R. Pesch and R. Schnackenburg (eds.), *Jesus und der Menschensohn*. FS Anton Vögtle (Freiburg: Herder, 1975), pp. 267-82. Reprint in idem, *Lukas, Theologe der Heilsgeschichte. Aufsätze zum lukanischen Doppelwerk*. BBB 59 (Bonn: Peter Hanstein, 1985), pp. 98-113.

Scholten, Wessel, *Specimen hermeneutico-theologicum. De appellatione τοῦ υἱὸς τοῦ ἀνθρώπου, qua Iesus se messiam professus est* (Traiecti ad Rhenum: Paddenburg & Schoonhoven, 1809).

Schreiber, Stefan, 'Henoch als Menschensohn. Zur problematischen Schlußidentifikation in den Bilderreden des äthiopischen Henochbuches (äthHen 71,14)'. *ZNW* 91 (2000), pp. 1-17.

Schröter, Jens, 'Zur Menschensohnvorstellung im Evangelium nach Maria'. In Stephen Emmel, Martin Krause, Siegfried G. Richter and Sofia Schaten (eds.), *Ägypten und Nubien in spätantiker und christlicher Zeit*. Akten des 6. Internationalen Koptologenkongresses Münster, 20.–26. Juli 1996. Vol. 2: Schrifttum, Sprache und Gedankenwelt. SKCO 6.2 (Wiesbaden: Reichert Verlag, 1999), pp. 178-88.

—, 'Jesus, der Menschensohn. Zum Ansatz der Christologie in Markus und Q'. In idem, *Jesus und die Anfänge der Christologie. Methodologische und exegetische Studien zu den Ursprüngen des christlichen Glaubens*. Biblisch-theologische Studien 47 (Neukirchen–Vluyn: Neukirchener Verlag, 2001), pp. 140-79. English: 'The Son of Man as the Representative of God's Kingdom: On the Interpretation of Jesus in Mark and Q'. In Michael Labahn and Andreas Schmidt (eds.), *Jesus, Mark and Q: The Teaching of Jesus and its Earliest Records*. JSNTSup 214 (Sheffield: Sheffield Academic Press, 2001), pp. 34-69.

Schürmann, Heinz, 'Beobachtungen zum Menschensohn-Titel in der Redequelle. Sein Vorkommen in Abschluß- und Einleitungswendungen'. In R. Pesch and R. Schnackenburg (eds.), *Jesus und der Menschensohn*. FS Anton Vögtle (Freiburg: Herder, 1975), pp. 124-47. Reprint in idem, *Gottes Reich—Jesu Geschick: Jesu Ureigener Tod im Licht seiner Basileia-Verkündigung* (Freiburg: Herder, 1983), pp. 153-82. English: 'Observations on the Son of Man Title in the Speech Source: Its Occurrence in Closing and Introductory Expressions'. In J. Kloppenborg (ed.), *The Shape of Q* (Minneapolis: Fortress Press, 1994), pp. 74-97.

Schulthess, F., 'Zur Sprache der Evangelien. Anhang. C. "Menschensohn"'. *ZNW* 21 (1922), pp. 247-50.

Schulz, Sigfried, *Untersuchungen zur Menschensohn-Christologie im Johannes-evangelium. Zugleich ein Beitrag zur Methodengeschichte der Auslegung des 4. Evangeliums* (Göttingen: Vandenhoeck & Ruprecht, 1957).

Schulze, Ludwig Theodor, *Vom Menschensohn und Logos. Ein Beitrag zur biblischen Theologie* (Gotha: Perthes, 1867).

Schwarz, Günther, *Jesus 'der Menschensohn'. Aramaistische Untersuchungen zu den synoptischen Menschensohnworten Jesu*, BWANT NF 19 (Der ganzen Sammlung 119) (Stuttgart: Kohlhammer, 1986).

Schweitzer, Albert, 'Die Bedeutung der Logosspekulation für die historische Darstellung des Lebens Jesu im 4. Evangelium mit besonderer Berücksichtigung des Ausdrucks "Menschensohn". Antrittsvorlesung an der theologischen Fakultät zu Straßburg 1/3. 1902. First published in idem, *Straßburger Vorlesungen*. Edited by Erich Gräßer and Johann Zürcher. Werke aus dem Nachlaß (München: Beck, 1998), pp. 27-41.

Schweizer, Eduard, 'Der Menschensohn (Zur eschatologischen Erwartung Jesu)'. *ZNW* 50 (1959), pp. 185-209. Reprint in idem, *Neotestamentica* (Zürich-Stuttgart: Zwingli, 1963), pp. 56-84.

—, 'The Son of Man'. *JBL* 79 (1960), pp. 119-29.

—, 'The Son of Man Again'. *NTS* 9 (1962–63), pp. 256-61. Reprint in idem, *Neo-testamentica* (1963), pp. 85-92.

—, 'Menschensohn'. *Die Zeichen der Zeit* 22 (1963), pp. 361-63.

—, 'Jesus – Menschensohn'. *Neue Zürcher Zeitung* 15.11.1972 (Mittagsausgabe). Reprint in R. Pesch and G. Stachel (eds.), *Augstein's Jesus. Eine Dokumentation* (1972), pp. 55-64.

—, 'Menschensohn und eschatologischer Mensch im Frühjudentum'. In R. Pesch and R. Schnackenburg (eds.), *Jesus und der Menschensohn*. FS Anton Vögtle (Freiburg: Herder, 1975), pp. 100-16. Reprint in idem, *Neues Testament und Christologie im Werden*. Aufsätze (Göttingen: Vandenhoeck & Ruprecht, 1982), pp. 104-20.

Seethaler, Paula, 'Kleine Studie über den "Menschensohn"'. *BuK* 11 (1956), pp. 85-87.

Seitz, O.J.F., 'The Future Coming of the Son of Man: Three Midrashic Formulations in the Gospel of Mark'. *SE* 4 (= TU 112, 1973), pp. 478-94.

Sharman, Henry Burton, *Son of Man and Kingdom of God: A Critical Study* (New York: Harper & Bros 1943, 2nd ed. 1944).

Sheldon, Martin E., 'The Eschatological *Son of Man* in Jewish and Christian Literature'. *Evangelical Journal* 17 (1999), pp. 60-75.

Shepherd, David, see Owen, Paul.

Shepherd, M.B., 'Daniel 7:13 and the New Testament Son of Man'. *WThJ* 68 (2006), pp. 99-111.

Sierig, Hartmut (ed.), *Mensch und Menschensohn*. FS Karl Witte (Hamburg: Friedrich Wittig Verlag, 1963).

Sidebottom, E.M., 'The Son of Man in the Fourth Gospel'. *ET* 68 (1956–57), pp. 231-35, 280-83.

—, 'The Ascent and the Descent of the Son of Man in the Gospel of St. John'. *AThR* 39 (1957), pp. 115-22.

Sieber, F., 'Über die Selbstbezeichnung Jesu als des Sohn des Menschen'. In G. Schnedermann, *Jesu Verkündigung und Lehre vom Reiche Gottes in ihrer geschichtlichen Bedeutung* (Leipzig: Deichert, 1895), I, pp. 257-69.

Sieg, Fr., 'Ὅμοιον υἱον ἀνθρώπου (Offb 1,13): Schlussfolgerungen aus der Unter suchung (Offb 1,13-16.17c.18; 2,1.8.12.18; 3,1.7.14)'. *Filologia Neotestamentica* 7 (1994), pp. 3-15.
—, 'The Son of Man, the Messiah, the Son of God and Simon Peter (Mt 16,13-20)'. *Bobolanum* 6 (1995), pp. 27-47.
Simonsen, Hejne, 'Dansk disputats om udtrykket "menneskesønnen"'. *SEÅ* 51–52 (1986–87), pp. 219-28 (practically identical with *Præsteforeningens Blad* 74 [1984], pp. 717-22).
Sjöberg, Erik, 'Känna 1 Henok och 4 Esra tanken på den lidande Människosonen?' *SEÅ* 5 (1940), pp. 163-83.
—, 'Frågan om den lidande Människosonen i 1 Henok'. *SEÅ* 7 (1942), pp. 141-44.
—, *Der Menschensohn im äthiopischen Henochbuch*. SHVL 41 (Lund: Gleerup, 1946).
—, 'Människosonen i judendom och urkristendom'. *Tjugoåttonde svenska läroverks läremötet i Stockholm 2-5 januari 1946 och dess förhandlinger* (1946), pp. 254-70.
—, 'Människosonen och Israel i Dan. 7'. *Religion och Bibel* 7 (1948), pp. 1-16.
—, 'Uttrycket "Människosonen" i Gamla Testamentet'. *STK* 26 (1950), pp. 35-44.
—, 'בן אדם und בר אנש im Hebräischen und Aramäischen'. *AcOr* 21 (1953), pp. 57-65, 91-107.
—, *Der verborgene Menschensohn in den Evangelien*. SHVL 53 (Lund: Gleerup, 1955).
Skibniewski, Stephan Leo Ritter Corvin von, *De bar nasha. Filio hominis* (Vienna: Méchitaristes, 1908).
Slater, Thomas B., '*Homoion huion anthropou* in Rev 1.13 and 14.14'. *BiTr* 44 (1993), pp. 359-60.
—, 'One Like a Son of Man in First-Century CE Judaism'. *NTS* 41 (1995), pp. 183-98.
—, 'Comparisons and the Son of Man'. *Bible Bhashyam* 24 (1998), pp. 67-78. Cf. *NTA* 43 (1998), 1214.
Smalley, Stephen S., 'The Johannine Son of Man Sayings'. *NTS* 15 (1968–69), pp. 278-301.
Smith, David, 'The Nickname "Son of Man"'. *ET* 18 (1906–1907), pp. 553-55.
Smith, Mahlon H., 'No Place for a Son of Man'. *Forum* 4 (1988), pp. 83-107.
—, 'To Judge the Son of Man: The Synoptic Sayings'. *Forum* 7 (1991), pp. 207-42.
Smith, Mark S., 'The "Son of Man" in Ugaritic'. *CBQ* 45 (1983), pp. 59-60.
Smyth, Kevin 'Heavenly Man and Son of Man in St Paul'. In *Studiorum Paulinorum Congressus Internationalis Catholicus 1961*. AnBib 17-18/1 (Rome: E. Pontificio instituto biblico, 1963), pp. 219-30.
Somerwell, R. 'The Son of Man'. *ET* 29 (1917–18), pp. 522-23.
Stalker, James, 'Son of Man, The'. *The International Standard Bible Encyclopaedia* V (1915, 2nd ed. 1925), cols. 2828-30.
Stanley, David, 'The Quest of the Son of Man'. *The Way* 8 (1968), pp. 3-17.
Stauffer, Ethelbert, 'Messias oder Menschensohn?' *NT* 1 (1956), pp. 81-102.
Stephenson, T., 'The Title "Son of Man"'. *ET* 29 (1917–18), pp. 377-78.
Stevens, B.A, 'Why "Must" the Son of Man Suffer? The Divine Warrior in the Gospel of Mark'. *BZ* NF 31 (1987), pp. 101-10.
Stott, Wilfrid, '"Son of Man"—A Title of Abasement'. *ET* 83 (1971–72), pp. 278-81.
Stowasser, Martin, 'Mk 13,26f und die urchristliche Rezeption des Menschensohns: Eine Anfrage an Anton Vögtle'. *BZ* NS 39 (1995), pp. 246-52.
Straton, Hillyer H., 'The Son-of-Man and the Messianic Secret'. *The Journal of Religious Thought* 24 (1967), pp. 31-49.

Stuckenbruck, Loren T., '"One like a Son of Man as the Ancient of Days" in the Old Greek Recension of Daniel 7,13: Scribal Error or Theological Translation?' *ZNW* 86 (1995), pp. 268-76. Greek: 'Ο υιός του ανθρώπου ως παλαιός των ημερών. Στο βιβλίο του Δανιήλ και την Αποκαλυψη του Ιωάννη'. *DBM* 15 (1996), pp. 8-14.

Sturch, R.L., 'The Replacement of "Son of Man" by a Pronoun'. *ET* 94 (1982–83), p. 333.

Sulzbach, Maria Furth, 'Who was Jesus? The Theology of the Son of Man'. *Religion in Life* 30 (1961), pp. 179-86.

Svedlund, Gerhard, 'Notes on *bar nash* and the Detrimental Effects of its Transformation into the Title "The Son of Man"'. In Tryggve Kronholm and Eva Riad (eds.), *On the Dignity of Man*. FS Frithiof Rundgren (= OrSuec 33-35 [1984–86]) (Stockholm: Almqvist & Wiksell, 1986), pp. 401-13.

Sæbø, Magne, 'Messias—Herrens tjener og menneskesønn'. In Thorleiv Austad and Øyvind M. Wee (eds.), *Hvem er Jesus?* (Oslo: Luther, 1984), pp. 19-30.

Taylor, Joan E., '*Ho huios tou antropou*, 'The Son of Man'. Some remarks on an androcentric convention of translation'. *The BiTr* 48 (1997), pp. 101-109.

Taylor, Vincent, 'The 'Son of Man' Sayings Relating to the Parousia'. *ET* 58 (1946–47), pp. 12-15. Reprint in idem, *New Testament Essays* (London: Epworth, 1970), pp. 119-26.

Teeple, Howard M., 'The Origin of the Son of Man Christology'. *JBL* 84 (1965), pp. 213-50.

Ternier, A., *Een eeuw filologisch onderzoek naar de term 'mensenzoon'*. Unpublished licentiate thesis (Leuven, 1991). Cf. Jean-Claude Loba Mkole, 'The Kiswahili mwana wa mtu and the Greek ho huios tou anthrópou'. In Gerald O. West and Musa W. Dube (eds.), *The Bible in Africa: Transactions, Trajectories and Trends* (Leiden: Brill, 2000), pp. 557-66.

Teutem, H.N. van, 'Van waar, dat Jezus zich bij Voorkeur den Zoon des Menschen neemde?' *Geloof en Vrijheid. Tweemaandelijksch Tidsschrift* 2 (1868), pp. 301-29.

Theisohn, Johannes, *Der auserwählte Richter. Untersuchungen zum traditionsgeschichtlichen Ort der Menschensohngestalt der Bilderreden des Äthiopischen Henoch* (SUNT 12; Göttingen: Vandenhoeck & Ruprecht, 1975).

Theobald, Michael, 'Gottessohn und Menschensohn. Zur polaren Struktur der Christologie im Markusevangelium'. SNTU/A 13 (Linz, 1988), pp. 37-79.

Thompson, G.H.P., 'The Son of Man: The Evidence of the Dead Sea Scrolls'. *ET* 72 (1960–61), p. 125.

—, 'The Son of Man—Some further Considerations'. *JThS* NS 12 (1961), pp. 203-209.

Thorion, Yochanan, 'אדם und בן אדם in den Qumrantexten'. *RdQ* 10 (1980), pp. 305-308.

Tidemann, J., 'De Zoon des Menschen'. *Waarheid in Liefde. Een godgeleerd Tijdsschrift, voor beschaafde Christenen, naar de Behoefte dezer Dagen* (1862), pp. 559-86.

Tijssen, H.H., 'De Zoon des Menschen'. *Geloof en Vrijheid. Tweemaandelijksch Tijdsschrift* 2 (1868), pp. 1-22.

Tillmann, Fritz, *Der Menschensohn. Jesu Selbstzeugnis für seine messianische Würde. Eine biblisch-theologische Untersuchung*. Biblische Studien 12,1-2 (Freiburg: Herder, 1907).

—, 'Hat die Selbstbezeichnung Jesu "der Menschensohn" ihre Wurzel in Dn 7,13?' *BZ* 5 (1907), pp. 35-47.

—, *Jesus, der Menschensohn.* Biblische Zeitfragen I, 11 (Münster in Westfalen: Altendorffschen Buchhandlung, 1908).

Tinsley, E.J., 'The Way of the Son of Man. The "Imitation of Christ" in the Gospel Tradition'. *Interp.* 7 (1953), pp. 418-25.

—, 'The Sign of the Son of Man'. *SJTh* 8 (1955), pp. 297-306.

Tödt, Heinz Eduard, *Der Menschensohn in der synoptischen Überlieferung* (Gütersloh: Mohn, 1959, 2. Aufl., 1963). English: *The Son of Man in the Synoptic Tradition.* Translated by Dorothea M. Barton (London: SCM Press/Philadelphia: Westminster Press, 1965).

Tödt, Ilse, 'Der "Menschensohn" und die Folgen'. In Christofer Frey and Wolfgang Huber (eds.), *Schöpferische Nachfolge.* FS Heinz Eduard Tödt. Texte und Materialien der Forschungsstätte der evangelischen Studiengemeinschaft Reihe A Nr. 5 (Heidelberg, 1978), pp. 541-61.

Toll, Christopher, 'Zur Bedeutung des aramäischen Ausdruckes *bar nas*'. In T. Kronholm and E. Riad (eds.), *On the Dignity of Man.* FS Frithiof Rundgren (= OrSuec 33-35 [1984–86]) (Stockholm: Almqvist & Wiksell, 1986), pp. 421-28.

—, 'The Meaning of the Aramaic Expression "Son of Man": An Addition to J.-C. Loba Mkole's "synthèse d'opinions philologiques"'. *JNSL* 23 (1997), pp. 225-26.

Torris, J., 'Le Fils de l'homme dans le Livre d'Henoch'. *Bulletin du Cercle Ernest Renan* 91, 92 (1962).

Tremel, Y.-B., 'Le Fils de l'homme selon saint Jean'. *Lumiere et Vie* 12 (1963), pp. 65-92.

Trenkle, Franz Sales, *Der Menschensohn. Eine exegetisch-kritische Untersuchung* (Freiburg, 1888).

Treves, Marco, 'Le Fils de l'homme et le pontificat de Judas'. *Cahiers du Cercle Ernest Renan* no. 112 (1979), pp. 147-51.

Troadec, H., 'Le Fils de l'homme est maître même du sabbat (Marc 2,23–3,6)', *BVC* 21 (1958), pp. 73-83.

Tuckett, Christopher M., 'Recent Work on the Son of Man'. *Scripture Bulletin* 12 (1981), pp. 14-18.

—, 'The Present Son of Man'. *JSNT* 14 (1982), pp. 58-81.

—, 'The Son of Man in Q'. In Marinus C. de Boer (ed.), *From Jesus to John: Essays on Jesus and New Testament Christology.* FS Marinus de Jonge. JSNTSup 84 (Sheffield: Sheffield Academic Press, 1993), pp. 196-215.

—, 'The Lukan Son of Man'. In C. Tuckett (ed.), *Luke's Literary Achievement.* JSNTSup 116 (Sheffield: Sheffield Academic Press, 1995), pp. 198-217.

—, 'Q 12,8: Once again "Son of Man" or "I"?'. In Jon A. Asgeirsson, Kristin de Troyer and Marvin W. Meyer (eds.), *From Quest to Q.* FS James M. Robinson. BEThL 146 (Leuven: Peeters/Leuven University Press, 2000), pp. 171-88.

—, 'The Son of Man and Daniel 7: Q and Jesus'. In A. Lindemann (ed.), *The Sayings source Q and the Historical Jesus.* BEThL 158 (Leuven: University Press-Peeters, 2001), pp. 371-94.

—, 'The Son of Man and Daniel 7: Inclusive Aspects of Early Christologies'. In Kieran J. O'Mahony (ed.), *Christian Origins: Worship, Belief and Society.* JSNTSup 241 (London: Sheffield Academic Press/Continuum, 2003), pp. 164-90.

Turnbull, Ralph G., *Profile of the Son of Man* (Grand Rapids: Baker Book House, 1969).

Tyler, W.S., 'The Son of Man'. *BS* 22 (1865), pp. 51-78.

Uemura, Shizuka, 'The Origin of the "Son of Man" as a Messianic Title: A Philological and Tradition-Historical Study'. *Annual of the Japanese Biblical Institute* 28 (2002), pp. 3-32.

Uloth, C.E.B., 'De beteeekenis van de uitdrukking "Zoon des menschen"'. *Godgeleerde Bijdragen* 36 (1862), pp. 467-87.

Ussing, Henry, *Menneskesønnens Liv paa Jorden* (København: Haase & Søn, 1936).

Usteri, Johann Martin, 'Die Selbstbezeichnung Jesu als des Menschen Sohn'. *Theologische Zeitschrift aus der Schweiz* 3 (1886), pp. 1-23.

Vaage, Leif E., 'The Son of Man Sayings in Q'. In John S. Kloppenborg and Leif E. Vaage (eds.), *Early Christianity, Q and Jesus.* Semeia 55 (Atlanta, GA: Scholars Press, 1992), pp. 103-29.

Valentine, C.H., 'The Son of Man Coming in the Clouds. Mark xiii.26; Matthew xxiv.30; Luke xxi.27'. *Theology* 23 (1931), pp. 14-21.

VanderKam, J.C.: 'Righteous One, Messiah, Chosen One, and Son of Man in Enoch 37–71'. In James H. Charlesworth (ed.), *The Messiah: Developments in Earliest Judaism and Christianity*. The First Princeton Symposium on Judaism and Christian Origins (Minneapolis: Fortress Press, 1992), pp. 169-91. Reprint in idem, *From Revelation to Canon: Studies in the Hebrew Bible and Second Temple Literature* (Boston/Leiden: Brill, 2002), pp. 413-38.

Vannutelli, Primo, *Il Figlio dell'Uomo. Studio sugli Evangeli* (Rome: Libreria di scienze e lettere, 1923).

—, '"Il Figlio dell'Uomo" (Critica ad una critica)'. *La Scuola Cattolica* (1925), pp. 456-60.

Vattioni, F., 'La prima menzione aramaica di "figlio dell' uomo"'. *Biblos-Press* 6 (1965), pp. 6-7.

Vermes, Geza, 'The Use of בר נשא/בר נש in Jewish Aramaic'. In Matthew Black (ed.), *An Aramaic Approach to the Gospels and Acts* (Oxford: Clarendon Press, 3rd ed. 1967) Appendix E, pp. 310-28. Reprint in idem, *Post-Biblical Jewish Studies*. SJLA 8 (Leiden: Brill, 1975), pp. 147-65.

—, 'The "Son of Man" Debate'. *JSNT* 1 (1978), pp. 19-32.

—, 'The Present State of the "Son of Man" Debate'. *JJS* 29 (1978), pp. 123-34. Reprint in idem, *Jesus and the World of Judaism* (London: SCM Press, 1983), pp. 89-99, 175-80.

Vielhauer, Philipp, 'Gottesreich und Menschensohn in der Verkündigung Jesu'. In W. Schneemelcher (ed.), *FS Günther Dehn* (Neukirchen–Vluyn: Erziehungsverein, 1957), pp. 51-79. Reprint in idem, *Aufsätze zum Neuen Testament*. ThB 31 (München: Kaiser, 1965), pp. 55-91.

—, 'Jesus und der Menschensohn. Zur Diskussion mit Heinz Eduard Tödt und Eduard Schweizer'. *ZThK* 60 (1963), pp. 133-77. Reprint in idem, *Aufsätze zum Neuen Testament* (1965), pp. 92-140.

Vignolo, R., see Pagazzi, G.C.

Viljoen, Francois P., 'Mark, the Gospel of the Suffering Son of Man: An Encouragement Directed to a Despondent Religious Minority in the City of Rome'. *In die Skriflig* 36 (2002), pp. 455-74.

Vögtle, Anton, 'Die Adam-Christus-Typologie und "der Menschensohn"'. *Trierer Theologische Zeitschrift* 60 (1951), pp. 309-28.

—, 'Menschensohn'. *Lexikon für Theologie und Kirche* VII (2. Aufl. 1962), pp. 297-300.

—, '"Der Menschensohn" und die paulinische Christologie'. *Studiorum Paulinorum Congressus Internationalis Catholicus 1961*. AnBib 17-18, 1 (Rome: E. Pontificio instituto biblico, 1963), pp. 199-218.
—, 'Bezeugt die Logienquelle die authentische Redeweise Jesu vom "Menschensohn"?' In Joël Delobel (ed.), *Logia. Les paroles de Jésus—The Sayings of Jesus*. Mémorial Joseph Coppens. BEThL 59 (Leuven: Peeters/Leuven University Press, 1982), pp. 77-99. Reprint in idem, *Offenbarungsgeschehen und Wirkungsgeschichte* (Freiburg: Herder, 1985), pp. 50-69.
—, 'Eine überholte "Menschensohn"-Hypothese?' In Kurt Aland and Siegfried Meurer (eds.), *Wissenschaft und Kirche*. FS Eduard Lohse. Texte und Arbeiten zur Bibel 4 (Luther-Verlag: Bielefeld, 1989), pp. 70-95.
—, *Die 'Gretchenfrage' des Menschensohnproblems. Bilanz und Perspektive*. Quaestiones Disputatae 152 (Freiburg: Herder, 1994).
Völter, Daniel, 'Der Menschensohn in Dan 7,13'. *ZNW* 3 (1902), pp. 173-74.
—, *Jesus der Menschensohn oder das Berufsbewusstsein Jesu* (Strassburg: Heitz, 1914).
—, 'Opmerkingen tot de Menschensohn-kvestie'. *NThT* 3 (1914), pp. 379-83.
—, 'Noch ein Wort über den Menschensohn. Neutestamentliche Streitfragen III'. *NThT* 4 (1915), pp. 143-47.
—, *Die Menschensohn-Frage neu untersucht* (Leiden: Brill, 1916).
—, 'Die Gesichte vom Adler und vom Menschen im 4. Esra nebst Bemerkungen über die Menschensohn-Stellen in den Bilderreden Henochs'. *NThT* 8 (1919), pp. 241-73.
Vogel, 'Der johanneische Menschensohn'. *Deutsch-amerikanische Zeitschrift für Theologie und Kirche* (It has not been possible to identify the article, the reference to 1904 being wrong in F. Tillmann, *Der Menschensohn* [1907], p. 108).
Vosté, J.M., 'The Title "Son of Man" in the Synoptic Gospels'. *The American Ecclesiastical Review* 120 (1949), pp. 310-26; 121 (1950), pp. 18-33.

Wagner, M., 'Der Menschensohn'. *NKZ* 36 (1925), pp. 245-78.
—, 'Der Menschensohn des 80. Psalms'. *ThStKr* 104 (1932), pp. 84-93.
Walck, Leslie, *The Son of Man in Matthew and the 'Similitudes of Enoch'*. Unpublished PhD dissertation (University of Notre Dame, 1999).
Walker, William O., 'The Kingdom of the Son of Man and the Kingdom of the Father in Matthew. An Exercise in *Redaktionsgeschichte*'. *CBQ* 30 (1968), pp. 573-79.
—, 'The Origin of the Son of Man Concept As Applied to Jesus'. *JBL* 91 (1972), pp. 482-90.
—, 'The Son of Man Question and the Synoptic Problem'. *NTS* 28 (1982), pp. 374-88. Reprint in William Reuben Farmer (ed.), *New Synoptic Studies* (Macon, GA: Mercer University Press, 1983), pp. 261-301.
—, 'The Son of Man: Some Recent Developments'. *CBQ* 45 (1983), pp. 584-607. Reprint in William Reuben Farmer (ed.), *New Synoptic Studies* (Macon, GA: Mercer University Press, 1983), pp. 261-301.
—, 'John 1:43-51 and "The Son of Man" in the Fourth Gospel'. *JSNT* 56 (1994), pp. 31-42.
Wansbrough, Henry, 'Jesus of Galilee: The Son of Man'. *Clergy Review* 60 (1975), pp. 760-66. Part of a series of articles in idem, 'Jesus of Galilee: Who Did he Think he Was?' *Clergy Review* 60 (1975), pp. 647-57, 760-66; 61 (1976), pp. 136-42.
Weiß, Hans-Friedrich, 'Menschensohn'. In *RGG*, IV (3rd ed. 1960), cols. 874-76.

Weist, Christoph, *Wer ist dieser Menschensohn? Die Geschichte der Exegese zum Menschensohn-Begriff.* Typewritten dissertation (Wien, 1972).

Wellhausen, Julius, 'Des Menschen Sohn'. In idem, *Skizzen und Vorarbeiten* VI (Berlin: Reimer, 1899), pp. 187-215.

Wifall, Walter, 'Son of Man—A Pre-Davidic Social Class?' *CBQ* 37 (1975), pp. 331-40.

Wilckens, Johann Christoph, 'Betrachtung über die im N.T. so gewöhnliche Benennung Christi des Menschen Sohn'. *Heßisches Heb-Opfer*. Theologischer und Philologischer Anmerckungen. 3. Band, 28. Stück (Gießen: Johann Philipp Krieger, 1741), pp. 696-715.

Wilckens, Ulrich, 'Christus, der "letzte Adam", und der Menschensohn. Theologische Überlegungen zum überlieferungsgeschichtlichen Problem der paulinischen Adam-Christus-Antithese'. In R. Pesch and R. Schnackenburg (eds.), *Jesus und der Menschensohn*. FS Anton Vögtle (Freiburg: Herder, 1975), pp. 387-403.

Willaert, B., 'Jezus, de Mensenzoon'. *Collationes Brugenses et Gandavenses* 5 (1959), pp. 515-36.

Willis, Clint (ed.), *Son of Man: Great Writing About Jesus Christ* (New York: Thunder Mouth Press, 2002).

Wilson, Frederick M., 'The Son of Man in Jewish Apocalyptic Literature'. *Studia biblica et theologica* 8 (1978), pp. 28-52.

Wilson, William E., 'The Coming of the Son of Man'. *The Modern Churchman* 36 (1946), pp. 56-66.

Winckler, Hugo, 'Des menschen sohn = erlöser'. In idem, *Altorientalische Forschungen* III,2 (Leipzig: Pfeiffer, 1904–1905), pp. 296-301.

Windisch, Hans, 'Angelophanien um den Menschensohn auf Erden. Ein Kommentar zu Joh 1,51'. *ZNW* 30 (1931), pp. 215-33.

Wink, Walter, '"The Son of the Man" in the Gospel of John'. In Robert T. Fortna and Tom Thatcher (eds.), *Jesus in Johannine Tradition* (Louisville: Westminster John Knox Press, 2001), pp. 117-23.

—, *The Human Being: Jesus and the Enigma of the Son of the Man* (Philadelphia: Fortress Press, 2002).

Winstanley, E.W., 'Days of the Son of Man'. *ET* 24 (1912–13), pp. 533-38.

Wogstad, M.D., 'Recent NT Research and the "Son of Man" in Mk 14:62 (par)'. *Shensüeh yü Chiaohui* 10,1 (1971–72), pp. XXII-XXXVII. Chinese: Chintai hsinyüeh Shengching chih T'anchiu chi Mak'e fuyin 14:62 chung chih 'Jentzu'. Op. cit. pp. 5-17 (*Bib.* 53 [1972] Elenchus 2729).

Wrede, William, 'Zum Thema "Menschensohn"'. *ZNW* 5 (1904), pp. 359-60.

Wright, G.F., 'The Term "Son of Man" as Used in the New Testament'. *The Bibliotheca Sacra* 44 (1887), pp. 575-601.

Xeravitz, Géza, 'Does the Figure of the "Son of Man" have a Place in the Eschatological Thinking of the Qumran Community?' *Louvain Studies* 26 (2001), pp. 334-45.

Young, Edward J., *Daniel's Vision of the Son of Man* (1958). Reprint in J.H. Skilton (ed.), *The Law and the Prophets*. FS Oswald Thompson Allis (Nutley, NJ: Presbyterian & Reformed Pub. Co., 1974), pp. 425-51.

Zalampis, M., 'The Relation of Eschatology to the Son of Man and the Kingdom of God'. *Review and Expositor* 53 (1956), pp. 326-31.

Zehrer, Franz, 'Jesus, der Menschensohn'. *Bibel und Liturgie* 47 (1974), pp. 165-76.

Zeller, D., 'Entrückung zur Ankunft als Menschensohn (Lk 13,34f; 11,29f)'. In *A cause de l'Evangile*. FS Jaques Dupont. LecDiv 123 (Paris: Éditions du Cerf, 1985), pp. 513-30.

Zenner, J.K., 'Der Menschensohn'. *Zeitschrift für katholische Theologie* 16 (1892), pp. 567-73.

Zorn, R.O., 'The Significance of Jesus' Selfdesignation, "the Son of Man"'. *Vox Reformata* 34 (1980), pp. 1-21.

Zuurmond, R., 'Vlees en bloed van de Mensenzoon: Opmerkingen bij Johannes 6:53'. *Amsterdamse Cahiers* 13 (1994), pp. 88-96.

C. *Other Secondary Literature*

Albright, William Foxwell, *From Stone Age to Christianity: Monotheism and the Historical Process* (Baltimore, 1940, 4th ed. 1946).

Allen, Willoughby C., *A Critical and Exegetical Commentary on the Gospel According to S. Matthew*. ICC (Edinburgh: T. & T. Clark, 1907, 3rd ed. 1912).

Allison, Dale, *Jesus of Nazareth: Millenarian Prophet* (Minneapolis: Fortress Press, 1998). See also under Davies, W.D.

Altaner, Berthold and Stuiber, Alfred, *Patrologie. Leben, Schriften und Lehre der Kirchenväter* (Freiburg: Herder, 7. Aufl., 1966).

Ammon, Christoph Friedrich von, *Die Geschichte des Lebens Jesu mit steter Rücksicht auf die vorhandenen Quellen dargestellt* I-III (Leipzig: Weidmann, 1842, 1844, 1847).

Andel, C.P. van, *De structuur van de Henoch-traditie en het Niuwe Testament*. STRT 2 (Utrecht, 1955).

Baird, William, *History of New Testament Research*. I. *From Deism to Tübingen* (Minneapolis: Fortress Press, 1992). II. *From Jonathan Edwards to Rudolf Bultmann* (Minneapolis: Fortress Press, 2003).

Bakel, H.A. van, 'De Carne Christi'. *NThT* 3 (1914), pp. 254-87.

Baldensperger, W., *Das Selbstbewusstsein Jesu im Lichte der messianischen Hoffnungen seiner Zeit* (Strassburg: Heitz & Mündel, 1888, 2. Aufl. 1892). 3rd ed. with the new title: *Die messianisch-apokalyptischen Hoffnungen des Judentums* (1903).

Balz, Horst Robert, *Methodische Probleme der neutestamentlichen Christologie*. WMANT 25 (Neukirchen–Vluyn: Neukirchener Verlag, 1967).

Bammel, Ernst, 'Matthäus 10,23'. *StTh* 15 (1961), pp. 79-92.

—, 'Erwägungen zur Eschatologie Jesu'. *SE* 2.2 = TU 88 (Berlin: Akademie-Verlag, 1964), pp. 3-32.

Bampfylde, G. 'The Similitudes of Enoch: Historical Allusions'. *JSJ* 15 (1984), pp. 9-31.

Barker, Margaret, *The Lost Prophet: The Book of Enoch and its Influence on Christianity* (Nashville: Abingdon Press, 1988).

Barrett, Charles Kingsley, 'The Background of Mark 10:45'. In A.J.B. Higgins (ed.), *New Testament Essays: Studies in Memory of T.W. Manson* (Manchester: Manchester University Press, 1959), pp. 1-18.

Barth, Karl, *Die Kirchliche Dogmatik*. III,2. *Die Lehre von der Schöpfung* (Zürich: Zollikon 1948) and IV,2. *Die Lehre von der Versöhnung* (1955). English: *Church Dogmatics*. III.2. *The Doctrine of Creation*. Translated by H. Knight et al.

(Edinburgh: T. & T. Clark, 1960). *Church Dogmatics* IV.2. *The Doctrine of Reconciliation*. Translated by G.W. Bromiley (Edinburgh: T. & T. Clark, 1958).

Bauer, Bruno, *Kritik der evangelischen Geschichte der Synoptiker* I-III (Leipzig: Wiegand, Braunschweig: Otto, 1841–42). Vol. III with the addition in the title: *und des Johannes*.

Bauer, Georg Lorenz, *Biblische Theologie des Neuen Testamentes* I-IV (Leipzig: Weygand, 1800–1802).

Bauer, Walter, *Die Briefe des Ignatius von Antiochia und der Polykarpbrief*. HNT 18 (Tübingen: Mohr [Siebeck], 1920).

Baumgärtner, W., 'Ein Vierteljahrhundert Danielforschung'. *ThR* 11 (1939), pp. 59-83, 125-44, 201-28.

Baur, Ferdinand Christian, *Das Christentum und die christliche Kirche der drei ersten Jahrhunderte* (Tübingen: Fues, 1853). English: *The Church History of the First Three Centuries*. Translated by Allan Menzies. 2 vols. Theological Translation Fund Library (3rd ed., London: Williams & Norgate, 1887).

—, *Vorlesungen über neutestamentliche Theologie*. Edited by F.F. Baur (Leipzig: Fues, 1864).

Beale, Gregory K., *The Use of Daniel in Jewish Apocalyptic Literature and in the Revelation of St. John* (University Press of America, 1984).

Beasley-Murray, G.R., 'The Interpretation of Daniel 7'. *CBQ* 45 (1983), pp. 44-58.

Beer, Georg, 'Das Buch Henoch'. In Emil Kautzsch (ed.), *Die Apokryphen und Pseudepigraphen des Alten Testaments* II (Tübingen: Mohr [Siebeck], 1900, 2nd ed. 1921), pp. 217-310.

Behrmann, Georg, *Das Buch Daniel*. Handkommentar zum Alten Testament III.3 (Göttingen: Vandenhoeck & Ruprecht, 1894).

Ben-Chorin, Schalom, *Bruder Jesus: Der Nazarener in jüdischer Sicht* (Munich: List, 1967).

Bengel, Johann Albrecht, *Gnomon Novi Testamenti in quo nativa verborum vi simplicitas, profunditas, concinnitas, salubritas sensum coelestium indicatur* (Tübingen: Schramm, 1742). English: *Gnomon of the New Testament*. Translated by J. Bandinel and A.R. Fausset. Edited by A.R. Fausset. 5 vols. (6th ed. Edinburgh: T. & T. Clark, 1866).

Bentzen, Aage, *Daniel*. HAT 19 (Tübingen: Mohr [Siebeck], 1937, 2nd ed. 1952).

— , *Det sakrale Kongedømme*. Bemærkninger i en løbende diskussion om de gammeltestamentlige Salmer. Festskrift udgivet af Københavns Universitet (København, 1945).

— , 'Kan ordet "Messsiansk" anvendes om Salmernes kongeforestillinger?' *SEÅ* 12 (1947), pp. 36-50.

—, 'King Ideology—"Urmensch"—"Troonsbestijgingsfeest". *StTh* 3 (1950–51), pp. 143-57.

Bernard, J.H., *A Critical and Exegetical Commentary on the Gospel According to St. John* I-II. Edited by A.H. McNeile. ICC (Edinburgh: T. & T. Clark, 1928).

Bertholdt, L., *Daniel aus dem Hebräisch-Aramäischen neu übersetzt und erklärt* I-II (Erlangen: Johann Jakob Palm, 1806–1808).

Beyschlag, Willibald, *Die Christologie des Neuen Testaments. Ein biblisch-theologischer Versuch* (Berlin: Rauh, 1866).

—, *Neutestamentliche Theologie oder Geschichtliche Darstellung der Lehren Jesu und des Urchristenthums nach den neutestamentlichen Quellen* I-II (Halle: Strien 1891). English: *New Testament Theology* I-II (Edinburgh: T. & T. Clark, 1894).

Beza, Theodor, ΤΗΣ ΚΑΙΝΗΣ ΔΙΑΘΗΚΗΣ ΑΠΑΝΤΑ. *Novum Iesu Christi Domini nostri Testamentum latine iam olim a veteri interprete nunc denuo a Theodore Beza versum: cum eiusdem annotationibus* (Zürich, 1559).

Birdsall, J. Neville, 'Problems of the Clementine Literature'. In J.D.G. Dunn (ed.), *Jews and Christians: The Parting of the Ways A.D. 70 to 135*. WUNT 66 (Tübingen: Mohr [Siebeck], 1992), pp. 347-61.

Black, Matthew, *An Aramaic Approach to the Gospels and Acts* (Oxford: Clarendon Press, 1946, 2nd ed. 1954, 3rd ed. 1967).

—, 'The Eschatology of the Similitudes of Enoch'. *JThS* NS 3 (1952), pp. 1-10.

—, 'The Messianism of the Parables of Enoch: Their Date and Contributions to Christological Origins.' In James H. Charlesworth (ed.), *The Messiah: Developments in Earliest Judaism and Christianity*. The First Princeton Symposium on Judaism and Christian Origins (Minneapolis: Fortress Press, 1992), pp. 145-68.

Bloch, Ernst, *Atheismus im Christentum. Zur Religion des Exodus und des Reichs*. Gesamtausgabe Band 14 (Frankfurt am Main: Suhrkamp, 1968). English: *Atheism in Christianity. The Religion of Exodus and the Kingdom* (New York: Herder & Herder, 1972).

Boers, Hendrikus, 'Where Christology is Real: A Survey of Recent Research on New Testament Christology'. *Interp.* 26 (1972), pp. 300-27.

Bolten, Johann Adrian, *Der Bericht des Matthäus von Jesu dem Messia. Uebersetzt und mit Anmerkungen begleitet* (Altona, 1792).

Boman, Thorleif, *Die Jesus-Überlieferung im Lichte der neueren Volkskunde* (Göttingen: Vandenhoeck & Ruprecht, 1967).

Borg, Marcus, *Jesus in Contemporary Scholarship* (Valley Forge, PA: Trinity, 1994).

Boring, M. Eugene, *Sayings of the Risen Jesus: Christian Prophecy in the Synoptic Gospels*. SNTSMS 46 (Cambridge: Cambridge University Press, 1982).

Bornhäuser, Karl, *Das Wirken des Christus durch Taten und Worte*. BFChTh 2/2 (Gütersloh: Bertelsmann, 1921).

Bornkamm, Günter, *Jesus von Nazareth*. Urban Taschenbücher 19 (Stuttgart: Kohlhammer, 1956, 7th ed. 1965). English: *Jesus from Nazareth* (New York: Harper & Row, 1960).

—, 'Der Auferstandene und der Irdische. Mt 28,16-20'. In E. Dinkler (ed.), *Zeit und Geschichte*. FS Rudolf Bultmann (Tübingen: Mohr [Siebeck], 1964), pp. 171-91.

Borsch, F.H., 'Mark XIV.62 and I Enoch LXII.5'. *NTS* 14 (1967–68), pp. 565-67.

Bousset, Wilhelm, *Jesu Predigt in ihrem Gegensatz zum Judentum. Ein religionsgeschichtlicher Vergleich* (Göttingen: Vandenhoeck & Ruprecht, 1892).

—, *Die jüdische Apokalyptik: Ihre religionsgeschichtlicher Herkunft und ihre Bedeutung für das neue Testament* (Berlin: Reuther & Richard, 1903).

—, *Die Religion des Judentums im neutestamentlicher Zeitalter* (Tübingen: Mohr [Siebeck], 1903, 2nd ed. 1906. 3rd ed. with the new title *Die Religion des Judentums im späthellenistischen Zeitalter*. Hg von Hugo Gressmann = HNT 21 (1926 = 4th ed. 1966).

—, *Was wissen wir von Jesus?* (Halle: Gebauer-Schwetschke 1904).

—, *Jesus*. RV I,1-3 (Tübingen: Mohr [Siebeck], 1904, 3rd ed. 1907).

—, 'R. Reitzenstein, Poimandres. Studien zur griech.-ägypt. und frühchristl. Literatur, 1904'. *GGA* 167 (1905), cols. 692-712.

—, *Die Offenbarung Johannis*. KEK XVI (Göttingen: Vandenhoeck & Ruprecht, 1906).

—, *Hauptprobleme der Gnosis*. FRLANT 10 (Göttingen: Vandenhoeck & Ruprecht, 1907).

—, *Kyrios Christos. Geschichte des Christusglaubens von den Anfängen des Christentums bis Irenäus*. FRLANT 21 (Göttingen: Vandenhoeck & Ruprecht, 1913, 2nd ed. 1921 [= 3rd ed. 1967]). English: *Kyrios Christos. A History of the Belief in Christ from the Beginnings of Christianity to Irenaeus*. Translated by John E. Stanley (New York: Abingdon Press, 1970).

—, *Jesus der Herr*. Nachträge und Auseinandersetzungen zu Kyrios Christos. FRLANT 25 (Göttingen: Vandenhoeck & Ruprecht, 1916).

Bowman, John Wick, *The Intention of Jesus* (London: SCM Press, 1945).

Box, G.H., 'IV Ezra'. In R.H. Charles (ed.), *The Apocrypha and Pseudepigrapha of the Old Testament* II (Oxford: Clarendon Press, 1913, 6th ed. 1969), pp. 542-624.

Brandenburg, Egon, *Adam und Christus. Exegetisch-religionsgeschichtliche Untersuchung zu Röm. 5,12-21* (1. Kor. 15). WMANT 7 (Neukirchen–Vluyn: Neukirchener Verlag, 1962).

Brandt, Wilhelm, *Die evangelische Geschichte und der Ursprung des Christenthums auf Grund einer Kritik der Berichte über das Leiden und die Auferstehung Jesu* (Leipzig: Reisland, 1893).

Braun, Herbert, *Jesus. Der Mann aus Nazareth und seine Zeit*. Themen der Theologie 1 (Stuttgart: Kreuz Verlag, 1969).

Brekelmans, C.H.W., 'The Saints of the Most High and their Kingdom'. *OTS* 14 (1965), pp. 305-29.

Broer, Ingo, 'Das Ringen der Gemeinde um Israel. Exegetischer Versuch über Mt 19,28'. In R. Pesch and R. Schnackenburg (eds.), *Jesus und der Menschensohn*. FS Anton Vögtle (Freiburg: Herder, 1975), pp. 148-65.

Brown, Raymond E., *Introduction to New Testament Christology* (New York: Paulist Press, 1994).

Brox, Norbert, 'Das messianische Selbstbewusstsein des historischen Jesus'. In Kurt Schubert (ed.), *Vom Messias zum Christus. Die Fülle der Zeit in religionsgeschichtlicher und theologischer Sicht* (Freiburg: Herder, 1964), pp. 165-201.

Bruce, Frederick F., 'The Oldest Greek Version of Daniel'. In H.A. Brongers et al. (eds.), *Instruction and Interpretation*. OTS 20 (Leiden: Brill, 1977), pp. 22-40.

Brun, Lyder, *Jesu Evangelium. En historisk fremstilling av Jesu forkyndelse* (Oslo: Aschehoug, 1917, 2nd ed. 1926).

Bucer, Martin, *In sacra quatuor Evangelia, Enarrationes perpetuæ* (Strasbourg: Hervag, 1553).

Buchanan, George Wesley, *To the Hebrews*. AB 36 (New York: Doubleday, 1972, 2nd ed. 1976).

Buhl, Frants, *De messianske Forjættelser i det gamle Testament* (København: Gyldendal, 1894).

—, 'Daniel, der Prophet'. *RE* 4 (3rd ed. 1898), pp. 445-57.

Bullinger, Heinrich, *In sacrosanctum Jesu Christi Domini nostril Euangelium secundum Matthaeum, commentariorum libri XII* (Zürich, 1542).

Bullock, C. Hassell, 'Ezekiel, Bridge Between the Testaments'. *JEThS* 25 (1982), pp. 23-31.

Bultmann, Rudolf, *Die Geschichte der synoptischen Tradition*. FRLANT 19 (Göttingen: Vandenhoeck & Ruprecht, 1921, 2nd ed. 1931 (= 6th ed. 1964). English: *The History of the Synoptic Tradition*. Translated by John Marsh (Revised ed., Peabody, MA: Hendrickson, 1963).

—, 'Die Bedeutung der neuerschlossenen mandäischen und manichäischen Quellen für das Verständnis des Johannesevangeliums'. *ZNW* 24 (1925), pp. 100-146. Reprint in idem, *Exegetica. Aufsätze zur Erforschung des Neuen Testaments*. Edited by Erich Dinkler (Tübingen: Mohr, 1967), pp. 55-104.

—, 'Zur Frage der Christologie'. *Zwischen den Zeiten* 5 (1927), pp. 41-69. Reprint in idem, *Glauben und Verstehen. Gesammelte Aufsätze* I (Tübingen: Mohr [Siebeck], 1933, 2nd ed. 1954), pp. 85-113.

—, *Das Evangelium des Johannes*. KEK II (Göttingen: Vandenhoeck & Ruprecht, 1941).

—, 'Die Frage nach der Echtheit von Mt 16,17-19'. *ThBl* 20 (1941), pp. 265-79. Reprint in idem, *Exegetica* (1967), pp. 255-77.

—, *Theologie des Neuen Testaments* (Tübingen: Mohr [Siebeck], 1948–53, 5th ed. 1965. English: *Theology of the New Testament* I-II. Translated by Kendrick Grobel (New York: Charles Scribner's Sons, 1951–55).

—, *Das Urchristentum im Rahmen der antiken Religionen* (Zürich: Artemis-Verlag, 1949). English: *Primitive Christianity in its Contemporary Setting*. Translated by R.H. Fuller (London: Thames & Hudson, 1956; in the Fontana Library, 1960).

Burkitt, Francis Crawford, *Jesus Christ: An Historical Outline* (London: Blackie & Son, 1932).

Burnier-Genton, Jean, *Le rêve subversif d'un sage: Daniel 7* (Geneva: Labor et fides, 1993).

Cadoux, Cecil John, *The Historic Mission of Jesus: A Constructive Re-examination of the Eschatological Teaching in the Synoptic Gospels*. Lutterworth Library 12 (London: Lutterworth, 1941).

Caird, G.B., *New Testament Theology*. Completed and edited by L.D. Hurst (Oxford: Clarendon Press, 1994, paperback edition, 1995).

Cajetan, Jakob de Vio (Dominican name: Thomas), *Evangelia cum commentario in quatuor Evangelia et Acta Apostolorum* (1530).

Calov(ius), Abraham, *Biblia illustrata Novi Testamenti simul Hugonis Grotii annotationes in libros N.T.* I-II (Dresden-Leipzig: Zimmermann, 1676).

Calvin, Johannes, *Institutio christianæ religionis* (Geneve, 1536, 8th ed. 1559). Reprint in Peter Barth (ed.), *Joannis Calvini Opera Selecta* I-III (München: Kaiser, 1926–28).

—, *In Evangelium secundum Ioannem Commentarius* (Geneve, 1553). Reprint in idem, *Harmonia ex tribus Euangelistis composita, Matthæo, Marco, & Luca: adjuncto seorsum Iohanne, quod pauca cum aliis communia habet* (Geneve, 1555, 2nd ed. 1560).

—, *Praelectiones in librum propheticarum Danielis* (Geneve, 1561, 2nd ed. 1571).

Camerarius, Joachim, *Notatio figurarum sermonis in libris quatuor evangeliorum, et indicata verborum significatio, et orationis sententia, ad illorum scriptorum intelligentiam certiorem studio* (Leipzig: Andreas Schneider, 1572).

Cappel(lus), Jaques., *Observationes in Novum Testamentum, exceptis Actibus Apostolorum et Apocalypsi D. Ioannis* (edited by Ludwig Cappel, Amsterdam, 1657).

Carpenter, J. Enslin, *The First Three Gospels*. Their Origin and Relations (Boston: American Unitarian Association, 1890, 4th ed. 1906).

Case, Shirley Jackson, *Jesus: A New Biography* (Chicago: University of Chicago Press, 1927).

—, 'The Alleged Messianic Consciousness of Jesus'. *JBL* 46 (1927), pp. 1-19.

Casey, P. Maurice, 'Porphyry and the Origin of the Book of Daniel'. *JThS* NS 27 (1976), pp. 15-33.

—, 'Culture and Historicity: the Plucking of the Grain (Mark 2.23-28)'. *NTS* 34 (1988), pp. 1-23.

—, 'Porphyry and Syrian Exegesis of the Book of Daniel'. *ZNW* 81 (1990), pp. 139-42.

—, *From Jewish Prophet to Gentile God: The Origins and Development of New Testament Christology* (Cambridge: James Clarke & Co., 1991).

—, *Aramaic Sources of Mark's Gospel*. SNTSMS 102 (Cambridge: Cambridge University Press, 1998).

Casey, R.P., 'The Earliest Christologies'. *JThS* NS 9 (1958), pp. 253-77.

Catchpole, D.R., 'The Answer of Jesus to Caiaphas'. *NTS* 17 (1970–71), pp. 213-26.

Cellarius, Christoph, *Exercitii oratorii de humana Christi natura contra haereticos quosvis defenda* (1680). Reprint in idem, *Programmata varii argumenti oratoriis exercitiis in citicensi Lyceo praemissa* (Leipzig, 1689), pp. 128-36.

Ceroke, C.P., 'Is Mk 2,10 a Saying of Jesus?' *CBQ* 22 (1960), pp. 369-90.

Charles, Robert Henry, 'Messianic Doctrine of the Book of Enoch, and its Influence on the New Testament'. *ET* 4 (1892–93), pp. 301-303.

—, *The Book of Enoch* (Oxford: Clarendon Press, 1893).

—, 'Book of Enoch'. In R.H. Charles (ed.), *The Apocrypha and Pseudepigrapha of the Old Testament* II (Oxford: Clarendon Press, 1913, 6th ed. 1969), pp. 163-277.

—, *A Critical and Exegetical Commentary on the Revelation of St. John* I-II. ICC (Edinburgh: T. & T. Clark, 1920).

—, *A Critical and Exegetical Commentary on the Book of Daniel* (Oxford: Oxford University Press, 1929).

Charlesworth, J.H., 'Seminar Report. The SNTS Pseudepigrapha Seminars at Tübingen and Paris on the Books of Enoch'. *NTS* 25 (1979), pp. 315-23.

—, *Jesus Within Judaism: A New Light from Exciting Archaelogicial Discoveries* (New York: Doubleday, 1988).

Chemnitz, Martin, *Harmoniae evangelistae* I-III. Edited by Polycarpo Lyserum (Frankfurt, 1593, new ed. 1615).

Chibici-Revneanu, Nicole, 'Ein himmlischer Stehplatz: Die Haltung Jesu in der Stephanusvision (Apg 7.55-56) und ihre Bedeutung'. *NTS* 53 (2007), pp. 459-88.

Christensen, Torben, *The Divine Order. A Study in F.D. Maurice's Theology*. AThD 11 (Leiden: Brill, 1973). Translation from Danish: *Logos og Inkarnation. En Studie i F.D. Maurice's Teologi* (København: I kommission hos Bethesdas Boghandel, 1954).

Clemen, Carl, *Religionsgeschichtliche Erklärung des Neuen Testaments. Die Abhängigkeit des ältesten Christentums von nichtjüdischen Religionen und philoso phischen Systemen* (Gießen: Töpelmann, 1909).

Cocceius, Johannes, *Observationes ad Danielem* (1666). Reprint in idem, *Opera omnia theologica, exegetica, didactica, polemica, philologica* I-VIII (Amsterdam, 1675, 2nd ed. 1689), III.

—, *Scholia in Evangelium secundam Matthaeum*. Reprint in idem, *Opera omnia theologica, exegetica, didactica, polemica, philologica* I-VIII (Amsterdam, 1675, 2nd ed. 1689), IV, pp. 3-43.

Cölln, Daniel Georg Conrad von, *Biblische Theologie* I-II. Mit einer Nachricht über des Verfassers Leben und Wirken. Edited by D. Schulz (Leipzig: Barth, 1836).

Colani, Timothée, *Jésus-Christ et les croyances messianiques de son temps* (Strasburg: Treuttel & Wurz, 1864). Swedish: *Jesus Christus och de messianska troslärorna på hans tid* (Stockholm: Häggströms Förlag, 1865).

Collins, Adela Yarbro, 'Daniel 7 and Jesus'. *Journal of Theology* 93 (1989), pp. 5-19.

—, 'Daniel 7 and the Historical Jesus'. In H.W. Attridge, J.J. Collins and T.H. Tobin (eds.), *Of Scribes and Scrolls*. FS John Strugnell (Lanham, MD: University Press of America, 1990), pp. 181-93.

—, 'The Influence of Daniel on the New Testament'. In John J. Collins, *Daniel*. Hermeneia (Minneapolis: Fortress Press, 1993).

Collins, John J., *The Apocalyptic Vision of the Book of Daniel*. HSM 16 (Missoula, MT: Scholars Press, 1977), pp. 90-123.

—, *The Apocalyptic Imagination. An Introduction to Jewish Apocalyptic Literature*. The Biblical Resource Series (1984, 2nd ed. Grand Rapids: Eerdmans, 1998).

—, *Daniel*. Hermeneia (Minneapolis: Fortress Press, 1993).

—, 'The *Son of God* Text from Qumran'. In M. de Boer (ed.), *From Jesus to John: Essays on Jesus and New Testament Christology*. FS M. de Jonge (1993), pp. 65-82; a later version in idem, *The Scepter and the Star: The Messiahs of the Dead Sea Scrolls and Other Ancient Literature* (1995), pp. 154-72.

—, 'Jesus and the Messiahs of Israel'. Hubert Cancik, Hermann Lichtenberger and Peter Schäfer (eds.), *Geschichte—Tradition—Reflexion. Band III. Frühes Christentum*. FS Martin Hengel zum 70. Geburtstag (Tübingen: Mohr [Siebeck] 1996), pp. 287-302.

Colpe, Carsten, *Die religionsgeschichtliche Schule. Darstellung und Kritik ihres Bildes vom gnostischen Erlösermythus*. FRLANT 78 (Göttingen: Vandenhoeck & Ruprecht, 1961).

—, 'New Testament and Gnostic Christology'. In Jacob Neusner (ed.), *Religions in Antiquity: Essays in Memory of E.R. Goodenough*. Studies in the History of Religion 14 (Leiden: Brill, 1968), pp. 227-43.

—, 'Der Spruch von der Lästerung des Geistes'. In Eduard Lohse (ed.), *Der Ruf Jesu und die Antwort der Gemeinde*. FS Joachim Jeremias (Göttingen: Vandenhoeck & Ruprecht, 1970), pp. 63-79. Photographic reprint in idem, *Kleine Schriften*. Dritter Band. Abteilung E. Menschensohn und Gottessohn, ed. by Christoph Elsas and Christiane Nasse (Berlin: Universitätsbibliothek der Freien Universität, 1996), pp. 184-200.

—, 'Traditionsüberschreitende Argumentationen zu Aussagen Jesu über sich selbst'. In Gert Jeremias, Heinz-Wolfgang Kuhn and Hartmut Stegemann (eds.), *Tradition und Glaube*. FS K.G. Kuhn (Göttingen: Vandenhoeck & Ruprecht, 1971), pp. 230-45. Photographic reprint in idem, *Kleine Schriften*. Dritter Band, pp. 201-16.

—, 'Gottessohn'. *RAC* XII (1983), pp. 19-58. Photographic reprint in idem, *Kleine Schriften*. Dritter Band, pp. 243-62.

Cone, Orello, 'Jesus' Self-Designation in the Synoptic Gospels'. *The New World* 2 (1893), pp. 492-518.

Conzelmann, Hans, 'Gegenwart und Zukunft in der synoptischen Tradition. *ZThK* 54 (1957), pp. 277-96. Reprint in idem, *Theologie als Schriftauslegung. Aufsätze zum Neuen Testament*. BETh 65 (München: Kaiser, 1974), pp. 42-61.

—, 'Jesus Christus'. In *RGG*, III (3rd ed. Tübingen: Mohr [Siebeck], 1959), cols. 619-53. English: *Jesus*. Translated by J. Raymond Lord (Philadelphia. Fortress Press, 1973).

—, 'Jesu självmedvetande'. *SEÅ* 28-29 (1963–64), pp. 39-53. German: 'Das Selbstbewusstsein Jesu'. In idem, *Theologie als Schriftauslegung*, pp. 30-41.
—, *Grundriss der Theologie des Neuen Testaments* (München: Kaiser, 1967). English: *An Outline of the New Testament Theology* (London: SCM Press, 1969).
Coppens, Joseph, 'Le chapitre VII de Daniel'. *EThL* 39 (1963), pp. 87-94.
—, 'Les Saints du Très-haut sont-ils a identifier avec les Milices célestes?' *EThL* 39 (1963), pp. 94-100.
—, 'Les saints dans le Psautier'. *EThL* 39 (1963), pp. 485-500. Reprint in idem, BEThL 61 (1983), pp. 78-93.
—, 'Un nouvel essai d'interpréter Dan., VII'. *EThL* 45 (1969), pp. 122-25.
—, 'Daniel VII, un rituel d'intronisation?' *EThL* 46 (1970), pp. 112-16.
—, 'La Vision du Très-Haut en Dan., VII et Hén. éthiop. XIV'. *EThL* 53 (1977), pp. 187-89.
—, 'Le chapitre VII de Daniel. Lecture et commentaire'. *EThL* 54 (1978), pp. 301-22. Reprint in idem, BEThL 61 (1983), pp. 28-49.
Cornelius a Lapide, *Commentarius in quatuor evangelia* I-II (Antwerpen: Jacob Meursium, 1639).
Creed, J.M., 'The Heavenly Man'. *JThS* 26 (1925), pp. 113-36.
Cross, Frank M., *The Canaanite Myth and Hebrew Epic: Essays in the History of Religion of Israel* (Cambridge, MA: Harvard University Press, 1973).
Cullmann, Oscar, *Die Christologie des Neuen Testaments* (Tübingen: Mohr [Siebeck], 1957, 3rd ed. 1963). English: *The Christology of the New Testament*. Translated by Shirley C. Guthrie and Charles A.M. Hall (London: SCM Press; Philadelphia: Westminster Press, 1959).
Curtis, W.A., *Jesus Christ the Teacher: A Study of His Method and Message Based on the Earliest Gospels* (New York: Oxford University Press, 1943, 3rd ed. 1945).

Dalman, Gustav, *Die Worte Jesu mit Berücksichtigung des nachkanonischen jüdischen Schrifttums und der aramäischen Sprache* I. *Einleitung und wichtige Begriffe* (Leipzig: Hinrichs 1898, 2nd ed. 1930 (= 3rd ed. Darmstadt: Wissenschaftliche Buchgesellschaft, 1965). English: *The Words of Jesus. Considered in the Light of Post-Biblical Jewish Writings and the Aramaic Language.* I. *Introduction and Fundamental Ideas* (Edinburgh: T. & T. Clark, 1902).
Davidsen, Ole, *The Narrative Jesus: A Semiotic Reading of Mark's Gospel* (Århus: Aarhus University Press, 1993).
Davies, W.D., *Paul and Rabbinic Judaism: Some Rabbinic Elements in Pauline Theology* (London: SPCK, 1948).
Davies, W.D., and Allison, Dale, *The Gospel According to Saint Matthew* II. ICC (Edinburgh: T. & T. Clark, 1991).
Day, John, *God's Conflict with the Dragon and the Sea: Echoes of a Canaanite Myth in the Old Testament*. University of Cambridge Oriental Studies 35 (Cambridge: Cambridge University Press, 1985).
Delcor, M., 'Les sources du chapitre VII de Daniel'. *VT* 18 (1968), pp. 290-312.
Delitzsch, Franz, *Commentar über den Psalter* I (Leipzig: Dörffling & Franke, 1859).
Dequeker, L., 'Daniel VII et les Saints de Très-Haut'. *EThL* 36 (1960), pp. 353-92 (= *ALBO* III.23 [1961], pp. 15-54).
—, 'The "Saints of the Most High" in Qumran and Daniel'. *OTS* 18 (1973), pp. 108-87.

Dexinger, Ferdinand, *Das Buch Daniel und seine Probleme*. SBS 36 (Stuttgart: Katholisches Bibelwerk, 1969).

Dibelius, Martin, *Jesus*. SG 1130 (Berlin: De Gruyter 1939, 2nd ed. 1949, 3rd ed. mit einem Nachtrag von W.G. Kümmel, 1960).

Díez Macho, A., 'L'usage de la troisième personne au lieu de la première dans le Targum'. In P. Casetti et al. (eds.), *Mélanges Dominique Barthélemy* (Göttingen: Vandenhoeck & Ruprecht, 1981), pp. 61-89.

Dillmann, August, *Das Buch Henoch* (Leipzig: Vogel, 1853).

Dodd, Charles Harold, *According to the Scriptures. The Substructure of New Testament Theology* (London: Nisbet, 1952).

—, *The Interpretation of the Fourth Gospel* (Cambridge: Cambridge University Press, 1953).

—, *The Founder of Christianity* (London: Collins, 1971).

Drachmann, Anders Bjørn, 'Messiasproblemet'. *Tilskueren* 1908. Reprint in idem, *Udvalgte Afhandlinger* (Kjøbenhavn/Kristiania: Gyldendalske Boghandel, 1911), pp. 108-23.

Drummond, James, *The Jewish Messia:. A Critical History of the Messianic Idea among the Jews from the Rise of the Maccabees to the Closing of the Talmud* (London: Longmans, Green, 1877).

Dumbrell, W.J., 'Daniel 7 and the Function of Old Testament Apocalyptic'. *RThR* 34 (1975), pp. 16-23.

Dunn, James D.G., *Christology in the Making: An Inquiry into the Origins of the Doctrine of the Incarnation* (London: SCM Press, 1980, 2nd ed. 1985).

—, 'Messianic Ideas and Their Influence on the Jesus of History'. In James H. Charlesworth (ed.), *The Messiah: Developments in Earliest Judaism and Christianity*. The First Princeton Symposium on Judaism and Christian Origins (Minneapolis: Fortress Press, 1992), pp. 365-81.

—, *Jesus Remembered*. Christianity in the Making 1 (Grand Rapids-Cambridge, UK: Eerdmans, 2003).

Duplacy, J. 'Marc, 2,10, Note de syntaxe'. In *Mélanges bibliques*. FS A. Robert. Travaux de l'Institut catholique de Paris 4 (Paris: Bloud & Gray, 1957), pp. 420-27.

Dupont, Jaques, 'Le logion des douze trones (Mt 19,28: Lc 22,28-30)'. *Bib.* 45 (1964), pp. 355-92.

Edwards, R.A., 'The Eschatological Correlative as a *Gattung* in the New Testament'. *ZNW* 60 (1969), pp. 9-20.

Eggler, J., *Influences and Traditions Underlying the Vision of Daniel 7:2-14: The Research History from the End of the 19th Century to the Present*. OBO 177 (Freiburg, Schweiz-Göttingen: Universitätsverlag, 2000).

Engnell, Ivan, 'Adam. 1 *G.T.*' In *SBU*, I (1948), cols. 13-15, 2nd ed. (1962), cols. 18-21.

—, 'Die Urmenschvorstellung und das Alte Testament'. *SEÅ* 22-23 (1957–58), pp. 265-89.

Episcopius, Simon, 'Notae breves in xxiv. priora capita Matthaei'. In idem, *Opera theologica* II (Amsterdam: Blaev, 1650).

Erasmus, Desiderius, *Annotationes Novi Testamenti* (1516, 2nd ed. 1535) = Facsimile-reprint: Anne Reeve (ed.), *Erasmus' Annotations on the New Testament: The Gospels* (London: Duckworth, 1986).

Evans, Craig A., 'Defeating Satan and Liberating Israel: Jesus and Daniel's Visions'. *Journal for the Study of the Historical Jesus* 1 (2003), pp. 161-70.

Fatum, Lone, 'Jesu "selvbevidsthed" og kristologien'. *DTT* 30 (1967), pp. 147-82.
Feine, Paul, *Theologie des Neuen Testaments* (Leipzig: Hinrichs, 1910, 2nd ed. 1911, 8th ed. by Kurt Aland, 1948). Reprint Berlin: Evangelische Verlagsanstalt, 1953.
Ferch, Arthur J., 'Daniel 7 and Ugarit: A Reconsideration'. *JBL* 99 (1980), pp. 75-86.
—, 'Porphyry: An Heir to Christian Exegesis?' *ZNW* 73 (1982), pp. 141-47.
Feuillet, A., 'Les origines et la signification de Mt 10,23b. Contribution a l'étude du probleme eschatologique'. *CBQ* 23 (1961), pp. 182-98.
Fitzmyer, Joseph A., 'Further Light on Melchizedek from Qumran Cave 11'. *JBL* 86 (1967), pp. 301-26.
Flacius, Matthias, *Clavis Scripturæ s. seu Sermone Sacrarum Literarum* (Basle: Quecum 1567, 2nd ed. 1609).
Fletcher-Louis, Crispin H.T., 'The High Priest as Divine Mediator in the Hebrew Bible: Dan 7:13 as a Test Case'. In *SBL 1997 Seminar Papers* (Atlanta, GA: Scholars Press, 1997), pp. 161-93.
Ford, Joan Massingberd, 'The Epithet "Man" for God'. *IThQ* 38 (1971), pp. 72-76.
France, R.T., *Jesus and the Old Testament: His Application of Old Testament Passages to Himself and His Mission* (Grand Rapids: Baker, 1971).
Fridrichsen, Anton, *Vem ville Jesus vara? Kristustrons historiska grundval enligt nutida bibelforskning*. Studentföreningens Verdandis Småskrifter 346 (Stockholm: Bonniers, 1931).
Friedrich, Gerhard, 'Ein Tauflied hellenistischer Judenchristen'. *ThZ* 21 (1965), pp. 502-16.
Fritzsche, Carl Friedrich August, *Evangelium Matthaei*. Quatuor N.T. Evangelia I (Leipzig: Fleischer, 1826).
Fuchs, Ernst, 'Jesus und der Glaube'. *ZThK* 55 (1958), pp. 170-85. Reprint in idem, *Zur Frage nach dem historischen Jesus*. Gesammelte Aufsätze II (Tübingen: Mohr [Siebeck], 1960, 2nd ed. 1965), pp. 238-57.
Fuller, Reginald H., *The Mission and Achievement of Jesus: An Examination of the Presuppositions of New Testament Theology*. SBTh 12 (London: SCM Press, 1954, 6th ed. 1970).
—, 'The Clue to Jesus' Self-understanding'. *SE* 2.2 = TU 88 (Berlin: Akademie Verlag, 1964), pp. 58-66.
—, *The Foundations of New Testament Christology* (London: Lutterworth, 1965).
Funk, Robert W., *Honest to Jesus: Jesus for a New Millenium* (San Francisco: Harper, 1996).

Gall, August Freiherrn von, ΒΑΣΙΛΕΙΑ ΤΟΥ ΘΕΟΥ. *Eine religionsgeschichtliche Studie zur vorkirchlichen Eschatologie*. Religionswissenschaftliche Bibliothek 7 (Heidelberg: Winter, 1926).
Gaston, Lloyd, *No Stone on Another: Studies in the Significance of the Fall of Jerusalem in the Synoptic Gospels*. NTSupp 23 (Leiden: Brill, 1970).
Gataker, Thomas, *De novi instrumenti stylo dissertatio* (London, 1648).
Génébrard, Gilbert, *De s. Trinitate libri tres contra huius ævi Trinitarios, Antitrinitarios, & Autotheanos* (Paris 1569, 2nd ed. 1585).

Gerhard, Johann, *Loci [communes] theologici, cum pro astruenda veritate tum pro destruenda quorumvis contradicentium falsitate per theses nervose solide et copiose explicati* I-IX (Jena, 1610–22).

Glassius, Salomo, *Philologia sacra, qua totius ss. Veteris et Novi Testamenti scripturae tum stylo et literature, tum sensus et genuinae interpretationis ratio et doctrina libris quinque expenditure ac traditur* (1623–36; later edition by Gottfred Olearius; Leipzig, 1705).

Glasson, T. Francis, *The Second Advent*: *The Origin of the New Testament Doctrine* (London: Epworth, 1945, 2nd ed. 1947).

—, 'Mark xiii and the Greek Old Testament'. *ET* 69 (1957–58), pp. 213-15.

—, 'The Reply to Caiaphas (Mark XIV.62)'. *NTS* 7 (1960–61), pp. 88-93.

Gnilka, Joachim, *Theologie des Neuen Testaments*. HThKNT Supplementsband 5 (Freiburg: Herder, 1994).

Goguel, Maurice, *Jésus* (Paris: Payot, 1932, 2nd ed. 1950).

Goppelt, Leonhard, *Typos. Die typologische Deutung des Alten Testament im Neuen*. BFChTh 2 Reihe Band 43 (Gütersloh: Bertelsmann, 1939; reprint Darmstadt: Wissenschaftliche Buchgesellschaft, 1973).

—, *Theologie des Neuen Testaments* 1-2. Edited by Jürgen Roloff (Göttingen: Vandenhoeck & Ruprecht, 1976). English: *Theology of the New Testament* I-II. Translated by John E. Alsup (Grand Rapids: Eerdmans, 1981–82).

Goulder, Michael D., *Midrash and Lection in Matthew* (London: SPCK, 1974, 2nd ed. 1977).

Grau, Rudolf Friedrich, *Das Selbstbewußtsein Jesu* (Nördlingen: Beck, 1887).

Greensfield, J.C., and Stone, M.E., 'The Enochic Pentateuch and the Date of the Similitudes'. *HThR* 70 (1977), pp. 51-65.

Grelot, Pierre, 'Le Messie dans les Apocryphes de l'Ancien Testament. État de la question'. In Édourd Massaux (ed.), *La Venue du Messie. Messianisme et Eschatologie*. RechBib 6 (Bruges, 1962), pp. 19-50.

Gressmann, Hugo, *Der Ursprung der israelitisch-jüdischen Eschatologie*. FRLANT 6 (Göttingen: Vandenhoeck & Ruprecht, 1905).

—, 'Das religionsgeschichtliche Problem des ursprungs der hellenistischen Erlösungsreli gion. Eine kritische Auseinandersetzung mit Reitzenstein II'. *ZKG* 41 NF 4 (1922), pp. 154-80.

—, *Der Messias*. FRLANT 43 (Göttingen: Vandenhoeck & Ruprecht, 1929).

Grotius, Hugo, *Annotationes in libros evangeliorum* (Amsterdam: Cornelius Blaev, 1641).

—, *Annotationes ad Vetus Testamentum* II (Amsterdam: Cornelius Blaev, 1644).

Grundtvig, Nikolai Frederik Severin, *Om den sande Christendom og Om Christendommens Sandhed* (2nd ed. København: Schønberg, 1865; originally in *Theologisk Maanedsskrift* 4–9 [1826–27]).

Gunkel, Hermann, *Schöpfung und Chaos in Urzeit und Endzeit. Eine religionsgeschichtliche Untersuchung über Gen 1 und Ap Joh 12* (Göttingen: Vandenhoeck & Ruprecht, 1895).

—, 'Aus Wellhausen's neuesten apokalyptischen Forschungen. Einige principielle Erörterungen'. *ZWTh* 42 NF 7 (1899), pp. 581-611. Reprint in Klaus Koch and Johann Michael Schmidt (eds.), *Apokalyptik*. WdF 365 (Darmstadt: Wissenschaftliche Buchge sellschaft, 1982), pp. 67-90.

—, 'Das vierte Buch Esra'. In Emil Kautzsch, *Die Apokryphen und Pseudepigraphen des Alten Testaments* II (Tübingen: Mohr [Siebeck], 1900, 2nd ed. 1921), pp. 331-401.

Hackspann, Theodor, *Notarum philologico-theologicarum in varia et difficilia scripturæ loca* I-III (Altdorf: Hagen, 1664).
Hävernick, Heinrich Andreas Christoph, *Commentar über das Buch Daniel* (Hamburg: Perthes, 1832).
Hahn, Ferdinand, *Christologische Hoheitstitel. Ihre Geschichte im frühen Christentum*. FRLANT 83 (Göttingen: Vandenhoeck & Ruprecht, 1963, 3rd ed. 1966). English: *The Titles of Jesus in Christology*. Translated by Harold Knight and George Ogg (London: Lutterworth, 1969).
Haller, Max, 'Das Alter vom Daniel 7'. *ThStKr* 93 (1920–21), pp. 83-87.
Hammershaimb, Erling, 'Første Enoksbog'. In E. Hammershaimb, Johannes Munck, Bent Noack and Paul Seidelin (eds.), *De gammeltestamentlige Pseudepigrafer i oversættelse med indledning og noter* I (København: Gads Forlag, 1953–63), pp. 69-174.
Hampel, Volker, '"Ihr werdet mit den Städten Israels nicht zu Ende kommen". Eine exegetische Studie über Matthäus 10,23'. *ThZ* 45 (1989), pp. 1-31.
Hanhart, Robert, 'Die Heiligen des Höchsten'. In B. Hartmann (ed.), *Hebräische Wortforschung*. FS Walter Baumgartner. VT.S 16 (Leiden: Brill, 1967), pp. 90-101.
Hansen, P.O. Ryberg, see Ryberg Hansen, P.O.
Hardouin, Jean, *Commentarius in Novum Testamentum* (Amsterdam: Sauzet, 1741).
Harnack, Adolf von, *Das Wesen des Christentums* (Leipzig: Heinrichs, 1900 and many later editions).
—, *Marcion. Das Evangelium vom fremden Gott* (2. Aufl. Leipzig: J.C. Hinrichs, 1924 = 3. Ausg. Darmstadt: Wissenschaftliche Buchgesellschaft, 1960).
Harris, Horton, *The Tübingen School* (Oxford: Clarendon Press, 1975).
Hartman, L.F., and Di Lella, A.A., *The Book of Daniel*. AB 23 (New York: Doubleday, 1978).
Hase, Karl von, *Das Leben Jesu*. Theologisch akademische Lehrschriften 1 (Leipzig: Breitkopf & Härtel, 1829, 3rd ed. 1840). English: *Life of Jesus: A Manual for Academic Study*. Translated by James Freeman Clarke (Boston: Walker, Wise & Co., 1860).
—, *Geschichte Jesu*. Nach akademische Vorlesungen (Leipzig: Breitkopf & Härtel 1876).
Hasel, G.F., 'The Identity of "The Saints of the Most High" in Daniel 7'. *Bib.* 56 (1975), pp. 173-92.
Hasler, Viktor, 'Jesu Selbstzeugnis und das Bekenntnis des Stephanus vor dem hohem Rat. Beobachtungen zur Christologie des Lukas'. *SThU* 36 (1969), pp. 36-47.
Hegel, Georg Friedrich Wilhelm, 'Der Geist des Christentums und sein Schicksal' [1798–99]. H. Nohl (ed.), *Hegels theologische Jugendschriften* (Tübingen, 1907, 2nd ed. Frankfurt am Main, 1966), pp. 241-342.
—, *Vorlesungen über die Philosophie der Religion. Nebst einer Schrift über die Beweise vom Daseyn Gottes* I-II. Edited by Phillip Marheineke (1832) = Georg Friedrich Wilhelm Hegel's Werke 11-12 (Berlin: Duncker & Humbolt, 1832).
Heitmüller, Wilhelm, *Jesus* (Tübingen: Mohr [Siebeck], 1913).
Hengel, Martin, 'Zwischen Jesus und Paulus. Die "Hellenisten", die "Sieben" und Stephanus (Apg 6,1-5; 7,54–8,3)'. *ZThK* 72 (1975), pp. 151-205. English: 'Between Jesus and Paul. The "Hellenists", the "Seven" and Stephen (Acts 6.1-15; 7.54–8.3)', in idem, *Between Jesus and Paul: Studies in the Earliest History of Christianity* (London: SCM Press, 1983), pp. 1-29.

—, 'Christological Titles in Early Christianity'. In James H. Charlesworth (ed.), *The Messiah: Developments in Earliest Judaism and Christianity*. The First Princeton Symposium on Judaism and Christian Origins (Minneapolis: Fortress Press, 1992), pp. 425-48.

—, '"Setze dich zu meiner Rechten!" Die Inthronisation Christi zur Rechten Gottes und Psalm 110,1'. In M. Philonenko (ed.), *Le Trône de Dieu*. WUNT 69 (Tübingen: Mohr [Siebeck], 1993), pp. 108-94.

—, 'Jesus der Messias Israels'. In idem and Anna Maria Schwemer, *Der messianische Anspruch Jesu und die Anfänge der Christologie*. WUNT 138 (Tübingen: Mohr [Siebeck], 2001), pp. 1-80.

Hengstenberg, Ernst Wilhelm, *Christologie des Alten Testamentes und Commentar über die Messianischen Weissagungen* I-III (Berlin: Ludwig Oehmigke, 1829–35, 2nd ed. 1854–57). English: *Christology of the Old Testament* (Edinburgh: T. & T. Clark, 1854–57).

Herder, Johann Gottfried, *Vom Erlöser der Menschen. Nach unser drei ersten Evangelien*. Christliche Schriften 2 (1796). In Bernard Suphan (ed.), *Herders Sämmtliche Werke* 19 (Berlin: Weidmann, 1880), pp. 135-252.

—, *Von Gottes Sohn, der Welt Heiland. Nach Johannes Evangelium. Nebst einer Regel der Zusammenstimmung unsrer Evangelien aus ihrer Entstehung und Ordnung*. Christliche Schriften 3 (1797). *Herders Sämmtliche Werke* 19 (1880), pp. 253-424.

Héring, Jean, *Le royaume de Dieu et sa venue. Étude sur l'espérance de Jésus et de l'apotre Paul*. EHPhR 35 (Neuchâtel: Delachau & Niestle 1937, 2nd ed. 1959).

Hertlein, Eduard, *Der Daniel der Römerzeit* (Leipzig: Heinsius, 1908).

Heß, Johann Jacob, *Geschichte der drey letzten Lebensjahre Jesu* I-III (Tübingen: Franck & Schramm, 1768, 3rd ed. 1773).

Heumann, Christoph August, *Erklärung des Neuen Testaments I Theil, in welchem die Geschichte des Herrn, wie sie Matthäus und Marcus beschreiben, betrachtet und erläutert wird* (Hannover, 1750).

Hilgenfeld, Adolf, *Die jüdische Apokalyptik in ihrer geschichtlichen Entwickelung. Ein Beitrag zur Vorgeschichte des Christenthums nebst einem Anhange über das gnostische System des Basilides* (Jena 1857; reprint Amsterdam: Rodopi, 1966).

—, 'Die Evangelien und die geschichtliche Gestalt Jesu'. *ZWTh* 6 (1863), pp. 311-40.

—, 'Jüdische Apokalyptik und Christenthum'. *ZWTh* 31 (1888), pp. 488-98.

—, 'Hans Lietzmann. Der Menschensohn. Ein Beitrag zu der Neutestamentlichen Theologie'. *Berliner philologische Wochenschrift* 17 (1897), cols. 1520-25.

—, 'Johannes und Jesus nach J. Wellhausen's Darstellung'. *ZWTh* 41 (1898), pp. 481-501.

—, 'Der Evangelist Marcus und Julius Wellhausen'. *ZWTh* 47 (1904), pp. 180-228, 289-332, 462-524.

Hindley, J.C., 'Towards a Date for the Similitudes of Enoch: An Historical Approach'. *NTS* 14 (1967–68), pp. 551-65.

Hitzig, Ferdinand, *Das Buch Daniel*. Kurzgefasstes exegetisches Handbuch zum Alten Testament 10 (Leipzig: Weidmann, 1850).

Hölscher, G., 'Die Entstehung des Buches Daniel'. *ThStKr* 92 (1919), pp. 113-38.

Hoffmann, Andreas Gottlieb, *Das Buch Henoch* (Jena: Croeker, 1833–38).

Hoffmann, Paul, *Studien zur Theologie des Logienquelle*. NTA NF 8 (Münster: Aschendorf, 1972).

Hofius, Otfried, 'Ist Jesus der Messias? Thesen'. In *Messias*. JBTh 8 (1993), pp. 103-29.

—, 'Der Septuaginta-Text von Daniel 7,13-14. Erwägungen zu seiner Gestalt und seiner Aussage'. *ZAW* 117 (2005), pp. 73-90.
Hofmann, Johann Christian Konrad, *Weissagung und Erfüllung im alten und im neuen Testamente. Ein theologischer Versuch* I-II (Nördlingen: C.H. Beck'schen Buchhandlung, 1841–44).
Hollmann, G., *Welche Religion hatten die Juden, als Jesus auftrat?* RV I/7 (Tübingen: Mohr [Siebeck], 1905, 2nd ed. 1910).
Holsten, Carl, 'Biblisch theologische Studien IV. Zur Entstehung und Entwicklung des Messiasbewußtseins in Jesus'. *ZWTh* 34 (1891), pp. 385-449.
Holtzmann, Heinrich Julius, *Die Synoptiker*. Hand-Commentar zum Neuen Testament I/1 (Tübingen: Mohr [Siebeck], 1890, 3rd ed. 1901).
—, *Das messianische Bewußtsein Jesu*. Ein Beitrag zur Leben-Jesu-Forschung (Tübingen: Mohr [Siebeck], 1907).
—, *Lehrbuch der neutestamentlichen Theologie* I-II (Tübingen: Mohr [Siebeck], 1896–97, 2nd ed. by A. Jülicher and W. Bauer, 1911).
Horton, F.L., *The Melchizedek Tradition*. SNTSMS 30 (Cambridge: Cambridge University Press, 1976).
Hübner, Hans, *Biblische Theologie des Neuen Testaments 3. Hebräerbrief, Evangelien und Offenbarung. Epilegomena* (Göttingen: Vandenhoeck & Ruprecht, 1995).
Hübner, Reinhard M., 'Thesen zur Echtheit und Datierung der sieben Briefe des Ignatius von Antiochien'. *ZAC* 1 (1997), pp. 44-72.
Hyldahl, Jesper, 'Har gnosticismen en filosofisk oprindelse?—det litteraære forhold mellem Eugnostos' brev og Sophia Jesu Christi belyst'. *DTT* 62 (1999), pp. 203-15.

Isaac, E., '1 (Ethiopic Apocalypse of) Enoch'. In James Charlesworth (ed.), *The Old Testament Pseudepigrapha* I (New York: Doubleday, 1983), pp. 5-89.

Jackson, Foakes J.F., and Lake, Kirsopp (ed.), *The Beginnings of Christianity*. Part I. *The Acts of the Apostles*. I. *Prolegomena* I. *The Jewish, Gentile and Christian Backgrounds* (London: Macmillan, 1920).
Jacobsen, August, 'Die Johannes-Apocalypse und die canonischen Evangelien'. *PKZ* 33 (1886), pp. 563-68, 583-88, 606-11, 630-33.
Jahn, Johann, *Einleitung in die Göttlichen Bücher des Alten Bundes* II. Theil (Wien: Wappler & Beck, 2nd ed. 1803).
Jansen, Cornelius, *Tetrateuchus, sive Commentarius in sancta Jesu Christi evangelia* (Louvain: Seger, 1639, 2nd ed. 1697).
Jansen, Herman Ludin, *Die Henochgestalt. Eine vergleichende religionsgeschichtliche Untersuchung*. SNVAO II. Hist.-Filos Klasse 1939 (Oslo: Dybwad, 1939).
Jeremias, Joachim, 'Die Berufung des Nathanael'. *Angelos* 3 (1928), pp. 2-5.
—, 'Erlöser und Erlösung im Spätjudentum und Urchristentum'. *Deutsche Theologie* 2 (Göttingen: Vandenhoeck & Ruprecht, 1929), pp. 106-19.
—, *Jesus als Weltvollender*. BFChTh 33, 4 (Gütersloh: Evangelischer Verlag, 1930).
—, 'Ἀδάμ'. *ThWNT* I (Stuttgart: Kohlhammer, 1933), pp. 141-43.
—, 'Die aramäische Vorgeschichte unserer Evangelien'. *ThLZ* 74 (1949), cols. 527-32.
—, 'παῖς θεοῦ'. *ThWNT* V (1954), pp. 676-713. Reprint in idem, *Abba*. Studien zur neutestamentlichen Theologie und Zeitgeschichte (Göttingen: Vandenhoeck & Ruprecht, 1966), pp. 191-216.

— , *Neutestamentliche Theologie*. Erster Teil. Die Verkündigung Jesu (Gütersloh: Gütersloher Verlagshaus, 1971). English: *New Testament Theology*. Translated by John Bowden (London: SCM Press, 1971).

Johansson, Nils, *Parakletoi. Vorstellungen von Fürsprechern für die Menschen vor Gott in der alttestamentlichen Religion, im Spätjudentum und Urchristentum* (Lund: Gleerup, 1940).

Jonge, Marinus de, and A.S. van der Woude, '11Q Melchizedek and the New Testament'. *NTS* 12 (1965–66), pp. 301-26.

Joüon, Paul, *L'Evangile de Notre-Seigneur Jésus-Christ* (Paris: Beauchesne, 2nd ed. 1930).

Juel, Donald, *Messianic Exegesis: Christological Interpretation of the Old Testament in Early Christianity* (Philadelphia: Fortress Press, 1988).

Jüngel, Eberhard, *Paulus und Jesus. Eine Untersuchung zur Präzisierung der Frage nach dem Ursprung der Christologie*. HUTh 2 (Tübingen: Mohr [Siebeck], 1962, 2nd ed. 1964).

Jung, Carl Gustav, *Ein moderner Mythus von Dingen die am Himmel gesehen werden* (Zürich. Rascher, 1958). Reprint in idem, *Zivilisation im Übergang*. Gesammelte Werke 10. Band (Olten und Freiburg im Breisgau: Walter-Verlag, 1974), pp. 337-474. English translation in idem, *Civilization in Transition*. Collected Works 10 (1974), pp. 307-433.

—, *Antwort auf Hiob* (1952/1961). In idem, *Gesammelte Werke* 11 (Zürich & Stuttgart: Rascher Verlag, 1963), pp. 385-506.

Junker, Hanstein, *Untersuchungen über literarische und exegetische Probleme des Buches Daniel* (Bonn, 1932).

Kähler, Martin, *Der sogenannte historische Jesus und der geschichtliche, biblische Christus* (Leipzig: Deichertschen Verlagsbuchhandlung, 1892). Reprint as ThB 2 (München: Kaiser,1956). English: *The So-Called Historical Jesus and the Historic, Biblical Christ*. Translated by Carl E. Braaten (Philadelphia: Fortress Press, 1964).

— , 'Christologie, Schriftlehre'. In *RE*, 4 (3rd ed. 1898), pp. 4-16.

Käsemann, Ernst, *Das wandernde Gottesvolk. Eine Untersuchung zum Hebräerbrief.* FRLANT 55 (Göttingen: Vandenhoeck & Ruprecht, 1939). English: *The Wandering People of God. An Investigation of the Letter to the Hebrews*. Translated by Roy A. Harrisville and Irving L. Sandberg (Minneapolis: Augsburg, 1984).

—, 'Das Problem des historischen Jesus'. *ZThK* 51 (1954), pp. 125-53. Reprint in idem, *Exegetische Versuche und Besinnungen* I (Göttingen: Vandenhoeck & Ruprecht, 1960, 4th ed. 1965), pp. 187-214. English: 'The Problem of the Historical Jesus'. In idem, *Essays on New Testament Themes*. SBTh 41 (London: SCM Press, 1964), pp. 15-47.

— , 'Neutestamentlicher Sammelbericht'. *VF* 9 (Theologischer Jahresbericht 1958/59) (1960–62), pp. 97-108.

Kant, Immanuel, 'Beantwortung der Frage: Was ist Aufklärung?' (1784). In *Kants Werke*. Akademia-Textausgabe VIII (1912; reprint Berlin: De Gruyter, 1968), pp. 33-42.

— , *Die Religion innerhalb der Grenzen der blossen Vernunft* (1793, 2nd ed. 1794). Reprint ed. by K. Vorländer, Philosophische Bibliothek 45 (Hamburg: Felix Meiner, 7th ed. 1961).

Karrer, Martin, *Jesus Christus im Neuen Testament*. Grundrisse zum Neuen Testament. NTD Ergänsungsreihe 11 (Göttingen: Vandenhoeck & Ruprecht, 1998).

Kattenbusch, Ferdinand, 'Das Messiastum Jesu'. *ZNW* 12 (1911), pp. 270-86.

—, 'Der Quellort der Kirchenidee'. *Harnack-Ehrung* (Leipzig: Hinrichs, 1921), pp. 143-72.

Kearns, Rollin, 'Die Historisierung des Traditionsgefüges um den Weltenherrn'. *Mutmaßungen zur Christologie* Heft 8 (Tübingen: Privdruck, 2006).

Keck, Leander E., 'Toward the Renewal of New Testament Christology'. *NTS* 32 (1986), pp. 362-77.

Keim, Theodor, *Der geschichtliche Jesus. Drei Reden mit Rücksicht auf die neuesten Werke und mit literarischen Beigaben*. Zweite vielfach umgearbeitete Auflage der Schriften 'Menschliche Entwickelung Jesu' und 'Geschichtliche Würde Jesu' (Zürich: Orelli & Füßli, 1865).

—, *Geschichte Jesu von Nazara in ihrer Verkettung mit dem Gesammtleben seines Volkes II, Das galiläische Lehrjahr* (Zürich: Orelli & Füßli, 1871). English: *The History of Jesus of Nazara* 1-6 (London: Williams & Norgate, 1876–83).

Kittel, Gerhard, 'Jesu Worte über sein Sterben'. *Deutsche Theologie*. Monatschrift für die Deutsche Evangelische Kirche 3 (1936), pp. 166-89.

Klausner, Joseph, *Jesus of Nazareth: His Life, Times and Teaching*. Translated from the original Hebrew by Herbert Danby (London: George Allen & Unwin, 1925).

—, *The Messianic Idea in Israel from Its Beginning to the Completion of the Mishnah* (London: George Allen & Unwin, 1956). This volume contains as Part III, pp. 387-517, *Die messianischen Vorstellungen des jüdischen Volkes im Zeitalter der Tannaiten* (Heidelberg, 1904).

Kloppenborg, John S., 'The Sayings Gospel Q and the Quest of the Historical Jesus'. *HThR* 89 (1996), pp. 307-44.

Knibb, M.A., 'The Date of the Parables of Enoch: A Critical Review'. *NTS* 25 (1978–79), pp. 345-59.

Knox, John, *The Death of Christ: The Cross in New Testament History and Faith* (New York: Abingdon Press, 1958).

Koch, Klaus, together with T. Niewisch and J. Thubach, *Das Buch Daniel*. EdF 144 (Darmstadt: Wissenschaftliche Buchgesellschaft, 1980).

Köcher, Johann Christoph, *Analecta philologica et exegetica in quatuor s. evangelia* (Altenburg: Richter, 1766).

Kraeling, Emil Gottlieb Heinrich, 'Some Babylonian and Iranian Mythology in the Seventh Chapter of Daniel'. In Jal Dastur Cursetji Pavry, *Oriental Studies*. FS Cursetji Erachji Pavry (London: Oxford University Press, 1933), pp. 228-31.

Kramer, Werner, *Christos Kyrios Gottessohn*. AThANT 44 (Zürich/Stuttgart: Zwingli Verlag, 1963).

Krarup, Frederik Christian, *Om forholdet mellem det guddommelige og menneskelige i Kristi person. En fremstilling af kristologien* (København: C.A. Reitzel, 1885).

Kreplin, Matthias, *Das Selbstverständnis Jesu. Hermeneutische und christologische Reflexion. Historisch-kritische Analyse*. WUNT 2. Reihe 141 (Tübingen: Mohr [Siebeck], 2001).

Kümmel, Werner Georg, 'Die Eschatologie der Evangelien. Ihre Geschichte und Sinn'. *ThBl* 15 (1936), pp. 225-41. Reprint in idem, *Heilsgeschehen und Geschichte. Gesammelte Aufsätze 1933–1964*. Marburger Theologische Studien 3 (Marburg: Elwert, 1965), pp. 48-66.

—, *Kirchenbegriff und Geschichtsbewußtsein in der Urgemeinde und bei Jesus*. SyBU I (Uppsala-Zürich, 1943, 2nd ed. Göttingen: Vandenhoeck & Ruprecht, 1968).

—, Die Theologie des Neuen Testaments nach seinem Hauptzeugen, Jesus—Paulus—Johannes. Grundrisse zu Neuen Testament. NTD Ergänzungsreihe Band 3 (Göttingen: Vandenhoeck & Ruprecht, 1969). English: *The Theology of the New Testament According to its Major Witnesses* (Nashville: Abingdon Press, 1973).

—, 'Jesusforschung seit 1965. V. Der persönliche Anspruch Jesu'. *ThR* NF 45 (1980), pp. 40-84. Reprint in idem, *Dreissig Jahre Jesusforschung (1950–1980)*, ed. von Helmut Merklein. BBB 60 (Bonn: Hanstein, 1985), pp. 330-74.

—, 'Jesusforschung seit 1965: Nachträge 1975–1980. V. Der persönliche Anspruch Jesu'. *ThR* NF 47 (1982), pp. 370-78. Reprint in idem, *Dreissig Jahre Jesusforschung (1950–1980)* (1985), pp. 519-28. Reprint in idem, *Vierzig Jahre Jesusforschung (1950–1990)*. Edited by Helmut Merklein. BBB 91 (Weinheim: Beltz Athenäum, 1994), pp. 661-90

—, 'Jesusforschung seit 1981. V. Der persönliche Anspruch sowie der Prozeβ und Kreuzestod Jesu'. *ThR* NF 56 (1991), pp. 391-420.

Künzi, Hans Martin, *Das Naheerwartungslogion Matthäus 10,23. Geschichte seiner Auslegung* (Tübingen: Mohr [Siebeck], 1970).

Küppers, W., 'Das Messiasbild der spätjüdischen Apokalyptik'. *IKZ* 23 (1933), pp. 193-256; 24 (1934), pp. 47-72.

Kvanvig, Helge, 'Struktur und Geschichte in Dan. 7,1-14'. *StTh* 32 (1978), pp. 95-117.

—, 'An Akkadian Vision as Background for Dan 7?' *StTh* 35 (1981), pp. 85-89.

Lacocque, A., *Le Livre de Daniel*. CAT (Neuchâtel: Delachaux & Niestlé, 1976).

Lagarde, Paul de, *Gesammelte Abhandlungen* (Leipzig: Brockhaus, 1866).

—, 'Die religion der zukunft'. In idem, *Deutsche Schriften* I (Göttingen: Dietrich, 1878), pp. 217-55.

—, 'Havet, Ernest: Études d'histoire religieuse. La Modernité des prophètes, 1891'. *GGA* 2 (1891), cols. 497-520.

Lagrange, Marie-Joseph, *Le Messianisme chez les Juifs (150 av. J.-C. à 200 ap. J.-C.)* (Paris, Gabalda, 1909).

—, *Le Judaïsme avant Jésus-Christ* (Paris: Gabalda, 2nd ed. 1931).

Lange, Joachim, *Das Erscheinen des Auferstandenen im Evangelium nach Mattäus. Eine traditions- und redaktionsgeschichtliche Untersuchung zu Mt 28,16-20*. FzB 11 (Würzburg: Echter Verlag, 1973).

Larsen, A.C., *Profeten Daniel og Esters Bog oversatte og forklarede for Lægfolk* (Kjøbenhavn: Philipsens Forlag, 1893).

Le Déaut, Roger, 'Le substrat araméen des Évangiles: Scolies en margie de l'*Aramaic Approach* de Matthew Black'. *Bib.* 49 (1968), pp. 388-99.

Leivestad, Ragnar, *Christ the Conqueror: Ideas of Conflict and Victory in the New Testament* (London: SPCK, 1954).

—, *Hvem ville Jesus være?* (Oslo: Land og Kirke/Gyldendal, 1982). English: *Jesus in His Own Perspective: An Examination of His Sayings, Actions, and Eschatological Titles* (Minneapolis: Augsburg, 1987).

Lengerke, Caesar von, *Das Buch Daniel. Verdeutscht und ausgelegt* (Königsberg: Bornträger, 1835).

Lietzmann, Hans, *Der Weltheiland* (Bonn: Marcus & Weber, 1909). Reprint in idem, *Kleine Schriften* I. *Studien zur spätantiken Religionsgeschichte*. TU 67 (Berlin: Akademie-Verlag, 1958), pp. 25-62.

—, *Geschichte der alten Kirche 1. Die Anfänge* (Berlin: De Gruyter, 1932, 4th ed. 1961).

Lightfoot, John, *Harmoniæ Quatuor Evangelistarum, tum inter se, tum cum Veteri Testamento* I-III (1644–50). Reprint in idem, *Opera Omnia* I (Rotterdam: Regner Leers, 1686), pp. 233-548.

—, *Horæ Hebraicæ et Talmudicæ II. In Evangelium S. Matthæi* (1658). Reprint in idem, *Opera Omnia* II (Rotterdam: Regner Leers, 1686), pp. 165-392. English: *A Commentary on the New Testament from the Talmud and Hebraica*. II. *Matthew–Mark* (Grand Rapids: Baker, 1979).

Lindars, Barnabas, 'Jesus as Advocate: A Contribution to the Christology Debate'. *BJRL* 62 (1979–80), pp. 476-97.

—, 'Enoch and Christology'. *ET* 92 (1980–81), pp. 295-99.

Linton, Olof, *Das Problem der Urkirche in der neueren Forschung. Eine kritische Darstellung.* Uppsala Universitets Årsskrift 1932 (Uppsala: Almqvist & Wiksell, 1932).

Lövestam, Evald, *Spiritus blasphemia. Eine Studie zu Mk 3,28f par Mt 12,31f, Lk 12,10.* SMHVL 1966–67:1 (Lund: Gleerup, 1968).

Lohmeyer, Ernst, *Kyrios Jesus. Eine Untersuchung zu Phil. 2,5-11.* SHAW Phil.-hist. Kl. Jahrgang 1927/28, 4. Abh. (Heidelberg: Carl Winter Universitätsverlag, 1928, 2nd ed. 1961).

—, *Galilä und Jerusalem.* FRLANT 52 (Göttingen: Vandenhoeck & Ruprecht, 1936).

—, *Das Evangelium des Markus.* KEK I,2 (Göttingen: Vandenhoeck & Ruprecht, 1937 = 16th ed. 1963).

—, *Gottesknecht und Davidssohn.* SyBU 5 (Uppsala/Lund: Gleerup, 1945). Later as FRLANT 61 (Göttingen: Vandenhoeck & Ruprecht, 1953).

Lohse, Eduard, *Grundriß der neutestamentlichen Theologie.* Theologische Wissenschaft 5 (Stuttgart: Kohlhammer, 1974, 2nd ed. 1979).

Longenecker, Richard N., *The Christology of Early Jewish Christianity.* SBTh SS 17 (London: SCM Press, 1970).

Lücke, Friedrich, *Commentar über die Schriften des Evangelisten Johannes* I-IV (Bonn: Weber, 1820–22).

Lust, J., 'Daniel 7,13 and the Septuagint'. *EThL* 54 (1978), pp. 62-69. Reprint in idem, *Messianism and the Septuagint.* Edited by K. Hauspie. BEThL 178 (Leuven: University Press 2004), pp. 1-8.

Luther: Martin Luther: *Werke. Kritische Gesamtausgabe* [Weimarer Ausgabe (*WA*)]. English: *Luther's Works* (Saint Louis: Concordia).

Maldonado, Juan, *Commentarii in quatuor evangelistas* (Mussiponti, 1596–97). English: *A Commentary on the Holy Gospels: St Matthew's Gospel* (London: Hodges, 1888).

Manson, Thomas Walter, *The Teaching of Jesus: Studies of its Form and Content* (Cambridge: Cambridge University Press, 1931, 8th ed. 1959).

—, 'Mark ii.27f.' *Coniectanea Neotestamentica* 11. FS Anton Fridrichsen (Lund: Gleerup, 1947), pp. 138-46.

—, *The Servant-Messiah: A Study of the Public Ministry of Jesus* (Cambridge: Cambridge University Press, 1953).

Manson, William, *Jesus the Messiah: The Synoptic Tradition of the Revelation of God in Christ: With Special Reference to Form-Criticism* (London: Hodder & Stoughton, 1943, 5th ed. 1948).

Marshall, I. Howard, *The Origins of New Testament Christology* (Downer's Grove, IL: InterVarsity Press, 1976).

—, *Jesus the Saviour: Studies in New Testament Theology* (London: SPCK, 1990).
Marti, Karl, *Das Buch Daniel*. KHC 18 (Tübingen: Mohr [Siebeck], 1901).
Marxsen, Willi, *Anfangsprobleme der Christologie* (Gütersloh: Gütersloher Verlag, 1960, 6th ed. 1969). English: *The Beginnings of Christology: A Study in its Problems*. Translated by Paul J. Achtemeier and Lorenz Nieting (Philadelphia: Fortress Press, 1969).
McArthur, H.K., 'Mark XIV.62'. *NTS* 4 (1957–58), pp. 156-58.
McDermott, John M., 'Luke, XII,8-9: Stone of Scandal'. *RB* 84 (1977), pp. 523-37.
—, 'Luc. XII,8-9: Pierre angulaire'. *RB* 85 (1978), pp. 381-401.
—, 'Mt. 10:23 in Context'. *BZ* NF 28 (1984), pp. 230-40.
Mearns, Christopher L., 'The Parables of Enoch—Origin and Date'. *ET* 89 (1977–78), pp. 118-19.
—, 'Dating the Similitudes of Enoch'. *NTS* 25 (1978–79), pp. 360-69.
Meier, John P., *A Marginal Jew: Rethinking the Historical Jesus*. III. *Companions and Competitors* (New York: Doubleday, 2001).
Melanchthon, Philipp, *Loci communes* (1521). Robert Stupperich (ed.), *Melanchthons Werke in Auswahl* (Gütersloh: G. Bertelsmann, 1952).
Merz, Annette, see Theissen, Gerd.
Metzger, Bruce M., 'The Fourth Book of Ezra'. In James Charlesworth (ed.), *The Old Testament Pseudepigrapha* I (New York: Doubleday, 1983), pp. 517-59.
Meyer, Arnold, *Jesu Muttersprache. Das galiläische Aramäisch in seiner Bedeutung für die Erklärung der Reden Jesu und der Evangelien überhaupt* (Freiburg im Breisgau/Leipzig/Tübingen: Mohr [Siebeck], 1896).
—, *Die moderne Forschung über die Geschichte des Urchristentums* (Freiburg im Breisgau/Leipzig/Tübingen: Mohr [Siebeck], 1898).
—, *Das 'Leben nach dem Evangelium Jesu'*. SgV 44 (Tübingen: Mohr [Siebeck], 1905).
Meyer, Eduard, *Ursprung und Anfänge des Christentums* I-III (Stuttgart-Berlin: Cotta, 1921–23).
Meyer, Heinrich August Wilhelm, *Kritisch exegetisches Handbuch über das Evangelium des Matthäus*. KEK I/1 (Göttingen: Vandenhoeck & Ruprecht, 1832, 5th ed. 1864).
Michaelis, Johann David, *Anmerkungen für Ungelehrte, zu seiner Uebersetzung des Neuen Testaments* I. *Anmerkungen zu Matthäus, Marcus und Lucas* (Göttingen: Vandenhoeck & Ruprecht, 1790).
Michaelis, Wilhelm, *Zur Engelchristologie im Urchristentum. Abbau der Konstruktion Martin Werners*. Gegenwartsfragen Biblischer Theologie I (Basel: Heinrich Majer, 1942).
Milik, J.T., 'Problèmes de la littérature Hénochique à la lumière des fragments araméens de Qumran'. *HThR* 64 (1971), pp. 333-78.
—, *The Books of Enoch: Aramaic Fragments of Qumrân Cave 4* (with the collaboration of M. Black) (Oxford: Clarendon Press, 1976).
Moffatt, James, *The Theology of the Gospels* (London: Duckworth, 1912, 5th ed. 1948).
Montefiore, C.G., *The Synoptic Gospels: Edited with an Introduction and a Commentary* I-II (London: Macmillan, 1909, 2nd ed. 1927).
Montgomery, J.A., *A Critical and Exegetical Commentary on the Book of Daniel*. ICC (Edinburgh: T. & T. Clark, 1927).
Moore, Georg Foot, *Judaism in the First Centuries of the Christian Era: The Age of the Tannaim* I-III (Cambridge, MA: Harvard University Press, 1927–30).

Morgenstern, Julian, *Some Significant Antecedents of Christianity*. StPB 10 (Leiden: Brill, 1966).

Mosca, Paul G., 'Ugarit and Daniel 7: A Missing Link'. *Bib.* 67 (1986), pp. 496-517.

Moulder, W.J., 'The Old Testament Background and the Interpretation of Mark X.45'. *NTS* 24 (1977–78), pp. 120-27.

Moule, C.F.D., 'From Defendant to Judge—and Deliverer: An Inquiry into the Use and Limitations of the Theme of Vindication in the New Testament'. *BSNTS* III (1952), pp. 40-53. Reprint in idem, *The Phenomenon of the New Testament*. SBTh SS 1 (London: SCM Press, 1967), pp. 82-99.

—, *The Origin of Christology* (Cambridge: Cambridge University Press, 1977).

Mowinckel, Sigmund, *Das Thronbesteigungsfest Jahwäs und der Ursprung der Eschatologie*. Psalmenstudien II. ANVAO II. Hist.-Filos. Klasse 1921. No. 6 (Oslo: Dybwad, 1922; reprint Amsterdam: Schippers, 1961, 3rd ed. 1966).

—, 'Henokskikkelsen i senjødisk apokalyptikk. Innlegg som 1ste ordinære opponent ved H. Ludin Jansens doktordisputas. Specimen: Die Henochgestalt. Eine vergleichende religionsgeschichtliche Untersuchung, 1939'. *NTT* 41 (1940), pp. 206-36.

—, 'Urmensch und "Königsideologie"'. *StTh* 2 (1949–50), pp. 71-89.

—, *Han som kommer. Messiasforventningen i Det gamle testament og på Jesu tid* (København: Gad, 1951). English: *He That Cometh*. Translated by G.W. Anderson, (Oxford: Blackwell, 1956).

Müller, Mogens, 'Der Jesus der Historiker, der historische Jesus und die Christusverkündigung der Kirche'. *KuD* 22 (1976), pp. 277-98.

—, 'The Hidden Context: Some Observations to the Concept of the New Covenant in the New Testament'. In Tord Fornberg and David Hellholm (eds.), *Texts and Contexts*. FS Lars Hartman (Oslo: Scandinavian University Press, 1995), pp. 649-58.

Münster, Sebastian, *Torat Hammaschiach: Evangelium secundum Matthaeum in lingua Hebraica cum versione Latina atque succinctis annotationibus* (Basle: Petrus, 1537).

Musculus, Wolfgang, *Commentariorum in evangelistam Ioannem*. Heptas prima (Basle: Hervag, 1545).

Neander, August, *Das Leben Jesu Christi in seinem geschichtlichen Zusammenhange und seiner geschichtlichen Entwickelung* (Hamburg, 1837). English: *The Life of Jesus Christ in its Historical Connexion and Historical Development* (London: Bell, 1888).

Neyrey, Jerome H., 'The Jacob Allusion in John 1:51'. *CBQ* 44 (1982), pp. 586-605.

Nickelsburg, George W.E., *Resurrection, Immortality, and Eternal Life in Intertestamental Judaism and Early Christianity*. Expanded edition. Harvard Theological Studies 56 (1st ed. 1972, Cambridge, MA: Harvard University Press, 2006).

Nietzsche, Friedrich, *Der Antichrist. Versuch einer Kritik des Christenthums*. Umwerthung aller Werthe. Erstes Buch (1888) 1895. Reprint in *Nietzsche's Werke*. Erste Abteilung Band VIII (Stuttgart: Kröner Verlag, 1906).

Noack, Bent, 'Fjerde Ezrabog'. In E. Hammershaimb, Johannes Munck, Bent Noack and Paul Seidelin (eds.), *De gammeltestamentlige Pseudepigrafer i oversættelse med indledning og noter* I (København: Gads Forlag, 1953–63), pp. 1-68.

Noth, Martin, 'Zur Komposition des Buches Daniel'.*ThStKr* 98/99 (1926), pp. 143-63.

—, '"Die Heiligen des Höchsten"'. *Interpretationes ad Vetus Testamentum*. FS Sigmund Mowinckel (Oslo: Land og Kirke, 1955), pp. 146-61 (= *NTT* 56 [1955], pp. 146-61.

Reprint in idem, *Gesammelte Studien zum Alten Testament*. ThB 6 (München; Kaiser, 1957), pp. 274-90.

Oertel, Eucharius Ferdinand Christian, *Antijosephinismus oder Kritik über eines Ungenannten schriftmäßigen Beweis daß Joseph der wahre Vater Christi sey* (1792).

—, *Christologie oder die Resultate der neuesten exegetischen Aufklärungen über den Artikel von der Gottheit Christi. Ein systematischer Versuch, besonders den iungen Theologen gewidmet* (1792).

Oesterley, W.O.E., *II Esdras (The Ezra Apocalypse)*. Westminster Commentaries (London: Methuen, 1933).

Olshausen, Hermann, *Die drei ersten Evangelien bis zur Leidensgeschichte*. Biblischer Commentar über sämmtliche Schriften des Neuen Testaments zunächst für Prediger und Studierende I (Königsberg: Unzer, 1830, 3rd ed. 1837). English: *Biblical Commentary on the New Testament* (New York: Sheldon, Blakeman, 1858).

O'Neill, J.C., 'The Silence of Jesus'. *NTS* 15 (1968–69), pp. 153-67.

Orelli, Conrad von, 'Messias'. In *RE* 12 (3rd ed. 1903), pp. 723-39.

Otto, Rudolf, *Leben und Wirken Jesu nach historisch-kritischer Auffassung* (Göttingen: Vandenhoeck & Ruprecht, 1902).

Owen, H.P., 'Stephen's Vision in Acts VII.55-6'. *NTS* 1 (1954–55), pp. 224-26.

Paul, Ludwig, *Die Vorstellungen vom Messias und vom Gottesreich bei den Synoptikern* (Bonn, 1895).

Paulus, Heinrich Eberhard Gottlob, *Philologisch-kritischer und historischer Commen tar über das neue Testament* I. Die drey ersten Evangelien erster Hälfte (Lübeck: Bohn, 1800, 2nd ed. 1804).

Percy, Ernst, *Die Botschaft Jesu. Eine traditionsgeschichtliche und exegetische Untersuchung*. LUÅ NF Avd. 1 Bd. 49/5 (Lund: Gleerup, 1953).

Perrin, Norman, *The Kingdom of God in the Teaching of Jesus* (London: SCM Press, 1963, 2nd ed. 1966).

—, 'Mark XIV.62: The End Product of a Christian Pesher Tradition?'. *NTS* 12 (1965–66), pp. 150-55. Reprint with Postscript in idem, *A Modern Pilgrimage in New Testament Christology* (Philadelphia: Fortress Press, 1974), pp. 10-22.

—, *Rediscovering the Teaching of Jesus* (London: SCM Press, 1967).

—, 'The Christology of Mark: A Study in Methodology'. *JR* 51 (1971), pp. 173-87. Reprint in idem, *A Modern Pilgrimage in New Testament Christology* (Philadelphia: Fortress Press, 1974), pp. 104-21.

Pesch, Rudolf, *Die Vision des Stephanus. Apg 7,55-56 im Rahmen der Apostelgeschichte*. SBS 12 (Stuttgart: Katholisches Bibelwerk, 1966).

—, 'Über die Autorität Jesu. Eine Rückfrage anhand des Bekenner- und Verleugnerspruchs Lk 12,8f par.' In Rudolf Schnackenburg, Josef Ernst and Joachim Wanke (eds.), *Die Kirche des Anfangs*. FS Heinz Schürmann. Erfurter theologische Studien (Leipzig: St Benno, 1978), pp. 25-55.

Pétrement, Simone, *Le Dieu séparé. Les origines du gnosticisme* (Paris: Éditions du Cerf, 1984).

Pfleiderer, Otto, *Das Urchristenthum, seine Schriften und Lehren, in geschichtlichem Zusammenhang* (Berlin: Reimer, 1887, 2nd ed. In two volumes, 1902). English: *Primitive Christianity: Its Writings and Teachings in their Historical Connections*

(New York: G.P. Putnam's Sons, 1906–11; reprint in 4 vol., Clifton, NJ: Reference Book, 1965).
—, *Die Entstehung des Christentums* (München: J.F. Lehmann, 1905). English: *Christian Origins*. Translated by Daniel A. Huebsch (New York: B.W. Huebsch, 1906).
Pfochenius, Sebastian, *Diatribe de lingua Graeca N. Test. Puritate* (Amsterdam, 1648),
Piscator (Fischer), Johannes, *Commentarius in omnes libros Novi Testamenti* (Herborn, 1621).
Plöger, Otto, *Theokratie und Eschatologie*. WMANT 2 (Neukirchen–Vluyn: Neukirchener Verlag, 1959).
—, *Das Buch Daniel*. KAT 18 (Gütersloh: Gütersloher Verlag, Gerd Mohn, 1965).
Polag, Athanasius, *Die Christologie der Logienquelle*. WMANT 45 (Neukirchen–Vluyn: Neukirchener Verlag, 1977).
Porteous, Norman W., *Das Danielbuch*. ATD 23 (Göttingen: Vandenhoeck & Ruprecht, 1962).
Poythress, V.S., 'The Holy Ones of the Most High in Daniel VII'. *VT* 26 (1976), pp. 208-13.
Procksch, Otto, 'Christus im Alten Testament'. *NKZ* 44 (1933), pp. 57-83.
Prostmeier, Ferdinand Rupert, *Der Barnabasbrief*. KAV 8 (Göttingen: Vandenhoeck & Ruprecht, 1999).

Quenstedt, Johann Andreas, *Theologia didactico-polemica, sive systema theologicum, in duas sectiones, didacticam et polemicam, divisum* I-VI (Wittenberg: Quenstedt & Haeredes, 1685).
Quispel, Gilles, 'Der gnostische Antropos und die jüdische Tradition'. *Eranos-Jahrbuch* 22 1953 (1954), pp. 195-234.

Rawlinson, A.E.J., *The New Testament Doctrine of the Christ* (London: Longmans, Green, 1926, 2nd ed. 1929).
Reimarus, Hermann Samuel, *Vom Zwecke Jesu und seiner Jünger* (Braunschweig, 1778). Reprint in *Fragmente des Wolfenbüttelschen Ungenannten*. Edited by Gotthold Ephraim Lessing (1774–78, 5th ed. Berlin: Reimer, 1895), pp. 1-127, 263-98. English: *The Goal of Jesus and His Disciples* (Leiden: Brill, 1970).
Reitzenstein, Richard, *Poimandres. Studien zur griechisch-ägyptischen und frühchristlichen Literatur* (Leipzig: Teubner, 1904).
—, *Das mandäische Buch des Herrn der Größe und die Evangelienüberlieferung*. SHAW Phil.-hist. Kl., 1919, 12. Abhandlung (Heidelberg: Carl Winther, 1919).
—, *Das iranische Erlösungsmysterium. Religionsgeschichtliche Untersuchungen* (Bonn: Weber, 1921).
Renan, Ernest, *Vie de Jésus* (Paris: Levy, 1863). English: *The Life of Jesus*. The Thinker's Library 53 (London: Watts & Co., 1935).
Rese, Martin, 'Überprüfung einiger Thesen von Joachim Jeremias zum Thema des Gottesknechtes im Judentum'. *ZThK* 60 (1963), pp. 21-41.
Reuss, Eduard Wilhelm Eugen R., *Histoire de la théologie chrétienne au siècle apostolique* I-II (Strasbourg: Treuttel & Wurtz, 1852, 3rd ed. 1864). English: *History of Christian Theology in the Apostolic Age* I-II. Translated from 3rd ed. by Annie Harwood, with Preface and Notes by R.W. Dale (London: Hodder & Stoughton, 1872).

Rhees, Rush, 'A "Striking Monotony" in the Synoptic Gospels'. *JBL* 17 (1898), pp. 87-102.

Rhodes, A.B., 'The Kingdoms of Men and The Kingdom of God: A Study of Daniel 7:1-14'. *Interp.* 15 (1961), pp. 411-30.

Richardson, Alan, *An Introduction to the Theology of the New Testament* (London: SCM Press, 1958).

Riesenfeld, Harald, *Jésus transfiguré. L'arriére-plan du récit évangélique transfiguration de notre-seigneur.* ASNU 16 (København: Munksgaard, 1947).

—, 'The Mythological Background of New Testament Christology'. In W.D. Davies and David Daube (eds.), *The Background of the New Testament and its Eschatology.* FS Charles Harold Dodd, 1954, 2nd ed. 1964), pp. 81-95.

Riessler, Paul, *Das Buch Daniel.* Kurzgefasster wissenschaftlicher Commentar zu den heiligen Schriften des Alten Testaments III,3,2 (Wien: Verlag von Mayer & Co., 1902).

Robinson, James M., *A New Quest of the Historical Jesus.* SBTh 25 (London: SCM Press, 1969, 4th ed. 1966). Enlarged German ed.: *Kerygma und historischer Jesus* (Zürich. Zwingli, 2nd ed. 1967).

Robinson, John A.T., 'The Second Coming—Mark xiv.62'. *ET* 67 (1955–56), pp. 336-40.

Rordorf, Willy, 'Gen 28,10ff und John 1,51 in der patristischen Exegese'. In Martin Rose (ed.), *Johannes-Studien: Interdisziplinäre Zugänge zum Johannes-Evangelium.* FS Jean Zumstein (Neuchâtel: Secrétariat de l'Université, 1990), pp. 39-46.

Rosenmüller, Johann Georg, *Scolia in Novum Testamentum I. Evangelia Matthaei et Marci* (Nuremberg: Felsecker, 1777).

Rowland, Christopher, 'John 1.51, Jewish Apocalyptic and Targumic Tradition'. *NTS* 30 (1984), pp. 498-507.

Rowley, H.H., *Darius the Mede and the Four World Empires in the Book of Daniel. A Historical Study of Contemporary Theories* (Cardiff: University of Wales Press, 1935).

—, *The Relevance of Apocalyptic: A Study of Jewish and Christian Apocalypses from Daniel to the Revelation* (London: Lutterworth, 1944, 2nd ed. 1947).

—, 'The Suffering Servant and the Davidic Messiah'. *OT* 8 (1950), pp. 100-136. Reprint in idem, *The Servant of the Lord and other Essays on the Old Testament* (London: Lutterworth, 1952), pp. 59-88.

Rudolph, Kurt, 'Urmensch'. In *RGG*, VI (3rd ed. 1962), cols. 1195-97.

Russell, D.S., The *Method and Message of Jewish Apocalyptic 200 BC–AD 100* (London: SCM Press, 1964).

Ryberg Hansen, P.O., *Evangelierne som Kilder til Jesu Liv. Hovedtræk af den nyere Forskning* (Copenhagen: Gyldendalske Boghandel, 1904).

Sabourin, Leopold, 'About Jesus' Self-Understanding'. *Religious Studies Bulletin* 3 (1983), pp. 129-34.

Sahlin, Harald, 'Antiochus IV. Epiphanes und Judas Mackabäus. Einige Gesichtspunkte zum Verständnisse des Danielbuches'. *StTh* 23 (1969), pp. 41-68.

—, 'Paulus och Danielsboken'. *SEÅ* 46 (1981), pp. 95-110.

Schaberg, Jane. 'Daniel 7,12 and the New Testament Passion-Resurrection Predictions'. *NTS* 31 (1985), pp. 208-22.

Schaik, A.P. van, '῎Αλλος ἄγγελος in Apk 14'. In J. Lambrecht (ed.), *L'Apocalypse johannique et l'Apocalyptique dans le Nouveau Testament*'. BETHL 53 (Gembloux: Duculot; Leuven: University Press, 1980), pp. 217-28.

Schelkle, K.H., *Theologie des Neuen Testaments II. Gott war in Christus.* Kommentare und Beiträge zum Alten und Neuen Testament (Düsseldorf: Patmos Verlag, 1973).

Schenke, Hans-Martin, *Der Gott 'Mensch' in der Gnosis* (Göttingen: Vandenhoeck & Ruprecht, 1962).

Schenkel, Daniel, *Das Charakterbild Jesu. Ein biblischer Versuch* (Wiesbaden: Kreidel, 1864, 2nd ed. 1864). English: *A Sketch of the Character of Jesus* (London: Long-mans, Greens, 1869).

Schlatter, Adolf, *Die Theologie des Neuen Testaments I: Das Wort Jesu* (Stuttgart: Calwer Verlag, 1909).

—, *Der Evangelist Matthäus. Seine Sprache, sein Ziel, seine Selbständigkeit* (Stuttgart: Calwer Verlag, 1929, 5th ed. 1959).

Schleiermacher, Friedrich, *Der christliche Glaube nach den Grundsätzen der evangelischen Kirche im Zusammenhange dargestellt* I-II (Halle an der Saale: Hendel, 1821–22, 2nd ed. 1830–31). English: *The Christian Faith.* Translated by H.R. Mackintosh and J.S. Stewart (Philadelphia: Fortress Press, 1976).

—, *Einleitung ins neue Testament.* Aus Schleiermacher's handschriftlichem Nachlasse und nachgeschriebenen Vorlesungen, mit einer Vorrede von Friedrich Lücke. Edited by G. Wolde. Friedrich Schleiermacher's sämmtliche Werke. 1. Abt. Zur Theologie. Achter Band (Berlin: Reimer, 1845).

—, *Das Leben Jesu.* Vorlesungen an der Universität zu Berlin im Jahr 1832. Edited by K.A. Rütenik. Friedrich Schleiermacher's sämmtliche Werke. 1. Abt. Zur Theologie. 6. Band (Berlin: Reimer, 1864).

Schmid, Christian Friedrich, *Biblischer Theologie des Neuen Testamentes.* Edited by Carl Weizsäcker, I-II (Stuttgart: Samuel Gottlieb Liesching, 1853, 2nd ed. 1859). English: *Biblical Theology of the New Testament* (Edinburgh: T. & T. Clark, 1870).

Schmidt, Johann Michael, *Die jüdische Apokalyptik. Die Geschichte ihrer Erforschung von den Anfängen bis den Textfunden von Qumran* (Neukirchen–Vluyn: Neukirchener Verlag, 1969, 2nd ed. 1976).

Schmidt, Karl Ludwig, 'Die Kirche des Urchristentums. Eine lexicographische und biblisch-theologische Studie'. *Festgabe für Adolf Deissmann* (Tübingen: Mohr [Siebeck], 1926–27, pp. 258-319.

—, 'Jesus Christus'. In *RGG*, III (2nd ed. Tübingen: Mohr [Siebeck], 1929), cols. 101-51. English translation by R.A. Wilson in Jeroslav Pelikan (ed.), *Twentieth Century Theology in the Making.* I. *Themes of Biblical Theology* (London: William Collins' Sons, 1969), pp. 93-168.

—, 'ἐκκλησία'. In *ThWNT*, III (1938), pp. 502-509.

Schmidt, Nathaniel, *The Prophet of Nazareth* (New York-London: Macmillan, 1905).

Schmidt, Paul Wilhelm, *Die Geschichte Jesu* I-II (Freiburg im B.: Mohr, 1899–1904).

Schmithals, Walter, *Die Gnosis in Korinth. Eine Untersuchung zu den Korintherbriefen.* FRLANT 66 (Göttingen: Vandenhoeck & Ruprecht, 1956, 2nd ed. 1965, 3rd ed. 1969).

—, *Die Apokalyptik. Einführung und Deutung* (Göttingen: Vandenhoeck & Ruprecht, 1973).

Schnackenburg, Rudolf, *Gottes Herrschaft und Reich. Eine biblisch-theologische Studie* (Freiburg: Herder, 1959, 4th ed. 1965). English: *God's Rule and Kingdom* (2nd ed. London-New York, 1968).

—, *Das Johannesevangelium*. I. Teil. HThKNT IV.1 (Freiburg: Herder, 1965, 2. Aufl., 1967).

—, *Die Person Jesu Christi im Spiegel der vier Evangelien*. HThKNT. Supplementsband 4 (Freiburg: Herder, 1993).

Schnedermann, Georg, *Jesu Verkündigung und Lehre vom Reiche Gottes in ihrer geschichtlichen Bedeutung* I-II (Leipzig: Deichert, 1893–95).

Schoeps, Hans Joachim, *Theologie und Geschichte des Judenchristentums* (Tübingen: Mohr [Siebeck], 1949).

Schoettgen, Christian, *Horae Hebraicae et Talmudicae in universum Novum Testamentum quibus Horae Io. Lightfooti in libri historicis supplentur, epistolae et Apocalypsis eadem modo illustrantur* (Dresden & Leipzig: Heckel, 1733).

Schousboe, Johannes, *Om den christne Eschatologis Forhold til den jødiske* (Aarhus og København: Albert Bayers Forlag, 1915).

Schreiner, Josef, 'Das 4. Buch Esra'. In Werner Georg Kümmel (ed.), *JSHRZ* V/4 (Gütersloher Verlagshaus Gerd Mohn, 1981), pp. 287-412.

Schubert, Kurt, 'Die Entwicklung der eschatologischen Naherwartung im Frühjudentum'. In Kurt Schubert (ed.), *Vom Messias zum Christus. Die Fülle der Zeit in religionsgeschichtlicher und theologischer Sicht* (Freiburg: Herder, 1964), pp. 1-54.

Schürer, Emil, *Geschichte des jüdischen Volkes im Zeitalter Jesu Christi* I-III (Leipzig: Hinrichs, 1874, 4th ed. 1901–1909. New English edition: *The History of the Jewish People in the Age of Jesus Christ*. Revised and edited by Geza Vermes Fergus Millar and Matthew Black (Edinburgh: T. & T. Clark, 1973–87).

—, *Das messianische Selbstbewusstsein Jesu Christi* (Göttingen: Dietrich, 1903).

Schürmann,. Heinz, 'Zur Traditions- und Redaktionsgeschichte von Mt 10,23'. *BZ* NF 3 (1959), pp. 82-88.

Schweitzer, Albert, *Das Messianitäts- und Leidensgeheimnis. Eine Skizze des Lebens Jesu* (Tübingen: Mohr [Siebeck], 1901, 3rd ed. 1956). English: *The Mystery of the Kingdom of God. The Secret of Jesus' Messiahship and Passion*. Translated by Walter Lowrie (New York: Macmillan, 1914, as Schocken paperback, 1964).

—, *Geschichte der Leben-Jesu-Forschung*. Zweite, neu bearbeitete und vermehrte Auflage des Werkes 'Von Reimarus zu Wrede', 1906 (Tübingen: Mohr [Siebeck], 1913, 3rd ed. 1921). English: *The Quest of the Historical Jesus*. First Complete Edition. Edited by John Bowden (London: SCM Press, 2000).

—, *Die psychiatrische Beurteilung Jesu. Darstellung und Kritik* (Tübingen: Mohr [Siebeck], 1913, 2nd ed. 1933).

—, *Reich Gottes und Christentum*. Edited by Ulrich Luz, Ulrich Neuenschwander and Johann Zürcher. Werke aus dem Nachlaß (München: Beck 1995).

Schweizer, Eduard, *Erniedrigung und Erhöhung bei Jesus und seinen Nachfolgern*. AThANT 28 (Zürich: Zwingli Verlag, 1955, 2nd ed. 1962).

—, *Jesus Christus im vielfältigen Zeugnis des Neuen Testaments*. Siebenstern Taschenbuch 126 (München und Hamburg: Siebenstern Taschenbuchverlag, 1968).

—, 'υἱός κτλ. D. Neues Testament'. In *ThWNT*, VIII (1969), pp. 364-95.

—, 'Jesus Christus I'. *TRE* 16 (1987), pp. 670-726.

Scott, R.B.Y., '"Behold, he cometh with Clouds"'. *NTS* 5 (1958–59), pp. 127-32.

Seidelin, Paul, 'Der Ebed Jahwe und die Messiasgestalt im Jesajatargum'. *ZNW* 35 (1936), pp. 194-231.

Semler, Johann Salomo, *Periphrasis Evangelii Iohannis, cum notis, et Cantabrigiensis codicis latino textu* I-II (Halle, 1771–72).

Sjöberg, Erik, 'Ville Jesus vara Messias? Bestridandet av Jesu messiasmedvetande i det sista seklets forskning'. *SEÅ* 10 (1945), pp. 82-151.

Smalley, Stephen S., 'Johannes 1,51 und die Einleitung zum vierten Evangelium'. In R. Pesch and R. Schnackenburg (eds.), *Jesus und der Menschensohn*. FS Anton Vögtle (Freiburg: Herder, 1975), pp. 300-313.

Soden, Hermann Freiherr von, *Die wichtigsten Fragen im Leben Jesu* (Berlin: Alexander Duncker, 1904).

Staerk, Willy, *Soter. Die biblische Erlösererwartung als religionsgeschichtliches Problem. Eine biblisch-theologische Untersuchung I: Der biblische Christus*. BFChTh 2. Rh. 32 (Güterloh: Bertelsmann, 1933).

—, 'Jesu Stellung zum jüdischen Messiasbegriff'. *PrM* 6 (1902), pp. 297-309.

—, *Die Erlösererwartung in den östlichen Religionen. Untersuchungen zu den Ausdrucksformen der biblischen Christologie* (Soter II) (Güterloh: Bertelsmann, 1938).

Stanton, Graham N., *Jesus of Nazareth in New Testament Preaching*. SNTSMS 27 (Cambridge: Cambridge University Press, 1974).

Stauffer, Ethelbert, *Die Theologie des Neuen Testaments* (Stuttgart: Kohlhammer, 1941, 4th ed. 1948). English: *New Testament Theology*. Translated by John Marsch (New York: Macmillan, 1955).

—, *Jesus. Gestalt und Geschichte*. Dalph-Taschenbücher 332 (Bern: Francke Verlag 1957).

Steen, Henrik, *Jesu ställning til judafolkets nationella messiasförhoppningar enligt synoptikerna* (Uppsala: Akademiska Bokförlaget, 1910).

Stefanovic, Zdravo, 'The Use of the Aramaic Word *bar* ("son") as a Noun of Relation in the Book of Daniel'. *Asia Advent Seminary Studies* 6 (2003), pp. 77-81.

Stephanus, Robert, *In Euangelium secundum Matthaeum, Marcum, et Lucam commentarii ex ecclesiasticis scriptoribus collecti. Novae glossae ordinariae specimen, donec meliora dominus* (1553).

Stier, Fridolin, *Gott und Engel im Alten Testament*. Alttestamentliche Abhandlungen 12,2 (Münster im Westphalen: Aschendorffschen Verlagsbuchhandlung, 1934).

Stone, Michael, 'The Concept of the Messiah in IV Ezra'. In Jacob Neusner (ed.), *Religions in Antiquity. Essays in Memory of E.R. Goodenough*. Supplements to Numen (Leiden: Brill, 1968), pp. 295-312.

—, *Fourth Ezra: A Commentary on the Book of Fourth Ezra*. Hermeneia (Minneapolis: Fortress Press, 1990).

See also Greenfield.

Strauss, David Friedrich, *Das Leben Jesu, kritisch bearbeitet* I-II (Tübingen: Osiander, 1835–36). English: *The Life of Jesus Critically Examined*. Translated by George Eliot after 4th ed. 1840 (New York: Blanchard, 1860). New edition ed. by Peter C. Hodgson (one volume; Fortress Press, 1972; reprint Ramsey, NJ: Sigler Press, 1994).

—, *Das Leben Jesu für das deutsche Volk bearbeitet* (Stuttgart: Kröner, 1864). English: *The Life of Jesus for the People* I-II (2nd ed. London: Williams & Norgate, 1879).

Strecker, Georg, *Das Judenchristentum in den Pseudoklementinen*. TU 70 (Berlin: Akademie-Verlag, 1958).

—, *Theologie des Neuen Testaments*. Bearbeitet, ergänzt und herausgegeben von Friedrich Wilhelm Horn (Berlin: De Gruyter, 1996). English: *Theology of the New Testament*. Translated by M. Eugene Boring (Louisville: Westminster John Knox Press, 2000).

Strobel, August, *Kerygma und Apokalyptik. Ein religionsgeschichtlicher und theologischer Beitrag zur Christusfrage* (Göttingen: Vandenhoeck & Ruprecht, 1967).

Ström, Åke V., *Vetekornet. Studier över individ och kollektiv i Nya Testamentet med särskild hänsyn till Johannesevangeliets teologi Joh. 12:20-33*. ASNU 11 (Stockholm: Svenska Kyrkans Diakonistyrelses Bokförlag, 1944).

Stuhlmacher, Peter, 'Das Bekenntnis zur Auferweckung Jesu von den Toten und die Biblische Theologie'. *ZThK* 70 (1973), pp. 365-403; reprint in idem, *Schriftauslegung auf dem Wege zur biblischen Theologie* (Göttingen: Vandenhoeck & Ruprecht, 1975), pp. 128-66.

—, 'Existenzvertretung für die Vielen: Mk 10,45 (Mt 20,28)'. In Rainer Albertz, Hans Peter Müller, H.H. Wolff and Walter Zimmerli (eds.), *Werden und Wirken des Alten Testaments*. FS Claus Westermann (Göttingen: Vandenhoeck & Ruprecht/ Gütersloh: Gütersloher Verlagshaus, 1980), pp. 412-27. Reprint in idem, *Versöhnung, Gesetz und Gerechtigkeit*. Aufsätze zur biblischen Theologie (Göttingen: Vandenhoeck & Ruprecht, 1981), pp. 27-42.

—, *Biblische Theologie des Neuen Testaments*. Band 1. *Grundlegung. Von Jesus zu Paulus* (Göttingen: Vandenhoeck & Ruprecht, 1992).

Suter, David Winston, *Tradition and Composition in the Parables of Enoch*. SBLDS 47 (Missoula, MT: Scholars Press, 1979).

—, 'Weighed in the Balance: The Similitudes of Enoch in Recent Discussion'. *Religious Studies Review* 7 (1981), pp. 217-21.

Talbert, Charles H., 'The Myth of a Descending–Ascending Redeemer in Mediterranean Antiquity'. *NTS* 22 (1975–76), pp. 418-40.

Taylor Vincent, *The Gospel According to St. Mark* (London: Macmillan, 1952).

—, *The Names of Jesus* (London: Macmillan, 1953).

Theissen, Gerd, and Merz, Annette, *Der historische Jesus. Ein Lehrbuch* (Göttingen: Vandenhoeck & Ruprecht, 1996). English: *The Historical Jesus: A Comprehensive Guide* (Minneapolis: Fortress Press, 1998).

Tholuck, Augustus, *Commentar zum Evangelio Johannis* (Hamburg: Perthes, 1827, 5th ed. 1837). English: *Commentary on the Gospel of St John* (Edinburgh: T. & T. Clark, 1860 (from 7th ed. Gotha: Perthes, 1857)).

Tindal, Matthew. *Christianity as Old as the Creation: Or, the Gospel, a Republication of the Religion of Nature* (1730).

Toledo, Francesco, *In sacrosanctum Ioannis Evangelium commentarii* I-II (Kölln: Agripp, 1589).

Torm, Frederik, 'Hvad mente Jesus af Nazareth om sig selv?' *Theologisk Tidsskrift for den danske Folkekirke* 11 (1896), pp. 557-605; 12 (1887), pp. 1-47.

Troje, Louise, 'Urmensch'. In *RGG*, V (2nd ed. 1931), cols. 1416-17.

Tuckett, Christopher, *Q and the History of Early Christianity: Studies on Q* (Edinburgh: T. & T Clark, 1996).

Uhlig, Siegbert, 'Das Äthiopische Henochbuch'. In Werner Georg Kümmel (ed.), *JSHRZ* V/6 (Gütersloher Verlagshaus Gerd Mohn, 1984), pp. 459-780.

VanderKam, James C. 'Daniel 7 in the Similitudes of Enoch (*1 Enoch* 37–71)', in Charlotte Hempel and Judith Lieu (eds.), *Biblical Traditions in Transmission.* FS Michael A. Knibb. SupJSJ 111 (Leiden: Brill, 2006), pp. 291-307.

Vawter, B., 'Ezekiel and John'. *CBQ* 26 (1964), pp. 450-58.

Veit, M., *Die Auffassung von der Person Jesu im Urchristentum nach den neuesten Forschungen.* Unpublished dissertation (Marburg, 1946).

Venema, H., *Dissertationes ad vaticinia Danielis emblematica Cap. II, VII, et VIII. De quatuor orientis regnis, ordien sibi successuris, et quinto Messiæ* (Leiden, 1745).

Vermes, Geza, *Jesus the Jew: A Historian's reading of the Gospels* (London: Collins, 1973).

Violet, Bruno, 'Die "Verfluchung" des Feigenbaums'. *ΕΥΧΑΡΙΣΤΙΟΝ.* FS Hermann Gunkel. FRLANT 36/2 (Göttingen: Vandenhoeck & Ruprecht, 1923), pp. 135-40.

Vögtle, Anton, 'Das christologische und ekklesiologische Anliegen von Mt. 28,18-20'. *SE* 2 = TU 87 (Berlin: Akademie-Verlag, 1964), pp. 266-94.

Völter, Daniel, *Das messianische Bewusstsein Jesu* (Strasburg: Heitz, 1907).

—, *Die Grundfrage des Lebens Jesu* (Stuttgart: A. Bonz' Erben, 1936).

Volkmar, Gustav, *Die Evangelien oder Marcus und die Synoptiker als der kanonischen und ausserkanonischen Evangelien nach dem ältesten Text mit historisch-kritischem Commentar* (Leipzig: Fues, 1870).

—, Jesus *Nazarenus und die erste christliche Zeit, mit den beiden ersten Erzählern* (Zürich: Schmidt, 1882).

Volz, Paul, *Jüdische Eschatologie von Daniel bis Akiba* (Tübingen: Mohr [Siebeck], 1903). Second edition as *Die Eschatologie der jüdischen Gemeinde im neutestamentlichen Zeitalter. Nach den Quellen der rabbinischen, apokalyptischen und apokryphen Literatur* (1934 = reprint Hildesheim: Georg Olms, 1966).

Vorst(ius), Johannes, *De Hebraismis Novi Testamenti Commentarius* I-II (Leipzig, 1665).

Walker, William O., 'Daniel 7:13-14'. *Interp.* 39 (1985), pp. 176-81.

[Walter, Ernst Johann Konrad], *Versuch eines schriftmäßigen Beweises, daß Joseph der wahre Vater Christi sey* (Berlin—Stralsund, 1792).

Wedderburn, A.J.N., 'Philo's "Heavenly Man"'. *NT* 15 (1973), pp. 310-26.

Wegscheider, Julius August Ludwig, *Institutiones theologicae christianae dogmaticae* (Halle: Gebauer, 1815, 2nd ed. 1817).

Weimar, Peter, 'Daniel 7. Eine Textanalyse'. In R. Pesch and R. Schnackenburg (eds.), *Jesus und der Menschensohn.* FS Anton Vögtle (Freiburg: Herder, 1975), pp. 11-36.

Weinel, Heinrich, *Biblische Theologie des Neuen Testaments. Die Religion Jesu und des Urchristentums.* Grundrisse der Theologischen Wissenschaften III/2 (Tübingen: Mohr [Siebeck], 1911, 3rd ed. 1921).

Weiser, Alfons, *Theologie des Neuen Testaments II. Die Theologie der Evangelien* (Stuttgart: Kohlhammer, 1993).

Weiss, Bernhard, *Lehrbuch der Biblischen Theologie des Neuen Testaments* (Berlin: Hertz, 1868, 5th ed. 1895). English: *Biblical Theology of the New Testament* I-II (Edinburgh: T. & T. Clark, 1893).

—, *Das Leben Jesu* I-II (Berlin: Hertz, 1882, 3rd ed. 1888).

—, *Die Religion des Neuen Testaments* (Stuttgart/Berlin: Cotta, 1903).

Weiss, Johannes, *Die Predigt Jesu vom Reiche Gottes* (Göttingen: Vandenhoeck & Ruprecht, 1892, 2nd ed. 1900, 3rd ed. 1964 'erweitert um einen Anhang mit wichtigen Stücken aus der ersten Auflage von 1892'). English: *Jesus' Proclamation of the Kingdom of God*. With a critical and historical introduction by Richard Hyde Hiers and David Latimore Holland (London-Philadelphia: Fortress Press, 1971; reprint Sigler Press, 1999).

—, *Das Urchristentum*. Posthumously ed. by Rudolf Knopf (Göttingen: Vandenhoeck & Ruprecht, 1917). English: *Earliest Christianity: A History of the Period A.D. 30–150* I-II. Edited by Frederick C. Grant (New York: Harper & Brothers, 1959).

Weisse, Christian Hermann, *Die evangelische Geschichte kritisch und philosophisch bearbeitet* I-II (Leipzig: Breitkopf & Härtel, 1838).

—, *Die Evangelienfrage in ihrem gegenwärtigen Stadium* (Leipzig: Breitkopf & Härtel, 1856).

Weizsächer, Carl, *Untersuchungen über die evangelische Geschichte ihre Quellen und den Gang ihrer Entwicklung* (Gotha: Besser, 1864, 2nd ed. 1901).

Wellhausen, Julius, *Israelitische und Jüdische Geschichte* (Berlin: Reimer, 1894, 2nd ed. 1895, 3rd ed. 1897, 4th ed. 1901, 5th ed. 1904, 6th ed. 1905, 7th ed. 1914).

—, 'Zur apokalyptische Literatur'. In idem, *Skizzen und Vorarbeiten* VI (Berlin: Reimer, 1899), pp. 215-49. Reprint in Klaus Koch and Johann Michael Schmidt (eds.), *Apokalyptik*. WdF 365 (Darmstadt: Wissenschaftliche Buchgesellschaft, 1982), pp. 58-66.

—, *Das Evangelium Marci* (Berlin: Reimar, 1903, 2nd ed. 1909).

—, *Einleitung in die drei ersten Evangelien* (Berlin: Reimer, 1905, 2nd ed. 1911).

Wendt, Hans Hinrich, *Die Lehre Jesu* I-II (Göttingen: Vandenhoeck & Ruprecht, 1886–90, 2nd ed. 1901). English: *The Teaching of Jesus* I-II (New York: Scribner's, 1892).

Werner, Martin, *Die Entstehung des christlichen Dogmas problemgeschichtlich dargestellt* (Bern, Leipzig: P. Haupt, 1941; 2nd ed. Bern: P. Haupt, Tübingen: Katzmann-Verlag, 1954). English: *The Formation of the Christian Dogma* (Boston: Beacon Press, 1965).

Wernle, Paul, *Jesus* (Tübingen: Mohr [Siebeck], 1916, 2nd ed. 1916).

Westcott, Brooke Foss, *The Gospel According to St. John. The Authorised Version with Introduction and Notes* (London: John Murray, 1882, 18th ed. 1937).

Westermann, Claus, 'Sinn und Grenze religionsgeschichtlicher Parallelen'. *ThLZ* 90 (1965), cols. 490-96.

Wette, Wilhelm Martin Leberecht de, *Lehrbuch der christlichen Dogmatik, in ihrer historischen Entwickelig dargestellt. Erster Theil. Biblische Dogmatik Alten und Neuen Testaments. Oder kritische Darstellung der Religionslehre des Hebraismus, des Judenthums und Urchristenthums* (Berlin: Georg Reimer, 1813, 3rd ed. 1831).

—, *Kurze Erklärung des Evangelium Matthäi*. Kurzgefasstes exegetisches Handbuch zum Neuen Testament I/1 (Leipzig: Weidmann, 1836, 2nd ed. 1838).

Wettstein, Johann Jacob, *Novum Testamentum Graecum. Editionis receptae cum lectionibus variantibus codicorum mss., editionum aliarum, versionum et patrum nec non commentario plenirore ex scriptoribus hebraeis, Graecis et Latinis* I-II (Amsterdam: Dommerian, 1751–52; reprint Graz: Akademische Druck- und Verlagsanstalt, 1962).

Windisch, Hans, *Der Barnabasbrief*. HNT 19 (Tübingen: Mohr [Siebeck], 1920).

Winter, Paul, 'Norman Perrin, Rediscovering the Teaching of Jesus'. *Deutsche Literaturzeitung* 89 (1968), cols. 783-85.

Witherington, Ben, III, *The Christology of Jesus* (Minneapolis: Fortress Press, 1990).

Wittichen, Carl, *Die Idee des Menschen, zweiter Beitrag zur biblischen Theologie hauptsächlich der synoptischen Reden Jesu* (Göttingen: Dietrich, 1868).

—, *Das Leben Jesu in urkundlicher Darstellung* (Jena: Dufft, 1876).

Wolf, Johann Christoph, *Curae philologicae et criticae in IV. ss. evangelia et actus apostolicos* I-II (Hamburg, 1725, 3rd ed. 1739).

Wolfburg, Morten Caspar, *Observationes sacrae in Novum Testamentum seu Annotationes theologico-criticae in voces plerasque N.T. ordine alphabetico, et dicta praecipua tam veteris quam novi foederis*. Edited by Eduard Leigh (København, 1717, 2nd ed. 1738).

Woude, A.S. van der, 'Melchisedek als himmlische Erlösergestalt in den neugefundenen eschatologischen Midraschim aus Höhle XI'. *OTS* 14 (1965), pp. 354-73.

Wrede, William, *Das Messiasgeheimnis in den Evangelien. Zugleich ein Beitrag zum Verständnis des Markusevangeliums* (Göttingen: Vandenhoeck & Ruprecht, 1901, 3rd ed. 1963). English: *The Messianic Secret*. Translated by J. C.G. Greig. Library of Theological Translations (London: James Clarke & Co., 1971).

Wrege, H.-Th., 'Zur Rolle des Geisteswortes in frühchristlichen Traditionen (LC 12,10 parr.)'. In Joël Delobel (ed.), *Logia. Les paroles de Jésus—The Sayings of Jesus*. Mémorial Joseph Coppens. BEThL 59 (Leuven: Peeters/Leuven University Press, 1982), pp. 373-77.

Zahn, Theodor, *Das Evangelium des Matthäus*. KNT 1 (Leipzig: Deichert, 1903, 3rd ed. 1910).

Zevit, Z., 'The Structure and Elements of Daniel 7'. *ZAW* 80 (1968), pp. 385-96.

Zimmern, Heinrich, 'II. Religion und Sprache'. In Eberhard Schraeder, *Die Keilinschriften und das Alte Testament*. 3. Auflage mit Ausdehnung auf die Apokryphen, Pseudepigraphen und das Neue Testament neu bearbeitet von H. Zimmern und H. Winckler (Berlin: Reuther & Reichard, 1903), pp. 343-653.

Zwingli, Ulrich, *Annotationes in Evangelistarum & Apostolorum scripta* (Zürich, 1531) = Tomus IV of *Opera d. Huldrychi Zvinglii*. Edited by Leonem Iudae (Zürich, 1545).

NB. After finishing the work I discovered that by mistake the following authors (and their articles) only figure in the Bibliography: T.Y. Cho, Jean Cruvellier, Pietro D'Aquino, Guiseppe de Rosa, P.D. Early, J.C. Greensfield and M. Stone, Howard Jacobsen, E.G. Jay, Joachim Kügler and Barclay M. Newman.

Indexes

Index of References

Index of Authors, Ancient and Modern (editors not included)

Lightning Source UK Ltd.
Milton Keynes UK
28 March 2010

152029UK00001B/3/P

9 781845 533359